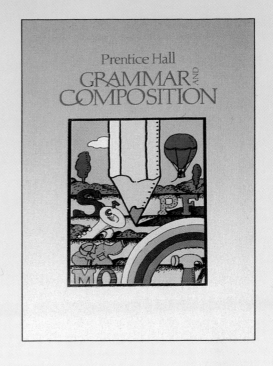

INTRODUCING
PRENTICE HALL
GRAMMAR AND
COMPOSITION

6-8

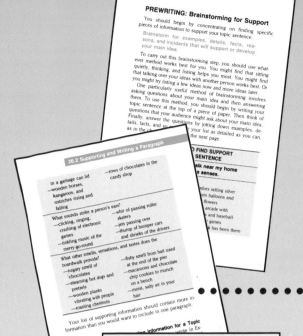

PREWRITING: Brainstorming for Support

You should begin by concentrating on finding specific pieces of information to support your topic sentence.

Brainstorm for examples, details, facts, reasons, and incidents that will support or develop your main idea.

To carry out this brainstorming step, you should use whatever method works best for you. You might find that sitting quietly, thinking, and listing helps you most. You might find that talking over your ideas with another person works best. Or you might try listing a few ideas now and more ideas later.

One particularly useful method of brainstorming involves asking questions about your main idea and then answering them. To use this method, you should begin by writing your topic sentence at the top of a piece of paper. Then think of questions that your audience might ask about your main idea. Finally, answer the questions by jotting down examples, details, facts, and so on. Make your list as detailed as you can, as in the ch... the next page.

...O FIND SUPPORT
...SENTENCE
...alk near my home
...e senses.

26.2 Supporting and Writing a Paragraph

	rows of chocolates in the candy shop
in a garbage can lid	
—wooden horses,	
kangaroos, and	
ostriches rising and	
falling	

What sounds strike a person's ears?
—clicking, ringing, / —whir of passing roller
crashing of electronic / skaters
games / —jets passing over
—tinkling music of the / —thump of bumper cars
merry-go-round / and shrieks of the drivers

What other smells, sensations, and tastes does the
boardwalk provide? / —fishy smell from bait used
—sugary smell of / at the end of the pier
chocolates / —macaroons and chocolate
—steaming hot dogs and / chip cookies to munch
pretzels / on a bench
—wooden planks / —moist, salty air in your
vibrating with people / hair
—roasting chestnuts

Your list of supporting information should contain more information than you would want to include in one paragraph.

...ting Information for a Topic

EXERCISE A:
Sentence. Re... wrote in Ex
ercise D of Se...
your paper a...
mation using...

1. Think ...
with ...
come ...
spec...

ASSIGNMENT 2

Topic Tracking Your Moods

Form and Purpose Journal entries that describe and explain emotional moods

Audience Yourself

Length At least one entry each day over a two-week period

Focus Write daily journal entries about a mood you felt during the day. In each entry, identify the mood, describe your exact feelings, and try to explain what brought on the mood.

Sources Yourself

Prewriting At the end of each day, id...
that you had. Th...

Prentice Hall Grammar and Composition

Springboards for Writing

Purpose

Tres Riches Heures Du Duc
De Berry (October)

The Lombourg Brothers

FLEXIBLE APPROACHES TO WRITING FOR GRADES 6-8

Students frequently come to a middle school from two or more elementary schools within a district. They bring to your classes a wide variety of writing abilities.

That's why you need a text offering many paths to good writing: Grammar and Composition 6-8.

SPECIFIC APPLICATIONS

Each writing unit begins with a general overview of the writing process. Chapters model how the process can be tailored to particular writing types. Your students then examine each model and imitate its parts. In this way they make the models their own.

PLENTIFUL ASSIGNMENTS

Writing Workshops are guided assignments that end every chapter—over 60 per grade level! Topics are rich and varied, often cutting across content areas. Additional workshops appear as blackline masters in the Teacher's Resource Book.

EXCITING VISUALS

Each Writing Workshop asks students to respond to photos, artwork or cartoons to motivate writing.

Or, use one of the beautiful fine art reproductions in the Writing Model Transparencies binder—sure to motivate remarkable work from young writers.

SOLID SKILLS DEVELOPMENT FOR GRADES 6-8

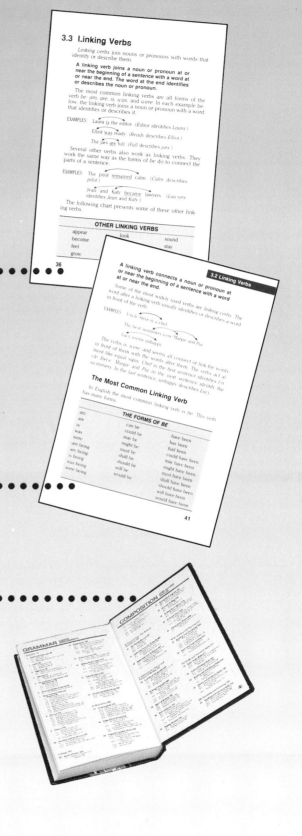

Middle school is the last chance for many students to master English fundamentals. That's why you need a text with strong grammar, usage and mechanics units: Grammar and Composition 6-8.

CLEAR, COMPLETE CONTENT

No other program comes close with depth and scope of skills coverage. Lessons have a simple, consistent structure:
- rule or key instruction, with verbal explanation
- visual restatement, with charts or diagrams
- immediate, hands-on application

You'll find plentiful exercises in every text and hundreds more in the Computer Exercise Bank.

SENSIBLE PACING

Middle school students can be overwhelmed by skills instruction. That's why the program presents digestible chunks of information at grade 6, then reviews and expands at grades 7-8.

CONVENIENT FORMAT

A handbook is a handy book, one that encourages students to become independent users of their texts. (A skill they'll need in high school.)

The whole organization of the text is laid out inside each back cover. The simple number code for each chapter subsection also appears as a clear cross-reference for all program components.

With Prentice Hall, students will quickly find what they need to know.

INTEGRATION OF SKILLS AND WRITING FOR GRADES 6-8

Middle school students often need to know why something is important. For instance, they must see an application or use for a basic skill. <u>Grammar and Composition 6-8</u> provides just the right context: students' own writing.

DEVELOPING WRITING SKILLS

These valuable activities appear throughout every grammar, usage and mechanics chapter. Each allows a student to tie the specific skill just taught to writing—either original writing or revision of a supplied model.

APPLYING SKILLS

Both you and your students will enjoy the full page of activities ending every skills chapter:

• The Skills Review always involves revision of a supplied model for a specific purpose.
• The Writing Workshop is a paced assignment, always on an exciting topic. Students are guided to revise/rewrite their work with a close eye to that chapter's focus.

CHECKLISTS FOR REVISING

These handy summaries appear in every writing chapter and invite students to evaluate their writing for clarity, conciseness and correctness.

(Inset page — 10.2 Avoiding Run-ons, p. 187)

10.2 Avoiding Run-ons

14. I am amused by the different beverage fads in this country now bottled water has become popular in many places.
15. Nathan Hale is undoubtedly the most famous spy from the Revolutionary War era, however, Lydia Darrah, another spy during that period, is credited with actually saving Washington's army on one occasion.
16. Franklin loves to make soup he told me that there are three basic soup stocks: chicken, meat, and fish.
17. Fables are stories that teach a moral sometimes they are about animals that speak and act like humans.
18. Edgar Allan Poe was an orphan at two, the rest of his life was also tragic.
19. Gershwin wrote the music for *Porgy and Bess*, many experts consider it America's first great folk opera.
20. The robin is the state bird of Michigan, the state flower is the apple blossom.

DEVELOPING WRITING SKILLS: Correcting Run-ons in a Composition. Three of the sentences in the following paragraph are run-ons. Rewrite the entire paragraph and correct each run-on. Do not use the same method to correct all the run-ons.

EXAMPLE   American pioneers ran into many different problems one of them was housing.

American pioneers ran into many different problems. One of them was housing.

(1) Early settlers on the prairie had problems finding timber to build homes. (2) Sod houses first appeared about 1830, in one period about 90 percent of the people west of the Missouri [...] these mud huts. (3) The settlers learned to build [...] in the Plains Indians they had long made their [...] earth. (4) Sod houses had walls three feet [...] were dark and poorly ventilated they were [...] cool in summer.

187

(Inset page — Skills Review and Writing Workshop, p. 215)

Skills Review and Writing Workshop

Using Verbs

CHECKING YOUR SKILLS
Rewrite the paragraph below, correcting all errors in verb usage.

(1) The cast members were not froze in terror on opening night. (2) They knowed that they had rose above being nervous. (3) First, two cast members busted their legs in a skiing accident. (4) Then the director catched the measles and was out for a week. (5) Two days before the show opened, the costume rental agency admitted that the costumes were still laying on a stage in a neighboring state! (6) The agency assured them, however, that an employee had went to pick the costumes up. (7) Yet it become clear that all these difficulties had drew the cast together. (8) On opening night they set down and went over their efforts. (9) They shaked hands and rose, determined to make the show a success. (10) When the show begun, the audience saw a confident cast.

USING USAGE SKILLS IN WRITING
Describing Action
Many experts say that an author's choice of verbs is crucial to successful writing, especially in descriptions of action. Follow the steps below to create a paragraph describing an action.

Prewriting: Focus on the preparation for some event, such as for a party or practicing for a game. List all the activities that went into the preparation.

Writing: In chronological order describe the activities that led up to the event. In the last sentence reveal the effect of these activities. Was the event successful?

Revising: First, check your verbs. Make sure they are all correct and specific. Then check for other improvements you can make. After you have revised, proofread carefully.

215

(Inset page — Checklist for Revising a Paragraph, p. 490)

Look at your writing after some time has passed, and use a checklist to help rethink your ideas and pinpoint problems.

In order to improve your writing, try to approach it from a new perspective. Leaving some time between writing and revising can help you see things you may have overlooked while writing. Sometimes hearing another person read your writing aloud can also help you be objective.

Once you are ready to take a fresh look at your writing, a checklist can help you find ways to make your writing stronger by pointing out some of the weaknesses discussed in this section. When you use a checklist, you should read each question and then reread your paragraph and think about that specific checklist item.

CHECKLIST FOR REVISING A PARAGRAPH

1. Does the topic sentence clearly express the main idea of the paragraph? If not, should you expand or narrow the focus of the topic sentence?
2. Have you included enough support to develop your topic sentence?
3. Can you find any generalizations and weak opinions that should be replaced with specific supporting information?
4. Are there any unnecessary pieces of information that your paragraph would be stronger without?
5. Would another order be better for your ideas? Would any of the ideas be clearer if they were introduced by transitions? Would a concluding sentence tie your paragraph's ideas together?
6. Could you make your paragraph more suited to your audience and purpose?
7. Could any of the sentences be lengthened, shortened, or combined for smoothness?
8. Are there any mistakes in grammar, usage, mechanics, or spelling?

490

A L L   T H E LANGUAGE ARTS FOR GRADES 6-8

All middle school programs must develop a student's total use of language, not just the ability to write well. <u>Grammar and Composition 6-8</u> presents balanced coverage of the related skills of English.

VOCABULARY AND SPELLING

Every text contains chapters on improving spelling and vocabulary.

A unique feature at every level is the chapter on word choice. Students learn to use specific, precise language and avoid slang or worn-out phrases.

STUDY AND RESEARCH

Successful high school students have solid study habits. Middle school is the time to develop study skills, using the unit in <u>Grammar and Composition 6-8</u> as a foundation.

Students learn library and dictionary skills and test-taking tips.

They develop critical thinking skills that may be applied to any subject area.

SPEAKING AND LISTENING

Because so many teachers use peer response groups to revise student writing, student oral skills have become increasingly important. Every text in <u>Grammar and Composition 6-8</u> presents a unit stressing classroom use of speaking/listening skills.

Chapter **21**

Improving Your Use of Words

Accurate, interesting writing depends on careful word choices. Words chosen with care can make your ideas seem both clear and fresh to your audience.

21.1 Choosing Precise Words

Whenever you concentrate on what you want to write, you will discover that many possible word choices are open to you. This section will show you how to avoid weak or dull word choices. It will also provide you with some new ways to find the most suitable words to express your ideas.

Using Action Words

Verbs are essential parts of your sentences. As you know from your study of grammar, some verbs are action verbs; other verbs are linking verbs. In addition verbs can be either in the active voice or in the passive voice. In general the more

406

52.1 Separating Fact from Opinion

The first step in analyzing and judging information is to decide how reliable it is. You need to determine how much of it you can accept as true. To do this, you must be able to tell fact from opinion.

Learn how to tell the difference between fact and opinion.

A statement of fact is one that is either true or false. A statement of fact can be proved true or false by measurement, by observation, by consulting reliable reference books or other records, by scientific experiment, or by the word of an eyewitness or expert.

The following two sentences are examples of statements of fact.

FACT: Joe's brother is five feet ten inches tall.
FACT: It is raining now.
FACT: Plants need both water and sunlight to survive.

You could easily test the first statement by measuring Joe's brother. You could test the second statement by looking out the window and observing the weather. You could check the third statement by consulting books, performing experiments, or talking with an expert on the subject.

The following chart lists questions to ask yourself to help you identify a statement of fact.

RECOGNIZING STATEMENTS OF FACT

1. Can you test the statement by direct observation or measurement?
2. Can you test the statement by ...
3. Can you test the ...

Chapter **41**

Speaking and Listening Skills

You listen and speak every day. They are both part of one process. When you speak, someone else listens. If you speak well, you can express your ideas clearly. If you listen well, you can remember more of what you hear.

41.1 Informal Speaking Skills

Informal speaking skills include talking with friends or family, discussing in class, giving directions, and making introductions. This section will help you improve these skills.

Speaking in Class Discussions

You can improve both your speaking and listening skills by taking part in class discussions. If you plan what you want to say before you say it and practice taking part in class often, you will increase your skills and confidence as well.

Develop confidence about participating in class through preparation and practice.

690

TOTAL
TEACHING SUPPORT
FOR GRADES 6-8

A Transparency Binder with over 100 transparencies will supplement your writing program. It includes:

SPRINGBOARDS FOR WRITING

Over 25 transparencies of fine art and photos provide starting points for writing. Each reproduction comes with a complete Lesson Plan showing how the artwork reinforces the writing process, plus suggestions for teaching different ability groups. A blackline master Writing Assignment is there to guide the student.

MODEL TRANSPARENCIES

Do your students know what good writing is? MODEL TRANSPARENCIES provide solid examples for the types of longer writing covered at grades 6-8: essay, report, short story, friendly and business letter. Each model has three parts: first draft, revised draft, proofread draft—so your students can see one writer's process step by step.

AN ANNOTATED TEACHER'S EDITION

provides your recipe for success:

- Lesson plans for each section of every chapter, in side-columns next to the student pages
- Objectives, lesson starts, critical thinking references for every exercise
- Suggestions for teaching the writing process
- Activities to individualize the program for three ability groups, to meet the varied needs of middle schoolers.

A COMPUTER EXERCISE BANK

that brings the convenience of the computer into your classroom. The bank allows you to choose from among over 500 exercises for each of three ability levels. Individualized instruction and make-up tests are easy when you can

- Create custom activities to fit student needs
- Add, edit and delete exercise items
- Scramble questions and answers

All exercises correlate to chapters and sections in the textbook.

A TEACHER'S RESOURCE BOOK

within a three-ring binder provides all the tools necessary to support a successful writing program, including:

- Evaluation Forms for teacher, peer, or self-evaluation
- Blackline masters to practice or reteach writing
- Listening/Speaking worksheets

PRENTICE HALL GRAMMAR AND COMPOSITION

6-8

GRADE 6   GRADE 7   GRADE 8

TOP RATED BY USERS*

✔ OVERALL SERIES QUALITY

✔ INTEGRATION OF COMPOSITION AND SKILLS

✔ LIVELY WRITING STYLE

• Based on a 1987 survey of over 2200 teachers, users of Prentice Hall Grammar and Composition were more satisfied than users of any other 6-12 language arts program on each of these key attributes.

For more information please call TOLL FREE 1-800-848-9500

PRENTICE HALL
School Division of Simon & Schuster
Englewood Cliffs, NJ 07632

136-93573-7

Prentice Hall

GRAMMAR AND COMPOSITION

ANNOTATED TEACHER'S EDITION

Prentice Hall

GRAMMAR AND COMPOSITION

Grade 8

Prepared by Gary Forlini
Senior Author of the Series

PRENTICE HALL
Englewood Cliffs, New Jersey
Needham, Massachusetts

ANNOTATED TEACHER'S EDITION

PRENTICE HALL Grammar and Composition

Fourth Edition

Cover art: courtesy of Myron Grossman

ISBN 0-13-712670-0

10 9 8 7 6 5 4 3 2

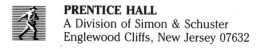

PRENTICE HALL
A Division of Simon & Schuster
Englewood Cliffs, New Jersey 07632

Contents

The Program

THE STUDENT TEXT. The Prentice Hall Grammar and Composition student text is designed to help students develop a better understanding and command of the English language. The text comprises two strong composition units and units on grammar, usage, and mechanics. In addition to these units, the text contains a vocabulary and spelling unit, a study and research skills unit, and a speaking and listening skills unit. By putting these eight together in one text, the Prentice Hall Grammar and Composition student text provides students with a comprehensive approach to building better English skills.

Because there is a simple, consistent format for each chapter, each section, and each subsection, the text will be immediately accessible to your students. Whether the book is being used in class or is being consulted as a reference tool, a student's understanding will also be enhanced by the fact that (1) all rules appear in colored type, (2) all examples and models are clearly labeled, and (3) numerous charts are used to present important concepts in an easy-to-grasp form. The text also provides three reference aids: the Table of Contents at the front of the book, a fully cross-referenced index, and a key of major concepts covered in the text.

Each subsection in the text ends with at least one set of basic exercises giving students immediate feedback, allowing you to conclude a day's lesson at any point, and assuring that no concept is overlooked. Each chapter, with the exception of the Writing Process Chapter and the chapters in the Forms and Process Composition unit, ends with a Skills Review and Writing Workshop that provides students with a review of the skills covered in the chapter in addition to a related writing activity. The Writing Process Chapter and each of the chapters in the Forms and Process unit end with one or more Writing Workshops that provide students with writing activities designed to strengthen their composition skills.

THE ANNOTATED TEACHER'S EDITION. The Annotated Teacher's Edition is designed to offer not only general strategies for course planning and evaluation but also specific section-by-section teaching suggestions that can be used on a daily basis. In the side-columns of the Annotated Teacher's Edition are objectives to help you plan your coverage of individual sections, suggestions for adapting each section for more advanced and less advanced students, page references for additional exercises included in each of the ancillaries to the text, and a correlation of critical-thinking skills involved in the exercises contained in each section. The objectives, which are correlated on a one-to-one basis with each subsection, should prove especially useful in planning which areas to emphasize and which exercises to assign to meet the particular needs of your students. The Annotated Teacher's Edition also includes an in-depth overview of the writing process that is designed to help you gain a better understanding of the writing process and aid you in teaching your students how to use the writing process. Finally, the Annotated Teacher's Edition contains a bibliography of general reference books that may prove useful in teaching a course in grammar and composition.

THE TEACHER'S RESOURCE BOOK. The Teacher's Resource Book includes five ancillaries—the Writing Process Activities, the Speaking and Listening Activities, the Practice Pages, the Test Program, and the Writing Workshops—that are designed to supplement the Prentice Hall Grammar and Composition text. These ancillaries make it possible for you to teach grammar and composition in the most comprehensive way possible. The Teacher's Resource Book also includes a time-allocation chart that gives suggested time allocations for each section of the course. The following paragraphs offer details about each of the ancillaries included in the Teacher's Resource Book.

THE WRITING PROCESS ACTIVITIES. The Writing Process Activities are designed to supplement the Composition units of the text. Fact sheets focusing on each of the steps involved in the writing process are included to provide students with straightforward and easily accessible sources of information. Additionally, the Writing Process Activities include prewriting worksheets which are designed to help students create and develop their own topics for writing assignments. Worksheets are also included for each of the major forms of writing covered in the text. In each one of the worksheets, students are provided with a writing situation that they must develop within the context of the form being studied. Finally, the Writing Process Activities include five evaluation sheets that are designed to provide teachers with a choice of fast, efficient, and thorough methods for evaluating students' work. These evaluation sheets are appropriate for peer evaluations and self-evaluations as well as teacher evaluations.

THE SPEAKING AND LISTENING ACTIVITIES.

The Speaking and Listening Activities are designed to supplement the Speaking and Listening unit of the text. Fact sheets and worksheets provide students with a means of reinforcing and mastering the communication skills covered in the text. The Speaking and Listening Activities also include comprehensive lesson plans that provide teachers with the information needed to relate the Speaking and Listening Activities to the text. The lesson plans also offer teaching suggestions and ideas for follow-up activities. The Speaking and Listening Activities also contain evaluation sheets that provide teachers with a quick and reliable method for evaluating students' work. Finally, an audio cassette designed to be used in conjunction with the Speaking and Listening Activities is included with the grade 12 Speaking and Listening Activities.

THE PRACTICE PAGES.

The Practice Pages are designed to reinforce the material covered in the Prentice Hall Grammar and Composition text by providing students with exercises to supplement the activities in the text. All eight units of the text are covered in the Practice Pages. The numbered heads in the Practice Pages correspond with those in the text to make it easy for students and teachers to locate exercises to supplement material being covered at a particular time during the school year. To assist students in learning to use the writing process within the context of a particular form of writing being studied, the Practice Pages also include Writing Process Pages for each of the major forms of writing covered. These pages are designed to lead the students through a writing assignment step by step. A Practice Pages Answer Key is provided to allow teachers to correct their students' work quickly and easily.

The Practice Pages may be easily removed from the Teacher's Resource Book so that you may copy them for students' use.

THE TEST PROGRAM.

The Test Program offers a complete pretest and post-test for each unit in the text, as well as a mastery test for each chapter. The pretests are designed to help you identify students' strengths and weaknesses so that you will be able to decide which sections of the text to stress. The post-tests are designed to measure how well students have progressed through studying the material and completing the exercises in the text. Each test is divided into sections, which are clearly labeled with numbered heads that correspond to the section numbers in the text. This makes it easy for you to omit any parts of the test that cover material you have not taught. Although the focus of the test program is mainly on objective questions, the tests for the composition units include questions that call for writing. Answers for all the questions contained in the Test Program are provided in the answer key at the back of the Test Program.

THE WRITING WORKSHOPS.

Writing Workshops appear at the ends of chapters in the composition units of Prentice Hall Grammar and Composition. For each Writing Workshop in the textbook, an additional Writing Workshop is provided on a blackline master. Using these additional Writing Workshops provides reinforcement and extension of skills.

THE COMPUTERIZED EXERCISE BANK.

A Computerized Exercise Bank which provides three additional exercises—one for less advanced students, one for average students, and one for above-average students—for each of the numbered sections in the Grammar, Usage, and Mechanics Units in the text is also available. The exercises in the Computerized Exercise Bank are stored on a disk that is compatible with Apple IIe and IBM PC computers and presented in an exercise book that accompanies the disk. The Computerized Exercise Bank makes it possible for you to create your own exercises by combining activities from different groups of exercises.

WRITING MODEL TRANSPARENCIES.

The Writing Model transparencies provide you with additional writing activities to reinforce and supplement composition skills taught in Prentice Hall Grammar and Composition. Having these activities on transparencies allows you to work easily with your class in small groups or as a whole and to guide their responses. The transparencies include Springboards for Writing, Paragraph Exercises, Models of most types of longer writing, and Checklists.

Teaching the Program

The Prentice Hall Grammar and Composition program provides you with a comprehensive treatment of grammar, composition, and allied skills. The program includes eight interrelated units: Grammar, Usage, Mechanics, Composition—The Writer's Techniques, Composition—Forms and Process of Writing, Vocabulary and Spelling, Study Skills, and Speaking and Listening Skills. These units work together to help students develop a thorough understanding of how the English language works and to teach them how to use their knowledge of the language to improve their writing and speaking skills.

The Prentice Hall Grammar and Composition program is also quite flexible. The program's flexibility makes it possible for you to consider a variety of options and possible teaching strategies. For example, you may choose to teach the complete course in the order presented in the text. You may, alternatively, choose to use the text in one of several other ways: as a grammar reference book, as a composition text, as a text used in conjunction with a literature text, as a resource book for teaching ideas, and as a handbook for correcting errors in composition.

TEACHING GRAMMAR AND COMPOSITION. Although the order in which the units are presented in the text works quite well for teaching grammar and composition, other orders can easily be followed. You may, for example, find it more useful to begin the year with the units Study and Research Skills and Speaking and Listening Skills. If you do choose to begin with grammar, you may want to start with the chapters on fragments and run-ons, then move into a quick coverage of the parts of speech, followed by a more leisurely progression through the chapters on sentence parts.

Still another popular and easily managed strategy is one that merges work on grammar and usage. For example, the usage chapters on verbs, pronouns, adjectives, and adverbs can be taught along with the corresponding chapters in the grammar unit.

Following any of these strategies, you will still face two basic choices on teaching composition. You may decide to leave all of the composition unit for later in the year, when you can give it your complete attention, or you may want to begin with composition and fit in chapters from Grammar, Usage, and Mechanics.

EMPHASIZING GRAMMAR, USAGE, AND MECHANICS. If your curriculum calls for an emphasis on grammar, you can either use the first few units of the text in the given order or combine or rearrange them in a number of ways. A good general strategy might be to emphasize usage and mechanics, which bear directly on writing, and use the chapters on grammar as a foundation for understanding the prescriptions for correct writing. Because there is a writing activity included in each of the Skills Review and Writing Workshops at the end of each chapter in the Grammar, Usage, and Mechanics Units in the text, your students will have a chance to do some work in composition even if time does not permit much attention to the Composition units in the text.

EMPHASIZING COMPOSITION. The two composition units in the text have been designed to present a thorough coverage of writing skills with emphasis not merely on rules, analysis, and special techniques but also on the way these can be combined with a more thorough understanding of the purposes involved and the steps and methods that can be used to achieve success. For a course that emphasizes composition, text material can be used in the given order, or it can be rearranged or divided in several other ways. For example, you may wish to start with the chapter on paragraphs, rather than with the Writing Process chapter, or you may want to start with the chapters on sentences.

The other units in the text will undoubtedly prove of value when you discover usage and mechanics problems in written work. You may find it important to have your students refer to the last chapter in the grammar unit on avoiding sentence errors. At the same time, you may find that some of the chapters in the Usage and Mechanics units will help your students learn to understand and avoid problems that they may be having in their writing. You may also want to spend some time on the Vocabulary and Spelling unit to help students improve their writing by expanding their vocabularies and learning to avoid spelling errors. Students will also benefit from the coverage of outlining and library skills in the study-skills unit when they undertake longer papers involving research.

TEACHING GRAMMAR AND COMPOSITION WITH LITERATURE. If you are using the text in a course that combines the study of literature and the study of grammar and composition, you may want to place special emphasis on the composition units. Students can learn about literature through the analysis of what good writing should be. They can also express their opinions about literature through writing.

The composition chapters on sentences should prove especially useful in helping students recognize the importance of the way in which authors use words. As the composition chapters increase the students' awareness of literary value, the study of literary models combined with those models already found in the text should expand the students' own ideas of what they can aspire to in their own writing.

Paragraphs, essays, and stories can be studied, not only for well-chosen words and phrases but also for logical organization. Although students will not always find topic sentences, thesis statements, or systematic supporting details, they will certainly find transitions, effective organization, and a general flow of ideas than can help them in their own writing.

TEACHING BASIC SKILLS. If your students have had little training in the basic skills needed to achieve success in English classes or in school in general, you may want to begin with the material on study and test-taking skills. Then, after thorough preteaching, you might select those chapters that deal with the more serious deficiencies you have discovered. The Practice Pages will prove useful for reinforcement.

CORRECTING ERRORS IN COMPOSITION.
If most of your students are above grade level and can already write with relative ease, you will find that the Prentice Hall Grammar and Composition program fits the reference needs of such students admirably. If you plan to use the text primarily as a reference tool, you may want to conduct a short workshop session on the use of a handbook sometime early in the course. Students can be asked to brainstorm for ideas about ways in which they might find a handbook useful—both in correcting mistakes and in developing ideas for compositions.

An Overview—Writing as Process

As teachers of English and language arts and therefore as the professionals who are responsible for teaching young people to write, we can appropriately be concerned about how they best learn this complex language activity. Writing skill is critically important to school success for young people, and it is deemed by society to be of central importance as a basic skill. Therefore, our best efforts, based on the most appropriate theory of learning to write, is the least these young people have a right to expect.

Traditional Theories About How Students Learn to Write

First, let us review some widely held theories of learning to write that both research and practice suggest are insufficient. You will probably recognize these theories in your own school experience, as both student and teacher.

The theory of frequency says that much writing practice—for instance, in journals and diaries—even if unmonitored and uncorrected will result in growth in writing skill. Yet the research shows that growth cannot be substantiated from frequency alone.

The grammatical theory of learning to write hypothesizes that knowledge of structures and the rules for combining them will result in students becoming writers. Neither a half-century of negative research evidence nor much pragmatic negative classroom experience has laid this notion entirely to rest.

Then there is the idea that students learn to write by having their writing corrected by the teacher. Classroom experience says students seem to gain little from the miles of red ink administered by their writing teachers; research fails to find a correlation between teacher correction and improvement in student writing ability.

Finally, some writing programs have been driven by the idea that students learn sentence types and paragraph models and phrase structures (the building blocks, if you will) and then organize them by some sort of plan into a coherent whole. This theory of instruction is found wanting because of its attention more to form than to substance.

Maybe these theories of teaching writing are not so much wrong as too narrow, leaving out too much while paying too much attention to fragments. Viewing writing as a process allows for a broader, more inclusive sense of the writing act as a basis for planning to teach it.

Writing as a Process

Today we think of writing as a complex process that involves the application of a wide range of thinking skills and language abilities. Thinking of the process as a series of steps, we can focus on the techniques and tools writers need, the knowledge they must develop, and the choices they must learn to make at each of these steps. From this understanding of what writers must be able to do, we can begin to devise some instructional strategies, some directed activities to teach appropriate skills and knowledge.

The process theory proposes that writers practice very different skills and undertake very different activities at each of the following three productive stages.

PREWRITING. Writers get warmed up, choose a focus, gather ideas and details, record, and begin to sort out their data, seeing how the data fit together in useful ways. This stage is a time of discovery and of invention. It is rich, productive, and extravagant. There are clearly ways to facilitate these events, ways that students must be taught if they are to achieve success.

WRITING. Writers need to get their ideas recorded in some sort of tentative, first-draft shape as easily and quickly as possible. Fluency with written English is critical to this stage, as is the knowledge of what choices are available to writers and what factors influence their judgment about these options. Therefore, writers must learn how to turn streams of thoughts and ideas into coherent, organized written streams, and they need to have much experience in making the choices and in having their judgments work effectively in the written piece. These tasks are specifically amenable to instruction.

REVISING. From revision that is supported by the positive, informed response of outside readers and by the rethinking and revising by the writers themselves, writers will learn that writing benefits from being scrutinized again (and again) after that first draft. This stage involves revising for sense and editing for word choice and sentence style. Writers need to learn how to review a draft with an eye to revision; they need to learn to be editors. In addition, they need to learn to proofread—to spot errors and make corrections in spelling, capitalization, punctuation, and grammar. These are complicated skills that require much learning and much teaching.

After a student's final draft is turned in, there is still opportunity for teaching and learning to occur. Students may be involved in evaluating their writing and the writing of others by using scoring sheets or rubrics and by emphasizing one of several different methods of scoring.

Finally, writing benefits when the classroom is a place where writing is valued as more than a pointless exercise, where it is honored, put on display, kept in a student file, presented in a classroom book, published.

Choices in Writing

Writing involves making informed choices about content, about organization, about linguistic structure, and about diction. A writer makes these many choices based on the internal logic of the piece and upon the dictates of the assignment. For example, the writer may decide that effective characterization requires the use of dialect, the establishment of a specific point of view, or a detailed description.

But these choices also depend upon external circumstances, such as purpose and intended audience. If persuasion is needed, the writer will use logic and present the best arguments. If the intended reader is markedly unsophisticated, simplicity of vocabulary and structure would be called for.

To develop the ability to make these choices effectively, the teacher must:
- make the range of choices explicit,
- explore the criteria governing choices,
- give student writers much experience in making these choices in specific writing situations, and
- develop a feedback structure so the writers develop a sense of how appropriate their choices have been.

Over the school years, experience and practice in writing can allow students to approach a maximum level of sophistication through experimentation, adjustment, and retrial.

The Writing Process Exemplified

To present the idea of the writing process in a more concrete and personal way, let us lead you through a hypothetical writing activity following the steps in the process.

You, the teacher, note a tendency for your students to overgeneralize, pronouncing the big idea but failing to support it with the rich details of experience. Therefore you decide to provide them an opportunity to practice developing an idea using specific details in a narrative-descriptive context.

You start them out with a model paragraph from Ray Bradbury's "The Sound of Thunder" where Bradbury imaginatively describes the first view of the terrible Tyrannosaurus Rex.

> It came on great, oiled, resilient, striding legs. It towered thirty feet above half of the trees, a great evil god, folding its delicate watchmaker's claws close to its oily, reptilian chest. Each lower leg was a piston, a thousand pounds of white bone, sunk in thick ropes of muscle, sheathed over in a gleam of pebbled skin like the mail of a terrible warrior. Each thigh was a ton of meat, ivory, and steel mesh. And from the great breathing cage of the upper body those two delicate arms dangled out front, arms with hands that might pick up and examine men like toys, while the snake neck coiled. And the head itself, a ton of sculptured stone, lifted easily upon the sky. Its mouth gaped, exposing a fence of teeth like daggers. Its eyes rolled, ostrich eggs, empty of all expression save hunger. It closed its mouth in a death grin. It ran, its pelvic bones crushing aside trees and bushes, its taloned feet clawing damp earth, leaving prints six inches deep wherever it settled its weight. It ran with a gliding ballet step, far too poised and balanced for its ten tons. It moved into a sunlit arena warily, its beautifully reptile hands feeling the air.

You ask the students in class discussion to infer the single effect produced by this paragraph; they identify the overwhelming might of the beast as the single dominant effect. Then you ask them to analyze the organization of the piece. They discover a bottom-to-top arrangement of details and a movement of the creature from far to near. They observe that this organization is significant in developing the single effect.

Then you pose a writing problem that will build on their observations about the model. You ask them to write about a time of great joy in their lives. In their writing they should use specific sensory details and figurative language to build the single effect of joy and organize these details in some clear and appropriate order, for example, chronological and/or spatial order.

First you ask them to brainstorm and list a series of joyful experiences from their own lives. Then you have them select one experience that would be the most appropriate for this particular assignment, the one that best offers specific details that could be definitely organized.

When they have identified their "moments," you ask them to cluster the remembered details. Encourage them to list more than they identified in their first response. Their clustering will likely produce eight or ten details about three or four aspects of the experience.

As the next step in the process, you ask them to design a chart that will produce both a plan of organization and a source of specific vocabulary. They each must determine a principle of organization that will make sense of their particular sets of data. Some might choose chronology, some spatial arrangement, and some a combination. Then they list their details in that order and, in a second column, list concrete and figurative words and terms that can be applied to each detail.

Details (in order)	Word Bank

Next students make decisions about organization and language. In this particular assignment, you might ask students to assume their own voice addressing an audience of peers and interested adults, all of whom are acquaintances or friends. You might ask them to write a narrative-descriptive paragraph that will be placed in a class book entitled "Our Moments of Joy." The book will be shared with classmates, classroom visitors, and parents and friends at open house.

Now the students are ready to begin the first draft, which you may assign as homework or which may be written in class.

On the due date of the first draft, you engage the class in two revision strategies. One is a small-group response to the oral reading by the writer of his or her draft. The discussion, led by the writer, focuses on what the problems were in organizing and writing the draft and is intended to ascertain if there are adequate concrete details to support the single effect of joy, to determine if the pre-selected organizational pattern worked, and to note if the piece was pleasing and successful.

The other revision strategy you choose is a written review by a partner using a critique sheet. On the sheet the partners are asked to identify the most successful details, perhaps classified by the five senses and by figures of speech. They are also asked for identification and response to any details that might damage the unity of the piece. The sheet might also call for comments on the logic of organization and the overall effect.

With these substantive reviews of content and organization in hand, but without any specific attention yet to mechanics or sentence structure, the writers are ready to begin revising their first drafts. Some of them will choose to make revisions on the draft itself; others may choose to produce a second draft. You challenge them to make the next version substantially different from or better than the first attempt. You also encourage them to edit for word choice and sentence structure.

When this revision is complete, you note or collect planning and preliminary drafts and give a process grade to each student that reflects on the thoroughness with which each student carried out the steps in the process.

To obtain a final draft, students rewrite their revised copies in ink or type them carefully and carry out final proofreading. They may move to the computer lab where they enter their texts in the computer. Their lab partners then act as proofreaders while the documents are being entered, or after the text is completed. Both reread the piece for typographical and mechanical errors. When the writers are satisfied that they have a near-perfect copy, they save and print their writing.

Because these final copies are to be placed in a class book, you do not mark any errors. (You might send a student back to the computer if his or her final copy seems too error-ridden or ask for another written or typed draft.) You set the following criteria to determine a letter grade for this project:

• specificity of language
• clear single effect
• adequacy of organization

- appropriateness to rhetorical stance
- correctness of spelling, punctuation, and word choice

The final drafts are assembled into the class book titled "Our Moments of Joy." The writings are arranged alphabetically by writers' names, a table of contents is prepared, and an attractive title page is designed. The book will be read by other members of the class and by visitors and parents. At the end of the year, the class book can be pulled apart and the "moments of joy" returned to their owners.

Let us now review what happened in this hypothetical writing activity. The prewriting phase contained modeling, brainstorming, and clustering, followed by some decision making that included specific activities related to organization and language. Students then began writing a first draft. Following the production of the first draft, post-writing revision included two activities: peer review and individual critiquing. Responding to the advice they received, students then changed the first draft or rewrote it. What followed was the production of a final draft and proofreading. The writing was evaluated and given a grade and finally published by placing in a class book.

The steps followed involved the students deeply in a process in which they had a reasonably good chance of success. It taught them how to make the process useful and operational in their own writing experience.

The Writing Process

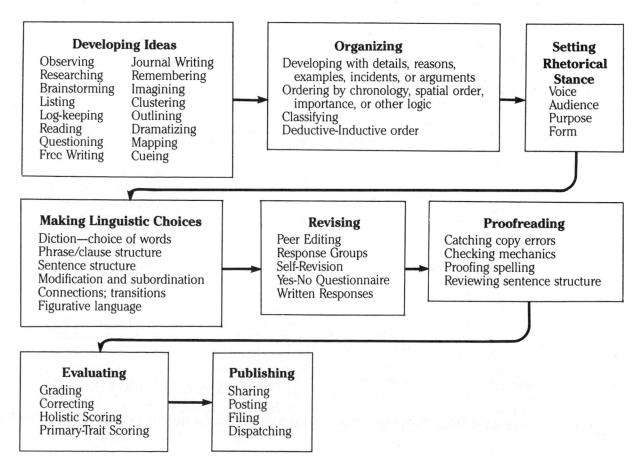

Developing Ideas

Observing	Journal Writing
Researching	Remembering
Brainstorming	Imagining
Listing	Clustering
Log-keeping	Outlining
Reading	Dramatizing
Questioning	Mapping
Free Writing	Cueing

Organizing

Developing with details, reasons, examples, incidents, or arguments
Ordering by chronology, spatial order, importance, or other logic
Classifying
Deductive-Inductive order

Setting Rhetorical Stance

Voice
Audience
Purpose
Form

Making Linguistic Choices

Diction—choice of words
Phrase/clause structure
Sentence structure
Modification and subordination
Connections; transitions
Figurative language

Revising

Peer Editing
Response Groups
Self-Revision
Yes-No Questionnaire
Written Responses

Proofreading

Catching copy errors
Checking mechanics
Proofing spelling
Reviewing sentence structure

Evaluating

Grading
Correcting
Holistic Scoring
Primary-Trait Scoring

Publishing

Sharing
Posting
Filing
Dispatching

The Writing Assignment

When one views the teaching of writing as the teaching of the process, the range of writing tasks must meet one more criterion in addition to those of maturity level, motivation, and appropriateness. A critical issue for the teacher is whether the assignments lead students through the process in a productive way. On the following pages some examples of writing activities are described that seem especially productive in permitting the student writer to utilize the process to move toward a higher quality final draft.

THE PLACE POEM. Students select a place about which they feel strongly and which they know very well. An excerpt from Whitman's *Leaves of Grass* extolling New York City is presented as a model. Students inductively determine that Whitman uses details of physical description, of climate, and of human activity for his content and a free, unrhymed kind of line with a refrain at the end as the poetic element. Students are then asked to cluster to the three content elements for their poem about their place, after which they are directed to try a rough draft of a poem of fourteen or more lines in which they express their sense of the place they have chosen. The teacher may model the revision session by presenting his or her rough draft on an overhead transparency and directing the students to critique the content and the poetic language by asking specific questions. Then student groups perform a similar critique session with classmates' poems, looking for content coverage, detail, sharp images, and personal connection. Final drafts are prepared with illustrations for inclusion in a class anthology. Note the use of a literary model, the clustering that serves an organizational function, the teacher's demonstration of the technique for obtaining revision advice, and the publication of results in a class anthology.

A TALK-WRITE COMPOSITION. After students have read James Thurber's "Snapshot of a Dog," focus their attention on the dog-fight sequence. Ask them to identify the key elements in the sequence of Rex's "attack" upon the other dog. Have them identify those who were witness to the event. Pose for the students certain pairs of characters:

- the streetcar conductor and his supervisor back at the car barn
- a fireman and his buddy at the station
- the owner of the other dog and his wife when he arrives home late for dinner
- the narrator and his father when the boy brings Rex home all wet

As a prewriting activity, have pairs of students role-play the conversations that might occur when a witness to the dog fight, prejudiced about what occurred, reports the event to a person who was not there. Have students discuss accuracy, verisimilitude, completeness, and approach. Then ask students to prepare their own version of the dialogue that might occur when other pairs come together. Revision would start with students reading aloud their dialogues with partners. Next, the group would critique dialogues based on criteria already established. Students would then revise in light of the comments. Publication would consist of dialogues performed for other classes. Note the use of literary stimulus, an oral prewriting activity, the establishment of criteria, and a revision advisory based on an oral presentation.

CREATE A MAGAZINE. This group-writing project asks groups of students to select a topic about which they are all knowledgeable and interested. Then they analyze several popular magazines and identify the "departments" which that publication features, noting the characteristics and style of each. These might include columns, articles, interviews, display ads, letters, reviews, and so forth. They then plan to build their own magazine on the subject they selected, subdividing the work to develop articles that would fit in the various departments. Each student would be responsible for the writing process on his or her particular assignment. Revision would be undertaken when students bring in their material and have their own group critique it. Each one would be responsible for the work of the others, and the grade on the project would apply to every student in the group. Note the use of the magazine as model, the application of process in the development of each article, and the critical role of group help in revision and final presentation.

The Classroom Writing Program

Sound writing practices will vary, depending on the nature of the specific learner, of the teacher, or of the class. How, then, can a selection of practices be crafted into a coherent, sensible program for a given universe of students in a specific school? Below are some principles to guide this selection.

- Writing can serve many functions, well beyond the common assumptions of writing as communication and writing as record. Writing more broadly viewed as an intellectual activity takes on functions of discovery, recall, organization, classification, connection, and evaluation, all important operations.
- Research suggests that neither guided composition on an occasional basis nor frequent unguided writing produces marked growth in writing skill. But experience would strongly argue for the combination of frequent, clearly purposeful, guided writing experience.
- Those who use the writing-process model and who explore appropriate variations on the process in their writing activities will experience its usefulness in all classrooms, with all students, whether students are heterogeneously grouped, ESL, special learners, or gifted. The writing-process model and its associated activities present themselves as vehicles for teaching and learning in classrooms, regardless of differing ranges of student ability.
- Writing is a tremendously complex activity involving the simultaneous application of a whole series of intellectual and physical activities. It is important in the classroom to break these activities into manageable segments so the learner has a chance to handle them successfully in some consecutive fashion (e.g., clustering for ideas, then seeking coherence through some logic of organization, then identifying controlling elements of stance, then drafting paragraphs for peer review, and finally revising in light of valid criticism).
- Students can profitably practice the steps in the writing process (prewriting, writing, and revising) separately, but they also need to experience the entire process on a single writing project in order to develop a sense of how to work from start to finish on a paper on their own. When the activities involving the steps in the process are each undertaken separately, teachers must help students see how each step can be independent but also integral in the production of a final written product.
- Since writing is a holistic act, one which requires the application of a whole range of skills to every writing project, following a recursive model would be appropriate. Such a model would give students

experience with most of what a writer does early on but then periodically would circle back to give the maturing learner another, perhaps more sophisticated, experience with the skill presented earlier.

- Students need to write more than a teacher of classes of 25 to 30 students can possibly evaluate carefully. Some compromise with the practice of thoroughly marking every paper is necessary.
- Although writing is a legitimate homework activity, it would be useful for all elements of the writing process to be undertaken at some time during the class period so the teacher can coach and monitor progress. Real teaching must continue after the assignment is set, through all stages of the process.
- Finally, it is important for teachers to understand and believe that writing can be taught and that students can indeed be "made" into writers by their serious application to thoughtful, appropriate learning activities set for them by well-intentioned teachers operating from well-informed theory.

Learning to write can be a rewarding, if challenging, scholastic adventure for students; teaching writing can offer teachers exhilaration without complete exhaustion. Writing can function productively in people's lives, even when they live in this marvelous age of electronic media and pushbutton magic.

A Creed for Writing Teachers

I believe that:
- Writing is a complex, unitary process that includes much more than the exercise of sub-skills; rather, it involves the application of an orderly step-by-step series of activities that must be learned.
- Writing requires an orderly integration of the random flow of thoughts and feelings.
- Students should write at a level appropriate to age and experience.
- Frequent guided writing experience is critical in a quality program of composition.
- Preparation for the act of writing is a decisive factor in the quality of the results.
- Students can benefit by working from oral to written forms.
- Application of sound grammatical principles is essential to quality writing. These principles are best developed in the context of writing.
- Every writing act benefits from the assumption of a rhetorical stance in which the writer makes

deliberate decisions regarding voice, audience, purpose, and form.

- Writing consists of the initial commitment to paper of a first draft, followed by a series of informed revisions.
- Writing "errors" are more likely to occur at the surface level in the convention of standard written English than in the deep linguistic structures of basic thought.
- Students are capable of intelligent responses to each other's writing; educational value accrues to both the student writer and the reader from these editing experiences.
- Teacher response and evaluation are basic parts of a good composition program.
- Learning to write effectively is a necessary and worthwhile activity for students and should be valued in the English classroom.

Prewriting

Prewriting is the first stage in the writing process. It includes any "experience, activity, or exercise that motivates a person to write, that generates material and ideas for writing, or that focuses a writer's attention on a particular subject. Prewriting stimulates and enlarges thought and moves writers from the stage of thinking about a writing task to the act of writing." *(Handbook for Planning an Effective Writing Program,* California State Department of Education). This stage in the writing process is frequently overlooked, but what writers do at the prewriting stage is likely to be even more important in generating quality than teacher "marking" at the end. In fact, the goal of prewriting is to develop the content and to explore the possibilities in the writing task so fully in the writers' minds (and on the pages in front of them) that the paper will virtually write itself. In the process of doing this planning, writers can discover more material than they need, one idea can lead on to another, details can be captured, and new approaches can emerge. The strategies that follow are designed to prepare the writer to get those words on paper.

Journals/Logs

JOURNALS. A journal is a written record of ideas, thoughts, questions, and impressions that come into a person's mind. Students keep their journals in a special book, which may be used later as resource material for writing assignments. In a journal students are free to develop ideas, speculate on events, plan projects, write poetry, reflect on personal matters, and draw and doodle. Their writing can be about anything they wish to write, or teachers may give a choice of two or three journal "starters." Generally, spelling, grammar, punctuation, and organization are not marked. Teachers merely record that the students wrote in their journal.

Value of Journals

- Preserves a student's experiences and impressions
- Encourages students to develop fluency in recording ideas and feelings
- Helps students discover the value of writing for themselves
- Examines thinking and promotes refining of ideas
- May provide the initial stimulus for a subsequent writing assignment

Journal Starters

1. Describe a favorite toy you had as a child. What made it special?
2. Describe the place where you feel (or have felt) most at home. What makes it a special place for you?
3. Write a list of at least fifty things that make you feel good.
4. Describe the perfect day. Put in as many details as you can. Make it a possible day, not a "dream" day.
5. Describe a "dream" day. How is it different from a possible day?
6. Who is the person from history that you would most like to meet and talk to? Why? What would you like to ask?
7. Who is the person alive today that you would most like to meet and talk to? Why? What would you like to ask?
8. Who is the person from literature that you would most like to meet and talk to? Why? What would you like to ask?
9. Compile a list of words that describe you as a child. Compile a second list that describes you as you are now. How are these lists the same? How are they different?

10. Are you a noun or a verb? Give evidence.
11. Finish this thought: "If I could change one thing about myself, I . . . " (If you can't think of anything, you might consider telling how you got to be perfect!)
12. Write a mini-biography using single words only, no phrases or sentences. (Born. Empty. Birthday. Four. Vague. Birthday. Five. Clearer. House. Pond. Hill. Kindergarten. Rhythm-band. Sand-table. And so on.)
13. Compile a list of inanimate or animate objects to which you might compare yourself metaphorically. (I am a windmill. I change direction or my thoughts whenever someone talks to me.)
14. Describe an animal that you identify with strongly. Why do you have a special feeling about this animal?
15. Tell about what triggers anger in you or in someone else.
16. Make a list of "I used to . . . but now . . ." statements. They need not be in any particular order or on any specific topic, but they should be true. Make another list of "I used to . . . but now . . ." statements. This list should be totally imaginative. Which list was more fun to make? What does this say about you?
17. Write about something that you wanted very much and perhaps worked long and hard for, but were unable to get. What were your feelings then? What are your feelings about it now?
18. Invent a monster and describe it. Tell where it lives, what it eats, and what it does.
19. What is your favorite kind of weather? Why?
20. Describe a time when you really felt fear. What made it a frightening time? How did you feel when it was over? (If you have never been afraid, what might frighten you?)
21. What is the best book you have ever read? Why did you like it? Did reading the book change you in any way? What way?
22. What is the best Halloween costume you have ever heard of? Tell about it and why it is special.
23. Write about what you *didn't* do this weekend.
24. Think of an incident that happened to you and exaggerate it in the telling. Make it into a tall tale.
25. If you were ruler of the world, what things would you banish absolutely for all time (rain on weekends, eggplant, and so forth)? Make a list. Use your imagination.

26. If you could go back in time anywhere and anytime, where/when would you go and why?
27. What law would you like to see enacted that would help people? How would it help?
28. What commercial on TV do you dislike beyond all others? What about it is particularly annoying to you?
29. What is your first vivid memory?
30. Design some gadget, machine, building, or other creation that might enrich future life. What does it look like? What does it do? How does it function? In what ways might it benefit people?
31. What current fashion in clothing do you particularly like or dislike?
32. Convince someone why music or art or computers are important in your life. Make them appreciate your viewpoint.
33. If you had $100,000, how would you spend it?
34. Be a building you know well. Talk about your life and memories.
35. Tell a person from a distant planet or from another era what pollution is. Make that person understand what causes it and why it is bad.
36. If you were one inch tall, what are some of the things you would do that you cannot do now?
37. If you could do something that you've never done before, what would it be? Why would you want to do it?
38. Begin a list of questions that you'd like to have answered. They may be about the future or the past.
39. What do you consider your greatest accomplishment to date and why?
40. Write one characteristic or habit about yourself that you like and describe it. Or write about one thing you don't like about yourself.
41. What is your hobby? Why do you enjoy it?
42. If you could go somewhere you've never gone before, where would you go? Why?
43. List as many reasons as you can for putting humans on the endangered species list.
44. You have been given the power to talk to animals. Which animal would you like to talk to? What questions would you ask?
45. Choose the first word that comes to mind and begin clustering. Where does your mind take you?
46. What, if anything, would you be willing to fight or even die for? Explain your answer.

47. If you could change one thing about the world, what would it be? Why would you make this change?
48. Tell about a dream you have had. If you cannot remember a dream, create one. If you can, try to analyze the dream.
49. What machine do you feel you could not live without? Explain.
50. Write about what you think you will be like and what you will be doing ten or twenty years from now.

LOGS.   A log is a multipurpose prewriting strategy that can be used in any class, where teaching, thinking, and learning take place. Logs focus students' attention on the writing activity to follow and allow students the opportunity to explore concepts in a divergent way prior to writing.

READING LOGS.   After reading (textbook, chapter, piece of literature, news article) students record their responses in expressive writing, jotting down any thoughts or questions related either to the content of the reading or to their own experiences. Logs may then be read aloud or by another student and questions, comparisons, or explanations shared.

LEARNING LOGS.   Especially useful as a prewriting and learning activity is to ask students to divide their paper in half and respond to questions about the learning that occurred in a given period. Example:

What did you learn today?

I learned that an expository essay has to have a clear, easy-to-follow thesis statement if I plan to write a good essay. I also learned that Julie is, surprisingly, a great writer. I really liked her thesis opener. She used a metaphor in it.

What questions do you still have?

Won't always having a three-part thesis statement be boring after a while? Why do I read essays by published writers who don't have a clear thesis statement at the beginning?

Other questions might be: What confused you? How would you use that information? What did you find helpful about the lesson? What was the point of today's discussion? What connections to your life can you make from today's discussion?

Suggestions for Implementing Logs

- Questions, focus, activities can be announced, posted, and/or read prior to the day's work.
- They need not be done every day.
- They generally require only 5 to 10 minutes of class time.
- Entries should not be longer than one-half page.
- Logs should be in a spiral binder or should be stapled sheets, so work can be kept in one place and easy reference can be made for earlier learning.
- They are not graded for mechanics, unless rewritten.
- The teacher may read logs and respond the next day to student comments, summarize logs, or reteach concepts for clarification as needed.
- Information in logs may be used for a more formal writing assignment or an exam.

Brainstorming/Word Bank/ Clustering/Mapping

BRAINSTORMING.   Brainstorming, a common prewriting technique, has students express randomly a variety of ideas, thoughts, opinions, and viewpoints about any given topic, either as an individual or group activity. Anyone may contribute any idea related to the topic; no value judgments, criticism, or alteration of ideas are made during brainstorming sessions. It is from this collection of contributions that the writer later discards and organizes to formulate a paper.

WORD BANK.   Word banks are lists of words. They depend upon listing words or ideas that come to mind about a specific topic and then categorizing the list or developing the categories first and then placing the words and ideas into the categories. The word bank can be a valuable tool for collecting the specific vocabulary useful to a writing activity.

CLUSTERING.   Clustering, a special application of brainstorming, retains the rich development of data or ideas that brainstorming offers while adding an organizational element to the collection. It triggers and focuses ideas as patterns emerge naturally within the cluster. The writers record a topic or concept in the middle of the page; then they gather ideas into clusters around the central concept. The visual character of the spatial "bubbling" of the ideas seems to stimulate the flow of association, and as a result, a large quantity of specific detail can be amassed quickly and used as a basis for an organized paper.

To demonstrate clustering, let's assume that students are asked to write a personal essay on a favorite object. The prompt suggests dealing with the physical description, the means by which it was obtained, and its value. For the student who interprets "object" as "animal" or "pet," clustering to gain the specifics about a pet dog would follow, as shown below.

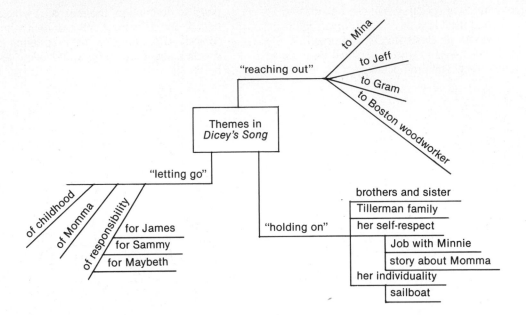

MAPPING. Mapping, similar to clustering, also adds a visual dimension that helps students gain greater control of and fluency in thinking and writing. Students first list words, then organize the words into categories as in a word bank. Next, students arrange these categories and words on a map of their own design. Many configurations may be developed, such as triangles, concentric circles, ladders, and road maps. The controlling topic or idea is placed in a dominant position, and the supporting ideas or words are written as extensions. New ideas often emerge during mapping, and additions and deletions are encouraged.

A student asked to write a short essay on the stated themes in Cynthia Voigt's *Dicey's Song* might produce a mapping activity such as the one above to develop ideas.

Direct Experience

The interview, opinion survey, field trip, and experiment or demonstration are prewriting strategies involving direct experience. Each involves the students in an activity that provides stimulus and information for writing. There are innumerable possibilities for teachers to direct or invent: the blind walk, classroom interviews on the first day of school, a planned field trip to the zoo or a play, demonstrating how to make a peanut butter and jelly sand-

wich, a survey to determine how students, faculty, and parents feel about a closed campus, or cleaning up the trash in the lunch room. Each activity can lead to a follow-up writing assignment.

Oral Activities

Drama, pantomime, debate, improvisation, discussion are all possibilities for motivation and prewriting. Again, teachers can direct or invent opportunities for verbal activities in which students participate or observe, thus providing stimulus for subsequent writing. Students may write about their own feelings as they participated, or about their observations as others communicated, or they may assume the role of someone or something else–a fly on the window, the clock on the wall—and respond from that posture.

Outlining

Traditionally, students have been expected to prepare an outline prior to writing a paper. However, with increased knowledge of the different ways students learn and the awareness of left and right brain functions, it is now acknowledged that clustering, word bank, mapping, and other prewriting activities are also acceptable ways for students to organize thoughts and prepare to write.

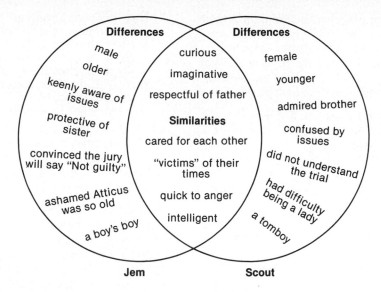

Differences   **Differences**

male

older

keenly aware of
issues

protective of
sister

convinced the jury
will say "Not guilty"

ashamed Atticus
was so old

a boy's boy

curious

imaginative

respectful of father

Similarities

cared for each other

"victims" of their
times

quick to anger

intelligent

female

younger

admired brother

confused by
issues

did not understand
the trial

had difficulty
being a lady

a tomboy

Jem   **Scout**

Venn Diagram

The Venn diagram, illustrated above, assists students in visualizing comparisons and contrasts. The information gathered and written on the diagram provides the basis for clear organization of thought and translation of information to a paper.

For example, a writer may use the Venn diagram to develop the ideas for a piece comparing Jem and Scout Finch, the two principal characters in Harper Lee's *To Kill a Mockingbird*. Very quickly the writer has available the qualities and characteristics they shared as well as some details for at least two addi-

tional paragraphs, one about how Jem was different from Scout and one about Scout's unique qualities.

Data Retrieval Chart

A data retrieval chart is used to collect and record data in a simple and convenient form so that it can be used later for analysis and interpretation. Because the chart allows students to gather the same kinds of information across two or more samples, comparisons and contrasts can be readily made. A limited and condensed sample of a data retrieval chart follows:

Data Retrieval Chart for Characters in *Romeo and Juliet*					
Characters	**Loyalty to Whom**	**Character Qualities**	**Ideas about Love**	**Center of What Conflict**	**Their Fate**
Romeo					
Juliet					
Benvolio					
Tybalt					
Nurse					
Friar L.					

When the data retrieval chart is filled in, it is then possible to ask a series of questions about the data that will help to establish relationships, inference, and meaning and involve students in many levels of thinking. The writing that follows will be organized, precise, and thoughtful. Question examples follow:

INFORMATION: What did you find out?
INTERPRETATION: What do you think this might mean?
COMPARISON: What similarities or differences do you see?
CLASSIFICATION: What items seem to be related to one another? How?
INFERENCE: What can you infer about this?
GENERALIZATION: What might be the reason for this?
What can you conclude from this?
What summary statements might you make?

Writing as Making Choices

Another stage of the writing process involves making choices. After writers have recalled, associated, related, and invented details, they are ready to make decisions about what they will write.

A major function of writing instruction is to teach writers about the choices that their language and the human thinking process make possible, about the criteria that direct the writers to the best decisions about these variables, and about how their decisions will affect the readers of their pieces. Writers gain skill and judgment in making these choices through specific instruction in the ranges of choice and in rich experience in applying them to specific writing situations.

ORGANIZING WRITING. An early problem facing the writer is the ordering of the material. What comes first? second? last? Frequently the prewriting activities have already suggested some grouping of detail; if not, sorting or classifying the data into groups may be a preliminary organizational strategy. Then the question of logical order occurs; usually the nature of the subject suggests an answer. Possible logical orders follow:

Logic of Time. Information is arranged in chronological order or reverse chronology. The *flashback* allows a variation here.

Logic of Space. Details are arranged according to their location, right to left, inside out, top to bottom, near to far (or the reverse).
Logic of Comparison. Data are organized by similar features and by differences.
Logic of Significance. Judgments are made about the importance of ideas, and then these ideas are arranged in ascending or descending order.

Clearly many other logical arrangements are possible. For example, the mystery writer deliberately withholds information. Writers need wide acquaintance with the possibilities for order, as well as some experience in testing them as they write.

STRATEGIC QUESTIONS. Writers might well learn to apply thinking strategies to their writing. For example, they might consider the use of an *inductive* order, where they build a body of facts from which they may draw a conclusion or state a generalization or principle. Or they might find that *deductive* order would be useful, where the generalization is stated first and the supporting details follow as an illustration or application of the principle.

Particularly useful is the application of a set of strategic questions to the potential content of a piece of writing. A simple, four-fold set of questions drawn from research into the thinking process and applied to the pirate episode in Mark Twain's *The Adventures of Tom Sawyer*, follows:

Restatement—a question asking for cognitive recall of the facts
Example: What superstitions did Tom know about?
Convergence—a question utilizing the information to prove a point or support a generalization
Example: Superstitions were significant to Tom's behavior and decisions. What evidence is there to support this statement?
Divergence—a question moving away from the universe of the situation in a possible but unexpected and personal way
Example: What superstitions have directed my behavior?
Evaluation—a question using the information to reach some kind of a value judgment
Example: Was it foolish for Tom to act upon the superstitions he believed?

Let's illustrate the application of strategic questions to a typical school writing assignment. A student has decided to respond to the topic, "My Summer Vacation," by writing about a mountain backpack trip she and her family had taken in the Washington Cascades. As a prewriting activity, she developed clusters on what they did to get ready and on the events of each of the five days. When she applied strategic questions, she came up with the following possibilities:

- What special equipment did this trip require? (restatement)
- What did I discover about myself on this trip? (convergence)
- How is this country like (or unlike) someplace else I have been? (divergent)
- What did I like best about this trip? (evaluative)

These questions (and their answers) will have uncovered for our writer the possibility of highlighting the special equipment of backpackers or of revealing the personal significance of the trip or of comparing this country to other places. She would have a focus for the paper.

MODES OF DISCOURSE.
Identifying modes of discourse through an extension of thinking skills strategies reveals new arenas of organizational choice for the writer. Teaching writing certainly includes acquainting writers with the range of choice in the many modes that exist in society's communication system.

The following modes of discourse, for example, are currently being considered for the direct writing assessment program in California:

Presentational Modes:

dialogue	fables
stories	interior monologues
poems	plays
scripts	song lyrics

Discursive Modes:

Socratic dialogue	autobiographical incident
firsthand biography	autobiographical phase
remembered places	firsthand chronicle
memoir—person or group	memoir—nature
reflective essay	observational record
report of information	summary
definition	description
analysis—causes	analysis—classification
analysis—effects	analysis—compare/contrast
interpretation	problem solution
controversial issue	support of generalization
evaluation	hypothesis

In spite of the length of the list above, it could be well argued that writers should become comfortable with this wide range of modes, to the point where they could wisely choose among the possibilities when approaching a writing task. Presumably such familiarity could best flow from having solved writing problems that required each mode.

ESTABLISHING A RHETORICAL STANCE.
Rhetorical stance is the position writers establish relative to the voice in which they speak, the audience they intend to address, the purpose for which they are writing, and the form in which the writing is most appropriate. In the typical school writing situation, the student writer assumes the *voice* of the uneasy student, addresses an *audience* of teacher and giver of grades, seems to have the *purpose* of getting as good a grade as possible (or alternately, to get the assignment done with a minimum of work), and uses whatever *form* the teacher has asssigned. Not much deliberation there!

What teachers expect is that each writing task would demand of the writer a thoughtful, considered judgment about each of the four elements of stance, which would then provide a basis for all kinds of important decisions about content, tone, organization, and complexity as the writing progresses.

Voice. One might assume that writers use their own voices, and that is that. But each of us fills many roles in real life, and we can imagine ourselves into many others. The eighth grader is a student in Mrs. H.'s class (known there as the genius or the dummy or the clown), she is a tolerant big sister to a rascally little brother, she is an obedient daughter, she is a good and loyal friend, she imagines herself a star ballerina, she is a busy babysitter, she can predict she will be a loving mother, she expects to be a bank executive.

The key questions that allow the writer to establish voice in the written piece follow:

Who am I in this situation?
How do I feel?
What is at stake for me?
How much do I know?
What more do I need to know?
What is my relationship to the situation?

Each writing occasion requires a redefinition of voice for the writer. As voice is defined, the writer will be better able to know what to write and how to write it. The writer of a complaint letter about a faulty product is going to use different vocabulary and a different tone than the writer of a love letter.

To establish a sensitivity to how voice affects writing, students can take on two different roles relative to the same subject matter: critic and supporter of a local election issue; themselves and a character in a story they've read discussing that character's behavior; or two of their inner selves arguing about some serious personal issue (getting bad grades, losing privileges).

Audience. Sensitivity to audience can also make important differences in how a written piece turns out. In considering their audience, writers need to consider

Who are the readers?
How well-informed on this subject are they?
How ready are they to receive this piece?
What help do I need to provide them?
What prejudices will they have?

Audience for any writing activity can be designated as part of the assignment, or it can grow naturally from the writing situation; audience can be real or simulated. Writers need to be deliberate in how they tune their message to their audiences. Writers might be asked to infer "audience" clues in each other's papers; questions about audience should certainly be posed at the revision time.

To develop a sense of audience, teachers might ask students to write variant versions of local events, one for the person who was temporarily absent from the scene and one for the person who knew nothing about it. Or they might be asked to write about the same problem to a person known to be sympathetic and one known to be antagonistic.

Purpose. When writers consider the real purposes of writing, as contrasted with the scholastic purpose of gaining a grade or credit, they soon realize that there are many potential purposes possible: inform-ing, confirming, explaining, recording, confusing, persuading, teasing, learning. And purpose affects the way a piece goes together. A comparative piece focuses on likenesses and differences, while a propaganda piece emphasizes only one side of a set of circumstances. When they choose their purpose, writers assume a responsibility to tailor their presentation to fit the purpose.

Instructional activities to give writers some experience with the variable of purpose include the following:
- Given a local issue known to students, ask them to write about it for two purposes, one to persuade a local official to take a particular stand and one to inform a friend who is away living in another town for the year.
- Use an advertisement for a product. Ask students to rewrite the information, both textual and pictorial, for the purpose of informing consumers objectively about the product.

Form. Writers also have a choice to make about the form in which their writing will be cast. There are a multiplicity of forms in our complicated modern society, and writers need to be able to choose across this wide range, based on what best fits with previous decisions about voice, audience, and purpose. Someone who was seeking a buyer for an old bike might properly select the form of a want ad in the local paper while someone intending to tell a humorous story about an old man for a senior citizens' magazine might choose the anecdote form.

To provide activities to help students become familiar with forms of writing and to aid them in choosing well, we might distribute copies of a wide variety of forms and ask students to report to their classmates about what the form is and how it works. We might give students a news item from the local paper and ask them to convert it first into a story and then into the question and answer for an advice column.

Possible Writing Assignments
Forms

ads	aphorisms	awards	billboards	brochures
advice columns	appendices		biographies	bulletins
allegories	applications	ballads	blurbs	bumperstickers
anecdotes	apologies	beauty tips	books	
announcements	assumptions	bedtime stories	book jackets	calendar quips
anthems	autobiographies	beginnings	book reviews	calorie charts

campaign speeches
cartoons
captions
cereal boxes
certificates
character sketches
children's stories
commercials
community bulletin
confessions
couplets
comparisons
conversation stoppers
comic strips
complaints
constitutions
contracts
conversations
critiques
cumulative stories

dialogue
data sheets
definitions
descriptions
diaries
dictionary
diets
directions
directories
documents
dramas
dream scripts

editorials
epilogues
encyclopedia entries
essays
evaluations
exaggerations
exclamations
explanations

fables
fairy tales
fantasies

films
flyers
folklore
fortunes

game rules
graffiti
good news-bad news
greeting cards
grocery lists
gossip

headlines
horoscopes

imitations of writers
impromptu speeches
insults
interviews
introductions
invitations

job applications
jokes
journals

labels
legends
letters (personal reactions,
   observations, persuasive
   to imaginary people from
   imaginary place)
lies
lists
love notes
lyrics

magazines
memos
memories
metaphors
menus
movie reviews
movie scripts

mysteries
myths

newscasts
newspapers
nursery rhymes

obituaries
opinions

palindromes
pamphlets
parodies
petitions
photo essay
plays
poems
policy papers
post cards
posters
prayers
problems
problem solutions
profiles and portraits
proposals
proverbs
puppet shows
puns

questionnaires
quotations

radio play
ransom notes
recipes
record covers
remedies
reminiscences and
   memoirs
research—a record of
   something learned
resumes
reviews (books, concerts,
   football games, dates,
   etc.)
riddles

satires
self-descriptions
sequels
sketches (notebooks
   jottings, gleanings)
sketches of famous
   people, places, ideas,
   events
slide show script
slogans
society news
songs
speeches
spoofs
sport accounts
stream-of-consciousness
   writing
superstitions

TV guides
TV programs
tall tales
telegrams
thank-you notes
theater programs
tongue twisters
traffic rules
travel folders
travel posters
tributes
trivia

underground newspaper
used car descriptions

want ads
wanted posters
warnings
wills
wise sayings
wishes
weather reports
weather forcasts
words—made up

yellow pages

An Application of Rhetorical Stance.
Demonstrated here is an application of the principle of rhetorical stance to that standard high school English Class assignment, the book report. This variation is probably better saved till near the end of the period of instruction, after students have had some experience both with the variables of rhetorical stance in composition and with understanding literature.

In this special book report, the writer is asked to assume at least two stances toward the book, producing a written piece for each. Possible stances include the following:

> The **researcher**, to produce a one-page fact sheet for a librarians' journal, records on a standard form the full bibliographic data, gives an analysis of the potential audience, and writes several one-sentence "theme" statements, a paragraph-long character sketch of a major character, and a one-paragraph description of one important event from the plot.

> The **psychologist**, to write an article for *Psychology Today*, does a character analysis of one main character, explaining how the character behaves and why the character behaves that way, identifying the most important features of the character's personality and using many specific examples from the book.

> The **film director**, to make a proposal to his producer in a memo, explains his plan for doing a full-length film of this book. His plan includes details of setting, costuming, and casting. Include a sample of the dialogue for one scene to give the producer an idea.

> The **critic**, to write a 300-word review for the book page of the local newspaper, makes a detailed and honest statement about the book, praising its strengths and revealing its weaknesses, using appropriate quotes from the book and making a clear recommendation about the reading of the book by readers the age of the writer.

Writing a First Draft

Once writers have worked through a deliberate prewriting experience, they are ready to write their first draft. Like the sketches of the artist or the rough drawings of the architect, this draft may be tentative, perhaps too rich or too poor in detail, or only partly developed. A goal in writing this draft will be to get it down quickly and easily with a minimum of fretting, expecting that many changes will ensue.

MAKING LINGUISTIC CHOICES. Choosing the right word, the right structure, the right sentence type are clearly major decisions for the writer, decisions that are repeated many, many times per page of writing. As the writer gains knowledge, skill, and experience, these decisions become more and more intuitive and automatic. But for a long time, they require information and thought and deliberate action. It is this kind of help that school English books are particularly well-suited to offer to the student writers, especially as the students need to expand their repertoire of sentence and phrase structures. Writers need to be trained to refer to dictionaries and thesauruses for specific help when they are confronting word-choice problems.

Specificity. A common fault of student writing is the unsupported generalization. Student papers abound in "It was neat" and "She was cool" and "He is gross." It is surely incumbent on the teacher of writing to make clear to students that the generalizing kind of sentence requires the details, the specific words to back it up.

Regular classroom experience in writing that specifies rather than generalizes would be appropriate. As a daily in-class activity, students could be asked to turn generalization sentences into specific paragraphs. Such sentences could include these:

> She acted weird.
> They were too crazy for me.
> It was the best game of the season.

Another possibility is to ask students to add the details to the barest of comparisons: Weekdays are different from Saturdays or junior high is different from high school.

Diction. Students also need to realize that the resources of a rich language like English gives them a great deal of choice in the selection of words. Part of the training of a writer needs to include the determination of the appropriateness of various synonyms, a sense of the shades of difference in meaning of words with similar definitions, and how selection of words helps to establish voice and audience and tone.

While formal exercises will help to establish the general principles here, a rich reading experience and regular reference to the word books—dictionary and thesaurus—will be important in building a real sense of diction.

Sentence Sense.   While sentence variety is stressed to student writers, it would be even better to help students build a sense of how different types of sentences function. Then they could select sentence type on the basis of what means of conveying information was most appropriate for that specific writing situation. For example, let's examine some standard sentence types as to function:

Simple. The sports car moved along the highway.
   Function: statement of the performance of the action

Expanded. The sleek sports car moved smoothly along the busy highway.
   Function: adds sensory detail to basic statement

Exclamatory. See the sports car move erratically along the highway!
   Function: alerts us to the danger the car poses

Interrogative. Is the sports car moving along the highway?
   Function: inquires if that is indeed what is happening

Compound. The sports car moved along the highway, and the highway patrol car followed closely.
   Function: combines two closely related actions

Complex. When the patrol car pulled out after it, the sports car moved more slowly along the highway.
   Function: relates two actions, showing one causing the other

Cumulative. The sports car moved along the highway, its chrome wheels flashing in the sun.
   Function: allows the accumulation of additional detail to support and amplify the initial assertion

The instructional goal here would be to move students along to where they could not only deal with the terminology and definitions but also utilize the appropriate sentence type for a given rhetorical situation.

A persistent problem for the student writer is mastering the unit of meaning called the sentence without leaving out essential sentence elements and creating a *fragment*, stringing sentences together into the monsters known as the *run-on,* or getting words confused and mislocated to the point that the sentence becomes *awkward* and loses its meaning.

A key to improvement here is moving past the definition of sentence problems and their identification to the practical revision of sentence faults. Given the sentence fault

My back yard is forest, deer come in it,

the student should be able to recognize that he or she is looking at a run-on, but the student should also be able to revise the sentence fault in at least one logical way, such as

Deer come into my back yard, which is forest.

He or she should recognize that this revision is preferable to the one that proposes

My back yard is forest. Deer come into it,

but that it may not be better than one that reads

Deer come into my forested back yard.

Improving Sentence Style.   Given the tremendous resources of the language, student writers do not need to be limited to simple sentence structures that fail to show relationships and order. However, given the number of students who are linguistically less mature than we might hope, including those for whom English is a second language, we do need some instructional techniques to help these students add sentence versatility to their writing repertoire. Several techniques that may broaden these students' resources follow.

Sentence Combining.   Students combine a group of source sentences into a single, well-formed English sentence.

Example:
   Source sentences. Bottles lie on every stream bed. Cans lie on every stream bed. They glint among the pebbles. (from Strong, *Sentence Combining*)

Solutions:
   Bottles and cans lie on every stream bed where they glint among the pebbles.
   Glinting among the pebbles, bottles and cans lie on every stream bed.
   Bottles and cans, which glint among the pebbles, lie on every steam bed.
   Bottles and cans lie on every stream bed, glinting among the pebbles.

Once the students' solutions, like those above or different ones, were proposed, then students would evaluate them. Any solutions that failed as grammatically correct sentences would be eliminated; those remaining would be evaluated on the basis of clarity, economy, and expressiveness. The goal would be to identify the best solution.

Sentence Modeling. Ask students to write sentences that are modeled structurally on well-written model sentences taken from literature. The teacher may specify the stubject matter of the sentences.

Example: Write a sentence about a vivid sunset, modeled after

"It blended so perfectly with the sand, driftwood, and seaweed that I might have passed it by." (William O. Douglas, *The Pacific Northwest*)

Possible solution: The alpenglow flared so brilliantly across the snowfields, the aspen grove, and the still surface of the lake that I might have thought it a painting.

Sentences from Starters. Ask students to complete sentences from starters that the teacher provides. These starters can demand predictable structures from the students; teachers need to plan carefully what kinds of structures they want to elicit. For example, a subordinate conjunction (*when, if, while,* etc.) demands a complex sentence. A short, simple sentence followed by a comma calls for the accumulation of detail in a cumulative sentence.

Examples: When . . . . , ...
The baby cried, ...

Framing Patterns. Framing patterns, growing out of the cloze technique in teaching reading, ask students to fill in the substantive words in frames that emphazise the structural elements. Once again this technique leads students to produce the complicated structures possible in English.

Examples:
Detail: Every time I'm out with Sammy, he does things to irritate me. For instance, once he _____. Another time he _____.
Besides he _____.
Frequently, he _____. Then

he _____. Finally
he _____ in spite
of _____.

Comparison: Your Aunt Sally often reminds me of my aunt. Both of them _____.
Also they _____. In addition, _____. Usually they both _____. Again, they _____.
Similary _____.

Cause and Effect: Relentlessly the flood waters rose and at midnight the dam broke.
Instantly, _____. Suddenly, the _____. At the same time, the _____. Immediately, the _____.
Then _____. Here and there _____.
Beyond _____.
Even _____.

Fluency In First-Draft Writing

To this point writing appears to be a deliberate act, the result of many decisions that are thoughtfully and carefully taken, based on sound criteria that are rigorously applied. However, as with many human activities, there is a contradictory consideration. There is the drive for fluency, for the easy, natural, fast flowing of words onto the page, without a lot of reasoning but rather with intuition. An analogy with speech suggests that the tension between the rational and the intuitive is natural. Speech is usually flowing and rapid, but it is clearly governed by rules that are automatically applied; as the speaker moves into more formal situations, the utterances seem to become more controlled.

It would seem reasonable to assume that writing also operates in tension between the poles of the rational and the intuitive. Therefore, it behooves teachers of writing to help their students achieve a fluency with the written language as well as a control over the principles of producing written English. Fluency can be developed by learning experiences. A few of these are described below.

Association chains: Writers free-associate with a starter term, seeing where their associations will take them in a given short length of time. They use single words only.

Stream-of-Thought: Students try to capture all their thoughts during a given time period. Phrases, words, dashes are okay. Neither organization nor mechanical accuracy is an issue.

Timed Writing: The emphasis here is to produce a coherent response, either to a teacher-directed stimulus or to a student-selected topic, in a given amount of time.

Journals: In regular journal sessions, students respond to what is going on in their lives or to stimuli in the classroom. The journal should appropriately include some affective response to events and people.

Revising

Revising—or what happens to student papers after they have generated ideas, made decisions about content, voice, and style, and written their first draft—includes several important stages: The first stage may involve revising content. The second stage, editing, may involve changing order, style, tone, vocabulary, focus, etc. This is followed by proofreading, or correcting mechanical errors of punctuation, spelling, capitalization, and grammar. Then follows evaluating, which means reading the papers, perhaps responding to them and assigning a mark or grade; and finally, publishing, or honoring, the papers by display or publication.

Revision, in terms of its etymological definition and its best application in the writing process, means "seeing again." Revision and rewriting, when properly executed and when regarded as a regular and important part of the process of writing, need not be viewed as a punishment or the price a student has to pay for a draft that is not acceptable the first time. If students incorrectly think of revision only in terms of correcting errors of grammar, punctuation, and spelling, or recopying an assignment neatly in ink, or simply of tidying up the writing to suit the whims of their English teacher, they may not develop a very respectful attitude toward the process. If students don't work at real revision, that is, viewing the whole work, considering elements of organization, style, tone, syntax, or impact, it may be laziness on their part, or it may be that they have not been taught how to revise, how to "see again."

Not all writing has to be revised, however. Impromptu essays, journal entries, logs, and a variety of other writing activities are designed simply to stimulate the flow of words and help students get into the habit of writing. Subjecting every word of these writings to revision would be inappropriate.

Quality revision can be a frustrating part of writing, both to teach and to learn, and unfortunately, many teachers do not appreciate the importance or the excitement of revision. It is not enough to tell students to "revise and resubmit." Rather

- Organize activities that will effectively teach the process of revision.
- Use revision strategies not just to find mistakes, but to show writers what they are doing right.
- Lead students through the problems uncovered in their written work to solutions that improve upon the draft.
- Help them discover which revision activities will solve which problems.
- Support them in applying the skills necessary to engage successfully in revision.

When students understand that increasing their vocabulary, engaging in sentence-combining exercises, and studying point of view, style, and voice can provide them with the tools they need to overcome inaccurate language, awkward syntax, disorganization, and inappropriate tone, they will be experiencing the motivating force and adventure of revision.

PEER EDITING/RESPONSE GROUPS. Student editing/response groups can be the most effective revision technique used in a classroom. When students know their peers will listen to, read, and respond to their writing, they exercise care because they are conscious of an audience whose opinions matter to them. During well-run editing sessions, writers see the effect of their work, sense the impact it could make with revision, and experience what it is like to be in a writer-audience relationship. Benefits accrue to the student-writer as well as to the student-editors. As group members read, edit, diagnose, and help solve the writing problems of others, they are developing similar skills for improving their own writings. They discover how many different ways there are to write well; they develop a critical sense that recognizes the components of good writing. In time, peer editing groups improve the learning environment of the classroom, creating an atmosphere of group inclusion, acceptance, support, reality-testing, collaboration, sharing, and trust.

After some time, peer editing groups can become so well organized and systematized, can provide such positive cooperative learning experiences, that sometimes the students become uncomfortable or embarrassed if the teacher moves to listen in or join their group. The students, having gained a sense of ownership of the process, see the teacher's role as just reading the final drafts and giving grades, not listening to their fumbling first drafts. They rely on their group to ask questions if meaning is unclear, to suggest better arrangement of ideas, to correct spelling and punctuation.

Two initial rules that enhance the revision process and that students should adhere to in editing/response groups follow.

1. Each student reads his or her own paper aloud to the group (no handing of papers to another to be read silently). As students read their own papers aloud, they will hear their own problems in syntax, organization, omissions, incompleteness, etc., and can immediately make changes.
2. The student who has read his or her paper should make the first evaluative response. It will be the natural inclination of the group members to say immediately, "That's good!" or "I liked it" before making suggestions for improvement or asking questions for clarification. However, self-evaluation is important and the writer/reader should respond first with remarks relative to the content or to his or her own feelings about the paper.

The following are suggestions of ways to ensure working and helpful editing/response groups:

- At the beginning of the year, establish trust in the classroom by emphasizing that there is value in each person's ideas, and specify that positive and specific comments and suggestions are more helpful than vague or inappropriate comments. For example, instead of saying "That was good!" a more specific response would be "I really liked your word choice in the conclusion." Instead of "It was too short!" say "It could have been improved if there'd been more information about the accident or a description of the scene."
- As students gain experience as editors/responders, they can be directed within the group to focus on some of the following questions:

1. What words and/or details were really effective?
2. What are the best sentences in the paper? Why?
3. Were there any parts that weren't clear? What needs to be added to make those parts clear?
4. Were there questions you wish the writer had answered?
5. Are more specific details needed to paint a clear picture? If so, where?
6. Would adding sensory impressions improve the paper?
7. Is there a place for figurative language?
8. Does the dialogue sound authentic?
9. Are there places where the addition of dialogue would make the paper more interesting? Where?
10. Should anything be changed to create the impression the writer was trying for? If so, what?
11. Is there anything that is clearly inappropriate in this paper?

- Demonstration of an editing/response session that includes the teacher should be conducted before the entire class so questions can be answered and rules clarified.
- Editing groups should be no more than three to five students. Students may choose their own group, or the teacher may assign students to groups, using whatever criteria seem appropriate for the classroom.
- Responses in the group may be oral, or students may use an editing/scoring sheet that is then attached to the paper for the writer to review and identify items for revision.
- Students may select a paper from their group that they feel best fulfills the assignment; these collected papers may then be read aloud to the class as examples of outstanding papers chosen in each editing group.

Editing groups will soon be running smoothly, efficiently, and effectively as students learn the value and pleasure of peer response to their writing.

WRITTEN REVISION ADVICE. In addition to peer-group editing, students can obtain written advice regarding their first drafts. This advice may be gathered informally in response to the list of criteria, or it may be programmed by use of a formal questionnaire or an editing sheet, an example of which is shown below.

Assignment: Write a Short Story.

_____
Writer of Story

_____
Editor (your name)

_____
Title of Story

	Yes	No	Somewhat
1. **Introduction:** Was striking and made me want to read on.			
2. **Characters:** Writing led me to have some feeling (sympathy, disgust, pity) about the characters.			
Writing gave sufficient information about the characters.			
What the characters said or did was consistent with the description.			
3. **Setting:** Where and when the events take place was clear.			
4. **Style:** Writing style was interesting and consistent.			
Foreshadowing was evident.			
There were striking expressions, similes, metaphors.			
5. **Plot:** The plot made sense sequentially.			
Conflict was intense, immediate, and clear.			
6. **Tone:** Tone in the writing was consistent with the plot and characters.			

The advisor will usually be the writer's classmates or the teacher, but on some occasions, the writer's parents, adult friends, or older family members may contribute. Students should be encouraged to seek advice widely. In any case, the purpose of revision needs to be made clear, and the advisor should be directed to view the job as looking primarily at content, detail, organization, and emphasis, and secondarily, at spelling, punctuation, and grammar.

It is useful to have the written record of this advice so the writer has it available for reference and also so the teacher can monitor how the student is responding to the advice.

SELF-REVISION. Students read aloud their own writing, listening carefully for any awkwardness, unclear or flawed meanings, or imprecise interpretations, at the same time watching for any mechanical deficiencies. They may respond on a critique sheet, usually looking for some specific items to assist them in revision, self-evaluation, and analysis.

Sample Self-Revision Sheet

Read your own paper. Then follow the directions.
A. Count the number of sentences on your paper. Record here _____.
B. List the first word in the first ten sentences.
   1.   6.
   2.   7.
   3.   8.
   4.   9.
   5.   10.
C. If you find that you repeated the same first word too many times, please make changes.
D. List the verbs in each of the first ten sentences.
   1.   6.
   2.   7.
   3.   8.
   4.   9.
   5.   10.
E. Could you substitute more active verbs? If so, do so.

YES-NO QUESTIONNAIRE. In a writing activity, the criteria, for both content and form, can be converted into a series of yes-no questions that even unsophisticated students can successfully answer about a fellow student's paper. The questions need to be worded so a "yes" answer reflects a satisfactory accommodation to the criterion. A negative answer marks a point where revision is necessary. The challenge to the writer in this strategy is to revise the paper to turn every no into a yes.

Yes-No Questionnaire

Read the story "The Kite" by Barnabas Ramon-Fortune and write a literary summary. Then respond to other students' papers on the basis of these questions.

_____ 1. Does the paragraph indicate the story took place on an island in the West Indies in recent times?

_____ 2. Does it indicate that Philip, the main character, is a young boy?

_____ 3. Does it indicate that the plot climax is Philip's destruction of the Dragon Kite?

_____ 4. Does it indicate the importance of Philip's father's encouraging him?

_____ 5. Does the paragraph refer to the special Ramdeen Kites that cost money?

_____ 6. Does it suggest that Philip lost several kites to the Dragon?

_____ 7. Does it indicate that a theme in the story is staying and fighting?

_____ 8. Does it suggest that the story is told in third person, focusing on the major character, Philip?

_____ 9. Does the paragraph include the title of the story?

_____ 10. Does the writer put the title in quotation marks?

DICTATION EXERCISE. A variation on the Yes–No Questionnaire is the Dictation Exercise, extremely useful in teaching student revision of mechanics. The teacher identifies two or three typical or repeated problem sentences from student papers and dictates them. The aim is for students to write them as dictated without any errors. Following the dictation, students number their papers for answers of yes or no to questions the teacher poses. An example of a typical dictation sentence and questions follows:

DICTATION: My mother, a writer of Spanish novels, exercises every day.

QUESTIONS: 1. Did you use a small letter "m" for mother, as it is a noun and not a title of address?

2. Did you surround the appositive "a writer of Spanish novels" with commas?

3. Did you capitalize Spanish, as it is considered a proper noun derived from the proper noun Spain?

4. Did you have _exercise_ correctly spelled e x e r c i s e?

5. Did you write _every day_ as two words indicating the noun "day" and its modifier "every"?

With a show of hands, students indicate how many yes answers they had. Then their goal is to make their sentences mechanically perfect. (It may be necessary to repeat the questions.) Papers are handed in and, generally, they are not graded on how many correct yes–no questions they answered originally, but rather on the accuracy of any revisions they needed to accomplish.

This revision activity fosters self-correction, provides immediate feedback, allows for exploration of the rules, and is easy to grade.

Proofreading

Proofreading is the job of cleaning up the paper, eliminating surface errors. Some writing teachers have taught that proofreading (looking for errors) _is_ revision, thus leaving students with the impression that learning to be a good writer is learning to avoid errors or correct them. The student then gets the faulty idea that a paper free from technical errors is a perfect paper, deserving an _A_.

Therefore, it is often advisable to allow a few minutes in class before final drafts are due for last-minute proofreading. Students may also utilize a few minutes to write a note telling the changes they made from the first to the final draft. When final drafts are turned in, the first draft(s) are stapled beneath the final copy. The teacher will be able to assess/grade the final draft, review and question the process the students used in revision, and comment positively on the improvements made from first to final draft.

Evaluation

If students have done a good job of utilizing the process of writing—using prewriting as a generating and organizing force, writing first drafts where ideas flow and fluency emerges, and revising for clarity, purpose, or emphasis—the task of evaluating/

grading/scoring/marking/correcting their papers will not be a heavy load. Papers will be turned in showing evidence of thoughtfulness, style, organization, sense of audience and purpose, and will be relatively free of mechanical errors. Many opportunities will be found for positive comments on the papers, and assigning a grade will be a pleasure and not a grind.

There is a distinction between evaluating, grading, and correcting.

Grading is the act of assigning a letter or number to represent the performance of the writer. However, a grade generally tells the student little about the specific strengths or weaknesses of the written work.
Correcting involves pointing out the student's mistakes; if done by the teacher with no further response from the student, it is probably a useless activity as it is not the teacher who needs experience in correcting mistakes; it is the student who needs to learn how to improve his or her own writing.
Evaluation may include grading and correcting, but it also implies an ongoing process designed to help students be aware of their strengths and their weaknesses.

Before evaluating students' written compositions, teachers should make known to the students the specific criteria by which the writing will be evaluated. For one assignment, content may be the specific objective; for another, emphasis may be placed on organization and diction. Evaluation should get to the heart of the writing, to its content and expression, and not exclusively to the conventions of punctuation, grammar, and spelling.

Involving students in the evaluation process is a way to accomplish the goals of evaluation. It can offer a satisfying learning environment and be an authentic avenue to their active participation in yet another facet of the learning process.

HOLISTIC SCORING. Holistic scoring is based on the idea that the whole composition is greater than the sum of its components, that no components may be judged apart from the whole, and all components should be judged simultaneously. Holistic scoring involves reading and scoring a paper based on the total effect of the first impression. It may be that clarity, forcefulness of expression, and originality will outweigh errors in punctuation, spelling, and grammar to create a positive impression. Or, it may

be that errors in syntax and mechanics may predominate to the point of obscuring the meaning and producing a negative impression of the paper.

Holistic scoring can be easily and profitably adapted to the classroom. In the procedure, students first write to the topic. Second, they help build a scoring guide with teacher advice and assistance. Third, students read the papers and score them. When sufficient time has elasped so that each student has read several papers, class time can valuably be used to discuss their observations about the papers: relevance to the topic, clarity of expression, diction, organization. As a result, students become increasingly aware of what makes good writing and they benefit from reading and scoring other students' papers, profiting from reading both the superior paper and the poor paper.

Sample Scoring Guide

4   clear, concise sentences
varied sentence structure
uses descriptive details
correct mechanics and paragraphing
special flair (uses imagination)
superior diction (effective word choice)
effective use of transition
writes to topic
well-organized

3   writes to topic
some transitions
mechanical problems do not interfere
clear, concise sentences
uses some details or imagination
adequate organization
appropriate paragraphing

2   lacks organization
partial development of topic
does not always use complete sentences
mechanical errors may interfere
faulty paragraphing

1   little or no organization
short and underdeveloped
many mechanical problems
wanders from topic

0   inappropriate
illegible
off topic
blank page

PRIMARY TRAIT SCORING is a way to score student writings by focusing only on one specific criterion related to the purpose of the writing. Decide what is the goal for a specific assignment, determine the various degrees of achieving the goal, and create a scoring guide. For instance, if the students are assigned a paper to argue for one side of a controversial issue and to defend it with at least four supporting reasons, the grading scale might look like this.

Excellent paper—defines a position and systematically defends it with at least four reasons that are logically and convincingly presented.

Good paper—defines a position and defends it with four reasons.

Weak paper—does not define a position nor defend it with reasons.

Average paper—defines a position but does not offer four points in support.

Additional traits, called Secondary and Tertiary Traits, which contribute to the success of a paper (organization, mechanics, etc.) may also be included in the evaluation so long as they are clearly defined. Scores may be weighted to show the relative importance of various traits and then totaled to indicate the overall quality of the paper. An example follows.

Scoring Guide
Halloween Mood Writing

PRIMARY TRAIT—MOOD

Excellent Vivid, specific words work together to make Halloween come alive and make the piece convincing. (20 points)

Good A Halloween mood is created with some vivid details so the reader has a sense of being there. (17 points)

Average The Halloween theme is present with many appropriate words but lacks vividness. (15 points)

Weak Some Halloween words are used to show that the author attempted to create a mood. (13 points)

SECONDARY TRAIT—ORGANIZATION

Excellent All the ideas are organized so one total impression of realism is created. (10 points)

Good Most of the ideas are organized for a specific mood. (8 points)

Average Paper has some organization to help create a mood. (7 points)

Weak Ideas are presented but in random order. (6 points)

TERTIARY TRAIT—MECHANICS

Excellent Errors in grammer, spelling, and punctuation are almost nonexistent. (5 points)

Good Paper has errors in grammar, spelling, or punctuation, but they do not hinder the mood created. (4 points)

Average Paper is difficult to understand at times because of errors in grammar, spelling, or punctuation. (3 points)

Weak Paper does not make sense because of errors in grammar, spelling, or punctuation. (2 points)

RESPONSE SHEETS are easily adapted for use in either the evaluation or revision stage and can be used by students or teacher. Pointing out the strengths and weaknesses of the papers is of extreme value to the student writers. It is important to designate what criteria were assessed or evaluated in the piece of writing. If students assist in designing the sheets, they have a clearer idea of the expectations of the assignment.

Assignment: The teacher leads the students in an imaginative journey. For example: "You are in a forest. What are the sounds you hear? What do you smell? Write about the forest."

_____

Author

_____

Editor (your name)

A. I thought the following section was the very best and written in the most interesting style:

_____ description of forest

_____ description of cup

_____ description of key

_____ description of house and body of water

_____ other _____

_____

_____

_____

B. I noted the following areas need improvement:
_____ spelling
_____ punctuation
_____ sentence variety
_____ consistency of tense
_____ descriptive details
_____ other _____
_____ no problems

C. An *example* of one noteworthy phrase or sentence:

_____

D. An *example* of one problem needing improvement (if any):

_____

E. I would award this paper _____

**** superior
 *** excellent
  ** good
   * poor

Publishing Student Writing

A final step in the writing process is to give credibility and value to the act of writing and to its product. Although honoring student writing can be done quite simply, it seems to be overlooked in many classrooms. It really means to demonstrate to the student that the written piece (and indirectly its author) is valued by other people. Several quick and easy means to accomplish the end of honoring the writers and their accomplishments are available to us.

Classroom management of final drafts can serve as a positive statement about the value of the writing activity. Have students read as many final drafts as they can in a given time period. Each student keeps a record of the papers read and some notable feature about each. Such an activity can make for a very interesting class period, and it also tells the writers that their pieces were important when they are appreciated by their classmates. The following form offers a management tool.

Rating: **** outstanding
 *** excellent
  ** good
   * poor

Name _____

Author	Something Memorable	Rating

The most outstanding paper I read today was by _____ for this (these) reason(s): _____
_____
_____
_____
_____
_____
_____

Maintaining an ongoing class writing file for each student is a way for the teacher to say that the written composition is important. The writing folder in a classroom file also offers fringe benefits of allowing the tracking of student progress or problems and of positive public relations with the families of the students. It also allows students to return to work in progress.

Classroom writing is too often viewed by students as exercise only; it is not seen as real. When the teacher can pose a writing opportunity with a real audience, with a real chance for response, writing immediately becomes more valuable in the eyes of the students.

There are many opportunities for "real" writing. A few of them are listed below, and the alert teacher can multiply this list several times over:

> fan letter
> public opinion letter
> letter to editor
> class correspondence
> school communications
> progress report to parents
> letter of inqury
> letter of appreciation
> pen pals

There is also the opportunity of publishing student writing—in the sense of making writing public. Publishing can range from a simple posting on a bulletin board or window wall to entering national competitions for publication in periodicals that reach a nationwide audience of readers and for prize money. Many teachers have success with classroom "publishing" in which they assemble student work into class anthologies. Schoolwide publications—newspapers, yearbooks, literary magazines—are an obvious next step.

The goal in all these ways to honor student writing is to help the students believe that they really do have something worthwhile to say and that they do possess the writing skills and resources to convey that meaningful message in an acceptable, even appreciated way. There is real power in the positive approach!

Jackie Proett
Kent Gill

Much of the information in "An Overview—Writing As Process" (pages 10–36) was adapted from the authors' work How to Succeed in Teaching Writing: A Handbook for Teachers *by Jackie Proett and Kent Gill, University of California, Davis, © 1984, published by NCTE.*

Bibliography

All About Letters. Urbana, IL: National Council of Teachers of English and the United States Postal Service, 1982.

Anderson, Philip M., ed. *Integrating Reading, Writing, and Thinking.* Urbana, IL: National Council of Teachers of English, 1983.

Armstrong, William B. *Study Tips.* Woodbury, NY: Barron's Educational Series, 1983.

Baker, Sheridan. *The Practical Stylist,* 3rd ed. New York: Crowell, 1973.

Barzun, Jacques. *Simple & Direct: A Rhetoric for Writers.* New York: Harper & Row, 1975.

Bates, Jefferson D. *Writing With Precision.* Washington, D.C.: Acropolis Books, 1983.

Buys, William E. and Copeland, James M. *Non-Competitive Speech Activities.* Lincolnwood, IL: National Textbook Company, 1985.

Copperud, R.H. *Webster's Dictionary of Usage and Style.* New York: Avenal Books, 1982.

Creative Word Processing in the Classroom Newsletter. P.O. Box 590727, San Francisco, CA 94159.

Dale, Edgar and O'Rourke, Joseph. *Living Word Vocabulary: A 43,000 Word Vocabulary Inventory.* Elgin, IL: Dome Press, 1979.

Devine, Thomas. *Teaching Study Skills.* Boston: Allyn & Bacon, 1981.

Follett, Wilson. *Modern American Usage.* New York: Hill and Wang, 1966.

Graves, Richard. *Rhetoric and Composition: A Sourcebook for Teachers and Writers.* Upper Montclair, NJ: Boynton Cook, 1984.

Lindemann, Erika. *A Rhetoric for Writing Teachers.* New York: Oxford University Press, 1982.

Memering, Dean and O'Hare, Frank. *The Writer's Work.* Englewood Cliffs, NJ: Prentice-Hall, 1980.

Miller, Walter James and Cluley, Elizabeth Morse. *How to Write Book Reports.* New York: Arco, 1984.

Murray, Donald. *Write to Learn.* New York: Holt, Rinehart and Winston, 1984.

Strong, William. *Practicing Sentence Options.* New York: Random House, 1984.

Strunk, William, Jr. and White, E.B. *Elements of Style.* New York: Macmillan, 1978.

Weidenborner, Stephen and Caruso, Domenick. *Writing Research Papers.* New York: St. Martin's Press, 1982.

Wresch, William, ed. *The Computer in Composition Instruction.* Urbana, IL: National Council of Teachers of English, 1984.

Student Edition

Prentice Hall

GRAMMAR AND COMPOSITION

SERIES CONSULTANTS

Grade 6
Joleen Johnson
Curriculum Writer, Office of
Secondary Instruction
San Bernardino City Unified Schools
San Bernardino, California

Grade 7
Ellen G. Manhire
English Consultant Coordinator
Fresno, California

Grade 8
Elizabeth A. Nace
Supervisor, Language Arts
Akron, Ohio

Grade 9
Jerry Reynolds
Supervisor, Language Arts
Rochester, Minnesota

Grade 10
Marlene Corbett
Chairperson, Department of English
Charlotte, North Carolina

Grade 11
Gilbert Hunt
Chairperson, Department of English
Manchester, Connecticut

Grade 12
Margherite LaPota
Curriculum Specialist
Tulsa, Oklahoma

CRITIC READERS

Sheila Bridges
J.L. Wilkinson Middle School
Middleburg, FL

John Elias
Wilkes-Barre Area School District
Wilkes-Barre, PA

Linda Fiddler
Pulaski County Schools
Little Rock, AR

Beverly J. Follendorf
Sweetwater Union High School
San Diego, CA

Jeri B. Jackson
Mt. Gap Middle School
Huntsville, AL

Druscilla L. Jones
Fayette County Public Schools
Lexington, KY

Wilbert J. Lindwall
San Diego City Schools
San Diego, CA

George Comer
Gary Public Schools
Gary, IN

Gloria A. Peirsol-Marino
Lockhart Junior High School
Orlando, FL

Starlyn M. Norman
Howard Junior High School
Orlando, FL

Dora H. Patterson
Meadowbrook Junior High School
Orlando, FL

Margaret A. Reed
Minneapolis Public Schools
Minneapolis, MN

Kathleen A. Sherman
Carroll High School
Fort Wayne, IN

Annette R. Van Dusen
Oklahoma City Public Schools
Oklahoma City, OK

Mary Ann Weathers
Shelby City Schools
Shelby, NC

Prentice Hall
GRAMMAR AND COMPOSITION

SERIES AUTHORS

Gary Forlini **Senior Author**
Pelham High School, Pelham, New York

Mary Beth Bauer Harris County Department of Education,
Houston, Texas

Lawrence Biener Locust Valley Junior-Senior High School,
Locust Valley, New York

Linda Capo Pelham Junior High School,
Pelham, New York

Karen Moore Kenyon Saratoga High School,
Saratoga, California

Darla H. Shaw Ridgefield School System,
Ridgefield, Connecticut

Zenobia Verner University of Houston,
Houston, Texas

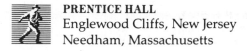
PRENTICE HALL
Englewood Cliffs, New Jersey
Needham, Massachusetts

SUPPLEMENTARY MATERIALS

Annotated Teacher's Edition

Teacher's Resource Book

Computer Exercise Bank

Writing Model Transparencies

Acknowledgments: page 783
Cover art: courtesy of Myron Grossman

PRENTICE HALL **Grammar and Composition**

Fourth Edition

ISBN 0-13-711839-2

10 9 8 7 6 5 4 3 2

PRENTICE HALL
A Division of Simon & Schuster
Englewood Cliffs, New Jersey 07632

Contents

Grammar   Usage   Mechanics

5

Composition and Allied Skills

IV Composition–The Writer's Techniques

16

18

UNIT I

Grammar

UNIT I
Grammar
(pp. 19–192)

This unit will help students explore and analyze both the eight parts of speech and the structure of sentences. The objectives of each section are detailed in the following pages. In the text itself, each objective is covered by a short subsection of explanatory text, followed by one or more sets of exercises. This arrangement will give the students a chance to test their understanding immediately.

Chapters 1–6 examine the parts of speech in a logical sequence: Nouns, pronouns, and verbs are covered first, followed by modifiers, prepositions, conjunctions, and interjections. The students in most classes will already be familiar with much of this material. They will then have a chance to review earlier work while concentrating on the more technical aspects of recognition and identification.

Chapters 7–10 examine the basic parts of sentences, the ways in which sentences can be expanded through the use of phrases and clauses, and the ways in which sentence errors can be corrected. Chapters 7, 8, and 9 end with sections on diagraming. Although the diagraming sections are optional, most students are likely to enjoy this activity. You may also find that diagraming helps many students see more clearly the relationships among the various sentence parts.

CHAPTER 1
Nouns and Pronouns

(pp. 19–37)

Section 1.1 discusses nouns, Section 1.2 deals with personal pronouns, and Section 1.3 considers demonstrative, relative, interrogative, and indefinite pronouns.

For a review of the entire chapter and a related writing activity, see the Skills Review and Writing Workshop on page 37.

1.1 Nouns

(pp. 20–25)

OBJECTIVES

After completing this section, students should be able to

- Identify nouns as the names of people, places, or things.
- Identify collective nouns.
- Identify compound nouns.
- Distinguish between common and proper nouns.

Chapter **1**

Nouns and Pronouns

Have you ever watched anyone build a stone wall? Building a sentence is a little like building a stone wall.

Words, like stones, must be chosen carefully and fitted together to make a sentence. The more you know about words, the easier it will be for you to do this.

One good way to begin learning about words is to look at the eight kinds of words in English, known as the *parts of speech*. The eight parts of speech are *nouns, pronouns, verbs, adjectives, adverbs, prepositions, conjunctions*, and *interjections*.

1.1 Nouns

Nouns are naming words. Nouns help people identify what they are talking or thinking about. *Grandfather, ice cream, loyalty*, and *Ohio* are all nouns.

A noun is the name of a person, place, or thing.

People, Places, and Things

Study the list of nouns in the chart. You may be surprised to find that some of these words are nouns.

1.1 Nouns

People	
farmer	Mrs. Wilson
Bostonians	pilot

Places

Chicago	waiting room
theater	Madison Square Garden

Things

Living and Nonliving Things That You Can See

flowers	ballpoint pen
goldfish	skyscraper
elephant	poem

Ideas and Things That You Cannot Usually See

success	revolution
happiness	fairness
anger	health

EXERCISE A: Classifying Nouns. All the words in the following list are nouns. Make three columns and label them as shown. Then place each word in the correct column.

EXAMPLE: <u>People</u> <u>Places</u> <u>Things</u>
                                         carrot

1. teacher people
2. grizzly bear things
3. sadness things
4. city places
5. basketball things
6. uprising things
7. Frank people
8. ranch places
9. heroism things
10. newspaper things
11. Maine places
12. fable things
13. flower things
14. justice things
15. countryside places
16. Mary Stuart people
17. vegetables things
18. silliness things
19. Atlantic Ocean places
20. truth things

TEACHING

Getting Started

Draw the following grid on the board. Elicit from students nouns that fit each of the categories, beginning with each of the letters at the left. Help students fill in any open boxes in the grid. For example, *T*ennessee River, *I*ceberg lettuce, *M*ercury, *E*instein, *s*eesaw.

	Rivers	Vegetables	Cars	Famous Last Names	Toys
T					
I					
M					
E					
S					

Use the grid to discuss the fact that nouns name people, places, and things.

Text Follow Through

Discuss text pages 20–25.

Assign Exercise A, page 21; Exercise B, page 22; Exercise C, page 23; Exercise D, page 24; Exercise E, page 24; and Developing Writing Skills, page 25.

Less advanced If students are having difficulty, begin the Developing Writing Skills activity, page 25, as a class activity. Have the class generate two or three examples for each item. Then have the students write sentences individually.

Average You might want to have each student bring a short newspaper clipping to class. Students can underline all the nouns in each clipping, list them on a piece of paper, and classify them according to the different categories presented in the section (common, proper, collective, or compound).

Advanced Using the model in Getting Started, have students construct their own grids to choose some categories that require common nouns and some that demand proper nouns. Set a ten-minute time limit for the completion of each grid and have students compare their answers when they are finished. Score 5 for each unique answer, 3 for each shared answer, and 0 for each blank.

Additional Practice

Practice Pages or Practice Book, pages 5–7

Less advanced Exercise Bank, Exercises A and B, pages 7–10

Average Exercise Bank, Exercises A, B, and C, pages 7–10

Advanced Exercise Bank, Exercises B and C, pages 7–10

TESTING

Test Program

Unit Pretest, page 5
Chapter Test, pages 13, 14
Unit Post-Test, page 33

RE-TEACHING

Practice Pages or Practice Book, pages 5–7

Collective Nouns

Certain nouns name groups of people or things. For example, a *jury* is a group of people; a *herd* is a group of animals. These nouns are called *collective nouns.*

A collective noun is a noun that names a group of individual people or things.

Following are some examples of collective nouns.

COLLECTIVE NOUNS		
team	committee	group
class	crowd	audience

EXERCISE B: Recognizing Collective Nouns. On your paper list the twenty nouns from the following sentences. Circle the five that are collective nouns.

Collective nouns are shaded.

EXAMPLE: Marie shocked the audience with her final words.

Marie (audience) words

1. A panel of scientists debated the probability of life on other planets.
2. An outlandish sketch of an imaginary Martian amused the audience.
3. The performance of the team improved tremendously after the speech given by the coach.
4. Pickett led his brigade in a daring charge at Gettysburg.
5. William Shakespeare wrote his plays for one particular company of actors.

Compound Nouns

You have probably used the words *soft* and *drink* separately many times. When both words are used together, however, they form a single noun that has a special meaning, as in "She drank a *soft drink.*"

THINKING SKILLS

Comprehension—*Explaining* whether a noun names a person, place, or thing (Exercise A, page 21)
Distinguishing collective nouns (Exercise B, page 22)
Distinguishing compound nouns (Exercise C, page 23)
Distinguishing between common and proper nouns (Exercises D and E, page 24)

Synthesis—*Composing* sentences with a variety of types of nouns (Developing Writing Skills, page 25)

1.1 Nouns

A compound noun is a noun made up of two or more words.

Compound nouns are usually written in one of three ways.

TYPES OF COMPOUND NOUNS		
Separate Words	**Hyphenated Words**	**Combined Words**
high school	cure-all	congresswoman
chief justice	cha-cha	framework
Empire State Building	mother-in-law	classroom

Check a dictionary for the spelling of unfamiliar compound nouns. If a word is not listed in the dictionary, spell it as separate words.

EXERCISE C: Recognizing Compound Nouns. The following paragraph has a total of ten compound nouns. Copy the paragraph onto your paper and underline each compound noun.

EXAMPLE: There is no way their <u>high school</u> can beat ours this year.

   (1) Yesterday in <u>homeroom</u>, Bob and I discussed sports in our <u>junior high school</u>. (2) We both agreed that our victory in <u>volleyball</u> was the <u>highlight</u> of the year. (3) Bob said he couldn't wait to go to <u>high school</u>, where we will be able to play <u>basketball</u>, <u>water polo</u>, and <u>baseball</u>. (4) I myself would like to be a <u>linebacker</u> playing <u>football</u>.

Common and Proper Nouns

All nouns can be divided into two large groups: *common nouns* and *proper nouns.*

A common noun names any one of a class of people, places, or things.

A proper noun names a specific person, place, or thing.

Common nouns are not capitalized. Proper nouns are always capitalized.

Common Nouns	Proper Nouns
author	Washington Irving
village	Tarrytown
story	"Rikki-tikki-tavi"

EXERCISE D: Identifying Common and Proper Nouns. Copy the following nouns. Place a *C* after each common noun and a *P* after each proper noun. Write a proper noun that gives an example of each common noun. Then, write a common noun that gives an example of a class to which each proper noun belongs.

Illustrations will vary; samples are given.

EXAMPLE: Mars

       Mars P planet

1. writer C—Kurt Vonnegut
2. Chicago P—city
3. Zeus P—god
4. river C—Amazon
5. street C—High Street
6. Louisa May Alcott
7. Jamaica P—country
8. horse C—Secretariat
9. automobile C—Ford
10. Blondie
11. state C—Maine
12. singer C—Elvis
13. Rockies P—mountains
14. relative C—Aunt Jo
15. team C—Dodgers
16. Washington P—state
17. book
18. ocean
19. May P—month
20. actress

6. P—writer 10. P—comic strip 17. C—Quo Vadis 18. C—Atlantic 20. C—Mary Tyler Moore

EXERCISE E: Distinguishing Between Common and Proper Nouns. Each of the following items contains three nouns, one of which is a proper noun that has not been capitalized. Write each proper noun correctly with capitals.

EXAMPLE: lion   leo   kitten

Leo

1. car   convertible   <u>oldsmobile</u> Oldsmobile
2. state   district   <u>dade county</u> Dade County
3. <u>lake erie</u>   ocean   river Lake Erie
4. magazine   <u>bible</u>   pamphlet Bible
5. nation   <u>ghana</u>   country Ghana
6. singer   songwriter   <u>john lennon</u> John Lennon
7. <u>aunt sally</u>   relative   woman Aunt Sally
8. character   <u>tom sawyer</u>   boy Tom Sawyer
9. cartoon   movie   <u>bambi</u> Bambi
10. poet   writer   <u>emily dickinson</u> Emily Dickinson

DEVELOPING WRITING SKILLS: Writing Sentences with Nouns. Write ten sentences of your own using each of the different types of nouns listed below. Underline these nouns.
Answers will vary; samples are given for the first two.
EXAMPLE: a compound noun

The carpenter constructed a <u>bookshelf</u> for my room.
1. Paris, France, is a lovely country. 2. I saw Mr. Jones yesterday.

1. a noun that names a place
2. a noun that names a person
3. a noun that names a thing you can see
4. a noun that names an idea
5. a collective noun
6. a compound noun made of separate words
7. a hyphenated compound noun
8. a combined compound noun
9. a proper noun that names a person
10. a proper noun that names a place

Pronouns 1.2

1.2 Pronouns
(pp. 25–30)

Pronouns are words that take the place of nouns. They are generally used when it would not make sense to repeat a noun over and over again. Imagine, for example, that you are writing about Aunt Jenny. If you were using only nouns, you might write the following sentence.

WITH NOUNS: Aunt Jenny was late because *Aunt Jenny* missed *Aunt Jenny's* train.

To avoid using Aunt Jenny's name too often, you would substitute pronouns.

WITH PRONOUNS: Aunt Jenny was late because *she* missed *her* train.

A pronoun is a word that takes the place of a noun or of a group of words acting as a noun.

Sometimes a pronoun takes the place of a noun in the same sentence.

EXAMPLE: My father opened *his* present first.

A pronoun can also take the place of a noun used in an earlier sentence.

EXAMPLE: My father opened his present first. *He* felt *he* couldn't wait any longer.

A pronoun may take the place of a whole group of words.

EXAMPLE: Trying to make the team is hard work. *It* takes hours of practice every day.

Antecedents of Pronouns

A pronoun is closely related to the noun it replaces. The noun that the pronoun takes the place of has a special name. It is called the *antecedent*.

An antecedent is the noun (or group of words acting as a noun) for which a pronoun stands.

1.2 Pronouns

The Latin prefix *ante* means "before," and most antecedents do come *before* the pronouns that take their place. In the preceding examples, *father* and *trying to make the team* are the antecedents of their pronouns.

EXAMPLES: My *father* opened *his* present first. *He* felt *he* couldn't wait any longer.

Trying to make the team is hard work. *It* takes hours of practice every day.

Once in a while an antecedent will come after the pronoun.

EXAMPLE: Since *she* is known as a fine soprano, *Lucy* was offered a part in the concert.

Finally, a pronoun will sometimes have no definite antecedent at all.

EXAMPLES: *Who* will represent the class?

Everything was lost in the flood.

In these examples the pronouns *who* and *everything* do not stand for any specific person or thing.

EXERCISE A: Recognizing Antecedents.
In each of the following sentences, a pronoun is underlined. Find the antecedent for each pronoun and write it on your paper.

Antecedents are shaded.

EXAMPLE: Somehow Jeff managed to lose <u>his</u> tuba.

Jeff

1. There is a zoo in Arkansas <u>that</u> trains and houses a remarkable group of animals.
2. Visitors at the zoo can see such marvels as Bert Backquack and <u>his</u> all-duck band.
3. The zoo also includes among <u>its</u> residents a roller-skating parrot.

Average   For students who need additional reinforcement, provide additional sentences similar to those in Exercises A and B. Have students circle each pronoun and draw an arrow from the pronoun to its antecedent.

Advanced   Ask each student to relate a personal anecdote or to describe a recent experience on paper. Have the students exchange papers and identify the personal pronouns in each story by person and number.

Additional Practice

Practice Pages or Practice Book, page 8

Less advanced   Exercise Bank, Exercises A and B, pages 11, 12

Average   Exercise Bank, Exercises A, B, and C, pages 11, 12

Advanced   Exercise Bank, Exercises B and C, pages 11, 12

TESTING

Test Program

Unit Pretest, page 5
Chapter Test, pages 13, 14
Unit Post-Test, page 33

RE-TEACHING

Practice Pages or Practice Book, page 8

THINKING SKILLS

Comprehension—*Inferring* antecedents of pronouns (Exercise A, page 27) *Giving* examples of pronouns and their antecedents (Exercise B, page 29)

Synthesis—*Writing* sentences using pronouns (Developing Writing Skills, page 30)

4. The trainers there believe that most animals behave intelligently if they are treated with respect.
5. Davy Crockett's tales made him a legend in his own time.
6. Davy went to Congress claiming that he had wrestled grizzly bears as a child.
7. Fashionable people found themselves competing for Davy's attention at parties.
8. As children, the Brontës created their own private world.
9. To avoid the prejudice against women who wrote, Charlotte and Emily Brontë took pen names.
10. Charlotte called herself "Currer Bell," and her sister became "Ellis Bell."

Personal Pronouns

The pronouns used most often are *personal pronouns.*

Personal pronouns refer to (1) the person speaking, (2) the person spoken to, or (3) the person, place, or thing spoken about.

Depending on whom or what a personal pronoun refers to, it is called a first-person, second-person, or third-person pronoun. The following chart lists these pronouns.

PERSONAL PRONOUNS		
	Singular	**Plural**
First Person	I, me, my, mine	we, us, our, ours
Second Person	you, your, yours	you, your, yours
Third Person	he, him, his she, her, hers it, its	they, them, their, theirs

First-person pronouns, such as *I, my, we,* and *our,* are used by the person or people actually speaking to refer to himself, herself, or themselves.

EXAMPLE: *I* waited for *my* package to arrive.

Second-person pronouns, such as *you* and *your,* have the same form whether they are singular or plural. They are used when a person is speaking directly to another person or to other people.

EXAMPLE: Sheila, *you* left *your* photos on the table.

Third-person pronouns have more forms than do the other types of personal pronouns. Note that there are separate masculine pronouns *(he, him, his)* and feminine pronouns *(she, her, hers)* for people and neuter pronouns *(it, its)* for things. Third-person pronouns are used to refer to someone or something that may not even be present.

EXAMPLE: I haven't seen my grandfather in a year. *He* will arrive from Florida tomorrow.

EXERCISE B: Identifying Personal Pronouns and Their Antecedents.

Each of the following sentences contains two personal pronouns. On your paper write each personal pronoun and its antecedent.

Personal pronouns are underlined; antecedents are shaded.

EXAMPLE: Jim, you forgot your hat.

        you   Jim   your   Jim

1. Mom, you forgot to call your sister.
2. "I tried to repair my stereo," said Carlos.
3. Since Meg moved, she has called her friends once a week.
4. Now, boys, you have to clean up your own mess.
5. James tried to reach the doctor, but she was not in her office.
6. My brothers quit the team when they found that their grades were suffering.

7. **Marge**, yesterday <u>you</u> promised to lend <u>your</u> album to Judy.

8. The **book** is not as exciting as <u>its</u> jacket suggests, but <u>it</u> has one suspenseful chapter.

9. The **McCurdys** said that <u>they</u> would volunteer some of <u>their</u> time.

10. **Uncle Dan** gave <u>his</u> favorite watch to <u>his</u> oldest nephew.

DEVELOPING WRITING SKILLS: Writing Sentences that Contain Personal Pronouns. Write a short sentence using a personal pronoun that fits each of the descriptions given in the following list. Underline the pronoun that you use.

Answers will vary; samples are given for the first two.

EXAMPLE: third person, plural pronoun

I folded the sheets and put <u>them</u> into the closet.

1. <u>I</u> hiked the length of the stream.   2. Did Bob see <u>him</u>?

1. first person, singular pronoun

2. third person, singular, masculine pronoun

3. a different third person, singular, masculine pronoun

4. first person, plural pronoun

5. a different first person, plural pronoun

6. third person, singular, feminine pronoun

7. second person, singular pronoun

8. second person, plural pronoun

9. third person, plural pronoun

10. a different third person, plural pronoun

1.3 Four Special Kinds of Pronouns
(pp. 30–36)

OBJECTIVES

After completing this section, students should be able to

- Identify demonstrative pronouns.
- Identify relative pronouns.
- Identify interrogative pronouns.
- Identify indefinite pronouns.

1.3 Four Special Kinds of Pronouns

Four other kinds of pronouns are important in our language: *demonstrative, relative, interrogative,* and *indefinite pronouns.*

Demonstrative Pronouns

Demonstrative pronouns are pointers.

A demonstrative pronoun points out a specific person, place, or thing.

1.3 Four Special Kinds of Pronouns

There are four demonstrative pronouns.

DEMONSTRATIVE PRONOUNS	
Singular	**Plural**
this that	these those

A demonstrative pronoun can come before or after its antecedent

BEFORE: *This* is the book I chose.

   Those are my new friends.

AFTER: Of all my stamps, *these* are the most valuable.

   We stopped in Bad Neustadt and Salz. *These* are the towns where our ancestors lived.

EXERCISE A: Recognizing Demonstrative Pronouns.
Each of the following items contains a demonstrative pronoun. On your paper write each demonstrative pronoun.

EXAMPLE: That is not the record I would have chosen.

   That

1. Those are the most expensive dresses in the store.
2. Of all the Beatles' records, these are their best.
3. Until recently a knowledge of Latin and Greek was considered essential to a liberal education. These are no longer even taught in many schools.
4. These are the three most popular exhibits.
5. Of all his ideas, those are the strangest.
6. This is the artist I want you to meet.
7. You may help by peeling carrots. That is your first chore.
8. He raises bromeliads. These are a kind of exotic plant.
9. That seems to be their busiest time of the year.
10. This was all she said before leaving: "I'll be back."

31

TEACHING
Getting Started

┌─ sentence bank ─┐
This sweatshirt is mine.
That book is torn.
I like those tapes.
└─────────────────┘

Write three sentences like those above on the board. Elicit from students the words in these sentences that point to some specific object. Discuss why these words are called demonstrative pronouns. Point out that demonstrative pronouns are only one of four special kinds of pronouns they will learn about in this section.

Text Follow Through
Discuss text pages 30–36.

Assign Exercise A, page 31; Exercise B, page 32; Exercise C, page 34; Exercise D, page 35; and Developing Writing Skills, page 36.

Less advanced These students might feel more confident working in pairs to complete the Developing Writing Skills activity on page 36.

Average In all the exercises, have students supply antecedents for the pronouns they select. If a pronoun has no antecedent, students can write *none*. Once again, you might have students who need additional reinforcement. Have them copy exercise sentences onto their papers, circle pronouns, and draw arrows to antecedents.

Advanced Have students write two original sentences for each of the four types of pronouns discussed in this section or attempt to write paragraphs that contain all four types of pronouns. Then have students exchange papers and underline and label each pronoun.

Additional Practice

Practice Pages or Practice Book, pages 9, 10

Less advanced   Exercise Bank, Exercises A and B, pages 13–16

Average   Exercise Bank, Exercises A, B, and C, pages 13–16

Advanced   Exercise Bank, Exercises B and C, pages 13–16

TESTING

Test Program

Unit Pretest, page 5
Chapter Test, page 14
Unit Post-Test, page 33

RE-TEACHING

Practice Pages or Practice Book, pages 9, 10

THINKING SKILLS

Knowledge—*Identifying* demonstrative pronouns in sentences (Exercise A, page 31)
Identifying relative pronouns in sentences (Exercise B, page 32)
Identifying interrogative pronouns in sentences (Exercise C, page 34)
Identifying indefinite pronouns in sentences (Exercise D, page 35)

Synthesis—*Writing* sentences, using each of the different types of pronouns (Developing Writing Skills, page 36)

Relative Pronouns

Relative pronouns are connecting words.

A relative pronoun begins a subordinate clause and connects it to another idea in the same sentence.

There are five relative pronouns.

RELATIVE PRONOUNS				
that	which	who	whom	whose

The following chart gives examples of relative pronouns connecting subordinate clauses to independent clauses. (See Section 9.1 for more information about relative pronouns and clauses.)

Independent Clauses	Subordinate Clauses
Here is the book	that Betsy lost.
Dino bought our old house,	which needs many repairs.
She is a singer	who has an unusual range.
Is this the man	whom you saw earlier today?
She is the one	whose house has a fire alarm.

EXERCISE B: Recognizing Relative Pronouns. Each of the following sentences contains a relative pronoun. On your paper write each relative pronoun.

EXAMPLE: The person who left has just volunteered.

who

1. A leader <u>whom</u> our nation will never forget is Lincoln.

2. She chose a hat <u>that</u> matched her gown.
3. I will spend the summer vacation with my cousin <u>who</u> lives in Kingston.
4. The pipe <u>that</u> had leaked for a month finally burst.
5. The woman <u>who</u> was chosen scientist of the year works as a biochemist.
6. We joined the club <u>whose</u> introductory offer was the best.
7. The experimental car, <u>which</u> runs on batteries, does not pollute the air.
8. The pupil <u>who</u> gets the scholarship must excel in mathematics.
9. The dancer <u>whom</u> we admired most performed two solos.
10. Can you find a button <u>that</u> matches the others?

Interrogative Pronouns

Some relative pronouns can also be used as *interrogative pronouns.*

An interrogative pronoun is used to begin a question.

All together there are five interrogative pronouns.

INTERROGATIVE PRONOUNS				
what	which	who	whom	whose

Interrogative pronouns often do not have antecedents. In the examples, two interrogative pronouns have antecedents.

EXAMPLES: *What* did she win at the bazaar?

Here are two choices. *Which* do you want?

Who is the owner of that cassette recorder?

Whom did they want to speak to?

Mine is finished. *Whose* is not?

EXERCISE C: Recognizing Interrogative Pronouns. Each of the following items contains an interrogative pronoun. On your paper write each interrogative pronoun.

EXAMPLE: Which of the colors goes best with this sweater?

Which

1. Which of Ernest Hemingway's novels takes place during the Spanish Civil War?
2. One President of the United States served as Chief Justice of the Supreme Court after he left office. Who was this President?
3. What are the main differences between the rules for professional football and the rules for college football?
4. Which is your favorite Joni Mitchell song?
5. A special symbol is hidden in this painting. What is the symbol?
6. Whom did Tom Sawyer and Becky Thatcher see when they were lost in the cave?
7. Who pitched the only perfect game in the history of the World Series?
8. What did Dorothy do to escape from the Wicked Witch of the West?
9. Who was the first woman to be elected to the United States Congress?
10. For whom did Lewis Carroll write *Alice in Wonderland?*

Indefinite Pronouns

You should learn to recognize one other kind of pronoun—the *indefinite pronoun.*

Indefinite pronouns refer to people, places, or things, often without specifying which ones.

In the chart on the following page, notice that a few indefinite pronouns can be either singular or plural, depending upon their use in the sentence.

1.3 Four Special Kinds of Pronouns

INDEFINITE PRONOUNS			
Singular		**Plural**	**Singular or Plural**
another	much	both	all
anybody	neither	few	any
anyone	nobody	many	more
anything	no one	others	most
each	nothing	several	none
either	one		some
everybody	other		
everyone	somebody		
everything	someone		
little	something		

Like interrogative pronouns, indefinite pronouns do not always have antecedents.

WITHOUT ANTECEDENTS: *Anyone* can volunteer to serve hot dogs at the game.

Many cheered when the President arrived.

WITH ANTECEDENTS: *All* of the students volunteered to sell hot dogs at the game.

The guests gathered eagerly. *Many* cheered when he arrived.

EXERCISE D: Recognizing Indefinite Pronouns.
Each of the sentences on the following page contains at least one indefinite pronoun. On your paper write the indefinite pronoun or pronouns from each sentence.

EXAMPLE: Nobody went to see that movie.

Nobody

Writing Across the Curriculum

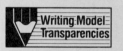

For additional practice with using nouns and pronouns in writing, use the art transparency, lesson plan, and writing assignment for *Self-Portrait*, pages 11–16. This assignment provides a writing across the curriculum activity in the content area of English.

Developing Writing Skills

Have students practice using pronouns in sentences by completing the following assignment.

Writing Across the Curriculum

The field of medicine has advanced greatly in recent years, and doctors continue to make strides toward curing some of the most common and deadly sicknesses and diseases.

Prewriting Imagine that you are a research physician and that you have just found the cure for one of humankind's illnesses. Prepare a news release to announce your discovery. The release must answer the five W's: Who? What? When? Where? Why? Your name is the answer to the first question, and the cure you found for the illness is the answer to the second question. Use your imagination to decide when and where you made your discovery. Finally, to answer the ''Why'' question, jot down the benefits that curing the illness will have. Arrange the list of benefits in order of importance.

Writing Write the first draft of the news release. Be sure to include answers to the five W's and to list the benefits of your discovery in order of importance.

Revising Make sure that you have answered each of the five W's. Have you identified yourself? Have you identified the disease or illness to which you have found a cure? Have you explained where and when you made the discovery? Finally, have you listed the benefits of your discovery?

1. <u>Everyone</u> applauded the winner of the marathon.
2. The coach asked <u>all</u> of the girls to prepare thoroughly for the match.
3. <u>Most</u> of the students are interested in computers, but <u>few</u> know how they actually work.
4. <u>Few</u> of my classmates knew <u>anything</u> about Susan B. Anthony.
5. The auditorium was so dark that we could see <u>nothing</u>.
6. Did <u>someone</u> remember to turn on the lights?
7. <u>Somebody</u> has taken one of the dictionaries.
8. <u>Neither</u> wanted to go, but it was important for <u>both</u> to attend.
9. <u>Little</u> is known about the people who built Stonehenge.
10. <u>No one</u> knew why <u>some</u> of the pages had been torn from his diary.

DEVELOPING WRITING SKILLS: Writing Sentences with Pronouns. Write ten sentences of your own using each of the different types of pronouns listed below. Underline the pronouns.

Answers will vary; samples are given for the first two.

EXAMPLE: *who* as a relative pronoun.

The room was crowded with people <u>who</u> were applauding wildly.

1. We laughed at <u>that</u> joke.

1. a singular demonstrative pronoun
2. a plural demonstrative pronoun that comes after its antecedent
3. *that* as a relative pronoun
4. *who* as a relative pronoun
5. *whose* as an interrogative pronoun
6. *which* as a relative pronoun
7. *which* as an interrogative pronoun
8. an indefinite pronoun with an antecedent
9. an indefinite pronoun without an antecedent
10. a relative pronoun and an indefinite pronoun

2. Of all my birthdays, <u>those</u> were the most memorable.

Skills Review and Writing Workshop

Nouns and Pronouns

CHECKING YOUR SKILLS

Write the two nouns or pronouns in each sentence.
1. Rain, jungle 2. Monkeys, vines 3. waters, crocodiles 4. this, Africa

(1) Rain is pouring down on a steaming tropical jungle. (2) Monkeys chatter and swing on vines. (3) In the sunny waters crocodiles sleep. (4) Is this deep inside Africa? (5) No, you are in the Bronx Zoo. (6) The exhibit is called Jungle World. (7) Also included is a 40-foot-high waterfall in a lush, tropical setting. (8) The animals, however, are the true stars around here. (9) Bats and anteaters can be seen flying and strolling about. (10) Here everyone can see, hear, smell, touch, and taste a real tropical jungle atmosphere. 5. you, zoo 6. exhibit, World 7. waterfall, setting 8. animals, stars 9. Bats, anteaters 10. everyone, atmosphere

USING GRAMMAR SKILLS IN WRITING
Writing a Description of a Place

Writers know that the use of vivid, specific nouns and clear pronouns in descriptive writing can capture the readers' interest. Write a description of an unusual place you have visited or would like to visit. Follow the steps below to create a descriptive paragraph that will make its readers want to go instantly to the place you are describing.
Answers will vary.

Prewriting: Picture the place you are describing. List those things that make the place unusual and memorable. Try to include at least five.

Writing: Begin your description with a detail that is unusual and so will capture your readers' attention. Add other details, arranged in a logical order. End with a topic sentence that tells the name of the place you are describing.

Revising: Look at the nouns and pronouns you used and change any that could be more vivid or interesting. Read the entire paragraph, looking for improvements you can make. After you have revised, proofread your paragraph carefully.

Checking Your Skills

In the Checking Your Skills assignment, students have identified nouns and pronouns in sentences. Explain to students that pronouns are essential in good writing to eliminate redundancy.

Critical Thinking

Have students cut out one-paragraph articles from discarded magazines and newspapers. Tell students to bring their articles to class. In class, ask for student volunteers to write the paragraph on the chalkboard. Then, have the student work with the rest of the class to identify all the nouns, pronouns, and antecedents of pronouns. The student should circle nouns, underline pronouns, and use an arrow to indicate the antecedent of each pronoun. The rest of the class should assist the student when necessary. You might want to have students identify the types of nouns and the types of pronouns in the paragraph.

Using Grammar Skills in Writing

Prewriting Before students begin writing, you might have them narrow the focus to convey one dominant impression of the subject in their descriptions. Students should state this dominant impression in the topic sentence and support it with vivid details and words appealing to the senses.

CHAPTER 2
Verbs
(pp. 38–50)

Each section of this chapter considers a different kind of verb: Section 2.1 looks at action verbs, Section 2.2 deals with linking verbs, and Section 2.3 discusses helping verbs. Understanding each type of verb is essential to students' work with sentence structure and will also help students to resolve a number of usage problems.

For a review of the entire chapter and a related writing activity, see the Skills Review and Writing Workshop on page 50.

2.1 Action Verbs
(pp. 38–42)

OBJECTIVES

After completing this section, students should be able to

- Identify action verbs that represent visible action and mental action.
- Identify transitive action verbs.
- Identify intransitive action verbs.

Chapter **2**

Verbs

The *verb* is a necessary part of every sentence. It helps tell whether an event is taking place in the present, past, or future. Verbs do more, however, than just tell time. Some verbs express action. Other verbs provide a link between two parts of a sentence. Still others simply point out that something exists.

This chapter will describe the two main kinds of verbs—*action verbs* and *linking verbs*—and will show you how these verbs can be used with another kind of verb—*helping verbs.*

2.1 Action Verbs

The following are verbs that are used all the time: *see, plan, run, eat, shout, tell,* and *sit.* All these verbs have one thing in common. They all express *action.*

An action verb tells what action a person or thing is performing.

In the sentence, "My father *waited* at the station for the train," the verb *waited* tells what *father* did. In the sentence "The swans *float* gracefully on the water," the verb *float* tells what *swans* do. The performers of the action *(father, swans)* are the *subjects* of the verbs. (See Chapter 7 for information about subjects.)

2.1 Action Verbs

Visible and Mental Action

It is useful to be able to recognize the different kinds of action that action verbs can express. Some actions are *visible*. You can see, for example, a group of swans flying or swimming. You can also see swans floating, even though little movement is going on. You can also see someone waiting.

Some other actions can be seen only with difficulty, if at all. These are usually *mental* actions. Compare the two kinds of action in the following chart.

Visible Action		Mental Action	
walk	spin	wonder	remember
stand	sing	think	dream
put	slide	believe	consider
open	chase	worry	decide

EXERCISE A: Recognizing Action Verbs. On your paper write the action verb from each sentence. After each verb write *visible* or *mental* to identify the kind of action the verb shows. Note that half are visible and half are mental.

EXAMPLE: People once believed in goblins.

    believed   mental

1. The *Concorde* flies quickly across the Atlantic. visible
2. For many weeks Columbus and his crew worried about reaching land. mental
3. Juan dreamed of his family in Cuba. mental
4. The quarterback threw a long pass. visible
5. The receiver barely caught the ball. visible
6. Elizabeth Kenny developed a treatment for polio. visible
7. She considered warmth and exercise to be the best therapy.
8. He remembers many events from World War II. mental
9. Weeds suddenly sprouted all over our front lawn. visible
10. She believed in justice and freedom for all. mental

7. mental

39

TEACHING

Getting Started

Discuss with students the examples of action verbs on page 38. Have students look up the verbs in a thesaurus and list on the board synonyms for each. Using this bank of action verbs, students can write additional example sentences on the board.

Text Follow Through

Discuss text pages 38–42.

Assign Exercise A, page 39; Exercise B, page 40; Exercise C, page 41; and Developing Writing Skills, page 41.

Less advanced When students complete the Developing Writing Skills activity, page 41, review their sentences individually, helping them to distinguish between transitive and intransitive verbs. Have students draw arrows from each transitive verb to its object, as they did in Exercise B.

Average For additional reinforcement, have the students work with the visible-action verbs in the chart on page 39, writing a sentence for each verb and then labeling each verb transitive or intransitive.

Advanced Have students write a pair of sentences—one transitive and one intransitive—for each of the following verbs:

    break   climb   run
    throw   wash

Additional Practice
Practice Pages or Practice
Book, pages 11, 12

Less advanced Exercise Bank,
Exercises A and B, pages 17–19

Average Exercise Bank, Exercises A, B, and C, pages 17–19

Advanced Exercise Bank, Exercises B and C, pages 17–19

TESTING
Test Program
  Unit Pretest, page 5
  Chapter Test, page 15
  Unit Post-Test, pages 33, 34

RE-TEACHING
Practice Pages or Practice
Book, pages 11, 12

THINKING SKILLS
Comprehension—*Distinguishing*
action verbs in sentences and
explaining the kind of action
each shows (Exercise A, page
39)
Distinguishing transitive verbs
and their objects (Exercise B,
page 40)
Distinguishing intransitive
verbs and *explaining* why they
are intransitive (Exercise C,
page 41)

Synthesis—*Writing* sentences
illustrating the same verbs as
transitive and intransitive
(Developing Writing Skills,
page 41)

Transitive Verbs

Some action verbs are *transitive*.

**An action verb is transitive if the receiver of the
action is named in the sentence.**

The receiver of the action is called the *object* of the verb.

EXAMPLES: Sandy *opened* the window with great difficulty.

The truck suddenly *hit* the pedestrian.

In the first example, *window* receives the action of the verb
opened. Opened is transitive because the sentence has an object *(window)* that tells *what* Sandy opened. In the second example, *hit* is transitive because the sentence includes a word
that tells *whom* the truck hit. This word is *pedestrian.* (See
Section 7.5 for more information about objects of transitive
verbs.)

EXERCISE B: Recognizing Transitive Action Verbs. Copy
the sentences. Underline the transitive action verb in each sentence and draw an arrow from the verb to its object.
Verbs are underlined; objects are shaded.

EXAMPLE: Andy hit a home run on her first try.

1. Lightning struck the new building.
2. Later in the day, Beth prepared the entire report.
3. Congress bought its first two navy vessels on October 13,
   1775.
4. The train reached the station two hours late.
5. According to legend, Lincoln wrote the Gettysburg Address
   while on his way to Pennsylvania.
6. Tom chopped enough wood to last through January.
7. At noon the flood waters reached the top of the barrier.
8. Jan put the groceries away.
9. Louise uses a kerosene heater in her room.

Developing Writing Skills

Have students practice using action verbs in writing by completing the following assignment.

Writing Across the Curriculum

Have you ever participated in or witnessed an exciting sporting event? A dramatic, game-winning home run in the ninth inning of a baseball game? A dazzling, nearly perfect routine to win a gymnastics meet?

Prewriting Think about the most exciting sporting event you ever participated in or witnessed. Select the crucial moments in the event and free write about them for several minutes. Look over your free writing and select details to include in a narrative passage describing this dramatic sports moment. Arrange the details in chronological order.

Writing Write the first draft of an article for **Great Moments in Sports** magazine. Begin with a topic sentence that grabs your audience's attention. Include a brief summary of the action up to the moment that you are describing. Then, use the details from your free writing to build your narrative to a dramatic climax. You should conclude your description with an explanation of the outcome of the event.

Revising Make sure that you have included all the important details concerning the sporting event. Is your description vivid? Have you used action verbs to make the description lively? Will your audience be compelled to read the entire passage? Proofread your description and prepare a final draft.

---

10. My parents <u>planted</u> various flowers near the entrance to our house.

Intransitive Verbs

An action verb can also be *intransitive.*

An action verb is intransitive if no receiver of the action is named in the sentence.

A sentence with an intransitive verb will not have an object.

EXAMPLES: My sister *smiled.*

The bus *raced* through the traffic light.

EXERCISE C: Recognizing Intransitive Action Verbs. On your paper write the intransitive action verb in each sentence. Be prepared to explain why the verb is intransitive.

EXAMPLE: He runs faster in the morning.

runs

1. Her ring <u>fell</u> between the planks of the boardwalk.
2. My brother <u>laughed</u> for an hour at the joke.
3. The explorers <u>traveled</u> along the banks of the river.
4. We <u>talked</u> for hours after dinner.
5. Fort Pierre <u>grew</u> slowly from a small trading post near Bad River in Missouri.
6. The spider <u>hovered</u> near the top of the lamp.
7. I <u>awoke</u> before dawn.
8. Pieces of glass <u>tinkled</u> to the floor after the accident.
9. Her magnificent voice <u>soared</u> across the auditorium.
10. The tiny poodle <u>stepped</u> daintily around the patches of mud.

DEVELOPING WRITING SKILLS: Writing Sentences with Action Verbs. The following ten verbs can be used as either

2.2 Linking Verbs
(pp. 42–46)

OBJECTIVES

After completing this section, students should be able to

- Identify forms of *be* as linking verbs.
- Identify other linking verbs.
- Distinguish between action verbs and linking verbs.

TEACHING

Getting Started

---
sentence bank

These socks are mine.
He looked great.
Sara is a student.

Write the Sentence Bank sentences on the board. Then introduce the word *linking* and ask students what it means. Explain that some verbs join ideas from the beginning of a sentence with ideas at the end. These verbs are called "linking

transitive verbs or intransitive verbs. Use each of the ten verbs in *two* sentences of your own, once as a transitive verb and once as an intransitive verb. Label your sentences *transitive* or *intransitive* and underline the verbs.

Answers will vary; samples are given for the first one.

EXAMPLE: read

He <u>read</u> the novel in a week.   transitive

After lunch, he <u>read</u> until dinner.   intransitive

1. Frogs <u>eat</u> insects.   trans / We usually <u>eat</u> in the dining room.   intrans

1. eat	3. grow	5. visit	7. finish	9. shout
2. jump	4. write	6. swim	8. play	10. drop

2.2 Linking Verbs

A few widely used verbs do not show action. These are *linking verbs*.

A linking verb connects a noun or pronoun at or near the beginning of a sentence with a word at or near the end.

Study the words before and after the linking verbs in the following examples. Note that the words after the linking verbs identify or describe the words that come before the verbs.

EXAMPLES: Rita *is* a dentist.

The winners *were* Tony and I.

He *looks* old.

The linking verbs *is*, *were*, and *looks* act almost as equal signs between the words they link.

Forms of *Be*

The verb *be* is the most commonly used linking verb in English. You should learn all of its many forms.

2.2 Linking Verbs

THE FORMS OF *BE*		
am	can be	have been
are	could be	has been
is	may be	had been
was	might be	could have been
were	must be	may have been
am being	shall be	might have been
are being	should be	must have been
is being	will be	shall have been
was being	would be	should have been
were being		will have been
		would have been

EXERCISE A: Recognizing Forms of *Be* as Linking Verbs.

Copy each of the following sentences onto your paper. Underline the form of *be* in each. Then draw a double-headed arrow connecting the words that are linked by the verb.

Verbs are underlined; linked words are shaded.

EXAMPLE: Edgar Allan Poe was a writer of great imagination.

1. Ringo Starr was the drummer for the Beatles.
2. The National League has been victorious in most recent All-Star games.
3. Edgar Allan Poe was for a short time a cadet at West Point.
4. The writer of supernatural tales might have been a strange general.
5. Marie Curie was the winner of two Nobel Prizes.
6. Your first choice should be the new Rod Stewart album.
7. Halley's Comet will be visible from parts of the United States in 1986.
8. Americans were fearful and excited about its last visit in 1910.
9. Ethel Barrymore was part of a famous theatrical family.
10. This family of actors had been successful on the stage before working in movies.

---

verbs." Discuss with students how linking verbs act almost as equal signs between the words they link. Rewrite the sentences using the equal sign: e.g.,

These socks = mine.

Text Follow Through

Discuss text pages 42–46.

Assign Exercise A, page 43; Exercise B, page 44; Exercise C, page 45; and Developing Writing Skills, page 46.

Less advanced   Make sure students can recognize most of the forms of *be* listed in the chart on page 43. Also help students to understand how the verbs on page 44 can be either action or linking verbs. Remind students to apply the "*am, is, are*" test (page 45) to each sentence in Exercise C before deciding on their answers. If students are still having difficulties, you might have them do the Developing Writing Skills activity on page 46 as an in-class group activity.

Average   Have students rewrite the first five sentences in Exercise C, keeping the subject the same but using each linking verb as an action verb and vice versa. Also, you might ask students in turn to read any one of the sentences they wrote for the Developing Writing Skills activity and have their classmates identify the type of verb in each sentence.

Other Linking Verbs

In addition to the verb *be,* a number of other verbs can be used as linking verbs.

OTHER LINKING VERBS					
appear	feel	look	seem	sound	taste
become	grow	remain	smell	stay	turn

These verbs often set up the same relationship between words as the linking verb *be* does. The words after the verbs identify or describe the words that come before the verbs.

EXAMPLE: Rita *became* a dentist.

Everything *smells* damp and musty.

He *looks* very old.

EXERCISE B: Identifying Other Linking Verbs. Copy each of the following sentences onto your paper. Underline the linking verb in each. Then draw a double-headed arrow connecting the words that are linked by the verb.

Verbs are underlined; linked words are shaded.

EXAMPLE: The chili tastes delicious.

1. The plant grew sturdy in the hothouse.
2. Gold coins seem a better investment.
3. Although far apart the sisters remained good friends.
4. The new chorus sounds even better than the old.
5. Sometimes Alex feels weak and tired.
6. That plant turns brown in the fall.
7. The roast goose looks sensational.
8. At the moment he appears very unhappy.
9. Both sponges smell sour.
10. The noises from the empty house sound strange.

Action Verb or Linking Verb?

Most of the twelve verbs in the chart on page 44 can be used as either linking verbs or action verbs.

LINKING: Richard *felt* sad.

ACTION: The doctor *felt* my pulse.

LINKING: The cake *tasted* too sweet.

ACTION: The chef *tasted* the stew.

To see whether a verb is a linking verb or an action verb, substitute *am, is,* or *are* for the verb. If the sentence still makes sense and if the new verb links a word before it to a word after it, then the original verb is a linking verb.

Linking	Action
The teacher *looked* angry.	The teacher *looked* for chalk.
(The teacher *is* angry?)	(The teacher *is* for chalk?)
Yes, it's a linking verb	No, it's an action verb

EXERCISE C: Distinguishing Between Action Verbs and Linking Verbs. On your paper write the verb from each sentence. After each action verb write *AV* and after each linking verb write *LV.*

EXAMPLE: Lucy smells a rat.

   smells   AV

1. My aunt in Iowa grows wheat and corn. AV
2. Just home from the hospital, my sister looked pale. LV
3. The ghost supposedly appears every night at twelve. AV
4. The guests stayed at the cottages near the lake. AV
5. For some reason he remains angry and depressed. LV
6. The apple and peach pies look absolutely delicious. LV

7. Lucinda <u>remained</u> at the convention in California for a full week. ^{AV}

8. Suddenly the valley <u>became</u> dark and misty. ^{LV}

9. The butter <u>turned</u> rancid. ^{LV}

10. Felix <u>seems</u> happy and rested. ^{LV}

DEVELOPING WRITING SKILLS: Writing Sentences with Action and Linking Verbs. Use each of the following verbs in two sentences of your own. Use the verb as a linking verb in the first sentence and as an action verb in the second sentence.

Answers will vary; samples are given for the first one.

EXAMPLE: sound

> Jenny sounds too happy this morning.

> The bell sounded over the loudspeakers.

1. That cake smells delicious. Ferdinand smells the flowers.

1. smell   3. appear   5. taste
2. feel   4. grow

2.3 Helping Verbs

A verb is sometimes just a single word. At other times, however, one verb may be made up of two, three, or four words. This kind of verb is called a *verb phrase.*

Helping verbs are added before another verb to make a verb phrase.

In the following examples, the *helping verbs* are italicized. Notice how they help to change the meaning of *opened,* the key part of the verb.

EXAMPLES: opened

> *has* opened

> *will have* opened

> *could have been* opened

> *is being* opened

2.3 Helping Verbs
(pp. 46–49)

OBJECTIVES

After completing this section, students should be able to

• Recognize helping verbs.
• Locate helping verbs in sentences.

TEACHING
Getting Started

word bank		
do	does	did
can	could	
may	might	must
will	shall	would
has	have	had

Recognizing Helping Verbs

Forms of the verb *be* are often used as helping verbs. Review the forms of *be* in the chart on page 43. In the following chart, the forms of *be* used as helping verbs are italicized.

SOME FORMS OF *BE* USED AS HELPING VERBS	
Helping Verbs	**Verbs**
is	opening
was being	trained
should be	written
had been	sent
might have been	played

Some other verbs can also be used as helping verbs.

OTHER HELPING VERBS			
do	have	shall	can
does	has	should	could
did	had	will	may
		would	might
			must

Many different verb phrases can be formed using one or more of these helping verbs. The chart shows just a few.

VERB PHRASES	
Helping Verbs	**Verbs**
does	find
had	gone
should	see
will have	talked
might have	told

Put the above words on the board. Elicit from students verb phrases combining each word with a different main verb. Write the verb phrases on the board as students dictate them. Point out that the Word Bank verbs are called "helping verbs." Discuss how each helping verb changes the meaning of the main verb in the phrase.

Text Follow Through

Discuss text pages 46–49.

Assign Exercise A, page 48; Exercise B, page 49; and Developing Writing Skills, page 49.

Less advanced You might review the forms of *be* from the chart on page 43 of Section 2.2. Help students to recognize when a form of *be* is a linking verb and when it is a helping verb in a verb phrase. You might also allow students to compare their answers in Exercise A. Call on students in turn to read the helping verbs they supplied and ask if anyone chose different helping verbs.

Average For additional reinforcement, have students rewrite the sentences in Exercise A with different helping verbs. Discuss how changing the helping verbs changes the meaning of the new sentences from the first ones they wrote. Where no variation occurs, as is likely to happen in sentence 9, students can discuss why only one choice seems appropriate.

Advanced In order to make the Developing Writing Skills activity more challenging, have students rewrite several of their sentences as questions so that one of the helping verbs will appear before the subject.

Additional Practice

Practice Pages or Practice Book, page 15

Less advanced Exercise Bank, Exercises A and B, pages 23, 24

Average Exercise Bank, Exercises A, B, and C, pages 23, 24

Advanced Exercise Bank, Exercises B and C, pages 23, 24

TESTING

Test Program

Unit Pretest, page 6
Chapter Test, page 16
Unit Post-Test, page 34

RE-TEACHING

Practice Pages or Practice Book, page 15

THINKING SKILLS

Knowledge—*Identifying* the complete verb phrase in sentences (Exercise B, page 49)

Application—*Using* helping verbs to create verb phrases in sentences (Exercise A, page 48)

Synthesis—*Writing* sentences with verb phrases (Developing Writing Skills, page 49)

EXERCISE A: Supplying Helping Verbs. Each of the following sentences contains one or more blanks. Write the sentences on your paper and fill in each blank with an appropriate helping verb.
Answers will vary; samples are given.

EXAMPLE: Ian _____ _____ _____ told not to ask that question.

Ian should have been told not to ask that question.

1. Jose ___has___ decided to go away to college.
2. She ___had___ ___been___ waiting at the station for more than two hours.
3. ___Have___ you chosen a topic for your report?
4. She ___is___ going to St. Louis on business tomorrow.
5. In another half-hour, she ___will___ ___have___ ___been___ sleeping for twelve hours.
6. My brother ___might___ perform the leading role in the show next week.
7. ___Can___ you explain why you are late?
8. When ___should___ the winners ___be___ notified?
9. This ___has___ been an almost unbelievable day.
10. He ___has___ ___been___ telling all sorts of stories about you.

Finding Helping Verbs in Sentences

Sometimes the words making up a verb phrase are separated by other words, such as *not, slowly,* and *carefully.* In certain types of questions, the parts of the verb phrase are usually separated. In the following examples, the parts of each verb phrase are italicized.

WORDS TOGETHER: She *could have been reached* by phone earlier.

WORDS SEPARATED: She *could* certainly *have been reached* by phone earlier.

This *has* not *happened* before.

Did you ever *expect* to win?

2.3 Helping Verbs

EXERCISE B: Locating Helping Verbs. On your paper write the complete verb phrase from each of the following sentences. Include all parts of the helping verb, but do *not* include any words that separate the parts of the verb phrase.

EXAMPLE: Patty did not leave until after four.

did leave

1. Uncle Bob <u>should have reached</u> Boston by now.
2. <u>Have</u> you ever <u>wanted</u> to ski at Mount Washington?
3. She <u>had</u> carefully <u>arranged</u> her plans a week in advance.
4. Sailboats <u>are</u> often <u>seen</u> on the lake in summer.
5. She probably <u>would have given</u> you her phone number later.
6. Traders <u>would</u> often <u>exchange</u> tools, weapons, and utensils for pelts of fur.
7. That book <u>has been</u> on the best-seller list for ten weeks.
8. <u>Do</u> you <u>know</u> the name of the first state?
9. You <u>should</u> not even <u>have attempted</u> that difficult somersault.
10. Those plants <u>have</u> not <u>been watered</u> in more than a week.

DEVELOPING WRITING SKILLS: Writing Sentences with Helping Verbs. Use each of the following verb phrases in a complete sentence. Underline all parts of the verb phrase in each sentence. If you wish you can put the word *not* or some other word between parts of the verb phrase.

Answers will vary; samples are given for the first two.
EXAMPLE: have been

My favorite books <u>have</u> always <u>been</u> about horses.
1. The new shop <u>will open</u> next week. 2. <u>Could</u> the butler <u>have been</u> behind the screen?

1. will open
2. could have been
3. has been told
4. can be reached
5. have been talking

6. must be tried
7. will leave
8. has decided
9. are hoping
10. may be taken

Writing Across the Curriculum

Writing Model Transparencies

For additional practice with using verbs in writing, use the art transparency, lesson plan, and writing assignment for *Full Moon Riders Along the Little Big Horn River*, pages 17–22. This assignment provides a writing across the curriculum activity in the content area of history.

Checking Your Skills

In the Checking Your Skills assignment, students have identified verbs and verb phrases in sentences. Explain to students that good writers take care to choose appropriate verbs in their writing. Ask students why this might be especially important for adventure stories.

Collaborative Learning

Divide the class into groups. Have each group select an action-packed story. Then, have the groups look through their stories carefully and select ten vivid action verbs. After they have selected the verbs, have each group write ten sentences using the verbs they selected from the stories. When students have completed this task, have a member of each group identify for the class the ten verbs the group selected, explain why they are vivid, and read the new sentences written by the group.

Using Grammar Skills in Writing

Publishing You might want to collect students' narratives to publish in a class magazine. If so, encourage students to include illustrations or photographs to enhance their narratives. Work together with the class to think of a title, design a cover, and arrange the order of the narratives for the magazine. Place the completed magazine where students can read it during their free time.

Skills Review and Writing Workshop

Verbs

CHECKING YOUR SKILLS

Write the verb or verb phrase in each sentence.
1. has heard 2. would recognize 3. was 4. had been warned 5. lived

(1) Every American has heard of Paul Revere's famous ride during the American Revolution. (2) But not many would recognize the name of our "Female Paul Revere." (3) She was Sibyl Luddington, the sixteen-year-old daughter of a colonel in the revolutionary army. (4) Colonel Luddington had been warned of an impending attack by some British troops in nearby Danbury, Connecticut. (5) His own troops lived on farms all around the countryside. (6) Someone had to warn them about the attack. (7) Sibyl could ride her horse as well as an adult. (8) And so she mounted her horse and became a messenger to the troops. (9) She galloped all over the countryside through the night. (10) By morning, thirty-seven American soldiers had assembled at the Luddingtons', ready for combat. 6. had to warn 7. could ride 8. mounted and became
9. galloped 10. had assembled

USING GRAMMAR SKILLS IN WRITING
Writing a Narrative

Good narrative writers use strong, vivid verbs to make their stories gripping. Think of a brief narrative, real or imaginary. Follow the steps below to create an intriguing story.
Answers will vary.

Prewriting: A good narrative should have a *beginning* that builds to a *climax* and then *ends*. List these three points for the narrative you are going to write. Be sure to arrange them in the order in which they happened.

Writing: Begin by setting the stage for your narrative. Introduce the characters, setting, and the conflict. Then build to the climax, and write a concluding sentence.

Revising: Look at the verbs you used, and change any that could be stronger. Read the entire narrative, looking for other improvements you can make. Revise proofread carefully.

Chapter 3

Adjectives

Adjectives
(pp. 51–63)

This chapter discusses a number of different types of adjectives. Section 3.1 considers descriptive adjectives, articles, nouns used as adjectives, proper adjectives, and compound adjectives. Section 3.2 deals with the various types of pronouns used as adjectives.

For a review of the entire chapter and a related writing activity, see the Skills Review and Writing Workshop on page 63.

Have you ever tried to describe an animal that you saw at a zoo? You may have used words such as *huge, heavy, gray, rough.* With these words you painted a picture of a specific animal—an elephant—so that other people could see the animal in their minds. The words you used are called *adjectives.*

There are many kinds of adjectives. This chapter will cover some of the most common of them.

Adjectives as Modifiers 3.1

Adjectives are used with two other parts of speech.

An adjective is used to describe a noun or a pronoun.

Some examples of adjectives used with nouns are: "*sleek* jets," "*clear, violet* eyes," "*tall, majestic* oaks."

Adjectives with Nouns and Pronouns

To *modify* means to "change slightly." Adjectives are modifiers because they slightly change the meaning of nouns and pronouns. Adjectives modify meaning by adding information

3.1 Adjectives as Modifiers
(pp. 51–58)

OBJECTIVES

After completing this section, students should be able to

- Identify adjectives as modifiers of nouns and pronouns in sentences.
- Distinguish between definite and indefinite articles.
- Identify proper adjectives.
- Identify compound adjectives.

TEACHING

Getting Started

Write on the board the adjectives and nouns on page 51:

sleek jets
clear, violet eyes
tall, majestic oaks

Have students identify the adjectives and nouns in each phrase. Discuss how the adjectives add extra meaning to the nouns and make them seem more interesting. Then, using a thesaurus, students should look up each of the adjectives and find adjective synonyms that could be substituted to modify the nouns.

Text Follow Through

Discuss text pages 51–58.

Assign Exercise A, page 52; Exercise B, page 54; Exercise C, page 55; Exercise D, page 56; Exercise E, page 57; and Developing Writing Skills, page 58.

Less advanced Go over the questions on page 52 to make sure students understand the kind of information that adjectives add to nouns. You might have students explain what question each underlined adjective in Exercise A answers. You might also have students exchange papers after they complete the Developing Writing Skills activity on page 58 and list each adjective and the word it modifies.

Average Have students bring to class short descriptive paragraphs from magazines or newspapers. Have them copy the paragraphs, substituting a blank space for each descriptive adjective. Then have them exchange papers and fill in the

that answers one of four questions: *What kind? Which one? How many? How much?* In the following chart, notice how adjectives answer these questions.

What Kind?	
brick house	*white* sheets
Which One?	
that man	*each* answer
How Many?	
one daffodil	*several* roses
How Much?	
no time	*enough* raisins

An adjective usually comes before the noun it modifies, as all the adjectives in the chart do. Sometimes, however, adjectives come after the nouns they modify.

EXAMPLE: The light, *white* and *shining*, fascinated her.

Adjectives that modify pronouns usually come after linking verbs. Sometimes, however, adjectives come before pronouns.

EXAMPLE: She was *tall* and *beautiful*.

Tall and *beautiful*, she walked into the ball.

EXERCISE A: Recognizing Adjectives and the Words They Modify.
Copy each of the following sentences onto your paper. Draw an arrow pointing from each underlined adjective to the noun or pronoun it modifies.

Modified words are shaded.

EXAMPLE: His sharp, witty remark was hardly appropriate.

3.1 Adjectives as Modifiers

1. The <u>many</u> rings of Saturn glowed in the <u>blurry</u> photograph.
2. The <u>tired</u> <u>old</u> man stumbled down the road.
3. <u>Several</u> books have been written about the <u>last</u> days of Roman power.
4. Willie Mays leaped for the <u>high</u> <u>fly</u> ball and made a <u>brilliant</u> catch.
5. Her <u>third</u> attempt was <u>good</u>, but in her <u>fourth</u> and <u>final</u> try, she broke a <u>ten-year-old</u> record.
6. The house, <u>dreary</u> and <u>uninviting</u>, has not been lived in for <u>seventeen</u> years.
7. Irving Berlin wrote <u>many</u> <u>wonderful</u> songs.
8. The <u>feathery</u> fins of the angel fish drifted in the <u>clear</u> <u>blue</u> water.
9. The <u>marble</u> statue was <u>pale</u> and <u>dramatic</u> against the <u>dark</u> <u>velvet</u> curtains.
10. The <u>crusty</u> <u>little</u> turtle crawled across the <u>deserted</u> parking lot.

Articles

Three commonly used adjectives are called *articles—the, a,* and *an.* These three words are adjectives because they come before nouns and answer the question *Which one?* Because of the way it modifies nouns, *the* is called the *definite* article.

The, the definite article, refers to a specific person, place, or thing.

EXAMPLES: *the* President   *the* auditorium   *the* green hat

The other two articles, *a* and *an,* are not as specific as *the.*

A and an, the indefinite articles, refer to any one of a class of people, places, or things.

EXAMPLES: *a* president   *an* auditorium   *a* green hat

A is used before consonant sounds. *An* is used before vowel sounds. Notice that you choose between *a* and *an* based on

53

blanks with appropriate adjectives. They can then compare their adjective choices with the ones originally used in the paragraphs.

Advanced Extending the same activity as for average students, have students list on the board the adjectives from the original paragraph and indicate any that are nouns used as adjectives, proper adjectives, or compound adjectives.

Additional Practice

Practice Pages or Practice Book, pages 16–18

Less advanced Exercise Bank, Exercises A and B, pages 25–29

Average Exercise Bank, Exercises A, B, and C, pages 25–29

Advanced Exercise Bank, Exercises B and C, pages 25–29

TESTING

Test Program

Unit Pretest, page 6
Chapter Test, pages 17, 18
Unit Post-Test, page 34

RE-TEACHING

Practice Pages or Practice Book, pages 16–18

THINKING SKILLS

Comprehension—*Explaining* which words adjectives modify in sentences (Exercise A, page 52)
Distinguishing nouns used as adjectives in sentences (Exercise C, page 55)
Distinguishing proper adjectives and the nouns they modify in sentences (Exercise D, page 56)

Distinguishing compound adjectives and the nouns they modify in sentences (Exercise E, page 57)

Application—*Using* definite and indefinite articles in sentences (Exercise B, page 54)

Synthesis—*Rewriting* sentences by adding different types of adjectives (Developing Writing Skills, page 58)

sound. The letter *h*, a consonant, may sound like either a consonant or a vowel. *O* and *u* are vowels, but they may sometimes sound like consonants.

USING *A* AND *AN*	
Consonant Sounds	**Vowel Sounds**
a *c*andy cane	an *e*gg
a *h*ome run (*h* sound)	an *h*onor (no *h* sound)
a *o*ne-way road (*w* sound)	an *o*men (*o* sound)
a *u*niform (*y* sound)	an *u*nhappy child (*u* sound)

EXERCISE B: Distinguishing Between Definite and Indefinite Articles. On your paper write the article that will correctly complete each of the following sentences. The word in parentheses tells you which kind of article.

EXAMPLE: What ___(indefinite)___ unusual subject!

What an unusual subject!

1. Did you see ___(definite)___ mayor yet? the
2. She bought ___(indefinite)___ new dress and ___(indefinite)___ umbrella. a/an
3. Our history teacher mentioned ___(definite)___ emperor. the
4. ___(Indefinite)___ old man and ___(indefinite)___ young woman slowly approached. An/a
5. She was given ___(indefinite)___ once-in-a-lifetime opportunity. a
6. ___(Definite)___ road we must take to ___(definite)___ bridge is blocked. The/the
7. He was eager to make friends because he was ___(indefinite)___ only child. an
8. Read ___(indefinite)___ book on World War II and then write ___(indefinite)___ report. a/a
9. Where did you put ___(definite)___ combination to ___(definite)___ safe? the/the

10. Some say ____(indefinite)____ apple a day keeps __(definite)__
    doctor away. an/the

Nouns Used as Adjectives

Nouns are sometimes used as adjectives. When a noun is used as an adjective, it comes before another noun and answers the question *What kind?* or *Which one?*

Nouns	Used as Adjectives
dinner	*dinner* party (*What kind* of party?)
morning	*morning* classes (*Which* classes?)

EXERCISE C: Identifying Nouns Used as Adjectives. Each of the following sentences contains one noun used as an adjective. Write the modifying noun on your paper, and next to it write the noun it modifies.

Nouns used as adjectives are underlined; modified nouns are shaded.

EXAMPLE: Fifteen baby buggies were blocking the path.

      baby   buggies

1. They brought a long grocery list to the market.
2. Did you attend the evening performance?
3. Guitar music soothes me.
4. Have the street lights been repaired yet?
5. The local bus will take you right to the train station.

Proper Adjectives

Some *proper adjectives* are simply proper nouns used as adjectives. Others are adjectives made from proper nouns.

A proper adjective is (1) a proper noun used as an adjective or (2) an adjective formed from a proper noun.

When a proper noun is used as an adjective, its form does not change.

Proper Nouns	Used as Proper Adjectives
Arizona	*Arizona* desert (*What kind* of desert?)
Tuesday	*Tuesday* morning (*Which* morning?)
Churchill	*Churchill* memorial (*Which* memorial?)

When an adjective is formed from a proper noun, the noun form changes.

Proper Nouns	Proper Adjectives Formed from Proper Nouns
Elizabeth	*Elizabethan* literature (*What kind* of literature?)
Boston	*Bostonian* architecture (*What kind* of architecture?)

All proper adjectives, as you can see from both charts, are capitalized.

EXERCISE D: Recognizing Proper Adjectives. Find the proper adjective in each sentence and write it on your paper. Next to it write the noun it modifies.
Proper adjectives are underlined; modified nouns are shaded.
EXAMPLE: Some Victorian antiques are rather ugly.

        Victorian   antiques

1. My brother is studying Jacksonian democracy in his history class.
2. Indian jewelry made of silver is very popular.
3. The weather department predicts a February blizzard.
4. My uncle has four rolls of silver Washington quarters.
5. Reporters watch the first Presidential primaries very carefully.
6. The Thanksgiving dinner was bountiful.

7. A *Newsweek* editor called several hours ago.
8. The January meeting of our club was canceled because of the ice storm.
9. When do you study American history in your school?
10. A Shakespearean comedy is fun to watch.

Compound Adjectives

Just as there are compound nouns, there are also *compound adjectives.*

A compound adjective is made up of more than one word.

Most compound adjectives are written as hyphenated words. Sometimes, however, they are written as combined words. If you are uncertain about which way to write a compound adjective, consult a dictionary for the correct spelling.

COMPOUND ADJECTIVES	
Hyphenated	**Combined**
one-sided opinion	*newborn* calf
so-called expert	*heartbreaking* news
worn-out clothing	*nearsighted* professor

EXERCISE E: Recognizing Compound Adjectives. Find the compound adjective in each sentence and write it on your paper. Next to the adjective, write the noun it modifies.
Compound adjectives are underlined; modified nouns are shaded.
EXAMPLE: Do you think that story is old-fashioned?

old-fashioned   story

1. Joanne was an unusually sweet, bright-eyed baby.
2. The Parents Council planned a schoolwide festival.
3. Joe Louis was a popular heavyweight champion.
4. My mother sees well, but my father is farsighted.

Developing Writing Skills

Have students practice using adjectives in writing by completing the following assignment.

Writing Across the Curriculum

How would you describe the area in which you live to a pen pal in a foreign country? Write a letter describing the area.

Prewriting Working with a partner, brainstorm for a list of words and phrases that describe your area. Think about the physical features of the region, the types of homes and buildings, the population, the weather, and anything else that will provide a complete description. Look over your list and choose the words and phrases that will provide the most complete and accurate description. Arrange the details describing any physical features in spatial order, and other information in order of importance.

Writing Write the first draft of a letter to your pen pal. You might want to describe the physical features of your area first, followed by any other information you want to include.

Revising Make sure that your pen pal will be able to visualize your area in his or her imagination. Have you included plenty of adjectives to make the description clearer and more vivid? Have you arranged the information logically?

3.2 Pronouns Used as Adjectives

(pp. 58–62)

5. The <u>hit-and-run</u> driver was later captured by the police.
6. An <u>offside</u> penalty cost our team five yards.
7. A <u>four-inch</u> steel latch protects the office safe.
8. She tells funny stories about her <u>absent-minded</u> friend.
9. That region of New Hampshire has several mountains with <u>snow-covered</u> peaks.
10. Achilles drove his spear into Hector's <u>bloodstained</u> armor.

DEVELOPING WRITING SKILLS: Writing Sentences with Adjectives. Rewrite the following paragraph adding two or more adjectives to each sentence. Use at least one noun as an adjective, one proper adjective, and one compound adjective in the paragraph. Then underline the adjectives that you have added.

Answers will vary; sample is given for the first one.

EXAMPLE: One night hailstones pounded on the roof of our house.

One <u>dark</u> <u>July</u> night <u>huge</u> hailstones pounded on the roof of our <u>vacation</u> house.

1. While traveling . . . the Maine coast . . . I saw a wind-blasted beach . . . .

(1) While traveling along the coast one day, I saw a beach covered with rocks and shells. (2) Scores of seagulls circled the beach, their cries echoing in the air. (3) Each time a gull spotted a fish under the water, it dove toward the water and brought out a fish within its beak. (4) I found a spot among the rocks from which to watch the battle between birds and fish. (5) On the highway behind me, trucks and cars raced by, their drivers unaware of the events that were happening just off to their right.

3.2 Pronouns Used as Adjectives

Pronouns, like nouns, can sometimes be used as adjectives.

A pronoun is used as an adjective if it modifies a noun.

3.2 Pronouns Used as Adjectives

Four kinds of pronouns are sometimes used as adjectives. They are *personal, demonstrative, interrogative,* and *indefinite pronouns.*

Possessive Adjectives

The following personal pronouns are often called *possessive adjectives: my, your, his, her, its, our,* and *their.* Because they have antecedents, they are considered to be pronouns. They are also adjectives because they answer the question *Which one?*

EXAMPLE: Anna is doing *her* homework.

This example shows that *her* is an adjective modifying the noun *homework. Her* is also a pronoun because it has an antecedent, *Anna.*

EXERCISE A: Identifying Possessive Adjectives. In each of the following sentences, a possessive adjective is underlined. On your paper make three columns as shown in the example. Write the underlined word in the first column. Then find the noun it modifies and its antecedent and put them in the second and third columns.

Modified words are underlined; antecedents are shaded.

EXAMPLE: Lincoln gave his life for his country.

Possessive Adjective	Noun Modified	Antecedent
his	life	Lincoln

1. Dori finished washing the dishes and then worked on her report.
2. Leaving his office, Mr. Cruz took a cab to the station.
3. Mary Louise will exhibit some of her watercolors in the village library.
4. My friends were late and could not keep their appointment.
5. Grabbing their lunches, the twins raced from the house.

OBJECTIVES

After completing this section, students should be able to

- Identify possessive adjectives.
- Identify demonstrative adjectives.
- Identify interrogative adjectives.
- Identify indefinite adjectives.

TEACHING

Getting Started

word bank		
my	our	her
your	his	its
their	whose	another
both	this	which

Write the Word Bank pronouns on the board. Point out that they have already learned in Sections 1.2 and 1.3 that each of these words is a pronoun. Yet the words can also be used as adjectives. Then elicit from students sentences using several of the pronouns as adjectives. Write the sentences on the board and then discuss with students how each of the pronouns modifies a noun.

Text Follow Through

Discuss text pages 58–62.

Assign Exercise A, page 59; Exercise B, page 60; Exercise C, page 60; Exercise D, page 62; and Developing Writing Skills, page 62.

Less advanced These students may need additional help in learning to distinguish between pronominal and adjectival uses. Remind students that when demonstrative, interrogative, and indefinite pronouns are used as adjectives, the noun modified follows immediately. If a noun or pronoun does not follow immediately, the word is being used as a pronoun.

Average Working in pairs, have students look for sentences in their reading assignments that illustrate each of the four kinds of pronouns used as adjectives. They should list the sentences on paper and exchange them with other pairs who will underline the adjectives and draw arrows to the words they modify.

Advanced Have these students do the same activity as average students, but have them do it independently. They should list their sentences, leaving blanks where the adjectives should go. Then have them exchange sentences, fill in the blanks in their classmates' sentences, and compare their choices to the originals.

Additional Practice

Practice Pages or Practice Book, pages 19, 20

Less advanced Exercise Bank, Exercises A and B, pages 30–33

Average Exercise Bank, Exercises A, B, and C, pages 30–33

Advanced Exercise Bank, Exercises B and C, pages 30–33

TESTING

Test Program

Unit Pretest, page 6
Chapter Test, page 18
Unit Post-Test, page 34

RE-TEACHING

Practice Pages or Practice Book, pages 19, 20

Demonstrative Adjectives

The four demonstrative pronouns—*this, that, these,* and *those*—can be used as *demonstrative adjectives.*

PRONOUN: I saw *this.*

ADJECTIVE: I'll buy *this* watch.

PRONOUN: I want *those.*

ADJECTIVE: Buy *those* peanuts.

EXERCISE B: Recognizing Demonstrative Adjectives.
Find the word *this, that, these,* or *those* in each of the sentences and copy it. If it is used as a pronoun, write *pronoun* after it. If it is used as an adjective, write the noun it modifies.

EXAMPLE: That is her decision.

That   pronoun

1. This room is always light and airy. room
2. After thinking it over, he took those. pron
3. Have you read that article yet? article
4. These photos are among the best I've seen. photos
5. I just can't believe that. pron

Interrogative Adjectives

Three interrogative pronouns—*which, what,* and *whose*—can be used as *interrogative adjectives.*

PRONOUN: *What* did he want?

ADJECTIVE: *What* name did he give?

PRONOUN·   *Whose* is that?

ADJECTIVE: *Whose* umbrella is that?

EXERCISE C: Recognizing Interrogative Adjectives. Find the word *which, what,* or *whose* in each of the sentences and

THINKING SKILLS

Comprehension—*Explaining* which words possessive adjectives modify and which words are their antecedents in sentences (Exercise A, page 59)
Distinguishing between demonstrative adjectives and demonstrative pronouns (Exercise B, page 60)
Distinguishing between interrogative adjectives and interrogative pronouns (Exercise C, page 60)
Distinguishing between indefinite adjectives and indefinite pronouns (Exercise D, page 62)

Synthesis—*Writing* original sentences with pronouns used as adjectives (Developing Writing Skills, page 60)

3.2 Pronouns Used as Adjectives

copy it. If it is used as a pronoun, write *pronoun* after it. If it is used as an adjective, write the noun it modifies.

EXAMPLE: What are you going to do?

What   pronoun

1. Which route did he decide to take? route
2. What can be done now to stop them? pron
3. At whose house shall we have the party? house
4. What movie do you want to see this weekend? movie
5. Which of the routes is the fastest to your house? pron

Indefinite Adjectives

A number of indefinite pronouns can also be used as *indefinite adjectives.*

Some indefinite adjectives can be used only with singular nouns, some only with plural nouns, and some with either singular or plural nouns.

INDEFINITE ADJECTIVES		
Used with Singular Nouns	**Used with Plural Nouns**	**Used with Singular or Plural Nouns**
another	both	all most
each	few	any other
either	many	more some
neither	several	

The following examples show the words in the chart used first as pronouns and then as adjectives.

PRONOUN: I bought one of *each.*

ADJECTIVE: *Each* album costs six dollars.

PRONOUN: *Both* of them called.

ADJECTIVE: *Both* girls called.

PRONOUN: I don't want *any*.

ADJECTIVES: I don't want *any* help.

   I don't want *any* string beans.

EXERCISE D: Recognizing Indefinite Adjectives. Find the indefinite pronoun or adjective in each of the following sentences and copy the word onto your paper. If it is used as a pronoun, write *pronoun* after it. If it is used as an adjective, write the noun it modifies after it.

EXAMPLE: Both children adored playing in the mud.

   Both   children

   1. <u>Several</u> people phoned the police after the accident. people
   2. <u>Both</u> appeared at the hotel for the contest. pron
   3. <u>More</u> apples in the bushel have spoiled. apples
   4. <u>Few</u> winners claimed their prizes. winners
   5. <u>Neither</u> of the choices was acceptable. pron

DEVELOPING WRITING SKILLS: Writing Sentences with Pronouns Used as Adjectives. Write ten sentences of your own. In each sentence use one of the following words to modify a noun. Then draw an arrow pointing from each adjective to the word it modifies.
Answers will vary; samples are given for the first two.

EXAMPLE: that

   Bobby will never get that role in the play.

1. this	5. which	9. their
2. whose	6. those	10. these
3. both	7. either	
4. her	8. our	

1. This drawing might win first prize.   2. Whose idea was it?

Writing Across the Curriculum

Writing Model Transparencies

For additional practice in using adjectives in writing, use the art transparency, lesson plan, and writing assignment for *Waterfall*, pages 23–28. This assignment provides a writing across the curriculum activity in the content area of nature.

Skills Review and Writing Workshop

Adjectives

CHECKING YOUR SKILLS

Write the two adjectives in each sentence. Do not include articles.

1. sealed, icy 2. enough, underwater 3. famous, prison 4. several, dangerous

(1) He could escape from a sealed crate in an icy stream. (2) He had enough courage to try underwater tricks that few had dared. (3) He became famous for escaping from chains, handcuffs, and prison cells. (4) Several tricks were extremely dangerous. (5) However, he was careful to keep himself physically fit. (6) He was an outstanding professional in his work. (7) What kind of person was this man? (8) He had been born Ehrich Weiss in Budapest, Hungary, and had taken Houdini as a stage, or professional, name. (9) Houdini spent years trying to expose fake mediums who claimed to have supernatural powers. (10) He was the greatest magician and escape artist the world had ever seen.

5. careful, fit 6. outstanding, his 7. What, this 8. stage, professional 9. take, supernatural 10. greatest, escape

USING GRAMMAR SKILLS IN WRITING
Writing a Character Sketch

Good writers use adjectives to write clear descriptions. Follow the steps below to write a short essay about an unusual person.

Answers will vary.

Prewriting: Choose a person who has outstanding traits. List at least three. Support each trait with an example or incident.

Writing: Begin your character sketch with the trait that is most likely to capture your readers' attention. Follow with one or more examples or incidents that point up the trait. Then add the other traits, supporting *them* with specific information.

Revising: Look at the adjectives you used and change any that could be stronger. Then read the entire sketch, making improvements. After you have revised, proofread carefully.

Checking Your Skills

In the Checking Your Skills assignment, students have identified adjectives in sentences. Explain to students that adjectives are important to clarify and bring to life the meaning of nouns and pronouns.

Speaking and Listening

Have students select a paragraph from a story or a non-fiction selection and replace the adjectives with other adjectives that will change the meaning of the paragraph to some degree. They should list the adjectives they replaced on a separate sheet of paper. In class, have students share their rewritten paragraphs. After a student finishes reading the paragraph, the class should guess what the original adjectives were. The student should then write the original adjectives on the chalkboard and the class can discuss how adjectives can change the tone and even the meaning of a paragraph.

Using Grammar Skills in Writing

Revising You might want students to exchange papers with a partner for the revising stage of this assignment. Partners should read the character sketches and comment on the impression the sketch gives of the subject. The writers should compare this impression with the impression they were trying to convey. Partners should then work together to revise their sketches.

CHAPTER 4
Adverbs

(pp. 64–71)

Chapter 4 consists of two short sections. Section 4.1 discusses the three types of words that adverbs modify, while Section 4.2 helps students find adverbs in sentences and distinguish them from adjectives.

For a review of the entire chapter and a related writing activity, see the Skills Review and Writing Workshop on page 71.

4.1 Adverbs as Modifiers

(pp. 64–67)

OBJECTIVES

After completing this section, students should be able to

- Identify adverbs that modify verbs.
- Identify adverbs that modify adjectives.
- Identify adverbs that modify other adverbs.

Chapter **4**

Adverbs

Like adjectives, *adverbs* modify words in sentences. Consider this sentence: *In the afternoon Judy worked.*

Judy could have worked *hard, happily,* or *unwillingly.* All of these words are adverbs. They tell how Judy worked.

The first section in this chapter will explain which parts of speech adverbs can modify. The second will give practice in recognizing adverbs in sentences.

4.1 Adverbs as Modifiers

Adverbs modify three different parts of speech.

An adverb modifies a verb, an adjective, or another adverb.

To recognize adverbs, you need to know how they modify each of these three parts of speech.

Adverbs Modifying Verbs

An adverb modifying a verb will answer one of four questions about the verb: *Where? When? In what manner?* or *To what extent?*

4.1 Adverbs as Modifiers

ADVERBS MODIFYING VERBS	
Where?	
drove *down*	stay *nearby*
is *here*	jump *away*
When?	
report *later*	come *tomorrow*
will leave *soon*	appeared *suddenly*
In What Manner?	
cautiously approached	walk *quietly*
smiled *happily*	tell *unwillingly*
To What Extent?	
nearly won	had *almost* left
hardly counted	*scarcely* escaped

EXERCISE A: Recognizing Adverbs That Modify Verbs.
Make and label four columns as shown. Then find the adverb in each sentence and write it in the appropriate column.

EXAMPLE: The dog slept quietly by the stove.

<u>Where?</u>   <u>When?</u>   <u>In What Manner?</u>   <u>To What Extent?</u>
quietly

3. When? 5. In what manner? 9. To what extent?

1. The bus traveled <u>rapidly</u> into the night. In what manner?
2. Does he <u>fully</u> understand what is expected? To what extent?
3. She <u>immediately</u> described the accident to a police officer.
4. The guests arrived <u>late</u> but found nobody at home. When?
5. <u>Silently</u>, the detective climbed the stairs to the attic.
6. Bud has <u>almost</u> finished his model. To what extent?
7. Do you expect to move <u>away</u> from Albuquerque? Where?
8. He is <u>always</u> creating problems. When?
9. The shopping center has <u>nearly</u> been completed.
10. My sister <u>quickly</u> cleaned the cage. In what manner?

TEACHING
Getting Started

┌─ sentence bank ─────────┐
We hope to see you soon.
Jane is getting dressed
  upstairs.
She angrily slammed the
  door.
He was somewhat surprised.
└──────────────────────┘

Put the Sentence Bank sentences on the board and underline the adverbs.

Elicit from students how the underlined words answer one of these questions about the verb: Where? In what manner? When? or To what extent? Point out that these words are called "adverbs." Adverbs can modify not only verbs but adjectives and other adverbs as well.

Text Follow Through
Discuss text pages 64–67.

Assign Exercise A, page 65; Exercise B, page 66; Exercise C, page 67; and Developing Writing Skills, page 67.

Less advanced You might have students work in pairs to generate adverbs that can be used in the Developing Writing Skills sentences. Then have students write the sentences independently and have their partners check them over.

Average For more practice, have students write three sentences to add to Exercises A, B, and C. They should exchange their sentences with classmates who will follow the exercise directions, identifying adverbs and the words they modify.

Advanced Have students find a passage in their reading that contains numerous adverbs. They should copy the passage, circle each adverb, and draw an arrow to the word it modifies.

Additional Practice

Practice Pages or Practice Book, pages 21, 22

Less advanced Exercise Bank, Exercises A and B, pages 34–36

Average Exercise Bank, Exercises A, B, and C, pages 34–36

Advanced Exercise Bank, Exercises B and C, pages 34–36

TESTING

Test Program

Unit Pretest, page 6
Chapter Test, pages 19, 20
Unit Post-Test, page 35

RE-TEACHING

Practice Pages or Practice Book, pages 21, 22

THINKING SKILLS

Comprehension—*Distinguishing* adverbs and *inferring* what information each provides (Exercise A, page 65)
Distinguishing adverbs and the adjectives or adverbs they modify (Exercise B, page 66; Exercise C, page 67)

Synthesis—*Composing* sentences with adverbs that modify verbs, adjectives, and adverbs (Developing Writing Skills, page 67)

Adverbs Modifying Adjectives

When an adverb modifies an adjective, it answers the question *To what extent?*

ADVERBS MODIFYING ADJECTIVES		
almost right	*not* sad	*unusually* rich

EXERCISE B: Recognizing Adverbs That Modify Adjectives. On your paper write the adverb from each sentence. After each adverb write the adjective it modifies.

Adverbs are underlined; adjectives are shaded.
EXAMPLE: She was very happy with the results.

very   happy

1. We examined an almost new tape recorder.
2. He was somewhat unwilling to answer our questions.
3. Sue was very glad to accept his invitation.
4. These baked potatoes are especially good.
5. He made the whipped cream too sweet.
6. An often noisy crowd waited outside the courtroom.
7. An unusually tall actress is needed for that role.
8. The patient looked decidedly ill.
9. That teacher is remarkably knowledgeable in her field.
10. This trip will be rather dangerous.

Adverbs Modifying Other Adverbs

When adverbs modify other adverbs, they again answer the question *To what extent?*

ADVERBS MODIFYING ADVERBS	
traveled *less slowly*	move *very cautiously*
lost *too easily*	lived *almost happily*

4.1 Adverbs as Modifiers

EXERCISE C: Recognizing Adverbs That Modify Other Adverbs. In each sentence, find an adverb that modifies another adverb by answering the question *To what extent?* Write this adverb and after it write the adverb it modifies.

Modifying adverbs are underlined; modified adverbs are shaded.

EXAMPLE: The movers arrived too early in the day.

       too   early

1. She worked too slowly to finish in time.
2. After his experience, he climbed trees rather cautiously.
3. The train should pull into the station quite soon.
4. After living for years in Japan, the child had almost totally forgotten how to speak English.
5. The vase was almost completely uncracked.
6. Do you think you can talk less rapidly?
7. My best friend has moved far away.
8. Although he lost, the knight fought very bravely.
9. He has been told that he speaks Spanish extremely well.
10. She was only slightly tired after the long race.

DEVELOPING WRITING SKILLS: Writing Sentences with Adverbs. Write five sentences using an adverb that fits each description below. Underline the adverb and draw an arrow from it to the word it modifies.

Answers will vary; samples are given for the first two.

EXAMPLE: an adverb that modifies a verb and answers the question *To what extent?*

       The driver of the car narrowly avoided an accident.

1. an adverb that modifies a verb and answers the question *Where?* Bob's pet mouse has run away.
2. an adverb that modifies a verb and answers the question *When?* Our guests arrived early.
3. an adverb that modifies a verb and answers the question *In what manner?*
4. an adverb that modifies an adjective
5. an adverb modifying another adverb

Developing Writing Skills

Have students practice using adverbs in writing by completing the following assignment.

Writing Across the Curriculum

Have you ever wondered what it would be like to witness a historic event? Chances are, on television or perhaps even first-hand, you have witnessed such an event. For example, the inauguration of a President, the launching of a space shuttle, or the signing of a peace treaty are all regarded as historic events.

Prewriting   Jot down a list of events that you have witnessed first-hand or on television that might someday be written about in history books. Choose one event and use the five W's cueing technique to brainstorm for details about it. The five W's include the following: Who? What? When? Where? and Why? You might have to do a little research to answer some of these questions. Arrange the details in order of importance.

Writing   Write the first draft of a news release describing the historic event. Be sure to include aswers to the five W questions in the first few sentences of the release. Then describe some of the less important details.

Revising   Make sure that you have described the event completely and accurately. Have you answered the five W's? Have you used adverbs to modify verbs, adjectives, and other adverbs? Proofread your news release and prepare a final draft.

4.2 Adverbs Used in Sentences
(pp. 68–70)

OBJECTIVES

After completing this section, students should be able to

- Locate adverbs in sentences.
- Distinguish between adjectives and adverbs.

TEACHING

Getting Started

Have students turn to page 68, and as a class, discuss the chart Location of Adverbs in Sentences, so that students understand the various positions adverbs can have in a sentence. Ask students to suggest additional example sentences for each adverb location listed in the chart.

Text Follow Through

Discuss text pages 68–70.

Assign Exercise A, page 68; Exercise B, page 70; and Developing Writing Skills, page 70.

Less advanced Do Exercise B as a class, asking students to identify the word that each underlined word modifies and the part of speech of the modified word. Remind students that adjectives modify nouns or pronouns, while adverbs modify verbs, adjectives, or other adverbs.

4.2 Adverbs Used in Sentences

Adverbs can be located in almost any part of a sentence.

Finding Adverbs in Sentences

Learning where to look for adverbs will help you to identify them. The following chart shows some of the positions in which adverbs can appear. The arrows point from the adverbs, to the words that they modify.

LOCATION OF ADVERBS IN SENTENCES	
Location	**Example**
At the Beginning of a Sentence	*Quickly,* they gathered the firewood.
At the End of a Sentence	They gathered the firewood *quickly.*
Before a Verb	He *cautiously* approached the dog.
After a Verb	She walked *slowly* from the room.
Between Parts of a Verb	They had *quickly* gathered the firewood.
Before an Adjective	He was *rather* glad about the results.
Before Another Adverb	She walked *rather* slowly from the room.

EXERCISE A: Locating Adverbs in Sentences. Each of the following sentences contains one or two adverbs. Copy the sentences onto your paper and underline the adverbs. Then draw arrows from the adverbs to the words they modify.

Adverbs are underlined; modified words are shaded.

68

4.2 Adverbs Used in Sentences

EXAMPLE: The poet <u>happily</u> inserted the perfect word.

1. She <u>tearfully</u> told us about the accident.
2. <u>Suddenly</u> the whistle sounded, and the train <u>slowly</u> left.
3. Bobby has <u>almost</u> finished his piano practice.
4. He has <u>never</u> asked for help.
5. My mother moved the couch <u>slowly</u> to the left.
6. The lifeguard does <u>not</u> think the pool will be open <u>soon</u>.
7. <u>Cautiously</u>, the police approached the building.
8. The wall was <u>brightly</u> painted in yellow and white.
9. He spun <u>too</u> <u>quickly</u> and lost his balance.
10. In 1860 Senator William M. Gwin and several others pushed <u>vigorously</u> for a pony-express route.

Adverb or Adjective?

Some words can be either adverbs or adjectives. An adverb always modifies a verb, an adjective, or another adverb. An adjective modifies a noun or pronoun.

ADVERB MODIFYING VERB: He drove too *fast.*

ADJECTIVE MODIFYING NOUN: He is a *fast* driver.

ADVERB MODIFYING ADJECTIVE: She is *much* happier now.

ADJECTIVE MODIFYING NOUN: I ate too *much* food.

Although many adverbs end in *-ly,* not all words ending in *-ly* are adverbs. Some adjectives are formed by adding *-ly* to nouns.

Nouns	Adjectives with *-ly* Endings
a beautiful *home*	a *homely* animal
an *elder* in the church	an *elderly* man
his true *love*	*lovely* flowers

Average   Refer students to Exercise A in Section 2.1 (page 39) and have them add at least one adverb to each sentence. Suggest that they try to place their adverbs in different locations within the sentences. Have students compare their choices and note the different positions in which they placed their adverbs.

Advanced   Have students bring in some of their favorite stories or articles from magazines or newspapers. Then have them list the adverbs used in the various readings, and indicate the part of speech each adverb modifies and the question each answers about the word it modifies.

Additional Practice

Practice Pages or Practice Book, page 23

Less advanced   Exercise Bank, Exercises A and B, pages 37, 38

Average   Exercise Bank, Exercises A, B, and C, pages 37, 38

Advanced   Exercise Bank, Exercises B and C, pages 37, 38

TESTING
Test Program

Unit Pretest, page 6
Chapter Test, pages 19, 20
Unit Post-Test, page 35

RE-TEACHING
Practice Pages or Practice Book, page 23

THINKING SKILLS

Comprehension—*Distinguishing* adverbs in sentences (Exercise A, page 68)
Distinguishing between adjectives and adverbs in sentences (Exercise B, page 70)

Synthesis—*Composing* sentences that contain adverbs (Developing Writing Skills, page 70)

Writing Across the Curriculum

For additional practice using adverbs in writing, use the art transparency, lesson plan, and writing assignment for *Self-Portrait*, pages 29–34. This assignment provides a writing across the curriculum activity in the content area of arts and crafts.

EXERCISE B: Distinguishing Between Adverbs and Adjectives. On your paper indicate whether the underlined word in each of the following sentences is an adverb or an adjective.

EXAMPLE: The poster was <u>finally</u> finished.

        adverb

1. My grandfather was a <u>kindly</u> man who always helped his grandchildren. adj
2. Aunt Millie drives <u>regularly</u> to Los Angeles to shop. adv
3. I always work <u>hard</u> on my class reports. adv
4. Mother had a <u>hard</u> time reaching the doctor. adj
5. The senator <u>bitterly</u> criticized his opponents. adv
6. My science teacher is an unusually <u>friendly</u> person. adj
7. Does the <u>early</u> bird catch the worm? adj
8. I jog <u>daily</u>. adv
9. Taking a coffee break is a <u>daily</u> practice in our company. adj
10. Has the engine been running <u>smoothly</u>? adv

DEVELOPING WRITING SKILLS: Writing Sentences with Adverbs. Write twenty sentences of your own using the adverbs in the following list. After writing each sentence, draw an arrow pointing from the adverb to the word or words that the adverb modifies.

Answers will vary; samples are given for the first two.

EXAMPLE: not

      She has not given us her answer.

1. beautifully	8. almost	15. quickly
2. slowly	9. happily	16. yesterday
3. regularly	10. smoothly	17. loudly
4. amazingly	11. seldom	18. completely
5. never	12. very	19. always
6. soon	13. away	20. usually
7. sleepily	14. now	

1. The dancer soared beautifully into the darkness.   2. We drove slowly on the wet road.

Skills Review and Writing Workshop

Adverbs

CHECKING YOUR SKILLS

Write the two adverbs in each sentence.

1. today, actually 2. unusually, suddenly 3. quickly, later 4. exceedingly, rather

(1) Some of the technology we take for granted today was actually presented to the general public in the 1930s. (2) At that time, two unusually imaginative comic strips suddenly appeared in many newspapers. (3) They were "Buck Rogers" and "Flash Gordon," both of which won popularity quickly and were later made into movies. (4) Buck and Flash drove exceedingly fast cars and rode on rather high-tech monorails. (5) Flash can be clearly seen watching a TV set and wielding a ray gun that looks uncannily like a laser beam. (6) There is a carefully drawn atomic power plant in Buck's city, as well as something that almost resembles a lie detector. (7) Rocket ships traveled more quickly in these 1930s strips than ours do. (8) Surely ours will soon catch up with those fictional ones. (9) Meanwhile, sci-fi movies today may be subtly presenting a picture of *our* future. (10) Could this very imaginative movie future actually turn out to be true?

5. clearly, uncannily 6. carefully, almost 7. more, quickly 8. Surely, soon

USING GRAMMAR SKILLS IN WRITING

Writing About Tomorrow's World

Good writers use adverbs to help give a clear sense of when, how, and where things are happening. Write a short essay about tomorrow's technology. Follow the steps below.

Answers will vary.

Prewriting: List four items you plan to include. Think of supporting details or reasons for each one.

Writing: Begin with your most unusual item. Arrange the others logically. Write a strong concluding sentence.

Revising: Look at your adverbs and change any that could be more specific, and make improvements. After you have revised, proofread carefully.

9. Meanwhile, subtly 10. very, actually

Checking Your Skills

In the Checking Your Skills assignment, students have identified adverbs in sentences. Remind students that adverbs enable writers to clarify the meaning of their sentences by answering the questions *Where? When? In What Manner?* and *To What Extent?*

Collaborative Learning

Divide the class into small groups of relatively equal ability. Have each group choose a three-paragraph excerpt from a short story or nonfiction selection. Each group should work together to identify the adverbs in the passage, the part of speech each adverb modifies, and the question each adverb answers. Each group should select a recorder to record the information. When the groups have completed the assignment, have someone other than the recorder read the passage aloud and share the results of the group's work.

Using Grammar Skills in Writing

Prewriting You might want students to free write for several minutes, imagining how technology will advance in the future. What new discoveries will be made? What new machines will be available to the public? How will these machines change our lives? After they have completed free writing, students can go back and select four items to include in their essays.

CHAPTER 5
**Prepositions,
Conjunctions, and
Interjections**
(pp. 72–83)

Each section in this chapter considers one of the remaining parts of speech: Section 5.1 discusses prepositions, Section 5.2 looks at conjunctions, and Section 5.3 deals with interjections.

For a review of the entire chapter and a related writing activity, see the Skills Review and Writing Workshop on page 83.

5.1 Prepositions
(pp. 72–76)

OBJECTIVES

After completing this section, students should be able to

- Identify one-word and compound prepositions.
- Identify prepositional phrases.
- Distinguish between prepositions and adverbs in sentences.

Chapter **5**

Prepositions, Conjunctions, and Interjections

Prepositions, conjunctions, and *interjections* all play special roles in sentences.

5.1 Prepositions

Prepositions are words such as *against, among, at, beyond, during, of,* and *on.*

A preposition relates the noun or pronoun following it to another word in the sentence.

Words Used as Prepositions

The chart lists fifty of the most commonly used prepositions.

5.1 Prepositions

FREQUENTLY USED PREPOSITIONS

about	behind	during	off	to
above	below	except	on	toward
across	beneath	for	onto	under
after	beside	from	opposite	underneath
against	besides	in	out	until
along	between	inside	outside	up
among	beyond	into	over	upon
around	but	like	past	with
at	by	near	since	within
before	down	of	through	without

Prepositions consisting of two or three words are called *compound prepositions.* Some of them are listed in the following chart.

COMPOUND PREPOSITIONS

according to	by means of	instead of
ahead of	in addition to	in view of
apart from	in back of	next to
aside from	in front of	on account of
as of	in place of	on top of
because of	in spite of	out of

The choice of preposition affects the way the other words in a sentence relate to each other. In the following example, read the sentence using each preposition. Notice how each preposition changes the relationship between *stopped* and *school.*

EXAMPLE:

The bus stopped
- at
- near
- opposite
- in back of
- next to

the school.

Average Most students should have little difficulty with the material in this section. For additional practice, have students rewrite their Developing Writing Skills sentences, using a different preposition in each (as in Exercise A).

Advanced Have students work in pairs. Each student should write five sentence pairs similar to those in Exercise C for a partner to identify the prepositions, prepositional phrases, and adverbs.

Additional Practice

Practice Pages or Practice Book, pages 24, 25

Less advanced Exercise Bank, Exercises A and B, pages 39–41

Average Exercise Bank, Exercises A, B, and C, pages 39–41

Advanced Exercise Bank, Exercises B and C, pages 39–41

TESTING

Test Program

Unit Pretest, page 7
Chapter Test, page 21
Unit Post-Test, page 35

RE-TEACHING

Practice Pages or Practice Book, pages 24, 25

THINKING SKILLS

Knowledge—*Identifying* prepositional phrases (Exercise B, page 75)

Comprehension—*Distinguishing* between prepositions and adverbs (Exercise C, page 75)

Application—*Modifying* sentences by using different prepositions (Exercise A, page 74)

EXERCISE A: Recognizing Prepositions. Find the preposition in each of the following sentences and write it on your paper. Then rewrite the sentence using a different preposition.

New prepositions will vary; samples are given.

EXAMPLE: They left the house at dawn.

at   They left the house before dawn.

1. The florist left a box outside the house. in
2. After breakfast I walk the dogs. Before
3. The baby crawled under the table. around
4. He warned us of the danger. about
5. The taxi drove in front of the delivery truck. behind
6. There is a round window near the entrance. above
7. She hid her bicycle in back of the fence. behind
8. What are those flowers growing on the hillside? near
9. Put these papers on top of my desk. on
10. Three deer loped through the woods. out of

Prepositional Phrases

A preposition must always be followed by a noun or pronoun. The group of words beginning with the preposition and ending with the noun or pronoun is called a *prepositional phrase*. The noun or pronoun that follows the preposition is called the *object of the preposition*.

PREPOSITIONAL PHRASES	
Prepositions	**Objects of Prepositions**
in	the *house*
with	*us*
in front of	the old dilapidated *barn*

Most prepositional phrases are brief. However, phrases with compound prepositions or with adjectives modifying the object can be longer.

Synthesis—*Writing* sentences with prepositional phrases (Developing Writing Skills, page 76)

5.1 Prepositions

EXERCISE B: Identifying Prepositional Phrases. On your paper write the prepositional phrase appearing in each of the following sentences.

EXAMPLE: She opened the gate in the fence.

in the fence

1. She waited all morning near the store.
2. In the morning Mom and Dad prepare breakfast and pack our lunches.
3. They reached the campsite by means of a steep, rocky path.
4. Uncle Steve brought a present for me.
5. According to Mr. Wilson, the math test has been postponed.
6. After much excitement we reached the airport five minutes early.
7. I stored my gear inside my best friend's locker.
8. In front of my house stands a weathered blue spruce.
9. When is she coming home from school?
10. Edith planted flowers in front of the shrubs.

Preposition or Adverb?

Some words can be either prepositions or adverbs, depending on how they are used in a sentence. To be a preposition, a word must be part of a prepositional phrase. If a word modifies a verb and has no object, it is an adverb.

OBJ

PREPOSITION: The jet flew *over* the house.

ADVERB: The entire family came *over*.

OBJ

PREPOSITION: They walked *along* the waterfront.

ADVERB: Won't you come *along*?

Developing Writing Skills

Have students practice using prepositional phrases in writing by completing the following assignment.

Writing Across the Curriculum

Every day we hear weather forecasts on the radio and television. One of the common topics of conversation with people is the weather. Why is weather so important to people? How does the weather affect the daily lives of the people in your community?

Prewriting Jot down a short summary of the weather in your area over the course of a year. Now, think about how the weather affects the daily lives of people in your community. How does it affect their dress? Their work? Their leisure? Think about temperature, precipitation, wind, and any noteworthy weather events, such as hurricanes, droughts, or violent thunder and lightning storms.

Writing Write the first draft of an explanation of how the weather affects the lives of the people in your community. Begin with a topic sentence that sums up the influence of weather. Then, briefly summarize the weather during spring and explain how it influences the people's lives. In chronological order, follow the same procedure for the other three seasons.

Revising Make sure that you have given a brief summary of the weather for each season along with its effect on the lives of the people in your community. Is your explanation clear? Proofread your paper and prepare a final draft.

EXERCISE C: Distinguishing Between Prepositions and Adverbs. In each of the following pairs of sentences, one sentence contains a word used as a preposition and the other contains the same word used as an adverb. Find which words appear in both sentences. If the word acts as a preposition, write the prepositional phrase on your paper. If the word acts as an adverb, write *adverb*.

Prepositional phrases are shaded; adverbs are underlined.

EXAMPLE:　We found the keys in the car.
　　　　　They came in and dinner began.

　　　　　in the car　　adverb

1. The rabbit would not come near.
　The rose bush is near the white fence.
2. You will find the house if you continue past the traffic light.
　The old man would often walk past in the evening.
3. Turn the lights on before it gets dark.
　The shopping center is two blocks farther on the right.
4. Several vultures soared around gracefully.
　Go completely around the traffic circle.
5. He and his baggage were thrown out the door.
　We all went out to celebrate our parents' anniversary.

DEVELOPING WRITING SKILLS: Writing Sentences with Prepositional Phrases. Write ten sentences of your own, each containing a prepositional phrase that begins with one of the prepositions listed below. Underline the preposition and circle its object.

Answers will vary; samples are given for the first two.

EXAMPLE:　instead of

　　　　　Voters elected a newcomer instead of the (incumbent.)

1. We rowed against the (current)　2. May I get ahead of (you?)

1. against
2. ahead of
3. among
4. because of
5. beneath
6. except
7. in addition to
8. in spite of
9. since
10. within

Conjunctions 5.2

Conjunctions work like cement between bricks. Words such as *and, but, as,* and *when* connect individual words or groups of words. They are the cement of sentences.

A conjunction connects words or groups of words.

Conjunctions fall into three groups. There are *coordinating conjunctions, correlative conjunctions,* and *subordinating conjunctions.*

Coordinating Conjunctions

Coordinating conjunctions connect words of a similar kind, for example, two or more verbs. They can also connect larger groups of words, such as prepositional phrases, or even entire sentences.

COORDINATING CONJUNCTIONS			
and	for	or	yet
but	nor	so	

In the following examples, the coordinating conjunctions are circled. The words they connect are italicized.

CONNECTING NOUNS: My *cousin* (and) his *wife* arrived yesterday for a visit.

CONNECTING ADJECTIVES: He had a choice of a *tan, red,* (or) *blue* shirt.

CONNECTING VERBS: The St. Bernard *chewed* (and) *swallowed* its food ravenously.

CONNECTING PREPOSITIONAL PHRASES: Put the package *on the doorstep* (or) *in the garage.*

77

5.2 Conjunctions
(pp. 77–81)

OBJECTIVES
After completing this section, students should be able to

- Identify coordinating conjunctions.
- Identify correlative conjunctions.
- Identify subordinating conjunctions.

TEACHING
Getting Started

sentence bank
Pat and my brother are friends. (nouns)
Pat likes bright red or orange T-shirts. (adjectives)
Pat runs and swims daily. (verbs)
Pat runs around the lake or through the park. (prepositional phrases)
Pat prefers running, but I like swimming better. (sentences)

Introduce the term *coordinating conjunction* by explaining that a conjunction connects words or groups of words and that a coordinating conjunction connects similar words or groups of words. Write the Sentence Bank sentences on the chalkboard. Point out the two nouns and the coordinating conjunction in the first sentence, and then have volunteers point out the coordinating conjunctions and the connected words in the other sentences. Volunteers might want to supply other sentences with coordinating conjunctions for classmates to identify the coordinating conjunction and the words being connected.

Text Follow Through

Discuss text pages 77–81.

Assign Exercise A, page 78; Exercise B, page 79; Exercise C, page 80; Exercise D, page 81; and Developing Writing Skills, page 81.

Less advanced You might want to have students complete Exercise D and the Developing Writing Skills activity in a classroom workshop session. Have students share ideas for sentences and suggest improvements to one another's efforts.

Average Students should have no difficulty identifying the conjunctions in the exercises. For additional practice, students can exchange the sentences they have written for the Developing Writing Skills activity. They can then circle the conjunction in each sentence and underline the words or groups of words each conjunction joins. Students can also be asked to write at the end of each sentence the kind of conjunction they circled.

Advanced Students might be asked to identify the kinds of conjunctions used in Exercise D and in the Developing Writing Skills activity.

CONNECTING TWO SENTENCES: *Alison wanted to go shopping, (but) she decided to do her homework first.*

EXERCISE A: Recognizing Coordinating Conjunctions.

Copy the following sentences onto your paper and circle the coordinating conjunction in each. Then underline the words or groups of words connected by the conjunction.

Conjunctions are shaded.

EXAMPLE: We nibbled on <u>cheese</u> (and) <u>crackers</u>.

1. We bought a <u>small</u> yet <u>comfortable</u> car.
2. The experiments are conducted <u>in the morning</u> and <u>in the evening</u>.
3. The actor was <u>handsome</u> but <u>untalented</u>.
4. I must <u>catch the train at noon</u>, for <u>I have a doctor's appointment in the city</u>.
5. The eagle <u>soared</u>, <u>swooped</u>, and <u>landed</u> on its nest.

Correlative Conjunctions

Correlative conjunctions connect the same kinds of words or groups of words as do coordinating conjunctions. Correlative conjunctions are different, however, because they come in pairs.

CORRELATIVE CONJUNCTIONS		
both . . . and	neither . . . nor	whether . . . or
either . . . or	not only . . . but also	

CONNECTING NOUNS: He opened (both) his *present* (and) her *present.*

CONNECTING PRONOUNS: (Either) *you* (or) *I* will be the lead runner.

CONNECTING VERBS: The sick python would (neither) *eat* (nor) *drink.*

Additional Practice

Practice Pages or Practice Book, pages 26, 27

Less advanced Exercise Bank, Exercises A and B, pages 42–44

Average Exercise Bank, Exercises A, B, and C, pages 42–44

Advanced Exercise Bank, Exercises B and C, pages 42–44

TESTING

Test Program

Unit Pretest, page 7
Chapter Test, page 21
Unit Post-Test, page 35

RE-TEACHING

Practice Pages or Practice Book, pages 26, 27

THINKING SKILLS

Knowledge—*Identifying* coordinating conjunctions and the words they connect (Exercise A, page 78)
  Identifying correlative conjunctions and the two groups of words they connect (Exercise B, page 79)
  Identifying subordinating conjunctions and dependent ideas (Exercise C, page 80)

Synthesis—*Writing* sentences using conjunctions provided (Exercise D, page 81)
  Composing original sentences with conjunctions (Developing Writing Skills, page 81)

5.2 Conjunctions

CONNECTING PREPOSITIONAL PHRASES: He will keep the appointment; (whether) *at one* (or) *at two,* he couldn't say.

CONNECTING TWO SENTENCES: (Not only) *is Lila a talented artist,* (but) *she is* (also) *a fine writer.*

EXERCISE B: Recognizing Correlative Conjunctions. Copy the following sentences onto your paper and circle the correlative conjunction in each. Then underline the two words or the two groups of words connected by the conjunction.
Conjunctions are shaded.
EXAMPLE: I can ask (neither) my father (nor) my mother for permission.

1. I don't care whether Marla or Lisa represents us.
2. She trains for the marathon both in the morning and in the afternoon.
3. Not only was he a fine athlete, but he was also a fine student.
4. Neither Michael nor she could explain the strange noises.
5. Grandfather was either reading or napping.

Subordinating Conjunctions

To *subordinate* means to "place below another in rank." *Subordinating conjunctions* connect two ideas by making one idea dependent on the other.

FREQUENTLY USED SUBORDINATE CONJUNCTIONS			
after	as though	since	until
although	because	so that	when
as	before	than	whenever
as if	even though	though	where
as long as	if	till	wherever
as soon as	in order that	unless	while

You will find that the subordinating conjunction always comes before the dependent idea. The subordinating conjunction connects the dependent idea to the main idea.

EXAMPLES:

MAIN IDEA   DEPENDENT IDEA
I did the planting (after) he prepared the soil.

DEPENDENT IDEA   MAIN IDEA
(When) he phoned this morning, he was unable to reach the senator.

The examples show that the main idea can come at the beginning or at the end of the sentence. Notice the important difference in punctuating the two examples. When the dependent idea comes first, it must be separated from the main idea with a comma. (See Section 9.2 for more information about subordinating conjunctions.)

EXERCISE C: Recognizing Subordinating Conjunctions.

Copy the following sentences onto your paper and circle the subordinating conjunction in each. Then underline the dependent idea following the conjunction and label it *Dependent*. Conjunctions are shaded.

DEPENDENT
EXAMPLE: (If) he asks my permission, I will grant it.

1. Since they want to join our club, I will nominate them.
2. They all went fishing while their father slept.
3. The stamps will be available whenever you wish to pick them up.
4. As if she didn't have enough trouble, she has lost her wallet.
5. As long as I can remember, we have spent part of the summer in Vermont.
6. She went home as soon as she heard the news.
7. I sometimes eat more than I should.
8. He lost his way because he forgot to take a map.
9. I can do it if you help me.
10. You look as though you need a rest.

Writing Across the Curriculum

For additional practice in using prepositions, conjunctions, and interjections in writing, use the art transparency, lesson plan, and writing assignment for *Mountain Landscape*, pages 35–40. This assignment provides a writing across the curriculum activity in the content of area earth science.

5.3 Interjections

EXERCISE D: Writing Sentences Using Conjunctions.

Fill in the blanks with words that will complete each sentence. Use as many words as necessary to complete each thought, but keep each conjunction in the position shown.

Answers will vary; samples are given.

EXAMPLE: _____ as though _____.

She acted as though she didn't really want to go.

1. Both ___Cheryl___ and ___I jumped up___.
2. If ___you can do the work___ , ___go ahead___.
3. ___I hope you can___ because ___I can't___.
4. Although ___the twins are here___ , ___their brother is not___.
5. Not only does she ___ski___ , but she also ___climbs mountains___.
6. ___Felix raised his hand___ , but ___you didn't see him___.
7. When ___we arrived___ , ___the party seemed to be over___.
8. Either ___Jane___ or ___Diane will bring crackers___.
9. ___I was surprised___ even though ___I knew the story___.
10. While ___you were fixing the car___ , ___we found the map___.

DEVELOPING WRITING SKILLS: Writing Original Sentences with Conjunctions.
Write sentences of your own using each of the following conjunctions.

Answers will vary; samples are given for the first two.

EXAMPLE: both . . . and

Both Irving and Poe wrote short stories.

1. You don't have to come unless you want to.
1. unless
2. or
3. when
4. neither . . . nor
5. although
6. even though
7. but
8. wherever
9. as if
10. whether . . . or

2. Grace or Mel can give you directions.

Interjections 5.3

The *interjection* is the part of speech that is used the least. Its only use is to express feelings or emotions.

81

5.3 Interjections
(pp. 81–82)

OBJECTIVE
After completing this section, students should be able to

• Identify interjections.

TEACHING

Getting Started

┌─ sentence bank ──────────┐
Hurrah! We won! (joy)
Oh, I didn't see you there. (surprise)
Ouch! That pan is hot! (pain)
Stop! Don't say another word! (impatience)
Uh, I'm not sure. (hesitation)
└──────────────────────────┘

Explain that interjections are used to express feelings or emotions. Write the Sentence Bank sentences on the chalkboard, omitting the words in parentheses. Elicit or point out the emotions or feelings indicated in the parentheses. You might have students read the sentences aloud to help them recognize the emotion implied by each interjection.

Ask for volunteers to write other interjections on the chalkboard and have them tell what emotion or feeling is expressed by each.

Text Follow Through

Discuss text pages 81–82.

Assign the Exercise, page 82, and Developing Writing Skills, page 82.

Less advanced You might want to let students choose any five of the words in the Developing Writing Skills activity for their sentences. Have students read their sentences aloud, emphasizing the implied feeling while other students try to guess the feeling.

Average Students should be able to complete this section with little difficulty. For additional practice, you might have students write brief dialogues in which the speakers use many interjections. For example:
He: Oh, I hope the teacher doesn't call on me.
She: Uh, I think she's looking this way.
He: Help! She is looking right at me.

Advanced To introduce the point that interjections should be used infrequently in formal writing, you may want to have students search for interjections in their reading assignments and then discuss the results.

Additional Practice

Practice Pages or Practice Book, page 28

Less advanced Exercise Bank, Exercises A and B, page 45

Average Exercise Bank, Exercises A, B, and C, page 45

Advanced Exercise Bank, Exercises B and C, page 45

TESTING

Test Program

Unit Pretest, page 7
Chapter Test, page 22
Unit Post-Test, page 35

RE-TEACHING

Practice Pages or Practice Book, page 28

THINKING SKILLS

Application—*Using* interjections that express given feelings (Exercise, page 82)

Synthesis—*Producing* sentences with interjections (Developing Writing Skills, page 82)

An interjection expresses feeling or emotion and functions independently of a sentence.

An interjection has no grammatical relationship to any other word in a sentence. It is, therefore, set off from the rest of the sentence with a comma or an exclamation mark.

Interjections can express different feelings or emotion.

JOY: *Wow!* I can't believe I won.

SURPRISE: *Oh,* I didn't expect to hear from you.

PAIN: *Ouch!* That hurts.

IMPATIENCE: *Tsk!* How long do they expect to wait?

HESITATION: I, *uh,* think you should leave.

EXERCISE: Recognizing Interjections. Rewrite each of the following sentences using an appropriate interjection in place of the feeling shown in parentheses.
Answers will vary; samples are given.

EXAMPLE: (Anger) I wanted to watch the footall game.

Darn! I wanted to watch the football game.

1. (Surprise) I never expected this. Oh!
2. (Impatience) We have to catch the train. Hey!
3. (Dislike) I don't like that hat at all. Yuck!
4. (Pain) I caught my finger in the door. Ow!
5. (Joy) We're all thrilled you came. Wow!

DEVELOPING WRITING SKILLS: Using Interjections in Sentences. Use the following interjections with commas or exclamation marks in sentences of your own.
Answers will vary; samples are given for the first two.

EXAMPLE: uh

My excuse is, uh, not what you might expect.
1. Ouch! I just stubbed my toe.

1. ouch	5. whew	9. ugh
2. gee	6. wow	10. hey
3. oh	7. darn	
4. goodness	8. ah	

2. Gee, I wish you could come.

Skills Review and Writing Workshop

Prepositions, Conjunctions, and Interjections

CHECKING YOUR SKILLS

Write the underlined words. Next to each word, tell whether it is a preposition, a conjunction, or an interjection.

1. prep, conj. 2. conj. 3. interj. 4. prep., prep. 5. conj. 6. prep. 7. conj.,

(1) <u>Until</u> Krakatoa, an island <u>between</u> Java and Sumatra, exploded, not much was known about volcanoes. (2) At the time, <u>neither</u> Krakatoa's recent history <u>nor</u> its current behavior had given any indication of what was about to happen. (3) <u>Oh</u>, a few rumblings had been heard. (4) Then, <u>on</u> August 27, 1883, Krakatoa exploded in what was the largest volcanic eruption <u>in</u> recorded history. (5) People nearly 3000 miles away heard the noise <u>and</u> saw the darkened sky. (6) They were <u>in</u> awe. (7) <u>When</u> ashes began falling, people thought the end <u>of</u> the world had come. (8) Over 40,000 people were killed <u>or</u> hurt. (9) <u>Because</u> of the dust in the atmosphere, sunsets were amazingly colorful <u>for</u> almost a year. (10) Krakatoa's explosion led scientists to find out more <u>about</u> volcanic eruptions. prep. 8. conj. 9. prep. 10. prep.

USING GRAMMAR SKILLS IN WRITING
Writing About a Disaster

Good writers use prepositions and conjunctions effectively for smooth writing. Imagine you are a witness to a disaster of some kind. You must write a brief account for radio. Follow the steps below to write a clear and accurate account.

Prewriting: Write down the most important information first. Then add other details in order of descending importance.

Writing: Begin by summing up the most important information. Add details to make your account colorful. Close with a sentence that indicates more news will follow.

Revising: Carefully check your prepositions and conjunctions for clarity and correctness. Then proofread carefully.

Checking Your Skills

In the Checking Your Skills assignment, students have identified prepositions, conjunctions, and interjections in sentences. Explain to students that the following speaking and listening activity will provide them with additional practice.

Speaking and Listening

Divide students into groups of four. Tell each group to write a dialogue that takes place among four characters who are discussing the eruption of Krakatoa one week after it occurred. The information in the Checking Your Skills paragraph should be revealed through the dialogue. Instruct students to use prepositions, conjunctions, and interjections in their dialogue. When they have finished writing, ask for volunteers to read their dialogues to the class.

Using Grammar Skills in Writing

Revising You might want students to work in peer editing groups when revising their radio accounts. Students should read their accounts aloud to the group, who should offer constructive suggestions. Suggestions might cover the order in which the information is delivered, the colorfulness of the language, or the clarity of the report.

CHAPTER 6
Reviewing Parts of Speech

(pp. 84–89)

This chapter expands and reinforces the concept that a word's part of speech is determined by its use in a sentence. Students who have covered the earlier chapters will have already seen the use of nouns and pronouns as adjectives, the use of a single word as an adverb or an adjective, and the use of a single word as a preposition or an adverb. This chapter extends the idea by showing other words that can be used as many different parts of speech.

For a review of the entire chapter and a related writing activity, see the Skills Review and Writing Workshop on page 89.

6.1 Determining Parts of Speech

(pp. 84–88)

OBJECTIVE

After completing this section, students should be able to

- Identify a word's part of speech from its use in a sentence.

Chapter # 6

Reviewing Parts of Speech

The preceding chapters have introduced each of the eight parts of speech. Being able to identify the part of speech of each word in a sentence is an important skill.

6.1 Determining Parts of Speech

English would be easier if it were possible to say, "This word is always a noun," "This word is always an adverb," and so on. Language, however, is flexible. To identify what part of speech a word is, consider how the word is used in each sentence.

How a word is used in a sentence determines its part of speech.

Some words can be used as several different parts of speech. In the four sentences that follow, you can see how the word *past* is used as a different part of speech in each sentence.

AS A NOUN: The *past* is often a guide for the future.

AS AN ADJECTIVE: His *past* actions trouble us.

AS AN ADVERB: A hummingbird just darted *past*.

AS A PREPOSITION: She drove *past* our house.

6.1 Determining Parts of Speech

Identifying Parts of Speech in Sentences

The following charts can help you identify the eight parts of speech. The middle column—"Questions to Ask Yourself"—should be particularly helpful to you in determining parts of speech.

Nouns and Pronouns. A noun names a person, place, or thing. A pronoun stands for a noun.

Part of Speech	Questions to Ask Yourself	Examples
Noun	Does the word name a person, place, or thing?	*Sue* received a *present* from her *aunt*.
Pronoun	Does the word stand for a noun?	*Each* gets *one* of *them*.

Verbs. A verb generally shows an action or a condition.

Part of Speech	Questions to Ask Yourself	Examples
Verb	Does the word tell what someone or something did?	She *bought* a cake.
	Does the work link a noun or pronoun before it with a noun or adjective that follows?	She *is* the captain. He *seems* sick.

Adjectives. An adjective modifies a noun or pronoun.

Part of Speech	Questions to Ask Yourself	Examples
Adjective	Does the word tell what kind, which one, how many, or how much?	*Several large, heavy* packages arrived.

Emphasize that some words can be used as several different parts of speech. Write the Sentence Bank sentences on the chalkboard. To identify the use of round as a noun, ask, "Does round name a person, place, or thing?" To identify the use of round as a verb, ask, "Does round tell what the van did (or didn't do)?" To identify the use of round as an adjective, ask, "Does round tell what kind?" To identify round as a preposition, ask, "Is round part of a phrase that ends in a noun or pronoun?"

Have volunteers use the following words in sentences as indicated:

1. paint—noun and verb
2. low—adjective, adverb, and verb
3. fast—noun, verb, adjective, and adverb

Text Follow Through
Discuss text pages 84–88.

Assign Exercise A, page 87; Exercise B, page 87; and Developing Writing Skills, page 88.

Less advanced Have students analyze step by step the parts of speech of three other words in the example sentence on page 87: *team* (noun), *finished* (verb), and *early* (adverb). After the students have identified the parts of speech, using the questions in the charts, they can be asked to use *team* as a verb, *finish* as a noun, and *early* as an adjective.

Average Students might return to Exercise A and write original sentences using the underlined words in sentences 4–7 as different parts of speech. If necessary, suggest that students use the dictionary to find the meanings of these words when they are used as different parts of speech.

Advanced Students can be asked to think of other words that can be used as different parts of speech and to use each of them in sentences illustrating as many parts of speech as possible. You might discuss where to locate part-of-speech information in dictionary entries and have students use dictionaries to discover the words for their sentences.

Additional Practice

Practice Pages or Practice Book, page 29

Less advanced Exercise Bank, Exercises A and B, page 46

Average Exercise Bank, Exercises A, B, and C, page 46

Advanced Exercise Bank, Exercises B and C, page 46

TESTING

Test Program

Unit Pretest, page 7
Chapter Test, page 23
Unit Post-Test, page 36

Adverbs. An adverb modifies a verb, an adjective, or another adverb.

Part of Speech	Questions to Ask Yourself	Examples
Adverb	Does the word tell where, when, in what manner, or to what extent?	Go *there!* You can go to our house *later.* She works *very quickly.* They are *nearly* ready.

Prepositions, Conjunctions, and Interjections. A preposition relates the noun or pronoun following it to another word. A conjunction connects words or groups of words. An interjection expresses feeling or emotion.

Part of Speech	Questions to Ask Yourself	Examples
Preposition	Is the word part of a phrase that ends in a noun or pronoun?	*In* the morning he often jogs. Sit *behind* them during the school assembly.
Conjunction	Does the word connect other words in the sentence?	Bill *and* Mary arrived. He will *either* go *or* stay behind. This is *as* it should be.
Interjection	Does the word express feeling or emotion?	*Gee!* I'm happy to see you. *Whew!* I'm glad that's over.

RE-TEACHING
Practice Pages or Practice
Book, page 29

THINKING SKILLS
Knowledge—*Identifying* nouns,
pronouns, verbs, and adjectives in sentences (Exercise
A, page 87)
Identifying adjectives, adverbs, prepositions, and conjunctions in sentences (Exercise B, page 87)

Synthesis—*Writing* sentences
using words as different parts
of speech (Developing Writing
Skills, page 88)

6.1 Determining Parts of Speech

Using these questions as a guide, you should be able to identify correctly what part of speech a particular word is. Consider the italicized words in the following sentence.

EXAMPLE: The team finished *practice* early since *everyone* arrived on time.

You might begin by wondering whether *practice* is a noun or a verb, since it can be used as either. Does the word name a person, place, or thing, or does it tell what the team did? *Practice*, in this sentence, names something. It is a noun.

At first glance *everyone* may seem to be a noun, but does it actually name a person? No. Does it stand for a noun? Yes, it stands for the names of the team members. Therefore, *everyone* has to be a pronoun.

Now try to analyze *team, finished,* and *early* in the same sentence. The more you rely on the questions in the charts, the easier this analysis should be.

EXERCISE A: Identifying Nouns, Pronouns, Verbs, and Adjectives. On your paper identify the underlined word in each sentence as a *noun, pronoun, verb,* or *adjective.*

EXAMPLE: They <u>drink</u> iced tea in July.   verb

1. The trip <u>lasted</u> for two weeks. verb
2. I think the <u>wooden</u> desk can be refinished. adj
3. This <u>rhinoceros</u> seems quite ferocious. noun
4. The window frame was <u>green</u>. adj
5. The tourist season <u>reaches</u> its peak in January. verb
6. These <u>stains</u> cannot be removed easily. noun
7. An <u>interested</u> parent can help a student greatly. adj
8. Will <u>they</u> agree on a choice? pron
9. His <u>idea</u> deserves more discussion. noun
10. It will be an <u>unhappy</u> day when she leaves. adj

**EXERCISE B: Identifying Adjectives, Adverbs, Preposi-
tions, and Conjunctions.** On your paper identify the under-

Developing Writing Skills

Have students use different parts of speech in writing by completing the following assignment.

Writing Across the Curriculum

There are many things in life that we all take for granted. For example, can you imagine a world in which numbers and counting did not exist? How would life be different without these concepts?

Prewriting Imagine that you are an astronaut and that you have landed on the planet Skugluck. The planet is inhabited by friendly, intelligent humanoids who have no notion of numbers or counting. Brainstorm for ideas about how you will explain these concepts. Look over your ideas and choose the best way to explain numbers and counting to the Skugluckians. Add any details and examples that will clarify your explanation. Arrange your explanation in a logical order.

Writing Write the first draft of your explanation. Try to make your explanation clear and concise. Use transitions to indicate relationships between the ideas in your explanation. Include an example or two to illustrate your explanation.

Revising Make sure that your explanation is clear and easy to follow. Have you used transitions to indicate the relationships between ideas? Have you included examples? Will the Skugluckians be able to grasp the concepts of numbers and counting? Prepare a final draft.

lined word in each sentence as an *adjective, adverb, preposition,* or *conjunction.*

EXAMPLE: <u>Before</u> she arrives, we will have left.   conjunction

1. She hasn't said a word <u>since</u> dinner. prep
2. She hasn't said a word <u>since</u> they arrived this morning. conj
3. He arrived last week and has been here ever <u>since</u>. adv
4. They were afraid they would be left <u>behind</u>. adv
5. You will find an old broom <u>behind</u> the cellar door. prep
6. He staggered <u>about</u> after bumping his head. adv
7. She strolled <u>about</u> the botanical gardens. prep
8. The garden apartment has an <u>outside</u> entrance. adj
9. The tool shed is just <u>outside</u> the door. prep
10. Would you like to walk <u>outside</u>? adv

DEVELOPING WRITING SKILLS: Using Words as Different Parts of Speech. Each of the following words can be used as at least two different parts of speech. Write two sentences for each word, using the word as a different part of speech each time.

Answers will vary; samples are given for the first one.

EXAMPLE: question

Her question was very strange.

Do you always question the results?

1. stop	5. jump	9. hope
2. past	6. dry	10. lemon
3. opposite	7. mail	
4. after	8. in	

1. Does the Number 5 bus stop here?   New Haven is the last stop for this train.

Skills Review and Writing Workshop

Reviewing Parts of Speech

CHECKING YOUR SKILLS

Write the part of speech of each underlined word or word group.

1. pronoun, noun 2. conjunction 3. verb, preposition 4. adverb 5. adjective,

(1) <u>She</u> is known to the world as <u>Nellie Bly</u>. (2) <u>Not only</u> was this courageous young woman one of America's first newspaperwomen, <u>but</u> she was <u>also</u> one of its first inquiring reporters. (3) At nineteen, Nellie <u>was digging</u> up news stories <u>for</u> the paper for which she worked. (4) She <u>particularly</u> wanted to show how badly women were treated in the 1880s. (5) To expose the <u>terrible</u> conditions of women in factories, Nellie got a job in <u>one</u> of the worst ones. (6) <u>Later</u>, she uncovered the horrible <u>conditions</u> existing in a home for insane women. (7) Eventually, Nellie Bly became <u>famous</u>. (8) In 1889 she decided to beat the record of a man <u>who had gone</u> around the world in 80 days. (9) People's interest in Nellie's journey <u>was</u> amazing. (10) <u>Well</u>, she did beat the record by completing her trip in 72 days!

pronoun 6. adverb, noun 7. adjective 8. verb 9. verb 10. interjection

USING GRAMMAR SKILLS IN WRITING

Writing a Travelogue

Knowing how to use the parts of speech correctly is the basis for good writing. Imagine you are on a long journey and must send your school newspaper brief accounts of the places you visit. Follow the steps below to write about a place that particularly impresses you.

Answers will vary.

Prewriting: Write at least three reasons why the place appeals to you. List specific details to support your reasons.

Writing: Begin with a general statement about the place. Then add your reasons, ending with the most important.

Revising: Look at the words you used and change any that seem weak. Then look for other improvements you can make. After you have revised, proofread carefully.

Checking Your Skills

In the Checking Your SKills assignment, students have identified parts of speech in sentences. Inform students that the following speaking and listening activity will provide them with additional practice.

Speaking and Listening

Prepare for this activity by making a spinner like those used for many board games. Divide the base of the spinner into eight sections. In each section, write one of the parts of speech: noun, pronoun, verb, adjective, adverb, conjunction, preposition, interjection. Bring the spinner to class and inform students that they are going to play the game "Know Your Parts of Speech." Ask for a student volunteer to begin. First, have the student spin the spinner. Then dictate a sentence, possibly from a story, for the student to write on the chalkboard. The sentence must include the part of speech indicated by the spinner. The student must then find the part of speech in the sentence. Set a time limit for the task and award a point for the correct answer. If you can not make a spinner, you might use a pair of dice, assigning a part of speech to each of the numbers three through ten.

Using Grammar Skills in Writing

Publishing You might want to collect students' travelogues into an anthology. Students can contribute photographs or illustrations of the place they wrote about. Display the collection where students can look through it.

CHAPTER 7
**Basic
Sentence Parts
and Patterns**
(pp. 90–132)

This chapter will provide students with an understanding of basic sentence elements; the ideas presented here will then be enlarged upon in subsequent chapters. Section 7.1 deals with the need for a subject and a verb in a sentence. Section 7.2 discusses complete subjects and predicates. Section 7.3 covers compound subjects and verbs, and Section 7.4 covers special problems with subjects. Sections 7.5 and 7.6 present direct and indirect objects, and Section 7.7 deals with subject complements. Section 7.8 considers the classification of sentences by function, and Section 7.9 introduces sentence diagraming as a tool for viewing relationships among sentence elements.

For a review of the entire chapter and a related writing activity, see the Skills Review and Writing Workshop on page 132.

7.1 The Basic Sentence
(pp. 90–95)

OBJECTIVES

After completing this section, students should be able to

- Identify a sentence as a group of words containing a subject and a verb.
- Distinguish between complete thoughts and incomplete thoughts.

Chapter **7**

Basic Sentence Parts and Patterns

By assembling the eight parts of speech in various patterns, you can express your ideas and communicate them to others. Patterns of words that communicate ideas are called *sentences.*

7.1 The Basic Sentence

There are many kinds of sentences. Sentences can be short, long, or complicated. But all sentences, in order to be sentences, must have certain ingredients.

The Two Basic Elements of a Sentence

All sentences must contain two basic elements.

A sentence must contain a subject and a verb.

7.1 The Basic Sentence

Both of these ingredients are necessary in order to have a sentence. If either one is missing, what remains is not a sentence.

The Subject. Every sentence must have a *subject.* Most subjects are nouns or pronouns found near the beginning of a sentence.

The subject of a sentence is the word or group of words that answers the question *Who?* or *What?* before the verb.

In the following examples, the subjects have been underlined and the verbs have been labeled.

EXAMPLES: <u>Father</u> bought a present for us.
           ^V

           Our new <u>car</u> was in the garage.
                    ^V

           <u>She</u> tried to be good to them.
              ^V

The noun *father* is the subject in the first example. It tells us *who* bought a present. The noun *car* in the second example tells *what* was in the garage. *Car,* therefore, is the subject of the sentence. In the third example, the pronoun *she* tells *who* tried to be good. *She* is the subject.

Not all subjects are this easy to find. Some are more than one word. Some may not appear at the beginning of the sentence. But the subject will always answer *Who?* or *What?* before a verb. (See Section 7.4 for more information about finding subjects in sentences.)

The Verb. As one of the two essential parts of a sentence, a *verb* simply tells something about a subject.

The verb in a sentence tells what the subject does, what is done to the subject, or what the condition of the subject is.

In the examples on the following page, the verbs have been underlined twice and the subjects have been labeled.

91

Average For additional practice, have students return to the sentences they wrote for Exercise B, substitute either a new subject or new verb in each sentence, and underline the subject once and the verb twice in each sentence.

Advanced Have students work with partners. Have one partner write five subjects for the other partner to make into complete sentences by adding the verbs. Partners can then reverse roles.

Additional Practice

Practice Pages or Practice Book, page 30

Less advanced Exercise Bank, Exercises A and B, pages 47, 48

Average Exercise Bank, Exercises A, B, and C, pages 47, 48

Advanced Exercise Bank, Exercises B and C, pages 47, 48

TESTING

Test Program
  Unit Pretest, page 8
  Chapter Test, page 24
  Unit Post-Test, page 36

RE-TEACHING

Practice Pages or Practice Book, page 30

THINKING SKILLS

Knowledge—*Labeling* subjects and verbs (Exercise A, page 92)

Application—*Modifying* incomplete sentences to create complete thoughts (Exercises B and C, page 94)

Synthesis—*Writing* complete sentences (Developing Writing Skills, page 95)

EXAMPLES: Bobby <u>gave</u> an unforgettable speech.

Their prize poodle <u>was stolen</u>.

She <u>has been</u> blue all day.

Gave is the verb in the first example. It tells what the subject, *Bobby,* did. In the second example, *was stolen* tells what was done to the subject *poodle. Has been* in the third example is a linking verb. It tells something about the condition of the subject by linking *she* to the word *blue.*

EXERCISE A: Recognizing Subjects and Verbs. Copy each of the following sentences onto your paper. Underline each subject once and each verb twice.

EXAMPLE: One Greek <u>hero</u> <u>spent</u> ten years trying to reach home.

1. The <u>ferry</u> <u>crosses</u> the river twice a day.
2. Our <u>teacher</u> <u>has been</u> more than fair with us.
3. My <u>sister</u> <u>bakes</u> delicious vanilla cookies.
4. The old <u>bridge</u> <u>creaks</u> occasionally under a heavy load.
5. The <u>book</u> <u>describes</u> the causes of the Great Depression.
6. Maybe the old <u>road</u> <u>will be opened</u> in the spring.
7. His <u>handwriting</u> <u>is</u> unreadable.
8. <u>They</u> <u>have told</u> us only half the story.
9. The old <u>rocker</u> <u>was repaired</u> just last week.
10. Without question <u>Cicely Tyson</u> <u>is</u> a brilliant actress.

The Need to Express a Complete Thought

In addition to having a subject and a verb, a sentence must express a *complete thought.* Difficulty in deciding whether a group of words is a sentence often comes down to difficulty in recognizing a complete thought.

7.1 The Basic Sentence

A group of words with a subject and verb expresses a complete thought if it can stand by itself and still make sense.

Making sure that your words express complete thoughts is especially important when you write.

Incomplete thoughts will leave readers with questions in their minds. Consider the group of words in the following example.

INCOMPLETE THOUGHT: The girl in the green bathing suit.

"What about the girl in the green bathing suit?" a reader may ask. "What did she do?" Standing by itself, this group of words obviously makes no sense. An important element is missing—the verb. Using *girl* as a subject, you can turn this incomplete thought into a sentence by adding any number of different verbs.

COMPLETE THOUGHTS
S   V The girl in the green bathing suit swims beautifully.
S   V The girl in the green bathing suit left.
S   V The girl in the green bathing suit is lying by the pool.

Notice that each of the examples in the chart has all of the ingredients necessary for a sentence: Each has a *subject* and a *verb* and each expresses a *complete thought.* Each sentence makes sense by itself.

Sometimes an incomplete thought may be a group of words with no word in it that can be used as a subject. Consider the following example.

INCOMPLETE THOUGHT: Near the stream by the roadside.

This incomplete thought is merely two prepositional phrases. *Both* a subject and a verb are needed.

                           S   V
COMPLETE: Wild <u>irises</u> <u>are growing</u> near the stream by the
             roadside.

In grammar incomplete thoughts are often called *fragments*. See Section 10.1 for more information about fragments and about how to avoid them in your writing.

EXERCISE B: Correcting Incomplete Thoughts. None of the following groups of words expresses a complete thought. On your paper correct each one by adding whatever words are needed to make a sentence.

Answers will vary; samples are given for the first two.

EXAMPLE: Three angry ducks in search of corn.

            Three angry ducks in search of corn waddled by.

1. The apple peeler is on top of the shelf in the kitchen.
  1. On top of the shelf in the kitchen.
  2. In the garage near the old newspapers.
  3. The clerk behind the counter.
  4. A police officer at the top of the hill.
  5. Because of all the wrong answers.

2. You must look in the garage near the old newspapers.

EXERCISE C: Recognizing Sentences. Only five of the following ten items are sentences. The rest are incomplete thoughts. If a group of words is a sentence, write *sentence* on your paper. If a group of words expresses an incomplete thought, add whatever words are needed to make a sentence. Then underline the subject once and the verb twice in each new sentence.

New sentences will vary; samples are given.

EXAMPLE: The suitcases from the plane.

            The <u>suitcases</u> from the plane <u>were unloaded</u>.

  1. She asked me about the next edition of the newspaper. sentence
  2. The <u>room</u> in the back of the house. <u>is used</u> for storage.
  3. In the desert, tall <u>cactuses</u>, <u>baked</u> in the sun.
  4. We understood her reasons. sentence
  5. From the observation deck at the rim of the canyon.
  6. The <u>teacher</u> on the third floor near the window. often <u>sits</u>

5. <u>we</u> <u>could see</u> many hiking groups.

7.2 Complete Subjects and Predicates

7. Walter opened the package quickly. sentence
8. He returns there every summer. sentence
9. Under the chair near the window. The <u>dog</u> <u>is</u>
10. His typewriter has an automatic carriage return. sentence

DEVELOPING WRITING SKILLS: Writing Sentences.
Write five complete sentences, using each of the nouns listed below as the subject of a sentence. Then write five sentences using each of the listed verbs. Underline the subjects once and the verbs twice in the ten sentences you have written.
Answers will vary; sample is given for the first one.
EXAMPLE: noun—tornado

> A <u>tornado</u> completely <u>destroyed</u> twenty-seven build-
> ings in the town.

Nouns	Verbs
1. supermarket	has
2. telephone	identified
3. camels	collapsed
4. senator	was
5. physician	traveled

1. The <u>supermarket</u> <u>sells</u> many types of food.

Complete Subjects 7.2 and Predicates

Every sentence is built around its two essential elements, the subject and verb. The subject and the verb together support the many details that a sentence may contain in expressing a complete thought.

DIFFERENT SENTENCES BUILT AROUND THE SAME SUBJECT AND VERB	
<u>People</u>	<u>swim</u>.
Many <u>people</u>	<u>swim</u> daily.
Many <u>people</u> in our town	<u>swim</u> daily at the pool.

7.2 Complete Subjects and Predicates
(pp. 95–97)

OBJECTIVE

After completing this section, students should be able to

• Identify complete subjects and complete predicates in sentences.

TEACHING

Getting Started

Write the following sentences on the chalkboard:

1. The paint dried.

2. The paint in the living room dried.

3. The paint in the living room dried completely in less than half an hour.

Draw a vertical line to divide the subject and the verb in the first sentence. Then underline the subject once and the verb twice. Have volunteers follow the same procedure with the next two sentences. They will note that each sentence contains the same subject and verb, yet the sentences are different. Point out that in sentences 2 and 3, *paint* plus the prepositional phrase *in the living room* is called the *complete subject* and in sentence 3, *dried* plus the adverb and two prepositional phrases is called the *complete predicate.*

Text Follow Through

Discuss text pages 95–97.

Assign the Exercise, page 96, and Developing Writing Skills, page 97.

Less advanced Students might complete the Developing Writing Skills activity in pairs, composing two different sentences with the same simple subject and simple predicate.

Average Students might want to make up ten subject-verb items similar to those in the Developing Writing Skills activity and then follow the same directions.

Advanced Students might write twenty sentences for the Developing Writing Skills activity rather than ten. To do this, they can be asked to expand each subject and verb separately instead of using the words in the pairs given in the text, or

Notice the space that divides the sentences. The words to the left of the space include the subject *people* and any other words that add details to it. In each sentence the words to the left of the space make up the *complete subject.* (The word *people* is often called, in contrast, the *simple subject.*)

The complete subject of a sentence consists of the subject and any words related to it.

As you can see in the preceding examples, a complete subject may be just one word—the subject itself—or it may be several words.

In the preceding examples, the words to the right of the space include the verb *swim* and any words that add details to it. This part of the sentence is called the *complete predicate.* (The verb itself, a word such as *swim* or a phrase such as *has swum,* is often called the *simple predicate.*)

The complete predicate of a sentence consists of the verb and any words related to it.

As you can see in the examples, a complete predicate may be just one word—a verb—or it may be several words.

EXERCISE: Recognizing Complete Subjects and Predicates. Copy each of the following sentences onto your paper. Underline the subject once and the verb twice. Then draw a vertical line between the complete subject and the complete predicate, as shown in the example.

EXAMPLE: The <u>man</u> in gray | <u>paced</u> in front of the statue.

1. A sudden <u>storm</u>|<u>swept</u> across the prairie.
2. Two old cargo <u>ships</u>|<u>collided</u> in the harbor.
3. <u>Bruce</u>|<u>described</u> his nervousness about the history test.
4. The lilac <u>bushes</u> in our front yard | <u>burst</u> into flower overnight.
5. <u>Rosalyn</u>|<u>sews</u> all her own clothing.

6. A rather strange <u>event</u> | <u>occurred</u> off the Atlantic coast of Maine.
7. Small white <u>spots</u> | <u>appeared</u> on the leaves of our plants.
8. <u>He</u> | <u>described</u> the accident in detail.
9. The local <u>museum</u> | <u>sits</u> on an acre of land near the river delta.
10. Many of the new <u>telephones</u> | <u>have</u> pushbuttons instead of dials.

DEVELOPING WRITING SKILLS: Developing Complete Subjects and Predicates. The first word in each of the following items is a noun or pronoun that can be used as a subject. The second word is a verb. Develop each item into a complete subject and predicate by adding details to the subject and verb. Write the new sentences on your paper.

Answers will vary; samples are given for the first two.

EXAMPLE: tree fell

The tree in our back yard fell during a storm last night.

1. The Missouri River flows into the Mississippi.

1. river flows	6. train arrived
2. comedians tried	7. cat jumped
3. everyone is	8. audience was
4. result was	9. answer is
5. storm lasted	10. kites soared

2. The two comedians tried their best to make us laugh.

Compound Subjects and Verbs 7.3

Many sentences have a single subject and a single verb. Some sentences, however, have more than one subject. Others have more than one verb.

Compound Subjects

A sentence with more than one subject is said to have a *compound subject.*

Additional Practice

Practice Pages or Practice Book, page 31

Less advanced   Exercise Bank, Exercises A and B, page 49

Average   Exercise Bank, Exercises A, B, and C, page 49

Advanced   Exercise Bank, Exercises B and C, page 49

TESTING

Test Program

   Unit Pretest, page 8
   Chapter Test, page 24
   Unit Post-Test, page 36

RE-TEACHING

Practice Pages or Practice Book, page 31

THINKING SKILLS

Knowledge—*Identifying* complete subjects and predicates (Exercise, page 96)

Application—*Producing* sentences using complete subjects and predicates (Developing Writing Skills, page 97)

7.3 Compound Subjects and Verbs

(pp. 97–101)

OBJECTIVES

After completing this section, students should be able to

• Identify compound subjects in sentences.

• Identify compound verbs in sentences.

TEACHING

Getting Started

Have students read the definition of a compound subject on page 98. Then write the following sentences on the chalkboard:

1. Daisies bloomed alongside the road.
2. Asters bloomed alongside the road.

Have a volunteer underline the subject of each sentence once and the verb twice. Ask for a volunteer to join the two sentences by using a compound subject joined by *and.* Then have the volunteer underline each part of the compound subject once and each verb twice. Continue by writing on the chalkboard other sentence pairs that could be combined into one sentence with a compound subject or a compound verb.

Text Follow Through

Discuss text pages 97–101.

Assign Exercise A, page 98; Exercise B, page 99; Exercise C, page 100; and Developing Writing Skills, page 100.

Less advanced Students might benefit from a brief study or review of conjunctions (Section 5.2) before undertaking the Developing Writing Skills activity.

Average If you wish to give students further practice in working with compound subjects and verbs, you might refer them to Exercise A in Section 7.1 (page 92). Ask the students to make the subjects compound in half the sentences and the verbs compound in the other half. If students have not yet

---

A compound subject is two or more subjects that have the same verb and are joined by a conjunction such as *and* or *or.*

The parts of the compound subjects in the following examples are underlined once. Each verb is underlined twice.

EXAMPLES: Ted and Louise are brother and sister.

My sister or she will represent our club.

Apples, peaches, and grapes are sold at the store.

EXERCISE A: Recognizing Compound Subjects. Each of the following sentences contains a compound subject. Copy the sentences onto your paper and underline the subjects that make up each compound subject.

EXAMPLE: Red, white, and blue are popular colors for flags.

1. Skaters and cyclists crowd the park each weekend.
2. After the dance Joan and I stopped for a milkshake.
3. All day wind and rain lashed the tiny island.
4. The coach, the team, and the cheerleaders boarded the bus for the game.
5. Both gorillas and orangutans are in danger of extinction.
6. Along the road daisies, buttercups, lilies, and dandelions grew in profusion.
7. Either the principal or the superintendent will introduce the speakers.
8. Adjectives and adverbs are modifiers.
9. Utah, Colorado, New Mexico, and Arizona touch borders at the same point.
10. San Marino and Monaco are two of the smallest nations.

Compound Verbs

A sentence with two or more verbs is said to have a *compound verb.*

studied subject-verb agreement, you may want to do this as an oral activity.

Advanced Students might want to make up five additional items similar to those in the Developing Writing Skills activity, and then have a partner complete the directions. Or you might have them look through their reading for examples of sentences with compound subjects or compound verbs. Have them copy the most interesting examples and bring them to class.

Additional Practice
Practice Pages or Practice Book, page 32

Less advanced Exercise Bank, Exercises A and B, pages 50, 51

Average Exercise Bank, Exercises A, B, and C, pages 50, 51

Advanced Exercise Bank, Exercises B and C, pages 50, 51

TESTING
Test Program

Unit Pretest, page 8
Chapter Test, page 25
Unit Post-Test, page 36

RE-TEACHING
Practice Pages or Practice Book, page 32

THINKING SKILLS
Knowledge—*Identifying* compound subjects (Exercise A, page 98)
Identifying compound verbs (Exercise B, page 99)
Identifying compound subjects and verbs (Exercise C, page 100)

7.3 Compound Subjects and Verbs

A compound verb is two or more verbs that have the same subject and are joined by a conjunction such as *and* or *or*.

EXAMPLES: He smiles often and frowns occasionally.
The plan will succeed or fail within a year.
She produces, directs, and often acts in her own productions.

Sometimes a sentence will have both a compound subject and a compound verb.

EXAMPLE: Jane and Sharon both sing and dance.

EXERCISE B: Recognizing Compound Verbs. Each of the following sentences contains a compound verb. Copy the sentences onto your paper, and underline the verbs that make up each compound verb.

EXAMPLE: Carol looked around and then laughed uproariously.

1. Our kite dipped suddenly and wrapped itself around a tree.
2. The workers first dug a hole and then carefully lowered the new shrub into it.
3. The dog turned around three times, settled into its bed, and yawned.
4. The coin slipped from my hand, rolled along the pavement, and dropped into a sewer drain.
5. My parents sold the station wagon and bought a new compact car.
6. I either left my door keys at home or lost them at school.
7. The conductor bowed to the audience, turned to the orchestra, and conducted Beethoven's Fifth Symphony.
8. The snake recoiled and then struck.
9. Jan finished her homework, prepared for bed, and settled down to her favorite TV show.
10. We gathered the corn and put it in bushel baskets.

EXERCISE C: Recognizing Compound Subjects and Verbs. Each of the following sentences contains a compound subject, a compound verb, or both. On your paper write the compound subjects and the compound verbs. Then label each compound subject and compound verb as in the example.

Compound verbs are underlined twice.

EXAMPLE: He and she are good friends.

He, she   compound subject

1. Our old <u>magazines</u> and <u>newspapers</u> are stored in the attic.
2. She <u>opened</u> the door and <u>rushed</u> out of the lobby.
3. My <u>mother</u> and <u>father</u> either <u>walk</u> or <u>drive</u> to the station.
4. The top <u>spun</u> for a minute, <u>teetered</u>, and finally <u>fell</u>.
5. <u>Trains</u>, <u>buses</u>, and <u>taxis</u> are three popular means of transportation in urban areas.
6. Neither <u>Cal</u> nor <u>Peter</u> liked Oliver's poem.
7. She <u>washes</u> and <u>scrubs</u> her face four times a day.
8. "<u>Bonny Barbara Allan</u>" and "<u>Lord Randal</u>" are two of the most popular English ballads.
9. <u>Michelle</u> and <u>she</u> <u>read</u> French well and often <u>translate</u> whole passages into English.
10. A tall <u>man</u>, three <u>girls</u>, and a little <u>boy</u> <u>appeared</u> at our door and <u>asked</u> for a "Mr. Malinowski."

DEVELOPING WRITING SKILLS: Developing Sentences with Compound Subjects and Verbs. The following items contain compound subjects and verbs. Expand these subjects and verbs into fully developed sentences by adding conjunctions, descriptive words, and other details. Write your complete sentences on your paper.

Answers will vary; samples are given for the first two.

EXAMPLE: cats, dogs   are

Large cats and small dogs are sometimes good friends.

1. That active toddler sometimes reaches up to the table and grabs the silverware.

1. toddler   reaches, grabs
2. food   was spoiled, could be eaten

2. After the power outage, the food was spoiled and could not be eaten.

3. Barbara, Lisa will agree
4. brother drove, walked
5. singer, musicians will record
6. uncle, aunt visited, stayed
7. Walt Whitman, Edgar Allan Poe have been
8. daffodils, irises were given, were put
9. snow, sleet fell, disrupted
10. friend learned, did

Special Problems with Subjects 7.4

In the first three sections of this chapter, each subject that you were asked to find appeared somewhere early in the sentence, with the verb following immediately or soon after. This pattern, a subject followed by a verb, is the pattern most often used in English. It is called *normal word order*. As long as the subject comes before the verb, it does not matter whether the subject and verb appear at the beginning, middle, or end of the sentence—the sentence is in normal word order.

NORMAL WORD ORDER:
The car raced toward the bridge.

Yesterday morning after breakfast,

Uncle George left on a flight for home.

Trapped by the bad weather, cold and hungry, she waited.

In several kinds of sentences, however, the subject and verb do not follow normal word order. In some sentences the subject may seem to be missing entirely. In others the subject may follow the verb or come between the parts of a verb phrase. This section will give you practice in recognizing sentences that do not follow normal word order. It will also help you find the subjects in these sentences.

7.4 Special Problems with Subjects
(pp. 101–107)

OBJECTIVES

After completing this section, students should be able to

- Identify subjects in sentences that give orders or directions.
- Find the subject in questions.
- Find the subject in sentences beginning with *there* or *here*.
- Find the subject in inverted sentences.

TEACHING

Getting Started

┌ **sentence bank** ─┐
1. Listen closely.
2. Where is my watch?
3. There are five cans of soup on the shelf.
4. Into the room walked the lost boy.
└────────────┘

Write the Sentence Bank sentences on the board and have students copy them on their papers. Ask students to underline the subject in each sentence with one line and the verb with two lines. Discuss any problems or unusual patterns that students encountered in the sentences. Point out to students that although in normal word order the subject comes before the verb, this order sometimes changes. They will learn four unusual patterns in this section.

Text Follow Through

Discuss text pages 101–107.

Assign Exercise A, page 102; Exercise B, page 104; Exercise C, page 105; Exercise D, page 106; and Developing Writing Skills, page 106.

Less advanced To make the Developing Writing Skills activity more accessible to students, you might supply sentences that correspond to the instructions in the text. Students can then underline the subjects once and the verbs twice. Then have them attempt writing sentences on their own or in pairs.

Average Have students bring to class particularly effective inverted-order sentences from their reading to share with the class. Volunteers can then identify the subjects and verbs in these sentences.

Advanced As a special challenge, you might ask students to rewrite some of the sentences in Exercise C in Section 7.3 (page 100) as follows. Warn students that a number of words may need to be changed slightly.

Sentence 1: Invert word order.
Sentence 2: Write as a question.
Sentence 7: Write as an order.
Sentence 8: Write as a question.
Sentence 10: Write as a question.

Subjects in Orders and Directions

Some sentences give orders or directions. In most of these sentences, the subject does not appear before the verb.

In sentences that give orders or directions, the subject is understood to be *you*.

On the left side of the following chart are three examples of sentences that give orders or directions. The verbs are underlined twice. On the right side, the same sentences appear with the understood subjects shown in parentheses.

Order or Direction	With Understood *You* Added
<u>Drive</u> carefully!	(You) <u>Drive</u> carefully!
After waiting a moment, <u>dial</u> the number again.	After waiting a moment, (you) <u>dial</u> the number again.
Lucy, <u>leave</u> the room.	Lucy, (you) <u>leave</u> the room.

EXERCISE A: Recognizing Subjects That Give Orders or Directions. Write the subject of each of the following sentences. Seven of the sentences give orders or directions. The other three are ordinary sentences in normal word order.

EXAMPLE: David, remember to turn out the lights.

(you)

1. Wash your face with soap and water. (You)
2. Tell us what happened, Frank. (You)
3. Marie, open the window about an inch. (you)
4. Paul tried to remove the splinter from Sue's finger. Paul
5. After raking the leaves, spread an even coat of lime on the lawn. (you)

Additional Practice
Practice Pages or Practice
Book, pages 33, 34

Less advanced Exercise Bank,
Exercises A and B, pages 52–55

Average Exercise Bank, Exercises A, B, and C, pages 52–55

Advanced Exercise Bank, Exercises B and C, pages 52–55

TESTING

Test Program

Unit Pretest, page 8
Chapter Test, page 25
Unit Post-Test, page 36

RE-TEACHING

Practice Pages or Practice
Book, pages 33, 34

THINKING SKILLS

Knowledge—*Identifying* subjects in sentences that give orders or directions (Exercise A, page 102)
Identifying the subject in questions (Exercise B, page 104)
Identifying the subject in sentences beginning with *There* or *Here* (Exercise C, page 105)
Identifying the subject in inverted sentences (Exercise D, page 106)

Synthesis—*Writing* sentences with subjects in various positions (Developing Writing Skills, page 106)

7.4 Special Problems with Subjects

6. Girls, help us carry these packages into the house. (you)
7. Measure the amount of rain that falls each morning. (You)
8. The bread jammed the toaster and burned. bread
9. Get the doctor at once! (You)
10. She bought a portable radio. She

Subjects in Questions

A sentence not in normal word order will generally be in *inverted word order*. The subject in such a sentence comes after its verb. This order is seen perhaps most often in questions.

In questions the subject often follows the verb.

Many questions begin with a verb or a helping verb. Others begin with such questioning words as *what, which, whose, who, when, why, where,* and *how.* In the following examples, notice that the subject sometimes comes between the parts of a verb phrase.

VERB FIRST: Are the apples very sour?

HELPING VERB FIRST: Have you opened your present?

QUESTIONING WORD FIRST: Where are the sour apples?

When will they begin the play?

If you have trouble finding the subject in a question, you can use a trick. Simply reword the question as a statement. The subject will then appear before the verb.

Question	Reworded as Statement
Are the apples very sour?	The apples are very sour.
Have you opened your present?	You have opened your present.
Where are the sour apples?	The sour apples are where.
When will they begin the play?	They will begin the play when.

Many questions use inverted word order, but some do not.

EXAMPLES: Whose <u>poems</u> <u>were selected</u> for the school literary magazine?

Who <u>has taken</u> my notebook?

EXERCISE B: Finding the Subject in Questions. Copy the following sentences onto your paper. Underline the subject in each.

EXAMPLE: Which Dickinson poem do <u>you</u> like best?

1. When did <u>she</u> call from her office?
2. Which book did <u>Billy</u> choose?
3. Has <u>Roberto</u> left for college yet?
4. Were the <u>flowers</u> delivered on time?
5. Which <u>team</u> has won the trophy?
6. How did <u>they</u> accept the news?
7. Where is the <u>signature</u> on this check?
8. Are <u>you</u> certain about the record?
9. <u>Who</u> took my pencil?
10. Why has <u>he</u> objected to the title of the play?

Subjects in Sentences Beginning with *There* or *Here*

Sentences beginning with *there* or *here* are usually in inverted word order.

There or here is never the subject of a sentence.

There can be used in two ways at the beginning of sentences. First, it can be used just to start the sentence.

SENTENCE STARTERS: There $\overset{\text{V}}{\underline{\text{are}}}$ two $\overset{\text{S}}{\underline{\text{astronauts}}}$ from NASA
in the office.

There $\overset{\text{V}}{\underline{\text{is}}}$ no good $\overset{\text{S}}{\underline{\text{reason}}}$ for our failure.

7.4 Special Problems with Subjects

There can also be used as an adverb at the beginning of sentences, as can the word *here*. As adverbs these two words point out where and modify the verbs.

ADVERBS: There $\overset{V}{\underline{goes}}$ the $\overset{S}{\underline{principal}}$.

Here $\overset{V}{\underline{are}}$ the $\overset{S}{\underline{invitations}}$ to the party.

Be alert to sentences beginning with *there* and *here*. They are probably in inverted word order. If you cannot find the subject, reword the sentence in normal word order. If *there* is just a sentence starter, it can be dropped from the sentence.

Sentence Beginning with *There* or *Here*	Reworded with Subject Before Verb
There <u>is</u> a <u>mistake</u> on your paper.	A <u>mistake</u> <u>is</u> on your paper.
Here <u>comes</u> the <u>captain</u> of the team.	The <u>captain</u> of the team <u>comes</u> here.

EXERCISE C: Finding the Subject in Sentences Beginning with *There* and *Here*. Copy the following sentences onto your paper. Underline the subject in each.

EXAMPLE: Here is the missing <u>piece</u>.

1. Here are the <u>notes</u> on the trip.
2. There were three <u>steps</u> to follow in the recipe.
3. There is a new sporting goods <u>store</u> in town.
4. There are the <u>magazines</u> on boating.
5. Here are three good mystery <u>novels</u> to read.
6. There is a bad winter <u>storm</u> approaching us.
7. There on the hill are the <u>ruins</u> of the ancient temple.
8. There can be only one <u>choice</u>.
9. Here sat the <u>ambassador</u> from Zimbabwe.
10. Here are your <u>assignments</u> for the next week.

Developing Student Writing

Have students practice writing sentences with subjects in various positions by completing the following assignment.

Writing Across the Curriculum

Almost everyone enjoys music of one kind or another. What is your favorite style of music? Country? Classical? Rock and Roll? Rap? Jazz? Blues? Have you ever really thought about why you prefer one style of music more than others?

Prewriting Think about your favorite style of music. Jot down a list of reasons why you prefer this style more than others. Your reasons should include why you like your style and why you dislike others. You might prefer more than one style of music. If so, jot down a list for each style. Arrange your list of reasons in a logical order.

Writing Write the first draft of an article for *Music Unlimited* magazine. In your article, explain why you prefer a particular style or styles of music more than others. Remember to present your views as opinions, not facts. Try to vary the length and structure of your sentences and also the position of the subject in some sentences.

Revising Make sure that you have provided both reasons why you enjoy your favorite style of music and reasons why you do not like other styles. Check to see that your ideas are presented as opinions and not facts. Have you varied the structure and length of your sentences? Proofread your article and prepare a final draft.

Subjects in Sentences Inverted for Emphasis

Sometimes a subject is intentionally put after its verb to draw attention to the subject.

In some sentences the subject follows the verb in order to receive greater emphasis.

In the following example, notice how the order of the words builds suspense by leading up to the subject.

EXAMPLE: In the midst of the crowd outside the theater

$$\overset{V}{\underline{stood}}\ \overset{S}{\underline{Muhammed\ Ali}}.$$

Sentences such as this one can be reworded in normal word order to make it easier to find the subject.

Inverted Word Order	Reworded with Subject Before Verb
In the midst of the crowd outside the theater stood Muhammed Ali.	Muhammed Ali stood in the midst of the crowd outside the theater.

EXERCISE D: Finding the Subject in Inverted Sentences. Copy the following sentences onto your paper. Underline the subject in each.

EXAMPLE: Far in the distance came the first roar of thunder.

1. High atop the tree on a dead branch perched a vulture.
2. All about the neighborhood lay the debris from the tornado.
3. Suddenly, into the clearing came three deer.
4. On that hill once stood a one-room schoolhouse.
5. Not far from the cabin was a clear, cold stream.

DEVELOPING WRITING SKILLS: Writing Sentences with Subjects in Various Positions. Write original sentences ac-

cording to the following directions. Add any missing subjects, using parentheses. Then underline the subject in each.
Answers will vary; samples are given for the first two.
EXAMPLE: Begin a sentence with *Were they.*

Were <u>they</u> really lost on a desert island?

1. Begin a sentence with *There are.*
2. Begin a sentence with *Choose.*
3. Begin a question with *What have.*
4. Begin a sentence with *How.*
5. Begin a sentence with *Here.*
6. Begin a question with *Did she.*
7. Begin a sentence with *There will be.*
8. Begin an order with *Stop.*
9. Write a sentence ending with the subject.
10. Write a question in which the subject comes before the verb.

1. There are four <u>apples</u> in the bowl.　2. <u>(You)</u> Choose your courses carefully.

Direct Objects 7.5

Often a subject and verb alone can express a complete thought. For example, "Birds fly" can stand by itself as a sentence even though it contains just a subject and a verb. In other sentences, however, the thought begun by a subject and its verb needs to be completed with other words. For example, the sentences "Toni bought," "The eyewitness told," "Our librarian is," and "Richard feels" all contain a subject and verb, but none expresses a complete thought. All these ideas need *complements.*

A complement is a word or group of words that completes the meaning of a subject and verb.

Complements are usually nouns, pronouns, or adjectives. They are located right after or very close to the verb. In the chart on the following page, the subjects are underlined once, the verbs twice, and the complements are boxed.

7.5 Direct Objects
(pp. 107–113)

OBJECTIVES
After completing this section, students should be able to

• Identify direct objects in sentences.
• Identify compound direct objects in sentences.
• Distinguish between direct objects, adverbs, and objects of prepositions.
• Locate direct objects in questions.

TEACHING
Getting Started
Tell students that direct objects are complements that are used after action verbs. They can be

found by asking *Whom?* or *What?* after an action verb, determining, in other words, *to whom* or *to what* the action occurred.

Write the following sentences on the chalkboard:

1. The principal shook my hand.
2. I thanked him for the award.

Have students read the sentences, and tell them to ask themselves, "Shook what?" and "Thanked whom?" to find the direct objects. Elicit that *hand* and *him* are the direct objects in the sentences. Point out that *award* in sentence 2 is the object of the preposition *for* and therefore cannot be the direct object. As a further test, have students answer the question "Thanked whom?" to see that *him* has to be the direct object.

Text Follow Through

Discuss text pages 107–113.

Assign Exercise A, page 108; Exercise B, page 109; Exercise C, page 111; Exercise D, page 112; and Developing Writing Skills, page 112.

Less advanced If students have difficulty with Exercise D, you might remind them to rewrite the questions in normal word order. These students might also work in pairs or in small groups to complete the Developing Writing Skills activity.

Average To reinforce recognition of direct objects, you might have students write answers to the first five questions in Exercise D. They can then underline the direct object in each of the new sentences.

Advanced You might instruct students to write the sentences in the Developing Writing Skills

---

DIFFERENT KINDS OF COMPLEMENTS
Toni bought cookies.
The eyewitness told us the story.
Our librarian is a poet.
Richard feels sad.

The next three sections will describe three types of complements: *direct objects, indirect objects,* and *subject complements.*

The Direct Object

Direct objects are complements that are used after action verbs.

A direct object is a noun or pronoun that receives the action of a transitive verb.

A direct object can be found by asking *Whom?* or *What?* after an action verb.

EXAMPLES: The message reached the lawyer. (DO)
(Reached *whom? Answer:* lawyer)

His landlord is raising the rent. (DO)
(Is raising *what? Answer:* rent)

In the examples *lawyer* and *rent* are the direct objects of the verbs. In the first sentence, the question is *Reached whom?* The answer is the *lawyer.* In the second example, the question is *Raised what?* The answer is the *rent.*

EXERCISE A: Recognizing Direct Objects. Each of the following sentences contains a direct object. Copy the sentences onto your paper and underline each direct object.

activity in any order they choose, as long as they use all the patterns. Students might then exchange papers and identify direct objects, adverbs, and prepositional phrases according to the instructions in Exercise C.

Additional Practice

Practice Pages or Practice Book, pages 35–37

Less advanced Exercise Bank, Exercises A and B, pages 56–59

Average Exercise Bank, Exercises A, B, and C, pages 56–59

Advanced Exercise Bank, Exercises B and C, pages 56–59

TESTING

Test Program

Unit Pretest, page 8
Chapter Test, page 25
Unit Post-Test, page 37

RE-TEACHING

Practice Pages or Practice Book, pages 35–37

THINKING SKILLS

Knowledge—*Identifying* direct objects in sentences (Exercise A, page 108)
Identifying compound direct objects in sentences (Exercise B, page 109)
Identifying direct objects in questions (Exercise D, page 112)

Comprehension—*Distinguishing* between direct objects, adverbs, and objects of prepositions in sentences (Exercise C, page 111)

Synthesis—*Writing* sentences with direct objects (Developing Writing Skills, page 112)

7.5 Direct Objects

EXAMPLE: She quickly opened the <u>letter</u>.

1. My aunt approached the <u>door</u> cautiously.
2. Sally gave our <u>puppy</u> to the Wilsons.
3. The patients take their <u>medicine</u> three times a day.
4. My mother sent the <u>clothing</u> to the Red Cross.
5. At night she often eats frozen <u>dinners</u>.
6. We received <u>oranges</u> from Florida.
7. I want <u>them</u> here now.
8. He winds his gold <u>watch</u> each morning.
9. After lunch she gave an <u>account</u> of the accident.
10. They did not serve any <u>dessert</u> after dinner.

Compound Direct Objects

Direct objects, like subjects and verbs, can be compound.

A compound direct object is two or more nouns or pronouns that receive the action of the same transitive verb.

If a sentence contains a compound direct object, asking *Whom?* or *What?* after the verb will give you more than one answer.

EXAMPLES: <u>Mother</u> <u>invited</u> Uncle Bill and Aunt Clara.
(Invited *whom? Answer:* Uncle Bill, Aunt Clara)

Our <u>host</u> <u>served</u> pie and ice cream for dessert.
(Served *what? Answer:* pie, ice cream)

EXERCISE B: Recognizing Compound Direct Objects.
Each of the sentences on the following page contains a compound direct object. On your paper write only the nouns or pronouns that make up each compound direct object.

EXAMPLE: Don't forget the carrots or the spinach.

carrots   spinach

1. At the market buy some <u>lettuce</u>, <u>carrots</u>, <u>squash</u>, and <u>tomatoes</u>.
2. After class Mr. Simpson complimented <u>Ned</u> and <u>him</u> on their project.
3. Did they buy a <u>sedan</u> or a <u>convertible?</u>
4. I shocked <u>Mary</u> and <u>Bob</u> with my story.
5. I saw <u>him</u> and <u>her</u> at the movies.
6. The train passed <u>New York</u>, <u>Providence</u>, and <u>Boston</u> while I slept.
7. Linda and Alan planted <u>marigolds</u> and <u>petunias</u> in their garden.
8. The poet Sylvia Plath wrote many <u>poems</u> and one <u>novel</u>.
9. She has always loved <u>ships</u> and the <u>sea</u>.
10. Sara bought a new <u>blouse</u> and a yellow <u>skirt</u> and blue <u>shoes</u>.

Direct Object, Adverb, or Object of a Preposition?

Not all action verbs have direct objects. Be careful not to confuse a direct object with an adverb or with the object of a preposition.

A direct object is never an adverb or the noun or pronoun at the end of a prepositional phrase.

Compare the following examples. Notice that the action verb *walked* has a direct object only in the first sentence.

EXAMPLES: <u>Joanne</u> <u>walked</u> her $\overset{\text{DO}}{\boxed{\text{dog.}}}$

<u>Joanne</u> <u>walked</u> briskly.

<u>Joanne</u> <u>walked</u> through the park.

Each example shows a very common sentence type. The first consists of a subject, a verb, and a direct object. The noun *dog* is the direct object of the verb *walked.* The second example consists of a subject, a verb, and an adverb. Nothing answers the question *What?* so there is no direct object. *Briskly* modifies the verb. The third example consists of a subject, a verb, and a prepositional phrase. Again, no noun or pronoun answers the question *What?* The prepositional phrase tells where Joanne walked.

Notice also that a single sentence can contain more than one of these three.

```
                       DO    ADV     PREP PHRASE
```
EXAMPLE: Joanne walked her dog briskly through the park.

EXERCISE C: Distinguishing Between Direct Objects, Adverbs, and Objects of Prepositions. Copy each of the following sentences onto your paper. Underline each direct object. Circle any adverbs or prepositional phrases. Not every sentence has all three.
Adverbs and prepositional phrases are shaded.
EXAMPLE: The dragon roared loudly in the night.

1. Fred drove the old truck into our driveway.
2. She opened the letter slowly and cautiously.
3. My mother attended the parade in the park.
4. The lion chased the frightened animals through the forest.
5. He practiced a new stunt for the competition.

Direct Objects in Questions

A direct object in a sentence in normal word order is found after the verb. In questions, which are often in inverted order, the position of a direct object in the sentence may change.

A direct object in a question is sometimes near the beginning of the sentence, before the verb.

Compare the position of the direct object in each of the sentences in the chart on the following page. The sentences in the first column are questions. In the second column, the questions have been reworded as statements in normal word order.

Questions	Normal Word Order
DO Whom did you ask for help?	DO You did ask whom for help.
DO What does he want from us?	DO He does want what from us.
DO Which book does he want from the library?	DO He does want which book from the library.

If you have trouble finding the direct object in a question, change the sentence into normal word order, as shown in the examples.

EXERCISE D: Finding Direct Objects in Questions. Copy each of the following sentences onto your paper and underline each direct object. Note that in two of the sentences, the direct objects follow the verbs.

EXAMPLE: <u>What</u> were you thinking?

1. Which <u>photograph</u> did she take?
2. <u>Whom</u> does he expect this evening?
3. <u>What</u> did you do with the package?
4. Where will you spend your <u>vacation</u>?
5. Which <u>books</u> have they read?
6. How many <u>records</u> did you buy?
7. Which <u>suggestions</u> have they considered so far?
8. <u>What</u> have you heard about the astronauts?
9. When will the judges announce the <u>awards</u>?
10. Which <u>color</u> have they chosen for the new curtains?

DEVELOPING WRITING SKILLS: Writing Sentences with Direct Objects. Write an original sentence for each of the following patterns. You may add additional words or details as long as you keep the assigned pattern.

Answers will vary; samples are given for the first two.

EXAMPLE: Subject + Verb + Direct Object + Direct Object

Becky collected both records and marbles.

1. My cousin borrowed my blue sweater.
   1. subject + verb + direct object
   2. subject + verb + direct object + prepositional phrase
   3. direct object + helping verb + subject + verb
   4. subject + verb + direct object + conjunction + direct object
   5. subject + verb + direct object + adverb + prepositional phrase
2. Dad is adding a toolshed to the garage.

Indirect Objects 7.6

Sentences that contain a direct object may also contain another kind of complement, called an *indirect object*.

The Indirect Object

A sentence cannot have an indirect object unless it first has a direct object.

An indirect object is a noun or pronoun that comes after an action verb and before a direct object. It names the person or thing that something is given to or done for.

An indirect object answers the question *To or for whom?* or *To or for what?* after an action verb. To find an indirect object, find the direct object first. Then ask the questions, as shown in the examples.

EXAMPLES:

           IO   DO
    I told them the story.
    (Told *to whom? Answer:* them)

                 IO   DO
    Dave gave each slide a new title.
    (Gave *to what? Answer:* slide)

In the first of the sentences above, *them* answers the question *To whom did I tell the story?* In the second example, *slide*

7.6 Indirect Objects
(pp. 113–116)

OBJECTIVES

After completing this section, students should be able to

- Identify indirect objects in sentences.
- Identify compound indirect objects in sentences.
- Distinguish between indirect objects and objects of prepositions.

TEACHING

Getting Started

Write the following pattern on the chalkboard: Subject + Verb + Indirect Object + Direct Object. Then below the pattern write this sentence: I gave Pat a record. Have students read the definition of an indirect object on page 113. Then ask for a volunteer to test the validity of the indirect object in the sentence by asking, "Gave to whom?" Have volunteers suggest other sentences that fit this sentence pattern, and write them on the chalkboard below the pattern.

answers the question *To what did Dave give a title?*

Keep in mind the following pattern: Subject + Verb + Indirect Object + Direct Object. An indirect object will almost always come between the verb and the direct object in a sentence.

EXERCISE A: Recognizing Indirect Objects. Each sentence contains a direct object and an indirect object. Copy the sentences and underline each indirect object.

EXAMPLE: Finally, she told <u>him</u> the news.

1. The coach gave <u>him</u> a special award.
2. We sent <u>her</u> a bouquet of flowers.
3. After dinner they told <u>us</u> the good news.
4. Have you shown <u>them</u> the new puppy?
5. Lucille lent her <u>brother</u> her umbrella.
6. I later wrote my <u>brother</u> an explanation for my behavior.
7. Pass your <u>sister</u> the vegetables.
8. Vasco taught <u>me</u> several Portuguese words.
9. I will order <u>you</u> some breakfast now.
10. Did you really sell <u>him</u> your record collection?

Compound Indirect Objects

Like a subject, verb, or direct object, an indirect object can be compound.

A compound indirect object is two or more nouns or pronouns that come after an action verb and before a direct object. It names the persons or things that something is given to or done for.

Compound indirect objects answer the same questions as single indirect objects: *To or for whom?* or *To or for what?*

EXAMPLE: Dave gave each slide and photo a new title.

(Gave *to what? Answer:* slide, photo)

7.6 Indirect Objects

EXERCISE B: Recognizing Compound Indirect Objects.

Each sentence contains a compound indirect object. Write the
nouns or pronouns that make up each one.

EXAMPLE: Will he tell Jay and Cathy the truth?

Jay   Cathy

1. Give him and her an equal amount.
2. Have you told Sally or Beth that story?
3. We gave the birds and the fish new homes.
4. Mother told the doctor and nurse our symptoms.
5. Did you get Marie and Steve their consent slips?
6. I gave the stairs and the porch a new coat of paint.
7. Have you told Mother and him the wonderful news?
8. Please read Bob and them the directions to the store.
9. In the morning I will give Joyce and her father our decision.
10. Take Uncle Bill and Aunt Lila a cold drink.

Indirect Object or Object of a Preposition?

Do not confuse an indirect object with the object of a
preposition.

**An indirect object never follows the preposition
to or *for* in a sentence.**

Compare the following examples.

EXAMPLES: Father bought him a present. (IO DO)

Father bought a present for him. (DO)

In the first example, *him* is an indirect object. It comes after
the verb and before the direct object. In the second, *him* is the
object of the preposition *for* and follows the direct object.

EXERCISE C: Distinguishing Between Indirect Objects and Objects of Prepositions.
Copy each sentence. Under-
line each indirect object. Circle each object of a preposition.
Objects of prepositions are shaded.

EXAMPLE: Strawberries gave <u>him</u> a rash.

1. Sheepishly, she told her <u>father</u> the story.
2. Raphael gave a bone to the collie.
3. Did you tell <u>him</u> the price?
4. Surprisingly enough, she gave her <u>aunt</u> the bracelet.
5. My mother brought her car to the repair shop.
6. I definitely will hold him to his promise.
7. In anger he gave <u>him</u> the money.
8. I did offer <u>her</u> a choice.
9. Please buy a new radio for them.
10. Have you shown your <u>mother</u> the test paper?

DEVELOPING WRITING SKILLS: Writing Sentences with Indirect Objects. Follow the directions to write five sentences.

Answers will vary; samples are given for the first two.

EXAMPLE: Write a sentence with three indirect objects.

Mary Beth told Cindy, Craig, and Joel her secret.

1. Mother Hubbard gave her dog a bone.

1. Write a sentence that fits this pattern: Subject + Verb + Indirect Object + Direct Object.
2. Using the same subject, verb, and direct object as in the first item, change the sentence to Subject + Verb + Direct Object + Prepositional Phrase.
3. Write a sentence with a compound indirect object connected by *and.*
4. Write a sentence with a compound indirect object connected by *or.*
5. Rewrite the sentence in the example, changing the compound indirect object to a prepositional phrase.

2. Mother Hubbard gave a bone to her dog.

7.7 Subject Complements

Both direct objects and indirect objects are complements

OBJECTIVES

After completing this section, students should be able to

- Identify predicate nouns and pronouns in sentences.
- Identify predicate adjectives in sentences.
- Identify compound subject complements in sentences.

TEACHING

Getting Started

Write the word *complement* on the board. Ask students to speculate on the meaning of the word. Explain that the first six letters will give them a hint. After students have defined *complement,* introduce the notion of a subject complement as a noun, pronoun, or adjective that follows a linking verb and helps to complete information about a subject.

Write the following sentences on the chalkboard:

1. Sheila is a good skier.
2. The girl in the blue jumpsuit is she.
3. The girl appeared frightened.

Ask for volunteers to identify first the subject and verb in each sentence and then the word after the verb that either identifies or describes the subject. Ask students to identify which subject complement is a noun, which is a pronoun, and which is an adverb.

Text Follow Through

Discuss text pages 116–121.

Assign Exercise A, page 118; Exercise B, page 119; Exercise C, page 120; and Developing Writing Skills, page 120.

7.7 Subject Complements

used with action verbs. Linking verbs, however, have a different kind of complement, called a *subject complement.*

A subject complement is a noun, pronoun, or adjective that follows a linking verb and tells something about the subject.

Nouns and pronouns that act as subject complements are *predicate nouns* and *predicate pronouns.* An adjective that acts as a subject complement is a *predicate adjective.*

Predicate Nouns and Pronouns

Both nouns and pronouns are sometimes used as subject complements after linking verbs.

A predicate noun or predicate pronoun follows a linking verb and renames or identifies the subject of the sentence.

It is easy to recognize *predicate nouns* and *predicate pronouns.* The linking verb acts much like an equal sign between the subject and the noun or pronoun that follows the verb. Both the subject and the predicate noun or pronoun refer to the same person or thing.

PREDICATE NOUNS AND PRONOUNS	
Examples	**Relationship of Words**
Ronnie will be the PN captain of our team.	The predicate noun *captain* renames the subject *Ronnie.*
North America's longest PN river is the Mississippi.	The predicate noun *Mississippi* identifies the subject *river.*
PRED PRON The two winners are they.	The predicate pronoun *they* identifies the subject *winners.*

Less advanced Students might work in pairs to write the sentences for the Developing Writing Skills activity. Then have them exchange papers with other pairs who will underline the subject complements and draw arrows pointing to the subject.

Average If students need further practice with subject complements, have them identify the type of subject complement in each sentence of Exercise A in Section 2.2 (page 43).

Advanced Students might be permitted to mix and match the subjects and predicates in the Developing Writing Skills activity and to compare their sentences to see the many variations possible.

Additional Practice

Practice Pages or Practice Book, pages 40, 41

Less advanced Exercise Bank, Exercises A and B, pages 63–65

Average Exercise Bank, Exercises A, B, and C, pages 63–65

Advanced Exercise Bank, Exercises B and C, pages 63–65

TESTING

Test Program

Unit Pretest, page 8
Chapter Test, page 26
Unit Post-Test, page 37

RE-TEACHING

Practice Pages or Practice Book, pages 40, 41

The verbs in these examples are all forms of the linking verb *be*. See Section 2.2 for a complete list of the forms of *be* and other linking verbs.

A predicate noun or pronoun will never be the object of a preposition. In the following example, the subject complement is *one*, not *stars*.

```
                    PRED PRON   OBJ OF PREP
EXAMPLE:   Diana Ross was │one│ of the │stars│ in The Wiz.
```

EXERCISE A: Recognizing Predicate Nouns and Pronouns.
Copy the following sentences onto your paper and underline each predicate noun or predicate pronoun.

EXAMPLE: That yellow shrub is a <u>forsythia</u>.

1. The capital of New Jersey is <u>Trenton</u>.
2. Peter Taylor is a notable short-story <u>writer</u>.
3. At this time Sheila appears the <u>front-runner</u>.
4. According to legend Prometheus was a <u>Titan</u>.
5. That young woman may someday become a fine <u>doctor</u>.
6. Many years ago Simla was the <u>capital</u> of British India.
7. Carlos and Juan have remained <u>buddies</u> for years.
8. The last person in line is <u>she</u>.
9. My favorite sport has always been <u>basketball</u>.
10. That camera was an excellent <u>choice</u>.

Predicate Adjectives

A linking verb can also be followed by a *predicate adjective*.

A predicate adjective follows a linking verb and describes the subject of the sentence.

A predicate adjective is considered part of the complete predicate of a sentence because it comes after a linking verb. In spite of this, a predicate adjective does not modify the words in the predicate. Instead, it describes the noun or pronoun that serves as the subject in front of the linking verb.

THINKING SKILLS

Knowledge—*Identifying* predicate nouns and pronouns (Exercise A, page 118)
Identifying predicate adjectives (Exercise B, page 119)
Identifying compound subject complements (Exercise C, page 120)

Synthesis—*Writing* sentences with subject complements (Developing Writing Skills, page 120)

7.7 Subject Complements

PREDICATE ADJECTIVES	
Examples	**Relationship of Words**
The <u>flight</u> to Houston <u>was</u> PA swift.	The predicate adjective *swift* describes the subject *flight*.
Our <u>congresswoman</u> PA <u>seems</u> very sensitive to the needs of her constituents.	The predicate adjective *sensitive* describes the subject *congresswoman*.

EXERCISE B: Recognizing Predicate Adjectives. Copy the sentences and underline each predicate adjective.

EXAMPLE: The sky is <u>murky</u>.

1. The scent of the flowers is very <u>sweet</u>.
2. Many of the houses are quite <u>old</u>.
3. I felt <u>sad</u> about his misfortune.
4. At night this road becomes particularly <u>dangerous</u>.
5. The smoke from the fire remained <u>heavy</u>.
6. This chemical smells <u>stronger</u> than any other.
7. The view from the mountaintop was <u>breathtaking</u>.
8. The old windmill in Aruba is very <u>attractive</u>.
9. The carton seems too <u>heavy</u> to carry.
10. He has always been <u>honest</u> about his shortcomings.

Compound Subject Complements

Like other sentence parts, subject complements can be compound.

A compound subject complement consists of two or more predicate nouns, pronouns, or adjectives.

EXAMPLES: My two best <u>friends</u> <u>are</u> Phil and Mark.

The other <u>speakers</u> <u>were</u> he and she.

The <u>highway</u> <u>seems</u> slick and icy.

EXERCISE C: Recognizing Compound Subject Complements.
Copy the following sentences onto your paper and underline each part of each compound subject complement. If a compound subject complement is made up of predicate adjectives, draw arrows pointing from each adjective to the subject. Subjects modified by predicate adjectives are shaded.

EXAMPLE: The icing was <u>rich</u> and <u>sweet</u>.

1. Vacations in state parks can be <u>interesting</u> and <u>inexpensive</u>.
2. My favorite poets are <u>Emily Dickinson</u> and <u>Langston Hughes</u>.
3. The old bridge seems <u>frail</u> and <u>dangerous</u>.
4. The organizers of the crafts fair were <u>Sonia</u> and <u>I</u>.
5. That imported cheese tastes <u>moldy</u> and much too <u>strong</u>.
6. This fish is either <u>flounder</u> or <u>sole</u>.
7. Are the sails <u>strong</u> and <u>seaworthy</u>?
8. Their hands became <u>raw</u> and <u>frostbitten</u> in the icy wind.
9. The soup is neither too <u>hot</u> nor too <u>cold</u>.
10. The flame first turned <u>orange</u>, then <u>blue</u>, and finally brilliant <u>white</u>.

DEVELOPING WRITING SKILLS: Writing Sentences with Subject Complements.
Use the following subjects and verbs to write sentences of your own. Include in each sentence the type of subject complement given in parentheses.
Answers will vary; samples are given.

EXAMPLE: poem was (compound predicate adjectives)

The poem was short but moving.

1. feet feel (predicate adjective) My/cold
2. Bob and Stan will be (predicate noun) lifeguards.
3. captains are (compound predicate pronouns) The/she and I.
4. dog is (compound predicate adjectives)
5. roast beef looks (predicate adjective) This/too rare.
6. cities are (compound predicate nouns)
7. cars appear (compound predicate adjectives)
8. precious metals are (compound predicate nouns)
9. music sounds (predicate adjective) His/old-fashioned.
10. cousins are (predicate noun and predicate pronoun)

4. The/mangy and dirty. 6. My favorite/Montreal and Denver. 7. These/clean and new. 10. My/Brenda and she.

The Four Functions 7.8 of Sentences

Sentences are often classified according to what they do. A sentence may be *declarative, interrogative, imperative,* or *exclamatory.*

A declarative sentence states an idea and ends with a period.

DECLARATIVE: A strong wind whipped through the valley.

Royale Street in New Orleans is filled with expensive shops and horse-drawn carriages.

The cost is three hundred dollars.

An interrogative sentence asks a question and ends with a question mark.

INTERROGATIVE: Where is the old city hall?

Have you ever attempted to make lasagna?

Who is he?

An imperative sentence gives an order or a direction and ends with either a period or an exclamation mark.

121

7.8 The Four Functions of Sentences
(pp. 121–123)

OBJECTIVE
After completing this section, students should be able to

- Identify sentences as declarative, interrogative, imperative, or exclamatory.

TEACHING
Getting Started
Tell students that sentences are classified according to what they do. Write the following sentences on the chalkboard:

My watch stopped.
Does it need a new battery?
Take it to the repair shop.
What will I do without a watch!

Step by step, analyze the function and features of each kind of sentence. Ask which one asks a question, which gives an order, which makes a statement, and which expresses a strong feeling. Point out the different punctuation marks used to end the sentences and ask how they affect the meaning of the sentence or the way it is read. You might want to have volunteers write on the chalkboard other examples of each kind of sentence for classmates to analyze and identify function.

Text Follow Through

Discuss text pages 121–123.

Assign the Exercise, page 122, and Developing Writing Skills, page 123.

Less advanced Have students work in pairs to complete the Developing Writing Skills activity. Have them exchange papers to compare how others handled the sentence-writing assignment.

Average Call on students in turn to read aloud in random order the sentences they wrote for the Developing Writing Skills activity while other students identify each sentence by function. You might also have students attempt to write sets of four different kinds of sentences, similar to the set in the Getting Started activity above.

Advanced Have students rewrite the sentences in the Exercise, changing each to another function. For example, sentence 1 could be changed to a declarative sentence: *It is wise to visit the dentist twice a year.* Other students might carry out the same activity orally.

Additional Practice

Practice Pages or Practice Book, page 42

Less advanced Exercise Bank, Exercises A and B, page 66

Many imperative sentences begin with a verb. When the subject of such a sentence is left out, it is understood to be *you.*

IMPERATIVE: Wrap the package carefully.

   Stop!

Imperative sentences, however, do sometimes have subjects. When they do, they sound very much like questions. But instead of ending with a question mark, they end with a period or exclamation mark. In the following examples, the subjects are italicized.

IMPERATIVE: Can *you* help us, please.

   Will *somebody* answer the phone!

An exclamatory sentence conveys strong emotion and ends with an exclamation mark.

EXAMPLES: What a terrible accident that was!

   He is a villain!

EXERCISE: Identifying the Use of Sentences. Read each of the following sentences and identify its use as *declarative, interrogative, imperative,* or *exclamatory.* After each answer, write the appropriate punctuation mark for that sentence.

EXAMPLE: What a mistake that was

   exclamatory   !

1. Have you visited the dentist yet this year inter ?
2. Choose the hat with the best fit imper .
3. Between 1629 and 1640, almost 60,000 people emigrated from England declar .
4. She worked very hard as governor declar .
5. Would you stand absolutely still now, please imper .
6. What are the other ingredients needed for the molasses cookies inter ?
7. I agree with the editorial in this newspaper declar .

Average Exercise Bank, Exercises A, B, and C, page 66

Advanced Exercise Bank, Exercises B and C, page 66

TESTING

Test Program

Unit Pretest, pages 8, 9
Chapter Test, page 26
Unit Post-Test, page 37

RE-TEACHING

Practice Pages or Practice Book, page 42

THINKING SKILLS

Knowledge—*Identifying* the use of sentences (Exercise, page 122)

Synthesis—*Writing* sentences with different uses (Developing Writing Skills, page 123)

---

8. What an excellent magazine this is exclam !
9. How much do they want for it now inter ?
10. Give two reasons supporting your opening statement imper .

DEVELOPING WRITING SKILLS: Writing Sentences with Different Uses. Write a sentence according to the directions given for each of the following items.
Answers will vary; samples are given for the first two.
EXAMPLE: Write an imperative sentence that ends with an exclamation mark.

Do it now!

1. Close the door behind you.
  1. Write an imperative sentence that begins with a verb.
  2. Write a question beginning with *Which.*
  3. Write a declarative sentence about your favorite hobby.
  4. Write an exclamatory sentence showing your surprise at something.
  5. Write a question beginning with a verb.

2. Which invitation should I accept?

Diagraming Basic 7.9 Sentence Parts

Diagraming is a visual way to explain how the parts of a sentence are related. In a diagram the words from a sentence are positioned on horizontal, vertical, and slanted lines. Each line stands for something different. This section will explain how you can draw diagrams for each of the sentence parts that were discussed in this chapter.

Subjects and Verbs

The basic parts of any sentence are the subject and its verb. In a diagram both the subject and verb are placed on a horizontal line. They are separated by a vertical line, with the subject on the left and the verb on the right.

7.9 Diagraming Basic Sentence Parts

(pp. 123–131)

OBJECTIVES

After completing this section, students should be able to

- Diagram sentences with subjects and verbs.
- Diagram sentences with adjectives, adverbs, and conjunctions.
- Diagram sentences with compound subjects and verbs.
- Diagram orders, sentences beginning with *There* or *Here,* and interjections.
- Diagram sentences with complements.

TEACHING

Getting Started

Explain that a sentence diagram is like other diagrams or blueprints. It shows all the parts of a sentence and how they fit together. Draw on the chalkboard a skeleton diagram for a basic subject-verb sentence. Then alongside the diagram write the following sentences:

1. Dogs barked.
2. Politicians spoke.
3. Records have been broken.

Diagram the first sentence for students, and then ask for volunteers to diagram the other sentences. Have students suggest other subject-verb sentences for classmates to diagram on the chalkboard. Note that students will learn to diagram much more complex sentences in this section.

Text Follow Through

Discuss text pages 123–131.

Assign Exercise A, page 124; Exercise B, page 125; Exercise C, page 127; Exercise D, page 128; Exercise E, page 131; Exercise F, page 131; and Developing Writing Skills, page 131.

Less advanced Students might be given skeleton diagrams to use in completing any or all of the exercises and the Developing Writing Skills activity. If you decide not to teach diagraming to these students, you can use the exercises for additional drill on parts of speech. Students can write the sentences and label subjects, verbs, modifiers, and complements.

EXAMPLE: Cars race.

Names and compound nouns are diagramed in the same way as *cars* in the preceding example. Verb phrases are diagramed as was the verb *race*.

EXAMPLE: Elizabeth Wilson has been called.

| Elizabeth Wilson | has been called |

EXERCISE A: Diagraming Subjects and Verbs. Each of the following sentences contains a subject and verb. Diagram each sentence, using the preceding examples as models.
Answers are on pages 126–127.

1. People grow.
2. Max spoke.
3. Mrs. Rodriguez has changed.
4. Oklahoma State Park has opened.
5. They have been notified.

Adjectives, Adverbs, and Conjunctions

Most sentences contain more than a subject and verb. Here are the ways to add adjectives, adverbs, and conjunctions to your basic diagrams.

Adding Adjectives. Adjectives are placed on slanted lines directly below the nouns or pronouns they modify.

EXAMPLE: A *strong, icy* wind appeared.

7.9 Diagraming Basic Sentence Parts

Adding Adverbs. Adverbs are also placed on slanted lines. They go directly under the verbs, adjectives, or adverbs they modify.

EXAMPLE: *Quite* nervous, Frank spoke *very hesitantly.*

Adding Conjunctions. Conjunctions are diagramed on dotted lines drawn between the words they connect.

EXAMPLE: The warm *and* friendly nurse spoke softly *but* firmly.

EXERCISE B: Diagraming Subjects and Verbs with Modifiers and Conjunctions. In addition to subjects and verbs, the following sentences contain adjectives, adverbs, and conjunctions. Diagram each sentence.

Answers are on page 127.

1. The old woman walked slowly.
2. The instructor spoke rapidly but quite distinctly.
3. The tiny but courageous dog yelped constantly.
4. The red and yellow tulips swayed very gently.
5. Extremely dense smoke was quickly drifting upward.

Compound Subjects and Verbs

It is necessary to split the horizontal line in order to diagram a sentence with either a compound subject or a compound verb.

Average You might want to supply skeleton diagrams for the first two items in each exercise. Then have students work independently on the others. Or you might have students work in pairs or groups to diagram odd-numbered sentences in class and diagram even-numbered sentences at home.

Advanced Many of the exercise sets found earlier in the chapter can be adapted to provide extra practice in diagraming. All prepositional phrases, appositives, and subordinate clauses must be removed, and the sentences should be checked carefully for other words that might give the students difficulty.

Additional Practice

Practice Pages or Practice Book, pages 43–46

Less advanced Exercise Bank, Exercises A and B, pages 67–71

Average Exercise Bank, Exercises A, B, and C, pages 67–71

Advanced Exercise Bank, Exercises B and C, pages 67–71

TESTING

Test Program

Unit Pretest, pages 11, 12
Chapter Test, page 26
Unit Post-Test, pages 39, 40

RE-TEACHING

Practice Pages or Practice Book, pages 43–46

THINKING SKILLS

Analysis—*Diagraming* subjects and verbs (Exercise A, page 124)

Diagraming subjects and verbs with modifiers and conjunctions (Exercise B, page 125)

Diagraming compound subjects and compound verbs (Exercise C, page 127)

Diagraming orders, sentences beginning with *There* and *Here,* and interjections (Exercise D, page 128)

Diagraming direct objects and indirect objects (Exercise E, page 131)

Diagraming subject complements (Exercise F, page 131)

Synthesis—*Writing* and *diagraming* sentences that contain a variety of components (Developing Writing Skills, page 131)

Answers for Exercise A, page 124

1.

2.

3.

Compound Subjects. A sentence with a compound subject has its subject diagramed on two levels.

EXAMPLE: Father and Mother are arriving.

In diagraming compound subjects, place any adjective directly under the word it modifies. If an adjective modifies the entire compound subject, place it under the main line of the diagram. In the following example, *several* modifies the entire compound subject. *Red* and *blue* modify separate subjects.

EXAMPLE: *Several red* balloons and *blue* kites floated overhead.

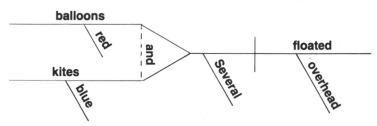

Compound Verbs. Sentences with compound verbs are diagramed similarly. In the following example, the adverb *magnificently* modifies both parts of the compound verb.

EXAMPLE: Jeffrey acts and sings *magnificently.*

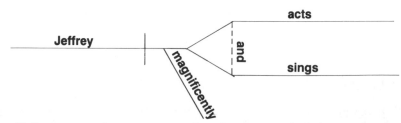

If the parts of a compound verb share a helping verb, the helping verb is placed on the main line of the diagram. If each

4.

5.

7.9 Diagraming Basic Sentence Parts

part of the compound verb has its own helping verb, then each helping verb is placed on the line with its own verb.

EXAMPLE: Betty will win or lose.

EXAMPLE: This project must grow or must shrink.

1.

EXERCISE C: Diagraming Compound Subjects and Compound Verbs. Correctly diagram each sentence.
Answers are on page 128.

1. Apples and grapes were served.
2. They can come or can stay.
3. The players, coaches, and parents cheered wildly.
4. The noisy crowd cheered, whistled, and applauded.
5. My brother and sister arrived early and left late.

2.

3.

Orders, Sentences Beginning with *There* and *Here,* and Interjections

Orders, sentences beginning with *there* or *here,* and interjections all follow special forms.

Orders. The subject of an order is usually understood to be *you*. The understood subject *you* is diagramed in the regular subject position, but in parentheses.

EXAMPLE: Stop now.

4.

5.

Answers for Exercise C, page 127

1.

2.

3.

4.

5.

Sentences Beginning with *There* and *Here*. *There* and *here* sometimes appear at the beginning of sentences and are mistaken for subjects. They are usually adverbs that modify the verb.

EXAMPLE: *Here* is your watch.

When *there* is used simply to start a sentence, it has no grammatical relation to the rest of the sentence. It is therefore placed on a short line above the subject.

EXAMPLE: *There* is an important meeting now.

Interjections. Like the word *there* used simply to start a sentence, interjections have no grammatical relation to the other words in a sentence. For this reason interjections are also placed on a short line above the subject.

EXAMPLE: *Wow!* I won.

EXERCISE D: Diagraming Orders, Sentences Beginning with *There* and *Here*, and Interjections. Diagram each of the following sentences. Answers are on page 129.

128

7.9 Diagraming Basic Sentence Parts

1. Begin now.
2. Here is my homework.
3. There once was a snake.
4. Whew! That hurt.
5. Gee! Watch out.

Complements

Direct objects, indirect objects, and subject complements are diagramed in three different ways.

Direct Objects. A direct object is placed on the same line as the subject and verb. The direct object follows the verb and is separated from it by a short vertical line.

EXAMPLE: Children drink milk.
           (DO above milk)

Children	drink	milk

A compound direct object is diagramed in a way similar to compound subjects and verbs. An adjective modifying both parts of the compound direct object is placed under the main line of the diagram. Otherwise, the adjective is placed directly under the word it modifies.

EXAMPLE: I have read five books and magazines.
           (DO above books, DO above magazines)

Indirect Objects. The indirect object is placed on a short horizontal line extending from a slanted line drawn directly below the verb.

EXAMPLE: The teacher gave them the good news.
           (IO above them)

1.
2.
3.
4.
5.

129

Answers for Exercise E, page 131

1.

2.

3.

4.

5.

A sentence with a compound indirect object is diagramed in the following way.

EXAMPLE: Mother bought Billy and me new gloves.

Subject Complements. The subject complements—predicate nouns, pronouns, and adjectives—follow linking verbs. All are diagramed in the same way. They are placed after the verb, separated from it by a short slanted line.

EXAMPLE: Julie will be our class president.

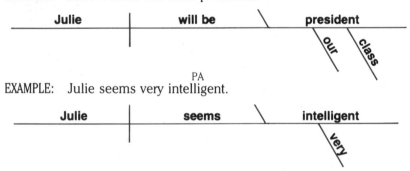

EXAMPLE: Julie seems very intelligent.

A compound subject complement is diagramed in the same way as a compound direct object, except that the separating line is slanted.

EXAMPLE: Those stamps are old and very valuable.

7.9 Diagraming Basic Sentence Parts

EXERCISE E: Diagraming Direct Objects and Indirect Objects. Diagram the following sentences. Some of the direct objects and indirect objects are compound.
Answers are on page 130.
1. My sister owes me a dollar.
2. Our teacher gave Brad and me a new assignment.
3. Father later bought lettuce, radishes, and cucumbers.
4. I will tell my mother the story tomorrow.
5. The gymnast showed us her new routine.

EXERCISE F: Diagraming Subject Complements. Diagram the following sentences. Some of the complements are compound.
Answers are in the margin.
1. The pool seems quite crowded.
2. The *Silver Streak* is a fine train.
3. Pat is the secretary and treasurer.
4. The river valley was unusually scenic.
5. Our new manager is honest and dependable.

DEVELOPING WRITING SKILLS: Writing and Diagraming Sentences. Follow the instructions below to write ten sentences of your own. Then correctly diagram each sentence. Keep your sentences simple.
Answers will vary.
EXAMPLE: Write a sentence that contains a direct object.

The actor memorized the entire script.

1. Write a sentence that contains at least one adjective and one adverb.
2. Write a sentence with a compound subject and verb.
3. Write a sentence that gives an order.
4. Write a sentence that contains a direct object.
5. Write a sentence with a compound subject complement.

1.

2.

3.

4.

5.

Checking Your Skills

In the Checking Your Skills assignment, students have identified parts of sentences. Explain to students that good writers use different sentence types and patterns to vary their sentence structures. This makes their writing smoother and more enjoyable to read.

Critical Thinking

Have students choose a paragraph from a short story. Students should diagram each of the sentences in the paragraph, identifying subjects and verbs, complements, adjective and adverb modifiers, and conjunctions. When they have finished diagraming the sentences, students should identify whether the sentences are declarative, interrogative, imperative, or exclamatory. Finally, students should look at all the sentences and decide whether the writer has varied the sentence structure in the paragraph. Students should find that in most of the paragraphs, the structure of the sentences is varied to some degree. If you wish, you might ask the class for examples of various types of sentences from their paragraphs.

Using Grammar Skills in Writing

Revising You might want students to form peer editing groups for the revision of their paragraphs. Each student should read his or her paragraph to the group, who should make constructive comments regarding the length and structure of the sentences, the logic of the ideas, and the clarity of the description.

Skills Review and Writing Workshop

Basic Sentence Parts and Patterns

CHECKING YOUR SKILLS

Write which sentence part each underlined word or word group is.

1. subject, direct object   2. subject, predicate adjective   3. predicate adjectives

(1) Too many people needlessly fear snakes of all kinds. (2) Actually, most of these legless reptiles are quite harmless. (3) They feel cool, smooth, and dry to the touch. (4) Western tradition and culture have given these creatures a bad reputation. (5) These often very beautiful animals can range in size from five inches to 30 feet. (6) The largest snake in South America is the anaconda. (7) For some unknown reason there are no native snakes at all in New Zealand. (8) Certain snakes, of course, are poisonous. (9) In the United States there are four poisonous types. (10) These are the rattlesnake, the water moccasin, the copperhead, and the coral snake.

4. verb, direct object   5. verb   6. predicate noun
7. predicate noun   8. verb   9. predicate noun   10. predicate nouns

USING GRAMMAR SKILLS IN WRITING
Writing a Science Paragraph

Writers know the importance of using clear and varied sentence patterns when they want to give the reader information. Write a paragraph for the science club about any animal that interests you. Follow the steps below to make your readers as interested in the creature as you are.

Answers will vary.

Prewriting: Picture the animal you are writing about. List at least six facts or details about its appearance and habits.

Writing: Begin your paragraph with a statement describing the animal. Add other intriguing information about its behavior and habits. End with a sentence that tells why you think the creature is special.

Revising: Check your sentences' construction, and make any changes that will add variety and strength to them. After you have revised, proofread carefully.

Chapter 8

Phrases

CHAPTER 8
Phrases
(pp. 133–154).

In this chapter students will build on their knowledge of the basic parts of a sentence by working with sentences that contain different kinds of phrases. In Sections 8.1 and 8.2, students will explore the functions of prepositional phrases and appositive phrases. In the next three sections, they will learn about verbal phrases. In Section 8.6 students will learn to incorporate prepositional and appositive phrases into basic sentence diagrams.

For a review of the entire chapter and a related writing activity, see the Skills Review and Writing Workshop on page 154.

Chapter 7 explained the basic parts of a sentence: subjects, verbs, and complements. Sentences are built with more than just these parts. *Phrases* of all kinds play an important role by adding information.

A phrase is a group of words that functions in a sentence as a single part of speech. Phrases do not contain a subject and verb.

There are several kinds of phrases: *prepositional, appositive, participial, gerund,* and *infinitive.* They get their names from the word that begins the phrase or from the most important word in it. You are probably most familiar with the prepositional phrase.

Prepositional Phrases 8.1

8.1 Prepositional Phrases
(pp. 133–138)

Section 5.1 explained that a *prepositional phrase* begins with a preposition and ends with a noun or pronoun called the object of the preposition.

EXAMPLES:
PREP OBJ   PREP OBJ   PREP OBJ
under the window   near them   at the store

OBJECTIVES

After completing this section, students should be able to

- Identify prepositional phrases used as adjectives.
- Identify prepositional phrases used as adverbs.

TEACHING

Getting Started

Tell students that prepositional phrases can be used like adjectives to modify nouns and pronouns. Write the following examples of adjective phrases on the chalkboard:

Modifying a subject The letter

on the table is yours.
Modifying a direct object
Julie sent two pictures

of her cat.
Modifying a predicate noun

My cat is the winner of a blue ribbon.
Modifying the object of a preposition The

owner of the car with the dented fender was angry.
Modifying the same word

The books about pets on this shelf are fiction.

Have students read each example and test each use of an adjective phrase by asking *What kind?* or *Which one?* Volunteers might want to supply additional examples of sentences with adjective phrases for classmates to identify the phrases. If a volunteer supplies a sentence with an adverb phrase, ask him or her to identify the kind of word modified. Emphasize that adjective phrases modify nouns and pronouns.

Prepositional phrases may also have compound objects.

EXAMPLE: near the flowers and the trees

In a sentence, a prepositional phrase can act as an adjective and modify a noun or pronoun. It can also act as an adverb and modify a verb, adjective, or adverb.

Prepositional Phrases That Act as Adjectives

A prepositional phrase that acts as an adjective is called an *adjective phrase.*

An adjective phrase is a prepositional phrase that modifies a noun or pronoun by telling what kind or which one.

The following chart compares adjective phrases to one-word adjectives. Notice that an adjective phrase usually follows its noun or pronoun.

Adjectives	Adjective Phrases
A *double-decker* bus skidded.	A bus *with a double deck* skidded.
The *blue-eyed* acrobat slipped and fell.	The acrobat *with the blue eyes* slipped and fell.

The adjective phrases answer the same questions as the one-word adjectives. *What kind* of bus skidded? A bus *with a double deck* did. *Which one* of the acrobats slipped and fell? The acrobat *with the blue eyes* did.

An adjective phrase can modify nouns and pronouns used in many ways: as subjects, direct and indirect objects, predicate nouns and pronouns, and so on.

8.1 Prepositional Phrases

MODIFYING A SUBJECT: Everyone *on the committee* objected.

MODIFYING A DIRECT OBJECT: She has a television *with remote control.*

MODIFYING A PREDICATE NOUN: Ted is the captain *of the team.*

When two adjective phrases appear together, the second phrase often modifies the object of the preposition in the first.

MODIFYING THE OBJECT
OF A PREPOSITION: The crack *at the top of the windshield* was caused by a pebble from the driveway.

At other times two or more adjective phrases may modify the same word.

MODIFYING THE SAME WORD: The bouquet *of roses on the table* arrived this morning.

EXERCISE A: Identifying Adjective Phrases.

Each of the following sentences contains at least one prepositional phrase used as an adjective. Copy the sentences onto your paper. Underline each adjective phrase and draw an arrow pointing from it to the word it modifies.

EXAMPLE: The room in the back is very damp.

1. Mr. Suarez bought a new car with a sun roof.
2. The book about Eleanor Roosevelt is inspiring.
3. Mary is the supervisor of all the nurses.
4. The house near the top of the hill has been sold.
5. The tree in the corner of the yard is a weeping cherry.
6. This is the way to the shopping mall.
7. The autographed picture of Reggie Jackson is one of my treasures.
8. The carton of eggs on the bottom of the pile has been crushed.

Text Follow Through

Discuss text pages 133–138.

Assign Exercise A, page 135; Exercise B, page 137; and Developing Writing Skills, page 137.

Less advanced   You might want to have students study or review the material on prepositions in Section 5.1 before beginning this section.

Average   Exercises A and B in Section 5.1 (pages 74–75) may be used as needed to give students additional practice in identifying prepositional phrases used as adjectives and adverbs. The sentences students wrote for the Developing Writing Skills Activity in Section 5.1 (page 76) can also be used in this way. Since the emphasis in the two exercises is on adverb phrases, you might want to instruct students to add a few adjective phrases of their own to the sentences.

Advanced   Have students complete Exercises A and B a second time, replacing as many phrases as possible with one-word modifiers. For example, the third sentence in Exercise A can be rewritten in the following way: *Mary is the nurses' supervisor.* Advise students that most sentences will need to change more radically, however. For example, sentence 1 might become *Mr. Suarez bought a sporty new car.*

Additional Practice

Practice Pages or Practice Book, page 47

Less advanced   Exercise Bank, Exercises A and B, pages 72, 73

Average Exercise Bank, Exercises A, B, and C, pages 72, 73

Advanced Exercise Bank, Exercises B and C, pages 72, 73

TESTING

Test Program

Unit Pretest, page 9
Chapter Test, page 27
Unit Post-Test, page 37

RE-TEACHING

Practice Pages or Practice Book, page 47

THINKING SKILLS

Knowledge—*Identifying* adjective phrases (Exercise A, page 135)
Identifying adverb phrases (Exercise B, page 137)

Synthesis—*Writing* sentences with adjective and adverb phrases (Developing Writing Skills, page 137)

9. The captain of the precinct gave a talk about gun control.
10. The front steps of many houses in Baltimore are white marble.

Prepositional Phrases That Act as Adverbs

Prepositional phrases can also be used as adverbs.

An adverb phrase is a prepositional phrase that modifies a verb, adjective, or adverb. Adverb phrases point out where, when, in what manner, or to what extent.

The examples in the following chart show that *adverb phrases* serve basically the same function that one-word adverbs do.

Adverbs	Adverb Phrases
The bus left *late.*	The bus left *after a two-hour delay.*
Put the package *there.*	Put the package *in the closet.*

In the first pair of examples, both *late* and *after a two-hour delay* answer the question *Left when?* In the second pair, *there* and *in the closet* answer the question *Put where?*

Like one-word adverbs, adverb phrases can modify verbs, adjectives, or adverbs.

MODIFYING A VERB: The diplomat chose her words *with great care.* (Chose *in what manner?*)

MODIFYING AN ADJECTIVE: She was angry *at my refusal.* (Angry *in what manner?*)

MODIFYING AN ADVERB: We talked late *into the night.* (Late *to what extent?*)

NOTE: Turn to page 152 for Exercise

Answers for Exercise A, page 152

8.1 Prepositional Phrases

Unlike adjective phrases, adverb phrases do not always appear close to the words they modify. They can appear in almost any position in a sentence, like one-word adverbs.

EXAMPLES: The legions of Roman soldiers left *in a hurry.*

About *two years later,* Caesar's army mounted another campaign.

Very often two or more adverb phrases in different locations will modify the same word in a sentence.

EXAMPLE: *After dinner* we drove *to the lake.*

EXERCISE B: Identifying Adverb Phrases. Each sentence contains at least one prepositional phrase used as an adverb. Copy the sentences onto your paper. Underline each adverb phrase and draw an arrow pointing from it to the word it modifies.

Modified words are shaded.

EXAMPLE: With increasing excitement she read the last chapter.

1. Our scout troop hiked through the forest.
2. At the traffic light, the road curves to the left.
3. They arrived early in the day.
4. Susan is upset about her science grades.
5. At the zoo many kinds of animals live in harmony.
6. The storm cleared by morning.
7. At noon the Museum of History opens for visitors.
8. They placed the berries in straw baskets.
9. Larger type would be easier on the eye.
10. At the first signal, the fire trucks raced from their stations.

DEVELOPING WRITING SKILLS: Writing Sentences with Adjective and Adverb Phrases. Write an original sentence using each of the prepositional phrases on the following page as an adjective or adverb according to the instructions in parentheses. Underline each phrase and draw an arrow pointing from it to the word it modifies.

Answers will vary; samples are given for the first two.

EXAMPLE: on the beach   (as an adverb phrase)

On the beach the bonfire burned brightly.

1. in the dark raincoat   (as an adjective phrase)
2. between dawn and dusk   (as an adverb phrase)
3. at her constant excuses   (as an adverb phrase)
4. near us   (as an adjective phrase)
5. from Congress   (as an adjective phrase)
6. with a great deal of hesitation   (as an adverb phrase)
7. to the department store   (as an adjective phrase)
8. under the bridge   (as an adjective phrase)
9. by a little-used side road   (as an adverb phrase)
10. of record albums   (as an adjective phrase)

1. The man in the dark raincoat was eating peanuts.

2. They hiked for miles between dawn and dusk.

8.2 Appositives in Phrases

Appositives, like adjective phrases, give information about nouns or pronouns.

An appositive is a noun or pronoun placed after another noun or pronoun to identify, rename, or explain the preceding word.

Appositives are very useful in writing because they give additional information using a minimum of words.

APPOSITIVES
The poet *Robert Frost* is much admired.
This antique car, a *Studebaker,* is worth thousands of dollars.
The song *"I Am a Rock"* is a classic.

OBJECTIVE

After completing this section, students should be able to

• Identify appositives and appositive phrases in sentences.

TEACHING

Getting Started

Have students read the definitions of an appositive and study the examples of appositives and appositive phrases (pages 138–139). Tell students that often in writing, sentences can be combined effectively by using an appositive phrase. Write the following on the

8.2 Appositives in Phrases

An appositive with its own modifiers creates an appositive phrase.

An appositive phrase is a noun or pronoun with modifiers. It stands next to a noun or pronoun and adds information or details.

The modifiers in the phrase can be adjectives or adjective phrases.

APPOSITIVE PHRASES

Mr. Wilkie, *an old, experienced scoutmaster,* knows every trail.

The painting, *a mural in many bright colors,* highlights the entrance.

The medicine, *a dark liquid with a horrible smell,* seems to work.

Appositives and appositive phrases can also be compound.

EXAMPLES: Volunteers, *boys* or *girls,* are wanted.

These poems, *"The Sea Gypsy"* and *"Before the Squall,"* are about love of the sea.

EXERCISE: Identifying Appositives and Appositive Phrases. Copy the following sentences onto your paper. Underline each appositive or appositive phrase and draw an arrow pointing from it to the noun or pronoun it renames. Renamed words are shaded.

EXAMPLE: Gwendolyn Brooks, an American poet, grew up on Chicago's South Side.

1. Our math teacher, Mrs. Cruz, helped us solve a puzzle.
2. Two O. Henry stories, "The Gift of the Magi" and "The Last Leaf," are my personal favorites.

chalkboard: *The Asian elephant is an endangered species. It can be bred successfully in captivity.* Ask for a volunteer to combine the sentences by using an appositive phrase. *(The Asian elephant, an endangered species, can be bred successfully in captivity.)* Supply other pairs of sentences that can be combined to form one sentence with an appositive phrase. Have volunteers write the new sentences on the chalkboard.

Text Follow Through

Discuss text pages 138–140.

Assign the Exercise, page 139, and Developing Writing Skills, page 140.

Less advanced Students might benefit from working in pairs to complete the Developing Writing Skills activity.

Average Have students bring to class at least one example of an appositive from a newspaper or magazine article. Then ask students to identify the appositives in each other's selections.

Advanced For the Developing Writing Skills activity, you can have students make at least three of the appositives rename direct objects. These students might also be encouraged to expand the appositives with additional modifiers.

Additional Practice

Practice Pages or Practice Book, page 48

Less advanced Exercise Bank, Exercises A and B, page 74

Average Exercise Bank, Exercises A, B, and C, page 74

Advanced Exercise Bank, Exercises B and C, page 74

**8.3 Participles in
Phrases**

(pp. 140–145)

3. Two low-calorie vegetables, kale and bean sprouts, are highly recommended.
4. George Patton, a general in World War II, was the subject of a prize-winning film.
5. The book *The Matarese Circle* pits an American spy against a Russian.
6. Beethoven wrote only one opera, *Fidelio.*
7. Senator Atkins, a wonderful speaker, made quite an impression.
8. Our destination, either Puerto Rico or Costa Del Sol, will be decided upon soon.
9. You must see Lincoln Center, the cultural mecca of New York.
10. The Beatles' movie *Yellow Submarine* won several awards.

DEVELOPING WRITING SKILLS: Writing Sentences with Appositives. Use the following words or phrases as apposi-tives in your own sentences.

Answers will vary; samples are given for the first two.

EXAMPLE: a real mistake

His choice, a real mistake, was greeted with laughter.

1. Dr. Dever, a fine teacher, will lead a tour of Spain this spring.

1. a fine teacher
2. the captain
3. a good driver
4. my oldest friend
5. a fascinating book
6. my favorite team
7. a restaurant in town
8. a beautiful song
9. a luscious dessert
10. a town landmark

2. Missy Sazonick, the captain, is the best swimmer on the team.

8.3 Participles in Phrases

The next three sections are about *verbals.* A *verbal* is a verb form that is used as another part of speech. There are three kinds of verbals: *participles, gerunds,* and *infinitives.* Each is used differently. Participles are used as adjectives, gerunds as nouns, and infinitives as nouns, adjectives, or adverbs.

140

OBJECTIVES

After completing this section, students should be able to

- Identify present and past participles.
- Distinguish between verbs and participles.
- Identify participial phrases.

8.3 Participles in Phrases

Verbals keep two important characteristics of verbs: (1) They can be followed by a complement, such as a direct object, and (2) they can be modified by adverbs and adverb phrases. A verbal with a complement or a modifier is called a *verbal phrase.* This section will discuss the first kind of verbal, the participle, and explain how it can be used in phrases.

Participles

Many of the adjectives you commonly use are actually *participles.*

A participle is a form of a verb that acts as an adjective.

There are two kinds of participles: *present participles* and *past participles.* You can recognize these two different kinds of participles by their endings. Present participles end in *-ing.*

PRESENT PARTICIPLES: going, playing, growing, telling, reading, jumping

Past participles usually end in *-ed,* although those formed from irregular verbs will have different endings such as *-t* or *-en.* (See Section 11.1 for a list of irregular verb endings.)

PAST PARTICIPLES: marked, jumped, moved, hurt, chosen, eaten

The following chart shows how both types of participles can be used as adjectives in sentences. Like other adjectives participles answer such questions as *What kind?* or *Which one?*

Present Participles	Past Participles
A *growing* baby sleeps much of the day.	Our *chosen* representative resigned.
Crying, he threw himself on the bed.	*Troubled,* she asked for advice.

TEACHING
Getting Started

Tell students that a participle is a form of a verb that acts like an adjective and that there are two kinds of participles: present participles and past participles. Explain that present participles end in *-ing,* and past participles end in *-ed* if they are formed from regular verbs or *-t* or *-en* if they are formed from irregular verbs. List the following participles on the chalkboard: *pasted, painted, covering, jumping, swooping, licensed, frightened, gliding, burning.* Have students identify each one orally as a present participle or a past participle, at a rapid pace. Choose one present participle and one past participle and use each in a sentence, both orally and on the board. Be certain students see how each functions as an adjective by telling which adjective question each answers in the sentence. Then ask for volunteers to use the other participles in original sentences.

Text Follow Through

Discuss text pages 140–145.

Assign Exercise A, page 142; Exercise B, page 142; Exercise C, page 144; and Developing Writing Skills, page 144.

EXERCISE A: Identifying Present and Past Participles. Write the participle from each sentence. Then write whether the participle is *past* or *present*.

EXAMPLE: The cracked vase cannot be repaired.

cracked past

1. A raging snowstorm struck the city. pres
2. Disturbed, she consulted her doctor about the symptoms. past
3. The police shined a glaring light on the robber. pres
4. Singing, she stepped from the shower. pres
5. The frozen pipe burst. past
6. Have you repaired the broken lamp? past
7. I have used reading glasses for some time now. pres
8. The story of the haunted house was very popular. past
9. Did you find the finished copies of the term paper? past
10. Laughing, she bowed several times to the audience. pres

Verb or Participle?

Sometimes verb phrases (verbs with helping verbs) are confused with participles. In the chart, however, note that a verb phrase always begins with a helping verb. A participle used as an adjective stands by itself and modifies a noun or pronoun.

Verb Phrases	Participles
The car *was racing* around the curve.	The *racing* car crashed into the wall.
I *was* greatly *disturbed* by the call.	The *disturbed* boy talked about his problem.

EXERCISE B: Distinguishing Between Verbs and Participles. Identify each underlined word as a *verb* or a *participle*. If the word is a participle, also write the word it modifies. Modified words are shaded.

142

8.3 Participles in Phrases

EXAMPLE: They found the <u>written</u> test easy to do.

participle   test

1. The doctor is <u>talking</u> to a patient.verb
2. She has a <u>growing understanding</u> of the problem.part
3. A <u>broken window</u> was part of the evidence.part
4. Brian has finally <u>chosen</u> a topic for his report.verb
5. Do you have a thick <u>marking pen</u>?part
6. We drove past a <u>deserted railroad terminal</u>.part
7. In exchange she is <u>asking</u> for another radio.verb
8. I bought three pounds of <u>ripened cheese</u>.part
9. She is always <u>playing</u> Mozart on her phonograph.verb
10. The prisoner was <u>brought</u> before the judge.verb

Participial Phrases

A participle can be expanded into a phrase by adding one or more modifiers or complements to it.

A participial phrase is a present or past participle that is modified by an adverb or adverb phrase or that has a complement. The entire phrase acts as an adjective in a sentence.

The examples in the following chart show a few of the ways that participles can be expanded into phrases.

PARTICIPIAL PHRASES
The diner, *chewing rapidly,* started to choke.
The old woman, *assisted by her daughter,* moved to a new house.
The clerks, *eating their lunch,* refused to answer the phone.

The first participial phrase is formed by adding the adverb *rapidly,* the second by adding the prepositional phrase *by her daughter,* the third by adding the direct object *lunch.*

TESTING

Test Program
  Unit Pretest, page 9
  Chapter Test, page 27
  Unit Post-Test, page 38

RE-TEACHING

Practice Pages or Practice Book, pages 49, 50

THINKING SKILLS

Knowledge—*Identifying* present and past participles (Exercise A, page 142)
  Identifying participial phrases (Exercise C, page 144)

Comprehension—*Distinguishing* between verbs and participles (Exercise B, page 142)

Synthesis—*Writing* sentences with participial phrases (Developing Writing Skills, page 144)

NOTE: Turn to page 153 for Exercise

Answers for Exercise B, page 153

1.

2.

3.

4.

5.

In these examples, notice that each participial phrase appears right after the noun it modifies. All three sentences could be reworded to move the phrases before the modified words.

EXAMPLES: *Chewing rapidly,* the diner started to choke.

   Assisted by her daughter, the old woman moved to a new house.

   Eating their lunch, the clerks refused to answer the phone.

EXERCISE C: Recognizing Participial Phrases. Each of the following sentences contains a participial phrase. Copy the sentences onto your paper. Underline each participial phrase and draw an arrow pointing from it to the word it modifies.
Modified words are shaded.

EXAMPLE: The frontier, underline spreading out endlessly to the west, excited the pioneers.

1. The plant, growing slowly, finally bloomed in June.
2. Chosen by the principal, Marie represented our school.
3. My father, walking the dog, met at old friend.
4. Laughing loudly, she ran from the room.
5. The coin, found in a cellar, proved to be valuable.
6. Telling her strange story, she began to giggle.
7. The detective, watching the suspect, discovered a clue.
8. Scolded by his father, he left the house and took a walk.
9. The students, listening carefully, followed the instructions perfectly.
10. The clipper, sailing majestically, reached the harbor in two hours.

DEVELOPING WRITING SKILLS: Writing Sentences with Participial Phrases. Write an original sentence using each of the participial phrases on the following page.
Answers will vary; samples are given for the first two.

EXAMPLE: hitting a home run

Hitting a home run, Chris tied the score.

1. Speaking slowly, the teacher repeated the question.

1. speaking slowly	6. reading a letter
2. reminded twice	7. frozen in the lake
3. opening the door	8. meeting often
4. speaking very slowly	9. choosing another way
5. followed by a puppy	10. thinking clearly

2. Ellen, reminded twice, still missed the bus.

Gerunds in Phrases 8.4

Like present participles, *gerunds* end in *-ing*. Present participles are used as adjectives. Gerunds are used as nouns.

A gerund is a form of verb that acts as a noun.

Gerunds

Like other nouns gerunds can be used as subjects, direct objects, predicate nouns, and objects of prepositions.

USE OF GERUNDS IN SENTENCES	
Subject	*Smoking* is not permitted in many public buildings.
Direct Object	Michael enjoys *painting*.
Predicate Noun	His favorite sport is *fishing*.
Object of a Preposition	Lucille never gets tired of *singing*.

EXERCISE A: Identifying Gerunds. Each sentence on the following page contains one gerund. Write the gerund from each sentence. Next to it write whether it is used as a *subject, direct object, predicate noun,* or *object of a preposition.*

145

8.4 Gerunds in Phrases
(pp. 145–147)

OBJECTIVES
After completing this section, students should be able to

- Identify gerunds used in sentences.
- Identify gerund phrases in sentences.

TEACHING
Getting Started

If students have just finished studying participles, they should be receptive to the idea that some verb forms can function as other parts of speech. Tell students that a gerund is a form of verb that acts as a noun. Write the following examples on the chalkboard:
Subject   Running is not allowed in the hallways.
Direct object   Many people enjoy jogging.
Predicate noun   My favorite activity is reading.
Object of a preposition   I earn money by baby-sitting.

Have volunteers write on the chalkboard other sentences with gerunds for classmates to identify.

Text Follow Through

Discuss text pages 145–147.

Assign Exercise A, page 145; Exercise B, page 147; and Developing Writing Skills, page 147.

Less advanced If you have chosen to omit Section 8.1 with your students, you should also omit this study of gerunds. Students whom you think ready for this section should have no great difficulty in identifying the gerunds in Exercise A. However, you may want to give them extra practice in determining each gerund's use in the sentence. Have these students begin by identifying the subject and verb of each sentence, covering only the first clause in sentence 4. Then students should identify any complements and any prepositional phrases, ignoring the infinitive phrase in sentence 8. At this point they should readily be able to identify the use of each gerund.

Average Students can be asked to rewrite the sentences in Exercise A so that each sentence contains a compound gerund. For example, the first sentence could become *Walking and jogging are excellent exercise.* Alternatively, you might use those same sentences and instruct the students to expand each gerund into a gerund phrase *(Walking at least a mile a day is excellent exercise.).*

EXAMPLE: Dancing is her favorite pastime.

Dancing   subject

1. Walking is excellent exercise. S
2. My little sister observes my birthday by phoning. obj of prep
3. This plant needs pruning. DO
4. Love is caring, and I always try to show I care. PN
5. Speeding led to the loss of her driver's license. S
6. Our goal has always been winning. PN
7. Don't you ever get tired of studying? obj of prep
8. Exercising is one way to burn up calories. S
9. After several months Frank's grandmother stopped writing. DO
10. The team finished practicing at five o'clock. DO

Gerund Phrases

A gerund can be part of a phrase.

A gerund phrase is a gerund with modifiers or a complement, all acting together as a noun.

The chart shows how gerunds are expanded.

GERUND PHRASES	
Gerund with Adjectives	*The loud, shrill howling* continued all morning.
Gerund with Direct Object	*Practicing the violin* is part of his daily routine.
Gerund with Prepositional Phrase	He helped the police by *telling about his experience.*
Gerund with Adverb and Prepositional Phrase	My father tries to stay fit by *walking rapidly to the station.*

Advanced You might give students some leeway in doing the Developing Writing Skills activity. Tell them that they must use two gerunds as objects of prepositions, two as subjects, and one as a direct object. They can then use the gerund phrases given in the activity in any order they wish.

Additional Practice

Practice Pages or Practice Book, page 51

Less advanced Exercise Bank, Exercises A and B, pages 78, 79

Average Exercise Bank, Exercises A, B, and C, pages 78, 79

Advanced Exercise Bank, Exercises B and C, pages 78, 79

TESTING

Test Program

Unit Pretest, page 9
Chapter Test, page 28
Unit Post-Test, page 38

RE-TEACHING

Practice Pages or Practice Book, page 51

THINKING SKILLS

Knowledge—*Identifying* gerunds (Exercise A, page 145) *Identifying* gerund phrases (Exercise B, page 147)

Synthesis—*Writing* sentences with gerund phrases (Developing Writing Skills, page 147)

8.5 Infinitives in Phrases
(pp. 147–151)

8.5 Infinitives in Phrases

EXERCISE B: Identifying Gerund Phrases. Write each gerund phrase. Next to it write whether the gerund phrase is used as a *subject, direct object, predicate noun,* or *object of a preposition.*

EXAMPLE: His favorite pastime was writing limericks.

writing limericks   predicate noun

1. Drinking large amounts of water can help clear the kidneys. S
2. His favorite hobby is raising guppies. PN
3. A loud knocking interrupted their dinner. S
4. Nothing can be gained by choosing sides. obj of prep
5. He enjoys composing all sorts of music. DO
6. The secretary kept perfect records by writing the dates of each event. obj of prep
7. Insulating older homes helps conserve energy. S
8. Tourists at the Acropolis are warned against taking stones for souvenirs. obj of prep
9. Traveling by air is the fastest way to get there. S
10. My plans for vacation include redecorating my room. DO

DEVELOPING WRITING SKILLS: Writing Sentences with Gerund Phrases. Use each of the gerund phrases in an original sentence according to the instructions in parentheses.
Answers will vary; samples are given for the first two.
EXAMPLE: singing in the shower   (as a subject)

Singing in the shower was her vocal exercise.
1. Andy frightened us by driving too fast.
1. driving too fast   (as the object of a preposition)
2. exercising in the morning   (as a subject)
3. collecting stamps and coins   (as a direct object)
4. cleaning her room thoroughly   (as the object of a preposition)
5. raising animals   (as a subject)
2. Exercising in the morning helps her to wake up completely.

Infinitives in Phrases 8.5

Infinitives can be used as three different parts of speech.

147

OBJECTIVES

After completing this section, students should be able to

• Identify the three uses of infinitives in sentences.
• Identify infinitive phrases in sentences.

TEACHING

Getting Started

Tell students that an infinitive is a form of a verb that comes after the word *to* and acts as a noun, an adjective, or an adverb. Write the following example sentences on the chalkboard:

Nouns
Subject To act is my goal.
Direct object I want to act.
Predicate noun My dream is to act.
Object of a preposition I have no goal except to act.
Appositive My goal, to act, is not an impossible one.

Adjectives
The person to see is the director.
She has the authority to hire.

Adverbs
Acting seems easy to do.
Ready to begin, I walked across the stage.

Be sure students understand the role each adverbial and adjectival infinitive plays in its sentence by having them tell what question it answers about the word it modifies. For example, *person to see* tells *which* person. Have volunteers write on the chalkboard other sentences with infinitives for classmates to identify.

An infinitive is the form of a verb that comes after the word *to* and acts as a noun, adjective, or adverb.

Three Uses of Infinitives

As a noun an infinitive can be used as a subject, direct object, predicate noun, object of a preposition, or appositive.

INFINITIVES USED AS NOUNS	
Subject	*To succeed* is a popular goal.
Direct Object	As soon as she gets home, she hopes *to write.*
Predicate Noun	His dream has always been *to travel.*
Object of a Preposition	They had no choice except *to leave.*
Appositive	Her decision, *to listen,* was a wise one.

Infinitives can be used as adjectives and adverbs. In the chart, infinitives answer the questions for adjectives and adverbs.

INFINITIVES USED AS ADJECTIVES AND ADVERBS	
Adjective	The person *to contact* is the dean. (*Which* person?)
	She has the ambition *to succeed.* (*What kind* of ambition?)
Adverb	This is easy *to do.* (Easy *in what manner?*)
	Ready *to leave,* they locked the door. (Ready *in what manner?*)

EXERCISE A: Identifying Infinitives. Find the infinitive in each of the following sentences and write it on your paper.

Text Follow Through
Discuss text pages 147–151.
Assign Exercise A, page 148;
Exercise B, page 150; and
Developing Writing Skills, page
150.

8.5 Infinitives in Phrases

EXAMPLE: They were always eager to answer.

  to answer

1. She wants to go.
2. Impossible to miss, the monument is right on the lake.
3. The recipe to try is on the package itself.
4. To listen is not easy with that uproar.
5. He wanted nothing except to sleep.
6. The librarian was happy to help.
7. His greatest wish, to fly, was never fulfilled.
8. This is the best reference book to consult.
9. Susan's dream is to dance.
10. To whistle is difficult for some people.

Infinitive Phrases

Infinitives, like gerunds and participles, can be combined with other words to form phrases.

An infinitive phrase is an infinitive with modifiers or a complement, all acting together as a single part of speech.

The chart shows how infinitives can be expanded.

INFINITIVE PHRASES	
Infinitive with Adverb	It will be important *to listen carefully.*
Infinitive with Prepositional Phrases	They like *to jog through the park at dawn.*
Infinitive with Direct Object	She hopes *to write a novel.*
Infinitive with Indirect and Direct Objects	I need *to give you my new telephone number.*

Less advanced If you decide these students are ready to comprehend this study of infinitives, you might give them some preliminary practice in distinguishing between the use of the word *to* as a preposition and its use at the beginning of an infinitive. Ask these students to identify the prepositional phrase in each of the following pairs of sentences. After they have told why they chose each phrase, you can introduce the idea of infinitives.

1. This is the best road to take. This is the best road to Claytonville.
2. I have a letter to mail. I wrote a letter to Mark.
3. Chris came to school late. Chris came to visit.
4. I made a promise to Lee. I made a promise to call back.

Average Students can be asked to use the following five infinitive phrases in sentences of their own. Students can then identify the functions of the infinitive phrases in each other's work either by reading sentences aloud to one another or by exchanging papers:

1. to be well liked
2. to play the role of Juliet
3. to miss the train
4. to overcome a fear of heights
5. to finish painting the house by the end of the week

Advanced As they complete the exercises, students might be asked to give the function of each infinitive used as a noun and to identify the use of other infinitives as adverbial or adjectival.

Additional Practice

Practice Pages or Practice Book, page 52

Less advanced Exercise Bank, Exercises A and B, pages 80, 81

Average Exercise Bank, Exercises A, B, and C, pages 80, 81

Advanced Exercise Bank, Exercises B and C, pages 80, 81

TESTING

Test Program

Unit Pretest, page 9
Chapter Test, page 28
Unit Post-Test, page 38

RE-TEACHING

Practice Pages or Practice Book, page 52

THINKING SKILLS

Knowledge—*Identifying* infinitives (Exercise A, page 148)

Identifying infinitive phrases (Exercise B, page 150)

Synthesis—*Writing* sentences with infinitive phrases (Developing Writing Skills, page 150)

EXERCISE B: Identifying Infinitive Phrases. Each of the following sentences contains one infinitive phrase. On your paper write each infinitive phrase.

EXAMPLE: To reach the peak was not possible in the blizzard.

   To reach the peak

1. To graduate a year early is my goal.
2. The teacher to ask for a reference is Miss Stevens.
3. I find it difficult to talk with strangers.
4. Her ambition is to direct a musical at school.
5. This is an offer to take very seriously.
6. To get home during the storm was quite difficult.
7. Our plan was to reach southern Maine by noon.
8. She was told to reorganize her composition.
9. The person to ask about that is James.
10. They want to wait another week before acting.

DEVELOPING WRITING SKILLS: Writing Sentences with Infinitive Phrases. Write an original sentence using each of the following infinitive phrases according to the directions in parentheses.

Answers will vary; samples are given for the first two.
EXAMPLE: to please Uncle Pete   (as an adverb)

   It was difficult to please Uncle Pete.

1. To succeed in English requires attention and practice.

1. to succeed in English   (as a subject at the beginning of the sentence)
2. to go into business for yourself   (as a direct object with the verb *want*)
3. to reach the station   (as an adverb after the adjective *easy*)
4. to become a lawyer   (as a predicate noun after the verb *is*)
5. to ask for advice   (as an adjective after the noun *teacher*)
6. to study carefully   (as a subject at the beginning of a sentence)
7. to leave for a vacation   (as an adverb after the adjective *happy*)

2. Next year they want to go into business.

8. to travel to France and Italy   (as a predicate noun after *was*)
9. to call home   (as a direct object after the verb *forgot*)
10. to go to college   (as an appositive after the noun *wish*)

Diagraming Prepositional 8.6 Phrases and Appositives

Section 7.9 explained how to diagram subjects, verbs, complements, and modifiers. You may want to study or review the diagrams in that section before studying the diagrams presented here for two of the most essential phrases, prepositional and appositive phrases.

Prepositional Phrases

The diagram for a prepositional phrase is drawn under the word it modifies. The diagram has two parts: a slanted line for the preposition and a horizontal line for the object of the preposition. Any adjectives that modify the object are placed beneath the object.

Adjective Phrases. The diagram for an adjective phrase is placed directly under the noun or pronoun that the phrase modifies.

EXAMPLE: The person *in the first office* will help you.

Adverb Phrases. The diagram for an adverb phrase is placed directly under the verb, adjective, or adverb that the phrase modifies.

151

8.6 Diagraming Prepositional Phrases and Appositives
(pp. 151–153)

OBJECTIVES

After completing this section, students should be able to

- Diagram sentences with prepositional phrases.
- Diagram sentences with appositives and appositive phrases.

TEACHING

Getting Started

Write the following sentences on the chalkboard:

The conductor of the school band is retiring.
She will travel around the world.

Ask for volunteers to identify the prepositional phrase in each sentence and then its function as adjectival or adverbial. Draw a skeleton diagram of both sentences on the chalkboard and have volunteers complete them. You may want to complete the diagram of the first sentence yourself and then have students complete the second diagram. Have students suggest other sentences with prepositional phrases for class-mates to diagram.

Text Follow Through

Discuss text pages 151–153.

Assign Exercise A, page 152; Exercise B, page 153; and Developing Writing Skills, page 153.

Less advanced You may want to review Exercise A orally before students begin diagraming. Be sure the students can identify both the prepositional phrases and the words they modify. You might give students skeleton diagrams to use in completing the exercises and the Developing Writing Skills activity. If you decide not to teach diagraming to these students, the exercises may be used for additional drill material.

Average Depending upon the class, your students might benefit from practice in filling in skeleton diagrams before they complete exercises. You may want to have students work as a group to complete two or three items in each exercise before having them continue independently.

Advanced Students might enjoy diagraming some of the sentences they have written for the Developing Writing Skills activity in Sections 8.1 and 8.2.

Additional Practice

Practice Pages or Practice Book, pages 53, 54

Less advanced Exercise Bank, Exercises A and B, pages 82, 83

EXAMPLE: I spoke later *with my best friend.*

Compound Objects of a Preposition. A prepositional phrase with a compound object is diagramed in the following way.

EXAMPLE: We made a bouquet *of zinnias, asters, and roses.*

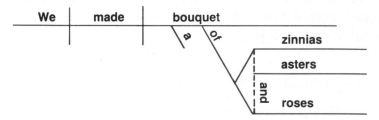

EXERCISE A: Diagraming Prepositional Phrases. Each of the following sentences contains one or two prepositional phrases. Diagram each sentence, using the preceding examples as models.

Answers are on page 137.

1. The man in the brown hat is my cousin.
2. I awoke suddenly at dawn.
3. A car with a faulty muffler roared up the street.
4. They moved to an apartment with two bedrooms, a large kitchen, and a balcony.
5. During the night he wrote a poem about loneliness.

Appositives

To diagram an appositive, place it in parentheses next to the noun or pronoun it renames. Any adjectives or adjective phrases that modify the appositive are positioned directly beneath it.

Average Exercise Bank, Exercises A, B, and C, pages 82, 83

Advanced Exercise Bank, Exercises B and C, pages 82, 83

TESTING

Test Program
   Unit Pretest, pages 11, 12
   Chapter Test, page 28
   Unit Post-Test, pages 39, 40

RE-TEACHING

Practice Pages, pages 53, 54

THINKING SKILLS

Analysis—*Diagraming* sentences with prepositional phrases (Exercise A, page 152) *Diagraming* sentences with appositive phrases (Exercise B, page 153)

Synthesis—*Writing* and *diagraming* sentences with prepositional phrases and appositives (Developing Writing Skills, page 153)

Developing Writing Skills

Writing Across the Curriculum

Have you ever tried to write instructions for others to follow?

Prewriting Think about an activity with which you are familiar but may require instructions for someone else. Write down a list of instructions for your activity. Add any missing details, and arrange the items in chronological order.

Writing Write the first draft of your instructions. Be sure to explain each step clearly and precisely.

Revising Check that you have not missed any important steps in your instructions.

8.6 Diagraming Prepositional Phrases and Appositives

EXAMPLE: George Washington, *the first President of the*

United States, established many traditions.

EXAMPLE: I wrote about George Washington, *our first President.*

EXERCISE B: Diagraming Appositive Phrases. Each of the following sentences contains one appositive phrase. Diagram each sentence.
Answers are on page 144.

1. We have a new pet, a furry, little kitten.
2. Joe Louis, the world heavyweight champion for twelve years, was an American hero.
3. The articles of Sylvia Porter, a financial columnist, appear in hundreds of daily newspapers.
4. We will be going to Zagreb, the capital of Yugoslavia.
5. This is a sonnet, a poem of fourteen lines.

DEVELOPING WRITING SKILLS: Writing and Diagraming Sentences with Prepositional Phrases and Appositives.

Write ten sentences of your own. Five sentences should contain prepositional phrases, and five should contain appositives. Then diagram your sentences according to the examples in this section.
Answers will vary.

154

Checking Your Skills

In the Checking Your Skills assignment, students have identified phrases in sentences. Explain to students that phrases are essential to good, clear writing and, whether they are aware of it or not, their own writing contains many phrases.

Critical Thinking

Have students choose one of the writing assignments they completed before learning the material from this chapter. Students should look over one or two paragraphs of the old writing assignment and, on a separate sheet of paper, write down all the sentences with phrases. Next, students should identify the types of phrases they used. Have students discuss their findings in class. Do students use many phrases in their writing? Do they seem to use one type of phrase more than others? Did students realize that they were using phrases when they wrote the paper? How important are phrases to clear writing? Finally, you might want to challenge students to rewrite their paragraphs clearly and logically without using any phrases. Students should find this task very difficult to accomplish successfully.

Using Grammar Skills in Writing

Prewriting You might want students to brainstorm to generate facts and ideas for their biographies. They can then choose five facts from these ideas. Also, have students arrange the five facts and their supporting examples and incidents in a logical order.

Skills Review and Writing Workshop

Phrases

CHECKING YOUR SKILLS

Write *adverb phrase, adjective, phrase, appositive phrase, participial phrase, gerund phrase,* or *infinitive phrase* for each underlined phrase below.

1. adjective phrase 2. appositive phrase 3. adjective phrase 4. adverb phrase

(1) Certain rare people are shining examples of human nobility. (2) Such a spirit was John Merrick, a late-nineteenth-century Englishman. (3) Merrick, deformed by a terrible disease, became known as the Elephant Man. (4) After many years, the disease had caused his face, skin, and body to resemble that of an elephant. (5) For a while he earned a meager living by appearing in side shows. (6) When Merrick was about 25, Sir Frederick Treves, a kindly physician with an interest in rare diseases, became Merrick's benefactor. (7) Merrick was allowed to live at the medical college at which Treves taught. (8) Merrick, mistreated horribly for most of his life, might have turned out angry, bitter, and depressed. (9) In a few months, however, Treves discovered that his patient was highly intelligent, gentle, pleasant, and uncomplaining. (10) Both a play and a movie about this extraordinary spirit were highly successful.

5. adverb phrase 6. appositive phrase 7. infinitive phrase 8. adjective phrase

USING GRAMMAR SKILLS IN WRITING

Writing a Biography

Write a brief biography for a local paper. Choose an historical person, or someone you know. Follow the steps below.

Answers will vary.

Prewriting: Write down at least five facts about the person, and note an example or incident to support each fact.

Writing: Begin with an attention-getting statement. Add your facts and incidents in chronological order. Consider ending by quoting something the person said.

Revising: Change any phrases that could be more effective. After you have revised, proofread carefully.

9. adverb phrase 10. adjective phrase

154

Each of the first two sections in this chapter introduces a different kind of subordinate clause: Section 9.1 discusses adjective clauses, Section 9.2 deals with adverb clauses, Section 9.3 then explores the classification of sentences by structure. Section 9.4 completes the instruction in diagraming and helps students see more clearly the relationships among the clauses they have been working with.

For a review of the entire chapter and a related writing activity, see the Skills Review and Writing Workshop on page 174.

Chapter **9**

Clauses

This chapter will explain the last important sentence element, the *clause.*

A clause is a group of words with its own subject and verb.

There are two basic types of clauses, and there is an important difference between them. The first type is called an *independent clause.*

An independent clause has a subject and a verb and can stand by itself as a complete sentence.

The length of a clause has little to do with whether it can stand alone. Each of the following examples can stand alone because it expresses a complete thought.

INDEPENDENT
CLAUSES:

The reporter shouted.

Mother wrote a letter to my cousin.

At dawn the caravan began to cross the desert in an effort to reach the town before dark.

The second type of clause is called a *subordinate clause.* Like an independent clause, it contains both a subject and a verb. A subordinate clause, however, is not a sentence.

A subordinate clause has a subject and a verb but cannot stand by itself as a sentence. It is only part of a sentence.

A subordinate clause does not express a complete thought even though it contains a subject and a verb.

                                    S   V
SUBORDINATE CLAUSES: when the phone rang
                              S   V
                        whom I often admired
                                  S   V
                        since the constitution was amended at
                        the last meeting

Each of these clauses has a subject and a verb, but each lacks something. Examine, for example, the first clause: *when the phone rang. When the phone rang,* what happened? More information is needed to make the thought complete.

Why does a subordinate clause not express a complete thought? The answer often can be found in the first word of the clause. Some subordinate clauses begin with subordinating conjunctions, words such as *if, since, when, although, because,* and *while.* Others begin with relative pronouns such as *who, which,* or *that.* These words are clues that the clause may not be able to stand alone. Compare, for example, the independent clauses and the subordinate clauses in the following chart. Notice how the addition of subordinating words changes the meaning of the independent clauses.

COMPARING TWO KINDS OF CLAUSES	
Independent	**Subordinate**
S V He arrived this morning.	S V *since* he arrived this morning
S V The room is not clean.	S V *if* the room is not clean

In order to make sense, a subordinate clause usually needs to be combined with an independent clause. In the following examples, the subordinate clauses are italicized; the independent clauses are not.

S   V   S   V

EXAMPLES: *Since he arrived this morning,* he has been working

at top speed.

             S   V

I will call the manager of the hotel tomorrow *if the*

        S   V

room is not clean.

This chapter will explain how subordinate clauses work with independent clauses to make complete sentences. It will also explain how subordinate clauses can act within sentences either as adjectives or as adverbs.

Adjective Clauses 9.1

Some subordinate clauses act as adjectives.

An adjective clause is a subordinate clause that modifies a noun or pronoun.

Adjective clauses, like one-word adjectives or adjective phrases, answer the questions *What kind?* or *Which one?*

Recognizing Adjective Clauses

Most adjective clauses begin with one of the five relative pronouns: *that which, who, whom,* and *whose.* Sometimes an adjective clause will begin with an adverb such as *when* or *where.*

Study the examples in the chart on the following page. The adjective clauses are italicized. The arrow in each sentence points to the word in the independent clause that the adjective clause modifies. Note also that an adjective clause usually comes right after the word it modifies.

157

9.1 Adjective Clauses
(pp. 157–160)

OBJECTIVES

After completing this section, students should be able to

- Identify adjective clauses in sentences.
- Use adjective clauses to combine sentences.

TEACHING
Getting Started

Remind students that a word or a phrase can function as an adjective. Ask how they think a clause might be able to function as an adjective. (By modifying a noun or pronoun.) Then write the following sentences on the board:

1. The Edgeville Eagles is a <u>snazzy</u> band.
2. The Edgeville Eagles is the band <u>with blue and gray uniforms</u>.
3. The Edgeville Eagles is the band <u>that won the Battle of the Bands</u>.

First, ask for a volunteer to identify the function of each underlined portion of a sentence. Have volunteers show how each tells *which band*. In sentence 3, have a volunteer locate the subject and verb of the subordinate clause. Then ask which word is modified by the subordinate clause. Elicit that *band,* a noun, is modified by the clause; therefore, the subordinate clause is an adjective clause. Have volunteers suggest other sentences with adjective clauses for classmates.

Text Follow Through

Discuss text pages 157–160.

Assign Exercise A, page 158; Exercise B, page 159; and Developing Writing Skills, page 160.

Less advanced Although the section should not prove particularly troublesome for most students, these students might benefit from looking more closely at the words that introduce adjective clauses. Ask students to list the words that introduce each adjective clause in Exercise A. Have each new word recorded on the board as it is given. Leave the list on the board so that students can refer to it when completing Exercise B and the Developing Writing Skills activity.

ADJECTIVE CLAUSES

She wrote the story *that won first prize.*

That British stamp, *which depicts Queen Victoria,* will be sold at auction.

The man *who opened the door* is my brother-in-law.

Marcia is the student *whom we chose to represent us in the debate.*

The boy *whose book I borrowed* is the class president.

In the period *since the war ended* much has happened.

This is the time *when I like to read.*

EXERCISE A: Identifying Adjective Clauses. Each of the following sentences contains an adjective clause. Copy the sentences onto your paper and underline each adjective clause. Be prepared to identify the word each clause modifies.
Modified words are shaded.
EXAMPLE: I like science fiction books <u>that are believable</u>.

1. The tailor <u>who shortened my skirt</u> is very reasonable.
2. This museum, <u>which is described in our travel guide</u>, was built in 1876.
3. The man <u>whose dictionary I borrowed</u> is a retired teacher.
4. Have you found a show <u>that you would like to see</u>?
5. In the month <u>since he had the accident</u>, his condition has improved greatly.
6. Have you visited the plaza <u>where the statue was dedicated</u>?
7. The painter <u>whom she most admires</u> is Georgia O'Keeffe.
8. The book <u>that you wanted</u> is no longer in print.
9. A play <u>that I particularly liked</u> was *All My Sons.*
10. That package, <u>which just arrived</u>, is for you.

9.1 Adjective Clauses

Combining Sentences with Adjective Clauses

Two sentences sometimes can be combined into one by changing one of them into an adjective clause. Such a combination is useful when the information in both sentences is closely related. Notice how the two sentences in the following example are changed into one sentence. The new sentence consists of an independent clause and an adjective clause.

TWO SENTENCES: My history teacher has written books on John Adams, Thomas Jefferson, and Benjamin Franklin. My teacher is considered by many scholars to be an expert on the American Revolution.

SENTENCE WITH
ADJECTIVE CLAUSE: My history teacher, *who is considered by many scholars to be an expert on the American Revolution,* has written books on John Adams, Thomas Jefferson, and Benjamin Franklin.

EXERCISE B: Using Adjective Clauses to Combine Sentences. Change the second sentence in each of the following groups into an adjective clause. Then make the adjective clause part of the first sentence. You will need to add a comma before and after each of these adjective clauses.
Answers will vary; samples are given for the first two.

EXAMPLE: Phillis Wheatley was an early American poet. She was born in Africa.

Phillis Wheatley, who was born in Africa, was an early American poet.

1. John Steinbeck, who won the Nobel Prize in 1962, wrote. . . .
1. John Steinbeck wrote *The Grapes of Wrath* and *The Pearl.* He won the Nobel Prize in 1962.

2. Albany has changed greatly in the last twenty-five years. It now boasts the lavish Empire State Plaza.

3. This hotel room will be more expensive. It has a view of the mountains.
2. Albany, which now boasts the lavish Empire State Plaza, has. . . .

RE-TEACHING

Practice Pages or Practice
Book, pages 55, 56

THINKING SKILLS

Knowledge—*Identifying*
adjective clauses (Exercise A,
page 158)

Application—*Using* adjective
clauses to combine sentences
(Exercise B, page 159)

Synthesis—*Writing* sentences
that contain adjective clauses
(Developing Writing Skills,
page 160)

9.2 Adverb Clauses
(pp. 160–164)

---

4. Katharine Hepburn won an Academy Award for her performance in *The Lion in Winter*. Her film career spans fifty
years.

5. My mother recently bought a small economy car. She had
always preferred large sedans.

**DEVELOPING WRITING SKILLS: Writing Sentences with
Adjective Clauses.** Write ten sentences containing adjective
clauses, as specified. Underline each adjective clause and
draw an arrow from the clause to the word it modifies.
Answers will vary; samples are given for the first two.

EXAMPLE: Write a sentence with a clause that begins with
whom.

Thomas Jefferson, whom we know mainly as a
statesman, was also a talented architect.

1. My friend who moved to Oklahoma will visit us next summer.

1. Write a sentence with a clause that begins with *who*.

2. Write a sentence with a clause that begins with *that*.

3. Write a sentence with a clause that begins with *which*.

4. Write a sentence with a clause that begins with *whose*.

5. Write a sentence with a clause that begins with *whom*.

6. Use an adjective clause beginning with *when* in a sentence.

7. Use an adjective clause beginning with *since* in a sentence.

8. Write two short sentences. Then combine them with an adjective clause that begins with *who*.

9. Write two short sentences. Then combine them with an adjective clause that begins with *whose*.

10. Write two short sentences. Then combine them with an adjective clause that begins with *that*.

2. The story that she told me was unbelievable.

9.2 Adverb Clauses

Some subordinate clauses act as adverbs.

**An adverb clause is a subordinate clause that
modifies a verb, an adjective, or an adverb.**

Adverb clauses can answer any of the following questions about the words they modify: *Where? When? In what manner? To what extent? Under what condition?* or *Why?*

Recognizing Adverb Clauses

Adverb clauses begin with subordinating conjunctions. Knowing the most common ones can help you recognize adverb clauses.

SUBORDINATING CONJUNCTIONS				
after	because	in order that	though	whenever
although	before	since	unless	where
as	even though	so that	until	wherever
as if	if	than	when	while
as long as				

In the following chart, the adverb clauses are italicized. The arrows point to the words that the clauses modify. Notice that each clause begins with a subordinating conjunction.

ADVERB CLAUSES	
Modifying Verbs	Sit *where I can see you.*
	The boys arrived *after the parade had begun.*
	He is acting *as if he had something to hide.*
	If you care, donate your time.
Modifying an Adjective	I was upset *because she forgot my birthday.*
Modifying an Adverb	The movie lasted longer *than I had expected.*

OBJECTIVES

After completing this section, students should be able to

- Identify adverb clauses in sentences.
- Identify elliptical adverb clauses in sentences.

TEACHING

Getting Started

Tell students that an adverb clause is a subordinate clause that modifies a verb, an adjective, or an adverb. Write the following sentences on the board:

1. We will leave before it gets dark out.
2. I'm sad because you're leaving.
3. You're leaving sooner than I had expected.

Have volunteers identify the independent clause and the subordinate clause in each sentence. Then ask which word is modified by each subordinate clause. Elicit that *will leave,* a verb; *sad,* an adjective; and *sooner,* an adverb, are the words modified; therefore, the subordinate clauses are adverb clauses. If some students have difficulty, remind them of the questions an adverb answers. In sentence 1, the clause tells *when* someone will leave; in sentence 2, the clause tells *why* someone is sad; in sentence 3, the clause tells *how much* sooner someone is leaving. Have volunteers suggest other sentences with adverb clauses for classmates to identify.

Text Follow Through

Discuss text pages 160–164.

Assign Exercise A, page 162; Exercise B, page 163; and Developing Writing Skills, page 164.

Less advanced It is not advisable to ask these students to attempt the subsection Elliptical Adverb Clauses. You may want to allow students to refer to the chart of subordinating conjunctions on page 161 when they work on the Developing Writing Skills activity. If you wish, you may provide students with a specific subordinating conjunction for each sentence, stressing the way relationship between two ideas is clarified as students combine sentences.

Average If students need more practice in working with adverb clauses, you can give them copies of the following sentences:

1. We cooperate more than they.
2. Alice always tries to remain as fair as she can.
3. Many in the audience fidgeted while they waited for the curtain to rise.
4. Bruno can be vicious when he is angry.
5. Our phone rings as often as theirs.

Ask students to copy each adverb clause and to complete in parentheses any elliptical clauses.

Advanced Students might enjoy comparing the sentences they write for the Developing Writing Skills activity. They should note the variations in emphasis resulting both from their choices of subordinating

---

Each of these clauses answers one of the questions for adverb clauses. The first clause, for example, answers the question *Where?*

Most adverb clauses occur either at the beginning or at the end of a sentence. If an adverb clause follows the independent clause, no punctuation is required.

EXAMPLES: Marie phoned *when she reached the station.*

Bob keeps more active *than anyone else I know.*

When an adverb clause begins a sentence, however, a comma is used.

EXAMPLES: *When I reviewed his message,* I rushed to the telephone.

Since she accepted the new assignment, she has had second thoughts.

EXERCISE A: Identifying Adverb Clauses.

Each of the following sentences contains an adverb clause. Copy the sentences onto your paper and underline each adverb clause. Be prepared to identify the verb, adjective, or adverb each clause modifies.

Modified words are shaded.

EXAMPLE: Before she married, Pearl Buck's name was Pearl Sydenstricker.

1. Before we left on vacation, we took the dogs to the kennel.
2. Although you have explained your reasons, I must vote according to my own beliefs.
3. The plant will thrive as long as you do not overwater it.
4. The baby is sleepier than I have ever seen her.
5. If you can make the trip, you will enjoy the scenery.
6. Barbara reads more rapidly than anyone in our class.
7. I finished dinner at seven so that I could watch the movie.

9.2 Adverb Clauses

8. My best friend is much wiser than most of us ever realized.
9. She acted as if she didn't expect to win the scholarship.
10. While I generally respect your ideas, I cannot agree with your present plan.

Elliptical Adverb Clauses

In certain adverb clauses, words are left out. These clauses are said to be *elliptical.*

In an elliptical adverb clause, the verb or the subject and verb are understood rather than actually stated.

Many elliptical adverb clauses are introduced by one of two subordinating conjunctions: *as* or *than.* In the following examples, the understood words have been added in parentheses. The first elliptical adverb clause is missing a verb; the second is missing a subject and a verb.

EXAMPLES: My brother can eat as much *as I (can).*

I liked this book more *than (I liked) that one.*

EXERCISE B: Recognizing Elliptical Adverb Clauses.
Each of the following sentences contains an elliptical adverb clause. Draw two columns on your paper as shown in the example. In the first column, write the elliptical clause. In the second write out the full adverb clause, adding the understood words.

EXAMPLE: She is stronger than I.

Elliptical Clause	Full Clause
than I	than I am

1. Our sports car is faster than his. is.
2. This book is just as interesting as that one. is.
3. Mrs. Wilson is as pleasant as Miss Grogan. is.
4. Jennifer gave more to him than to her. she gave
5. We are more willing to serve than they. are.

Additional Practice
Practice Pages or Practice Book, pages 57, 58

Less advanced   Exercise Bank, Exercises A and B, pages 86, 87

Average   Exercise Bank, Exercises A, B, and C, pages 86, 87

Advanced   Exercise Bank, Exercises B and C, pages 86, 87

TESTING
Test Program

Unit Pretest, pages 9, 10
Chapter Test, page 29
Unit Post-Test, page 38

RE-TEACHING
Practice Pages or Practice Book, pages 57, 58

THINKING SKILLS
Knowledge—*Identifying* adverb clauses (Exercise A, page 162)
Identifying elliptical adverb clauses (Exercise B, page 163)

Synthesis—*Writing* sentences with adverb clauses (Developing Writing Skills, page 164)

164

Developing Writing Skills

Have students practice using adverb clauses in sentences by completing the following assignment.

Writing Across the Curriculum

Have you ever had to miss a day of school due to illness or for other reasons? How did you find out the information you missed on that day?

Prewriting Imagine that a classmate from science class has missed the past two days of classes and has asked you to write a summary of what was covered. Look over your notes from your last two science classes and list the main ideas. Then look for examples, facts, and details to explain or support these main ideas.

Writing Write the first draft of the summary. Include all the main ideas covered in class, and provide details, facts, or examples to support or explain each one.

Revising Make sure that you have summarized all the main ideas from the two science classes. Have you supported each main idea with examples, details, or facts? Have you arranged your summary in a logical order? Will your classmate be able to understand and follow your summary? Proofread your summary and share the final draft with a science classmate.

9.3 Classifying Sentences by Structure

(pp. 164–170)

DEVELOPING WRITING SKILLS: Writing Sentences with Adverb Clauses. Combine each of the following pairs of sentences into a single sentence by making one of them an adverb clause. Write the new sentences on your paper and underline the adverb clause in each. Refer to the chart of subordinating conjunctions on page 161, if necessary.

Answers will vary; samples are given for the first two.

EXAMPLE: Joe stayed at school. The others went home.

Joe stayed at school <u>after the others went home</u>.

1. She left the house early <u>because she did not want to disturb anyone</u>.
1. She left the house early. She did not want to disturb anyone.
2. You went into the kitchen. Did you notice anything new?
3. Margie was very tired. She could not enjoy most of the game.
4. Yeats first studied art. He soon realized that his real talents lay in writing poetry.
5. We have finished all our homework. We want to go ice skating this afternoon.
6. Mr. Wilkens acted strangely all morning. He couldn't remember where he was.
7. They went to the shopping center. I returned home from school.
8. Your parents won't object. I will drive you to the bazaar.
9. I was in Spain last summer. I learned about the languages of the different regions.
10. The well-known author Richard Wright was born in Natchez, Mississippi. He later moved to Memphis, Tennessee.

2. <u>When you went into the kitchen</u> did you notice anything new?

9.3 Classifying Sentences by Structure

All sentences can be classified by the number of clauses and kinds of clauses that they contain. There are four basic sentence structures: *simple, compound, complex,* and *compound-complex.*

164

9.3 Classifying Sentences by Structure

The Simple Sentence

Most writers use *simple sentences* more than any other type.

A simple sentence consists of a single independent clause.

A simple sentence can be short or long. It must contain a subject and a verb. It may also contain complements, modifiers, and phrases. Some simple sentences contain various compounds—a compound subject or a compound verb or both. Other parts of the sentence may also be compound. A simple sentence, however, does not contain any subordinate clauses.

The following examples show a few of the many possible variations of the simple sentence. The subjects have been underlined once and the verbs twice.

ONE SUBJECT AND VERB: The siren sounded.

COMPOUND SUBJECT: Ice cream and cookies are my two favorite desserts.

COMPOUND VERB: My sister acts and sings in the play.

COMPOUND SUBJECT AND VERB: Frank and Bill crossed the mountain but failed to reach the campsite by nightfall.

WITH PHRASES AND COMPLEMENTS: At breakfast we gave them the news about his victory.

EXERCISE A: Recognizing Simple Sentences. Copy each of the simple sentences on the following page onto your paper and underline the subject once and the verb twice. Some of the subjects and verbs may be compound.

EXAMPLE: Many streets and schools are given the names of famous people.

OBJECTIVES

After completing this section, students should be able to

- Identify simple sentences.
- Identify compound sentences.
- Identify complex sentences.
- Identify compound-complex sentences.

TEACHING

Getting Started

Tell students that a simple sentence contains a single independent clause, and that one or more parts of a simple sentence may be compound. Write the following sentences on the chalkboard:

One subject and verb   Pat sings.
Compound subject   Pat and Kay sing in the choir.
Compound verb   Pat sings and plays the guitar.
Compound subject and verb Pat and Kay sing and play the guitar.

Have volunteers suggest other simple sentences for which classmates can identify the subjects and verbs. Then write a fifth sentence on the board: *Pat sings, and Kay plays the piano.* Ask students to locate subjects and verbs; they should see that this sentence consists of two independent clauses. Inform the class that this sentence is a compound sentence. Ask a volunteer to explain how a compound sentence differs from a simple sentence with compound parts.

Text Follow Through
Discuss text pages 164–170.

Assign Exercise A, page 165; Exercise B, page 166; Exercise C, page 166; Exercise D, page 167; Exercise E, page 168; Exercise F, page 168; Exercise G, page 169; Exercise H, page 169; Exercise I, page 169; and Developing Writing Skills, page 170.

Less advanced If students proceed in a step-by-step manner through the many exercises in the section, they should have a good understanding of the types of sentence structures by the time they are asked to distinguish among them in Exercise I. Before students begin the Developing Writing Skills activity, you may want to review and discuss in class their work on Exercise I. You might also consider working with these students to help them complete the Developing Writing Skills activity, or you might decide to exempt some students from it altogether.

Average To give the class additional practice in identifying sentence structure, you can have students read aloud in random order the sentences they wrote for the Developing Writing Skills activity, or you can present some of the best ones on a ditto master.

Advanced Students should apply what they have learned in their writing. Have them review several past compositions to locate examples of compound, complex, and compound-complex sentences. You may suggest that they try revising one or more to incorporate a variety of sentence structures. Or you may prefer to assign a new composition, requiring that they use all four structures.

1. He <u>swam</u> to the canoe and <u>paddled</u> the rest of the way to the shore.
2. Waiting near the bridge, <u>we</u> finally <u>spotted</u> the caravan of trucks.
3. <u>Jennie</u> <u>passed</u> French but <u>failed</u> algebra.
4. My <u>mother,</u> my <u>father,</u> and my <u>sister</u> all <u>attended</u> the play.
5. Both the <u>bus</u> and the <u>taxi</u> <u>had</u> engine trouble and <u>arrived</u> late.

EXERCISE B: More Work with Simple Sentences. In a book or magazine, find ten simple sentences. On your paper copy each sentence and mark it as in Exercise A.
Answers will vary.

The Compound Sentence

Independent clauses are the key elements in a *compound sentence.*

A compound sentence consists of two or more independent clauses.

The independent clauses in most compound sentences are joined by a comma and one of the coordinating conjunctions *(and, but, for, nor, or, so, yet).* Sometimes a semicolon (;) is used to join independent clauses in a compound sentence. Like simple sentences compound sentences contain no subordinate clauses.

EXAMPLES: The <u>roads</u> <u>are</u> relatively safe, but the <u>bridges</u> <u>are</u> icy.

She <u>visited</u> Cornell University this weekend; <u>she</u> also <u>spent</u> some time at Ithaca College nearby.

EXERCISE C: Recognizing Compound Sentences. Copy the following compound sentences. Underline the subject once and the verb twice in each independent clause.

Additional Practice
Practice Pages or Practice Book, pages 59, 60

Less advanced Exercise Bank, Exercises A and B, pages 88–91

Average Exercise Bank, Exercises A, B, and C, pages 88–91

Advanced Exercise Bank, Exercises B and C, pages 88–91

TESTING
Test Program
 Unit Pretest, page 10
 Chapter Test, page 29
 Unit Post-Test, page 38

RE-TEACHING
Practice Pages or Practice Book, pages 59, 60

THINKING SKILLS
Knowledge—*Identifying* subjects and verbs in simple sentences (Exercise A, page 165) *Identifying* subjects and verbs in compound sentences (Exercise C, page 166) *Identifying* subjects, verbs, and subordinate clauses in complex sentences (Exercise E, page 168) *Identifying* subjects, verbs, and subordinate clauses in compound-complex sentences (Exercise G, page 169) *Identifying* the structure of sentences (Exercise I, page 169)

9.3 Classifying Sentences by Structure

EXAMPLE: Bolivia has no seacoast; Paraguay is also landlocked.

1. Our first stop was the port of Hamilton in Bermuda; our second stop was at Nassau in the Bahamas.
2. Several tiles fell off the space shuttle during liftoff, but the craft nonetheless landed safely.
3. Susan baked the bread, and Ron prepared the salad.
4. Your argument is weak, for you have no proof to support your ideas.
5. Many islands dot the coast of Yugoslavia, yet few of them have inhabitants.

EXERCISE D: More Work with Compound Sentences. In a book or magazine, find ten compound sentences. On your paper copy each sentence and mark it as in Exercise C.
Answers will vary.

The Complex Sentence

A sentence with an adjective or adverb clause is called a *complex sentence.*

A complex sentence consists of one independent clause and one or more subordinate clauses.

The independent clause in a complex sentence is often called the *main clause* to distinguish it from the subordinate clause or clauses. The main clause and each subordinate clause have their own subjects and verbs. Those in the independent clause are called the *subject of the sentence* and the *main verb.*

EXAMPLE: SUBORDINATE CLAUSE   MAIN CLAUSE
When the fog lifted we continued our trip.
MAIN CLAUSE
SUBORDINATE CLAUSE
The person who will speak last is my sister.

In the first example, *we* is the subject of the sentence, and *continued* is the main verb. In the second example, *person* is the subject of the sentence, and *is* is the main verb.

EXERCISE E: Recognizing Complex Sentences. The following are complex sentences. Copy each onto your paper. In each clause underline the subject once and the verb twice. Then put parentheses around each subordinate clause.

EXAMPLE: The player (who scores the most points) wins.

1. I will leave (after you are safely indoors.)
2. (Although he is a marvelous science student,) he is weak in mathematics.
3. The noise (that shattered the window) was a sonic boom.
4. You may sit here (if you like.)
5. The museum (that we wanted to visit) is not open today.

EXERCISE F: More Work with Complex Sentences. In a book or magazine, find ten complex sentences. On your paper copy each sentence and mark it as in Exercise E.

Answers will vary.

The Compound-Complex Sentence

A *compound-complex sentence*, as the name indicates, contains the elements of both a compound sentence and a complex sentence.

A compound-complex sentence consists of two or more independent clauses and one or more subordinate clauses.

EXAMPLE: SUBORDINATE CLAUSE   INDEPENDENT CLAUSE
As he was leaving for school, Larry remembered

to take his lunch, but he forgot the report

INDEPENDENT CLAUSE

SUBORDINATE CLAUSE
that he had finished the night before.

9.3 Classifying Sentences by Structure

EXERCISE G: Recognizing Compound-Complex Sentences. The following are compound-complex sentences. Copy each onto your paper. In each clause underline the subject once and the verb twice. Then put parentheses around each subordinate clause that you find.

EXAMPLE: The <u>person</u> (<u>who</u> <u>knows</u> it best) <u>is</u> not here, but

<u>we</u> <u>can try</u> it anyway.

1. The mountain <u>areas</u> <u>are</u> barren, but the <u>valleys</u> <u>are</u> fertile (since <u>they</u> <u>are irrigated</u> daily)
2. The <u>musicians</u>(<u>who</u> <u>appeared</u> for the audition) <u>were</u> generally excellent, but a <u>few</u> <u>were</u> real amateurs.
3. (Since the <u>blizzard</u> <u>ended,</u>) the <u>schools</u> <u>have remained</u> closed, but <u>shops</u> in town <u>have reopened.</u>
4. Our school <u>band</u> <u>seems</u> ready for the concert, and the <u>chorus</u> <u>will</u> again <u>be</u> in top shape(because its leading <u>tenor</u> <u>has returned</u> after a long illness.)
5. (<u>Although</u> the two-hundred-year-old <u>house</u> <u>has been declared</u> a landmark,) its <u>plumbing</u> <u>is</u> nearly in ruins, and few <u>people</u> <u>have shown</u> any interest in buying it.

EXERCISE H: More Work with Compound-Complex Sentences. In a book or magazine, find five compound-complex sentences. On your paper copy each sentence and mark it as in Exercise G.
Answers will vary.

EXERCISE I: Identifying the Structure of Sentences. Identify the structure of each of the following sentences as either *simple, compound, complex,* or *compound-complex.*

EXAMPLE: Without thinking, we asked again.

simple

1. If this offense is reported, he will receive a severe fine. cpx
2. The apples, peaches, and pears are in the refrigerator. smp

1.

2.

3.

4.

5.

3. Father will fly home from Dallas tomorrow, or he will phone the family. cpd
4. Antoinette carefully described the people that she had seen. cpx
5. The room is dark in the morning, but sunlight floods it in the afternoon. cpd
6. Gilberto left suddenly in the middle of the school committee meeting and did not reappear until more than two hours later. smp
7. She gave him a battered copy of *Bartlett's Familiar Quotations,* and he used it until his fiancée gave him a new dictionary of quotations. cpd-cpx
8. The book is very long; it does, nevertheless, have many interesting passages. cpd
9. Marco Polo was born on the walled island of Korcula in the Adriatic. smp
10. She described the method that she had used to save her brother's life. cpx

DEVELOPING WRITING SKILLS: Writing Sentences with Different Structures. Write original sentences according to the following instructions.

Answers will vary; samples are given for the first two.

EXAMPLE: Write a complex sentence that ends with an adverb clause.

Louisa May Alcott kept a diary when she was young.

1. Chub caught his kite in the tree and began to cry.
1. Write a simple sentence with a compound verb.
2. Write a complex sentence that begins with an adverb clause.
3. Write a compound-complex sentence consisting of two independent clauses followed by a subordinate clause.
4. Write a complex sentence in which the adjective clause comes right after the subject in the independent clause.
5. Write a compound sentence in which the two independent clauses are joined by a comma and the conjunction *but.*

2. Until I saw it for myself, I didn't believe the size of the statue.

Diagraming Clauses 9.4

The previous sections on diagraming dealt with different forms of simple sentences. This section will introduce diagrams for clauses in compound and complex sentences.

Compound Sentences

A compound sentence is a combination of two or more independent clauses. To diagram a compound sentence, begin by diagraming each clause separately, one above the other. Then join the clauses at the verbs using a dotted line shaped like a step. Place the conjunction or semicolon on the horizontal part of the step.

EXAMPLE: Mary slowly opened the package, and then she smiled happily.

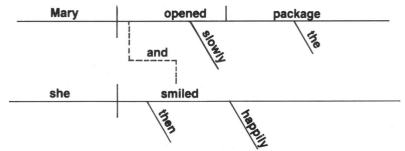

EXERCISE A: Diagraming Compound Sentences. On your paper, diagram each of the following compound sentences.
Answers are on page 170.

1. The roads are safe, but the bridges are icy.
2. Richard left for Boston yesterday; Gregory will leave today.
3. She wrote herself a note, yet she still forgot her appointment.
4. We must paint the fence; otherwise, it may rot.
5. We will give him three guesses; she will then tell him the answer.

171

9.4 Diagraming Clauses
(pp. 171–173)

OBJECTIVES

After completing this section, students should be able to

- Diagram compound sentences.
- Diagram sentences containing subordinate clauses.

TEACHING

Getting Started

Write the following sentence on the board: *We planted pumpkin seeds, but they never sprouted.* Have volunteers identify the subject and verb in each independent clause, the direct object in the first independent clause, the adjective and adverb modifiers, and the conjunction. Then provide a skeleton diagram for the sentence and help students complete the diagram. Have volunteers suggest other compound sentences for classmates to diagram.

Text Follow Through

Discuss text pages 171–173.

Assign Exercise A, page 171; Exercise B, page 173; and Developing Writing Skills, page 173.

Less advanced As in previous diagraming sections, you might want to provide skeleton diagrams for students to use in completing the exercises and the Developing Writing Skills activity. If you decide not to

172

teach diagraming to these students, you might want to use the exercise material to provide extra drill work on clauses.

Average Some students will benefit from your provision of skeleton diagrams for the first several sentences in each exercise. This should give them the practice and familiarity necessary to continue independently. If you wish to provide further practice in diagraming compound and complex sentences, you might ask students to diagram selected sentences from Exercises C and E of Section 9.3 (pages 166–168).

Advanced Students might be given the challenge of diagraming some of the compound-complex sentences in Exercise G of Section 9.3 (page 169).

Additional Practice

Practice Pages or Practice Book, pages 61, 62

Less advanced Exercise Bank, Exercises A and B, pages 92, 93

Average Exercise Bank, Exercises A, B, and C, pages 92, 93

Advanced Exercise Bank, Exercises B and C, pages 92, 93

TESTING

Test Program

Unit Pretest, pages 11, 12
Chapter Test, page 30
Unit Post-Test, page 39, 40

RE-TEACHING

Practice Pages or Practice Book, pages 61, 62

THINKING SKILLS

Analysis—*Diagraming* compound sentences (Exercise A, page 171)

Subordinate Clauses

A complex sentence contains one independent clause and one or more subordinate clauses. In a diagram of a complex sentence, each clause is placed on a separate horizontal line.

Adjective Clauses. A subordinate adjective clause is placed on a horizontal line of its own beneath the independent clause. The two clauses are then connected by a dotted line. This dotted line connects the noun or pronoun being modified in the independent clause with the relative pronoun in the adjective clause.

EXAMPLE: The person *whom you described* is the principal.

EXAMPLE: This is the man *whose car was stolen.*

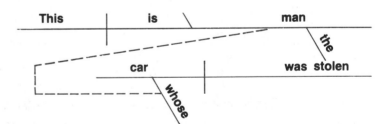

Adverb Clauses. A subordinate adverb clause is diagramed in the same way a subordinate adjective clause is. The adverb clause is also written on a horizontal line of its own beneath the independent clause. In a diagram of an adverb clause, however, the subordinating conjunction is written along the dotted line. This line extends from the modified verb, adverb, or adjective in the independent clause to the verb in the adverb clause.

172

9.4 Diagraming Clauses

EXAMPLE: They left *before the parade began.*

Answers for Exercise B, page 173

EXERCISE B: Diagraming Subordinate Clauses. Each of the following sentences contains an adjective or an adverb clause. Diagram each sentence.
Answers are in the margin.

1. I discovered the culprit who had caused the problem.
2. We left the theater before the play began.
3. The milk that I bought is sour.
4. When the judge entered, everyone rose.
5. The plans that they discussed remain a mystery.

DEVELOPING WRITING SKILLS: Writing and Diagraming Compound and Complex Sentences. Start with this simple sentence: *Rain fell for two hours.* Expand the simple sentence according to the instructions below to form compound and complex sentences. Then diagram each new sentence.
Answers will vary.

EXAMPLE: Form a compound sentence by adding *but* and a second independent clause.

Rain fell for two hours, but we finished the game.

1. Form a compound sentence by adding *so* and another independent clause.
2. Form a compound sentence by adding a semicolon and another independent clause.
3. Add an adverb clause at the beginning to form a complex sentence.
4. Add an adverb clause at the end to form a complex sentence.
5. Add an adjective clause after *Rain* to form a complex sentence.

Checking Your Skills

In the Checking Your Skills assignment, students have identified clauses in sentences. Explain to students that the following speaking and listening activity will provide them with additional practice with clauses.

Speaking and Listening

For homework, have students write two simple sentences, two compound sentences, two complex sentences, and two compound-complex sentences. Students should use both adverb and adjective clauses. Next, have students identify the independent and subordinate clauses in each of their sentences. They should also indicate whether the subordinate clauses are adjective or adverb clauses. In class, have a student to volunteer read a sentence aloud for the class. Have the class copy the sentence on a piece of paper, classify it, identify the types of clauses included, and indicate whether subordinate clauses are adjective or adverb clauses. The student reader should then ask other students for their answers. The reader can call on students of his or her choice, ask for volunteers, or have a class discussion.

Using Grammar Skills in Writing

Publishing You might ask for student volunteers to read their descriptions aloud to the class. The class should listen carefully and write down the solution for each description. The class should then be informally quizzed on the solutions to each of the descriptions to assess their listening skills.

Skills Review and Writing Workshop

Clauses

CHECKING YOUR SKILLS

Identify each underlined word group as an *independent clause*, an *adjective clause* or an *adverb clause*.

1. independent 2. adverb 3. adjective 4. adverb 5. adverb 6. adjective

(1) <u>For a long time, scientists assumed that animals could not use tools</u>, and they only recently began to find some examples of tool use in the animal world. (2) <u>If we study animal behavior closely</u>, we see some remarkable facts. (3) One animal that uses a simple tool is the chimpanzee, <u>which can use a twig to dislodge ants from an anthill</u>. (4) Many monkeys can open coconuts almost <u>as easily as people can</u>. (5) They throw the coconuts on the ground <u>until they crack open</u>. (6) The sea otter, <u>which is considered a highly intelligent animal</u>, has an unusual method of opening clams and oysters. (7) <u>It floats on its back with a small rock on its chest</u>, and then it bangs the clam or oyster against the rock. (8) <u>When they have trouble opening shellfish</u>, gulls drop them onto large rocks. (9) <u>The impact breaks open the shellfish</u>. (10) Some animals are quite adept at using objects as tools, but <u>only human beings are able to manufacture complicated equipment to make work easier</u>.

7. independent 8. adverb 9. independent 10. independent

USING GRAMMAR SKILLS IN WRITING
Writing About Animals

Follow the steps below to describe how an animal solved a problem in a clever way.

Answers will vary.

Prewriting: List the steps of the animal's actions in the order in which they occurred.

Writing: Relate how the animal went about solving the problem it faced. Save the animal's solution for the end.

Revising: Could any of your sentences be combined by using adjective or adverb clauses? Look for other improvements you could make. After revising, proofread.

Chapter **10**

Avoiding Sentence Errors

A knowledge of sentence structure can help you avoid writing either incomplete or overcrowded thoughts.

This chapter will discuss three common sentence errors and give you practice in correcting them.

Avoiding Fragments 10.1

A fragment is only part of a sentence.

A fragment is a group of words that does not express a complete thought.

A fragment cannot stand alone.

Recognizing Fragments

A sentence must contain a subject *and* a verb. If it does not, the result is a fragment. Often the fragment will be made up of one or more phrases. A fragment may also include a verb with-

This chapter concludes students' formal work with sentence parts and asks them to apply their knowledge of grammar in correcting a number of common writing problems. Sections 10.1 and 10.2 deal with the common structural errors of fragments and run-ons. Section 10.3 shows students how to identify and correct misplaced modifiers.

For a review of the entire chapter and a related writing activity, see the Skills Review and Writing Workshop on page 192.

10.1 Avoiding Fragments
(pp. 175–182)

OBJECTIVES

After completing this section, students should be able to

- Identify sentence fragments.
- Identify and correct phrase fragments.
- Identify and correct clause fragments.

TEACHING

Getting Started

Emphasize that a sentence must have a subject and a verb. If it doesn't, it is a sentence fragment. Tell students that a good way to spot a fragment is to read the words aloud; their ear should tell them if the words are a complete sentence or not. Read the following to the students, and ask them to identify each as a sentence or a fragment.

1. the kittens in the basket
2. Ask for information about student discounts.
3. launched on the first Saturday in December
4. discovering something brand new
5. Are there any new sources of energy?

You may then want to write each of these groups of words on the board and have students discuss which vital sentence part is missing from each.

Text Follow Through

Discuss text pages 175–182.

Assign Exercise A, page 177; Exercise B, page 179; Exercise C, page 181; and Developing Writing Skills, page 181.

Less advanced Students may become confused about verbal phrases. If you have opted to omit a study of participles, gerunds, and infinitives, you will want to avoid fragments using these, instead providing more practice in correcting prepositional phrase fragments. You may wish to work closely with students in analyzing the sentences in Exercise A. Students can compare the fragments they

out a subject or a word that could be used as a subject without a verb. A fragment might even include a subject and a word that could be used as *part* of a verb. A subordinate clause is a fragment even though it includes a subject and a verb. Missing in this case are the *main* subject and verb.

FRAGMENTS
About five o'clock.
Should have left by now.
The man in the dark overcoat.
The car swerving around the corner.
If she expects me to finish the job.

One good way to spot a fragment is to read the words aloud. Read each fragment in the preceding chart and listen carefully. Your ear will tell you that something is missing. Now compare these fragments with the complete sentences in the following chart. The original fragments are printed in italics.

COMPLETE SENTENCES
My uncle arrived *about five o'clock.*
We *should have left by now.*
The man in the dark overcoat knocked on the door.
The car was *swerving around the corner.*
If she expects me to finish the job, she will have to give me more time.

Notice what was added in each case to make a complete sentence from the fragment. The first fragment became complete with the addition of a subject and verb. The second became complete with the addition of a subject, while the third became complete with the addition of a verb and a modifying phrase. The fourth became complete when a helping verb was added. The fifth, a subordinate clause, needed a full independent clause.

10.1 Avoiding Fragments

EXERCISE A: Recognizing Sentence Fragments. Each of the following groups of words is either a sentence or a fragment. For each group write *F* if it is a fragment and *S* if it is a complete sentence.

EXAMPLE: Near the end of the story.   F

1. On top of the hill. F
2. A policeman standing on the corner. F
3. The money stolen from the largest bank in town. F
4. This road leads to the state assembly building. S
5. The person waiting for us at the bus stop. F
6. When Aunt Millie stepped from the plane. F
7. Near the ledge by the window in the living room. F
8. Backed into the billboard. F
9. Because she waited too long to call for help. F
10. The robber rattled by the noises in the attic. F
11. A beautiful baby smiling at us. F
12. Should report to the manager's office. F
13. Although I always try to be on time. F
14. Between you and me. F
15. A severe winter storm raged for more than a day. S
16. A man identifying himself as a CIA agent. F
17. Since my last visit to Chile and Peru. F
18. Only a part of the sentence. F
19. The two top brands are about equal in quality. S
20. Two or three miles down the highway at the traffic light. F

Phrase Fragments

You can easily learn to recognize many different types of fragments. One of the most common types is the *phrase fragment.* Since a phrase does not contain a subject and a verb, it cannot stand alone as a sentence.

A phrase should not be capitalized and punctuated as if it were a sentence.

find with those in the chart on page 176 and try to determine what is missing in each.

Average   Students must have a grasp of prepositions, participles, gerunds, and infinitives and the phrases using each if they are to succeed in the subsection Phrase Fragments. Some may be puzzled until they recall that verbals are filling another role in the sentence; they are no longer verbs. If students need more practice in correcting fragments, you can have them write complete sentences using the fragments in Exercise A.

Advanced   Students can draw one chart showing types of phrase fragments and one showing the types of clause fragments. They can then supply original examples to illustrate each type of fragment.

Additional Practice

Practice Pages or Practice Book, pages 63, 64

Less advanced   Exercise Bank, Exercises A and B, pages 94–96

Average   Exercise Bank, Exercises A, B, and C, pages 94–96

Advanced   Exercise Bank, Exercises B and C, pages 94–96

TESTING

Test Program

Unit Pretest, page 10
Chapter Test, page 31
Unit Post-Test, page 38, 39

RE-TEACHING

Practice Pages or Practice Book, pages 63, 64

THINKING SKILLS

Four kinds of phrases—prepositional, participial, gerund, and infinitive—are sometimes used alone by mistake as fragments. If you recognize that a phrase fragment has been treated as a sentence, you should correct it. Often the fragment can be added to a nearby sentence in the passage.

PREPOSITIONAL PHRASE FRAGMENT: My uncle arrived after a long trip. *On a specially chartered plane.*

ADDED TO NEARBY SENTENCE: My uncle arrived after a long trip *on a specially chartered plane.*

PARTICIPIAL PHRASE FRAGMENT: *Walking in the rain.* I developed a sore throat.

ADDED TO NEARBY SENTENCE: *Walking in the rain,* I developed a sore throat.

Sometimes it is not possible to add a phrase fragment to a nearby sentence. In such a case, you must make a complete sentence from the fragment itself. You will often have to add both a subject and a verb as well as any other words that are needed to make a sentence that expresses a complete thought.

GERUND PHRASE FRAGMENT: Growing flowers successfully.

COMPLETED SENTENCES: *Growing flowers successfully* requires great skill.

He enjoys *growing flowers successfully.*

In the first corrected sentence, a verb and an object have been added. In the second sentence, a subject and a verb have been added.

Look at another example, this one using an infinitive phrase.

INFINITIVE PHRASE FRAGMENT: To swim well.

COMPLETED SENTENCES: *To swim well* was her ambition.

Her ambition was *to swim well.*

10.1 Avoiding Fragments

In the first corrected sentence, a verb and a complement have been added. In the second sentence, a subject and a verb have been added.

The variety of phrase fragments possible is almost endless. If you think a sentence is actually a fragment, check for three things: a subject, a verb, and a complete thought.

EXERCISE B: Changing Phrase Fragments into Sentences. Use each of the following phrase fragments in a sentence. You may use the phrase at the beginning, at the end, or in any other position in the sentence.
Answers will vary; samples are given for the first two.
EXAMPLE: In Chicago and St. Louis.

Major fairs have been held in Chicago and St. Louis.
1. We saw a baseball bat near the broken window.
1. Near the broken window.
2. Chewing gum.
3. Lost for several hours.
4. In the kitchen.
5. Chosen by the committee.
6. To eat too fast.
7. Holding my grandmother's hand.
8. In the morning after breakfast.
9. Crossing the street carefully.
10. To read a newspaper.
2. Chewing gum is not permitted in many classes.

Clause Fragments

A clause, as you may remember, has a subject and a verb. But not every clause can stand alone as a sentence. Some are *clause fragments*.

A subordinate clause should not be capitalized and punctuated as if it were a sentence.

Subordinate clauses are among the most common types of fragments. Because they contain subjects and verbs, a writer may sometimes think that subordinate clauses express complete thoughts. But a subordinate adjective or adverb clause by itself is *not* a complete thought. It must be joined to, or made into, an independent clause.

An adjective clause usually begins with a relative pronoun such as *that, which, who, whom,* or *whose.* The best way to correct an adjective clause fragment used as a sentence is to add the entire adjective clause to an independent clause.

ADJECTIVE CLAUSE FRAGMENTS: That you explained to me.

Whom you decided to pick.

COMPLETED SENTENCES: This is the agreement *that you explained to me.*

The girl *whom you decided to pick* won't serve on the committee.

An adverb clause usually begins with a subordinating conjunction such as *since, although, if, while, because,* or *when.*

ADVERB CLAUSE FRAGMENTS: If I can reach him soon.

Since you offered him another chance.

This type of fragment can usually be corrected in either of two ways. One way to correct this type of fragment is to drop the subordinating conjunction.

SENTENCES: I can reach him soon.

You offered him another chance.

If taking away the conjunction changes your intended meaning, then add the entire subordinate clause to an independent clause.

COMPLETED SENTENCES: *If I can reach him soon,* I will drive him to the game.

He agreed to try again *since you offered him another chance.*

10.1 Avoiding Fragments

EXERCISE C: Changing Clause Fragments into Sentences. Use each of the following clause fragments in a sentence.
Answers will vary; samples are given for the first two.

EXAMPLE: If I ever see Paris.

    If I ever see Paris, I will send you a post card.
1. When the delivery man rang the bell, the dogs began to bark.

1. When the delivery man rang the bell.
2. Who reserved rooms in the new motel.
3. That he wanted to use.
4. Which she had saved for over a year.
5. That he intends to carry out.
6. Whom he later married.
7. Although she has collected old silver coins for a long time.
8. Since the electricity has been off for the last two days.
9. If they decide to travel by railroad.
10. When the chimney in back of the school began to smoke.
2. These are the people who reserved rooms in the new motel.

DEVELOPING WRITING SKILLS: Changing Fragments into Sentences. Use each of the following fragments as part of a complete sentence.
Answers will vary; samples are given for the first two.

EXAMPLE: Thinking about you every day.

    I have been thinking about you every day.
1. Opening the door to the garage, he hurt his thumb.

1. Opening the door to the garage.
2. With soft rolls, white bread, and vanilla cookies.
3. Since I received his letter last week.
4. On the top shelf of the closet.
5. Taken from the top drawer in the desk.
6. Buying buttons, snaps, and zippers.
7. Which reached us the next morning.
8. Replacing a cylinder in the old engine.
9. Whose house he rented.
10. Because I won't accept his advice.
11. If we can't reach them by Monday.
12. To report to the principal.
2. The bakery cases were filled with soft rolls, white bread, and vanilla cookies.

13. In a map of the old part of town.
14. Waiting for more than an hour at the bus stop.
15. Whose book I borrowed yesterday.
16. When the delivery truck pulled up.
17. Smiling and showing their approval.
18. Under the pile of papers on the bookcase.
19. While I am willing to do my part.
20. With roses and marigolds.

10.2 Avoiding Run-ons
(pp. 182–187)

OBJECTIVES

After completing this section, students should be able to

- Identify two kinds of run-on sentences.
- Use appropriate punctuation or coordination to correct run-on sentences.

TEACHING

Getting Started

Direct students' attention to the definition of a run-on sentence on page 182. Write the following on the board:

no punctuation Some plants are sources of medicine others are sources of fuel.

comma only Every weekend, guides lead tours of the botanical gardens, the tours are free with the standard admission fee.

Ask for volunteers to read the run-on sentences aloud. Tell them to listen for the end of a complete thought and to identi-

10.2 Avoiding Run-ons

Fragments lack essential parts that would make them sentences. Another kind of sentence error is found in sentences that are crowded with too much information. An overcrowded sentence is called a *run-on.*

A run-on is two or more complete sentences that are not properly joined or separated.

Run-ons are usually the result of haste. The writer fails to take the time to see where one sentence ends and a new sentence begins.

Two Kinds of Run-ons

Learn to recognize run-ons when you see them. One type consists of two sentences that are not joined or separated by any punctuation at all. An even more frequent kind of run-on consists of two sentences punctuated only with a comma.

RUN-ONS	
With No Punctuation	**With Only a Comma**
The hall was dark and dreary-looking a row of chairs was placed against the far wall.	The coach welcomed the new players, he explained his rules for practice.

fy each complete sentence. Have volunteers write on the board other sentences for classmates to identify as full sentences or run-ons.

10.2 Avoiding Run-ons

A good way to distinguish between a run-on sentence and a correct sentence is to read the words aloud. Hearing the words will help you decide whether they express one complete thought or more than one complete thought.

EXERCISE A: Recognizing Run-ons. Some of the following items are full sentences; others are run-ons. On your paper write *S* if the item is a complete sentence and *RO* if the item is a run-on.

EXAMPLE: Her horse fell, she ended in a ditch.   RO

1. A comedy of manners usually deals with the behavior of people these witty plays are often about middle- and upper-class men and women. RO
2. The Johnstown Flood was brought about by the collapse of the Conemaugh Reservoir in Pennsylvania, it occurred during a period of very heavy rainfall. RO
3. In an attempt to correct the leak, he actually caused much more damage. S
4. Beethoven's Seventh Symphony has often been called the *Dance Symphony,* the composer himself conducted the first performance of it in Vienna in 1813. RO
5. A highlight of a trip through the coastal region of Norway usually is a cruise through the beautiful fjords. S
6. He had read all of Jack London's books the first one was *Call of the Wild.* RO
7. Cigar smoking is now prohibited on most airline flights, cigarette smoking, however, is still permitted in special sections. RO
8. Irrigation of arid land was first begun in the United States by the Mormons sometime before the Civil War. S
9. The storm flooded major highways, motorists were warned to stay at home. RO
10. In 1700 the Natchez Indians lived between the Yazoo and Pearl rivers on the east side of the Mississippi. S

Text Follow Through

Discuss text pages 182–187.

Assign Exercise A, page 183; Exercise B, page 186; and Developing Writing Skills, page 187.

Less advanced Go over each exercise aloud. Allow students to hear the connection between punctuation marks and meaning in a sentence. If some students do not alter oral interpretation for added punctuation, read the sentences to them both ways yourself.

Average Have students compare answers to Exercise B. They can then discuss the varieties of ways to correct run-on sentences, and how the correction affects meaning.

Advanced Give students the option of using subordinating conjunctions as they complete Exercise B. Students can look for lengthy sentences in their outside reading, copy them down, and bring them to class. The sentences can then be analyzed to show how ideas in long sentences can be correctly coordinated or subordinated.

Additional Practice

Practice Pages or Practice Book, pages 65, 66

Less advanced Exercise Bank, Exercises A and B, pages 97, 98

Average Exercise Bank, Exercises A, B, and C, pages 97, 98

Advanced Exercise Bank, Exercises B and C, pages 97, 98

TESTING

Test Program

Unit Pretest, page 11
Chapter Test, pages 31, 32
Unit Post-Test, page 39

RE-TEACHING

Practice Pages or Practice
Book, pages 65, 66

THINKING SKILLS

Knowledge—*Identifying* run-ons
(Exercise A, page 183)

Application—*Changing*
sentences, correcting run-ons
(Exercise B, page 186)

Synthesis—*Revising* to correct
run-ons in a composition
(Developing Writing Skills,
page 187)

Three Ways to Correct Run-ons

Once you have spotted a run-on, there are three relatively simple ways to correct it.

Using End Marks. End marks are periods, question marks, and exclamation marks.

Use an end mark to separate a run-on into two sentences.

An end mark breaks a run-on into two shorter but complete sentences. Use whichever end mark is needed at the end of the first sentence.

RUN-ON: Last Friday this traffic light was not working an emergency crew repaired it the same day.

CORRECTED SENTENCES: Last Friday this traffic light was not working. An emergency crew repaired it the same day.

RUN-ON: Stop complaining, it won't make things any better.

CORRECTED SENTENCES: Stop complaining! It won't make things any better.

Using a Comma and a Coordinating Conjunction. If the ideas in both parts of a run-on are related, you can usually change the run-on into a compound sentence.

Use a comma and a coordinating conjunction to combine two independent clauses into a compound sentence.

The five most frequently used coordinating conjunctions are *and, but, or, for,* and *nor.* In using this method, it is important to remember that both a *comma* and a *coordinating conjunction* are needed.

RUN-ON: My father eats a full breakfast each morning, my mother has only juice and coffee.

CORRECTED SENTENCE: My father eats a full breakfast each morning, *but* my mother has only juice and coffee.

RUN-ON: I enjoy belonging to different clubs I expect to join the community center soon.

CORRECTED SENTENCE: I enjoy belonging to different clubs, *and* I expect to join the community center soon.

Using Semicolons. A semicolon can also be used to punctuate the two parts of a run-on.

Use a semicolon to connect two closely related ideas.

Semicolons should not be used too often. In addition, they should be used only when some type of relationship exists between the ideas in both parts of the sentence.

RUN-ON: The first speaker outlined some general ideas, the second filled in the details.

CORRECTED SENTENCE: The first speaker outlined some general ideas; the second filled in the details.

A semicolon is often used when the second part of a run-on includes such words as *however, for example,* or *moreover.* When a semicolon comes before one of these words, a comma is used after the word to separate the word from the rest of the clause. Study the following corrected example carefully for the positions of both the semicolon and the comma.

RUN-ON: His suggestions are not always sound, for example he wanted to spend all that money without doing any research first.

CORRECTED SENTENCE: His suggestions are not always sound; for example, he wanted to spend all that money without doing any research first.

EXERCISE B: Correcting Run-ons. Rewrite each of the following run-ons using any of the three methods described in this section. Use each method at least four times.

Answers will vary; samples are given for the first two.

EXAMPLE: They were in a hurry, the crowd was enormous.

They were in a hurry, but the crowd was enormous.

1. The first rocket launching was unsuccessful, but the second fulfilled all our

1. The first rocket launching was unsuccessful the second fulfilled all our expectations.

2. Tell the truth, it is easier than lying.

3. My father watches football, basketball, and baseball on TV my mother prefers to watch comedies, concerts, and documentaries.

4. I think the book itself was poor, the film version was a disaster.

5. The Marquis de Lafayette reached New York on August 16, 1824, he had been invited by President Monroe.

6. I hope to visit Denmark and Sweden this summer, however, I will have to see how expensive it will be.

7. The plants in our garden are not doing well they seem dry and lifeless.

8. Lotteries go back to pre-Revolutionary times, even then they were used to raise money for schools, roads, and bridges.

9. My brothers and I always crave dessert all my parents ever have is black coffee.

10. The first English settlers brought a primitive loom to this country, a better Dutch loom with a fly shuttle soon replaced the English loom.

11. The American author Harriet Beecher Stowe wrote *Uncle Tom's Cabin* before the Civil War, she did not die until 1896.

12. I am saving for a new turntable, however, my old one still works well.

13. "The Playground of the World" is what Atlantic City likes to call itself it does have beautiful hotels, casinos, and a fine beach.

expectations.   2. Tell the truth; it is easier than lying.

14. I am amused by the different beverage fads in this country now bottled water has become popular in many places.

15. Nathan Hale is undoubtedly the most famous spy from the Revolutionary War era, however, Lydia Darrah, another spy during that period, is credited with actually saving Washington's army on one occasion.

16. Franklin loves to make soup he told me that there are three basic soup stocks: chicken, meat, and fish.

17. Fables are stories that teach a moral sometimes they are about animals that speak and act like humans.

18. Edgar Allan Poe was an orphan at two, the rest of his life was also tragic.

19. Gershwin wrote the music for *Porgy and Bess,* many experts consider it America's first great folk opera.

20. The robin is the state bird of Michigan, the state flower is the apple blossom.

DEVELOPING WRITING SKILLS: Correcting Run-ons in a Composition. Three of the sentences in the following paragraph are run-ons. Rewrite the entire paragraph and correct each run-on. Do not use the same method to correct all the run-ons.

Corrections for 2, 3, and 5 may vary; a sample is given for 2.

EXAMPLE: American pioneers ran into many different problems one of them was housing.

American pioneers ran into many different problems. One of them was housing.

(1) Early settlers on the prairie had problems finding timber to build homes. (2) Sod houses first appeared about 1830, in one period about 90 percent of the people west of the Missouri River lived in these mud huts. (3) The settlers learned to build sod houses from the Plains Indians they had long made their winter homes from earth. (4) Sod houses had walls three feet thick. (5) These huts were dark and poorly ventilated they were warm in winter and cool in summer.

2. Sod houses first appeared about 1830; in one period about 90 percent of the people west of the Missouri River lived in these mud huts.

Developing Writing Skills

Have students practice avoiding run-on sentences in writing by completing the following assignment.

Writing Across the Curriculum

Art is all around us. Paintings, sculptures, movies, architecture, and photographs are just some of the common forms of art that we see every day. What is your favorite type of art?

Prewriting Imagine that your community is planning an art exhibition. Think about the type of art that you would like to see exhibited. Choose one and free write about why you especially enjoy it and why it would be appropriate for a community exhibition. Look over your free writing, circle the ideas you wish to include in a letter to the planning committee, and arrange the ideas in order of importance.

Writing Write the first draft of a letter to the exhibition planning committee. In the topic sentence, indicate which type of art you would prefer to have shown. In the body of the letter, list your reasons for this preference. You might want to list your strongest reason last.

Revising Make sure that you have clearly stated the type of art you would prefer to have exhibited and that you have provided reasons for this choice. Is the tone of the letter polite and respectful? Have you listed your reasons in order of importance, with the strongest reason last? Have you avoided any run-on sentences? Proofread your letter and prepare a final draft.

10.3 Avoiding Misplaced Modifiers
(pp. 188–191)

OBJECTIVES

After completing this section, students should be able to

- Identify misplaced modifiers.
- Correct misplaced modifiers by moving them closer to the words they modify.

TEACHING

Getting Started

Review the fact that a modifier acts as an adjective or an adverb. Emphasize that modifiers placed too far from the words they modify are called *misplaced modifiers.* Write the following sentence on the chalkboard: *I borrowed a book from the library with seven hundred pages.* Ask students what has seven hundred pages, the library or a book. Have a volunteer place the modifier closer to *book (I borrowed a library book with seven hundred pages).* Tell students that moving a modifier closer to the word it modifies is one correction, but that sometimes other methods are needed. Write the following on the chalkboard: *Holding out her hand, Lee's new ring was admired by everyone.* Ask students who was holding out a hand. Elicit that *Lee* was holding out her hand, and that the sentence should be rewritten to include her name as the word

10.3 Avoiding Misplaced Modifiers

When phrases and clauses that act as adjectives or adverbs are placed too far from the words they modify, confusion can result. A modifier that is placed incorrectly is called a *misplaced modifier.*

A modifier should be placed as close as possible to the word it modifies.

Recognizing Misplaced Modifiers

When a modifier is placed too far from the word it modifies, the sentence may be difficult to understand.

MISPLACED MODIFIER: I bought a stereo at the store *with push-button controls.*

The misplaced modifier above is the phrase *with pushbutton controls.* In the sentence it sounds as though the store, and not the stereo, has pushbutton controls. The sentence can be improved by placing this modifier closer to the word *stereo* and placing the other phrase at the beginning of the sentence.

CORRECTED SENTENCE: At the store I bought a stereo *with push-button controls.*

Look now at a slightly different kind of misplaced modifier.

MISPLACED MODIFIER: *Suffering from a cold,* her test mark was poor.

Here the problem is more complicated. The sentence begins with the phrase *suffering from a cold.* That phrase should modify a person. Instead it incorrectly modifies the word *mark.* The sentence should be rewritten to include the name of the person who has a cold.

10.3 Avoiding Misplaced Modifiers

CORRECTED SENTENCE: *Suffering from a cold,* Diana did poorly
on the test.

EXERCISE A: Recognizing Misplaced Modifiers. Some of the following sentences are correct, but most of them contain misplaced modifiers. If the sentence is correct, write *C* on your paper. If the sentence contains a misplaced modifier, write *MM.*

EXAMPLE: Writing a letter, his signature is almost always illegible.   MM

1. Crossing the bridge, a tollbooth was hit by the car. MM
2. I always prefer a room in a motel with a window. MM
3. Choosing his words carefully, the school principal began to speak. C
4. Having had our dinner, the boat continued the journey. MM
5. Having received a medal, my dream was fulfilled. MM
6. She gave the letter to Mr. Gross with the envelope. MM
7. Driven to the station early, we decided to have lunch. C
8. I chose that hat for my mother with the flower. MM
9. Reaching the end of the road, the farm came into view. MM
10. Frightened by the noise, my screams were heard down the hall. MM

Correcting Misplaced Modifiers

Three kinds of modifiers that are commonly misplaced are prepositional phrases, participial phrases, and adjective clauses. For each of these modifiers, the rule is the same: Place the modifier as close as possible to the word it modifies.

A misplaced prepositional phrase usually occurs in a sentence with two or more phrases in a row. The misplaced prepositional phrase should be moved closer to the word it modifies. Any other phrases that might also be confused should be moved as well.

being modified *(Holding out her hand, Lee let everyone admire her ring).*

Text Follow Through

Discuss text pages 188–191.

Assign Exercise A, page 189; Exercise B, page 190; and Developing Writing Skills, page 191.

Less advanced If you feel that students need extra help in correcting misplaced modifiers, you can guide them through the required revisions of the first five sentences in Exercise B. You may also want to work with these students in carrying out the revisions called for in the Developing Writing Skills activity.

Average To provide additional reinforcement, you might ask students to return to Exercise A and correct the misplaced modifiers.

Advanced Have students bring to class examples of misplaced modifiers they have found in newspaper and magazine articles. Have students read their sentences for classmates to identify the misplaced modifiers and correct them.

Additional Practice

Practice Pages or Practice Book, pages 67, 68

Less advanced Exercise Bank, Exercises A and B, pages 99, 100

Average Exercise Bank, Exercises A, B, and C, pages 99, 100

Advanced Exercise Bank, Exercises B and C, pages 99, 100

MISPLACED PHRASE: My brother chose a car at the

showroom *without optional equipment.*

CORRECTED SENTENCE: At the showroom my brother chose

a car *without optional equipment.*

Participial phrases are often used at the beginning of sentences. The word that the phrase modifies should appear right after the phrase. Sometimes it is necessary to rephrase the sentence to get the modified word next to the phrase.

MISPLACED PHRASE: *Driving into the park,* the statue of Eisenhower was seen.

Who did the driving? Who saw the statue? Someone performed both these actions. The sentence should be rephrased to show who did the driving.

CORRECTED SENTENCE: *Driving into the park,* we saw the statue of Eisenhower.

A misplaced adjective clause should also be brought closer to the word it modifies. In the following example, the clause is too far away from *man.*

MISPLACED CLAUSE: The police arrested a man after a long

investigation *that was seen often in the vicinity.*

CORRECTED SENTENCE: After a long investigation, the police

arrested a man *that was seen often in the vicinity.*

EXERCISE B: Correcting Misplaced Modifiers. Rewrite the following sentences, eliminating the misplaced modifiers. Underline the modifier that was misplaced in the original and draw an arrow pointing from the modifier to the word it modifies.

Answers may vary; samples are given for the first two.

10.3 Avoiding Misplaced Modifiers

EXAMPLE: Swimming leisurely, his worries were left behind.

Swimming leisurely, he left his worries behind.

1. The book that he wanted was not available.

1. The book was not available that he wanted.
2. Entering the movie, my best friend was seen in the last row.
3. We are sending you a package of seeds by parcel post with planting instructions.
4. The man was really very stingy that many people admired.
5. Eating lunch rapidly, my trip was soon continued.
6. Mother bought strawberries at the supermarket that tasted delicious.
7. Swimming as fast as possible, the drowning girl was reached.
8. The train was unusually late that I always take into the city.
9. Told to remain silent, the crying of the baby grew even louder.
10. I welcomed my old friend as soon as he arrived with great affection.

2. My best friend was seen entering the movie in the last row.

DEVELOPING WRITING SKILLS: Correcting Misplaced Modifiers in a Composition. Three of the sentences in the following composition contain misplaced modifiers. Rewrite the entire paragraph and correct these errors.

Answers will vary.

EXAMPLE: Herodotus is best remembered for his works about history by many people.

By many people Herodotus is best remembered for his works about history.

(1) Except for his writings, little is known of Herodotus' life. (2) Born about 490 B.C., several years of his early adulthood were spent by him in travel. (3) He must have been filled by the lands he visited—Egypt, Mesopotamia, Palestine, southern Russia—with awe. (4) At Thurii in southern Italy, he wrote his famous *History,* where he had retired. (5) Reading Herodotus' accounts, one almost envies the life of the man who is called the Father of History.

Checking Your Skills

In the Checking Your Skills assignment, students have corrected errors in sentence structure. Discuss with students how sentence errors such as run-on sentences, misplaced modifiers, and fragments would affect the reading of good literature.

Critical Thinking

Prepare for this activity by choosing an excerpt from a short story or nonfiction selection that students have recently read for class. Rewrite the exerpt, eliminating all the punctuation marks. Duplicate the rewritten exerpt for distribution to the class. In class, have students read the rewritten excerpt carefully and insert punctuation where they believe it belongs. Have volunteers read their punctuated exerpts to the class. Along with the class, check these exerpts for fragments or run-on sentences. Students will probably find that the volunteers punctuated the exerpt in different ways and that there is more than one correct way to punctuate the narrative. However, they will also find that different punctuation of the same passage can not only change the flow of the narrative but even change the meaning. Now read the exerpt as it was originally punctuated. Have students discuss the differences in the flow and in the meaning of the differently punctuated narratives.

Using Grammar Skills in Writing

Publishing You might want to select several of the reviews to submit to the school or a local newspaper.

Skills Review and Writing Workshop

Avoiding Sentence Errors

CHECKING YOUR SKILLS

Answers will vary; samples are given for 1 and 3.
Rewrite the paragraph, correcting errors in sentence structure.

1. The work of William Shakespeare, who was born in 1564, . . . masterpiece. He. . . .

(1) Born in 1564, the work of William Shakespeare contains a larger number of masterpieces, he is undoubtedly our greatest playwright. (2) Shakespeare's literary output includes a total of thirty-seven plays. (3) Among them, sixteen comedies, ten history plays, and eleven tragedies, which include the powerful dramas of *Hamlet*, *Othello*, *King Lear* and *Macbeth*. (4) Very little is known to scholars living in the twentieth century of Shakespeare's early life. (5) As the son of a glove maker, Shakespeare was given an education that was adequate but not extensive. (6) Though he may have served as a schoolmaster in his youth. (7) At the age of eighteen, he married Anne Hathaway they had three children. (8) For a period of seven years, he disappeared during which he may have gone to London. (9) As an actor in a touring company. (10) Shakespeare emerged from these "lost" years as a respected actor and a playwright with a growing reputation around 1592.

3. Among them are. . . .

USING GRAMMAR SKILLS IN WRITING
Writing a Television Review

Imagine you are writing a review of a television movie for your newspaper. Follow the steps below to write a review that has correctly structured and interesting sentences.

Answers will vary.
Prewriting: Outline at least three reasons that support your opinion about a particular movie.

Writing: State your opinion of the movie. Give your reasons and support them with examples. End with a recommendation.

Revising: Look at the structure of your sentences. Make sure there are no fragments, run-ons, or misplaced modifiers. After revising, proofread carefully.

UNIT II

Usage

UNIT II
Usage
(pp. 193–294)

This unit deals with the principal parts, tenses, and voices of verbs; the case forms of pronouns; agreement of subjects and verbs and of pronouns and antecedents; the degrees of adjectives and adverbs; and such usage pitfalls as double negatives. Since so much of this material requires an understanding of grammar and syntax, you may wish to deal with these chapters after you have taught Unit I. Alternately, you may choose to teach the chapters in Unit II along with the chapters in Unit I that offer the necessary background information.

Students learn most nonstandard usage by hearing and speaking nonstandard forms, not by reading them. As a result, oral practice can help many students master the standard English forms. For this reason the teaching suggestions that follow frequently recommend oral drill. You should feel free, however, to use this method at any point in the unit. As often as possible, have students read aloud and repeat completed exercise sentences using standard forms so they become accustomed to hearing the forms used by educated speakers and writers.

CHAPTER 11
Levels of Usage
(pp. 194–198)

This chapter identifies levels of usage in the English language. It presents a number of examples of standard and of nonstandard English. As you follow the text with your students, you may want to provide a more detailed perspective, identifying the circumstances under which the usage of each level of language is appropriate and acceptable.

For a review of the entire chapter and a related writing activity, see the Skills Review and Writing Workshop on page 198.

11.1 Two Levels of Standard English
(pp. 194–197)

OBJECTIVES

After completing this section, students should be able to

- Identify examples of standard formal and informal English usage.
- Use formal and informal English in their own writing.

Chapter

11
Levels of Usage

The customary way that a word or expression is used in speaking or writing is known as usage. Correct usage is language that is appropriate for the occasion. Standard English is used by most educated people. Nonstandard English includes dialect, or language used by a particular social, regional, or ethnic group. It includes slang.

11.1 Two Levels of Standard English

Standard English may be either formal or informal. Formal English is used in serious speaking and writing. Informal English is used in conversation and in casual writing.

Formal English

In formal English, sentences are precisely worded and grammatically correct.

Formal English uses traditional standards of correctness. Its sentence structures are often complex, and it uses a wide vocabulary.

The next chart lists some characteristics of formal English.

11.1 Two Levels of Standard English

FORMAL ENGLISH

1. No contractions are used. For example, *do not* is used instead of *don't*, and *it is* is used instead of *it's*.

2. Slang is never used. Words such as *phony* are not acceptable.

3. The pronoun *you* is never used to mean "a person." A specific noun or the pronoun *one* is used instead.

4. Precise wording and correct grammatical structure are used. A sentence that sounds like everyday conversation is generally not formal English.

Below is an example of formal English. Notice the absence of contractions, the complicated sentence structure, and the use of words not generally found in ordinary conversation.

EXAMPLE: Always the path of American destiny has been into the unknown. Always there arose enough of reserves of strength, balances of sanity, portions of wisdom to carry the nation through to a fresh start with ever-renewing vitality.—Carl Sandburg

EXERCISE A: Recognizing Formal English. From each pair of sentences below, choose the more formal sentence.

EXAMPLE: a. She's our new math teacher.

b. She is our new mathematics teacher.

b

1. a. The officer told the children to leave. a
   b. The officer told the kids to go away.
2. a. My pals and I are crazy about sports.
   b. My friends and I enjoy sports very much. b
3. a. Almost half our class flunked the test.
   b. Almost half of our class failed the test. b
4. a. They did not like our suggestion. a
   b. They didn't like our suggestion.

TEACHING

Write on the board the following:

(a) Good morning, Mr. Fiore. I hope you are feeling better today.
(b) Morning. How's the cold today?

Ask students to comment about who might say each greeting, and in what circumstances. Discuss with students that either is correct, but the first is appropriate for a more formal situation, whereas the latter would be used in casual conversation with a friend or acquaintance. To introduce the concept of standard English, add a third greeting on the board: *Hey, man, what's happenin'?* Elicit from students that this greeting uses slang, which is nonstandard English. Students should understand that nonstandard usage can be appropriate in very informal situations, but that they should learn the rules of standard usage and when the rules apply in writing and speaking. To reinforce the teaching of these concepts, add another three sentences such as the ones below and have students label each as formal, informal, or nonstandard English.

(a) Club's plumb broke.
(b) The treasury's empty.
(c) Club funds are depleted.

Text Follow Through

Discuss text pages 194–197.

Assign Exercise A, page 195; Exercise B, page 197; and Developing Writing Skills, page 197.

Less advanced If much of the class makes frequent errors in standard usage, you may wish to devote time to practice correct informal usage of words and phrases which the class misuses most persistently. For example, if double negatives and subject-verb agreement are the most important errors made by the class, time should be spent in drill to replace the nonstandard phrases with informal standard ones.

Average It is important for students to realize the importance of occasion to deciding whether to use informal or formal English. While eighth graders do not often need to use formal English, they should feel comfortable using it. To provide practice, write on separate slips of paper a number of different situations and types of communication, such as the following:

1. Phone call to your mom, asking to stay overnight at a friend's house.
2. Letter to the editor of a newspaper expressing feelings about teachers' strike.
3. Acceptance speech upon winning election for president of student council.
4. Asking a teacher (or neighbor) to help chaperone a club party on a school night.

Have each student draw a slip and orally or in writing create sentences appropriate for the situation.

Advanced Provide students with excerpts from several famous speeches (Presidential, Nobel acceptance, etc.) or literary essays and ask them to rewrite each in informal English, trying for humorous effect. Have students then exchange

5. a. I've got to have that bike.
   b. I must have that bicycle. b
6. a. Most of the kids are going on the class trip.
   b. Most of the students are going on the class trip. b
7. a. She's always been good at history.
   b. She has always excelled at history. b
8. a. Several hundred people attended the game. a
   b. Several hundred people showed up for the game.
9. a. I've just about decided to take biology next year.
   b. I have almost decided to take biology next year. b
10. a. You'd expect warmer weather in this part of the country.
    b. One would expect warmer weather in this region. b

Informal English

Most conversations are held in informal English. Friendly letters, casual notes, and many stories, newspaper, and magazine articles are written in informal English.

Informal English is conversational in tone. It uses a smaller vocabulary than formal English, and the sentence structure is less complex.

Informal English is just as correct as formal English, but the grammatical structure may be looser. Sentences tend to be shorter and simpler, and many words and phrases that are not acceptable in formal English may be used in informal English.

The following chart lists some characteristics of informal English.

INFORMAL ENGLISH
1. Contractions are acceptable in informal English.
2. Words and phrases used in friendly conversations, specialized vocabulary such as sports terms, and popular expressions, if not overused, are acceptable.
3. The pronoun *you* may be used in a general way.

11.1 Two Levels of Standard English

4. Sentences can be looser and more conversational, more humorous, or more personal. Most of the words used are ordinary, everyday ones.

Below is an example of informal English. Notice the use of contractions and the simple vocabulary.

EXAMPLE: The toughest thing about success is that you've got to keep on being a success. Talent is only a starting point in this business. You've got to keep on working that talent. Someday, I'll reach for it and it won't be there.—Irving Berlin

EXERCISE B: Recognizing Formal and Informal English.

Identify each sentence below as either formal or informal.

EXAMPLE: You never know what's going to happen around here.

informal

1. Pull up a chair and make yourself at home. I
2. Some of the students were detained after school. F
3. We'll have to call off the game because it's raining so hard. I
4. The jury listened impassively to the witness's testimony. F
5. I've got to get to the store before it closes. I
6. We all contributed money to buy my uncle a present. F
7. The teacher emphasized over and over the importance of one's own hard work. F
8. Feel free to drop in whenever you're in town. I
9. Many scientists consider dolphins intelligent. F
10. It is impossible to predict when the volcano will erupt again. F

DEVELOPING WRITING SKILLS: Writing Formal and Informal English.
Write five sentences of your own in formal English, following the rules on page 195. Then use the suggestions on page 196 and above to change your five sentences into informal English. Avoid the overuse of slang.
Answers will vary.

rewrites and attempt to reconstruct the original excerpt in formal English. (To make sure each student reconstructs an excerpt he or she has not seen yet, divide the class into groups, each of which receives a different excerpt. Then have students exchange papers with someone from another group.)

Comparisons of rewrites with the original excerpts could provide interesting discussion about vocabulary and syntax choices.

Additional Practice

Practice Pages or Practice Book, page 69

Less advanced Exercise Bank, Exercises A and B, pages 101, 102

Average Exercise Bank, Exercises A, B, and C, pages 101, 102

Advanced Exercise Bank, Exercises B and C, pages 101, 102

TESTING

Test Program

Unit Pretest, page 41
Chapter Test, page 44
Unit Post-Test, page 53

RE-TEACHING

Practice Pages or Practice Book, page 69

THINKING SKILLS

Comprehension—*Distinguishing* between formal standard English usage and informal English (Exercise A, page 195; Exercise B, page 197)

Synthesis—*Writing* sentences using formal and informal standard English (Developing Writing Skills, page 197)

Checking Your Skills

In the Checking Your Skills assignment, students rewrote a paragraph using formal English. Tell students that the following collaborative learning activity will provide them with additional practice with formal and informal English.

Collaborative Learning

Divide the class into groups. Have each group work together to brainstorm for slang words and other informal uses of English. From these words, have the groups create humorous dialogues that use as many slang words as possible as well as other forms of informal English. For example, students might create a dialogue between a person who speaks only in slang and a person who speaks only in formal English. The humor would arise from the misunderstanding of the person who does not understand slang; this person would be perplexed by the literal meaning of many of the slang words. Students could include a third character who "translates" the slang into formal English for the person who does not understand slang. When all the groups have prepared their dialogues, have them perform them for the rest of the class.

Using Usage Skills in Writing

Prewriting If students are unsure of the proper form of a friendly letter, refer them to the section on friendly letters in their textbooks, pages 598–603.

Skills Review and Writing Workshop

Levels of Usage
CHECKING YOUR SKILLS
Answers will vary.
Rewrite the following paragraph using formal English.

(1) We're all worried about air pollution and water pollution. (2) But we're not too concerned about noise pollution. (3) In some neighborhoods near jet airports, you can't sleep at night. (4) On city streets, car engines and horns make a lot of noise. (5) Hot-rodders and motorcyclists do more than their share. (6) If you're really unlucky, you'll have to listen to a construction crew's jackhammer. (7) And there are always the kids with their portable tape players. (8) Scientists say that listening to loud noises can damage your hearing. (9) Even loud music can do it. (10) Some youngsters in their twenties already have hearing problems.

USING USAGE SKILLS IN WRITING
Writing a Letter

Informal English is considered appropriate for personal letters. Write a letter to an imaginary friend in another country, following the steps below.
Answers will vary.
Prewriting: Think of what your friend might want to know about your school activities and home life. Make a list of recent events. Note which of your experiences may differ from your friend's.

Writing: Make up a heading and salutation. Then write the body of your letter. You might want to write one paragraph about each of the events or descriptions you chose to focus on.

Revising: Revise your letter to make sure you have used informal but correct English. Would your letter be understood by someone whose background and customs are different? After you have revised, proofread the letter carefully.

Chapter 12

Using Verbs

CHAPTER 12
Using Verbs
(pp. 199–231)

Chapter 12 shows how verbs express time and voice. It also demonstrates the correct use of verbs. Students must have the appropriate grammar background in order to understand the content of this chapter. Study or review of Section 2.3 on the helping verbs will help students understand Section 12.1 on the principal parts of verbs. Before moving on to verb conjugation in Sections 12.2 and 12.3, students should be familiar with first-, second-, and third-person forms of personal pronouns discussed in Section 1.2. Study or review of Sections 2.1 and 2.2 on action and linking verbs will help students gain a better understanding of Section 12.4 on active and passive voice. Students should also understand subjects and predicates in sentences, as covered in Chapter 7, before learning about the passive voice. Section 12.5, which summarizes some of the major problems that students encounter in verb usage, also depends to some extent on students' knowledge of the basic parts of sentences.

For a review of the entire chapter and a related writing activity, see the Skills Review and Writing Workshop on page 231.

Over the years rules have been established that reflect the way most educated Americans use their language. The rules in this and the following chapters are those of standard English. They are the rules that you will probably be expected to apply in most of the writing and speaking you do in school.

Verb usage is an area that causes many problems. Since verbs have many forms and uses, you may find yourself occasionally making mistakes with them. This chapter will help you learn their various forms and will give you guidance in using them correctly in your speaking and writing.

The Principal Parts of Verbs 12.1

Verbs have different forms to express time. The form of the verb *talk* in the sentence "She *talks* about her plans" expresses action in the present. In "She *talked* about her plans," the verb shows that the action happened in the past. These forms of verbs are known as *tenses*. To use the various tenses of verbs correctly, you must know how to form the *principal parts* of a verb.

12.1 The Principal Parts of Verbs
(pp. 199–208)

A verb has four principal parts: the *present*, the *present participle*, the *past*, and the *past participle*.

Here are the four principal parts of the verb *talk*.

PRINCIPAL PARTS OF *TALK*			
Present	**Present Participle**	**Past**	**Past Participle**
talk	(am) talking	talked	(have) talked

Notice in the chart the first principal part, the present. This is the form of the verb that you would find listed in a dictionary. Notice also the second and fourth principal parts and the words before them in parentheses. When these two principal parts are used as verbs in sentences, helping verbs are always used with them.

Here are four sentences, each using one of the principal parts of the verb *talk*.

EXAMPLES: I sometimes *talk* too much.

   We *were talking* to the guidance counselor.

   They *talked* together for hours.

   He *has talked* about a trip to Greece.

By looking at the third and fourth principal parts of a verb, you can learn whether the verb is *regular* or *irregular*.

Regular Verbs

Most verbs in English are *regular*.

The past and past participle of a regular verb are formed by adding -ed or -d to the present form.

The past and past participle of such regular verbs as *lift* and *contain*, which do not end in *-e*, are formed by adding *-ed* to

12.1 The Principal Parts of Verbs

the present form. With regular verbs that end in *-e,* such as *save* and *change,* you simply add *-d* to the present form.

PRINCIPAL PARTS OF REGULAR VERBS			
Present	**Present Participle**	**Past**	**Past Participle**
lift	(am) lifting	lifted	(have) lifted
contain	(am) containing	contained	(have) contained
save	(am) saving	saved	(have) saved
change	(am) changing	changed	(have) changed

EXERCISE A: Recognizing the Principal Parts of Regular Verbs. On your paper write the verb or verb phrase from each of the following sentences. Then identify the principal part used to form the verb.

EXAMPLE: Frank was serving dinner when he heard the news.

was serving   present participle

1. I <u>practice</u> my music every day. pres
2. Antonio <u>rubbed</u> his hiking boots carefully with saddle soap. past
3. Celia <u>has wanted</u> to meet my twin cousins for a long time. past part
4. The twins <u>are competing</u> against each other in the debate next week. pres part
5. Henry <u>mailed</u> the letter without a stamp and without a ZIP code. past
6. <u>Were</u> you <u>laughing</u> at the actress's joke or at her costume? pres part
7. Because of the thunderstorm, we <u>postponed</u> our trip to the beach. past
8. Lawrence <u>had</u> already <u>changed</u> his mind twice before breakfast. past part
9. Those dogwood trees in the park always <u>blossom</u> in the spring. pres
10. What <u>is</u> she <u>placing</u> over the door? pres part

RE-TEACHING

Practice Pages or Practice Book, pages 70, 71

THINKING SKILLS

Knowledge—*Labeling* principal parts of verbs (Exercise A, page 201)

Listing the principal parts of irregular verbs (Exercise C, page 205)

Application—*Using* the principal parts of regular verbs in sentences (Exercise B, page 202)

Using the past tense form of irregular verbs (Exercise D, page 206)

Using the past participle form of irregular verbs (Exercise E, page 206)

Using the correct principal part of irregular verbs (Exercise F, page 207)

Synthesis—*Writing* a narrative using the different principal parts of verbs (Developing Writing Skills, page 208)

EXERCISE B: Using the Principal Parts of Regular Verbs.

Copy each of the following sentences onto your paper, writing the correct form of the word given in parentheses.

EXAMPLE: The caterpillar has ___(change)___ into a moth.

The caterpillar has changed into a moth.

1. Meredith is ___(lift)___ weights to increase her strength. lifting
2. Edgar had already ___(straighten)___ his tie six times before the interview began. straightened
3. The baby tipped over the cup and ___(spill)___ the milk on his feet. spilled
4. I am happy that they still ___(visit)___ me every summer. visit
5. Alexandra is ___(design)___ a special table for her work room. designing
6. Car chases in movies have always ___(frighten)___ me. frightened
7. Had you ___(finish)___ your newspaper before the bus arrived? finished
8. His grandmother has ___(create)___ her own exotic desserts for years. created
9. Who is ___(knock)___ at the back door? knocking
10. He has ___(base)___ the character in his story on his Uncle Robert. based

Irregular Verbs

Most verbs in the English language are regular. Many of the most commonly used English verbs, however, are *irregular*.

The past and past participle of an irregular verb are *not* formed by adding *-ed* or *-d* to the present form.

The third and fourth principal parts of irregular verbs are formed in different ways and must be memorized. Some irregular verbs with the same past and past participles and some irregular verbs with the same present, past, and past participles are shown in the charts on the following page.

12.1 The Principal Parts of Verbs

SOME IRREGULAR VERBS WITH THE SAME PAST AND PAST PARTICIPLE

Present	Present Participle	Past	Past Participle
bring	(am) bringing	brought	(have) brought
build	(am) building	built	(have) built
buy	(am) buying	bought	(have) bought
catch	(am) catching	caught	(have) caught
fight	(am) fighting	fought	(have) fought
find	(am) finding	found	(have) found
get	(am) getting	got	(have) got *or* (have) gotten
hold	(am) holding	held	(have) held
lay	(am) laying	laid	(have) laid
lead	(am) leading	led	(have) led
lose	(am) losing	lost	(have) lost
pay	(am) paying	paid	(have) paid
say	(am) saying	said	(have) said
sit	(am) sitting	sat	(have) sat
spin	(am) spinning	spun	(have) spun
stick	(am) sticking	stuck	(have) stuck
swing	(am) swinging	swung	(have) swung
teach	(am) teaching	taught	(have) taught

SOME IRREGULAR VERBS WITH THE SAME PRESENT, PAST, AND PAST PARTICIPLE

Present	Present Participle	Past	Past Participle
bid	(am) bidding	bid	(have) bid
burst	(am) bursting	burst	(have) burst
cost	(am) costing	cost	(have) cost
hurt	(am) hurting	hurt	(have) hurt
put	(am) putting	put	(have) put
set	(am) setting	set	(have) set

SOME IRREGULAR VERBS THAT CHANGE IN OTHER WAYS

Present	Present Participle	Past	Past Participle
arise	(am) arising	arose	(have) arisen
be	(am) being	was	(have) been
begin	(am) beginning	began	(have) begun
blow	(am) blowing	blew	(have) blown
break	(am) breaking	broke	(have) broken
choose	(am) choosing	chose	(have) chosen
come	(am) coming	came	(have) come
do	(am) doing	did	(have) done
draw	(am) drawing	drew	(have) drawn
drink	(am) drinking	drank	(have) drunk
drive	(am) driving	drove	(have) driven
eat	(am) eating	ate	(have) eaten
fall	(am) falling	fell	(have) fallen
fly	(am) flying	flew	(have) flown
freeze	(am) freezing	froze	(have) frozen
give	(am) giving	gave	(have) given
go	(am) going	went	(have) gone
grow	(am) growing	grew	(have) grown
know	(am) knowing	knew	(have) known
lie	(am) lying	lay	(have) lain
ride	(am) riding	rode	(have) ridden
ring	(am) ringing	rang	(have) rung
rise	(am) rising	rose	(have) risen
run	(am) running	ran	(have) run
see	(am) seeing	saw	(have) seen
shake	(am) shaking	shook	(have) shaken
sing	(am) singing	sang	(have) sung
sink	(am) sinking	sank	(have) sunk
speak	(am) speaking	spoke	(have) spoken
spring	(am) springing	sprang	(have) sprung
swear	(am) swearing	swore	(have) sworn

12.1 The Principal Parts of Verbs

swim	(am) swimming	swam	(have) swum
take	(am) taking	took	(have) taken
tear	(am) tearing	tore	(have) torn
throw	(am) throwing	threw	(have) thrown
wear	(am) wearing	wore	(have) worn
write	(am) writing	wrote	(have) written

EXERCISE C: Completing the Principal Parts of Irregular Verbs. Without looking back at the charts in this section, write the missing principal parts for the following irregular verbs on your paper.

EXAMPLE:

Present	Present Participle	Past	Past Participle
———	writing	———	———
write	writing	wrote	written

	Present	Present Participle	Past	Past Participle
1.	freeze	freezing	froze	frozen
2.	run	running	ran	run
3.	lie	lying	lay	lain
4.	swing	swinging	swung	swung
5.	set	setting	set	set
6.	hold	holding	held	held
7.	teach	teaching	taught	taught
8.	pay	paying	paid	paid
9.	bring	bringing	brought	brought
10.	lay	laying	laid	laid
11.	go	going	went	gone
12.	drink	drinking	drank	drunk
13.	know	knowing	knew	known
14.	ride	riding	rode	ridden
15.	shake	shaking	shook	shaken
16.	do	doing	did	done
17.	catch	catching	caught	caught

18.	rise	rising	rose	risen
19.	tear	tearing	tore	torn
20.	burst	bursting	burst	burst

EXERCISE D: Using the Past of Irregular Verbs. For each of the following sentences, choose the correct verb from the choices in parentheses and write it on your paper.

EXAMPLE: We (freezed, froze) the vegetables.

froze

1. The camping trip was fun, but my sister (catched, <u>caught</u>) a bad cold.
2. The pitcher (<u>threw</u>, throwed) the ball to third base.
3. This bicycle (costed, <u>cost</u>) much more than my last one.
4. After dinner Earl (<u>lay</u>, lied) down for a rest.
5. Maggie's father (<u>built</u>, builded) their house himself.
6. Ron (<u>swore</u>, sweared) that he would never go near that highway again.
7. Jessie (blowed, <u>blew</u>) the balloons up for Seth's party.
8. The bear quickly (<u>put</u>, putted) her paw into the beehive.
9. The baseball (<u>broke</u>, breaked) the new bay window of the shoe store.
10. Last winter we (flied, <u>flew</u>) down to Orlando to visit my grandmother.

EXERCISE E: Using the Past Participle of Irregular Verbs. For each of the following sentences, choose the correct verb from the choices in parentheses and write it on your paper.

EXAMPLE: Angel Clare should not have (spoke, spoken) to Tess that way.

spoken

1. Has the sun (rose, <u>risen</u>) yet?
2. Gary has (<u>drawn</u>, drew) these designs for our parade float.

12.1 The Principal Parts of Verbs

3. I had (ran, <u>run</u>) home to meet you, but you never came.
4. Since moving to the city, Colleen and Marcie have (ate, <u>eaten</u>) many unfamiliar foods.
5. The bell had already (<u>rung</u>, rang) when the new teacher walked into the room.
6. I have (came, <u>come</u>) to study, not to waste time.
7. Don must have (<u>grown</u>, grew) four inches in the last year.
8. Joyce had (wore, <u>worn</u>) a bathing suit to the picnic.
9. The sandbar had already (<u>sunk</u>, sank) out of sight by the time we arrived.
10. I was pleased that you had (chose, <u>chosen</u>) that album.

EXERCISE F: Supplying the Correct Principal Part of Irregular Verbs. Copy each of the following sentences onto your paper, writing the correct past or past participle form of the verb given in parentheses.

EXAMPLE: Sandy had ___(draw)___ up a plan of attack.

Sandy had drawn up a plan of attack.

1. The spider had ___(spin)___ a lovely web in the corner of the empty room. spun
2. In the first place, you should never have ___(swing)___ the bat so hard. swung
3. For her birthday Karen's aunt ___(give)___ her a pair of skis. gave
4. Lenny ___(begin)___ to work on this puzzle three days ago. began
5. Who ___(be)___ that masked man? was
6. If you had not ___(fall)___ down, you wouldn't have noticed that flower. fallen
7. The two athletes have already ___(shake)___ hands. shaken
8. The truth has always ___(lie)___ somewhere between the two positions. lain
9. Dressed in silver, the dancer ___(spring)___ out of the shadows. sprang
10. The two families have always ___(take)___ their vacations at the same beach. taken

11. He had told it so many times that his story, though true, had ___(wear)___ thin. worn
12. Through the telescope Juanita ___(see)___ the rings of Saturn very clearly. saw
13. We have ___(throw)___ enough seeds and crumbs to that sparrow to make several loaves of bread. thrown
14. Deborah had never ___(sing)___ that song before. sung
15. Sam thought that we had ___(go)___ for the day since the office was locked. gone
16. As soon as Sue ___(drink)___ the cup of soup, she slept. drank
17. Barking urgently, the terrier ___(lead)___ us deeper into the woods. led
18. The two artists have ___(fight)___ over the years, but they always make up. fought
19. Jean's accusation ___(hurt)___ me, but I didn't know how to reply. hurt
20. The politician had ___(speak)___ the same words many times before. spoken

DEVELOPING WRITING SKILLS: Using the Principal Parts of Verbs. Write a brief account of something exciting or frightening that has happened to you recently. Use at least five of the verbs in the following list.
Answers will vary.

EXAMPLE: write

The letter that he had written was a real surprise.

1. rise	4. be	7. do	9. shake
2. say	5. frighten	8. run	10. escape
3. find	6. choose		

12.2 The Six Tenses of Verbs

In English verbs have six *tenses*.

A tense is a form of a verb that shows time of action or state of being.

OBJECTIVES

After completing this section, students should be able to

- Identify the basic forms of the six tenses of verbs.
- Conjugate the basic forms of verbs.

12.2 The Six Tenses of Verbs

Each of the six tenses has two categories: six *basic* forms and six *progressive* forms. This section will explain how the basic forms are made. The next section will explain the progressive forms.

The Basic Forms of the Six Tenses

The following chart shows the *basic* forms of the six tenses, using as an example the verb *speak*. As you can see in the third column, the six basic forms make use of just three of the principal parts: the present, the past, and the past participle.

BASIC FORMS OF THE SIX TENSES OF *SPEAK*		
Tense	**Basic Form**	**Principal Part Used**
Present	I speak	The Present
Past	I spoke	The Past
Future	I will speak	The Present
Present Perfect	I have spoken	The Past Participle
Past Perfect	I had spoken	The Past Participle
Future Perfect	I will have spoken	The Past Participle

Study the chart carefully. Learn what the tenses are called and which principal parts are needed to form them. Then learn to recognize the four tenses that need helping verbs.

EXERCISE A: Identifying the Basic Forms of Verbs. On your paper write the verb from each of the following sentences. Then identify the tense of the verb.

EXAMPLE: We have collected a ton of newspapers for recycling.

   have collected   present perfect

1. Gabriel will present his report first. fut
2. We lived in Idaho for ten years. past
3. They had notified us of their arrival. past perf

TEACHING

Getting Started

Ask a volunteer to recall the four principal parts of a verb. Explain that three of those parts (present, past, and past participle) are used to form the six basic tense forms. Have students refer to the chart on page 209. Explain how the formation of the perfect tenses differs from that of the regular present, past, and future tenses. (Perfect tenses use helping verbs *have* and *had* and indicate an action completed in the past or before a time indicated.)

Text Follow Through

Discuss text pages 208–213.

Assign Exercise A, page 209; Exercise B, page 212; Exercise C, page 212; and Developing Writing Skills, page 213.

Less advanced   Be sure students remember to look for verb phrases in this section, rather than one-word verbs. To reinforce the material on verb tense, write the following on the board. Point out that the second column shows how tense is used to tell different times or to indicate when something takes place.

Six Tenses | Tell When...
Present — it happens
Past — it happened
Future — it will happen
Present Perfect — it has happened
Past Perfect — it had happened
Future Perfect — it will have happened

Create a third column on the right, entitled "Helping Verb" and ask students to supply the helping verb used to form each tense. In a fourth column, labeled "Principal Part," volunteers can write the names of the principal parts used to form each tense. Then have students supply various verbs as examples.

Average The sentences students write in Developing Writing Skills can be used to provide further practice in identifying and forming tenses. Have students choose one of the six sentences they have written for each word and copy all of the chosen sentences on a separate sheet of paper. They can then exchange papers and identify the tense of the verb in each sentence that they receive. Finally, they can rewrite each sentence using a different verb in the same tense.

Advanced Introduce the idea of short conjugations—conjugations such as the one in the chart at the beginning of the section, using only a single pronoun. You might ask advanced students to write a short conjugation for each verb in Exercise A.

4. Elaine and June <u>practice</u> their figure skating for two hours every day. pres
5. Our dogs <u>have bitten</u> no one. pres perf
6. The family <u>will have finished</u> dinner by seven. fut perf
7. Linda and Alison <u>arrived</u> at school earlier than usual. past
8. We <u>have seen</u> that movie twice. pres perf
9. I <u>will stay</u> here no longer. fut
10. The Lochtefeld family <u>owns</u> an art gallery on Nantucket. pres

Conjugating the Basic Forms of Verbs

A helpful way to become familiar with all the forms of a verb is by *conjugating* it.

A conjugation is a list of the singular and plural forms of a verb in a particular tense.

Each tense in a conjugation has six forms that correspond to the first-, second-, and third-person forms of the personal pronouns. (See Section 1.2 for a review of personal pronouns.)

To conjugate any verb, begin by listing its principal parts.

PRINCIPAL PARTS OF *GO*			
Present	**Present Participle**	**Past**	**Past Participle**
go	going	went	gone

The conjugation in the chart below and on the next page shows all the basic forms of *go* in all six tenses.

CONJUGATION OF THE BASIC FORMS OF *GO*		
	Singular	**Plural**
Present	I go you go he, she, it goes	we go you go they go

Additional Practice

Practice Pages or Practice Book, page 72

Less advanced Exercise Bank, Exercises A and B, pages 105, 106

Average Exercise Bank, Exercises A, B, and C, pages 105, 106

Advanced Exercise Bank, Exercises B and C, pages 105, 106

TESTING

Test Program

Unit Pretest, page 41
Chapter Test, page 44
Unit Post-Test, page 53

RE-TEACHING

Practice Pages or Practice Book, page 72

THINKING SKILLS

Knowledge—*Identifying* the tense of verbs (Exercise A, page 209)

Application—*Producing* the basic forms of verbs (Exercise B, page 212)
Using the correct tense of verbs in sentences (Exercise C, page 212)

Synthesis—*Writing* sentences using the basic forms of the six tenses of verbs (Developing Writing Skills, page 213)

12.2 The Six Tenses of Verbs

Past	I went	we went
	you went	you went
	he, she, it went	they went
Future	I will go	we will go
	you will go	you will go
	he, she, it will go	they will go
Present Perfect	I have gone	we have gone
	you have gone	you have gone
	he, she, it has gone	they have gone
Past Perfect	I had gone	we had gone
	you had gone	you had gone
	he, she, it had gone	they had gone
Future Perfect	I will have gone	we will have gone
	you will have gone	you will have gone
	he, she, it will have gone	they will have gone

An important verb to learn to conjugate is the verb *be*. It is both the most common and the most irregular verb in English.

PRINCIPAL PARTS OF *BE*

Present	Present Participle	Past	Past Participle
be	being	was	been

CONJUGATION OF THE BASIC FORMS OF *BE*

	Singular	Plural
Present	I am	we are
	you are	you are
	he, she, it is	they are

Past	I was you were he, she, it was	we were you were they were
Future	I will be you will be he, she, it will be	we will be you will be they will be
Present Perfect	I have been you have been he, she, it has been	we have been you have been they have been
Past Perfect	I had been you had been he, she, it had been	we had been you had been they had been
Future Perfect	I will have been you will have been he, she, it will have been	we will have been you will have been they will have been

EXERCISE B: Conjugating the Basic Forms of Verbs. On your paper conjugate each of the following verbs. The first two verbs are regular; the second two are irregular. Use the conjugation of *go* on pages 210–211 as your model. Begin each of your conjugations by listing the principal parts of the verb.

   1. ask   2. move   3. speak   4. begin

EXERCISE C: Supplying the Correct Tense. Supply the basic form of the verb as directed in parentheses.

Answers should follow the model given.

EXAMPLE: Helen Keller (speak—past) her first word when she was an infant.

               Helen Keller spoke her first word when she was an infant.

12.3 The Progressive Forms of Verbs

1. We (ask—past) the police officer for directions to the museum. asked
2. The Johnsons (move—present perfect) three times in the past year. have moved
3. They (see—past perfect) everything they wanted to by the end of their vacation. had seen
4. Lou always (begin—present) his homework after dinner. begins
5. By the end of their tour, the group (perform—future perfect) in eleven cities. will have performed
6. We (visit—future) the Uffizi Gallery when we go to Florence this summer. will visit
7. Sharon (talk—past perfect) to her counselor earlier in the day. had talked
8. He never (do—present) what he is told to do. does
9. We (grow—present perfect) very fond of our new neighbors. have grown
10. She (give—past) you a chance yesterday to play. gave

DEVELOPING WRITING SKILLS: Using the Basic Forms of the Six Tenses. Write six sentences of your own for each verb in the following list using a different tense in each.
Answers will vary; samples are given for the first one.
EXAMPLE: give

1. The door needs a new lock. The door needed a new lock, and we bought one.
   She gives us flowers every spring.

   She gave us flowers last year.

   (and so on)

The door will need a new lock eventually. The door has needed a new lock for a

1. need   2. walk   3. sing   4. draw   5. be

long time. The door had needed a new lock for years before it was fixed. By tomorrow, the door will have needed a new lock for exactly one month.

The Progressive Forms of Verbs 12.3

Section 12.2 gave the six tenses in their basic forms. Each of these tenses also has a *progressive* form. All six of the progressive forms of a verb are made using just one principal part: the present participle. This is the principal part that ends in -*ing*.

12.3 The
Progressive Forms
of Verbs
(pp. 213–217)

Recognizing Progressive Forms

The chart shows the progressive forms of the six tenses.

PROGRESSIVE FORMS OF THE SIX TENSES OF *SPEAK*

Tense	Progressive Form	Principal Part Used
Present	I am speaking	
Past	I was speaking	
Future	I will be speaking	
Present Perfect	I have been speaking	The Present Participle
Past Perfect	I had been speaking	
Future Perfect	I will have been speaking	

EXERCISE A: Identifying the Tense of Progressive Forms of Verbs. Study the preceding chart, which shows the progressive form of the six tenses of speak. Then identify the tense of each of the following verbs.

EXAMPLE: was thinking   past

1. will be going   fut
2. have been seeing   pres perf
3. am helping   pres
4. will have been hiking
5. was carrying   past
6. had been visiting
7. am leaving   pres
8. will be making   fut
9. was playing   past
10. had been practicing
11. have been buying   pres perf
12. will have been trying
13. was teaching   past
14. am writing   pres
15. had been catching   past perf
16. will be singing   fut
17. have been putting   pres perf
18. was sitting   past
19. will have been waiting
20. am collecting   pres

4. fut perf   6. past perf   10. past perf   12. fut perf   19. fut perf

12.3 The Progressive Forms of Verbs

Conjugating the Progressive Forms of Verbs

Conjugating the progressive forms of any verb is easy if you know how to conjugate the basic forms of the verb *be*.

To conjugate the progressive forms of a verb, add the present participle of the verb to a conjugation of the basic forms of *be*.

A complete conjugation of the basic forms of *be* is shown on pages 211 and 212. Compare that conjugation with the following conjugation of the progressive forms of *go*. To form the progressive forms of a verb, you must know the basic forms of *be*.

CONJUGATION OF THE PROGRESSIVE FORMS OF *GO*

	Singular	Plural
Present Progressive	I am going you are going he, she, it is going	we are going you are going they are going
Past Progressive	I was going you were going he, she, it was going	we were going you were going they were going
Future Progressive	I will be going you will be going he, she, it will be going	we will be going you will be going they will be going
Present Perfect Progressive	I have been going you have been going he, she, it has been going	we have been going you have been going they have been going

Less advanced For additional practice, have individual or pairs of students develop sentences with many of the verb phrases in Exercise A. Then have them exchange papers and indicate the tense of each verb as it is now used in context.

Average Use of the progressive forms has little meaning out of context. To give students practice in using the six tenses, provide a set of sentence beginnings and instruct them to complete the sentences in a way that makes the ongoing condition of the action logical.

He is studying . . .
He was studying . . .
He will be studying . . .
He has been studying . . .
He had been studying . . .
He will have been studying . . .

If students seem puzzled, complete one or two of the sentences orally with them. For example, *He is studying for the test. He will have been studying for two hours when the bell rings.*

Advanced Students can write short conjugations, as suggested for Section 12.2, using a single pronoun, this time giving the progressive forms for ten of the verbs in Exercise A. The idea of the "principal parts bee" introduced in the TE for Section 12.1 may be adapted and used to provide more drill. You might include basic as well as progressive verb forms. Call out the verb first, then a subject, tense, and form.

Question: *draw,* she—future progressive
Answer: she will be drawing

Additional Practice

Practice Pages or Practice
Book, page 73

Less advanced Exercise Bank,
Exercises A and B, pages 107,
108

Average Exercise Bank, Exercises A, B, and C, pages 107,
108

Advanced Exercise Bank, Exercises B and C, pages 107, 108

TESTING

Test Program

Unit Pretest, page 41
Chapter Test, page 45
Unit Post-Test, page 53

RE-TEACHING

Practice Pages or Practice
Book, page 73

THINKING SKILLS

Knowledge—*Identifying* the
tense of progressive forms of
verbs (Exercise A, page 214)

Application—*Producing*
conjugations of the
progressive forms of verbs
(Exercise B, page 216)
Using the progressive form of
the verb in the correct tense
(Exercise C, page 216)

Synthesis—*Writing* sentences
using the progressive forms
of the six tenses (Developing
Writing Skills, page 217)

| Past Perfect Progressive | I had been going you had been going he, she, it had been going | we had been going you had been going they had been going |
| Future Perfect Progressive | I will have been going you will have been going he, she, it will have been going | we will have been going you will have been going they will have been going |

EXERCISE B: Conjugating the Progressive Forms of Verbs. On your paper conjugate the progressive forms of each of the following verbs. Use the chart on page 215 and above showing the progressive forms of *go* as your model.
Answers should follow the model given.
   1. move   2. freeze

EXERCISE C: Supplying the Correct Tense. Copy each of the following sentences onto your paper, supplying the progressive form of the verb as directed in parentheses.

EXAMPLE: He (go—present progressive) to Alabama to visit his relatives.

He is going to Alabama to visit his relatives.

1. I (write—past progressive) to you when you telephoned me. was writing
2. Clarissa (study—future progressive) music at a special camp this summer. will be studying
3. Reggie (carry—present perfect progressive) a heavy course load this year. has been carrying
4. Despite her height, Kate (hope—present progressive) to make the basketball team. is hoping
5. I was very relieved because I (expect—past perfect progressive) a much lower grade. had been expecting

6. The rain (ruin—present progressive) all of our plans. is ruining
7. He (swim—future perfect progressive) for two hours by noon.
8. Nick (have—present perfect progressive) second thoughts about the concert. has been having
9. The last ferry (leave—future progressive) soon. will be leaving
10. We (watch—past perfect progressive) the dancer carefully all evening. had been watching

7. will have been swimming

DEVELOPING WRITING SKILLS: Using the Progressive Forms of the Six Tenses. Write six sentences of your own for each verb in the following list. Use a different tense in the progressive form in each of your sentences.

Answers will vary; samples are given for the first one.

EXAMPLE: ask

1. We are moving our headquarters to a new building. We were moving when the

We are asking for three tickets.

We were asking about their dog.

(and so on)

car bumped us. We will be moving to San Antonio next week. We have been

1. move 2. have 3. say 4. give 5. think

moving away from that policy for a while now. We had been moving in the wrong direction until we changed course. We will have been moving furniture for six hours by lunch time.

Active and Passive Voice 12.4

Just as verbs change tense to show time, they may also change form to show whether or not the subject of the verb is performing an action. In English most verbs have two *voices*, one to show that the subject is performing an action and one to show that the subject is having an action performed upon it.

A voice is a form of a verb that shows whether or not the subject is performing the action.

Two Voices

The two voices are called *active* and *passive*.

Active Voice. Any action verb can be used in the *active* voice.

217

12.4 Active and Passive Voice
(pp. 217–222)

OBJECTIVES

After completing this section, students should be able to

- Distinguish between the active and the passive voice.
- Conjugate verbs in the passive voice.
- Use active and passive voices appropriately.

TEACHING
Getting Started

┌─ sentence bank ─────────┐
The hot sun melted the ice
cream.
The ice cream was melted
by the hot sun.
└─────────────────────────┘

To introduce the concept of *voice,* write the Sentence Bank sentences on the chalkboard.

Ask a volunteer to underline the verb in each sentence with two lines, and the subject with one line. Elicit in which sentence the subject actively does something. Explain that a verb in the active voice is expressing some action that the subject actually does, while a verb in the passive voice expresses an action that is done to or received by the subject. You might also link the notion of voice to being an active or passive person, if you wish.

Text Follow Through
Discuss text pages 217–222.

Assign Exercise A, page 218; Exercise B, page 220; Exercise C, page 221; and Developing Writing Skills, page 221.

Less advanced You may want to begin by discussing subjects and direct objects. Write the following sentence on the board: *John painted the boat.* Ask students to come to the board to complete the following steps:

1. Underline the verb.
2. Circle the subject.
3. Draw a box around the direct object.

A verb is active when its subject performs the action.

ACTIVE VOICE: Sharon *told* a long story about her summer vacation.

Bob *left* early.

In each of these examples, the subject performs the action. Sharon did the telling; Bob did the leaving. Notice also in the examples that an active verb may or may not have a direct object.

Passive Voice. Most action verbs can also be used in the *passive* voice.

A verb is passive when its subject does not perform the action.

PASSIVE VOICE: The long story about her summer vacation *was told* by Sharon.

Bob *was left* with the bill.

In each of these examples, the subject is the receiver rather than the performer of the action. In the first sentence, the performer is named: Sharon. *Sharon,* however, is the object of the preposition *by* and is no longer the subject. In the second sentence, the performer of the action is not named. The sentence does not tell *who* left Bob with the bill. Notice finally that neither of these sentences has a direct object. An active verb may or may not have a direct object, but a passive verb almost never does.

EXERCISE A: Distinguishing Between Active and Passive Voice. On your paper write the verb or verb phrase from each of the sentences on the following page. Then identify the voice of the verb or verb phrase as either *active* or *passive*.

218

Students can then be asked to try to rewrite the sentence, making the direct object into the subject. The results can lead into a discussion of active and passive voice.

12.4 Active and Passive Voice

EXAMPLE: Those flowers were sent without a card.

were sent   passive

1. Ted <u>was hurt</u> by Julie's reaction to his song. pass.
2. The play <u>was pronounced</u> a great success by the producer and the critics. pass.
3. Unfortunately, nobody <u>believed</u> him. act.
4. That sapling <u>was bent</u> by last December's unexpected ice storm. pass.
5. Hot, tired, and out of breath, Kim finally <u>reached</u> the top of the Statue of Liberty. act.
6. The desk clerk <u>directed</u> us to the hotel dining room. act.
7. The note <u>was left</u> in this bottle more than fifty years ago. pass.
8. Simon <u>jumped</u> over the porch railing into the lilac bush. act.
9. After a long wait, Jill <u>was admitted</u> to the club. pass.
10. Sam <u>befriended</u> me on my first day here, more than five years ago. act.

Forming the Tenses of Passive Verbs

A passive verb always has two parts.

A passive verb is always a verb phrase made from a form of *be* plus a past participle.

Here is a short conjugation of the passive forms of the verb *report* with the pronoun *it*.

CONJUGATION OF THE PASSIVE FORMS OF *REPORT*

Tense	Passive Form
Present	it is reported
Past	it was reported
Future	it will be reported
Present Perfect	it has been reported
Past Perfect	it had been reported
Future Perfect	it will have been reported

You may also want to limit the work to the first objective, distinguishing between the active and the passive voice. If so, students need complete only Exercise A. You might then emphasize the greater value of the active voice in most sentences and have students answer Exercise C orally.

Average Students can work again with Exercise A for further practice. Ask them to rewrite sentences, changing active voice to passive and vice versa. Then ask students to identify the subject in each of the original sentences and in their rewritten sentences.

Advanced Ask students to select a paragraph or two from their outside reading and to analyze the verbs in the paragraphs for use of active and passive voice. Students may then be asked for an evaluation of the relative effectiveness of each in different types of formal and informal writing.

Additional Practice
Practice Pages or Practice Book, pages 74, 75

Less advanced Exercise Bank, Exercises A and B, pages 109–111

Average Exercise Bank, Exercises A, B, and C, pages 109–111

Advanced Exercise Bank, Exercises B and C, pages 109–111

TESTING

Test Program

Unit Pretest, page 42
Chapter Test, page 46
Unit Post-Test, page 54

RE-TEACHING

Practice Pages or Practice
Book, pages 74, 75

THINKING SKILLS

Comprehension—*Distinguishing*
between active and passive
voice verbs (Exercise A,
page 218)

Application—*Producing*
conjugations of verbs in the
passive voice (Exercise B,
page 220)

Synthesis—*Rewriting* sentences
changing the voice of verbs
(Exercise C, page 221)
Modifying a paragraph by
changing some passive verbs
into active verbs (Developing
Writing Skills, page 221)

EXERCISE B: Conjugating Verbs in the Passive Voice.
Using the chart on page 219 as your model, conjugate the following two verbs in the passive voice. In each conjugation include the pronouns indicated in parentheses.
Answers should follow the model given.

1. do   (with *it*)   2. scold   (with *he*)

Using Active and Passive Voices

Each of the two voices has its proper use in English.

Use the active voice whenever possible.

Sentences with active verbs are less wordy and more forceful than those with passive verbs. Compare, for example, the following sentences. Notice the different number of words each sentence needs to report the same information.

ACTIVE: The movers *lugged* the piano up the steps.

PASSIVE: The piano *was lugged* up the steps by the movers.

Though you should aim to use the active voice in most of your writing, there will be times when you will need to use the passive voice.

Use the passive voice to emphasize the receiver of an action rather than the performer of the action.

In the following example, the receiver of the action is the subject *paintings*.

EMPHASIS ON RECEIVER: The three priceless paintings *were damaged* by vandals.

The passive voice should also be used when there is no performer of the action.

Use the passive voice to point out the receiver of an action when the performer is unknown or unimportant and is not named in the sentence.

12.4 Active and Passive Voice

PERFORMER UNKNOWN: The paintings *were stolen* sometime during the night.

PERFORMER UNIMPORTANT: The museum *was* quickly *ordered* closed while the police searched for clues.

EXERCISE C: Using the Active Voice. Rewrite each of the following sentences, changing the verb from the passive voice to the active voice and making whatever other changes are necessary.

Revisions may vary; samples are given for the first two.

EXAMPLE: This old watch was found by me in my grandmother's bureau.

I found this old watch in my grandmother's bureau.

1. We ate all the hamburgers in less than five minutes.

1. All the hamburgers were eaten by us in less than five minutes.
2. Television is hardly ever watched by Randy and Caroline.
3. The story was blurted out by the twins to everyone in the room.
4. A decision was suddenly reached by the President.
5. A home run was hit by Hank Aaron in his first time at bat.
6. Sequined tank suits were worn by the members of the precision swim team.
7. Many books have been read by me since I got a library card.
8. The javelin was forcefully hurled into the air by Don.
9. A remarkable opportunity was missed by you yesterday.
10. Four languages are spoken by him fluently.

2. Randy and Caroline hardly ever watch television.

DEVELOPING WRITING SKILLS: Correcting Unnecessary Use of the Passive Voice. Most of the underlined verbs in the paragraph on the following page are in the passive voice. Rewrite the paragraph changing as many of the passive verbs into active ones as you think necessary to improve the paragraph. It is not necessary to change every passive verb.

Answers will vary; sample is given in the margin.

Developing Writing Skills (pp. 214–215)

(1) After years of preparation and many delays, the United States launched the first space shuttle in 1981. (2) The shuttle had been designed by NASA engineers to make a number of voyages into outer space. (3) The spacecraft *Columbia* made the very first voyage on April 12, 1981. (4) Astronauts John Young and Robert Crippen manned the spaceship. (5) These men had been carefully trained for many years by NASA to participate in the space shuttle program. (6) The *Columbia* was lifted into space from Cape Canaveral by several rockets that could be reused by the space program. (7) The Navy later recovered these rockets from the Atlantic Ocean. (8) The spacecraft with its human cargo orbited the earth for two days. (9) Astronauts Young and Crippen finally guided it back to the earth and landed it on the ground at Bakersfield, California. (10) Millions of Americans heralded the successful flight as this country's return to outer space.

EXAMPLE: Vehicles of many different sorts <u>have been sent</u> into space by the United States.

The United States has sent vehicles of many different sorts into space.

(1) After years of preparation and many delays, the first space shuttle <u>was launched</u> by the United States in 1981. (2) The shuttle <u>had been designed</u> by NASA engineers to make a number of voyages into outer space. (3) The very first voyage <u>was made</u> by the spacecraft *Columbia* on April 12, 1981. (4) The spaceship <u>was manned</u> by astronauts John Young and Robert Crippen. (5) These men <u>had been</u> carefully <u>trained</u> for many years by NASA to participate in the space shuttle program. (6) The *Columbia* <u>was lifted</u> into space from Cape Canaveral by several rockets that <u>could be reused</u> by the space program. (7) These rockets <u>were</u> later <u>recovered</u> by the Navy from the Atlantic Ocean. (8) The spacecraft with its human cargo <u>orbited</u> the earth for two days. (9) It <u>was</u> finally <u>guided</u> back to the earth and <u>was landed</u> on the ground at Bakersfield, California, by astronauts Young and Crippen. (10) The successful flight <u>was heralded</u> by millions of Americans as this country's return to outer space.

12.5 Glossary of Troublesome Verbs
(pp. 222–230)

OBJECTIVE

After completing this section, students should be able to

• Use a number of problem verbs correctly.

12.5 Glossary of Troublesome Verbs

The following verbs cause problems for many speakers and writers. Some of the problems involve using the principal parts of certain verbs. Other problems involve learning to distinguish between the meanings of certain confusing pairs of verbs. As you read through the following list, note those verbs that have caused you difficulty in the past and concentrate on them. Use the exercises to test your understanding. When you are writing and revising your compositions, refer to this section to check your work.

(1) *ain't* *Ain't* is not considered correct English. Avoid using it in speaking and in writing.

12.5 Glossary of Troublesome Verbs

INCORRECT: He *ain't* going to the movies with Millicent and
her father.

CORRECT: He *isn't* going to the movies with Millicent and
her father.

(2) burst   This irregular verb has the same form for three of its principal parts. The present, past, and past participle of *burst* all are *burst*. *Bust* and *busted* are not considered correct. If you find you are using these incorrect forms, try replacing them with the present, past, or past participle of the verb *break*. *Break*, *broke*, or *broken* may be easier for you to use correctly.

INCORRECT: If you drop the model airplane, it *will bust*.

She *busted* the blister on her hand.

The radio in my dad's car *has been busted*.

CORRECT: If you drop the model airplane, it *will break*.

She *burst* (or *broke*) the blister on her hand.

This radio *has been broken*.

(3) did, done   Remember that *done* is a past participle and can be used as a verb only with a helping verb such as *have* or *has*. Instead of using *done* without a helping verb, use *did*. Otherwise you can add the helping verb before *done*.

INCORRECT: I already *done* my homework.

CORRECT: I already *did* my homework.

I *have* already *done* my homework.

(4) dragged, drug   *Drag* is a regular verb. Its principal parts are *drag*, *dragging*, *dragged*, and *dragged*. *Drug* is never correct as the past or past participle of *drag*.

INCORRECT: I *drug* the heavy suitcases up the stairs.

You *should have drug* the sack of potatoes out of the rain.

223

Average The verb pairs *sit-set, rise-raise,* and *lie-lay* give students the most trouble. Be sure students understand the differences in meaning between the two in each pair. They should also note which verb in each pair is usually followed by a direct object. It is a good idea to drill students first on each of the verbs separately, preparing sentences for written or oral answers, before mixing sentences requiring, say, both *lie* and *lay* in all their forms.

Advanced Pretesting may show that students need work with only a few of the troublesome verbs. The sentences students write for Developing Writing Skills can be used for a chapter review. Have each student read aloud one of his or her sentences. You can then ask the class to identify the verb in the sentence, its tense and form, and its voice.

Additional Practice

Practice Pages or Practice Book, page 76

Less advanced Exercise Bank, Exercises A and B, page 112

Average Exercise Bank, Exercises A, B, and C, page 112

Advanced Exercise Bank, Exercises B and C, page 112

TESTING

Test Program

Unit Pretest, page 42
Chapter Test, page 46
Unit Post-Test, page 54

RE-TEACHING

Practice Pages or Practice Book, page 76

CORRECT: I *dragged* the heavy suitcases up the stairs.

You *should have dragged* the sack of potatoes out of the rain.

(5) drowned, drownded *Drown* is a regular verb. Its past and past participle are formed simply by adding *-ed* to the present form: *drown-+-ed. Drownded* is wrong. Do not add the extra *d* either in speaking or in writing.

INCORRECT: The lemmings all raced into the sea and *drownded*.

CORRECT: The lemmings all raced into the sea and *drowned*.

(6) gone, went *Gone* is the past participle of *go* and can be used as a verb only with a helping verb such as *have* or *has. Went* is the past participle of *go* and can be used as a verb only with a helping verb such as *have* or *has. Went* is the past of *go* and is never used with a helping verb.

INCORRECT: Jean and Frank *gone* to the shopping mall.

We *should have went* along with them.

CORRECT: Jean and Frank *have gone* to the shopping mall.

Jean and Frank *went* to the shopping mall.

We *should have gone* along with them.

(7) have, of In conversation the words *have* and *of* often sound very similar. Be careful not to write *of* when you really mean the helping verb *have* or its contraction *'ve.*

INCORRECT: You should *of* stayed until the end of the show.

CORRECT: You should *have* stayed until the end of the show.

You *should've* stayed until the end of the show.

(8) lay, lie These verbs are troublesome to many people because they look and sound almost alike and have similar

THINKING SKILLS

Application—*Using* the correct verb of a troublesome pair (Exercise A, page 228; Exercises B and C, page 229)

Synthesis—*Writing* sentences using troublesome verbs correctly (Developing Writing Skills, page 230)

12.5 Glossary of Troublesome Verbs

meanings. The first step in learning to distinguish between *lay* and *lie* is to become thoroughly familiar with their principal parts. Memorize the principal parts of both verbs.

PRINCIPAL PARTS:	lay	laying	laid	laid
	lie	lying	lay	lain

The next step is to compare the meaning and use of the two verbs. *Lay* usually means "to put (something) down" or "to place (something)." This verb is almost always followed by a direct object.

EXAMPLES: Marie always *lays* her books and notes on her desk.

The workers *will be laying* new carpeting at our house soon.

This morning I *laid* my lab materials on the classroom floor.

The builders *have laid* the foundation for the new school.

Lie usually means "to rest in a reclining position." It also can mean "to be situated." This verb is used to show the position of a person, place, or thing. *Lie* is never followed by a direct object.

EXAMPLES: My mother usually *lies* down before fixing our dinner.

The dog *is lying* in front of the fire.

The ancient city of Palmyra *lay* in the Syrian desert.

The broken glass *has lain* in the alley for more than a week.

Pay special attention to one particular area of confusion between *lay* and *lie*. *Lay* is the present tense of *lay*. *Lay* is also the past tense of *lie*.

PRESENT TENSE OF LAY: I *lay* the mail on that table every morning.

PAST TENSE OF LIE: My visiting cousin *lay* down with a headache.

(9) *learn, teach* *Learn* means "to receive knowledge." *Teach* means "to give knowledge." Do not use *learn* in place of *teach*.

INCORRECT: Dan *learned* me how to ice-skate.

CORRECT: Dan *taught* me how to ice-skate.

(10) *leave, let* *Leave* means "to allow to remain." *Let* means "to permit." Do not reverse the meanings.

INCORRECT: *Leave* me finish!

Let the dog alone!

CORRECT: *Let* me finish!

Leave the dog alone!

(11) *raise, rise* *Raise* has several common meanings: "to lift (something) upward," "to build (something)," "to grow (something)," or "to increase (something)." This verb is usually followed by a direct object.

EXAMPLES: *Raise* the lamp just a bit.
DO

My uncle *has been raising* wheat and corn on his farm.
DO   DO

The town *raised* a monument to the heroes of the Vietnam War.
DO

Our volunteers *have raised* 1,500 dollars in a month.
DO

Rise, on the other hand, is not usually followed by a direct object. This verb means "to get up," "to go up," or "to be increased."

12.5 Glossary of Troublesome Verbs

EXAMPLES: We learned in third grade that the sun *rises* in the east.

Our neighbor's old, white rooster surely *will be rising* soon.

She *rose* for a moment and then dropped back into her seat.

Has the rate of inflation *risen* as sharply this month as last?

(12) saw, seen   *Seen* is a past participle and can be used as a verb only with a helping verb such as *have* or *has*. Instead of using *seen* without a helping verb, use *saw*. Otherwise you can add the helping verb before *seen*.

INCORRECT: I *seen* that show when it was in town for three weeks last year.

CORRECT: I *saw* that show when it was in town for three weeks last year.

(13) says, said   A common mistake in reporting what someone said is to use the present tense *says* rather than the past tense *said*.

INCORRECT: First he turned ghostly white, and then he *says,* "I need to sit down."

CORRECT: First he turned ghostly white, and then he *said,* "I need to sit down."

(14) set, sit   The first step in learning to distinguish between *set* and *sit* is to become thoroughly familiar with their principal parts.

PRINCIPAL PARTS: set   setting   set   set
                   sit   sitting   sat   sat

To avoid confusing these two verbs, understand the difference in their meanings. *Set* commonly means "to put (something) in a certain place or position." It is usually followed by a direct object.

EXAMPLES: Set (not *sit*) the vase down carefully.
                           DO

                           DO
             They *are setting* decoys out on the lake in prepara-
             tion for their hunting trip.

                           DO
             Frank *set* the table for dinner.

                           DO
             We *have set* those plants in direct sunlight for the
             winter.

Sit usually means "to be seated" or "to rest." In its usual meanings, the verb *sit* is not followed by a direct object.

EXAMPLES: The house where Grandmother was born *sits* (not *sets*) atop that hill.

             The delegates *have been sitting* in a hot room all day.

             Mona *sat* in the first seat.

             The owl *has sat* in the hemlock tree since sunset.

(15) *sneaked, snuck*   *Sneak* is a regular verb. Its principal parts are *sneak, sneaking, sneaked,* and *sneaked. Snuck* is sometimes heard in conversation in place of *sneaked.* You should avoid using *snuck,* however, in your writing.

INCORRECT: The cat *snuck* up, then sprang at the unwary
                bird.

CORRECT: The cat *sneaked* up, then sprang at the unwary
                bird.

**EXERCISE A: Avoiding Problems with Troublesome Verbs
1–5.** For each of the following sentences, choose the correct verb from the choices in parentheses and write it on your paper.

EXAMPLE: Amelia Earhart (did, done) what few other people
             dared to do.

             did

12.5 Glossary of Troublesome Verbs

1. The child (<u>dragged</u>, drug) his stuffed bear across the playground.
2. (Ain't, <u>Aren't</u>) you finished with your homework yet?
3. The happy guests (busted, <u>burst</u>) into the dining room.
4. The patriot said, "I (done, <u>did</u>) my best for my country."
5. Her answer was (<u>drowned</u>, drownded) in catcalls.
6. My bicycle is (busted, <u>broken</u>) and can't be fixed.
7. You look like something the cat (drug, <u>dragged</u>) in.
8. The workers (done, <u>have done</u>) everything on our list.
9. It (ain't, <u>isn't</u>) right to drop pennies from tall buildings.
10. The weak swimmer almost (<u>drowned</u>, drownded) in the brutal current.

EXERCISE B: Avoiding Problems with Troublesome Verbs
6–10. For each of the following sentences, choose the correct verb from the choices in parentheses and write it on your paper.

1. Ms. Barker should (of, <u>have</u>) given us more time to finish that job.
2. When we left, we (lay, <u>laid</u>) a blanket over the antique chair to protect it.
3. I wish you would (learn, <u>teach</u>) me how to water-ski.
4. (Let, <u>Leave</u>) your brother alone!
5. (<u>Let</u>, Leave) him go!
6. My mother would have (went, <u>gone</u>) to college if she had had the money.
7. Children, (<u>lie</u>, lay) still until I call you.
8. I am going to (<u>teach</u>, learn) myself how to cook in a Chinese wok.
9. You should (of, <u>have</u>) seen your face when they called out your name.
10. They (<u>went</u>, gone) away without saying goodbye.

EXERCISE C: Avoiding Problems with Troublesome Verbs
11–15. For each of the following sentences, choose the correct

Developing Writing Skills

Have students practice using verbs correctly in writing by completing the following assignment.

Writing Across the Curriculum

Almost everyone who has ever gone to school has wondered at times "Why do I need to know this subject? I can't imagine ever using this information in everyday life!" Yet, all school subjects have practical applications to activities outside of school.

Prewriting Jot down a list of reasons why mathematics is an important subject to learn. What are the applications of mathematics to activities you or people you know perform outside of school? Add to your list any activities you can think of that involve math.

Writing Write the first draft of an article for the school newspaper that explains the importance of learning mathematics. Your topic sentence should state the idea that mathematics is important to learn. To support the main idea, provide examples of the uses of mathematics in everyday life. Restate your main idea in the concluding sentence.

Revising Make sure that you have expressed your opinion in the topic sentence of your article and that you have given good examples to support it. Look over the article to make sure that you have used verbs correctly; be especially careful when you check any troublesome verbs.

verb from the choices in parentheses and write it on your paper.

1. The beam isn't balanced; (rise, <u>raise</u>) your end a little bit.
2. We (set, <u>sat</u>) down to a delicious lobster dinner.
3. The space shot was the most spectacular thing I've ever (saw, <u>seen</u>).
4. He pointed to the carrot and (<u>said</u>, says), "Let's feed the rabbit."
5. Harriet and Shirley (snuck, <u>sneaked</u>) back to the wings of the theater.
6. He was proud that I (seen, <u>saw</u>) how well he did.
7. Then the witch smiled and (says, <u>said</u>), "Look, I'll take a bite of the apple myself."
8. "(Sit, <u>Set</u>) the bird cage in that corner, please."
9. Inflation occurs when prices (raise, <u>rise</u>).
10. Allen (snuck, <u>sneaked</u>) a look at his birthday presents.

DEVELOPING WRITING SKILLS: Using Troublesome Verbs Correctly. Write an original sentence for each of the following verbs.

Answers will vary; samples are given for the first two.

EXAMPLE: seen

      She has seen many changes in the past eighty years.

1. The balloon burst when it hit the branch.   2. What have you done with my keys?

1. burst	8. lie	15. let
2. done	9. went	16. set
3. dragged	10. leave	17. rise
4. drowned	11. raise	18. said
5. gone	12. sneaked	19. sit
6. did	13. lay	20. saw
7. have	14. teach	

Skills Review and Writing Workshop

Using Verbs
CHECKING YOUR SKILLS
Rewrite the following paragraph, correcting all errors in verb usage. Change the passive voice to active voice throughout.
Answers will vary.
(1) The sun raised and set yesterday, but in between were strange changes. (2) The day begun with the sun shining cheerfully. (3) Soon, however, thick gray clouds snuck in, and I gave up my biking plans. (4) Yet the wind continued to blow, and by noon the clouds were dispersed. (5) I stepped outside but instantly swinged back around into the house when I seen the black clouds piling up in the west. (6) They were being churned eastward by the wind, stronger now. (7) Soon a furious thunderstorm breaked and raged. (8) I laid back in a chair near a window and watched in wonder. (9) For three hours the storm shaked the world but then blowed on as rapidly as it had came. (10) The sun bursted forth again and by sunset had erased all sign of the storm.

USING USAGE SKILLS IN WRITING
Writing About Weather
Each day is unique, but a writer must carefully choose details and verbs to convey that uniqueness. Follow the steps below to create a paragraph describing the weather.
Answers will vary.
Prewriting: Choose a recent day that had a dominant weather pattern—sun, wind, rain, or something else. List the details that made this day different from similar days.

Writing: In the first sentence describe the overall weather pattern of the day you chose. Then use details to provide a word picture of what the day was really like.

Revising: First, check your verbs. Make sure they are all correct and specific. Then check for other improvements you can make. After you have revised proofread carefully.

Checking Your Skills
In the Checking Your Skills assignment, students have corrected errors in verb usage. Explain to students that using the correct verb tense is important because it expresses the time of the action.

Collaborative Learning
Divide the class into groups of roughly equal ability. Explain to the groups that they will be playing the game "Conjugate Your Verb." Choose one group to go first and give them a regular verb. Within a certain time limit, the group must work together to conjugate the verb. The group earns one point for correctly identifying the four principal parts of the verb, two points for conjugating the basic forms of the verb, and three points for conjugating the progressive forms of the verb. You must act as judge to decide how many points to award a group who has partially completed the conjugation or whose conjugation is partially correct. After groups have completed one or two rounds with regular verbs, have them try irregular verbs.

Using Usage Skills in Writing
Revising As students revise, you might want them to check that their descriptions convey a dominant weather pattern and that the descriptions explain why this particular day was different from similar days. They should also make sure that all the details in their descriptions contribute to the single, dominant impression they wish to convey.

CHAPTER 13
Using Pronouns
(pp. 232–244)

This chapter builds on Chapters 7 through 9, which discuss basic sentence parts, phrases, and clauses. Students cannot choose appropriate case forms of personal pronouns in Section 13.1 or interrogative and relative pronouns in Section 13.2 without knowing sentence structure and syntax. You therefore might want to study or review the relevant grammar chapters before teaching this chapter.

For a review of the entire chapter and a related writing activity, see the Skills Review and Writing Workshop on page 244.

13.1 Cases of Personal Pronouns
(pp. 232–239)

OBJECTIVES

After completing this section, students should be able to

- Identify the case of personal pronouns.
- Use pronouns in the nominative case correctly.
- Use pronouns in the objective case correctly.
- Use pronouns in the possessive case correctly.

Chapter 13

Using Pronouns

Some pronouns change form depending on use. For example, in "I hit the ball," the pronoun *I* is a subject. But in "The ball hit me," *I* changes to *me* to show that the pronoun is now a direct object. The relation between a pronoun's form and its use is known as *case*.

This chapter will show you how to use the forms of pronouns correctly.

13.1 Cases of Personal Pronouns

The personal pronouns listed in Section 1.2 are arranged in three groups. Pronouns in the first group refer to the person speaking; those in the second group refer to the person spoken to; and those in the third to the person, place, or thing spoken about. Pronouns can also be grouped according to their *cases*.

English has three cases: *nominative, objective,* and *possessive*.

Three Cases

The chart on the following page shows the personal pronouns grouped according to the three cases.

232

13.1 Cases of Personal Pronouns

THE THREE CASES OF PERSONAL PRONOUNS

Nominative Case	Use in Sentence
I, we you he, she, it, they	Subject of a Verb Predicate Pronoun

Objective Case	Use in Sentence
me, us you him, her, it, them	Direct Object Indirect Object Object of a Preposition

Possessive Case	Use in Sentence
my, mine, our, ours your, yours his, her, hers, its, their, theirs	To Show Ownership

EXERCISE A: Identifying Case. On your paper identify the case of the personal pronouns that are underlined in the following sentences.

EXAMPLE   Melvin left the theater without <u>us</u>.

objective

1. <u>His</u> photograph was awarded second prize. poss
2. Frances wrote <u>me</u> about the party for Vickie. obj
3. The first actors onstage will be <u>he</u> and <u>I</u>. nom
4. The collie caught the Frisbee and ran away with <u>it</u>. obj
5. Laurent and <u>I</u> haven't finished the kite yet. nom
6. As soon as the lights came on, Rennie saw <u>them</u>. obj
7. Uncle Norman forgave <u>us</u> for playing that band's music. obj
8. According to <u>your</u> count, how many people came to the second performance? poss
9. Unfortunately, <u>he</u> was the last person to leave the house. nom
10. Don't tell <u>me</u> any more bad news. obj

233

TEACHING
Getting Started

Students will draw from their knowledge about sentence parts, structure, and syntax as they complete exercises in this section. They should have already studied Chapters 7–9, or you may wish to review those chapters before teaching this material.

Start off by explaining that personal pronouns can be divided into three groups, or *cases*; each case is used for a particular set of jobs in the sentence. Have students list all the personal pronouns they can that can be used in this sentence: _____ *enjoyed the party.* (A master list may be placed on the board.) Tell students that this group forms the *nominative case*—pronouns that serve as subjects and predicate pronouns.

Students may generate the list for the *objective* and *possessive* cases in a similar fashion, using the following sentences as a test for usability:

Mark gave _____ 50 cents.
This is _____ book; *and* that book is _____ .

Text Follow Through

Discuss text pages 232–239.

Assign Exercise A, page 233; Exercise B, page 235; Exercise C, page 236; Exercise D, page 238; Exercise E, page 238; and Developing Writing Skills, page 239.

Less advanced Correct use of pronoun cases is as much a matter of hearing the correct use as of practicing the writing of it. Have students read aloud as many exercise sentences as possible, and do plenty of example sentences on the board. To simplify terminology, you could refer to the nominative case as the subject form, and to the objective case as the object form.

You may also find it helpful to delay Exercise A until students have completed the other exercises.

Average Students can rewrite the sentences in Exercise A, using other personal pronouns in place of those that are underlined. To provide extra practice, divide the class into two teams; one taking the nominative case and the other the objective case. Each team member who makes up a sentence that contains a pronoun used correctly in his or her team's case gains one point for the team. Give two points for sentences demonstrating the pronoun used correctly in a compound subject or object.

Advanced Students might write additional sentences using pronouns listed in Developing Writing Skills but changing the sentence part called for wherever possible.

You might also have students write sentences with the pronouns described in the following list:

1. Nominative case as subject of verb
2. Nominative case as predicate pronoun
3. Objective case as direct object
4. Objective case as object of a preposition
5. Possessive case to show ownership

The Nominative Case

Personal pronouns in the *nominative case* have two uses.

Use the nominative case (1) for the subject of a verb and (2) for a predicate pronoun.

In the following examples, note that all of the predicate pronouns follow linking verbs.

SUBJECTS: *I* build model sailboats.

She hopes to become a surgeon.

With great glee *they* are planning a surprise party.

PREDICATE PRONOUNS: It was *I* who suggested a picnic.

$\overset{LV}{\text{The best dancers are}}$ *we* and *they*.

People seldom forget to use the nominative case for a pronoun that is used by itself as a subject. Problems sometimes arise, however, when the pronoun is part of a compound subject.

INCORRECT: John and *me* build model sailboats.

To make sure you are using the correct case of the pronoun in a compound subject, use just the pronoun with the verb in the sentence. Trying this test in the preceding example, you would see that "Me build" is obviously wrong. The nominative case *I* should be used instead.

CORRECT: John and *I* build model sailboats.

You should also note that in speaking and in casual writing people often use the objective case for any personal pronoun after a linking verb. In formal writing, however, you should still use the nominative case.

INFORMAL: "Who is it?" "It's *me*."

FORMAL: The organizers of the dance were Maria, Juan, and *I*.

Additional Practice
Practice Pages or Practice
Book, pages 77–79

Less advanced Exercise Bank,
Exercises A and B, pages
113–116

Average Exercise Bank, Exercises A, B, and C, pages
113–116

Advanced Exercise Bank, Exercises B and C, pages 113–116

13.1 Cases of Personal Pronouns

EXERCISE B: Using Pronouns in the Nominative Case.
Complete each of the following sentences by writing a nominative pronoun on your paper. Then tell how each pronoun is used in the sentence.

Pronouns may vary; samples are given.

EXAMPLE: Without question _____ had to care for the pony herself.

she   subject

1. After losing the match, __we__ boarded a bus and drove silently out of town. S
2. Georgina and __he__ both wanted something more extravagant. S
3. The winner of the first prize for the best essay would obviously be __she__ . pred pron
4. Only __he__ knows the spot where the best mushrooms grow. S
5. __They__ are sanding an old oak desk for the room we use to study in. S
6. Doris always answered the telephone very formally by saying, "It is __I__ ." pred pron
7. When the airport came into view, __we__ began to talk excitedly. S
8. The first person in line to buy tickets to the concert was __he__ . pred pron
9. In addition to that old letter, __we__ found two high-buttoned shoes. S
10. Unfortunately, __I__ can't possibly finish the job by tomorrow morning. S

The Objective Case

Personal pronouns in the *objective case* have three uses.

Use the objective case (1) for a direct object, (2) for an indirect object, and (3) for the object of a preposition.

TESTING
Test Program

Unit Pretest, page 42
Chapter Test, page 47
Unit Post-Test, page 54

RE-TEACHING
Practice Pages or Practice
Book, pages 77–79

THINKING SKILLS
Knowledge—*Identifying* the
case of personal pronouns
(Exercise A, page 233)

Application—*Using* pronouns in
the nominative case (Exercise
B, page 235)
Using pronouns in the objective case (Exercise C, page
236)
Using pronouns in the possessive case (Exercise D,
page 238)

Synthesis—*Revising* sentences
to use pronoun case correctly
(Exercise E, page 238)
Writing sentences using pronouns as specified sentence
parts (Developing Writing
Skills, page 239)

DIRECT OBJECTS: Frank's comment upset *me*.

Luis saw *us* in the library.

INDIRECT OBJECTS: Tell *her* the good news.

I sent *them* a postcard from Santa Barbara.

OBJECTS OF PREPOSITIONS: Take the packages from *them*.

The wasps swarmed around *me*.

Mistakes usually occur only when the object is compound.

INCORRECT: Frank's comment upset Kathy and *I*.

Tell Dorothy and *she* the good news.

The wasps swarmed around Lucy and *I*.

Again, to test whether the case of a pronoun is correct, use the pronoun by itself after the verb or preposition. In the preceding examples, "upset I," "Tell she," and "around I" all sound wrong. Objective pronouns are needed.

CORRECT: Frank's comment upset Kathy and *me*.

Tell Dorothy and *her* the good news.

The wasps swarmed around Lucy and *me*.

EXERCISE C: Using Pronouns in the Objective Case. Complete each of the following sentences by writing an objective pronoun on your paper. Then tell how each pronoun is used in the sentence.

Pronouns may vary; samples are given.

EXAMPLE: His grandmother's stories gave _____ ideas that he later used in his writing.

him   indirect object

1. Rain or shine, Ellen always brought happiness with ___her___ . obj of prep

2. Henry visited __us__ on his trip out West. DO

3. Please tell __me__ your problems. IO

13.1 Cases of Personal Pronouns

4. In the 1000-meter run, Jonathan timed __them__ with a stopwatch. DO
5. Richard dedicated his book to __her__ . obj of prep
6. The weather gives __us__ very little opportunity for swimming. IO
7. Caroline sent Max and __me__ a message about the change in plans. IO
8. Beth ran behind __him__ and hid the present. obj of prep
9. Jerry should show __them__ his prize lamb. IO
10. We left __him__ at home with the baby. DO

The Possessive Case

Personal pronouns in the *possessive case* all show ownership of one sort or another.

Use the possessive case of personal pronouns before nouns to show possession. In addition, recognize that certain personal pronouns may be used by themselves to indicate possession.

BEFORE NOUNS: The kitten licked *its* paws.

Chris held *my* hand.

BY THEMSELVES: Is this book *yours* or *mine?*

Hers was the best composition.

Personal pronouns in the possessive case are never written with an apostrophe. Keep this in mind especially with possessive pronouns that end in -*s.*

INCORRECT: Did you see *his'* new bicycle?

These seats are *our's,* not *their's.*

CORRECT: Did you see *his* new bicycle?

These seats are *ours,* not *theirs.*

When the pronoun *it* ends with an apostrophe and an -*s*, it is not a possessive pronoun but a contraction meaning *it is.*

CONTRACTION: *It's* going to rain.

POSSESSIVE PRONOUN: The parakeet feels safe in *its* cage.

EXERCISE D: Using Pronouns in the Possessive Case.
For each of the following sentences, choose the correct word from the choices in parentheses and write it on your paper.

EXAMPLE: Fortunately, the sinking boat was not (our's, ours).

　　　　　　ours

1. (His, His') exceptional voice brought Len to the conductor's attention.
2. The chimpanzee and (it's, its) master go for a walk in the park each afternoon.
3. I will never understand (you, your) joy in working on a stamp collection.
4. The bicycles were (theirs, their's).
5. (My, Me) last letter to him was ten pages long.
6. You may use this room while (your's, yours) is being painted.
7. The album was clearly (hers, her's).
8. The bird was so friendly that (its, it's) chirps ceased to irritate us.
9. George grabbed the pie and yelled, "(Its, It's) mine!"
10. Fred now felt he could call the house of his host (his', his) own.

EXERCISE E: Checking the Case of Personal Pronouns.
Some of the underlined pronouns in the following sentences are incorrect. On your paper identify each error and supply the correct form of the pronoun. For sentences without any errors, write *correct.*
Incorrect pronouns are shaded.

EXAMPLE: I sent invitations to Jeremy and he.

　　　　　　he　　him

1. The lion in the center ring kept looking at her and me. C

13.2 Cases of *Who* and *Whom*

2. Donald gave no real reason for leaving his' suitcase in the station. his
3. This room and it's furnishings were designed by my uncle's firm. its
4. He will probably decide to sit between you and I at the concert. me
5. The flowers wilting in the heat are theirs. C
6. The person on the other end of the line was him. he
7. Harry, Jessie, and me worked all afternoon. I
8. We will never forget the way that you told that joke. C
9. The students finally chosen were they and us. we
10. These books used to be Regina's, but now they are your's. yours

DEVELOPING WRITING SKILLS: Using Pronouns Correctly. Use each of the following pronouns in a sentence of your own according to the instructions in parentheses.

Answers will vary; samples are given for the first two.

EXAMPLE: her   (as the object of a preposition)

They left for the fair grounds without her.

1. The debate between us and them lasted for hours.
   1. us and them   (with a preposition)
   2. he and I   (as predicate pronouns)
   3. its   (to show possession)
   4. your   (to show possession)
   5. her   (as an indirect object)
   6. him   (as a direct object)
   7. hers   (to show possession)
   8. you and I   (as a subject)
   9. it's   (to mean *it is*)
   10. his   (to show possession)
2. The people for the job are he and I.

Cases of *Who* and *Whom* 13.2

The pronouns *who* and *whom* have two common uses in sentences. They can be used in questions, and they can be used to begin subordinate clauses in complex sentences.

OBJECTIVE

After completing this section, students should be able to

• Use *who* and *whom* correctly in sentences.

TEACHING

Getting Started

You may want to review *clauses* and *subordinate clauses* briefly with the class before beginning this section.

Write the following on the board:

_____ opened the window?
_____ did you write about?

Ask students to determine what sentence part is needed to fill each blank. If students have difficulty seeing that the second sentence needs an object of the preposition, rewrite it as: *You did write about _____?* Next explain to students that the pronouns *who* and *whom* also have case. Ask which students would use to fill in each blank. Elicit that *who* must be in the nominative case; *whom* in the objective.

Text Follow Through

Discuss text pages 239–243.

Assign Exercise A, page 242; Exercise B, page 242; and Developing Writing Skills, page 243.

Less advanced You may want to duplicate separate sets of sentences, one set requiring *who* and the other set requiring *whom*. Have students fill in the blank with the appropriate pronoun and then label the subject, verb, direct object, object of the preposition, and indirect object, if present, in each sentence.

Questions	Complex Sentences
Who is knocking at the door?	I don't know the person *who* is knocking at the door.
Whom did you invite to your party?	One guest *whom* you invited will not be able to attend.

Separate Uses in Sentences

Many people have problems deciding when it is correct to use *whom* instead of *who*. Like personal pronouns *who* and *whom* indicate case. *Who* is nominative; *whom* is objective.

The Nominative Case: Who. Just like the nominative personal pronouns, such as *I* or *she, who* is used as a subject.

Use *who* for the subject of a verb.

You will often find the word *who* used as the subject of a question.

SUBJECT IN A QUESTION: *Who* hit the most home runs?

Who may also be used as the subject of a subordinate clause in a complex sentence.

SUBJECT IN A SUBORDINATE CLAUSE: I admire the player *who* hit the most home runs.

In the example *who* is part of an adjective clause: *who hit the most home runs.* Within the clause itself, *who* is the subject of the verb *hit.*

The Objective Case: *Whom.* The uses of *whom* are similar to those of the objective personal pronouns, such as *me* or *him.*

Use whom (1) for the direct object of a verb and (2) for the object of a preposition.

13.2 Cases of *Who* and *Whom*

The following examples show *whom* used in questions.

DIRECT OBJECT: *Whom* did he meet at the movies?

OBJECT OF PREPOSITION: From *whom* did she receive the flowers?

Whom were you talking about?

Questions that include the word *whom* will generally be in inverted word order. If you reword the first example so that it follows normal word order, you will see that *whom* is the direct object of the verb *did meet: he did meet whom at the movies.* In the second example, it is easy to see that *whom* is the object of a preposition because it comes right after the preposition *from.* In the last sentence, *whom* is separated from its preposition *about.* Again, rewording may help: *you were talking about whom.* Rewording is also useful when *whom* is part of a subordinate clause.

DIRECT OBJECT: I wonder about the person *whom* he met at the movies.

OBJECT OF PREPOSITION: Janet thanked her aunt, from *whom* she had received a bracelet.

A subordinate clause that should begin with *whom* will always be in inverted word order. To check whether you have used the correct case of the pronoun, isolate the clause and put it in normal word order. In the first of the preceding examples, the subordinate clause is *whom he met at the movies.* In normal word order, the clause would be *he met whom at the movies.* The objective pronoun *whom* is a direct object.

In the second example, the subordinate clause is *from whom she had received a bracelet.* You can probably guess that *whom* is the object of a preposition since it follows *from.* In normal word order, the clause would be *she had received a bracelet from whom. Whom* is the object of the preposition *from.*

Average If students need further practice with this material, you can duplicate the following sentences from Section 1.3, omitting the interrogative and relative pronouns:

Exercise B: Sentences 1, 3, 5, 8, 9

Exercise C: Sentences 2, 6, 7, 9, 10

Advanced Students can write questions and complex sentences using both *who* and *whom*. They can then exchange sentences and identify the functions of the pronouns in each other's sentences.

Additional Practice

Practice Pages or Practice Book, page 80

Less advanced Exercise Bank, Exercises A and B, page 117

Average Exercise Bank, Exercises A, B, and C, page 117

Advanced Exercise Bank, Exercises B and C, page 117

TESTING

Test Program

   Unit Pretest, page 42
   Chapter Test, page 47
   Unit Post-Test, page 54

RE-TEACHING

Practice Pages or Practice Book, page 80

THINKING SKILLS

Comprehension—*Distinguishing* between *who* and *whom* in sentences (Exercise A, page 242)

Distinguishing the way *who* and *whom* are used in subordinate clauses (Exercise B, page 242)

Synthesis—*Writing* sentences with *who* and *whom* (Developing Writing Skills, page 243)

EXERCISE A: Using *Who* and *Whom* in Questions. For each of the following sentences, choose the correct pronoun from the choices given in parentheses and write it on your paper.

EXAMPLE: (Who, Whom) did you ask to the party?

　　　　　　Whom

1. To (who, <u>whom</u>) were you just speaking?
2. (<u>Who</u>, Whom) among us has met a famous person?
3. This article was written by (who, <u>whom</u>)?
4. (Who, <u>Whom</u>) were you helping in the cafeteria the other day?
5. Of the two, (<u>who</u>, whom) is more capable?
6. (<u>Who</u>, Whom) is your favorite singer?
7. (<u>Who</u>, Whom) wouldn't know you, even in that disguise?
8. (Who, <u>Whom</u>) did she leave with the children?
9. For (who, <u>whom</u>) should I ask at the Governor's office?
10. (<u>Who</u>, Whom) in this group could be at the theater by seven o'clock?

EXERCISE B: Using *Who* and *Whom* in Subordinate Clauses. On your paper, write the subordinate clause in each of the following sentences. Then indicate the way in which *who* or *whom* is being used in the subordinate clause.
Subordinate clauses are underlined.
EXAMPLE: What is the name of the person who is calling?

　　　　　　who is calling   subject

1. My sister Emily, <u>for whom I wrote this poem</u>, is hiding in the maple tree. obj of prep
2. I know the singer <u>who performed at your party</u>. S
3. I can introduce you to Walter, <u>whom you have been admiring from afar</u>. DO
4. We were eager to meet the woman <u>who will be our candidate.</u>
5. Guess the name of the person <u>who told me that</u>. S

13.2 Cases of *Who* and *Whom*

6. Give it to the person <u>whom you place the most trust in</u>. <small>obj of prep</small>
7. Guess what happened to the man <u>whom we met in the lobby at intermission</u>. <small>DO</small>
8. Gil is one person <u>whom I have absolute confidence in</u>. <small>obj of prep</small>
9. Please don't invite the person <u>who spilled the coffee last time</u>. <small>S</small>
10. I asked Jim to tell me the name of the person <u>who wrote the limerick</u>. <small>S</small>

DEVELOPING WRITING SKILLS: Writing Sentences with *Who* and *Whom*. Write five original sentences, each using *who* or *whom* according to the instructions given in parentheses.

<small>Answers will vary; sample is given for the first one.</small>

EXAMPLE: who (as subject in a subordinate clause)

> I spoke to the person who wanted information about tidal waves.

1. who (as subject in a question)
2. whom (as direct object in a question)
3. who (as subject in a subordinate clause)
4. whom (as direct object in a subordinate clause)
5. whom (as object of a preposition in a subordinate clause)

<small>1. Who lives here?</small>

Checking Your Skills

In the Checking Your Skills assignment, students have corrected errors in pronoun usage. Tell students that the following speaking and listening activity will provide them with additional practice.

Speaking and Listening

Tell the class that they will be playing the game "Know Your Pronouns." Divide the class into two groups of roughly equal ability. Each group should select ten sentences from literature that include one or more personal pronouns. In about one half of the sentences, students should substitute incorrect forms of the pronouns. The pronouns should be left in their correct form in the other sentences. Have one group read one of their sentences aloud to the other group. The other group must decide whether the pronouns in the sentence are used correctly or incorrectly. If their answer is correct, the group receives one point. They can receive a bonus point if they can supply the correct form of a pronoun that is incorrect. The group that reads the sentence receives a point if the other group's answer is incorrect.

Using Usage Skills in Writing

Prewriting Students might prefer to free write about the event. Instruct them to write down anything concerning the event that comes into their thoughts, whether it is appropriate or not. They can then go back and select those thoughts that are applicable for their journal entries.

Skills Review and Writing Workshop

Using Pronouns

CHECKING YOUR SKILLS

Rewrite the following paragraph, correcting all errors in pronoun usage.

Answers will vary.

(1) On the second essay Mr. Warner gave Gail and I top scores. (2) That was a surprise for Jason, who teachers ordinarily find no fault with. (3) The whole class, in fact, thought it would be him who would lead. (4) His work, after all, is usually held up as a model for we. (5) Perhaps Gail and me had really worked hard, while Jason is one of those people who simply assumed their excellence. (6) Jason, like those whom take things for granted, really hadn't tried his hardest. (7) The teacher, at any rate, saw something in the work of Gail and I that he didn't see in Jason's. (8) He told the class that it was us who showed the most thought. (9) I watched Jason reread his paper; later he asked to read ours'. (10) "Whom will Mr. Warner rank highest next time?" he asked, determination in his voice.

USING USAGE SKILLS IN WRITING
Writing a Journal Entry

Writers often use journals to explore themselves and their feelings. Follow the steps below to write a journal entry.

Answers will vary.

Prewriting: Think of a time when you learned something about yourself. Jot down the details of the event, and consider exactly what led to the self-knowledge.

Writing: Describe the event, stressing what happened to you. Lead up to a statement about the knowledge you gained from the experience.

Revising: First, look at your pronouns to make sure they are all correct. Then check for other improvements you can make. After you have revised, proofread carefully.

Sections 14.1 and 14.2 deal with subjects and verbs: Section 14.1 discusses agreement between subjects and verbs, and Section 14.2 considers special problems with subject-verb agreement. Section 14.3 covers agreement between pronouns and antecedents.

For a review of the entire chapter and a related writing activity, see the Skills Review and Writing Workshop on page 266.

Chapter # 14

Making Words Agree

Subjects and verbs work together in sentences. For example, you would never say, *"I are* the first in line," or *"Am you going* to the party?" You would hear that something is wrong with these sentences. The problem is that the subjects and verbs do not *agree*.

In most of the sentences you speak and write, you automatically make subjects and verbs agree. In some sentences, however, the mind can be tricked into making the verb agree with a word that is not the subject of the sentence. In such a case, check to find the real subject and make sure it agrees with its verb.

Pronouns too must agree with the words they stand for. This chapter will explain the importance of agreement and will give you practice making the parts of sentences work together.

Agreement Between Subjects 14.1 and Verbs

14.1 Agreement Between Subjects and Verbs
(pp. 245–254)

Subject and verb *agreement* has one main rule.

A subject must agree with its verb in number.

OBJECTIVES

After studying this section, students should be able to

- Identify the number of nouns and pronouns.
- Identify the number of verbs.
- Make verbs agree with singular and plural subjects.
- Make verbs agree with compound subjects.

TEACHING

Getting Started

Students need familiarity with the terms *number* and *agreement* as well as *singular* and *plural*. The concept of number in verbs is somewhat trickier than that in subjects. Have students turn to page 247 and study the chart. Elicit that singular verbs differ from singular nouns in that -s or -es added to a verb makes it singular. Students can test this themselves by substituting various verbs in sentences such as the following:

He *motions* to us.
They *motion* to us.
She *sings* beautifully.
We *sing* pretty well.

Text Follow Through

Discuss text pages 245–254.

Assign Exercise A, page 246; Exercise B, page 248; Exercise C, page 249; Exercise D, page 252; Exercise E, page 252; Exercise F, page 253; and Developing Writing Skills, page 254.

Less advanced In Exercise A you may wish to ask students to give the number of the nouns and personal pronouns only. The indefinite pronouns in the list (3, 6, 18, 20) may pose problems at this time; they will be

---

In grammar the concept of *number* is simple. The number of a word can be either *singular* or *plural*. A singular word indicates *one*. A plural word indicates *more than one*. Only nouns, pronouns, and verbs have number.

The Number of Nouns and Pronouns

The difference between the singular and plural forms of most nouns and pronouns is easy to recognize. Compare the singular and plural forms of the nouns below.

NOUNS	
Singular	**Plural**
girl	girls
bus	buses
child	children
goose	geese

Most nouns are made plural by adding -s or -es to the singular form (girl*s*, bus*es*). Some nouns become plural in other ways (child*ren*, g*ee*se). (See Section 34.2 for more information about making nouns plural.)

Sections 1.2 and 1.3 listed the singular and plural forms of the various kinds of pronouns. For example, *I, he, she, it, this,* and *anyone* are singular; *we, they, these,* and *both* are plural; and *you, who,* and *some* can be either singular or plural.

Being able to recognize the number of nouns and pronouns will help you to determine whether a subject is singular or plural.

EXERCISE A: Recognizing the Number of Nouns and Pronouns. On your paper indicate whether each of the following words is *singular* or *plural*.

EXAMPLE: mice   plural

treated separately in Section 14.2. Inability to identify subjects correctly may cause students trouble in Exercises C and E. Show example sentences for practice in locating subjects followed by prepositional phrases. Ask students to underline the subject once, circle the prepositional phrase, and select the appropriate verb to fill in the blank in sentences such as this one: *The sandwiches on the counter (is/are) for us.*

Average While students complete Exercises C through E, provide oral reinforcement by having students read the completed sentences aloud. Those students who have difficulty distinguishing subjects when prepositional phrases follow them can practice writing sentences in which they place brackets around the prepositional phrases. You could supply a list of phrases on the board for students to use in their sentences.

Advanced You may want to use Exercise F (page 253) as a diagnostic test to see which subsections students need to learn or review.

Additional Practice
Practice Pages or Practice Book, pages 81–83
Less advanced Exercise Bank, Exercises A and B, pages 118–121
Average Exercise Bank, Exercises A, B, and C, pages 118–121
Advanced Exercise Bank, Exercises B and C, pages 118–121

14.1 Agreement Between Subjects and Verbs

1. I sing
2. it sing
3. gas sing
4. we pl
5. they pl
6. others pl
7. bees pl
8. boxes pl
9. bird sing
10. mess sing
11. mouse sing
12. both pl
13. roses pl
14. each sing
15. those pl
16. houses pl
17. player sing
18. someone
19. women pl
20. friendship

18. sing 20. sing

The Number of Verbs

As shown in the conjugations in Sections 12.2 and 12.3, verbs have many forms to indicate tense. Few of these forms cause problems in agreement because most of them can be used with either singular or plural subjects (I *go*, we *go;* he *ran,* they *ran*). Problems involving the number of verbs usually occur only with third-person forms in the present tense and with forms of *be.*

The following chart shows all of the basic forms of two different verbs—*send* and *go*—in the present tense.

SINGULAR AND PLURAL VERBS IN THE PRESENT TENSE		
Singular		**Plural**
First and Second Person	**Third Person**	**First, Second, and Third Person**
(I, you) send	(he, she, it) send*s*	(we, you, they) send
(I, you) go	(he, she, it) go*es*	(we, you, they) go

Notice that the verb form changes only in the third-person singular column, where an *-s* or *-es* is added to the verb. Unlike nouns, which usually become *plural* when *-s* or *-es* is added, verbs with *-s* or *-es* added to them are singular.

The helping verb *be* may also indicate whether a verb is singular or plural. The chart on the following page shows only those forms of the verb *be* that are always singular.

TESTING

Test Program

Unit Pretest, page 43
Chapter Test, page 48
Unit Post-Test, page 55

RE-TEACHING

Practice Pages or Practice
Book, pages 81–83

THINKING SKILLS

Knowledge—*Identifying* the
number of nouns and pro-
nouns (Exercise A, page 246)

Comprehension—*Distinguishing*
between singular and plural
verbs to agree in number with
their subjects (Exercise B,
page 248; Exercise C, page
249; Exercise F, page 253)
Distinguishing between
singular and plural verbs to
agree with compound subjects
joined by *or, nor,* or *and*
(Exercises D and E, page 252)

Synthesis—*Writing* sentences
with verbs that agree in
number with singular, plural,
and compound subjects (Developing Writing Skills, page
254)

FORMS OF THE HELPING VERB *BE* THAT ARE ALWAYS SINGULAR

am	is	was	has been

EXERCISE B: Recognizing the Number of Verbs. For each of the following items, choose the verb from the choices in parentheses that agrees in number with the pronoun. After each answer write whether the verb is singular or plural.

EXAMPLE: he (begin, begins)

begins   singular

1. we (knows, <u>know</u>) pl
2. they (was, <u>were</u>) pl
3. she (<u>knows</u>, know) sing
4. I (is, <u>am</u>) sing
5. he (were, <u>was</u>) sing
10. pl
6. we (is, <u>are</u>) pl
7. they (<u>have</u>, has) pl
8. it (<u>was</u>, were) sing
9. she (have, <u>has</u>) sing
10. we (argues, <u>argue</u>)

Agreement with Singular and Plural Subjects

To check the agreement between a subject and a verb, begin by determining the number of the subject. Then make sure the verb has the same number.

A singular subject must have a singular verb.
A plural subject must have a plural verb.

In the following examples, the subjects are underlined once and the verbs twice.

SINGULAR SUBJECT AND VERB: <u>Larry</u> never <u>arrives</u> on time.

<u>She</u> <u>is</u> happy about her grade.

According to the announcement,
the <u>plane</u> <u>is preparing</u> to land.

14.1 Agreement Between Subjects and Verbs

PLURAL SUBJECT AND VERB: Those <u>boys</u> in my Spanish class never <u>arrive</u> on time.

According to the announcements, both <u>planes</u> <u>are preparing</u> to land.

In the preceding examples, the subjects stand next to or near their verbs. Often, however, a subject is separated from its verb by a prepositional phrase. In these cases it is important to remember that the object of a preposition is never the subject of a sentence.

A prepositional phrase that comes between a subject and its verb does *not* affect subject-verb agreement.

In the following examples, the correct subject is *poster;* the word *coins* is the object of the preposition *of.* Since *poster* is singular, it cannot agree with the plural verb *show.*

INCORRECT: This <u>poster</u> of the ancient coins <u>show</u> the portraits of all the Roman emperors.

CORRECT: This <u>poster</u> of ancient coins <u>shows</u> the portraits of all the Roman emperors.

EXERCISE C: Making Verbs Agree with Singular and Plural Subjects. For each of the following sentences, choose the correct verb of the two shown in parentheses and write it on your paper.

EXAMPLE: The books on the shelf (was, were) dogeared.

        were

1. The wind always (<u>makes</u>, make) the screen door rattle during the summer.
2. The keys to our house (is, <u>are</u>) on a ring just inside the garage.
3. The geese (migrates, <u>migrate</u>) north every year at this time.
4. My friends never (knows, <u>know</u>) what I will do next.

5. A famous painting of those trees and windmills (<u>hangs</u>, hang) in the art museum.
6. The parents of my best friend (has, <u>have</u>) invited me to the ballet.
7. The silence (<u>was</u>, were) deafening after the prosecution rested its case.
8. The secret of her many successes (<u>lies</u>, lie) in her diligence.
9. Red roses on a white wooden trellis (blooms, <u>bloom</u>) in my aunt's lovely garden.
10. The child with two sets of grandparents (<u>enjoys</u>, enjoy) the attention of many doting adults.

Agreement with Compound Subjects

A compound subject is two or more subjects that are joined by a conjunction, usually *or* or *and*. (See Section 7.3 for information about finding compound subjects in sentences.) A number of different rules govern the way in which verbs must agree with compound subjects.

Two or more singular subjects joined by *or* or *nor* must have a singular verb.

In the following example, the conjunction *or* joins two singular subjects. Although two names make up the compound subject, it does not take a plural verb. Either Alice or Mike will help, not both.

EXAMPLE: Either <u>Alice</u> or <u>Mike</u> <u>is going</u> to help us.

Problems often occur when the parts of a compound subject joined by *or* or *nor* are mixed in number.

When singular and plural subjects are joined by *or* or *nor,* the verb must agree with the closest subject.

In the following examples, notice how the verb depends on the subject that is closer to it.

14.1 Agreement Between Subjects and Verbs

SINGULAR SUBJECT CLOSER: Neither the <u>students</u> nor their home economics <u>teacher</u> <u>is waiting</u> for the two of us in the school auditorium.

PLURAL SUBJECT CLOSER: Neither the home economics <u>teacher</u> nor the <u>students</u> <u>are waiting</u> for the two of us in the school auditorium.

Compound subjects joined by *and* create still another situation for you to consider when you decide whether to use a singular or a plural verb.

A compound subject joined by *and* is usually plural and must have a plural verb.

And usually acts as a plus sign. Whether the parts of the compound subject are all singular, all plural, or are mixed in number, they usually add up to a subject that calls for a plural verb.

EXAMPLES: The <u>cup</u> and the <u>glass</u> <u>are</u> broken.

The <u>cups</u> and <u>glasses</u> <u>are</u> broken.

Three <u>cups</u> and one <u>glass</u> <u>are</u> broken.

This rule has two exceptions. If the parts of the compound subject are thought of as a single thing, then the compound subject is considered singular and must have a singular verb. The other exception involves the words *every* and *each*. Either of these words used before a compound subject in a sentence indicates the need for a singular verb in that sentence. Read the following examples carefully. They show all of these exceptions.

EXAMPLES: <u>Cucumbers</u> and <u>yogurt</u> <u>is</u> a popular Middle Eastern dish. (Cucumbers + yogurt = one dish)

Every <u>cup</u> and <u>glass</u> <u>is</u> broken.

Each <u>cup</u> and <u>glass</u> <u>is</u> broken.

EXERCISE D: Making Verbs Agree with Compound Subjects Joined by *Or* and *Nor*. For each of the following sentences, choose the correct verb from the choices in parentheses and write it on your paper.

EXAMPLE: Neither the soup nor the salad (was, were) ready.

   was

1. Either Mary or John (is, are) going in my place.
2. Neither Kate nor her parents (has, have) ever met anyone as eccentric as Ace.
3. Bread or fruit always (goes, go) well with cheese.
4. Neither the nails nor the hammer (was, were) there.
5. Either Joanna or Howard (takes, take) the children to school each day.
6. Neither the hat on that shelf nor the scarves on this one (belongs, belong) in a shop like yours.
7. Either the kittens or the dachshund (has, have) frightened the baby.
8. Fred or his brothers (watches, watch) the store at lunchtime.
9. Neither Emily nor Marian (knows, know) how to get to the library.
10. I suspect that either the maids or the butler (is, are) not telling the inspector the whole truth.

EXERCISE E: Making Verbs Agree with Compound Subjects Joined by *And*. For each of the following sentences, choose the correct verb from the choices in parentheses and write it on your paper.

EXAMPLE: Every knife and fork in the house (has, have) disappeared.

   has

1. Clocks and sundials (measures, measure) time.
2. Cake and pie (is, are) Murray's favorite desserts.

14.1 Agreement Between Subjects and Verbs

3. The gingham dog and the calico cat (does, <u>do</u>) not get along with each other.
4. The decorations and the centerpiece (was, <u>were</u>) beautiful.
5. Every book and record in this library (<u>shows</u>, show) signs of wear.
6. On this issue Congress and the President (finds, <u>find</u>) the present law to be inadequate.
7. Macaroni and cheese (<u>was</u>, were) served last night.
8. Each sheet and pillowcase in our hotel (<u>is</u>, are) freshly laundered every day.
9. Every student and teacher in this school (<u>knows</u>, know) what must be done to improve class attendance.
10. The horse and the mule (was, <u>were</u>) once the major means of transportation in this country.

EXERCISE F: Recognizing Subjects and Verbs That Agree. For each of the following sentences, choose the correct verb from the choices in parentheses and write it on your paper.

EXAMPLE: Either Elizabeth Blackwell or Amelia Earhart (is, are) the subject of her report.

is

1. Marcy and Julio (is, <u>are</u>) directing the class play.
2. Because of the wind, the doors in the deserted house next to the cemetery (creaks, <u>creak</u>) open and shut all night long.
3. Either Vanessa or Robert (<u>has</u>, have) enough votes to win the election.
4. To decorators a combination of red and green (<u>represents</u>, represent) Christmas.
5. Every cat and dog (<u>was</u>, were) adorned with a large ribbon.
6. Neither the walls nor the floor of your room (looks, <u>look</u>) very clean.
7. Spaghetti and meatballs (<u>is</u>, are) a popular dinner.

8. Each television and radio in the store (<u>was</u>, were) tuned to a different station.
9. Either my mother or my brothers (cleans, <u>clean</u>) the fish we catch.
10. The mice in our attic (scampers, <u>scamper</u>) when we sleep.

DEVELOPING WRITING SKILLS: Writing Sentences with Singular, Plural, and Compound Subjects. Using the list of subjects below, write ten sentences of your own. Choose one of the following verb forms for each sentence: (a) a form of *be*, (b) *has* or *have*, and (c) the present tense forms of verbs. Underline the subject(s) once and the verb(s) twice.

Answers will vary.

EXAMPLES: Three of them

               Either Rodney or Carl

               <u>Three</u> of them <u>are eating</u> here every Monday.

               Either <u>Rodney</u> or <u>Carl</u> <u>has</u> to write your campaign speech.

1. the dolphins in the story
2. ham and cheese
3. both the chairperson and the secretary of the company
4. neither the tennis coach nor the players
5. neither the players nor the tennis coach
6. she or they
7. he and I
8. pictures of the foggy swamp
9. Melanie or Sophia
10. every parent and child in the audience

14.2 Special Problems with Subject-Verb Agreement

(pp. 254–259)

14.2 Special Problems with Subject-Verb Agreement

Some sentences may cause you special problems when you check for agreement between subjects and verbs.

14.2 Special Problems with Subject-Verb Agreement

Agreement in Sentences with Unusual Word Order

In most sentences the subject comes before the verb. Sometimes, however, this normal word order is inverted, or turned around. (See Section 7.4 for more information about sentences with inverted word order.) In sentences that are inverted, look for the subject after the verb and apply the following rule.

When a subject comes after the verb, the subject and verb still must agree with each other in number.

Some sentences may be inverted for emphasis. Such a sentence usually begins with a prepositional phrase that is followed by the verb and then the subject. Always make sure the verb agrees with the subject, not with a word placed before the verb. In the following example, the plural verb *were growing* agrees with the plural subject *tulips.* The singular noun *sidewalk* is the object of a preposition.

EXAMPLE: Near the fence along the sidewalk <u>were growing</u>
          many bright-red <u>tulips</u>.

Sentences beginning with *there* or *here* are almost always in inverted word order. Again, look for the subject after the verb (or after the helping verb) and make sure that the subject and verb agree.

EXAMPLES: There <u>were</u> many <u>tulips</u> <u>growing</u> by the fence in the
            back yard.
            Here <u>is</u> the <u>magazine</u> I promised to lend you.

The contractions *there's* and *here's* contain the singular verb *is: there is, here is.* Do not use these contractions with plural subjects.

INCORRECT: Here<u>'s</u> the <u>magazines</u> I promised you.

CORRECT: Here <u>are</u> the <u>magazines</u> I promised you.

OBJECTIVES

After completing this section, students should be able to

- Make subjects and verbs agree in sentences with unusual word order.
- Make subjects and verbs agree in sentences that have indefinite pronouns as subjects.

TEACHING

Getting Started

┌ sentence bank ─────────┐
Here are the papers you
  dropped.
How lovely and pure is the
  new-fallen snow.
Why are they here?
└────────────────────────┘

Write on the board the Sentence Bank sentences. Ask volunteers to locate and underline the subject and verb in each sentence. Elicit that in these sentences the subject follows the verb. Explain that in such sentences, the verb still must agree with its subject.

Text Follow Through

Discuss text pages 254–259.

Assign Exercise A, page 256; Exercise B, page 257; Exercise C, page 258; and Developing Writing Skills, page 259.

Less advanced   You might suggest that students working with inverted sentences such as those in Exercise A mentally rewrite them in normal word order to check agreement. To give more work with indefinite pronouns, you can have students rewrite in the present tense sentences 1, 4, 8, and 10 of Exercise D in Section 1.3 (pages 35–36).

Average If students need more practice with the concepts in this section, you can have them work again with the sentences in Exercise C. Students can re-write the sentences, making the following changes:

Sent. 1: Change *Most* to *All.*
Sent. 2: Change *Some* to *One.*
Sent. 3: Change *ivy* to *the vines.*
Sent. 4: Change *Each* to *Several.*
Sent. 5: Change *the report and the book* to *the key.*
Sent. 6: Change *that story* to *those fairy tales.*
Sent. 7: Change *antiques* to *sheep.*
Sent. 8: Change *Everybody* to *No one.*
Sent. 9: Change *three reasons* to *one reason.*
Sent. 10: Change *total price of* to *total expenditures for.*

As students work on this activity, remind them that many of the original sentences are incorrect. Their job now, however, is to come up with ten sentences that are correct.

Advanced Have students scan articles and stories for inverted order sentences and sentences using indefinite pronouns. Have them copy ten such sentences onto a piece of paper. They can then exchange papers with other students and locate the verb and subject in each sentence they have received.

Additional Practice

Practice Pages or Practice Book, page 84

Less advanced Exercise Bank, Exercises A and B, pages 122, 123

Finally, many questions are in inverted word order. Check questions carefully to find the subject and make sure that it agrees with the verb.

INCORRECT: Where's the magazines you promised me?

CORRECT: Where are the magazines you promised me?

EXERCISE A: Checking Agreement in Sentences with Inverted Word Order. On your paper write the subject from each of the following sentences. Then choose the correct verb from the choices in parentheses.

Subjects are shaded.

EXAMPLE: There (is, are) the missing giraffes.

giraffes   are

1. Where in your desk (is, are) your yellow pencil?
2. Beyond this town and across the river (looms, loom) the Empire State Building.
3. Here (is, are) the letter I mentioned to you.
4. Why (is, are) all three outfielders looking the wrong way?
5. There (is, are) many possible reasons for their behavior.
6. Crawling behind the sofa (was, were) two loudly giggling children.
7. Here in this box (is, are) several toys from my childhood.
8. How often (does, do) he manage to take a break from his responsibilities?
9. How silently and softly (falls, fall) the rain.
10. There (is, are) no excuse for such table manners.

Agreement with Indefinite Pronouns

When used as subjects, indefinite pronouns can also cause problems.

Depending on its form and meaning, an indefinite pronoun can agree with either a singular or a plural verb.

Average Exercise Bank, Exercises A, B, and C, pages 122, 123

Advanced Exercise Bank, Exercises B and C, pages 122, 123

14.2 Special Problems with Subject-Verb Agreement

Look again at the list of indefinite pronouns in Section 1.3. Notice that some of the pronouns are always singular. Included here are those ending in *-one (anyone, everyone, someone)*, those ending in *-body (anybody, everybody, somebody)*, and those that imply one *(each, either)*. Other indefinite pronouns are always plural: *both, few, many, others,* and *several*. A few can be either singular or plural: *all, any, more, most, none,* and *some*.

The following examples show pronouns from each of the three categories. Notice in the first group that the prepositional phrases between the subjects and verbs do not affect agreement.

ALWAYS SINGULAR: One of the lamps is broken.

Everybody at the movies was frightened by the film.

Neither of your ideas seems workable.

ALWAYS PLURAL: Many are bringing their own lunches.

Others are buying their lunches at school.

Several eat at home.

EITHER SINGULAR
OR PLURAL: Most of the salad has been eaten.

Most of the apples have been eaten.

When an indefinite pronoun can be either singular or plural, the number of the pronoun's antecedent becomes the determining factor. In the first sentence of the last set of examples, the antecedent of *most* is *salad*. Since *salad* is singular, the verb is singular. In the second sentence, the antecedent of *most* is *apples*. Since *apples* is plural, the verb is plural.

EXERCISE B: Checking Agreement with Indefinite Pronouns. For each of the following sentences, choose the correct verb from the choices in parentheses, and write it on your paper.

TESTING

Test Program

Unit Pretest, page 43
Chapter Test, page 48
Unit Post-Test, page 55

RE-TEACHING

Practice Pages or Practice Book, page 84

THINKING SKILLS

Comprehension—*Distinguishing* between singular and plural verbs in inverted order sentences (Exercise A, page 256) *Selecting* the correct verb to agree with indefinite pronoun subjects (Exercise B, page 257) *Selecting* the correct verb to avoid problems in agreement (Exercise C, page 258)

Synthesis—*Writing* sentences that correctly match subjects and verbs to avoid special subject-verb agreement problems (Developing Writing Skills, page 259)

EXAMPLE: All of the trees in the garden (was, were) swaying in the wind.

were

1. Both of you (writes, <u>write</u>) well enough to enter the essay contest.
2. Everyone (<u>remembers</u>, remember) the day the emergency sprinklers flooded our classroom with six inches of water.
3. Most of the movie (<u>was</u>, were) shown at the wrong speed and couldn't be seen.
4. Some of the students (drives, <u>drive</u>) to school.
5. Few of those classroom television sets (works, <u>work</u>) properly.
6. Most of the books we read (expands, <u>expand</u>) our knowledge of the world.
7. (Does, <u>Do</u>) any of them play on the junior high field hockey team?
8. Some of the bread (<u>feels</u>, feel) stale.
9. Each of you (<u>deserves</u>, deserve) to receive the good citizenship award.
10. All of the subjects in the paper (has, <u>have</u>) been researched thoroughly.

EXERCISE C: Checking Special Problems in Agreement.
For each of the following sentences, choose the correct verb from the choices in parentheses and write it on your paper.

EXAMPLE: Here (is, are) the rings you asked to see.

are

1. Most of the students (comes, <u>come</u>) to every session.
2. Some of the tourists (doesn't, <u>don't</u>) speak English.
3. Over the roof and down the pillar (<u>creeps</u>, creep) the ivy.
4. Each of the boys (<u>has</u>, have) both oils and watercolors.
5. Here (is, <u>are</u>) the report and the book that were missing.
6. How often (<u>has</u>, have) that story been told?
7. One of the antiques (<u>was</u>, were) very valuable.

8. Everybody on the two teams (is, are) waiting.
9. There (is, are) at least three reasons why the dog must stay at home.
10. What (was, were) the total price of all of your purchases?

DEVELOPING WRITING SKILLS: Writing Sentences with Special Kinds of Subject-Verb Agreement. Write ten original sentences according to each of the following instructions. Underline the subject once and the verb twice.
Answers will vary.

EXAMPLE: Write an inverted-order sentence that begins with *Here is.*

Here is the pamphlet for the rally.

1. Write an inverted-order sentence with a plural subject.
2. Write an inverted-order sentence with a singular subject.
3. Write a sentence that begins with *There were.*
4. Write a sentence that begins with a prepositional phrase followed by the verb and then the subject.
5. Write a question beginning with *When are.*
6. Write another question beginning with *Where's.*
7. Write a sentence with a singular indefinite pronoun subject.
8. Write a sentence with a plural indefinite pronoun subject.
9. Write a sentence with an indefinite pronoun subject followed by a prepositional phrase.
10. Write a sentence that begins with *Here's.*

Agreement Between Pronouns 14.3 and Antecedents

An antecedent is the noun for which a pronoun stands. Sometimes a pronoun's antecedent is a group of words acting as a noun, or even another pronoun. This section will show you how pronouns agree with their antecedents. If you are not sure you can quickly recognize pronouns and antecedents, review Sections 1.2 and 1.3.

259

14.3 Agreement Between Pronouns and Antecedents
(pp. 259–265)

OBJECTIVES
After completing this section, students should be able to

- Make personal pronouns agree with their antecedents in person and number.
- Make personal pronouns agree with indefinite pronouns.

Making Personal Pronouns and Antecedents Agree

Personal pronouns should agree with their antecedents in two ways.

A personal pronoun must agree with its antecedent in both person and number.

Person indicates whether a pronoun refers to the person speaking (first person), the person spoken to (second person), or the person, place, or thing spoken about (third person). *Number* indicates whether a pronoun is singular (referring to one) or plural (referring to more than one). A personal pronoun must agree with its antecedent in both person and number.

EXAMPLE: *Lisa* presented *her* report on careers in medicine to the class yesterday.

In the example, the pronoun *her* is third person and singular. It agrees with its antecedent *Lisa,* which is also third person and singular.

Avoiding Shifts in Person. A common error in agreement occurs when a personal pronoun does not have the same person as its antecedent. This error usually involves the careless use of *you* with a noun in the third person.

INCORRECT: *Alexander* is practicing the backstroke, a stroke *you* need to master if *you* want to compete in the swim meet.

CORRECT: *Alexander* is practicing the backstroke, a stroke *he* needs to master if *he* wants to compete in the swim meet.

Whenever you use *you* in your writing, make sure it refers only to the person you are addressing (your reader). It should never be used to refer to the person you are writing about.

14.3 Agreement Between Pronouns and Antecedents

Avoiding Shifts in Number. Achieving agreement in number is sometimes a problem when the antecedent is a compound joined by *or* or *nor*.

Use a singular personal pronoun to refer to two or more singular antecedents joined by *or* or *nor*.

Two or more singular antecedents joined by *or* or *nor* must have a singular pronoun, just as they must have a singular verb.

INCORRECT: Either *Bob* or *Jim* is bringing *their* guitar to the picnic.

CORRECT: Either *Bob* or *Jim* is bringing *his* guitar to the picnic.

When a compound antecedent is joined by *and,* a plural personal pronoun is used.

EXAMPLE: *Andrea* and *Jane* brought *their* books.

EXERCISE A: Making Pronouns and Antecedents Agree.
Rewrite each of the following sentences, filling in the blank with an appropriate pronoun.

EXAMPLE: The trees had dropped _____ leaves all over the brick path.

The trees had dropped their leaves all over the brick path.

1. Philip and Carla were proud of __their__ new kitchen.
2. Each boy on the soccer team had __his__ own special memories of the game.
3. The people in the park all seemed to have smiles on __their__ faces.
4. Julie is going to Japan, a country __she__ has always wanted to visit.
5. Paul would never forget __his__ day at the fair.

Average Have students work at the board, writing their answers to Exercises A and B. After writing each sentence, they can show that the pronouns and their antecedents do agree by first drawing a circle around each pronoun and then drawing an arrow from the pronoun to its antecedent. Finally, they can list the person and number of the connected words.

Advanced You might have students make up sentences of their own similar to those in the exercises of this section. Each should be written on a separate slip of paper. All contributions can then be placed in a container and drawn out at random for a contest. Divide the class into two teams. Each team receives a point for supplying the correct pronoun in a sentence.

Additional Practice
Practice Pages or Practice Book, page 85

Less advanced Exercise Bank, Exercises A and B, pages 124, 125

Average Exercise Bank, Exercises A, B, and C, pages 124, 125

Advanced Exercise Bank, Exercises B and C, pages 124, 125

TESTING
Test Program

Unit Pretest, page 43
Chapter Test, page 48
Unit Post-Test, page 55

RE-TEACHING
Practice Pages or Practice Book, page 85

THINKING SKILLS

Comprehension—*Selecting* personal pronouns that agree with indefinite pronouns (Exercise C, page 263)

Application—*Using* pronouns that agree with antecedents (Exercise A, page 261)
Modifying sentences to correct shifts in person and number (Exercise B, page 262)

Synthesis—*Rewriting* sentences to correct errors in pronoun-antecedent agreement (Exercise D, page 264)
Rewriting a paragraph to correct errors in pronoun-antecedent agreement (Developing Writing Skills, page 264)

6. The poodle, a new mother, was carefully guarding ___her or its___ litter.
7. Either Sarah or Susan will certainly remember to bring ___her___ book.
8. The three children were proudly wearing ___their___ new boots.
9. All travelers can benefit from planning ___their___ trips ahead of time.
10. Neither Ian nor Peter was sure about ___his___ answer on the test.

EXERCISE B: Avoiding Shifts in Person and Number.

Each of the following sentences contains a single error in pronoun-antecedent agreement. On your paper rewrite each sentence correctly, underlining the pronoun that you have changed and its antecedent.
Incorrect pronouns are underlined; antecedents are shaded.
EXAMPLE: Bill wants to know where you can go to study art.

Bill wants to know where he can go to study art.

1. Alex has put together a racing bike you couldn't buy in a store. he
2. Neither Caroline nor Lee has decided whether they can come to the party. she
3. All Brownie leaders should gather with her troops at 3:15. their
4. Each bronco tried their luck at unseating the champion. its
5. Jill is going to a clinic where you can get a flu immunization shot. she
6. Terry and Gene forgot his lines in the play. their
7. Each sandwich was packed in their own vacuum-sealed wrapper. its
8. Either Loretta or Harriet will lend their textbook to Sal. her
9. Jeff lives in Chicago, where you can make many train and plane connections. he
10. All applicants must sign the register before you can take the examination. they

Agreement Between Personal Pronouns and Indefinite Pronouns

Indefinite pronouns (listed in Section 1.3) are words such as *each, everyone, neither,* and *one.* Pay special attention to the number of a personal pronoun when the antecedent is a singular indefinite pronoun.

Generally use a singular personal pronoun when its antecedent is a singular indefinite pronoun.

In making a personal pronoun agree with an indefinite pronoun, ignore the object of any prepositional phrase that might fall between them. In the first two of the following examples, *their* mistakenly agrees with *dogs* and *records.*

INCORRECT: *Neither* of the dogs has received *their* shots yet.

              Put *each* of the records in *their* cover.

CORRECT: *Neither* of the dogs has received *its* shots yet.

              Put *each* of the records in *its* cover.

EXERCISE C: Making Personal Pronouns and Indefinite Pronouns Agree. For each of the following sentences, choose the correct pronoun from the choices in parentheses and write it on your paper.

EXAMPLE: Each of the boys has (his, their) money in hand.

          his

1. Neither of the parakeets has eaten (<u>its</u>, their) food.
2. Not one of the apples had fallen from (<u>its</u>, their) branch.
3. Give each of the girls a lab coat of (<u>her</u>, their) own.
4. Several of the players were eating (his, <u>their</u>) lunches.
5. Fortunately, each of the books was filed in (<u>its</u>, their) correct location.
6. Neither of the students has written (<u>her</u>, their) paper yet.

Developing Writing Skills

Have students practice clear pronoun-antecedent agreement in writing by completing the following assignment.

Writing Across the Curriculum

Technology is advancing at an unprecedented rate. Consider the modern kitchen. Modern conveniences such as microwave ovens, electric dishwashers, and gas ovens would be truly incredible devices to someone who lived one hundred years ago.

Prewriting Imagine that you are a scientist who lived one hundred years ago. You have just been transported in time and have arrived in a modern kitchen. Select one modern appliance that you find particularly interesting or incredible. From the perspective of someone who lived one hundred years ago, free write about the appliance. Choose words and phrases for a description of the appliance's appearance and its uses.

Writing Write the first draft of a journal entry describing the kitchen appliance and its uses. Be sure that you write your entry from the point of view of a person who lived one hundred years ago.

Revising Make sure that your journal entry vividly describes the appliance. Does your entry include the appliance's uses? Is the entry written from the point of view of a scientist who lived one hundred years ago? Is there clear agreement between any pronouns and their antecedents? Prepare a final draft.

7. The director asked all of the actors to practice (his, their) lines.
8. Few of the musicians were playing (his, their) instruments correctly.
9. Some of the dogs actually resembled (its, their) masters.
10. Take all of these shoes and clean (it, them).

EXERCISE D: Checking Agreement Between Pronouns and Antecedents. Some of the following sentences contain errors in pronoun-antecedent agreement. On your paper rewrite the incorrect sentences, and write *correct* for those without errors.

EXAMPLE: Neither of the girls brought their parents.

Neither of the girls brought her parents.

1. Each of the flowers had closed their petals for the night. its
2. Only one of the women had given their real name. her
3. Some of the speakers were confused and forgot his points in the debate. their
4. Lee Anne is boarding a plane that will take you to Hawaii by way of San Francisco. her
5. Not one of the directors felt good about her work in the festival. C
6. Neither Henry nor Edwin has started their homework. his
7. All of the dogs obeyed their trainer. C
8. Every term paper was given their grade by the same teacher. its
9. Each one of the five men on the crew started their lunch break at the stroke of noon. his
10. Several of the stories were criticized for its blandness. their

DEVELOPING WRITING SKILLS: Writing a Paragraph with Clear Pronoun-Antecedent Agreement. The sentences in the following paragraph contain errors in pronoun-antecedent agreement. Rewrite the paragraph to correct the errors.
Errors are underlined; corrections are given after the paragraph.

14.3 Agreement Between Pronouns and Antecedents

EXAMPLE: Every young woman is likely to have a slightly different view of their own future.

Every young woman is likely to have a slightly different view of her own future.

(1) Neither Natalie nor Beth planned their future in ordinary terms. (2) Each of the two sisters had their own ambitious plans. (3) Natalie knew that you would have to work very
hard to become a writer. (4) She also knew that a good writer
cannot always earn a living from their work. (5) Beth wanted
to become a champion speed skater, although their path could
be difficult. (6) She knew you would have only a few years to
excel in this physically demanding discipline. (7) Both girls
knew that above all you would have to have confidence in
yourself. (8) They expected to be frustrated sometimes in
reaching her dreams. (9) Both also felt that her hopes had
some chance of being fulfilled. (10) Each one tried to outdo
the other in their hard work and dedication.

1. her 2. her 3. she 4. her 5. her 6. she 7. they/themselves 8. their
9. their 10. her

Checking Your Skills

In the Checking Your Skills assignment, students have corrected errors in agreement. Explain to students that the following critical thinking activity will provide them with additional practice.

Critical Thinking

For homework, have each student compose ten sentences with intentional agreement problems. Encourage students to incorporate a variety of agreement problems in their sentences. Students should also write the corrected form of the sentences on a separate sheet of paper. In class, group students in pairs. Have each pair of students exchange papers and correct the agreement problems in the ten sentences. When they have completed this, partners should exchange papers and correct each other's work. For any incorrect answers, partners should review together the rules concerning that particular usage problem. You might want to group your less advanced students with average or advanced partners for this activity.

Using Usage Skills in Writing

Publishing You can create a display for students' advice columns. You might display the columns on a bulletin board or in another prominent location for all students to read. If you do so, encourage students to include diagrams and other visual aids with their columns.

Skills Review and Writing Workshop

Making Words Agree
CHECKING YOUR SKILLS

Rewrite the paragraph below, correcting all errors in agreement.
Answers will vary.

(1) The debaters from Redwood was discussing its strategy for the finals. (2) They knew that you should plan carefully. (3) Although most of the contests were over, the scores of several schools was very close. (4) The Redwood students realized that neither they nor their greatest rival were able to afford a mistake in the finals. (5) Redwood's captain and co-captain was arguing about whether the team should choose to go first or last if Redwood won the toss. (6) Finally the co-captain said, "Everyone of us know that we face a battle. (7) There's mistakes we might make if we speak first. (8) If we speak after Lincoln, each of our debaters can plan their arguments more." (9) Nobody were able to disagree. (10) The next day the Redwood students were successful in its debate.

USING USAGE SKILLS IN WRITING
Writing a Paragraph of Advice

Newspaper advice columns give advice on subjects ranging from manners to gardening. Follow the steps below to write a paragraph of advice for a newspaper column.
Answers will vary.

Prewriting: Think of a question someone might ask you about a hobby you are familiar with. Take notes on how you would answer the question.

Writing: Write the question, and then write your answer from your notes. Be sure to be clear and specific.

Revising: First, eliminate any problems in verb or pronoun agreement. Then look for other improvements you can make. After you have revised, proofread carefully.

Chapter 15

Using Modifiers

Sections 15.1 through 15.4 deal with the correct use of modifiers. Section 15.1 on regular adjectives and adverbs discusses the usual ways of forming the comparative and superlative degrees of modifiers. Section 15.2 on irregular adjectives and adverbs lists the most common irregular modifiers and lists their comparative and superlative degrees. Sections 15.3 and 15.4 give information that will help students use the degrees of adverbs and adjectives correctly. Section 15.5 lists common problems that students encounter with modifiers and gives solutions for each problem.

For a review of the entire chapter and a related writing activity, see the Skills Review and Writing Workshop on page 283.

Adjectives and adverbs can be used to compare two or more people, places, or things that share the same basic qualities. These two parts of speech have different forms in sentences depending on the kind of comparison that is being made.

The following examples show how adjectives and adverbs change form:

ADJECTIVE: "Lena is *young. She is younger* than Roy, but Fran is the *youngest* of all."

ADVERB: "This engine runs *smoothly*. This engine runs *more smoothly* than that one. This engine runs *most smoothly* of all."

The different forms of adjectives and adverbs are known as *degrees of comparison.*

Most adjectives and adverbs have three degrees of comparison: the *positive,* the *comparative,* and the *superlative* degree.

The *positive* degree is used when no comparison is being made. This form is listed in a dictionary. The *comparative* degree is the form used when two things are being compared. The *superlative* degree is used when three or more things are being compared.

15.1 Regular Adjectives and Adverbs
(pp. 268–271)

OBJECTIVES
After completing this section, students should be able to

- Use *-er* and *-est* or *more* and *most* to form the comparative and superlative degrees of most one- and two-syllable modifiers.
- Use *more* and *most* to form the comparative and superlative degrees of all modifiers with more than two syllables.

TEACHING
Getting Started

To introduce the idea of comparison, write the following on the board:

Paula is quick, but Maria is the _____ of the two runners. That engine is powerful, but this V-8 is even _____ . Jack's room is _____ , but my room is _____ .

Have volunteers fill in the blanks in the first two sentences. Elicit that adjectives can change form in order to compare two things that have like qualities by adding *-er* or *more*. Then have students sug-

---

The first four sections in this chapter will explain how the three degrees are formed and will show you how different degrees should be used in sentences. The fifth section will discuss certain troublesome adjectives and adverbs and will give you practice using them correctly.

15.1 Regular Adjectives and Adverbs

Like verbs, adjectives and adverbs can be either *regular* or *irregular*. Happily, most adjectives and adverbs in English are regular. That is, their comparative and superlative degrees are formed in predictable ways.

Two rules govern *regular* modifiers. The first covers adjectives and adverbs of one or two syllables. The second concerns adjectives and adverbs of three or more syllables.

Modifiers of One or Two Syllables

The comparative and superlative degrees of most adjectives and adverbs of one or two syllables can be formed in either of two ways.

Use *-er* or *more* to form the comparative degree and *-est* or *most* to form the superlative degree of most one- and two-syllable modifiers.

Adding *-er* and *-est* is the most common way.

COMPARATIVE AND SUPERLATIVE DEGREES FORMED WITH *-ER* AND *-EST*

Positive	Comparative	Superlative
tall	taller	tallest
strong	stronger	strongest
happy	happier	happiest
friendly	friendlier	friendliest

15.1 Regular Adjectives and Adverbs

More and *most* can also be used to form the comparative and superlative degrees of most one- and two-syllable modifiers. They should not be used, however, when they sound awkward, as in "He is *more tall* than I am" or "This is the *most strong* rope we have." Notice in the following chart that two of the modifiers from the preceding chart, *happy* and *friendly*, can use *more* and *most* to form the comparative and superlative degrees. *More* and *most* are also used with most adverbs ending in *-ly* and with one- and two-syllable modifiers that would sound awkward with *-er* and *-est*.

COMPARATIVE AND SUPERLATIVE DEGREES FORMED WITH *MORE* AND *MOST*

Positive	Comparative	Superlative
happy	more happy	most happy
friendly	more friendly	most friendly
slowly	more slowly	most slowly
brisk	more brisk	most brisk

Try using *-er* and *-est* with the last two examples in this chart. Notice how awkward they sound. If you are in doubt about which form to use, say the words aloud. Then use the method that sounds better.

EXERCISE A: Forming the Comparative and Superlative Degrees of One- and Two-Syllable Modifiers. On your paper write the comparative and superlative degrees of the following modifiers. If the degrees can be formed in either way, write the *-er* and *-est* forms.

1. cloudier/cloudiest 2. sunnier/sunniest 3. more hopeful/most hopeful

EXAMPLE: sad

　　　　　sadder   saddest

4. more rapid/most rapid 5. more rudely/most rudely 6. more just/most just

1. cloudy   3. hopeful   5. rudely   7. narrow   9. lucky
2. sunny   4. rapid   6. just   8. strange   10. awkward

7. narrower/narrowest 8. stranger/strangest 9. luckier/luckiest
10. more awkward/most awkward

gest a variety of possible word pairs to fill the blanks in the third sentence. Discuss which fill-ins end in *-er* and which are preceded by *more*. Make sure students don't use both forms at once (e.g., *more prettier*).

Similar sentences can be used to elicit guidelines for changing adjectives to show comparison of more than two things.

Text Follow Through

Discuss text pages 268–271.

Assign Exercise A, page 269; Exercise B, page 270; and Developing Writing Skills, page 271.

Less advanced Students may require a brief review of the material on adjectives in Chapter 3 and on adverbs in Chapter 4 before beginning this section. To reinforce the material on degrees in the present section, you can place these columns on the board, having students supply the information shown in parentheses.

Degree	Formed by Adding...
Positive	(_____)
Comparative	(-er) or (more)
Superlative	(-est) or (most)

Students can then supply several different examples of regular adjectives and adverbs and their degrees in a third column to the right, labeled "Examples."

Average To give students additional practice with this material, refer them to Exercise B in Section 7.7 (page 119). Students can identify at least one adjective or adverb in each sentence and then write its comparative and superlative degrees. Note that the sentences contain a few words such as *very* that cannot be compared readily. You may wish to discuss these words.

Advanced Some modifiers that normally form the comparative and superlative with *-er* and *-est* will in some cases instead be compared with *more* and *most*. Encourage students to consult the dictionary, which will show both ways when both are acceptable.

Additional Practice

Practice Pages or Practice Book, page 86

Less advanced Exercise Bank, Exercises A and B, pages 126, 127

Average Exercise Bank, Exercises A, B, and C, pages 126, 127

Advanced Exercise Bank, Exercises B and C, pages 126, 127

TESTING

Test Program

Unit Pretest, page 43
Chapter Test, page 49
Unit Post-Test, page 55

RE-TEACHING

Practice Pages or Practice Book, page 86

THINKING SKILLS

Knowledge—*Naming* the comparative and superlative degrees of one- and two-syllable modifiers (Exercise A, page 269)
Naming the comparative and superlative degrees of modifiers with more than two syllables (Exercise B, page 270)

Modifiers of Three or More Syllables

When a modifier has three or more syllables, its comparative and superlative degrees are easy to form.

Use *more* and *most* to form the comparative and superlative degrees of all modifiers of three or more syllables.

Never use *-er* or *-est* with modifiers of more than two syllables.

DEGREES OF MODIFIERS WITH THREE OR MORE SYLLABLES		
Positive	**Comparative**	**Superlative**
eagerly	more eagerly	most eagerly
favorable	more favorable	most favorable
difficult	more difficult	most difficult

Less and *least*, which mean the opposite of *more* and *most*, can be used to form the comparative and superlative degrees of any of the modifiers in the chart. *Less* and *least* can also be used with modifiers of one or two syllables.

EXAMPLE:	eagerly	less eagerly	least eagerly
	favorable	less favorable	least favorable
	difficult	less difficult	least difficult

EXERCISE B: Forming the Comparative and Superlative Degrees of Modifiers with More than Two Syllables. Write the comparative and superlative degrees of the following modifiers. Use *more* and *most* and then *less* and *least* for each.

All words should follow the model given in the example.

EXAMPLE: happily

more happily   most happily

less happily   least happily

Synthesis—*Writing* pairs of sentences using comparative and superlative degrees of regular modifiers (Developing Writing Skills, page 271)

15.2 Irregular Adjectives and Adverbs

1. intelligent	6. industriously
2. effective	7. infamous
3. affectionate	8. popular
4. overburdened	9. intricate
5. glittery	10. protected

DEVELOPING WRITING SKILLS: Forming the Comparative and Superlative Degrees of Regular Modifiers. On your paper write two sentences for each of the following modifiers. Write one sentence using the comparative degree of the modifier and one sentence using the superlative degree.

Answers will vary; samples are given for the first one.

EXAMPLE: ambitious

Bernadette was always more ambitious than her sister Annemarie.

Maryellen, however, was the most ambitious one of all.

1. She is kinder than I. In fact, she is the kindest person I know.

1. kind	6. hopeless
2. lonely	7. simple
3. careful	8. adventurous
4. exciting	9. hard
5. handsome	10. windy

Irregular Adjectives and Adverbs 15.2

The comparative and superlative degrees of a few adjectives and adverbs are *irregular* in form. The only way to learn them is to memorize them.

Memorize the irregular comparative and superlative forms of certain irregular adjectives and adverbs.

The chart on the following page lists the most common irregular modifiers. Memorizing the degrees of these irregular adjectives and adverbs will help you use them correctly in your sentences.

271

15.2 Irregular Adjectives and Adverbs
(pp. 271–273)

OBJECTIVE

After completing this section, students should be able to

• Recognize the positive, comparative, and superlative degrees of the most common irregular modifiers.

TEACHING
Getting Started

Tell students that, as in every area of language study, there are exceptions to the rules they learned in the last section about forming comparative and superlative degrees of modifiers. Some modifiers do not form the comparative and superlative degrees with -er and -est or more and most. Read aloud sentences like the following. Students will immediately hear the comic result of attempting to use the regular endings with these modifiers.

That was the *baddest* I have ever done on a test.
I was not well yesterday; today I am *weller*.

Ask students if they can correct these sentences orally and make others to illustrate the superlative forms of these two modifiers. Have students think of any other examples of modifiers that form the comparative and superlative irregularly. Refer students to the chart on page 272 to find more examples and see how each modifier forms its comparative and superlative forms.

Text Follow Through

Discuss text pages 271–273.

Assign Exercise A, page 272; Exercise B, page 273; and Developing Writing Skills, page 273.

Less advanced Students are likely to benefit from oral drill on irregular adjectives and adverbs. Such practice will help them commit these forms to memory. First, drill students on the words alone; then, students can read their answers to the exercises aloud, correcting any mistakes.

Average If students need further practice, they can reuse the modifiers in Exercise A. Instruct students to divide their papers into three columns with the headings *Positive, Comparative,* and *Superlative.* Students can then write the underlined modifier from each sentence in

DEGREES OF IRREGULAR ADJECTIVES AND ADVERBS

Positive	Comparative	Superlative
bad	worse	worst
badly	worse	worst
far (distance)	farther	farthest
far (extent)	further	furthest
good	better	best
well	better	best
many	more	most
much	more	most

EXERCISE A: Recognizing the Degree of Irregular Modifiers. On your paper identify the degree of the underlined word in each of the following sentences.

EXAMPLE: After a short talk with the coach, Chris did not feel at all <u>bad</u>.

positive

1. Visitors to the Finger Lakes region in upstate New York can see <u>many</u> lovely lakes and waterfalls. pos
2. <u>Farther</u> out, white sails glinted in the sunlight. compar
3. Which is <u>worse</u>, being too hot or being too cold? compar
4. Actually, I dislike being wet <u>most</u> of all. super
5. The plowing was going <u>well</u> when the thunderstorm began. pos
6. Peter gave me the <u>worst</u> wrench in the toolbox and told me to remove the wheel. super
7. Mary Ellen likes field hockey <u>more</u> than any other sport. compar
8. Although the weather was <u>bad</u>, Shelly had a wonderful time. pos
9. José has never been in <u>better</u> form than he was in today's debate. compar
10. I thought that of all the speakers he handled the controversial issues <u>best</u>. super

15.2 Irregular Adjectives and Adverbs

EXERCISE B: Using the Comparative and Superlative Degrees of Irregular Modifiers. Copy each sentence, supplying the form of the modifier requested in parentheses.

EXAMPLE: Joanna feels (well—comparative) today.

better

1. Milt did (badly—comparative) on this test than on the previous one. worse
2. Jean can speak (many—comparative) languages than anyone else in our class. more
3. I always work (well—superlative) under pressure. best
4. Leonardo da Vinci is admired (much—superlative) for the versatility of his genius. most
5. Marilyn's (bad—superlative) fears were realized when she forgot to study for her history examination. worst
6. One thousand miles is the (far—superlative) I have ever been from home. farthest
7. Your antique car will look (good—comparative) after you polish it. better
8. Who found the (many—superlative) items in the scavenger hunt? most
9. Jan enjoys reading poetry (much—comparative) than any other kind of writing. more
10. Michael's (good—superlative) character trait is his honesty.
10. best

DEVELOPING WRITING SKILLS: Forming the Comparative and Superlative Degrees of Irregular Modifiers. On your paper write two sentences for each of the following modifiers, one using the comparative degree and one using the superlative degree.
Answers will vary; samples are given for the first one.
EXAMPLE: much

I like cider more than apple juice.

However, the drink I like most is papaya juice.

1. far   2. bad   3. many   4. well   5. good
1. This car can go farther on a gallon of gas than our old one. The farthest we have taken it is to Texas and back.

---

the appropriate column and fill in the other two degrees.

Advanced   Have students choose one sentence from each pair they have written for Developing Writing Skills, copy the chosen sentences on a separate sheet of paper, and exchange papers with partners. The students can then identify the degree in each sentence and write a compatible sentence for each, using the positive degree.

Additional Practice
Practice Pages or Practice Book, page 87

Less advanced   Exercise Bank, Exercises A and B, page 128

Average   Exercise Bank, Exercises A, B, and C, page 128

Advanced   Exercise Bank, Exercises B and C, page 128

TESTING
Test Program

Unit Pretest, page 43
Chapter Test, page 49
Unit Post-Test, page 55

RE-TEACHING
Practice Pages or Practice Book, page 87

THINKING SKILLS
Knowledge—*Identifying* the degree of irregular modifiers (Exercise A, page 272)

Application—*Using* the comparative and superlative degrees of irregular modifiers in sentences (Exercise B, page 273)

Synthesis—*Composing* sentences using the comparative and superlative degrees of irregular modifiers (Developing Writing Skills, page 273)

OBJECTIVE

After completing this section, students should be able to

- Use the comparative and superlative degrees of modifiers correctly.

TEACHING

Getting Started

Students should see that addition of both *more* or *most* and *-er* or *-est* to a modifier is unnecessary, as both add the same meaning. To demonstrate, write incorrect sentences on the board, such as the following:

You did a good job, but I think you can do more better yet. Which of these cities is most farthest away from our city? That was the most tragicest ending I have seen.

Ask a volunteer to cross out the unnecessary word or word ending and explain why it is not needed. A common error among students is the use of the superlative degree in comparison of two objects. Write the following on the board, and ask students how many things are being compared:

Which do you like best, swimming or jogging?

Discuss whether the comparative or superlative degree is needed for a two-item comparison.

Text Follow Through

Discuss text pages 274–276.

Assign the Exercise, page 275, and Developing Writing Skills, page 276.

Less advanced You may want to ask students to write only

15.3 Using Comparative and Superlative Degrees

Keep two rules in mind when you use the comparative and superlative degrees.

Use the comparative degree to compare *two* people, places, or things.

Use the superlative degree to compare *three or more* people, places, or things.

Usually you need not mention specific numbers when you are making a comparison. The other words in the sentence should help make it clear whether you are comparing two items or three or more items.

EXAMPLES: Joanna feels *better* today.

This is Gene's *best* drawing.

In the examples, the comparative degree *better* clearly compares Joanna's present condition to a single previous condition. The superlative degree *best* obviously compares one of Gene's drawings to all his others.

Pay particular attention to the modifiers you use when you are comparing just two items. Do not make the mistake of using the superlative degree.

INCORRECT: Of Gene's two drawings, that one is *best*.

This is the *most exciting* book of the two.

CORRECT: Of Gene's two drawings, that one is *better*.

This is the *more exciting* book of the two.

Pay attention also to the form of the modifiers you use in the comparative and superlative degrees. Do not make *double comparisons*. You should never use both *-er* and *more* to form the comparative degree or both *-est* and *most* to form the su-

15.3 Using Comparative and Superlative Degrees

perlative degree. Use one or the other method, but not both. Moreover, be sure you never use *-er* or *more* and *most* with an irregular modifier.

INCORRECT: Debbie and Rick are the *most happiest* couple we know.

The situation in that country could not be *more worse.*

CORRECT: Debbie and Rick are the *happiest* couple we know.

The situation in that country could not be *worse.*

EXERCISE: Correcting Errors in Degree. Some of the following sentences contain errors in degree. On your paper rewrite the incorrect sentences. Write *correct* if the sentence contains no errors.

1. Henrietta's watercolors were the <u>most palest</u> in the painting class. palest
2. Of the two jackets Betram bought yesterday, I like the tweed one <u>best</u>. better
3. That Hitchcock movie was one of the most frightening films I have ever seen. C
4. It was hard to say which of the two children looked <u>youngest</u>. younger
5. Joyce's words became even <u>more louder</u> when Ted refused to explain his actions. louder
6. Which of these three letterheads looks <u>more</u> informal to you? most
7. Hank was the <u>most</u> diligent of the twins, but Holly was the <u>smartest</u>. more/smarter
8. The mezzo soprano's voice carried better on high notes than low notes. C
9. That book would head my list of the ten <u>most worst</u> novels of all time. worst
10. Which of your parents do you and your brother resemble <u>most</u>? more

ten sentences for Developing Writing Skills. One way of doing this would be to instruct them to use the comparative degree of the first five words and the superlative degree of the second five words. Or you might have them write sentences for the first five words in pairs in class and sentences for the last five words independently at home.

Average   To give students additional practice in identifying and correcting poor comparisons and double comparisons, you can use the following phrases. Ask students to explain why each phrase is wrong and then to give a correct version.

1. most hottest afternoon
2. better photograph in the group
3. more sicker
4. best of the two
5. least worst
6. more better
7. the oldest of the two
8. most worst program
9. less farther
10. most saddest

Advanced   Some students need additional practice in using the degrees of *bad, badly,* and *well.* Provide sentences taken from student compositions in which errors in the use of these irregular modifiers have arisen. If that is not possible, you might ask students to write a paragraph about an illness they have had, being sure to use *bad, badly,* and *well* correctly in each of their degrees at least once.

Additional Practice

Practice Pages or Practice Book, page 88

Less advanced   Exercise Bank, Exercises A and B, page 129

Average Exercise Bank, Exercises A, B, and C, page 129

Advanced Exercise Bank, Exercises B and C, page 129

TESTING

Test Program

Unit Pretest, page 43
Chapter Test, page 49
Unit Post-Test, page 55

RE-TEACHING

Practice Pages or Practice Book, page 88

THINKING SKILLS

Application—*Modifying* sentences to correct degrees in error (Exercise, page 275)

Synthesis—*Writing* sentences using both the comparative and superlative degree of modifiers (Developing Writing Skills, page 276)

15.4 Making Logical Comparisons
(pp. 276–279)

OBJECTIVES

After completing this section, students should be able to

- Construct balanced comparisons.
- Use *other* and *else* correctly in comparisons.

TEACHING

Getting Started

To introduce the idea of balanced comparisons, write the following on the board:

The rapid transit system in New York is older than Washington, D.C.

By having a volunteer point out what two things are compared (a subway system and an entire

---

DEVELOPING WRITING SKILLS: Using the Comparative and Superlative Degrees. Write two sentences for each of the following modifiers, one using the comparative degree and one using the superlative degree.

Answers will vary; samples are given for the first one.

EXAMPLE: slowly

The molasses dripped more slowly than the maple syrup.

However, the honey dripped most slowly of the three.

1. Your pine tree is taller than ours. In fact, it's the tallest pine on the block.

1. tall	5. beautiful	9. quickly
2. ancient	6. strong	10. badly
3. difficult	7. much	
4. fearful	8. terrible	

15.4 Making Logical Comparisons

In most situations you will have no problems forming the degrees of modifiers and using them correctly in sentences. Sometimes, however, you may find that the way you have phrased a sentence makes your comparison unclear. You will then need to think about the words you have chosen and revise your sentence, making sure your comparison is logical.

Balanced Comparisons

Most comparisons make a statement or ask a question about the way in which basically similar things are either alike or different. For example, one sentence might compare the sound of two radios. Because the sentence compares sound to sound, the comparison is *balanced*. Problems can occur, however, when a sentence compares basically dissimilar things. For example, it would be illogical to compare the *sound* of one radio to the *size* of another radio. Sound and size are not basically similar things and cannot be compared meaningfully.

15.4 Making Logical Comparisons

Make sure that your sentences compare only items of a *similar* kind.

An unbalanced comparison is usually the result of carelessness. The writer generally has simply left out something. Read the following incorrect sentences carefully.

INCORRECT: This book's index is larger than that book.

Our classroom is larger than the sixth-graders.

In the first sentence, an *index* is mistakenly compared to an entire *book*. In the second sentence, a *classroom* is compared to *sixth-graders*. Both sentences can easily be corrected to make the comparisons balanced.

CORRECT: This book's index is longer than that book's index.

Our classroom is larger than the sixth-graders' classroom.

EXERCISE A: Making Balanced Comparisons. Rewrite each of the following sentences, making the illogical comparisons more balanced.

EXAMPLE: This dog's coat is shinier than that dog.

This dog's coat is shinier than that dog's coat.

1. Bernie's roller skates look newer than Jodie. Jodie's roller skates
2. This year's fair was better attended than last year. year's fair
3. Our morning newspaper's circulation is much larger than our afternoon newspaper. newspaper's circulation
4. Pia's project covered more material than Eddie. Eddie's project
5. Because he is dead, this painter's work is more valuable than that painter. painter's work
6. Andrea's family is smaller than Jane. Jane's family
7. My record collection is not as large as my sister.
8. My vegetable garden produced more tomatoes than Ed.
9. My mother's car looks better than my father. father's car
10. This pond's frogs are much noisier than that pond. pond's frogs

7. sister's record collection   8. Ed's vegetable garden

Additional Practice
Practice Pages or Practice
Book, page 89

Less advanced Exercise Bank,
Exercises A and B, pages 130,
131

Average Exercise Bank, Exercises A, B, and C, pages 130,
131

Advanced Exercise Bank, Exercises B and C, pages 130, 131

TESTING
Test Program

Unit Pretest, page 43
Chapter Test, pages 49, 50
Unit Post-Test, page 55

RE-TEACHING
Practice Pages or Practice
Book, page 89

THINKING SKILLS

Application—*Modifying*
sentences to make illogical
comparisons more balanced
(Exercise A, page 277)
Modifying sentences adding
other and *else* to make
comparisons more logical (Exercise B, page 278)

Synthesis—*Writing* sentences
that contain logical comparisons (Developing Writing
Skills, page 279)

Other and *Else* in Comparisons

Another common error in writing comparisons is to compare
something with itself.

**When comparing one of a group with the rest of
the group, make sure your sentence contains
the word *other* or *else*.**

Adding *other* or *else* in such situations helps make the comparison clear. For example, since Queen Victoria was herself a
British monarch, she cannot logically be compared to *all* British monarchs. She must be compared to all *other* British
monarchs.

Problem Sentences	Corrected Sentences
Queen Victoria reigned longer than any British monarch.	Queen Victoria reigned longer than any *other* British monarch.
The captain scored more touchdowns than anyone on the team.	The captain scored more touchdowns than anyone *else* on the team.

EXERCISE B: Using *Other* and *Else* in Comparisons. Rewrite each of the following sentences, adding *other* or *else* to
make the comparisons more logical.

EXAMPLE: George types faster than any student in his class.

George types faster than any other student in his class.

1. My mother sings more beautifully than <u>any</u> member of my family. any other
2. Theodore Roosevelt took office at a younger age than <u>any</u> American President. any other
3. Our English teacher is stricter than <u>anyone</u> on the faculty.
4. I like chocolate better than <u>any</u> food. any other

3. anyone else

15.5 Glossary of Troublesome Adjectives and Adverbs

5. Julie was funnier than <u>anyone</u> in the stunt show. anyone else

6. In the semifinals Carrie served more aces than <u>any</u> player in the whole tournament. any other

7. William Shakespeare is more admired than <u>any</u> English playwright. any other

8. *Roots* reached a wider audience than <u>any</u> television show.

9. In our house baseball is more popular than <u>any</u> sport. any other

10. Greta Garbo was more famous than <u>any</u> actress of her time.

8. any other   10. any other

DEVELOPING WRITING SKILLS: Writing Logical Comparisons. On your paper write a sentence that makes the comparison specified in each of the following items. Make sure that your comparisons are balanced and logical.

Answers will vary; a sample is given for the first one.

EXAMPLE: Compare the records of two basketball teams.

> Our basketball team's record is much better than their basketball team's record.

1. This book's events are much more exciting than that book's events.

1. Compare the events in two different books.
2. Compare the humor on two television shows.
3. Compare one President with all the rest, using the word *better*.
4. Compare one popular singer with all the rest, using the word *worse*.
5. Compare one city with all the rest.

Glossary of Troublesome 15.5 Adjectives and Adverbs

Certain commonly used adjectives and adverbs often cause people problems both in speaking and writing. As you read through the following list, make a note of those words that have puzzled you in the past and use the exercises to test your understanding. When you are writing and revising a composition, refer to this section to check your work.

Developing Writing Skills

Have students practice writing logical comparisons by completing the following writing assignment.

Writing Across the Curriculum

People enjoy making comparisons between just about everything. Have you ever compared two motion pictures?

Prewriting   Free write about two motion pictures that you have seen recently, noting some things you liked and things you disliked about both. Decide which film you enjoyed more. Circle words and phrases that you can use to compare the films. Be sure to select aspects for comparison that are found in both films.

Writing   Write the first draft of your comparison of the two films. Make sure that you present your comparison in a logical order. Conclude your comparison by stating your preference.

Revising   Make sure that you have presented your comparison as an opinion. Have you identified both films? Are all your comparisons logical? Have you stated your preference at the end of the comparison?

15.5 Glossary of Troublesome Adjectives and Adverbs
(pp. 279–282)

OBJECTIVE

After completing this section, students should be able to

- Avoid a number of common errors in adjective and adverb usage.

TEACHING

Getting Started

1. I didn't do _____ for my first skating lesson.
2. The scouts felt _____ about the canceled campout.
3. The meat appeared _____ , with a greenish hue around the edges.

Bad and *badly* present a dilemma to many students. Write the pair of words on the board and ask the part of speech of each. (*Bad* is an adjective; *badly* is an adverb.) Have the class review how each part of speech is used, then read aloud or place on the board sentences like those in the Sentence Bank, asking volunteers to complete the sentences with *bad* or *badly*.

Explain that students will turn now to a section that will help them clear up any confusions they have with this adjective/adverb pair and with others that are sometimes troublesome.

Text Follow Through

Discuss text pages 279–282.

Assign the Exercise, page 281, and Developing Writing Skills, page 282.

Less advanced You may wish to focus attention on *bad/badly* and *good/well*, the most common problem areas of this section. You might first want to review the material on linking verbs in Section 2.2. Then direct students to the Exercise. Relevant sentences in the Exercise include numbers 2, 4, 6, 7, 9,

(1) bad, badly   *Bad* is an adjective; *badly* is an adverb. Use *bad* after linking verbs, such as *appear, feel, look,* and *sound.* Use *badly* after action verbs, such as *act, behave, do,* and *perform.*

INCORRECT: I felt *badly* after the long hike in the rain.
(LV)

The small children behaved *bad* at the museum.
(AV)

CORRECT: I felt *bad* after the long hike in the rain.
(LV)

The small children behaved *badly* at the museum.
(AV)

(2) fewer, less   The adjective *fewer* answers the question "How many?" Use it to modify things that can be counted. The adjective *less* answers the question "How much?" Use it to modify amounts that cannot be counted.

HOW MANY: *fewer* calories, *fewer* doses, *fewer* worries

HOW MUCH: *less* starch, *less* medicine, *less* worry

(3) good, well   *Good* is an adjective. *Well* can be either an adjective or an adverb. Most mistakes in the use of these modifiers occur when *good* is placed after an action verb. Use the adverb *well* instead.

INCORRECT: I did *good* on the test.
(AV)

CORRECT: I did *well* on the test.
(AV)

As adjectives these words have slightly different meanings. *Well* usually is limited to a person's health.

EXAMPLES: I always feel *good* after jogging three miles.

The soup is especially *good* today.

Uncle Howard has not been *well* for several months.

(4) just   As an adverb *just* often means "no more than." When *just* has this meaning, make sure it is placed right before the word it logically modifies.

15.5 Glossary of Troublesome Adjectives and Adverbs

INCORRECT: I *just* want one slice of turkey.

CORRECT: I want *just* one slice of turkey.

(5) only   The position of *only* in a sentence sometimes affects the sentence's entire meaning. Consider the meaning of the following sentences.

EXAMPLES: *Only* he takes care of that dog. (Nobody else takes care of the dog.)

He *only* takes care of that dog. (He does nothing else for the dog.)

He takes care of *only* that dog. (He takes care of that dog and no other dog.)

Problems can occur when *only* is placed in a sentence in such a way that it makes the meaning imprecise.

IMPRECISE: *Only* mark your mistakes.

BETTER: Mark *only* your mistakes.

EXERCISE: Correcting Errors Caused by Troublesome Adjectives and Adverbs.
Some of the following sentences contain errors in the use of the modifiers discussed in this section. On your paper rewrite the faulty sentences, writing *correct* if a sentence contains no errors.

EXAMPLE: They sang good together.

They sang well together.

1. We found less seashells on the beach this year. fewer
2. Greg looked badly after running the marathon. bad
3. Our vacation begins in just two weeks. C
4. Ellen did good in the auditions, but Kathryn did better and won the role. well
5. I only want three things for my birthday this year. want only
6. The pineapple tasted especially well served with bananas and ice cream. good

11, 13, 16, 18, 20. Provide students with additional sentences for oral drill or written practice until they are comfortable with the use of these modifiers.

Average   For additional practice have students write original sentences using each of the following words correctly:

1. bad
2. badly
3. good
4. well
5. fewer
6. less
7. just
8. only

Advanced   Students should be sensitive to changes in word placement that change sentence meaning. Have them write three sentences, similar to those on page 281, using *only* in a different position, so that each sentence has a different meaning. Have them read the sentences orally, one by one, as other students explain how the meaning differs.

You might also want to emphasize *less* and *fewer*. Ask students to list as many nouns as possible in a five-minute period. Students should then create two columns on a sheet of paper, heading them with *Less* and *Fewer*, and place each noun under the heading which correctly modifies it.

Additional Practice

Practice Pages or Practice Book, page 90

Less advanced   Exercise Bank, Exercises A and B, page 132

Average   Exercise Bank, Exercises A, B, and C, page 132

Advanced   Exercise Bank, Exercises B and C, page 132

TESTING

Test Program

Unit Pretest, page 43
Chapter Test, page 50
Unit Post-Test, page 55

RE-TEACHING

Practice Pages or Practice Book, page 90

THINKING SKILLS

Application—*Modifying* sentences to correct errors caused by troublesome adjectives and adverbs (Exercise, page 281)

Synthesis—*Writing* sentences using troublesome adjectives and adverbs correctly (Developing Writing Skills, page 282)

7. Gramps has been responding well to treatment for arthritis. C

8. Mort <u>just needs</u> three more points to beat the scoring record in our league. needs just

9. Unfortunately, Roger is taking the news very <u>bad</u>. badly

10. <u>Less</u> than a hundred people came to the auction. fewer

11. Static made the rock group sound very <u>badly</u>. bad

12. They <u>only called</u> once. called only

13. Her recovery has taken a long time, but Maria is finally well. C

14. Ed <u>just had</u> fifteen minutes to finish his test. had just

15. Water actually occupies <u>fewer</u> space than ice. less

16. I can't understand why Jim ran so <u>bad</u> today. badly

17. I gained fewer pounds than I expected during summer vacation. C

18. His control of his voice is especially <u>well</u> today. good

19. You <u>only have</u> one chance to guess the right answer, so take your time. have only

20. Be good and you will look good. C

DEVELOPING WRITING SKILLS: Using Troublesome Adjectives and Adverbs Correctly. Write a sentence according to the directions given in each of the following items.
Answers will vary; samples given for the first two.
EXAMPLE: Use *badly* to describe some action.

Because his arm hurt, he threw the ball badly.

1. Only Simon finished the test in an hour.   2. I felt bad about spoiling the surprise.

1. Use *Only* at the beginning of a sentence.

2. Use *bad* with a linking verb.

3. Use *fewer* to compare two sets of items.

4. Use *less* to compare two sets of items.

5. Use *well* as an adverb.

6. Use *only* after a verb.

7. Use *well* as an adjective.

8. Use *good* as an adjective.

9. Use *badly* with an action verb.

10. Use *just* to mean "no more than."

Skills Review and Writing Workshop

Using Modifiers

CHECKING YOUR SKILLS

Rewrite the following paragraph, correcting all errors in adjective and adverb usage.

Answers will vary.

(1) We felt very well about ourselves when we finally reached the end of the trail. (2) The trail we had hiked was longest than any other trail in the state. (3) About half way Maria and Andy started feeling badly but then got their second wind. (4) Another problem was the fact that this trail was more steeper than others we had hiked. (5) Only we had gone a couple miles before our legs told us we were heading uphill! (6) Carlo was the more affected. (7) He had had less experiences than the rest of us. (8) The third and more serious difficulty was the roughness of the terrain. (9) In early spring, after winter rockfalls but before repairs, the stones and gullies made the trail the worse one we had ever hiked. (10) All of us were carefuller than usual, however, so no one fell or turned an ankle.

USING USAGE SKILLS IN WRITING
Writing about a Personal Experience

Both fiction and nonfiction writers sometimes use their personal experiences in their writing. Follow the steps below to write a paragraph about a personal experience.

Answers will vary.

Prewriting: Think of an experience in which you overcame some difficulty. Take notes on precisely what difficulty you overcame, how you did so, and how you felt.

Writing: Write a topic sentence that tells how you felt about your experience. Then describe the experience, emphasizing the specific events that posed the difficulty.

Revising: First, make sure your adjectives and adverbs are correct. After you have revised, proofread the paragraph.

Checking Your Skills

In the Checking Your Skills assignment, students have corrected errors in adjective and adverb usage. Tell students that the following speaking and listening activity will provide them with additional practice.

Speaking and Listening

Bring a single die to class. Tell students that they are going to play the game "Know Your Modifiers." Explain that each student will roll the die and will make up a sentence using the form of the modifier that corresponds to the number he or she has rolled. The numbers on the die correspond to the following forms: one, positive degree of comparison; two, comparative degree; three, superlative degree; four, a balanced comparison; five, a troublesome adjective or adverb; six, "wild"—you choose the form of modifier. After the student has rolled the die, you will provide him or her with a modifier that the student will use in a sentence. For example, a student rolls the die and it comes up three, which corresponds to the superlative degree. You would then supply the student with an adjective or adverb, and he or she would compose and recite a sentence using that modifier in the superlative degree.

Using Usage Skills in Writing

Revising When students are ready to revise their paragraphs, you might refer them to the Checklist for Revising a Paragraph, on page 490 of *Grammar and Composition*.

CHAPTER 16
**SOLVING
SPECIAL
PROBLEMS**
(pp. 284–294)

Section 16.1 deals with the correct use of negatives in sentences. Sentence 16.2 presents twenty pitfalls in usage, ranging from frequently confused words to unacceptable nonstandard usage.

For a review of the entire chapter and a related writing activity, see the Skills Review and Writing Workshop on page 294.

16.1 Double Negatives

(pp. 284–286)

OBJECTIVE

After completing this section, students should be able to

- Recognize and correct double negatives.

TEACHING

Getting Started

Most students will have encountered the double negative error in previous language classes. For those students who persist in such errors, it may be helpful to explain that such errors are not simply a fine point of grammar. Double negatives make the meaning of a sentence unclear, or just plain wrong. To say, *We couldn't have no parties this year* is to communicate the opposite of what is intended: *We could have parties*.

Text Follow Through

Discuss text pages 284–286.

Chapter **16**

Solving Special Problems

Many common errors in writing and speech involve the use of words or expressions that have traditionally been considered wrong in most kinds of writing. Other problems are caused by words that are spelled almost alike and so are easily confused.

16.1 Double Negatives

Negative words, such as *never* and *not,* are used in sentences to deny something or to say *no.* Many years ago, it was customary to use two or more negative words in one clause for emphasis. Today only one negative word is needed to give a sentence a negative meaning.

The Mistaken Use of Double Negatives

Some people mistakenly use *double negatives,* two negative words, when one alone is called for.

16.1 Double Negatives

Do not write sentences with double negatives.

In the following chart, the sentences on the left contain double negatives. Notice on the right how each sentence can be corrected in either of two ways.

Double Negatives	Corrected Sentences
We did*n't* see *no one*.	We did*n't* see anyone.
	We saw *no one*.
She has*n't no* money.	She has*n't* any money.
	She has *no* money.
You *never* gave me *nothing*.	You *never* gave me anything.
	You gave me *nothing*.

EXERCISE: Correcting Double Negatives. The following sentences contain double negatives. On your paper rewrite each sentence in *two* ways.

EXAMPLE: We didn't tell Frank nothing about the surprise.

We didn't tell Frank anything about the surprise.

We told Frank nothing about the surprise.

1. didn't see anybody/saw nobody   3. never suggests anything/suggests nothing

1. Jennifer <u>didn't see nobody</u> she knew at the conference.
2. Michael <u>couldn't find nothing</u> about his topic in the encyclopedia. couldn't find anything/could find nothing
3. Franklin <u>never suggests nothing</u> really original.
4. I <u>haven't never</u> eaten octopus. haven't ever/have never
5. <u>Don't say nothing</u> about the contest to Don.
6. Phyllis <u>hasn't no</u> extra time this term. hasn't any/has no
7. Chris <u>will not show Paul none</u> of her sketches.
8. <u>Don't never</u> ride your bicycle on that road. Don't ever/ Never
9. I <u>don't make no</u> excuses for my behavior.
10. William <u>can't remember nothing</u> about the accident.

5. Don't say anything/Say nothing   7. will not show Paul any/will show Paul none   9. don't make any/make no   10. can't remember anything/can remember nothing

Assign the Exercise, page 285, and Developing Writing Skills, page 286.

Less advanced Oral reinforcement can be of great benefit to students. Training students to proofread their writing by reading it aloud will be useful throughout their school careers. Often ears can pick up what eyes miss. You can have students read aloud both of their corrected versions of the sentences in Exercise A, correcting any continued mistakes as they read.

Average Ask students to write compound sentences containing a single negative in each clause. For example: *I said I couldn't attend, but she didn't hear me.*

For further practice, have students rewrite Sentences 2, 5, 7, and 8 from Developing Writing Skills, keeping the same meaning, but finding a different way to make each statement negative.

Advanced You may wish to introduce the words *hardly*, *barely*, and *scarcely* as negatives which are incorrect when used with *not*. Sentences like the following may be written on the board for correction:

I couldn't hardly hear the announcement.
She hasn't barely got time to rest between events.

Students should be able to see that the intended meaning is that the person *could* hear, although to a small degree; that the person *has* time to rest, but not much. Therefore, the word *not* is unnecessary.

Additional Practice

Practice Pages or Practice Book, page 91

Less advanced Exercise Bank, Exercises A and B, page 133

Average Exercise Bank, Exercises A, B, and C, page 133

Advanced Exercise Bank, Exercises B and C, page 133

TESTING

Test Program

Unit Pretest, page 43
Chapter Test, page 51
Unit Post-Test, page 56

RE-TEACHING

Practice Pages or Practice Book, page 91

THINKING SKILLS

Application—*Modifying* sentences to correct double negatives (Exercise, page 285)

Synthesis—*Writing* negative sentences correctly (Developing Writing Skills, page 286)

16.2 Twenty Common Usage Problems

(pp. 286–293)

OBJECTIVE

After completing this section, students should be able to

• Identify and avoid making a number of common usage errors.

TEACHING

Dictate to the class the following sentences, asking students to write the correct spelling of each italicized word:

Ginny gave me good *advise.*
Did the news *effect* her strongly?
My brother is three inches taller *then* I.

Then write the sentences on the board and have students check their spellings of the

---

DEVELOPING WRITING SKILLS: Writing Negative Sentences. Use each of the following words in a negative sentence.

Answers will vary; samples are given for the first two.

EXAMPLE: nobody

When I called her house, nobody answered.

1. wasn't
2. never
3. not
4. didn't
5. none
6. can't
7. nowhere
8. nothing
9. wouldn't
10. no

1. There wasn't any cereal left.   2. I have never seen a ring like yours.

16.2 Twenty Common Usage Problems

This section presents twenty usage problems in alphabetical order. Some of the problems are expressions that you should avoid entirely. Others are words that are often confused because they have a similar spelling or meaning.

As you read through the list, note especially those words that have caused you difficulty in the past. Then use the exercises for practice.

You may also wish to refer to this section for guidance when you are writing and revising your compositions. If you do not find the explanation of a problem anywhere in this section, check for it in the index at the back of the book.

(1) *accept, except*   Do not confuse these words, which sound alike but differ in spelling and in meaning. *Accept,* a verb, means "to take what is offered" or "to agree to." *Except,* a preposition, means "leaving out" or "other than."

VERB: We *accept* your plan.

PREPOSITION: No one *except* Betty Jane agreed to the idea of spending the summer at a dude ranch.

16.2 Twenty Common Usage Problems

(2) *advice, advise*   Do not confuse the spelling of these related words. *Advice* is a noun meaning "an opinion"; *advise* is a verb meaning "to give an opinion to."

NOUN: Ask your teacher for *advice* about the assignment.

VERB: Our teacher *advised* us about what to do.

(3) *affect, effect*   *Affect* is almost always a verb meaning "to influence" or "to bring about a change in." *Effect,* usually a noun, means "result." Occasionally, *effect* is a verb. Then it means "to cause."

VERB: The wrong kind of diet can *affect* a person's health.

NOUN: You should feel the *effect* of the medicine immediately.

VERB: The administration *effected* many changes in the budget.

(4) *all ready, already*   *All ready* is used as an adjective to mean "ready." *Already,* an adverb, means "by or before this time."

ADJECTIVE: We were *all ready* to leave.

ADVERB: The mail had *already* arrived.

(5) *among, between*   *Among* and *between* are both prepositions. *Among* always refers to three or more. *Between* usually refers to just two.

EXAMPLES: The kite became caught *among* the pin oak's branches.

Let's keep this secret *between* you and me.

(6) *at*   Do not use *at* after *where*. Simply eliminate the word *at.*

INCORRECT: I don't know *where* we're *at.*

CORRECT: I don't know *where* we are.

(7) *because*   Do not use *because* after *the reason.* Eliminate one or the other.

three words. Elicit that each of the three is only one letter different in spelling from another word (*advice, affect, than*) which differs in meaning but is often confused with the look-alike. Have students pronounce each word of the three pairs together, and ask for volunteers to use each in an oral sentence. Explain to the class that these are just three examples of words, phrases, or sets of words that they will focus on now in order to clear up possible confusion.

Text Follow Through

Discuss text pages 286–293.

Assign Exercise A, page 291; Exercise B, page 291; Exercise C, page 292; and Developing Writing Skills, page 293.

Less advanced   You might want to stop after reviewing each set of five items and have students complete and discuss the corresponding exercise. You might also encourage students to refer to the glossary when they explain their answers.

Average   Students can be asked to write original sentences using each of the following word pairs correctly:

1. among/between
2. beside/besides
3. in/into
4. like/as
5. than/then

Advanced   Have students review compositions or journal entries they have written previously to locate any examples of usage errors of the sort studied in this section. They should then write the sentences, with errors corrected, on a separate piece of paper. Another activity you might assign is to have students write paragraphs in which they use as many of the twenty pairs of words studied as possible. Students can then exchange papers and try to locate and correct any errors in each paragraph.

Additional Practice

Practice Pages or Practice Book, page 92

Less advanced Exercise Bank, Exercises A and B, page 134

Average Exercise Bank, Exercises A, B, and C, page 134

Advanced Exercise Bank, Exercises B and C, page 134

TESTING

Test Program

Unit Pretest, page 43
Chapter Test, pages 51, 52
Unit Post-Test, page 56

RE-TEACHING

Practice Pages or Practice Book, page 92

THINKING SKILLS

Comprehension—*Distinguishing* between troublesome word pairs to avoid errors in usage (Exercises A and B, page 291; Exercises C and D, page 292)

Synthesis—*Writing* sentences correctly using words that often cause usage problems (Developing Writing Skills, page 293)

INCORRECT: *The reason* for his absence is *because* he has a sore throat and fever.

CORRECT: He is absent *because* he has a sore throat and fever.

The reason he is absent is that he has a sore throat and fever.

(8) ***beside, besides*** As prepositions, these two words have different meanings and cannot be interchanged. *Beside* means "at the side of" or "close to." *Besides* means "in addition to."

EXAMPLES: Sit here *beside* me.

No one *besides* me knew the answer.

(9) ***different from, different than*** *Different from* is generally preferred over *different than*.

EXAMPLES: The movie was *different from* what I had expected.

This movie is *different from* that one.

(10) ***due to the fact that*** All these words are unnecessary. Use *since* or *because* instead.

INCORRECT: *Due to the fact that* you were late, we began without you.

CORRECT: *Since* you were late, we began without you.

(11) ***farther, further*** *Farther* usually refers to distance. *Further* means "additional" or "to a greater degree or extent."

EXAMPLES: The school I will attend next year is much *farther* away.

Lisa wanted *further* information.

(12) ***in, into*** *In* refers to position. *Into* suggests motion.

POSITION: Three baby rabbits are *in* my mother's vegetable garden.

MOTION: The dog chased the rabbits *into* the woods.

16.2 Twenty Common Usage Problems

(13) kind of, sort of   Do not use *kind of* and *sort of* to mean "rather" or "somewhat."

INCORRECT: Lorraine felt *kind of* good about her grades in English and Spanish.

CORRECT: Lorraine felt *rather* good about her grades in English and Spanish.

(14) like   *Like* is a preposition that usually means "similar to" or "in the same way as." It should be followed by an object. Do not use *like* before a subject and a verb. Use *as* or *that* instead.

PREPOSITION: The creature's hands looked *like* claws.
                                                    OBJ

              He was howling *like* a coyote.
                                          OBJ

INCORRECT: Your plan worked just *like* you said it would.
                                               S   V

              It seems *like* the movie has started.
                                    S   V

CORRECT: Your plan worked just *as* you said it would.

              It seems *that* the movie has started.

(15) than, then   *Than* is used in comparisons. Do not confuse it with the adverb *then*, which usually refers to time.

COMPARISON: Aunt Penelope is older *than* Alexander thought she was.

TIME: The party ended at six o'clock, and *then* we left for home.

(16) that, which, who   *That* can refer to either things or people. *Which* should be used only with things and *who* only with people.

THINGS: The book *that* (or *which*) you borrowed from the library is overdue.

PEOPLE: The person *that* (or *who*) delivered the speech is my teacher.

(17)   *their, there, they're*   *Their,* a possessive adjective, always modifies a noun. *There* can be used either as a sentence starter or as an adverb. *They're* is a contraction of *they are.*

POSSESIVE ADJECTIVE: Our guests forgot *their* coats.

SENTENCE STARTER: *There* are two ways to solve the mystery.

ADVERB: Put the books *there.*

CONTRACTION: *They're* leaving   for   Canada   and   Alaska tomorrow.

(18)   *this here, that there*   Avoid using these expressions by simply leaving out *here* and *there.*

INCORRECT: *This here* pair of designer jeans costs twenty-five dollars.

CORRECT: *This* pair of designer jeans costs twenty-five dollars.

(19)   *to, too, two*   *To* is a preposition used to begin a prepositional phrase or an infinitive. *Too* is an adverb that modifies adjectives and other adverbs. Do not forget its second *o.* *Two* is a number.

PREPOSITION: *to* the bank, *to* Chicago

INFINITIVE: *to* see, *to* receive

ADVERB: *too* short, *too* slowly

NUMBER: *two* friends, *two* canaries

(20)   *when, where, why*   Do not use *when, where,* or *why* directly after a linking verb. Reword the sentence.

INCORRECT: Parties *are when* I always have a good time.

The park *is where* we play baseball.

Because I need advice *is why* I am calling.

CORRECT: I always have a good time at parties.

We play baseball in the park.

I am calling because I need advice.

16.2 Twenty Common Usage Problems

EXERCISE A: Avoiding Usage Problems 1–5. For each of the following sentences, choose the correct form from the choices in parentheses and write it on your paper.

EXAMPLE: (Among, Between) the six of them, we should be able to find someone with a sense of humor.

   Among

1. Evelyn gave me some good (<u>advice</u>, advise).
2. The huge sandwich was divided (between, <u>among</u>) Kit, Mary, and Stan.
3. The team members were (<u>all ready</u>, already) for the game.
4. (Accept, <u>Except</u>) for Steven no one had any difficulty finding the restaurant.
5. Hot weather (<u>affects,</u> effects) people in different ways.
6. This place is (all ready, <u>already</u>) beginning to look more attractive.
7. The senator asked several experts to (advice, <u>advise</u>) her on the subject of energy.
8. Joan's words had a strange (affect, <u>effect</u>) on him: He fainted.
9. The conversation (among, <u>between</u>) the two sounded like a vaudeville routine.
10. It is always difficult to (<u>accept</u>, except) one's own limitations.

EXERCISE B: Avoiding Usage Problems 6–10. For each of the following sentences, choose the correct form from the choices in parentheses and write it on your paper.

1. The hayride was canceled (due to the fact that, <u>because</u>) rain was predicted.
2. I don't know where my algebra book could (<u>be</u>, be at).
3. The reason we came is (because, <u>that</u>) your letter alarmed us.
4. (Due to the fact that, <u>Since</u>) Janet has studied Italian, she will give the waiter our order.

5. (Beside, <u>Besides</u>) us, who will help decorate the gym?
6. Chris didn't want his new room to be any different (<u>from</u>, than) his old one.
7. Do you know where bait can be (<u>found</u>, found at)?
8. His reason for resigning was (because, <u>that</u>) his family needed him.
9. The girls moved the picnic table so that they could eat (<u>beside</u>, besides) the lake.
10. This version of the story is different (<u>from</u>, than) yours.

EXERCISE C: Avoiding Usage Problems 11–15. For each of the following sentences, choose the correct form from the choices in parentheses and write it on your paper.

1. Kathleen walked (in, <u>into</u>) the room and announced the name of the winner.
2. His progress in his studies was greater (<u>than</u>, then) his friends imagined.
3. It seems (like, <u>that</u>) you were expecting us all along.
4. Wynn looked (kind of, <u>rather</u>) green after eating all those peppers.
5. (<u>In</u>, Into) the closet Kelly found the missing keys.
6. Nathan has a good speaking voice, but he sings (as, <u>like</u>) a frog.
7. First I dropped the turkey, and (than, <u>then</u>) I spilled the gravy.
8. Andy wrote every day, just (like, <u>as</u>) she had promised.
9. It looks (sort of, <u>rather</u>) silly for you to leave after just arriving.
10. As you climb (<u>farther</u>, further) up the mountain, the trees become sparser.

EXERCISE D: Avoiding Usage Problems 16–20. For each of the following sentences, choose the correct form from the choices in parentheses and write it on your paper.

Developing Writing Skills

Have students practice correct usage in writing by completing the following assignment.

Writing Across the Curriculum

Although most people like the area in which they live, almost everyone enjoys seeing other parts of the country or the world. Do you have a place that you especially enjoyed visiting or that you would like to visit in the future?

Prewriting Think of a place that you have visited or that you would like to visit in the future. Free write about the place for several minutes. Choose the words and phrases that best describe the place and the reasons for its attraction. Add any other important details to your notes.

Writing Write the first draft of a travel brochure about your favorite vacation spot. Your purpose is to try to persuade others to visit this place. Include sensory details in your physical description that will appeal to more than one of the readers' senses. Also include the reasons why you find the place appealing.

Revising Make sure that your brochure follows the logical order you established in your prewriting. Check your description. Will someone who has never seen the vacation spot be able to imagine what it looks, sounds, and smells like? Have you included the reasons why you find the place particularly appealing? Does your brochure have any common usage problems? Prepare a final draft.

16.2 Twenty Common Usage Problems

1. Put (<u>this</u>, this here) cover on the bicycle.
2. The woman (which, <u>that</u>) wrote our textbook gave a lecture to the science club.
3. He has two sisters, but (their, <u>they're</u>) both engaged.
4. Twilight is (when, <u>the hour when</u>) everything seems most tranquil.
5. The dog (who, <u>that</u>) ran up to greet you is ten years old.
6. Independence Hall is (where, <u>the place where</u>) the Liberty Bell is displayed.
7. Mattie and Teresa built (they're, <u>their</u>) model dinosaur out of toothpicks.
8. Two hundred dollars is (to, <u>too</u>) high a price for this stereo.
9. He told me that (his cold is why he skipped practice, <u>he skipped practice because of his cold</u>).
10. The carpenter (which, <u>who</u>) built this room is skillful.

DEVELOPING WRITING SKILLS: Writing Sentences Using Certain Words Correctly. Write ten original sentences, each following one of the descriptions given below. Refer to pages 286–290.
Answers will vary.

EXAMPLE: Write a sentence using *different from.*

    Hillary's opinion is different from yours.

1. Write a sentence using the preposition *except.*
2. Write a sentence using the verb *accept.*
3. Write a sentence using *farther* in relation to distance.
4. Write a sentence using the noun *advice.*
5. Write a sentence using the verb *advise.*
6. Write a sentence using a verb that means "to influence."
7. Write a sentence using a preposition that means "at the side of."
8. Write a sentence using the preposition *like.*
9. Write a sentence using *further* to mean "additional" or "to a greater degree or extent."
10. Write a sentence with the preposition *besides.*

Checking Your Skills

In the Checking Your Skills assignment, students have corrected common usage problems in a paragraph. Explain to students that often the best way to remember correct usage is to find easy ways to remember the rules.

Collaborative Learning

Divide the class into ten groups of about the same ability level. Assign to each group two of the twenty common usage problems covered in this chapter. Have each group work together to come up with a fun and easy way to remember the usage rules for both of their problems. Suggest that students try to come up with short poems such as limericks, songs, riddles, jokes, fairy tales, fables, or even short skits. Explain that such brief and memorable explanations will make remembering the rules easier and hopefully more enjoyable. You will probably have to assist the groups to come up with ideas and to formulate their ideas into finished work. Have the groups present their finished work to the rest of the class, and display it in its written form on the class bulletin board.

Using Usage Skills in Writing

Revising Have students make sure that they have written their historical narratives from the first-person point of view, using the pronoun "I" when referring to themselves. Students should be sure that they used this point of view throughout the narrative.

Skills Review and Writing Workshop

Solving Special Problems

CHECKING YOUR SKILLS

Rewrite the following paragraph, correcting all usage errors.
Answers will vary.

(1) The marathon race was when Claudia disciplined herself farther than ever before. (2) She had always been sort of athletic, due to the fact that she had three brothers. (3) Her experiences hadn't been different than there's, and their was considerable rivalry between them all. (4) Claudia was the only one, however, which signed up for the marathon. (5) Her brothers said it would be to much for her, but she did not except their advise. (6) As she trained, Claudia noticed that her routine was also effecting her schoolwork. (7) Her concentration improved, and her grades hadn't never been better. (8) By race day Claudia felt like the marathon itself was less important then what she had learned from training. (9) Beside finishing, she was proud of her whole effort. (10) The real reason for her pride was because this time she had competed with no one accept herself.

USING USAGE SKILLS IN WRITING
Writing About a Historical Event

Writers often write about their involvements in historical events. Practice doing the same by following the steps below.
Answers will vary.

Prewriting: Choose a historical event with which you are familiar. Imagine you were one of the people involved in this event. Make notes on what it might have meant to be involved in it. List historical details to include.

Writing: Begin by identifying the event and the part you played. Using your notes and list, describe the event and how it affected your life.

Revising: Check your usage. Then look for other improvements to make. After revising, proofread carefully.

UNIT III

Mechanics

17 Using Capitals

18 Using Abbreviations

19 Using Punctuation Marks

UNIT III
Mechanics
(pp. 295–390)

This unit presents detailed explanations of capitalization, abbreviation, and punctuation. Although some of the material may be a review for many of your students, you may still want to plan to spend enough time on this unit to cover all the rules and exercises. Most students can benefit greatly from a review of basic points combined, as in the present unit, with new concepts and ideas. The broader view they will gain should help them see mechanics as a means of communicating more clearly.

The material on capitalization and abbreviation in Chapters 17 and 18 does not depend greatly on students' knowledge of grammar or sentence structure. Thus, you may teach the chapters at any time during the year. You can also choose to present sections of the chapters whenever students' compositions demonstrate a need for instruction in these areas.

Comprehension of the material on punctuation in Chapter 19, in contrast, does depend to a large extent on students' understanding of grammar and sentence structure. Therefore, if you wish to teach punctuation in conjunction with composition, you will first need to make sure that students understand the related concepts covered in Unit I. You can do this by skimming the section you wish to cover, noting any terms that the students may have difficulty with, and then studying or reviewing in class the appropriate material in Unit I.

CHAPTER 17
Using Capitals
(pp. 296–317)

Chapter 17 consists of a number of short sections that move from the most basic uses of capitals to more specialized uses of capitals. Sections 17.1 through 17.3 cover the most basic uses of capitals. Sections 17.4 through 17.6 cover more specialized uses of capitals.

For a review of the entire chapter and a related writing activity, see the Skills Review and Writing Workshop on page 317.

Chapter # 17

Using Capitals

Capital letters may signal the beginning of a sentence or an important word within a sentence. A sentence written without capitals is confusing: mr. bailey conducted the band from youngstown as they played a march by sousa.

With the addition of capitals, the same sentence is easier to read: Mr. Bailey conducted the band from Youngstown as they played a march by Sousa.

The meaning of a sentence is clearer when it is capitalized correctly.

To capitalize means to begin a word with a capital letter.

The six sections in this chapter present a number of rules that will help you capitalize correctly.

17.1 Capitals for First Words

17.1 Capitals for First Words
(pp. 296–300)

Capital letters are used for the first words in all sentences and in many quotations. They are also used for the word *I*, whatever its position in a sentence.

OBJECTIVES

After completing this section, students should be able to

- Capitalize the first word in a sentence correctly.
- Use capitals correctly in quotations.
- Capitalize the word *I* whenever it appears in a sentence.

17.1 Capitals for First Words

Sentences

One of the most common uses of a capital is to signal the beginning of a sentence.

Capitalize the first word in declarative, interrogative, imperative, and exclamatory sentences.

DECLARATIVE: Strong gusts of wind made it dangerous to drive on the bridge.

INTERROGATIVE: Who found the clue leading to the suspect's arrest?

IMPERATIVE: Think carefully before you decide.

EXCLAMATORY: What an amazing coincidence this is!

Sometimes only part of a sentence is written out. The rest of the sentence is understood. In these cases a capital is still needed for the first word.

EXAMPLES: When?   Why not?   Certainly!

EXERCISE A: Using Capitals to Begin Sentences. Copy the following items onto your paper, adding the missing capitals.

Underlined letters are to be capitalized.

EXAMPLE: great! when will we leave?

Great! When will we leave?

1. few students have shown more determination than she.
2. i left my book somewhere. but where?
3. what? would you repeat that?
4. please refer to an encyclopedia for a more detailed explanation.
5. next weekend? we thought the play opened tonight.
6. how talented you are!
7. stand at attention during the inspection.
8. when is the science project due?
9. wow! that was a surprise!
10. his bicycle is considerably older than he is.

TEACHING

Getting Started

Write on the board the following sentences: *"the mail will not be delivered today," i informed him. "it is a holiday, you know."* Ask a volunteer to come to the board and correct the sentence. Elicit from students that *the* and *it* must be capitalized because they begin new sentences; *i* must be capitalized because that word is by convention always capitalized. You might want to tie this section in with Section 19.6 (pages 363–371) to be sure students understand proper use of quotation marks before they attempt Exercise B and Developing Writing Skills in this section.

Text Follow Through

Discuss text pages 296–300.

Assign Exercise A, page 297; Exercise B, page 298; Exercise C, page 299; and Developing Writing Skills, page 299.

Less advanced You may want to work through the Quotations subsection with students, having students write the exercise sentences on the board and make any corrections necessary. For sentences 2, 3, 8, 9, and 10 of Developing Writing Skills, you may want to provide the introductory, concluding, or interrupting expressions *(they promised, He reminded,* etc.).

Average You may wish to ignore the subsections Sentences and The Word *I*, with which students will probably have no difficulty, and focus entirely on correct use of capitals in quotations. You might excerpt a portion of a literature selection read by the class, reproducing a section of dialogue but using lower-case letters for all words that begin sentences. Then ask students to underscore all words that should be capitalized.

Advanced Students can use this section for a quick review. If any students make careless errors in writing quoted sentences, suggest that they write half a page of dialogue between two people, being certain to use complete sentences, and to interrupt some quotations with the words of saying. They should exchange papers and have classmates check whether they have used capitals correctly.

Additional Practice

Practice Pages or Practice Book, page 93

Less advanced Exercise Bank, Exercises A and B, pages 135–137

Average Exercise Bank, Exercises A, B, and C, pages 135–137

Advanced Exercise Bank, Exercises B and C, pages 135–137

TESTING

Test Program

Unit Pretest, page 57
Chapter Test, pages 60, 61
Unit Post-Test, page 66

Quotations

A capital letter also signals the first word in a quoted sentence.

Capitalize the first word in a quotation if the quotation is a complete sentence.

In each of the following examples, the first word of the quotation is capitalized because it begins a complete sentence.

EXAMPLES: Several people shouted, "Stop the bus!"

"She really wants to play first base," Arlene confided.

When a quotation consists of one complete sentence in two parts, only one capital is needed.

EXAMPLE: "How much longer," asked Brian, "are you going to need that book?"

If a quotation contains more than one sentence, capitalize the first word of each sentence.

EXAMPLE: "Please distribute these maps to everyone," explained the director. "They show the location of each exhibit."

EXERCISE B: Using Capitals for Quotations. Copy each of the following sentences onto your paper, adding the missing capitals.
Underlined letters are to be capitalized.

EXAMPLE: "where did you find this one?" he asked.

"Where did you find this one?" he asked.

1. "begin tuning your instruments," the conductor told the musicians.
2. the telephone operator asked, "what number did you dial?"
3. "let me do the driving," said Earl. "sit back and relax."
4. "turnips are good for you," he stated as he served the steaming dish.

RE-TEACHING
Practice Pages or Practice
Book, page 93

17.1 Capitals for First Words

5. "cardinals devour the birdseed," she explained, "but wood-peckers prefer suet."
6. after an hour the audience began to shout, "we want Joe! we want Joe!"
7. "all the important documents are in the filing cabinet," the secretary explained. "notice, however, that they are not in alphabetical order."
8. Marty whispered, "let me borrow some paper."
9. "collecting rock samples," Jill told the class, "is a fascinating hobby."
10. "dependable equipment is a must," the instructor noted.

THINKING SKILLS

Application—*Using* correct capitalization in sentences and quotations (Exercise A, page 297; Exercise B, page 298; Exercise C, page 299)

Synthesis—*Writing* sentences and quotations to fit patterns, using correct capitalization (Developing Writing Skills, page 299)

The Word *I*

The pronoun *I* is always written as a capital.

Capitalize the word *I* wherever it appears in a sentence.

EXAMPLE: I worked two years as a clerk before I received the promotion.

EXERCISE C: Using the Pronoun *I*. Copy the following sentences onto your paper, adding the missing capitals.
Underlined letters are to be capitalized.
EXAMPLE: she and i were the last to arrive.

She and I were the last to arrive.

1. am i late?
2. i hope i answered the question correctly.
3. "sometimes," i told her, "i feel as discouraged as you do."
4. when they finally announced the winner, it was i.
5. the following pronouns are singular: i, she, and he.

DEVELOPING WRITING SKILLS: Using Capitals for First Words. Each of the following patterns represents a complete sentence. Write sentences that fit the punctuation of each pattern, using capitals where they are needed.
Answers will vary; samples are given.

EXAMPLE: _____! _____!

　　　　Darn! He let the cat in again!

1. _____Is the dog outside_____?
2. "_____I think so_____," ___he said___,
3. ___She asked___, "_____Are you going_____?"
4. _____What a day we had_____!
5. _____The rains began_____.
6. ___Wow___! _____Aren't you excited_____?
7. _____The dog is hungry_____. ___Why___?
8. "___Let's go___," ___I said___. "___We're late___."
9. "___Throw it___," ___he said___, "___now___."
10. _____Where is the party_____? ___When___?

17.2 Capitals for Proper Nouns

Because a proper noun names a specific person, place, or thing, it is capitalized.

Capitalize all proper nouns.

Names of People

One kind of proper noun that you will often see is the name of a specific person.

Capitalize each part of a person's full name.

EXAMPLES:　Michelle T. Como　　P.A. Sullivan

When a last name has two parts and the first part is *Mc, O',* or *St.,* the second part of the last name must also be capitalized.

EXAMPLES:　McMurphy　　O'Connor　　St. John

For two-part last names that do not begin with *Mc, O'* or *St.,* the capitalization varies. Check with a reliable source for the correct spelling.

300

17.2 Capitals for Proper Nouns
(pp. 300–307)

OBJECTIVES

After completing this section, students should be able to

- Capitalize the names of people correctly.
- Identify and capitalize correctly proper nouns that name geographical places.
- Identify and capitalize correctly a number of other proper nouns including those that name specific events and specific groups.

TEACHING

Getting Started

Prepare a television trivia quiz (to give students orally), being sure to include questions that require students to name people, places, specific events and times, and specific groups. A

17.2 Capitals for Proper Nouns

EXERCISE A: Using Capitals for Names of People. On your paper write each name that you find in the following sentences, adding the missing capitals.

Underlined letters are to be capitalized.

EXAMPLE: Her best friend was andrea mcmahon.

Andrea McMahon

1. We asked cindy to join us on our class trip.
2. This book by e.b. white is a children's classic.
3. My cousin, paul mcbride, is a talented trumpet player.
4. helen st. james invited us to her graduation party.
5. The firm is managed by t.l. johnson and her partner, b.r. whitaker.
6. She usually listens to the music of brahms or beethoven.
7. Short stories by o. henry were among his favorites.
8. The convention was organized by elizabeth cady stanton and susan b. anthony.
9. With a friendly smile, maria lopez invited the unexpected visitors to enter.
10. The patriot paul revere was an expert silversmith.

Geographical Places

The names of specific geographical places are proper nouns.

Capitalize geographical names.

Any place listed on a map should be capitalized.

GEOGRAPHICAL NAMES	
Streets	First Avenue, Spencer Road
Towns and Cities	Plainfield, Los Angeles, Tokyo
Counties	Orange County, Wayne County
States and Provinces	Oklahoma, Manitoba
Nations	France, Ecuador, Saudi Arabia
Continents	South America, Africa, Asia

multiple-choice quiz is preferable. Be sure students understand the quiz is not to be graded. When students have completed the quiz, have them place correct answers on the board. Ask students to check carefully to make sure answers are correctly capitalized. Ask volunteers to list examples of nouns that are capitalized. Elicit that all answers to the quiz are proper nouns and therefore must be capitalized.

Text Follow Through

Discuss text pages 300–307.

Assign Exercise A, page 301; Exercise B, page 302; Exercise C, page 306; and Developing Writing Skills, page 307.

Less advanced Students can be asked to supply additional examples for each of the charts in the section. You might also read aloud sets of items such as the following and ask students to write on their papers the proper noun in each set of words, using correct capitalization, of course:

1. ocean   body of water Isthmus of Panama
2. Sears Tower   skyscraper building

When they complete the Developing Writing Skills activity, you may want to have students work in small groups, providing each with a sample brochure to examine.

Average Students can work in pairs to complete the Developing Writing Skills activity. Encourage them to use encyclopedias, atlases, and other reference materials to find specific information to include in their descriptions. You might also ask students to find sentences containing proper nouns in magazine and newspaper articles. They can then copy the sentences, leaving out the capitals. In class, students can exchange papers with classmates and capitalize the sentences correctly.

Advanced It is unlikely that students need to review the entire section systematically. You might have students create quizzes for each other. Each quiz should contain sentences that fail to capitalize proper nouns in a wide range of subcategories. Have students leave a blank line after each sentence. Students should then exchange quizzes, make corrections, and beneath each write the category from one of the charts in this section that indicates the type of proper noun. For example, one item might read:

The *super bowl* will be played on *new year's day*, *wednesday*. (special event, holiday, day)

Additional Practice

Practice Pages or Practice Book, pages 94, 95

Less advanced Exercise Bank, Exercises A and B, pages 138–140

Average Exercise Bank, Exercises A, B, and C, pages 138–140

Advanced Exercise Bank, Exercises B and C, pages 138–140

TESTING

Test Program

Unit Pretest, page 57
Chapter Test, pages 60, 61
Unit Post-Test, page 66

Valleys and Deserts	Death Valley, the Mojave Desert
Mountains	the Rocky Mountains, Mount Rushmore
Sections of a Country	New England, the Southwest, the Northeast
Islands	Iceland, Pitcairn Island
Scenic Spots	the Everglades, Yosemite National Park
Rivers and Falls	the Colorado River, Rainbow Falls
Lakes and Bays	Lake Superior, Saginaw Bay
Seas and Oceans	the Dead Sea, the Indian Ocean

Compass points, such as north, southwest, or east, are considered proper nouns only when they name specific geographical locations. In those cases, they are capitalized. When they simply refer to directions, they are not.

EXAMPLES: We spent our vacation in the East.

Bitterly cold winds swept southeast across the mountains.

EXERCISE B: Using Capitals for Geographical Places. On your paper write each geographical place name that you find in the following sentences, adding all the capitals that are missing.

Underlined letters are to be capitalized.

EXAMPLE: They had seen niagara falls in 1954.

Niagara Falls

1. A few miles south of buckhorn lake is the cumberland national park.
2. The Blakes bought a cottage on lake drive in schuyler county.
3. Our tour included a visit to india and china, neighboring countries in asia.
4. The trip was extended to include a week's stay in ceylon, an island in the indian ocean.

RE-TEACHING
Practice Pages or Practice Book, pages 94, 95

THINKING SKILLS

Knowledge—*Identifying* names of people as capitalized proper nouns (Exercise A, page 301)
Identifying geographical places as capitalized proper nouns (Exercise B, page 302)
Identifying a variety of proper nouns that should be capitalized (Exercise C, page 306)

Synthesis—*Writing* a description including proper nouns from numerous categories (Developing Writing Skills, page 307)

17.2 Capitals for Proper Nouns

5. The st. johns river flows into the atlantic ocean near jacksonville, florida.
6. The sahara covers most of the land of north africa.
7. We lived in providence, rhode island, before moving to the west.
8. mount everest, the highest of the himalaya mountains, has claimed many lives.
9. During the summer we visited friends in toronto, canada.
10. The plane flew west over the atlantic ocean and landed in halifax, nova scotia, before flying on to bangor, maine.

Other Proper Nouns

Other kinds of proper nouns also require capital letters.

Capitalize the names of specific events and periods of time.

The following chart gives examples of events and times that are capitalized.

SPECIFIC EVENTS AND TIMES	
Historical Periods	the Golden Age, the Renaissance, the Industrial Revolution
Historical Events	the Boxer Rebellion, World War I
Documents	the Declaration of Independence, the Bill of Rights, the Homestead Act
Days	Friday, Sunday
Months	March, June
Holidays	Memorial Day, St. Valentine's Day, New Year's Day
Religious Days	Easter, Pentecost, Muharram
Special Events	the Orange Bowl, the State Fair of Texas

The names of seasons are an exception to this rule. Even though they represent specific times of year, they are not capitalized.

EXAMPLE: Last winter was the coldest in a decade.

Like specific events the names of specific groups are considered to be proper nouns.

Capitalize the names of various organizations, government bodies, political parties, races, and nationalities, as well as the languages spoken by different groups.

The following chart shows examples of each of these kinds of groups.

SPECIFIC GROUPS	
Clubs	the Lincoln School Camera Club, the Philadelphia Pioneer Track Club
Organizations	the International Red Cross, the Girl Scouts
Institutions	Georgia Institute of Technology, Tenakill School, Beth Israel Hospital
Businesses	Rolodex Corporation, L.L. Bean, Inc.
Government Bodies	the Congress of the United States, the Supreme Court, the Los Angeles City Council
Political Parties	the Republican Party, the Democratic Party
Races and Nationalities	Caucasian, Algerian, Japanese, Mexican, American
Languages Spoken by Different Groups	English, Portuguese, Arabic, Norwegian

17.2 Capitals for Proper Nouns

The names of religions and many religious terms are also proper nouns.

Capitalize references to religions, deities, and religious scriptures.

The following chart shows the words that the major religions use to refer to important religious figures and holy writings. Note that the name of each religion is also capitalized.

RELIGIOUS REFERENCES	
Christianity	God, the Lord, the Father, the Son, the Holy Ghost, the Bible, books of the Bible (such as Genesis, Exodus, Matthew, Mark)
Judaism	God, the Lord, the Father, the Prophets, the Torah, the Talmud, the Midrash
Islam	Allah, the Prophet, Mohammed, the Koran
Hinduism	Brahma, the Bhagavad-Gita, the Vedas
Buddhism	Buddha, Mahayana, Hinayana

An exception to this rule occurs when the word *god* or *goddess* is used in reference to ancient mythology. Do not use a capital for the word *god* or *goddess*.

EXAMPLE: the god Mars   the goddess Athena

Many other proper nouns also require capitalization.

Capitalize the names of other special places and items.

The following chart shows specific examples of these other kinds of proper nouns.

OTHER SPECIAL PLACES AND ITEMS	
Monuments	the Eiffel Tower, the Statue of Liberty
Memorials	the Tomb of the Unknown Soldier

Buildings	the Museum of Natural History
Celestial Bodies (except the moon, the sun, and generally the earth)	the Spiral Galaxy, Jupiter, Orion
Awards	the Pulitzer Prize, the Nobel Peace Prize
Air, Sea, Space, and Land Craft	*Air Force One*, the *Lusitania*, *Apollo 12*, a Ford Model A
Trademarks	Kellogg's Rice Krispies, Polaroid

EXERCISE C: Using Capitals for Other Proper Nouns.

On your paper write each proper noun that you find in the following sentences, adding the missing capitals.

EXAMPLE: The temple was dedicated to the goddess minerva.

   Minerva

1. The english and americans have been allied for many years.
2. Janet bought a box of hershey's to make cocoa for the ice-skating party.
3. Many cards sent on valentine's day picture the god cupid.
4. For Jed the most impressive monument in washington was the lincoln memorial.
5. In our country thanksgiving is traditionally celebrated on the last thursday in november.
6. After graduating from westchester community college, she worked for gaylord ad agency.
7. John was a democrat when he was first elected to the house of representatives.
8. In the spring christians celebrate easter.
9. Colorful fireworks blazed across the sky on that fourth of july.
10. The founder of the religion now known as islam was mohammed.

17.2 Capitals for Proper Nouns

11. Paul thoroughly enjoyed his visit to the museum of modern art.
12. Sheila sailed the *albatross* to victory in a race sponsored by the west shore yacht club.
13. The bill of rights guarantees freedom of religion, speech, and assembly.
14. During the winter our pantry shelves are stocked with boxes of cheerios.
15. A small statue of buddha was placed in a corner of the room.
16. In 1899 jane addams founded hull house, a settlement house that offered educational and health services to the poor.
17. During the renaissance a new interest in learning spread throughout europe.
18. The spacecraft *voyager 1* photographed saturn's many rings.
19. Jamie and her brother each won a national merit award.
20. To protest great britain's policy of taxation without representation, americans staged the boston tea party.

DEVELOPING WRITING SKILLS: Using Capitals for Proper Nouns.

Write a brief description of a real or fictional vacation area. Your description should include proper nouns from at least ten of the twelve categories in the following list. Try to make the area appeal to tourists by writing in the style of a travel brochure. Be sure to capitalize correctly.

Descriptions will vary; samples of proper nouns are given.

1. A town or city
2. A language   Spanish
3. A special event
4. A historical event or period   World War II
5. A body of water
6. A mountain   Mount Whitney
7. A building   the Sears Tower
8. A celestial body   Venus
9. A monument   Grant's Tomb
10. A month   May
11. A religious holiday   Christmas
12. A section of a country

1. Brownsville, Texas   3. the Danbury Fair   5. the Gulf of Mexico
12. the Southwest

307

Developing Writing Skills

Have students practice capitalizing proper nouns by completing the following assignment.

Writing Across the Curriculum

Have you ever wanted to be a DJ for a radio station and play your favorite songs for people? If you were assigned to play music for the rest of your school, what songs would you choose?

Prewriting   Imagine that your school is having a pep rally for an upcoming school event. You have been selected to choose appropriate music to play as students are coming into the school gym before the pep rally begins. Brainstorm for a list of songs that are appropriate for such an event. The purpose of the music is to get students in the proper mood for the rally. Look over your list and choose the five best songs for this purpose.

Writing   Write the first draft of a memo to the pep rally planning committee. In your memo, begin by explaining the mood you hope to set with the music you have selected. Then, list the songs you have chosen in the order in which you will play them. Now explain why these songs are appropriate.

Revising   Make sure that you have described the mood you hope to set with the songs you have chosen. Are the songs listed in the order in which they will be played? Have you capitalized all proper nouns? Proofread your memo and prepare a final draft.

17.3 Capitals for Proper Adjectives

(pp. 308–309)

OBJECTIVE

After completing this section, students should be able to

- Capitalize proper adjectives correctly.

TEACHING

Getting Started

To introduce the concept of *proper adjectives,* write on the board several proper nouns, such as *Labor Day, England, Shakespeare,* and *Mars.* Beside each, write a sentence such as the following.

1. We marched in the _____ parade.
2. My brother is studying _____ literature.
3. She was asked to direct the _____ festival.
4. Science-fiction film makers prefer to make _____ skin green.

Ask for volunteers to fill the blanks with a form of the word provided on the left or with the word itself. (*Labor Day, English, Shakespearean, Martian*) Explain to students that most proper adjectives are made from proper nouns. As with proper nouns, proper adjectives are capitalized.

Text Follow Through

Discuss text pages 308–309. *Assign* the Exercise, page 308, and Developing Writing Skills, page 309.

Less advanced For extra practice, provide a ditto of Exercise D in Section 3.1 (pages 56–57). Omit the capitals and have students capitalize correctly.

Average Have students compile lists of proper adjectives and the nouns they modify. Proper adjectives might include

17.3 Capitals for Proper Adjectives

Proper adjectives are proper nouns and proper noun forms that are used as adjectives to describe another word.

Proper Adjectives

A single capitalization rule applies to most of the proper adjectives.

Capitalize most proper adjectives.

In the following examples, notice that both proper nouns and proper adjectives are capitalized. Common nouns that are modified by proper adjectives, however, are not capitalized.

PROPER NOUNS: World War I

the Congress

PROPER ADJECTIVES: a World War I battle

a Congressional report

A trademark, the name of a company's product, is considered a proper noun. If you use only part of the trademark, the brand name, to describe a common noun, the brand name becomes a proper adjective. In this case capitalize only the proper adjective.

PROPER NOUN: Kellogg's Rice Krispies

PROPER ADJECTIVE: Kellogg's cereal

EXERCISE: Using Capitals for Proper Adjectives. Complete each of the following sentences by supplying a proper adjective that is correctly capitalized.
Answers will vary; samples are given.
EXAMPLE: Her most treasured possession was an antique

_____ sofa.

Victorian

17.4 Capitals for Titles of People

1. Philip's dog, an __Irish__ setter, won a prize.
2. The __London__ buses run twenty-four hours a day.
3. This Sunday we will have a __Halloween__ party.
4. I asked you to buy __Palmolive__ dish detergent.
5. The __American__ car proved to be the best buy.
6. Saul's parrot nibbled on the __Ritz__ cracker.
7. The librarian located a translation of the __French__ novel.
8. It is easier to write with a __Parker__ pen.
9. The __Wallis__ family attended a reunion in Maryland.
10. __Minnesota__ winters are usually long and cold.

DEVELOPING WRITING SKILLS: Using Capitals for Proper Adjectives. Use each of the following words as a proper adjective in an original sentence. Be sure to capitalize the proper adjectives correctly.

Answers will vary; samples are given for the first two.

EXAMPLE: italian

> He returned with many stories about the friendliness of the Italian people.

1. Sheila is fond of Mexican food.   2. That was a Biblical reference.

1. mexican
2. biblical
3. roman
4. kraft
5. californian
6. danish
7. canadian
8. new england
9. african
10. japanese

Capitals for Titles of People 17.4

Several rules govern the use of capitals for titles of people.

Social and Professional Titles

Social and professional titles may be written before a person's name or may be used when speaking directly to another person.

nationalities, geographical references, and particular months associated with the students' daily lives. Students might also include brand names of items found in local stores.

Advanced Students might be asked to search for and list examples of words that contain proper adjectives that are no longer regularly capitalized. They might start with the following three examples: *dutch oven, french fries,* and *russian dressing.* You can have students share the additional examples they find in printed materials.

Additional Practice

Practice Pages or Practice Book, page 96

Less advanced Exercise Bank, Exercises A and B, page 141

Average Exercise Bank, Exercises A, B, and C, page 141

Advanced Exercise Bank, Exercises B and C, page 141

TESTING

Test Program

> Unit Pretest, page 57
> Chapter Test, pages 60, 61
> Unit Post-Test, page 66

RE-TEACHING

Practice Pages or Practice Book, page 96

THINKING SKILLS

Application—*Using* appropriate proper adjectives in sentences (Exercise, page 308)

Synthesis—*Writing* sentences using correctly capitalized proper adjectives (Developing Writing Skills, page 309)

17.4 Capitals for Titles of People

(pp. 309–313)

OBJECTIVES

After completing this section, students should be able to

- Capitalize social and professional titles correctly.
- Capitalize family titles correctly.

TEACHING

Getting Started

Most students know that titles for people should be capitalized but become confused about appropriate situations for capitalization. To introduce this section, write the following sentences on the board:

1. As soon as he could, Professor Jacobs informed the other professors about the meeting.
2. After having served as president of the volunteer services for two years, Councilman Smith resigned.

Ask students why they think it is appropriate to capitalize *professor* in one instance in sentence 1 and not in the other; *councilman,* but not *president,* in sentence 2. Elicit from students that the title used as a part of the person's name is capitalized, whereas in general usage it is not.

Text Follow Through

Discuss text pages 309–313.

Assign Exercise A, page 311; Exercise B, page 312; and Developing Writing Skills, page 313.

Less advanced Students may need to discuss the meanings of the terms *possessive noun* and *possessive pronoun* before they can make decisions about the appropriate use of capitals in family titles. You might also have students look in newspapers for additional examples of capitalized and uncapitalized titles.

Capitalize the title of a person when it is followed by the person's name or when it is used in direct address.

The following chart gives examples of some of these titles.

TITLES OF PEOPLE	
Social	Mister, Madam or Madame, Miss, Sir
Business	Doctor, Professor, Superintendent
Religious	Reverend, Father, Rabbi, Bishop, Sister
Military	Private, Ensign, Captain, General, Admiral, Colonel
Government	President, Secretary of State, Ambassador, Senator, Representative, Governor, Mayor

Notice how these titles can be used both before a person's name and in direct address with or without the person's name.

BEFORE A NAME: Private Jacobson and Captain Wilkins arrived together.

DIRECT ADDRESS: Doctor Bennett, your patient needs you.

Please, Miss, hurry.

The titles of high government officials, such as the President of the United States, the Chief Justice of the Supreme Court, and the Queen of England, are generally capitalized even if no name or direct address is involved.

Capitalize the titles of certain high government officials even when the titles are not followed by a person's name or used in direct address.

WITH A PERSON'S NAME: Queen Victoria ruled England for over sixty years.

WITHOUT A PERSON'S NAME: The President greeted the Queen as she entered the room.

17.4 Capitals for Titles of People

The titles of lower government officials may also be capitalized when there is no name given, but only when they refer to the specific person who has that title.

SPECIFIC REFERENCE: Tell the members of the press the Mayor will speak with them now.

GENERAL REFERENCE: The mayor of a large city often has a difficult job.

See Section 18.1 for information about capitalizing abbreviated social and professional titles.

EXERCISE A: Using Capitals for Social and Professional Titles. If the title in each of the following sentences is correctly capitalized, write *correct* on your paper. If it is incorrectly capitalized, rewrite the title, correcting the error.

EXAMPLE: The president was seated in the Oval Office of the White House.

President

1. Pardon me, professor, but would you repeat that quotation? *Professor*
2. Several sermons given by reverend Donne have been published. *Reverend*
3. After serving the school district for ten years, superintendent Mills retired. *Superintendent*
4. There was limited television coverage of the President's last press conference. *C*
5. All of the army's Generals agreed that a military attack was not possible. *generals*
6. I heard that senator Carr is widely respected. *Senator*
7. Our teacher asked Sir Richard to speak to the class about British royalty. *C*
8. The queen of England will attend the celebration next month. *Queen*
9. Representative Wilkins voted against the revised plan. *C*
10. In 1898 admiral Dewey defeated the Spanish fleet. *Admiral*

Average Titles that often cause the most confusion for students are those used alone to refer to the person spoken about or to (e.g., *I watched Grandfather repair his car.*). Students may find it helpful to learn that these titles are capitalized because they stand for the person's name.

Advanced Students might be asked to add at least one additional title to each category in the chart on page 310.

Additional Practice

Practice Pages or Practice Book, page 97

Less advanced Exercise Bank, Exercises A and B, pages 142, 143

Average Exercise Bank, Exercises A, B, and C, pages 142, 143

Advanced Exercise Bank, Exercises B and C, pages 142, 143

TESTING

Test Program

Unit Pretest, page 57
Chapter Test, pages 60, 61
Unit Post-Test, page 66

RE-TEACHING

Practice Pages or Practice Book, page 97

THINKING SKILLS

Comprehension—*Distinguishing* between social and professional titles that should and should not be capitalized (Exercise A, page 311)

Application—*Using* capitals correctly for family titles (Exercise B, page 312)

Synthesis—*Writing* sentences using capitals correctly for titles of people (Developing Writing Skills, page 313)

Family Titles

A different rule is needed for titles that show family relationships.

Capitalize titles showing family relationships when the title is used with the person's name or in direct address. The title may also be capitalized in other situations when it refers to a specific person, except when the title comes after a possessive noun or pronoun.

BEFORE A NAME: We invited Aunt Rebecca to the party.

IN DIRECT ADDRESS: Watch out, Uncle, or you'll slip.

REFERRING TO A SPECIFIC PERSON: Is Grandmother going?

AFTER A POSSESSIVE NOUN: I helped Linda's aunt.

AFTER A POSSESSIVE PRONOUN: Your uncle is wonderful.

EXERCISE B: Using Capitals for Family Titles. Complete each of the following sentences by filling the blank with a family title or a title with a name.
Answers will vary; samples are given.

EXAMPLE: Please, _____ , send more pineapples.

Please, Grandfather, send more pineapples.

1. My _aunt_ likes to spend her spare time working on our car.
2. While the rest of us danced, _Grandpa_ played the fiddle.
3. His _brother_ is now on the junior varsity soccer team.
4. "Come quickly, _Mom_ !" Cindy cried.
5. Their _aunt_ knits sweaters for all the children.
6. Few people are as widely traveled as Randy's _father_ .
7. "Let me tell you, _Grandma_ , about that fish I almost caught," he said.
8. Before the race began, _Uncle Jay_ tried to remain calm.
9. I told Jill's _mother_ that we would be home later than usual.

10. Slowly ___Dad___ began to shovel a narrow path through the deep snow.

DEVELOPING WRITING SKILLS: Using Capitals for Titles of People. Write ten sentences of your own, using in each sentence one title as described in the following items. Be sure to capitalize correctly.

Answers will vary; samples are given for the first two.

EXAMPLE: A family member's title and name

We will visit Aunt Roberta this summer.

1. The group will be addressed by Doctor Jonas Bower.

1. A business or professional title and a specific name
2. A government title and a specific name
3. An English monarch's title
4. A military title and a specific name
5. A family member's title used in direct address
6. A reference to the President of the United States
7. A family member's title used with a possessive pronoun
8. A social title and a specific name
9. A government title not followed by a specific name
10. A family member's title used with a possessive noun

2. Senator Smith voted for the bill.

Capitals for Titles of Things 17.5

Titles of certain things must also be capitalized.

Works of Art

Works of art cover a variety of items, including written, printed, sung, drawn, painted, or sculpted materials. The titles of works of art should be capitalized properly.

Capitalize the first word and all the other important words in the titles of books, periodicals, poems, stories, plays, paintings, and other works of art.

17.5 Capitals for Titles of Things
(pp. 313–316)

OBJECTIVES
After completing this section, students should be able to

• Capitalize the titles of works of art correctly.
• Capitalize the titles of school courses when appropriate.

Getting Started

You may check students' recall of the rule for capitalizing titles of works of art and introduce the section as well by asking each student to think of one book, magazine, musical composition, poem, and painting (or sculpture) that each especially likes. Call on students to write one or two titles from their lists on the board. These examples can be used to initiate a discussion about which words should be capitalized in titles of works of art.

Text Follow Through

Discuss text pages 313–316.

Assign Exercise A, page 314; Exercise B, page 315; and Developing Writing Skills, page 315.

Less advanced If you find that students need more practice, you might write on the board or on a ditto master sentences 3, 4, 5, and 6 of Exercise A in Section 19.7 (page 373) and sentences 1, 4, 6, 7, 8, and 9 of Exercise B in Section 19.7 (page 375). Include underlining or quotation marks, but omit the capital letters in the titles.

Average For additional practice, prepare a survey in which you have each student write the title of his or her favorite work in each of the five categories presented on page 314. As you present survey results on the board, have students indicate which letters in each title should be capitalized.

Advanced Have students write sentences about the courses they plan to take in high school, using capitals appropriately.

All the words in a title should be capitalized except for articles (*a, an, the*) and conjunctions and prepositions of fewer than five letters. These words should be capitalized only when they are used as the first word of a title.

Notice the use of underlining and quotation marks in the following examples. See Section 19.7 for more information on the punctuation of these titles.

BOOK: <u>The Red Pony</u>

PERIODICAL: <u>National Geographic</u>

POEM: "Stopping by Woods on a Snowy Evening"

SHORT STORY: "The Gold Bug"

PAINTING: <u>A Girl with a Watering Can</u>

EXERCISE A: Using Capitals for Works of Art. Rewrite each of the following titles, adding the missing capitals. Use underlining and quotation marks as shown.

Underlined letters are to be capitalized.

EXAMPLE: <u>rose in bloom</u>

<u>Rose in Bloom</u>

1. <u>as you like it</u>
2. <u>the call of the wild</u>
3. "<u>jabberwocky</u>"
4. <u>better homes and gardens</u>
5. <u>tales of a wayside inn</u>
6. <u>the mystery of the old clock</u>
7. <u>field and stream</u>
8. <u>the old man and the sea</u>
9. "<u>the ransom of red chief</u>"
10. <u>in the rain</u>

School Courses

Sometimes titles of school courses are capitalized, and sometimes they are not.

17.5 Capitals for Titles of Things

Capitalize titles of courses when the courses are language courses or when the courses are followed by a number.

EXAMPLE: My schedule includes Latin, English, and Science 101.

Although languages are always capitalized, other school subjects should not be capitalized when discussed in a general manner.

EXAMPLE: This semester I will study typing, algebra, and Spanish.

EXERCISE B: Using Capitals for Courses. For each of the following, choose the correctly written course title from the choices in parentheses and write it on your paper.

EXAMPLE: My most difficult course is (german, German).

German

1. I signed up for Miss Albee's (earth science 201, <u>Earth Science 201</u>).
2. Susan is glad that she took an extra course in (<u>math</u>, Math).
3. In (english, <u>English</u>) we are studying lyric poetry.
4. The most popular elective course in our school is (cooking, <u>Cooking</u>).
5. Dennis found that (algebra I, <u>Algebra I</u>) was easier than he had thought.

DEVELOPING WRITING SKILLS: Using Capitals for Titles of Things. Copy each of the following sentences onto your paper, supplying a title as directed in parentheses. Use underlining and quotation marks as shown and be sure to capitalize correctly.

Answers will vary; samples are given.

EXAMPLE: (Play title) is my favorite play.

<u>The King and I</u> is my favorite play.

Point out to students the difference between a general course such as physical science and an actual class title such as Biology I. They may exchange their papers and correct any errors they find.

Additional Practice
Practice Pages or Practice Book, page 98

Less advanced Exercise Bank, Exercises A and B, pages 144, 145

Average Exercise Bank, Exercises A, B, and C, pages 144, 145

Advanced Exercise Bank, Exercises B and C, pages 144, 145

TESTING
Test Program

Unit Pretest, page 57
Chapter Test, pages 60, 61
Unit Post-Test, page 66

RE-TEACHING
Practice Pages or Practice Book, page 98

THINKING SKILLS
Comprehension—*Distinguishing* between titles for courses that should or should not be capitalized (Exercise B, page 315)

Application—*Modifying* titles of works of art to correct capitalization (Exercise A, page 314)

Synthesis—*Writing* correctly capitalized titles of things in sentences (Developing Writing Skills, page 315)

17.6 Capitals in Letters
(p. 316)

OBJECTIVE

After completing this section, students should be able to

• Capitalize letter salutations and closings correctly.

TEACHING

Getting Started

Provide a sample letter (perhaps a letter to the editor of a newspaper) to show appropriate letter form as well as the relevant capitalizations. Point out the salutation and closing of the letter.

Text Follow Through

Discuss text page 316.

Assign the Exercise, page 316, and Developing Writing Skills, page 316.

Less advanced Before students attempt the Developing Writing Skills activity, you may want to have them refer to the discussion of proper letter form in Section 31.1 (pages 598–608).

Average Students can exchange the invitations they write as part of the Developing Writing Skills Activity and write responses accepting or rejecting the invitations.

Advanced Students can write letters to government officials or local newspapers expressing their opinions about an issue of interest to the students.

Additional Practice

Practice Pages or Practice Book, page 99

Less advanced Exercise Bank, Exercises A and B, page 146

Average Exercise Bank, Exercises A, B, and C, page 146

1. Linda tried to read (<u>book title</u>) as the bus sped along the highway. <u>The Pearl</u>
2. Our local theater company presented (<u>play title</u>) last Saturday night. <u>Our Town</u>
3. Branden passed (course title) after getting a tutor's help. Geometry
4. To read ("short story title") takes only a few minutes. "A Day's Wait
5. I usually read every issue of (<u>magazine title</u>). <u>Newsweek</u>

17.6 Capitals in Letters

An additional rule applies specifically to the special parts of letters.

Capitalize the first word and all nouns in letter salutations and the first word in letter closings.

SALUTATIONS: Dear Mr. Perkins: Dear Aunt Maude,

My dear Friends,

CLOSINGS: Sincerely yours,   Yours truly,

Affectionately,

EXERCISE: Using Capitals for Letter Salutations and Closings. Rewrite each of the following letter parts, adding the missing capitals.
Underlined letters are to be capitalized.
EXAMPLE: dear cousin jo,

Dear Cousin Jo,

1. <u>m</u>y dear <u>a</u>nna and <u>f</u>red,
2. <u>d</u>ear <u>f</u>amily,
3. <u>d</u>ear <u>s</u>ir or <u>m</u>adam:
4. <u>w</u>ith deepest regret,
5. <u>r</u>espectfully yours,

DEVELOPING WRITING SKILLS: Using Capitals in Letters. Write a brief letter inviting a friend to a party. Use a salutation and closing that are different from the ones in the previous exercise. Capitalize correctly throughout the letter.
Answers will vary.

316

Skills Review and Writing Workshop

Using Capitals

CHECKING YOUR SKILLS
Rewrite the paragraph, correcting capitalization errors.
Underlined letters are to be capitalized.

(1) last friday my uncle ted and i toured tarrytown, new york, an interesting old village on the hudson river near the tappan zee bridge. (2) To the north, on the albany post road, is the old dutch church in sleepy hollow. (3) across from it is philipse manor, the restored home of the philipse family, who sided with the british during the american revolutionary war. (4) To the south is the home of washington irving, the author of the famous short story, "the legend of sleepy hollow." (5) Along main street is the historic tarrytown music hall. (6) When my uncle saw lyndhurst, an old castle, he remarked, "it looks as if vampires lived here." (7) The town is governed by a mayor and a board of trustees composed of republicans and democrats. (8) to the north, general motors operates an assembly plant. (9) The village contains the warner library. (10) It also has many shops, and an italian and a chinese restaurant.

USING MECHANICS SKILLS IN WRITING
Writing About Your Town

Publicity writers know that correct capitalization is necessary. Follow the steps below to write a brief brochure about your town for a new tourist office that is opening there.

Answers will vary.
Prewriting: Make a list of interesting, notable, or historic features of your town. Jot down points about each that would intrigue tourists.

Writing: Start with a general statement inviting your reader to visit the town. Briefly discuss each place on your list, using vivid descriptive details. End with a statement recommending your town as an enjoyable experience.

Revising: Check your capitalization. Read your brochure, making other improvements. Then, proofread carefully.

Checking Your Skills
In the Checking Your Skills assignment, students have corrected capitalization errors in sentences. Tell students that the following activity will provide additional practice.

Critical Thinking
Have students rewrite brief passages from short stories or nonfiction selections, changing all capital letters to lower case. Have students exchange papers with partners and correct the capitalization errors in the rewritten passages. Then students should check each other's work.

Using Mechanics Skills in Writing

Publishing You might want to select some of the brochures for submission to the Chamber of Commerce or for display in the local public library.

Advanced Exercise Bank, Exercises B and C, page 146
TESTING
Test Program
Unit Pretest, page 57
Chapter Test, page 61
Unit Post-Test, page 66

RE-TEACHING
Practice Pages, page 99

THINKING SKILLS
Application—*Modifying* letter salutations and closings to correct capitalization (Exercise, page 316)
Using capitalization correctly in a letter (Developing Writing Skills, page 316)

CHAPTER 18
Using Abbreviations
(pp. 318–332)

Chapter 18 covers abbreviations in four short sections. A number of the abbreviations in the chapter may already be familiar to your students. However, students may not realize that many of these abbreviations are not acceptable in formal writing. To help students build their awareness, each rule in the chapter includes information on when it is appropriate to use each abbreviation.

For a review of the entire chapter and a related writing activity, see the Skills Review and Writing Workshop on page 332.

18.1 Abbreviations of Titles of People
(pp. 318–323)

OBJECTIVES

After completing this section, students should be able to

- Abbreviate social titles correctly.
- Use abbreviations correctly for governmental, military, and professional titles before names and for social and professional titles after names.

Chapter **18**

Using Abbreviations

Most *abbreviations* are formed by using the first letter of a word along with a few other important letters in the word.

To abbreviate means to shorten a word or phrase.

Abbreviations can be valuable tools in writing if you know when and how to use them. They can be very helpful in informal writing situations—taking notes or writing lists, for example. However, only a few abbreviations can be used in formal writing.

18.1 Abbreviations of Titles of People

Perhaps the most common abbreviations are used with names.

Social Titles

Mr. and *Mrs.* are the most familiar of the abbreviations used for social titles.

Abbreviations of social titles before a proper name begin with a capital letter and end with a period. They can be used in any type of writing.

18.1 Abbreviations of Titles of People

SOCIAL TITLES: Mr.

                    Mrs. or Mme. (Madame)

                    Messrs. (plural of Mr.)

                    Mmes. (plural of Mrs. and Mme.)

EXAMPLES: Mr. Comstock sells furniture as a second job.

                    Mrs. Ridley made an appointment with the firm's auditors.

NOTE ABOUT MISS AND MS.: *Miss* and the plural form *Misses* are social titles used before the names of single women. They are not abbreviations and are not punctuated with a period. The title *Ms.* can be used before the name of a single or a married woman. Although *Ms.* is not the abbreviation of another word, it is followed by a period.

EXAMPLES: Miss Kelly requested a leave of absence.

                    His question was answered by Ms. Hartley.

EXERCISE A: Using Abbreviations of Social Titles. Copy the following sentences onto your paper, adding an abbreviation of an appropriate social title or the word *Miss, Misses,* or *Ms.* before each name or pair of names. Use at least five different abbreviations.
Answers will vary; samples are given.

EXAMPLE: The law firm was owned by _____ Ryan and James.

                    The law firm was owned by Messrs. Ryan and James.

1. __Mme.__ Zola modeled the designer's new line.
2. __Mr.__ York claims that his parking ticket was not deserved.
3. No one had foreseen __Miss__ Clark's reaction.
4. __Misses__ Black and Haynes wore identical costumes to the masquerade party.
5. My teacher, __Mr.__ Cole, assigns homework every night.

1. Mister Robinson was chosen to be our representative.
2. I wrote a letter to Representative Shirley Chisholm.
3. Did you know that Sergeant Lopez was promoted?
4. Rosemary Martino, Doctor of Philosophy, spoke to us about the responsibilities of a senator.
5. Doctor Fields sent the bill to James Bentley, Junior.

Average Students may be familiar with most of the abbreviations covered in this section. However, they may be surprised that they are not acceptable in most formal writings. In addition, students interested in the military might enjoy preparing a complete list of ranks and their abbreviations for a particular branch of the service.

Advanced Have students look through newspapers and magazines to discover examples of appropriately abbreviated titles. You may also wish to discuss the use of *Ms.* in written communications. For example, in letter salutations, when is it appropriate to use *Mr., Mrs., Miss,* or *Ms.?* Students may be interested to know that *Ms.* is a form that evolved for both practical and social reasons. Point out that Ms. is appropriate in a business letter salutation to a woman whose marital status you do not know. It is preferred by some women who feel that *Miss* and *Mrs.* are labels that overemphasize the importance of being married.

6. A solution to the problem was suggested by __Messrs.__ O'Keefe and Martinez.
7. We asked __Misses__ Dennison and D'Anastasio to lead the hike.
8. The jury waited for __Ms.__ Thomas to present the evidence.
9. __Messrs.__ Wheeler and Pine have both worked as foreign correspondents.
10. Even as an experienced secretary, __Mrs.__ Hawkins was dismayed by the stack of papers on the desk.

Other Titles

Many other titles can be written before a name to identify a person's business or profession.

Abbreviations of other titles used before proper names also begin with a capital letter and end with a period. These abbreviations are used less often in formal writing.

The following chart shows some abbreviations of governmental, military, and professional titles commonly used before names.

ABBREVIATIONS OF COMMON TITLES BEFORE NAMES					
Governmental		**Military**		**Professional**	
Supt.	Superintendent	Pvt.	Private	Dr.	Doctor
Rep.	Representative	Sgt.	Sergeant	Atty.	Attorney
Sen.	Senator	Lt.	Lieutenant	Prof.	Professor
Gov.	Governor	Capt.	Captain	Hon.	Honorable
Treas.	Treasurer	Col.	Colonel	Rev.	Reverend
Sec.	Secretary	Maj.	Major	Fr.	Father
Amb.	Ambassador	Gen.	General	Sr.	Sister
Pres.	President	Ens.	Ensign	Br.	Brother
		Adm.	Admiral		

18.1 Abbreviations of Titles of People

In most formal writing, these titles should be spelled out, especially when only the last name is written.

EXAMPLES: Governor Herrick was reelected twice.

Captain Bixby inspected the ship carefully.

The parish appreciated Father Perry's dedication.

In certain cases it is acceptable to use the abbreviated forms. *Dr.* may be used in formal writing if it comes before a proper name. Nonreligious titles may also be abbreviated if they are used along with a person's first name or initials.

EXAMPLES: Dr. Fenson was still on duty in the emergency room.

Prof. Mariana Peres requested several books at the library.

Sometimes the abbreviation of a title appears after a name.

Abbreviations of titles after a name start with a capital letter and end with a period. They can be used in any type of writing.

The following chart shows abbreviations of titles that come after names.

ABBREVIATIONS OF COMMON TITLES AFTER NAMES			
Social		**Professional**	
Jr.	Junior	D.D.S.	Doctor of Dental Surgery
Sr.	Senior	M.D.	Doctor of Medicine
		Ph.D.	Doctor of Philosophy
		R.N.	Registered Nurse

Notice that when an abbreviation is written after a name within a sentence, a comma is placed before and after the abbreviation. When an abbreviated title occurs at the end of a sentence, only the comma before the abbreviation is used.

Additional Practice

Practice Pages or Practice Book, page 100

Less advanced   Exercise Bank, Exercises A and B, page 147

Average   Exercise Bank, Exercises A, B, and C, page 147

Advanced   Exercise Bank, Exercises B and C, page 147

TESTING

Test Program

Unit Pretest, page 57
Chapter Test, pages 62, 63
Unit Post-Test, page 66

RE-TEACHING

Practice Pages or Practice Book, page 100

THINKING SKILLS

Application—*Using* abbreviations of social titles appropriately in sentences (Exercise A, page 319)
Using abbreviations of other titles appropriately in sentences (Exercise B, page 322)

Synthesis—*Writing* sentences using abbreviations of titles appropriately (Developing Writing Skills, page 322)

Developing Writing Skills

Have students practice using correct abbreviations in writing by completing the following assignment.

Writing Across the Curriculum

The job of elected officials is to carry out the will of the people. Officials often become aware of people's wishes and desires concerning issues and policies through letters.

Prewriting Free write about an issue or problem in your community or in the country that concerns you. Think about the reasons for your concern and the action you think elected officials should take. Circle words and phrases that would be appropriate to use in a letter to an elected official.

Writing Write the first draft of a business letter to an elected official. If your topic is of local concern, address your letter to a local official. If the problem is a state concern, address your letter to your state legislator. If the problem is a national concern, address the letter to your congressman. In your letter, identify the issue or problem and explain why it concerns you. If you have any suggestions or ideas concerning your topic, suggest them in a polite manner.

Revising Make sure that you have used the correct form for a business letter. If you are unsure, see pages 603–607 in your textbook. Have you identified the issue or problem? Have you explained why the issue or problem concerns you? Have you used abbreviations correctly?

EXAMPLES: Anthony Petri, Jr., attends Brighton Academy.

The psychology course will be taught by Eleanor Adams, Ph.D.

EXERCISE B: Using Abbreviations of Other Titles. Copy the following sentences, using the abbreviated form of each title.

EXAMPLE: The missing clue was found by Professor Ashley Crewes.

The missing clue was found by Prof. Ashley Crewes.

1. A sign on the door read, "Jacqueline Bartley, Doctor of Dental Surgery." D.D.S.
2. Jacob Schmidt, Doctor of Philosophy, teaches at the local college. Ph.D.
3. Lieutenant Daisy Murphy prepared her locker for inspection. Lt.
4. Arthur Schlesinger, Junior, is an expert in U.S. history. Jr.
5. Ambassador Sidney Rochester joined the speakers at the convention. Amb.
6. Our town's pediatrician, Doctor Whitaker, actually makes house calls. Dr.
7. The jury listened carefully as Attorney Arlene Clemens questioned the witness. Atty.
8. Professor William Anderson polished his glasses as he spoke to the class. Prof.
9. Janice Summers, Registered Nurse, discussed career opportunities with the students. R.N.
10. The club members waited until Secretary Chris Morganthal read the minutes. Sec.

DEVELOPING WRITING SKILLS: Using Abbreviations of Titles Correctly. Write a sentence for each of the following, correctly using an abbreviation of each of the titles described. Follow the rules for formal writing.
Answers will vary; samples are given for the first two.

EXAMPLE: A man who has the same name as his father

Percy Bysshe McCoy, Jr., always used his initials when signing his name.

1. I saw Mrs. Bernstein in the supermarket today.

1. A married woman
2. A club treasurer
3. A registered nurse
4. A man
5. A colonel

6. An ambassador
7. A lawyer
8. Two men
9. A medical doctor
10. Three married women

2. We listened to Treas. Robert Clark discuss our deficit.

Abbreviations for Time and Historical Dates 18.2

Abbreviations for time and historical dates are found in all types of writing.

Time

Abbreviations are used to express time before noon and after noon.

For abbreviations of time before noon and after noon, either capital letters followed by periods or small letters followed by periods are acceptable. These abbreviations can be used in any type of writing.

ABBREVIATIONS: A.M. *or* a.m. (*ante meridiem,* before noon)

P.M. *or* p.m. (*post meridiem,* after noon)

These abbreviations should only be used with numerals.

WITH NUMERALS: The first tremor registered at 7:20 a.m.

By 1:00 P.M. the train had crossed the Canadian border.

WITHOUT NUMERALS: At six o'clock each day, my family sits down to dinner.

18.2 Abbreviations for Time and Historical Dates
(pp. 323–326)

OBJECTIVES

After completing this section, students should be able to

• Use abbreviations correctly to express time before and after noon.
• Use abbreviations correctly to express historical dates before and after the birth of Christ.

TEACHING

Getting Started

┌ **sentence bank** ─────────
Report for practice at 7:30 *ante meridiem* sharp!
The festivities began at 8:00 *post meridiem.*
A vase made around 3500 *before Christ* sold for $500,000.
The Battle of Hastings was fought in 1066 *anno Domini.*

Write the Sentence Bank sentences on the board.

Have students speculate about the meaning of each underlined phrase and a possible abbreviation for each phrase. Have a volunteer rewrite each sentence using the appropriate abbreviation. Discuss why these four abbreviations are preferable to the spelled-out versions. (The long forms are unfamiliar and outdated.) Be sure students note the text notations on pages 323 and 324 that show the meanings of each time- and date-related term.

Text Follow Through

Discuss text pages 323–326.

Assign Exercise A, page 324; Exercise B, page 325; and Developing Writing Skills, page 325.

Less advanced You may want to indicate a preference for one of the two choices given for abbreviating time before and after noon (using capital or small letters) so that students won't be confused.

Average Stress the need for consistency in using a.m./p.m. or A.M./P.M. Students can use abbreviations for time in writing weekly study schedules, as suggested in Section 35.1.

Advanced You might ask each student to research and list five historical events that happened before the birth of Christ and five that happened after the birth of Christ. They can then write a paragraph to present the events in chronological order.

EXERCISE A: Using Abbreviations of Time. From the words given in parentheses, write the abbreviation or phrase that correctly expresses time in each of the sentences.

EXAMPLE: When going fishing, he always gets up at 4:30 (in the morning, A.M.).

A.M.

1. If we leave now, we can see the 7:30 (in the afternoon, P.M.) show.
2. The police sergeant arrived at his desk at five o'clock (in the morning, A.M.).
3. Set your alarm clock for 7:30 (in the morning, A.M.).
4. The cafeteria opens at five o'clock (in the morning, a.m.).
5. June punched her time card at exactly three o'clock (in the afternoon, P.M.).

Dates

Abbreviations can also be used to express historical dates before and after the birth of Christ.

Abbreviations for historical dates before and after the birth of Christ require capital letters followed by periods. They can be used in any type of writing.

ABBREVIATIONS: B.C. (before Christ)

A.D. (*anno Domini,* in the year of the Lord)

Use B.C. and A.D. with numerals that express the year. B.C. always follows the number. A.D. may be written after or before the number.

EXAMPLES: Alexander conquered Babylon in 331 B.C.

The death of Ptolemy in 180 A.D. halted the progress of astronomy for a time.

The Empress Theodora died in A.D. 548.

18.2 Abbreviations for Time and Historical Dates

EXERCISE B: Using Abbreviations of Historical Dates.
Copy the following sentences onto your paper, writing the abbreviated form for each historical date given in parentheses. Numbers and abbreviations are given.

EXAMPLE: According to one historian, Rome was founded in (753 before Christ).

According to one historian, Rome was founded in 753 B.C.

1. The Greek philosopher Socrates died in (399 before Christ). 399 B.C.
2. Eleanor of Aquitaine, queen of both France and England, died in (1204 in the year of the Lord). 1204 A.D. or A.D. 1204
3. In (1000 in the year of the Lord), Leif Ericsson is said to have landed on the coast of America. 1000 A.D. or A.D. 1000
4. Hannibal crossed the Alps in (218 before Christ). 218 B.C.
5. The ancient city of Pompeii was burned in (79 in the year of the Lord). 79 A.D. or A.D. 79

DEVELOPING WRITING SKILLS: Using Abbreviations of Time and Dates.
Write a sentence for each of the following items, including an abbreviation of the indicated time or date and using the information given in parentheses. Numbers and abbreviations are given.

EXAMPLE: eleven o'clock before noon (the British often have a coffee break)

At 11:00 A.M. the British often have a coffee break.

1. 1603 in the year of the Lord (Elizabeth I ended a reign of forty-five years) 1603 A.D. or A.D. 1603
2. 214 before Christ (the Great Wall of China was begun) 214 A.D.
3. two o'clock after noon (sirens summoned volunteer firefighters) 2:00 P.M. or p.m.
4. 54 before Christ (Julius Caesar invaded Britain) 54 B.C.
5. six o'clock after noon (newscasters described a local water shortage) 6:00 P.M. or p.m.
6. fifteen minutes past eight o'clock after noon (the baseball game was cancelled) 8:15 P.M. or p.m.

Additional Practice

Practice Pages or Practice Book, page 101

Less advanced Exercise Bank, Exercises A and B, pages 148, 149

Average Exercise Bank, Exercises A, B, and C, pages 148, 149

Advanced Exercise Bank, Exercises B and C, pages 148, 149

TESTING

Test Program

Unit Pretest, page 57
Chapter Test, pages 62, 63
Unit Post-Test, page 66

RE-TEACHING

Practice Pages or Practice Book, page 101

THINKING SKILLS

Comprehension—*Distinguishing* whether use of abbreviations of time is appropriate (Exercise A, page 324)

Application—*Using* abbreviations for historical dates in sentences (Exercise B, page 325)

Synthesis—*Writing* sentences using abbreviations of time and dates (Developing Writing Skills, page 325)

18.3 Geographical Abbreviations

(pp. 326–329)

OBJECTIVE

After completing this section, students should be able to

• Use geographical abbreviations correctly and appropriately.

TEACHING

Getting Started

Write on the board the names of several states, for example, *Texas, Michigan, Indiana, Nebraska, Massachusetts.* Ask for volunteers to write the abbreviations for each on the board. Some students will know that the postal service prefers its two-letter, all-capitalized abbreviation. Any inconsistencies in the way students abbreviate on the board can be used to initiate discussion of the differences between traditional and the postal service abbreviations and situations when each should be used.

---

7. 1431 in the year of the Lord (Joan of Arc died)
8. seven o'clock before noon (an airplane made an emergency landing) 7:00 A.M. or a.m.
9. 1215 in the year of the Lord (the Magna Charta was written)
10. ten o'clock before noon (the crafts fair started) 10:00 A.M. or a.m.

7. 1431 A.D. or A.D. 1431 **9.** 1215 A.D. or A.D. 1215

18.3 Geographical Abbreviations

Geographical terms and locations are often used in informal writing, such as notes and lists, and also in addressing envelopes.

Abbreviations for geographical terms before or after a proper noun begin with a capital letter and end with a period. They are seldom used in formal writing.

The following chart shows some of the most commonly used of these abbreviations.

ABBREVIATIONS OF GEOGRAPHICAL TERMS					
Ave.	Avenue	Ft.	Fort	Prov.	Province
Bldg.	Building	Hwy.	Highway	Pt.	Point
Blk.	Block	Is.	Island	Rd.	Road
Blvd.	Boulevard	Mt.	Mountain	Rte.	Route
Co.	County	Natl.	National	Sq.	Square
Dist.	District	Pen.	Peninsula	St.	Street
Dr.	Drive	Pk.	Park, Peak	Terr.	Territory

Each of the fifty states may also be abbreviated.

Traditional abbreviations for states begin with a capital letter and end with a period. They are seldom used in formal writing.

The following chart shows these abbreviations.

18.3 Geographical Abbreviations

TRADITIONAL ABBREVIATIONS FOR STATES

Ala.	Alabama	Me.	Maine	Okla.	Oklahoma
Alaska	Alaska	Md.	Maryland	Ore.	Oregon
Ariz.	Arizona	Mass.	Massachusetts	Pa.	Pennsylvania
Ark.	Arkansas	Mich.	Michigan	R.I.	Rhode Island
Calif.	California	Minn.	Minnesota	S.C.	South
Colo.	Colorado	Miss.	Mississippi		Carolina
Conn.	Connecticut	Mo.	Missouri	S. Dak.	South
Del.	Delaware	Mont.	Montana		Dakota
Fla.	Florida	Nebr.	Nebraska	Tenn.	Tennessee
Ga.	Georgia	Nev.	Nevada	Tex.	Texas
Hawaii	Hawaii	N.H.	New	Utah	Utah
Ida.	Idaho		Hampshire	Vt.	Vermont
Ill.	Illinois	N.J.	New Jersey	Va.	Virginia
Ind.	Indiana	N. Mex.	New Mexico	Wash.	Washington
Iowa	Iowa	N.Y.	New York	W. Va.	West
Kans.	Kansas	N.C.	North Carolina		Virginia
Ky.	Kentucky	N. Dak.	North Dakota	Wis.	Wisconsin
La.	Louisiana	O.	Ohio	Wyo.	Wyoming

The traditional abbreviation for the District of Columbia is D.C. Use the traditional abbreviation in formal writing whenever the abbreviation follows the word *Washington*.

EXAMPLE: We visited Washington, D.C., on our class trip.

In 1963 the Postal Service introduced a new set of abbreviations for state names.

The official Postal Service abbreviations for states require capital letters with no periods. They are generally not used in formal writing.

The Postal Service prefers that you use these abbreviations when you address envelopes or packages for mailing.

327

Text Follow Through
Discuss text pages 326–329.
Assign the Exercise, page 328, and Developing Writing Skills, page 329.

Less advanced You might permit students to refer to the charts in the text when completing the Exercise and the Developing Writing Skills activity. You may prefer to have students concentrate on learning postal service abbreviations, which they will probably use more often, rather than risk confusion in learning both types of abbreviations. Have students write post cards to two friends or relatives, address them appropriately, and mail them.

Average Students might take part in a spelling bee that tests their ability to give the correct abbreviations for geographical terms. Call out a city and state and have students spell out the state abbreviation in either traditional or postal service form.

Advanced Students might enjoy compiling a class list of places of birth, using abbreviations. For further practice in abbreviating geographical terms, students can also make address books listing friends and relatives.

Additional Practice
Practice Pages or Practice Book, page 102

Less advanced Exercise Bank, Exercises A and B, page 150

Average Exercise Bank, Exercises A, B, and C, page 150

Advanced Exercise Bank, Exercises B and C, page 150

OFFICIAL POSTAL SERVICE ABBREVIATIONS

AL	Alabama	ME	Maine	OK	Oklahoma
AK	Alaska	MD	Maryland	OR	Oregon
AZ	Arizona	MA	Massachusetts	PA	Pennsylvania
AR	Arkansas	MI	Michigan	RI	Rhode Island
CA	California	MN	Minnesota	SC	South
CO	Colorado	MS	Mississippi		Carolina
CT	Connecticut	MO	Missouri	SD	South
DE	Delaware	MT	Montana		Dakota
FL	Florida	NB	Nebraska	TN	Tennessee
GA	Georgia	NV	Nevada	TX	Texas
HI	Hawaii	NH	New	UT	Utah
ID	Idaho		Hampshire	VT	Vermont
IL	Illinois	NJ	New Jersey	VA	Virginia
IN	Indiana	NM	New Mexico	WA	Washington
IA	Iowa	NY	New York	WV	West
KS	Kansas	NC	North Carolina		Virginia
KY	Kentucky	ND	North Dakota	WI	Wisconsin
LA	Louisiana	OH	Ohio	WY	Wyoming

The Postal Service abbreviation for the District of Columbia is DC.

EXERCISE: Recognizing Geographical Abbreviations.
Write the traditional abbreviations for the geographical terms given in parentheses in each of the following sentences.

EXAMPLE: In April they will move from Johnson (Street) to Hastings (Boulevard).

       St.   Blvd.

1. The address is: 49 Wilmot (Avenue), Dorchester, (Nebraska). Ave
2. Few people live in (District) 6 of Tompkins (County). Dist./Co.

3. Follow (Route) 75 west until it crosses the (Ohio) border. Rte./O.
4. Sandy's brother is stationed at (Fort) Wayne. Ft.
5. We visited Dinosaur (National) Monument, (Colorado). Natl./Colo.
6. (Mount) Fuji erupted with sudden force. Mt.
7. We passed through Sullivan (County) on our way to the cabin. Co.
8. Remember this address: 16 Chamblee (Drive), Decatur, (Alabama). Dr./Ala.
9. Chincoteague (Island) is off the coast of (Maryland). Is./Md.
10. Alberta (Province) in Canada is north of (Montana). Prov./Mont.

DEVELOPING WRITING SKILLS: Understanding Geographical Abbreviations. Write ten sentences, each using the word that one of the following abbreviations stands for.
Sentences will vary; words abbreviations stand for are given.
EXAMPLE: Hwy.

The bank robbers sped along Highway 66.

1. UT   3. Me.   5. Natl.   7. Pk.   9. CA
2. Sq.   4. Blvd.   6. Okla.   8. Co.   10. Rd.

1. Utah 2. Square 3. Maine 4. Boulevard 5. National 6. Oklahoma 7. Park or Peak 8. County 9. California 10. Road

Abbreviations of Measurements 18.4

Using abbreviations for measurements makes technical writing easier.

Traditional Measurements

Periods are used with traditional measurements.

With traditional measurements use small letters and periods to form the abbreviations. These abbreviations are not used in formal writing except with numerals.

The following chart shows examples of these abbreviations. Notice that the *F.* for *Fahrenheit* is an exception to the rule about small letters.

18.4 Abbreviations of Measurements
(pp. 329–331)

OBJECTIVES

After completing this section, students should be able to

- Abbreviate traditional measurements correctly.
- Abbreviate metric measurements correctly.

TEACHING
Getting Started

idea bank

2.54 _____ = 1 _____
(inches and centimeters)
1 _____ = 2.2 _____
(pounds and kilograms)
454 _____ = 1 _____
(pounds and grams)

On the board write the Idea Bank equivalents. Parenthetical words inform students of the two measurements being compared. Ask volunteers to fill in the blanks appropriately with abbreviations for the measurements. As students fill in the abbreviations, there should be opportunity to point out that metric measurements are abbreviated without periods, whereas traditional English measurements do use them.

Text Follow Through

Discuss text pages 329–331.

Assign Exercise A, page 330; Exercise B, page 331; and Developing Writing Skills, page 331.

Less advanced You may need to stress that students should use periods with abbreviations of traditional measurements but *not* with abbreviations of metric measurements. The fact that a single abbreviation can be used for both singular and plural may also need extra attention.

Average You may wish, in conjunction with a science instructor who also works with these students, to have students prepare their own metric-English conversion charts for all relevant measurement categories they are asked to use. They can find many of these conversions in almanacs or in unabridged dictionaries. Students can then use the charts to convert such items as their weight, foot length, book weight, etc., from the traditional to the metric, using appropriate abbreviations.

Advanced Students may also complete their own conversion charts, as described above, us-

TRADITIONAL MEASUREMENTS					
in.	inch(es)	tsp.	teaspoon(s)	pt.	pint(s)
ft.	foot; feet	tbsp.	tablespoon(s)	qt.	quart(s)
yd.	yard(s)	oz.	ounce(s)	gal.	gallon(s)
mi.	mile(s)	lb.	pound(s)	F.	Fahrenheit

WITHOUT ABBREVIATION: The ball missed by eleven inches.

WITH ABBREVIATION: The ball missed by 11 in.

EXERCISE A: Using Abbreviations of Traditional Measurements.

On your paper write the abbreviations for the traditional measurements that are underlined in each of the following sentences.

EXAMPLE: The baby weighed six pounds, four ounces.

  6 lb. 4 oz.

1. Bought separately, four quarts of ice cream cost more than one gallon. 4 qt./1 gal.
2. Johanna is five feet, four inches tall. 5 ft./4 in.
3. Beat one teaspoon of vanilla into one pint of cream. 1 tsp./1 pt.
4. This week I lost two pounds, eight ounces. 2 lb./8 oz.
5. Sam said that the hundred yards he ran seemed like five miles. 100 yd./5 mi.

Metric Measurements

Abbreviations of metric measurements do not require periods.

With metric measurements use small letters and no periods to form the abbreviations. These abbreviations are not used in formal writing except with numerals.

Notice in the following chart that the abbreviations of *liter* and *Celsius* are exceptions to the small letter rule.

18.4 Abbreviations of Measurements

METRIC MEASUREMENTS

g	gram(s)	mm	millimeter(s)	L	liter
kg	kilogram(s)	cm	centimeter(s)	C	Celsius
		m	meter(s)		
		km	kilometer(s)		

WITHOUT ABBREVIATION: Last night the temperature was zero degrees Celsius.

WITH ABBREVIATION: Last night the temperature was 0°C.

EXERCISE B: Using Abbreviations of Metric Measurements. Write the abbreviation for the metric measurement that is underlined in each of the following sentences.

EXAMPLE: We traveled only <u>forty-two kilometers</u> that day.

42 km

1. Bob joked that he grew only <u>one millimeter</u> a year. 1 mm
2. As a model, Esther keeps her weight at <u>fifty kilograms</u>. 50 kg
3. The average body temperature is <u>thirty-seven degrees Celsius</u>. 37°C
4. Most paper clips are about <u>three centimeters</u> long. 3 cm
5. Did you know that a dollar bill weighs about <u>one gram</u>. 1g

DEVELOPING WRITING SKILLS: Using Abbreviations of Traditional and Metric Measurements. On your paper write ten sentences, each using one of the following measurements and measurement abbreviations.

Answers will vary; samples are given for the first two.

EXAMPLE: F.

His favorite temperature is 78°F.

1. We bought several pints of milk.   2. Water boils at 100°C.

1. pints
2. C
3. kilogram
4. oz.
5. gal.
6. meters
7. ft.
8. mm
9. lb.
10. grams

ing a science text as a reference point. After they have completed the charts, you might have the students solve some conversion problems which you supply (such as 12 ft. = _____ m) either orally or in writing. The written answers should use abbreviations correctly.

Additional Practice

Practice Pages or Practice Book, page 103

Less advanced   Exercise Bank, Exercises A and B, pages 151, 152

Average   Exercise Bank, Exercises A, B, and C, pages 151, 152

Advanced   Exercise Bank, Exercises B and C, pages 151, 152

TESTING

Test Program

Unit Pretest, page 57
Chapter Test, pages 62, 63
Unit Post-Test, page 66

RE-TEACHING

Practice Pages or Practice Book, page 103

THINKING SKILLS

Application—*Using* abbreviations of traditional measurements (Exercise A, page 330)
Using abbreviations of metric measurements (Exercise B, page 331)

Synthesis—*Writing* sentences using abbreviations of traditional and metric measurements (Developing Writing Skills, page 331)

Checking Your Skills

In the Checking Your Skills assignment, students have corrected abbreviation errors in sentences. Tell students that the following collaborative learning activity will provide them with additional practice.

Collaborative Learning

Divide students into groups. Explain to the groups that they will write a continuation of the story in the Checking Your Skills activity, imagining that Professor Crook escaped from the Sergeant with the statue. They should use as many abbreviations as possible. The finished story will be in an "abbreviation code." When they have finished, have a representative from each group read their continuation of the story to the rest of the class. After all groups have read their continuations, have the class as a whole vote on the best one, which can be displayed on the class bulletin board.

Using Mechanics Skills in Writing

Prewriting You might want students to decide on a topic for their news reports and free write about it for several minutes. Have students write whatever comes to mind, letting one idea suggest others. Remind them not to be concerned whether the ideas are good or bad, but simply to write down everything. They can then go over their free writing and choose the ideas that are appropriate for the reports. Once students have chosen their ideas, they can add any additional ideas or details that will add to their news reports.

Skills Review and Writing Workshop

Using Abbreviations

CHECKING YOUR SKILLS

1. a.m./Street   2. President/in the afternoon   3. 79 B.C./1937 A.D.   4. Pennsylvania

Rewrite the paragraph, correcting all abbreviation errors.

(1) Last Saturday Mr. Norman Goodman and Ms. Angela Bright, private detectives, met at 9:30 am on Market St.   (2) Angela told Norman that an ancient golden statue, a gift for the Pres., was to arrive by plane at one o'clock P.M.   (3) The statue had been made in B.C. 79, but had not been discovered until A D 1937.   (4) The statue, now worth millions of dollars, was to be stored in a warehouse in PA.   (5) The two detectives planned to guard the six-ft. statue by following it to the warehouse on Green Ave.   (6) A thief from Washington, D.C., had decided to steal the statue from the truck as it turned into the warehouse driveway.   (7) The thief, Prof. Crook, did steal the statue, right after the detectives left.   (8) But Crook had driven only 3 km when his car broke down.   (9) As he was arrested by Sgt Reynolds, Crook shouted that he wanted his atty.   (10) Reporter Diane Taknow covered the story for the local newspaper.

5. six-foot/Avenue   6. correct   7. Professor   8. three kilometers   9. Sergeant/attorney   10. correct

USING MECHANICS SKILLS IN WRITING

Writing a News Report

Using abbreviations correctly is an important writing skill. Follow the steps below to write a news report that has both action and suspense, as well as an unexpected ending.

Answers will vary.

Prewriting: Plan a news report based on an unusual incident—real or imaginary. List the events in the order in which they occur.

Writing: Begin by setting the stage. Mention place, time, and persons involved. Build to a climax step-by-step and then give the unexpected ending.

Revising: Make sure that any abbreviations you use are correct. After you have revised, proofread your report.

Chapter 19

Using Punctuation Marks

Chapter 19 is much longer than the other two chapters in this unit. It consists of nine sections, which present an in-depth study of all of the most common punctuation marks, beginning with end marks and commas.

The correct use of punctuation marks depends on a basic understanding of grammar and sentence structure. Therefore, you will want to make sure that students understand the concepts covered in Unit I before studying this chapter.

For a review of the entire chapter and a related writing activity, see the Skills Review and Writing Workshop on page 390.

Punctuation marks act as signals to readers. They tell readers when to pause or stop, when to read with a questioning tone, and when to read with excitement. Punctuation marks also connect ideas or set ideas apart.

Punctuation is a commonly accepted set of symbols used to convey specific directions to the reader.

The most common punctuation marks are shown below.

COMMON PUNCTUATION MARKS			
period	.	colon	:
question mark	?	quotation marks	" "
exclamation mark	!	hyphen	-
comma	,	apostrophe	'
semicolon	;		

This chapter will help you become more familiar with these punctuation marks and the rules for using them.

19.1 End Marks
(pp. 334–339)

OBJECTIVES

After completing this section, students should be able to

- Use periods correctly at the end of declarative and imperative sentences, indirect questions, and most abbreviations.
- Identify the need for question marks with direct questions, incomplete questions, and statements intended as questions.
- Recognize the need for exclamation marks with exclamatory sentences, forceful imperative sentences, and some interjections.

TEACHING
Getting Started

The importance of punctuation in clear communications can be demonstrated as a beginning activity for this chapter. Write sentences such as the following on the board and ask students to explain how the meaning of each differs.

How are you? Going to the bonfire and hayride tonight? How are you going to the bonfire and hayride tonight?
Stop! Children crossing.
Stop children crossing.

As the correct use of punctuation depends upon students' understanding of grammar and sentence structure, you may want to review some of the concepts in Unit I before assigning

19.1 End Marks

End marks signal the end or conclusion of a sentence, word, or phrase.

There are three end marks: the period [.], the question mark [?], and the exclamation mark [!]. They usually indicate the end of a sentence.

Uses of the Period

The *period* is the most frequently used of all the end marks. The following rules explain its use.

Use a period to end a declarative sentence, that is, to end a statement of fact or opinion.

STATEMENT OF FACT: Monticello was Thomas Jefferson's home in Virginia.

STATEMENT OF OPINION: I believe that we can be optimistic about the outcome.

A period is also used for imperative sentences, that is, sentences that give directions or issue a command.

Use a period to end an imperative sentence, that is, to end a direction or command.

DIRECTION: Turn left at the next intersection.

COMMAND: Come here.

Sometimes a declarative sentence contains an indirect question. An indirect question is one that does not require a response.

Use a period to end an indirect question.

INDIRECT QUESTION: Jackie asked what time it was.

The period is also used with many abbreviations.

Use a period to end most abbreviations.

Although some abbreviations do not end in periods, most of them do.

INITIALS: L. J. Fergusson

TITLES: Mr.   Mrs.   Dr.   Gen.

PLACE NAMES: St.   Mt.   Calif.   Mass.

When a sentence ends with an abbreviation that makes use of a period, it is not necessary to put a second period at the end.

EXAMPLE: The person she called on was Arthur Jones, Jr.

EXERCISE A: Using the Period. The following sentences do not have periods. Copy each of the sentences onto your paper, adding periods as needed.

EXAMPLE: Jacob Jones, Sr, was not pleased when his son ran
　　　　　　off to join the circus

　　　　　　Jacob Jones, Sr., was not pleased when his son ran
　　　　　　off to join the circus.

1. Straighten your tie and comb your hair.
2. I think Mrs. Berg gave the message to her son, Chris Berg, Jr.
3. Sgt. S. P. Casey wrote the speeding ticket that Mr. Gillespie received.
4. Fill out the form and sign it at the bottom.
5. Dr. Birch asked me if Sally Ryan, R.N., works at the hospital in Coral Springs.

Uses of the Question Mark

An interrogative sentence, which asks a question requiring an answer, ends with a *question mark*.

Use a question mark to end an interrogative sentence, that is, to end a direct question.

this section and others in the chapter. A cursory review of sentence types (declarative, imperative, exclamatory, and interrogative) may be helpful, too.

Text Follow Through
Discuss text pages 334–339.

Assign Exercise A, page 335; Exercise B, page 336; Exercise C, page 338; and Developing Writing Skills, page 338.

Less advanced   You may wish to incorporate into this section a study or review of sentence fragments and run-on sentences as presented in Sections 10.1 and 10.2. You may also wish to have students study or review the material on sentence functions in Section 7.8.

Average   Exercises in punctuation furnish many opportunities for review or introduction of points of grammar and usage. If any students have difficulty distinguishing indirect questions, write several examples on the board, discuss them, and then have students rewrite them as direct questions.

Advanced   Ask students to make the sentences they write for the Developing Writing Skills activity as difficult as possible. You can then place their sentences, omitting end marks, on the board or duplicate them to challenge other students in the class.

Additional Practice
Practice Pages or Practice Book, page 104

Less advanced   Exercise Bank, Exercises A and B, pages 153–155

Average Exercise Bank, Exercises A, B, and C, pages 153–155

Advanced Exercise Bank, Exercises B and C, pages 153–155

TESTING

Test Program

Unit Pretest, page 58
Chapter Test, page 64
Unit Post-Test, page 67

RE-TEACHING

Practice Pages or Practice Book, page 104

THINKING SKILLS

Application—*Using* periods correctly in sentences (Exercise A, page 335)
Using correct punctuation for direct, indirect, or incomplete questions (Exercise B, page 336)
Using exclamation marks appropriately in exclamatory and imperative sentences and interjections (Exercise C, page 338)

Synthesis—*Composing* sentences using appropriate end marks (Developing Writing Skills, page 338)

INTERROGATIVE SENTENCES: Where are you staying in Florida**?**

Was there a valid reason for her absence**?**

Do not confuse an interrogative sentence, which is a direct question, with an indirect question. An indirect question requires no answer and should end with a period.

Sometimes a single word or phrase is used to ask a question.

Use a question mark to end an incomplete question in which the rest of the question is understood.

EXAMPLE: Of course, I will meet you. When**?**

A question that shows surprise is sometimes phrased as a declarative sentence. Use a question mark to indicate that the sentence is a question.

Use a question mark to end a statement that is intended as a question.

EXAMPLES: There is no electricity**?**

You invited him for dinner**?**

EXERCISE B: Using the Question Mark. The following sentences do not have end marks. Some sentences are direct questions requiring question marks. Others are indirect questions requiring periods. Still others are statements intended as questions. Copy each of the sentences onto your paper, adding the correct punctuation mark.

EXAMPLE: She wondered if she would ever be famous

She wondered if she would ever be famous.

1. How many people attended the play the first night? The second night?
2. I wondered why my car would not start.

336

3. You lost the ten dollars I gave you for the tickets to the concert?

4. The students asked if any more assemblies will be scheduled.

5. Which doctor developed a successful vaccine for smallpox? When?

6. The children asked whether any refreshments would be served.

7. Which planet is the red one?

8. A stork built its nest on your chimney?

9. Would you repeat that?

10. The puppy scratched you?

Uses of the Exclamation Mark

The *exclamation mark* is used to indicate strong emotions such as anger or amazement.

Use an exclamation mark to end an exclamatory sentence, that is, to end a statement showing strong emotion.

EXAMPLES: I finally understand the problem!

That was a terrifying experience!

The exclamation mark may also be used to end an urgent imperative sentence.

Use an exclamation mark after an imperative sentence if the command is urgent and forceful.

EXAMPLE: Run for your life!

In addition, an exclamation mark often follows an interjection.

Use an exclamation mark after an interjection expressing strong emotion.

EXAMPLE: Oh! You've ruined the surprise.

Note About Using Exclamation Marks: Exclamation marks should not be used too often. Overusing them makes writing too emotional and less effective.

OVERUSED: I made brownies for dessert! They are made with semisweet chocolate, walnuts, and other rich ingredients! You will never taste better brownies!

CORRECT: I made brownies for dessert. They are made with semisweet chocolate, walnuts, and other rich ingredients. You will never taste better brownies!

EXERCISE C: Using the Exclamation Mark. Exclamation marks have been left out of each of the following items. Copy the items, adding exclamation marks as needed. Then identify each item that requires an exclamation mark as an *exclamatory sentence*, an *imperative sentence*, or an *interjection*.

EXAMPLE: Watch out

　　　　　　Watch out! imperative sentence

1. Surprise! We tricked you. interject
2. We broke the record for having the most people in a telephone booth! exclam
3. That's impossible! exclam
4. Don't touch! Those vases are priceless. imper
5. If only I could remember! exclam
6. Well! This is a deliberate insult. interject
7. He repaired the television in less than five minutes! exclam
8. I haven't eaten since yesterday! exclam
9. Foul! That was a double dribble. interject
10. Stop dragging your feet! imper

DEVELOPING WRITING SKILLS: Using End Marks Correctly in Sentences. Write ten original sentences according to the following instructions. Be sure to use the correct end marks for the sentences, words, or phrases that require them.
Answers will vary; samples are given for the first two.

EXAMPLE: Write a sentence beginning with an interjection.

　　　　　Wow! That's more what I had in mind.

1. We went to a movie last night.   2. I thought the movie was very funny.

1. Write a statement of fact.
2. Write a statement of opinion.
3. Write a declarative sentence followed by an interjection.
4. Write a direction.
5. Write a command.
6. Write an indirect question.
7. Write a declarative sentence containing the initials of a person's name.
8. Write a statement intended as a question.
9. Write an exclamatory sentence followed by an incomplete question.
10. Write an urgent command.

Commas That Separate Basic 19.2 Elements

A *comma* (,) in a sentence signals the reader to pause briefly. It is common practice either to neglect commas or to overuse them. If you use a comma only when you have a specific rule in mind, your writing will be smoother and clearer to your reader.

Generally, commas function in one of two ways: (1) to *separate* items, such as two independent clauses, from each other or (2) to *set off* items, such as introductory words, from the rest of the sentence. This section shows you how to use commas to *separate* items from each other.

Commas with Compound Sentences

A compound sentence consists of two or more independent clauses that are joined by a coordinating conjunction. Coordinating conjunctions include *and, but, for, nor, or, so,* and *yet.*

339

section. To introduce the use of the comma as a separator, write these sentences on the board:

1. Bring a sack lunch a warm coat gloves or mittens and a thermos of hot cocoa.
2. I have extra ice skates but I don't know if they will fit you.

Ask a volunteer to add punctuation to sentence 1 to make it easier to read. Elicit from students that the list of things is confusing without commas. (Where does one item leave off and the next begin?) If students want to place commas after *gloves* and *mittens,* help them to see that they are logically only one item in the list; both are not required.

In sentence 2, ask a student to underline the subject of each independent clause once; the verb, twice. Elicit from students that the comma is appropriate because it shows that the two thoughts are separate and equal yet indicates a lesser pause than a period. This reflects the connection between the related ideas when they are joined by the conjunction *but.*

Text Follow Through

Discuss text pages 339–345.

Assign Exercise A, page 340; Exercise B, page 342; Exercise C, page 344; and Developing Writing Skills, page 344.

Less advanced Do not attempt to teach more than one or two comma rules a day with students. The rules tend to be confusing if piled on top of one another. You may wish to study or review Section 9.3 just before students are asked to complete Exercise A. As they do Exercise C, you might remind students

---

Use a comma before the conjunction to separate two independent clauses in a compound sentence.

COMPOUND SENTENCES: I filled my canteen with fresh spring water**,** and we began the long hike back to town.

Storm clouds were gathering overhead**,** so the children brought their kites inside.

Use a comma before a conjunction only when there are complete sentences on both sides of the conjunction. Do not use a comma before a conjunction when a word, phrase, or subordinate clause appears on either side of the conjunction.

WORDS: *Glue* or *tape* will hold the sign in place.

PHRASES: We could go *to the movies* or *for a walk*.

SUBORDINATE CLAUSES: Try to buy a car *that has low mileage* and *that is in good condition*.

Sometimes the independent clauses in a compound sentence are so short and their meaning so clear that the comma may be left out.

EXAMPLE: Adam tried to speak but he could not.

EXERCISE A: Using Commas with Compound Sentences.

Commas have been left out of the following compound sentences. Read each sentence and decide where the comma goes. On your paper write the word before the comma, the comma, and the conjunction following the comma.

EXAMPLE: She was tired yet she was determined to finish the race.

tired, yet

1. The sheep bleated fearfully but the shears never cut their skin.

19.2 Commas That Separate Basic Elements

2. The freshly painted walls and newly waxed floors made the apartment pleasant, yet major repairs were still needed.
3. Lin is inclined to exaggerate, but her stories are entertaining.
4. Mr. Klein's kitchen has been remodeled, and it now contains many modern conveniences.
5. There were no trees growing on the desert island, nor was there any water.
6. We could hear music blaring inside the house, but no one answered when we knocked.
7. Tom hoed the soil, and Eliza trimmed the branches.
8. Wind rattled the windows of the cabin, yet the campers slept soundly.
9. She was forced to dismount, for her horse was lame.
10. Many people have reptiles as pets, but few of them know how to care for reptiles properly.

Commas Between Items in a Series

A series consists of three or more similar items.

Use commas to separate three or more words, phrases, or clauses in a series.

Notice that the number of commas used is one fewer than the number of items in the series. For example, in the first of the following sentences, *four* items in a series are separated by *three* commas.

SERIES OF WORDS: The buffet included *turkey*, *ham*, *roast beef*, and *lamb*.

SERIES OF PHRASES: The treasure map directed them *through the woods*, *over the mountain*, and *past the bridge*.

SERIES OF CLAUSES: The house was rather quiet *before she arrived*, *before her luggage was piled up in the hall*, and *before her three poodles took over*.

---

to apply both of the ways suggested on page 343 in determining whether or not to use a comma to separate adjectives.

Average   Students will be less familiar with the use of the comma to separate phrases and clauses in a series than with its use to separate single-word items. You may want to review the definitions of phrases and clauses and point out examples in the sentences of Exercise B.

Students may find deciding when to use commas to separate adjectives the most difficult aspect of this section. Be sure they understand the rule of thumb about inserting *and* between the adjectives. Since *and* is a separating word, they should find it logical that a comma is appropriate where *and* makes sense.

Advanced   Ask students to look through newspapers, textbooks, or other reading material to find five examples of adjectives separated by commas and five without commas. They can bring their examples to class and share them with their classmates. You might also choose sentences these students have written for the Developing Writing Skills activity and write them on the board, omitting the comma. Then you can call on other students to add the necessary punctuation.

Additional Practice

Practice Pages or Practice Book, page 105

Less advanced   Exercise Bank, Exercises A and B, pages 156–158

Average   Exercise Bank, Exercises A, B, and C, pages 156–158

Advanced Exercise Bank, Exercises B and C, pages 156–158

TESTING

Test Program

Unit Pretest, page 58
Chapter Test, page 64
Unit Post-Test, page 67

RE-TEACHING

Practice Pages or Practice Book, page 105

THINKING SKILLS

Application—*Using* commas in compound sentences (Exercise A, page 340)
Using commas between items in a series (Exercise B, page 342)
Using commas when appropriate to separate equal adjectives (Exercise C, page 344)

Synthesis—*Writing* sentences using commas when appropriate to separate basic elements (Developing Writing Skills, page 344)

One exception to the rule for commas with series occurs when each item is joined to the next by a conjunction. In this case no commas are necessary.

EXAMPLE: For this exam you will need two pencils *and* an eraser *and* a slide rule.

A second exception to the rule concerns words that are considered to be one item. Paired words such as *macaroni and cheese* should not be split by a comma.

EXAMPLE: Every table in the diner was set with *a knife and fork*, *a cup and saucer*, and *salt and pepper*.

EXERCISE B: Using Commas Between Items in a Series.

Copy each of the following sentences onto your paper, adding commas as needed.

EXAMPLE: Alex threw back the covers stamped across the room and pounced on the alarm clock.

Alex threw back the covers, stamped across the room, and pounced on the alarm clock.

1. The pioneers crossed deserts, scaled mountains, and forded rivers before they reached the West.
2. Silk, cotton, and wool are natural fibers.
3. I must mow the lawn, trim the hedges, and weed the garden.
4. Studying your notes, listening to directions, and feeling confident can help you do well on the exam.
5. The performers ran off the stage, down the aisles, and through the exit doors.
6. For dinner Lauren wanted spaghetti and meatballs, bread and butter, and ice cream and cake.
7. Becky first requested, then insisted on, and finally pleaded for permission to visit her cousin for the weekend.
8. Bring a wrench, a pair of pliers, and a hammer and nails out to the garage.

9. Elizabeth polished the silverware set the table and lit the candles.
10. Ted walked to the end of the diving board leaped into the air and dived gracefully into the pool.

Commas Between Adjectives

Sometimes two or more adjectives are placed before the noun they describe. Use the following rule to determine whether to use a comma between them.

Use commas to separate adjectives of *equal* rank.

There are two ways to decide if adjectives are of equal rank. First, if the word *and* can be placed between the adjectives without changing the meaning of the sentence, then the adjectives are of equal rank. Second, if the order of the adjectives can be changed, then they are equal.

After reading the following examples, try both methods of determining whether the adjectives are of equal rank.

EXAMPLES: She left *detailed, precise* instructions for the substitute.

A *smooth, round* stone was cupped in her hand.

As you can see, the adjectives in the examples are equal, and commas are necessary to separate them. Sometimes, however, placing *and* between the adjectives or changing their order can destroy the meaning.

Do not use commas to separate adjectives that must stay in a specific order.

In the following examples, you can see that either adding *and* or changing the order of the adjectives results in sentences that make no sense.

EXAMPLES: *Three brief* paragraphs will be enough.

In a *few short* hours, we will be finished.

Developing Writing Skills

Have students practice using commas to separate basic elements in writing by completing the following exercise.

Writing Across the Curriculum

People have always been fascinated by animals. Is there any kind of animal that you particularly enjoy?

Prewriting Free write about a favorite animal. You might choose a pet, an animal you have seen in the wild or at the zoo, or an animal that you have seen on television. Look over your free writing and choose words and phrases appropriate for a description of the animal's appearance and behavior. If you wish, do some research on your topic.

Writing Write the first draft of an article for the magazine *Animals! Animals! Animals!* In your article, be sure to give a clear and precise description of the appearance and behavior of your animal. Use vivid words that appeal to the senses. If the animal is a pet, try to give an idea of its personality through your description. Also include the reason why this animal is one of your favorites.

Revising Make sure that you have identified the animal at some point in the article. Have you described the animal's appearance and behavior clearly and precisely? If your subject is a pet, have you conveyed its personality? Have you used commas correctly and where necessary? Proofread your article and prepare a final draft.

NOTE ABOUT COMMAS WITH ADJECTIVES: Never use a comma to separate the last adjective in a series from the noun it modifies.

INCORRECT: A *yellow*, *long-stemmed*, rose lay on the table.

CORRECT: A *yellow*, *long-stemmed* rose lay on the table.

EXERCISE C: Using Commas Between Adjectives.
In each of the following sentences, two adjectives have been underlined. Copy the adjectives onto your paper, adding commas only where necessary.

EXAMPLE: The <u>two</u> <u>little</u> girls were playing jacks.

two little

1. Thomas and I noticed an <u>unfamiliar</u> <u>musky</u> odor inside the cave.
2. <u>Many</u> <u>shallow</u> pools formed on the beach after the light rain.
3. <u>Several</u> <u>faint</u> giggles brought the librarian to his feet.
4. On the door was a <u>heavy</u> <u>ornate</u> knocker in the shape of a wreath.
5. <u>Slow</u> <u>steady</u> rowing soon brought all of the team's boats to shore.

DEVELOPING WRITING SKILLS: Using Commas to Separate Basic Elements in Your Writing.
Follow the directions to write five sentences of your own. Use commas only where necessary.

Answers will vary; samples are given for the first two.

EXAMPLE: Write a sentence containing a series of clauses.

They finally relaxed when the meal was over, when the guests had left, and when they had cleared the table.

1. We tried repeatedly, yet we couldn't budge the rock.

1. Write a compound sentence using the conjunction *yet* to join two independent clauses.
2. Write a sentence containing a series of at least three nouns.

2. Leroy enjoys only music, art, and English.

3. Write a sentence containing three nouns, each joined to the next by *and*.
4. Write a sentence containing two adjectives of equal rank that modify the same noun.
5. Write a sentence containing two adjectives that belong in a specific order.

Commas That Set Off Added 19.3 Elements

In addition to separating similar kinds of words and word groups, such as adjectives or independent clauses, commas are also used to *set off* or isolate certain groups of words that are added to sentences. Included in this category are introductory words and phrases, words and groups of words inserted in the middle or at the end of a sentence, and a few special elements such as dates.

Commas After Introductory Material

Commas are often used to set off information at the beginning of a sentence.

Use a comma after an introductory word, phrase, or clause.

As you study the following chart, notice how a comma sets off the introductory word or words in each of the sentences.

KINDS OF INTRODUCTORY MATERIAL

Introductory Words	*No,* we don't need any.
	Fran, give me your camera quickly before the kitten moves.
	Smiling, the flight attendant greeted the passengers.

19.3 Commas That Set Off Added Elements
(pp. 345–355)

OBJECTIVES
After completing this section, students should be able to

- Use commas correctly to set off introductory words, phrases, and clauses in sentences.
- Use commas correctly to set off parenthetical expressions.
- Use commas correctly to set off nonessential expressions.
- Use commas as needed to set off dates and geographical names.
- Use commas correctly in other situations.

TEACHING
Getting Started

This is a very concentrated section. Proceed slowly, making sure students have mastered one rule before going on to the next. To introduce the idea of commas as a device to set off added elements, you might try writing several simple sentences on the board, and ask students to adapt one sentence to become an introductory element for a second sentence. For example, a sentence such as *The puppies tumbled down the hill after it* could be paired with *They spied a young rabbit.* Students might adapt the second sentence to become an introductory element in two ways:

When they spied a young rabbit, the puppies tumbled down the hill after it.
Spying a young rabbit, the puppies tumbled down the hill after it.

Have students discuss the logic of adding a comma after the introductory material. They should see that the introductory material must be set off by a slight pause to make the meaning of the sentence clear.

Text Follow Through

Discuss text pages 345–355.

Assign Exercise A, page 346; Exercise B, page 348; Exercise C, page 349; Exercise D, page 351; Exercise E, page 353; and Developing Writing Skills, page 354.

Less advanced You may prefer to skip the subsection Commas with Nonessential Expressions if you feel it is more likely to burden and confuse students than to enlighten them. A review of participial phrases and adjective clauses will probably be necessary before undertaking this section, and you will want to spend considerable time with the chart of essential and nonessential phrases on page 349. You can discuss with students why the expression in each example is or is not

Introductory Phrases	*Inside the warm and comfortable stable,* the calf struggled to its feet.
	Shattered into many sharp fragments, the window was now a hazard.
	To succeed in business, you must have perseverance.
Introductory Adverb Clauses	*When the huge elm tree became diseased,* we called a tree surgeon.
	Although the police responded quickly, they arrived too late.

An exception is made for short prepositional phrases. If an introductory prepositional phrase is only two or three words long, it generally will not need a comma to set it off.

EXAMPLE: *After the exam* Monica felt relieved.

EXERCISE A: Using Commas After Introductory Material.
Each of the following sentences needs a comma to set off introductory material. On your paper write the introductory word or words, the comma, and the word following the comma.

EXAMPLE: To get a better view Fran climbed to the top of the hill.

To get a better view, Fran

1. For better or for worse, we were committed to the task.
2. If you are easily frightened, don't see that movie.
3. Gripping the man's cuff in his jaws, the bulldog braced his legs and pulled.
4. Yes, these plastic treads should make the stairs safer.
5. To calm the jittery horse, Irene stroked its neck and spoke quietly.
6. Please, isn't there any way you could make an exception?

19.3 Commas That Set Off Added Elements

7. Remember, no one is admitted beyond this point.
8. With dry clothing and warm food, the climbers soon recovered.
9. After the brief intermission, we returned to our seats.
10. Marsha and Bill, will you please stop arguing?

Commas with Parenthetical Expressions

A *parenthetical expression* is a word or phrase that is not essential to the meaning of the sentence.

Use commas to set off parenthetical expressions.

Parenthetical expressions usually appear in the middle or at the end of a sentence. A parenthetical expression in the middle of a sentence needs two commas. A parenthetical expression at the end of a sentence needs only one.

The following chart shows some common kinds of parenthetical expressions. Notice that each of the sentences makes sense with or without the parenthetical expression.

KINDS OF PARENTHETICAL EXPRESSIONS	
Names of People Being Addressed	Listen carefully, *Bob and Lucinda,* while I explain.
	That's a logical conclusion, *Pete.*
Certain Adverbs	The other team, *therefore,* won the baseball game.
	Roberta will not be able to go with us, *however.*
Common Expressions	The math test, *I think,* will be very difficult.
	They believe in her ability, *of course.*
Contrasting Expressions	These apples, *not those,* are ripe enough to use.
	The decision should be mine, *not yours.*

essential and encourage students to try reading each example (and each sentence in Exercise C) without the underlined material to determine whether the material is essential or nonessential.

Average You may want to review appositives, participial phrases, and adjective clauses briefly with students. The rule for using commas with nonessential expressions will be new to most students. Proceed slowly, using plenty of examples on the board until you are sure students have grasped the nature of nonessential elements. Students will probably be familiar with the use of commas to separate parts of geographical and date information. However, they may be surprised to learn that the comma is needed *after* both, as well. Emphasize this point.

Advanced Students might enjoy collecting examples of sentences in which commas are especially important in making the meaning and relationships clear. Students can be asked to exchange the papers they write for the Developing Writing Skills activity and to check each other's work. Caution them to make sure that each student has followed the instructions and used commas correctly. Students can also review their own recent compositions to see if they have used commas correctly.

Additional Practice

Practice Pages or Practice Book, pages 106, 108

Less advanced Exercise Bank, Exercises A and B, pages 159–163

EXERCISE B: Using Commas with Parenthetical Expressions. Copy each of the following sentences onto your paper, adding commas as needed to set off the parenthetical expressions.

EXAMPLE: Her hope of course was that he would return.

Her hope**,** of course**,** was that he would return.

1. Check the yellow pages of the telephone directory,Melissa.
2. Charles,we believe,is the right man for the job.
3. Audrey's hair is black,not red.
4. We assumed,nevertheless,that you would still come to the party.
5. This kitten,however,believes your hen is its mother.
6. If you bring in the painting,Mr. Curtis,we can help you choose a frame.
7. Beth's grades,therefore,need improvement.
8. Hurry up,Armando,or we'll miss our bus.
9. Their younger son,not the older,showed an interest in the family business.
10. Everyone is eagerly anticipating the holiday,of course.

Commas with Nonessential Expressions

Some writers have trouble determining when a phrase or clause should be set off with commas. It helps to know whether the phrase or clause is *essential* or *nonessential* to the meaning of the sentence. Expressions that are essential cannot be left out without changing the meaning of the sentence. Expressions that are nonessential are additional phrases or clauses that, in contrast, can be left out.

Use commas to set off nonessential expressions.

The chart on the following page shows examples of essential and nonessential phrases and clauses. Notice that removing an essential expression alters the sentence's meaning; removing a nonessential expression does not.

19.3 Commas That Set Off Added Elements

ESSENTIAL AND NONESSENTIAL EXPRESSIONS	
Appositives and Appositive Phrases	
Essential	The famous dramatist *Ben Jonson* wrote these comedies.
Nonessential	Ben Jonson**,** *a famous dramatist***,** wrote these comedies.
	These comedies were written by Ben Jonson**,** *a famous dramatist*.
Participial Phrases	
Essential	The girl *waiting in the car* is my sister.
Nonessential	Pat**,** *waiting in the car***,** asked us to hurry.
	The time passed slowly for my sister**,** *waiting in the car*.
Adjective Clauses	
Essential	We need someone *who can play a harmonica and a guitar*.
Nonessential	Bob Dylan**,** *who can play a harmonica and a guitar***,** was applauded enthusiastically.
	We applauded enthusiastically for Bob Dylan**,** *who can play a harmonica and a guitar*.

EXERCISE C: Using Commas with Nonessential Expressions. Read each of the sentences on the following page carefully to determine whether the underlined expression is essential or nonessential. If the material is essential, write *E*. If the material is nonessential, copy the sentence onto your paper, adding any commas needed.

EXAMPLE: The New England poet <u>Emily Dickinson</u> lived a very quiet life.

     E

1. Our new kittens, who could not find their mother, meowed loudly.
2. Grandmother's old quilt, filled with soft eiderdown, was a family heirloom.
3. My favorite book is a spell-binding story written by the famous author Robert Louis Stevenson. E
4. My favorite author, Robert Louis Stevenson, wrote *Treasure Island*.
5. Only a person who was a genius could have formulated this theory. E
6. Albert Einstein, who was a genius, formulated the theory of relativity.
7. Our school newspaper, published twice a month, won an award.
8. The person wearing a new red coat boarded the plane. E
9. Fred, my younger brother, has just learned to swim.
10. I would like you to meet Miss Jorgenson, my new neighbor.

Commas with Dates and Geographical Names

Dates usually have several parts, such as months, days, and years. Commas prevent such dates from being unclear.

When a date is made up of two or more parts, use a comma after each item except in the case of a month followed by a day.

In the following examples, notice that commas follow most of the words and numbers in the dates. An exception is found in all cases where a month is followed by a day.

EXAMPLES:　Saturday, July 20, is their anniversary.

January 1, 1945, was the beginning of an exciting year for my grandfather.

On September 7, 1982, school began.

19.3 Commas That Set Off Added Elements

When dates contain only months and years, commas are optional.

EXAMPLES: Before February 1981 the house had no central heating system.

                    Before February, 1981, the house had no central heating system.

Geographical names may also consist of more than one part. Again, commas help prevent confusion.

When a geographical name is made up of two or more parts, use a comma after each item.

EXAMPLES: Our neighbors moved from Columbus, Ohio, to Temperance, Michigan.

                    This cheese was shipped from Montigny, Moselle, France, by my friend Robert.

EXERCISE D: Using Commas with Dates or Geographical Names. Copy each of the following sentences onto your paper, adding commas where they are needed.

EXAMPLE: The new student had come from San Juan Puerto Rico in March.

                    The new student had come from San Juan, Puerto Rico, in March.

1. On March 15, 1917, the Czar of Russia gave up his throne.
2. The exchange student explained that Nairobi, Kenya, is located almost directly on the Equator.
3. This recipe for clam sauce comes from a restaurant in Milan, Italy.
4. On Thursday, March 15, Lynn will give a party to celebrate her birthday.
5. Alexandra will leave for Geneva, Switzerland, on Monday, October 10.

Other Uses of the Comma

The following rules govern the use of commas in addresses, letter salutations and closings, numbers, and quotations. A final rule concerns using commas to avoid misunderstandings.

The first rule covers commas used in addresses.

Use a comma after each item in an address made up of two or more parts.

As you can see in the following example, commas are placed after the name, street, and city. No comma separates the state from the ZIP code.

EXAMPLE: Write to Maxwell Hunnicutt, 54 Monmouth Avenue, Dallas, Texas 75243.

Fewer commas are needed when an address is written on an envelope.

EXAMPLE: Maxwell Hunnicutt
54 Monmouth Avenue
Dallas, Texas 75243

Letter salutations and closings also make special use of commas.

Use a comma after the salutation in a personal letter and after the closing in all letters.

SALUTATIONS: Dear Bill,   My dear Aunt Harriet and Uncle Bill,

CLOSINGS: Sincerely,   With best wishes,   Very truly yours,

Another use of commas is to make it easier to read large numbers.

With numbers of more than three digits, use a comma after every third digit, counting from the right.

EXAMPLES: 1,750 feet   3,608,787 square miles

19.3 Commas That Set Off Added Elements

NOTE ABOUT COMMAS WITH NUMBERS: Do not use commas with ZIP codes, telephone numbers, page numbers, or serial numbers.

ZIP CODE: 14301

TELEPHONE NUMBER: (212) 555-2473

PAGE NUMBER: on page 1022

SERIAL NUMBER: 059 94 6106

Commas can also show where direct quotations begin and end.

Use commas to set off a direct quotation from the rest of a sentence.

As you read the following examples, notice that the correct location of the commas depends upon the "he said/she said" part of the sentence. (See Section 19.6 for more information about the punctuation used with quotations.)

EXAMPLES: Bret said, "Hold the door open."

"I can't," Lorna replied, "because my arms are full of books."

The final rule covers special situations when a comma is needed to avoid confusion.

Use a comma to prevent a sentence from being misunderstood.

Without any commas the following sentences are confusing. The addition of commas keeps the reader from having to puzzle over the meaning.

UNCLEAR: Beyond the mountains were clearly visible.

CLEAR: Beyond, the mountains were clearly visible.

UNCLEAR: After watching Zack asked to join the game.

CLEAR: After watching, Zack asked to join the game.

EXERCISE E: Using Commas in Other Situations. Commas have been left out of the following sentences and groups of words. Copy each item onto your paper, adding commas as needed.

EXAMPLE: There were 1407 people in the audience, all demanding an encore.

There were 1,407 people in the audience, all demanding an encore.

1. Send this postcard to Jimmy Murphy, 509 Cliff Street, Newfield, New York   14867.
2. The Zambian census taken in 1963 indicated a population of 3,405,788 Africans and 84,370 non-Africans.
3. In the spring Mandy planted 3,000 flowers.
4. Arlene advised, "Take the train instead of the bus."
5. While racing, John's dog developed a limp.
6. Maryann's permanent residence is 3 Hill Drive, Apartment 3E, New Milford, Connecticut 06776.
7. Inside, Mr. Martin took off his coat and warmed himself by the fire.
8. "Your request is unreasonable," Barry stated.
9. My dear Patricia,   Sincerely,

     Nathaniel
10. "The serial number," said Sue, "is 101 27 304."

DEVELOPING WRITING SKILLS: Using Commas to Set Off Added Elements. Write ten original sentences, each containing the material described in the following directions. Use commas when necessary.

Answers will vary; samples are given for the first two.

EXAMPLE: Use the word *however*.

Nothing, however, could have pleased them more.

1. The members of our team, listening to the weather report, feared the game

1. Use the phrase *listening to the weather report* as nonessential information.
2. Use the clause *who volunteered* as essential information.
3. Use the word *Oh* at the beginning of a sentence.
4. Indicate the full date, including the day of the week, of your next birthday.

would be canceled.   2. Everyone who volunteered was given a job.

5. Write a direct quotation consisting of one sentence interrupted by *Dennis said*.
6. Use your area code and telephone number.
7. Use the expression *not the green one*.
8. Use the phrase *Under the surface of the crystal-clear water* to begin a sentence.
9. Directly address *Cindy,* asking her a question.
10. Use the name and complete address of a friend.

The Semicolon 19.4

The *semicolon* looks like a period above a comma (;). Like the two punctuation marks that make it up, the semicolon includes a pause in a sentence. However, the semicolon is less final than a period and indicates more of a pause than a comma does.

Two basic functions of the semicolon are (1) to join related independent clauses and (2) to take the place of commas that would cause confusion for the reader.

Semicolons Used to Join Independent Clauses

Semicolons are used to join independent clauses only in specific situations.

Use a semicolon to join independent clauses that are *not* already joined by the conjunctions *and, or, nor, for, but, so, or yet*.

Two independent clauses joined by a conjunction usually require a comma before the conjunction.

CLAUSES WITH COMMA: Shelly's birthstone is an amethyst**,** *and* Faith's is an opal.

Sometimes no conjunction is used to join clauses. Then, the semicolon replaces both the comma and the conjunction.

OBJECTIVES

After completing this section, students should be able to

- Use semicolons correctly to join independent clauses.
- Use semicolons in sentences where additional commas would cause confusion.

TEACHING

Getting Started

To introduce the idea of independent clauses joined by a semicolon, review with students the use of commas and coordinating conjunctions in compound sentences. Students should see that just as the comma and conjunction join related ideas with an appropriate pause, the semicolon does the same. Stress, however, that the two ideas must be obviously related, since the relationship-showing conjunction is omitted. Also note that without a conjunction, a comma is not sufficient to separate the two independent clauses. Place several examples of compound sentences on the board, and have student volunteers rewrite them using semicolons. The use of conjunctive adverbs will be new for many students. Place several more example sentences on the board using *however, therefore, instead,* or other conjunctive adverbs to join independent clauses. Help students to see that such sentences need the stronger punctuation mark because the relationship-showing word is followed by a comma. The longer pause helps to clarify meaning.

Text Follow Through

Discuss text pages 355–360.

Assign Exercise A, page 357; Exercise B, page 359; and Developing Writing Skills, page 360.

Less advanced You might wish to review or study compound sentences (in Section 9.3) just before beginning this section. You might also decide to turn the Developing Writing Skills activity into a class activity. You may wish to omit the subsection Semicolons Used to Avoid Confusion, instead devoting more time to use of semicolons to join independent clauses.

Average For extra practice, ask students to write example sentences for each rule in the section. Students can also rewrite sentences 2 to 5 in Exercise C, Section 9.3 using semicolons instead of conjunctions.

CLAUSES WITH SEMICOLON: Marianne's birthstone is an amethyst; Faith's is an opal.

A semicolon should never be used simply as a shortcut. When two independent clauses are not closely related, a semicolon should not be used. Instead, the clauses should be written as separate sentences.

INCORRECT: The fire began with a casually tossed match; many years must pass before a forest can recover from a fire.

CORRECT: The fire began with a casually tossed match. Many years must pass before a forest can recover from a fire.

The fire began with a casually tossed match; one moment of carelessness resulted in terrible destruction.

Note that when a sentence contains three or more related independent clauses, they may still be separated with semicolons.

EXAMPLE: The birds vanished; the sky grew dark; the little pond was still.

Semicolons are also used when independent clauses are separated by certain special words.

Use a semicolon to join independent clauses separated by either a conjunctive adverb or a transitional expression.

Certain words or phrases—conjunctive adverbs and transitional expressions—establish the relationship between sentence parts.

CONJUNCTIVE ADVERBS: also, besides, furthermore, however, indeed, instead, moreover, nevertheless, otherwise, therefore, thus

Advanced Students might be asked to find in their reading additional examples of each type of sentence specified in the Developing Writing Skills activity.

Additional Practice
Practice Pages or Practice Book, page 109

Less advanced Exercise Bank, Exercises A and B, pages 164, 165

Average Exercise Bank, Exercises A, B, and C, pages 164, 165

Advanced Exercise Bank, Exercises B and C, pages 164, 165

TESTING
Test Program
  Unit Pretest, page 58
  Chapter Test, page 64
  Unit Post-Test, page 67

RE-TEACHING
Practice Pages or Practice Book, page 109

THINKING SKILLS
Application—*Using* semicolons to join independent clauses (Exercise A, page 357)
Using semicolons instead of commas to avoid confusion (Exercise B, page 359)

Synthesis—*Writing* sentences using semicolons (Developing Writing Skills, page 360)

19.4 The Semicolon

TRANSITIONAL EXPRESSIONS: as a result, at this time, consequently, first, for instance, in fact, on the other hand, second, that is

When these words separate two independent clauses, a semicolon generally goes before the conjunctive adverb or transitional expression.

EXAMPLE: We were very impressed with the child's knowledge of science; *indeed,* she was remarkably well-informed.

Remember to place a comma after the conjunctive adverb or transitional expression. The comma sets off the conjunctive adverb or transitional expression, which acts as an introductory expression to the second clause.

EXERCISE A: Using Semicolons to Join Independent Clauses.
Semicolons have been left out of the following sentences. Read each sentence and decide where one or more semicolons are required. On your paper write the word before each semicolon, the semicolon, and the word that follows it.

EXAMPLE: I like the color of the leaves in October however, I do not like raking them.

  October; however

1. Jeb hurried to finish his project;as a result, his work was slipshod and unacceptable.
2. Some of the volunteers were assigned the task of painting; others were responsible for repairing the playground equipment.
3. Lester sent the hamburger back;it was too rare.
4. The soup was cold;the salad was limp;the chicken was burned.
5. The prairie dog barked a warning;immediately, all the rodents scampered for safety.

6. Marge had a cast on her leg;nevertheless, she was the first one on the dance floor.
7. I expect you to be on time;furthermore, be ready to work hard.
8. Ornamental fans were arranged on the walls; large, comfortable cushions were scattered on the rug.
9. Mrs. Walker forgot to mail the payment;consequently, the electricity was turned off.
10. The fans droned overhead;the temperature rose steadily;the students sat listlessly at their desks.

Semicolons Used to Avoid Confusion

Occasionally a semicolon may be used in place of a comma.

Consider the use of a semicolon to avoid confusion when independent clauses or items in a series already contain commas.

In the following example, there are several commas in the first clause. Adding another comma before the word *but* would create unnecessary confusion for the reader. Therefore, the use of a semicolon is appropriate in this particular sentence.

EXAMPLE: This side of the lake, which has never had any public beaches, has always been a secluded, private retreat for our family; but we have now been forced to abandon it because of the increasingly high property taxes.

You may also use a semicolon to separate items in a series when the items already contain a number of commas. The semicolon shows where each *complete* item ends.

EXAMPLE: The waiter brought fresh shrimp, which was heaped on a bed of lettuce; herring, which had been marinated in a sour cream sauce; soft shell crabs, which had been sautéed in lemon and butter; and salmon, which had been poached with vegetables.

EXERCISE B: Using Semicolons to Avoid Confusion.
Read the following sentences and decide where semicolons should be used instead of commas. Copy each sentence onto your paper, making the necessary corrections.

EXAMPLE: Heather, who was eight, had always loved living in Aspen Park, a suburb of Detroit, but she faced the move without fear.

Heather, who was eight, had always loved living in Aspen Park, a suburb of Detroit; but she faced the move without fear.

1. In a house with poor insulation, heat escapes through the walls and the roof, but adding more insulation can help keep the heat inside and can thus lower fuel bills. roof; but

2. This delicatessen, which is only a few blocks away from our house, has delicious roast beef, ham, and corned beef sandwiches, so Jerry and I always come here for lunch.

3. The three puppies that we kept from our poodle's first litter were Coco, a light brown female, Snowflake, a white female, and Tippy, a gray male. female; Snowflake/female; and

4. Before the town restored this area, the street was lined with neglected homes, but now the houses, each with many rooms, have been remodeled as professional buildings.

5. In our family Christine, who is seventeen, plays the guitar, Julie, who is fifteen, plays the trombone, and Maxine, who is only nine, plays the bassoon. guitar; Julie/trombone; and

6. On Fridays and Saturdays, I work as a cashier first, from three-thirty to five o'clock, as a filling station attendant second, from five-thirty to seven o'clock, and as a baby sitter last, from eight o'clock until late in the evening.

7. Jenny, who rarely finds fault with anything, criticized the food, the company, and the entertainment, yet the rest of us were quite content. entertainment; yet

8. Even with his help, we had still not addressed all of the envelopes, not even all of those on the first list, and time was running out. list; and

2. sandwiches; so   4. homes; but   6. o'clock; as/o'clock; and

9. This car needs a new hood, a new grill, and new head-lights, but the engine, transmission, and interior are all in excellent condition. headlights; but

10. The wagon, sagging and missing a wheel, hardly seemed a bargain for the price, and Jack, disappointed but firm, re-fused to buy it. price; and

DEVELOPING WRITING SKILLS: Using Semicolons in Your Writing. Write five original sentences, each using semi-colons as indicated in the following directions.
Answers will vary; samples are given for the first two.

EXAMPLE: Use a semicolon in a sentence with a conjunctive adverb.

The Johnsons were pet lovers; indeed, they had three cats, six dogs, and a dozen hamsters.

1. The wind blew hard; the shutters rattled; the house shook.

1. Use two semicolons to join three independent clauses in the same sentence.
2. Use a semicolon to join two independent clauses separated by *on the other hand*.
3. Use a semicolon with two independent clauses that already contain commas.
4. Use two semicolons in a sentence to separate a series of three items that are already punctuated with commas.
5. Use a semicolon to join two independent clauses not joined by a conjunction.

2. The cake looks good; on the other hand, fruit would be a lighter dessert.

19.5 The Colon
(pp. 360–363)

OBJECTIVES

After completing this section, students should be able to

• Use colons correctly as in-troductory devices.
• Use colons correctly in special writing situations.

19.5 The Colon

The *colon* looks like one period placed above another (:). This mark directs attention to the information that follows it.

The Colon as an Introductory Device

As the following rule shows, one of the most important uses of the colon is to introduce a list of miscellaneous items.

Point out that a colon looks like two periods, but it is used differently from a period. Ask students to name some uses for colons. They will probably mention listings of time and salutations of business letters. Note that colons are also used in special kinds of sentences. Explain to students that in these sentences the colon not only indicates a pause but also is intended to direct the reader's attention to some important information to follow. One use is to call attention to a list. Give students an example of a sentence in which such a listing requires a colon and one in which a colon isn't needed.

1. Be sure to bring the following items on the day of the test: two number 2 pencils, a slide rule, and a good eraser.
2. In the supply box were plenty of pencils, pens, and erasers.

Point out that the first sentence consists of an independent clause followed by a list; it requires a colon as a connective element and signal. The second sentence consists of a simple sentence whose list is actually the subject. It does not make sense to set off the subject of a sentence from its verb.

Text Follow Through
Discuss text pages 360–363.

Assign Exercise A, page 361; Exercise B, page 362; and Developing Writing Skills, page 363.

19.5 The Colon

Use a colon before a list of items following an independent clause.

EXAMPLE: His disguise included the following touches: large sunglasses, a black wig, a handlebar mustache, and platform shoes.

Notice that an independent clause comes before the colon. Although it may include words that hint there is more to come, such as *the following,* the clause must make sense by itself. Never use a colon to introduce a list that does not follow an independent clause. A colon should never, for example, separate a verb or a preposition from its object.

INCORRECT: As additions to her spring wardrobe, she purchased: white cotton gloves, a straw hat, and a lightweight coat.

Her new spring wardrobe consisted of: white cotton gloves, a straw hat, and a lightweight coat.

CORRECT: She added three new items to her spring wardrobe: white cotton gloves, a straw hat, and a lightweight coat.

EXERCISE A: Using Colons as Introductory Devices. Colons have been left out of some of the following sentences. Write the word before each missing colon, the colon, and the word following the colon. Write *correct* for any sentence that does not need a colon.

EXAMPLE: José wanted three things a horse, a saddle, and boots.

things: a

1. We finally located several constellations: Orion, Taurus, Pisces, and Virgo.
2. Merry carried the following items on her first day of class: a pencil sharpener, an eraser, a box of crayons, and a lunch box.

Less advanced You may wish to omit the first part of this section entirely and have students study only the subsection on special uses of the colon. If so, omit the Developing Writing Skills activity. Instead, ask students to give five examples of the use of the colon in special situations.

Average Students might be asked to write one additional sentence for each of the items in the Developing Writing Skills activity. The sentences should be written in random order, and all colons should be omitted. Students can then exchange papers and punctuate each other's sentences.

Advanced Students could rewrite the sentences in Exercise B of Section 19.2 (page 342) so that each sentence consists of an independent clause followed by a list of items and punctuated with a colon.

Additional Practice

Practice Pages or Practice Book, page 110

Less advanced Exercise Bank, Exercises A and B, pages 166, 167

Average Exercise Bank, Exercises A, B, and C, pages 166, 167

Advanced Exercise Bank, Exercises B and C, pages 166, 167

TESTING

Test Program

Unit Pretest, page 58
Chapter Test, page 64
Unit Post-Test, page 67

3. It was once believed that the universe was made up of four elements:earth, water, air, and fire.
4. My favorite movies include *Star Wars, 2001,* and *Superman.* C
5. The value of our property increased because of several improvements: landscaping the yard, blacktopping the driveway, and insulating the house.

Special Uses of the Colon

A colon is used to indicate time with numerals, to end salutations in business letters, and to signal important ideas.

Use a colon in a number of special writing situations.

The following chart shows examples of these special uses of the colon.

SPECIAL USES OF THE COLON	
Numerals Giving the Time	3:04 P.M. 5:00 a.m.
Salutations in Business Letters	Gentlemen: Dear Ms. Langly:
Labels Used to Signal Important Ideas	Warning: If taken internally, consult a physician immediately. Notice: Shop is closed for repairs.

EXERCISE B: Using Colons in Special Situations. Colons have been left out of the following expressions. Copy each item onto your paper, adding colons as needed.

EXAMPLE: Note the beach closes at dusk.

Note: The beach closes at dusk.

1. Dear Colonel Landstrom:
2. 400 A.M.

RE-TEACHING
Practice Pages or Practice Book, page 110

THINKING SKILLS
Application—*Showing* where to place colons as introductory devices in sentences (Exercise A, page 361)
Showing where to place colons in special situations (Exercise B, page 362)

Synthesis—*Writing* sentences using colons (Developing Writing Skills, page 363)

3. Caution: Proceed at your own risk.
4. Dear Voter:
5. Warning: The Surgeon General has determined that cigarette smoking is dangerous to your health.

DEVELOPING WRITING SKILLS: Using Colons in Your Writing. Write five original sentences or examples according to the following directions, using colons as needed.
Answers will vary; samples are given for the first two.
EXAMPLE: Write a salutation of a business letter.

   Dear Senator Craig:
1. There are only three choices on the menu: steak, chicken, and fish.
   1. Write a list of items following an independent clause.
   2. Write a list of items following a verb.
   3. Write a list of items following a preposition.
   4. Write a sentence containing a numeral and an abbreviation giving the time.
   5. Write a label and an important idea it signals.
2. We visited Seattle, Vancouver, and Calgary.

Quotation Marks with Direct 19.6 Quotations

There are many reasons for using quotation marks. Sometimes you may want to show that you are repeating the exact words spoken by a person or printed in a book. At other times, in writing fiction, for example, you may want your characters to reveal themselves in their own words or to show action through dialogue.

Direct and Indirect Quotations

There are two types of quotations: *direct* and *indirect*. A direct quotation requires the use of special punctuation.

A direct quotation represents a person's exact speech or thoughts and is enclosed in quotation marks (" ").

19.6 Quotation Marks with Direct Quotations
(pp. 363–371)

OBJECTIVES
After completing this section, students should be able to
- Distinguish between direct and indirect quotations.
- Place quotation marks correctly in direct quotations accompanied by introductory, concluding, or interrupting expressions.
- Use commas and end marks correctly with direct quotations.
- Use quotation marks appropriately in dialogue.

TEACHING

Getting Started

Students must be able to distinguish between direct and indirect quotations to succeed in this section. Place examples such as the following on the board and ask a student to explain why quotation marks are needed in the first sentence but not in the second.

The captain answered, "We must reach the bridge by midnight."
The captain said that we must reach the bridge by midnight.

Students should see that the second sentence is not the captain's exact words but a secondhand report by someone else. You may want to review with students the use of capital letters in quotations, introduced in Section 17.1.

Text Follow Through

Discuss text pages 363–371.

Assign Exercise A, page 364; Exercise B, page 367; Exercise C, page 369; Exercise D, page 370; and Developing Writing Skills, page 371.

Less advanced Insist that students refer to the text rules and examples as they complete the exercises. You might also have students write exercise sentences on the board in order to illustrate correct punctuation and capitalization.

You may find that the Developing Writing Skills activity is too challenging for some students. If so, you might ask them to tape-record actual dialogues and then to transcribe them, adding ap-

EXAMPLES: Margo said, "Let me do it for you."

"Why didn't she call me?" Don wondered.

An indirect quotation, on the other hand, does not need special punctuation.

An indirect quotation reports the general meaning of what a person said or thought and does not require quotation marks.

EXAMPLES: Margo said that she would do it for me.

Don wondered why she hadn't called him.

EXERCISE A: Distinguishing Between Direct and Indirect Quotations. Read each of the following sentences carefully to determine whether it contains a direct quotation that requires quotation marks or an indirect quotation. If the sentence contains a direct quotation, write *D* next to the appropriate number on your paper. If it contains an indirect quotation, write *I*.

EXAMPLE: It was the same old story repeating itself, thought Bruce.

D

1. Carol complained that her sister was never on time. I
2. I have noticed that, commented Bruce. D
3. I wish she would hurry, continued Carol. D
4. Bruce thought that the delay might make them miss the movie. I
5. He said that they should probably leave without her. I
6. Maybe she has a reason, said Carol. D
7. I, however, object to the casual way she operates, she added. D
8. Beginning to worry, Bruce decided that he should try to remain calm. I
9. Let's give her five more minutes, he suggested. D
10. That's a good idea, Carol agreed. D

19.6 Quotation Marks with Direct Quotations

Direct Quotations with Introductory, Concluding, and Interrupting Expressions

A writer will generally identify a speaker by using words such as *he asked* or *she said* with a quotation. These expressions can introduce, conclude, or interrupt a quotation. The following rule shows how to punctuate sentences with introductory expressions.

When an introductory expression precedes a direct quotation, place a comma after the introductory expression and write the quotation as a full sentence.

EXAMPLES: The animal trainer explained, "All wild animals should be treated with caution."

Barney asked, "Is it difficult to train a lion to perform?"

When an explanatory expression comes at the end of a direct quotation, the punctuation changes.

When a concluding expression follows a direct quotation, write the quotation as a full sentence ending with a comma, question mark, or exclamation mark inside the quotation mark. Then write the concluding expression.

Notice that the comma in the first of the following examples is placed where a period would usually be appropriate. Since the sentence is not yet complete, the comma signals the reader to pause rather than stop.

EXAMPLES: "That depends on several factors," the trainer replied.

"Could you show us one of your lions?" interrupted Barney.

"Please!" everyone chorused.

propriate introductory, concluding, and interrupting expressions.

Average   Students should write their exercise answers on the board so that correct punctuation and capitalization can be seen. You might also ask students to rewrite each indirect quotation in Exercise A as a direct quotation and vice versa.

To give students additional practice in punctuating dialogue, select a short passage from a play in a literature anthology. Have students rewrite the section as dialogue. They should include introductory, concluding, and interrupting expressions to identify the speakers, and they may incorporate stage directions.

Advanced   Prepare slips of paper that outline situations appropriate for dialogue, with characters and situation described on each. Each student (or student pair) can draw a slip and prepare a dialogue. If possible, have students write their dialogues on transparencies to make sharing them with the class easier via overhead projector.

Additional Practice

Practice Pages or Practice Book, pages 111, 112

Less advanced   Exercise Bank, Exercises A and B, pages 168–171

Average   Exercise Bank, Exercises A, B, and C, pages 168–171

Advanced   Exercise Bank, Exercises B and C, pages 168–171

TESTING

Test Program

Unit Pretest, page 58
Chapter Test, page 65
Unit Post-Test, page 67

RE-TEACHING

Practice Pages or Practice
Book, pages 111, 112

THINKING SKILLS

Comprehension—*Distinguishing*
between direct and indirect
quotations (Exercise A, page
364)

Application—*Using* quotation
marks with uninterrupted and
interrupted direct quotations
(Exercise B, page 367)
Using end marks and quotation marks correctly in direct
quotations (Exercise C,
page 369)

Synthesis—*Revising* dialogue
by adding quotations marks,
other punctuation marks, and
indentations appropriately (Exercise D, page 370)
Writing dialogue following
numerous different quotation
rules (Developing Writing
Skills, page 371)

Notice also that the concluding expressions do not begin with capitals.

An expression that interrupts a quotation requires twice as many quotation marks.

When the direct quotation of one sentence is interrupted, end the first part of the direct quotation with a comma and a quotation mark. Place a comma after the interrupting expression, and then use a new set of quotation marks to enclose the rest of the quotation.

Each of the following examples consists of *one* sentence. As you study the quotations, pay special attention to these items: (1) the comma inside the quotation mark at the end of the first part of the quotation; (2) the small letter at the beginning of the interrupting expression; (3) the comma inserted after the interrupting expression; (4) the small letter at the beginning of the second part of the quotation; and (5) the end mark inside the last quotation mark.

EXAMPLES: "This," the trainer said, "is Rufus, a lion I trained."

"What would he do," asked Corrina, "if I tried to touch him?"

Often a quotation consists of two sentences, with a complete sentence on each side of the interrupting expression.

When two sentences in a direct quotation are separated by an interrupting expression, end the first quoted sentence with a comma, question mark, or exclamation mark and a quotation mark. Place a period after the interrupter, and then write the second quoted sentence as a full quotation.

Study the examples that follow and look closely at these items: (1) the varied punctuation at the end of the first quoted sentence; (2) the small letter used at the beginning of the in-

19.6 Quotation Marks with Direct Quotations

terrupting expression; (3) the period following the interrupting expression; (4) the capital at the beginning of the second quoted sentence; and (5) the end mark inside the last quotation mark.

EXAMPLES: "That would be dangerous**,**" the trainer quickly explained**.** "Rufus is usually very gentle, but he is not a house cat**."**

"Did you see those teeth**?**" asked Mark**.** "I wouldn't dream of touching him**."**

EXERCISE B: Using Direct Quotations with Introductory, Concluding, and Interrupting Expressions. The following direct quotations have not been correctly punctuated or capitalized. Copy each of the sentences onto your paper, making the necessary corrections.

Underlined letters are to be capitalized.

EXAMPLE: Elena said we will need at least twelve more

Elena said, "We will need at least twelve more."

1. "there will be no exceptions to this rule," the teacher announced.
2. brian added "after the wood is sanded, apply a thin coat of varnish."
3. "two heads are better than one" said Sandra.
4. "have you ever considered a permanent? the hairdresser politely inquired.
5. "do it now! shouted Jake.
6. "please go ahead," said Andy as he examined the broken chain on his bicycle. "I can't go anywhere until this is repaired."
7. "i think," speculated Denise, "that his summer job will be a good one."
8. repeatedly the young man insisted "I must have your answer."
9. "can't you wait for me? shouted Hector from the balcony. "I'll be ready in two minutes."
10. as the fog became thicker, Mother said "use your low beams."

Quotation Marks with Other Punctuation Marks

Sometimes it may be hard to decide whether to place another puncutation mark inside or outside a quotation mark. You have seen that a comma or period used with a direct quotation goes inside the final quotation mark. In some cases, however, an end mark comes after the quotation mark. The following rules can help you choose the correct placement.

The first rule applies to a quoted declarative sentence.

Always place a comma or a period inside the final quotation mark.

EXAMPLES: "This lawn needs attention," Mrs. Finch told her children.

She added, "This looks more like a field than a yard."

Question marks or exclamation marks used with quotation marks can be more confusing. Both the sense of the quotation and the sense of the entire sentence must be considered to determine whether the punctuation should go inside or outside the quotation marks.

Place a question mark or exclamation mark inside the final quotation mark if the end mark is part of the quotation.

The following examples are declarative sentences. The first example contains a quotation that asks a question; the second contains a quotation that shows strong emotion. The end mark in each case depends on the sense of the quotation.

EXAMPLES: Joseph asked, "Don't I mow the lawn every week?"

Salvatore, his brother, protested loudly to their father, "I mow the lawn a lot more often than you do!"

19.6 Quotation Marks with Direct Quotations

In the preceding examples, each complete sentence seems to call for a period. However, two final punctuation marks are unnecessary, so the period is dropped.

INCORRECT: Rodney asked, "Will you stop arguing?".

CORRECT: Rodney asked, "Will you stop arguing?"

Sometimes the entire sentence, not the quotation, requires a question mark or an exclamation mark. Then the order of the punctuation changes.

Place a question mark or exclamation mark outside the final quotation mark if the end mark is part of the entire sentence, not part of the quotation.

In the following examples, the quotations are declarative, but the sentences are not. The first sentence is a question, and the second is an exclamation.

EXAMPLES: Did anyone say, "You have been negligent"?

I'm shocked that you can say, "I'm not responsible"!

EXERCISE C: Using End Marks with Direct Quotations.

End marks have been left out of the following sentences. Read each sentence and decide if the missing punctuation goes inside or outside the quotation marks. Copy the sentences onto your paper and include the necessary punctuation.

EXAMPLE: Has anyone said, "Please"

Has anyone said, "Please"?

1. Noel commented, "I can't think of a better reason"
2. Who said, "Waste not, want not"?
3. How could the owner have said, "My dog is friendly"?
4. How dare you say, "You weren't invited"!
5. My friend asked, "Why does firing a pistol start the race?"
6. The pilot continued, "Is this your first flight?"

7. Zelda excitedly announced, "I got the job!"
8. Ben said, "All he had ever asked for was a fair chance."
9. Will anyone say, "That is not what I meant"?
10. As the artist sketched, he muttered, "This still isn't right."

Quotation Marks for Dialogue

Dialogue is direct conversation between two or more people.

When writing dialogue, begin a new paragraph with each change of speaker.

EXAMPLE: "Will you be going with us on the family camping trip this year?" Noreen asked her cousin.

Gwen hesitated before answering, "I'm afraid so. My parents think I enjoy the experience."

"You fooled me, too," Noreen replied. "Maybe the trip will be better this year."

"Well, at least it can't be any worse," sighed Gwen. "On the last trip, I got a case of poison ivy that lasted for weeks!"

Notice that each sentence is punctuated according to the rules discussed earlier in this section. When writing dialogue, you also need to remember to indent whenever a new speaker talks.

EXERCISE D: Using Quotation Marks with Dialogue. The following selection is a dialogue. However, it is missing some punctuation marks and paragraph indentations. Decide where quotation marks, other punctuation marks, and indentations are needed. Then copy the paragraphs onto your paper, making the necessary changes. Answers are in the margin.

(1) This is quite a large crowd Andrea whispered to her friends. (2) You're right answered Paul. (3) I understand that this speaker is a famous expert on the Old West. (4) Bill, who

Answers for Exercise D, page 370

(1) "This is quite a large crowd," Andrea whispered to her friends.

(2) "You're right," answered Paul. (3) "I understand that this speaker is a famous expert on the Old West."

(4) Bill, who was sitting on Andrea's left, joined the conversation by asking, "Why do you think that topic is so popular?"

(5) "It may have something to do with the programs on television," Andrea suggested.

was sitting on Andrea's left, joined the conversation by asking Why do you think that topic is so popular? (5) It may have something to do with the programs on television Andrea suggested.

DEVELOPING WRITING SKILLS: Using Quotation Marks in Your Writing. Choose one of the following topics or make up a topic of your own. Then write a dialogue consisting of at least fifteen sentences. Use as many different quotation rules as possible, and remember to punctuate and indent correctly.

Answers will vary.

A day at the beach   A situation to be avoided
A broken promise   A change of opinion
A moment of anger

Underlining and Other Uses of 19.7 Quotation Marks

Underlining and quotation marks help make titles and other special words and names stand out in your writing. *Underlining* is used only in handwritten and typed work. In printed materials *italics* take the place of underlining.

UNDERLINING: The Call of the Wild

ITALICS: *The Call of the Wild*

This section explains when it is correct to underline and when it is correct to use quotation marks.

When to Underline

One of the most common uses of underlining is for titles of long written works such as novels.

Underline the titles of long written works and the titles of publications that are published as a single work.

19.7 Underlining and Other Uses of Quotation Marks
(pp. 371–376)

OBJECTIVES

After completing this section, students should be able to

- Use underlining appropriately with certain titles, names, and words.
- Use quotation marks correctly with titles.

TEACHING

Getting Started

Make sure students understand that underlining is equivalent to italicizing. Place on the board titles of some novels, short stories, poems, television series, single TV episodes, magazines, and magazine articles with which most students are familiar. Explain that the rationale behind using underlining instead of quotation marks in titles is a matter of creating stronger emphasis. Italics or underlining is used with works that are published or produced by themselves (are larger, more encompassing, or more imposing or important in and of themselves); quotation marks are used with shorter works that tend to be published or produced as part of a larger work (are a subpart or take up less space).

Text Follow Through

Discuss text pages 371–376.

Assign Exercise A, page 373; Exercise B, page 375; and Developing Writing Skills, page 376.

Less advanced Students might benefit from supplying their own examples for each of the categories of titles presented in this section.

Average Students might be asked to write a paragraph including their favorite titles from at least three of the categories mentioned in the section.

Advanced You might choose some of the best sentences written for the Developing Writing Skills activity and place them on the board without underlining or quotations for students to punctuate correctly.

The following chart shows some of these kinds of titles.

WRITTEN WORKS THAT ARE UNDERLINED	
Title of a Book	The Adventures of Tom Sawyer
Title of a Play	A Raisin in the Sun
Title of a Long Poem	Paradise Lost
Title of a Magazine	Seventeen
Title of a Newspaper	The New York Times

NOTE ABOUT NEWSPAPER TITLES: The portion of the title that should be underlined will vary from newspaper to newspaper. The New York Times should always be fully capitalized and underlined. Other papers, however, can usually be treated in one of two ways: for example, either the Los Angeles Times or the Los Angeles Times. Unless you know the exact name of a paper, choose one of these two forms and use it consistently.

Certain other titles also need underlining.

Underline the titles of movies, television and radio series, and works of music and art.

The following chart illustrates some of these titles.

ARTISTIC WORKS THAT ARE UNDERLINED	
Title of a Movie	Rocky
Title of a Television Series	Scarecrow and Mrs. King
Title of a Long Work of Music	Surprise Symphony
Title of a Record Album	Elton John's Greatest Hits
Title of a Painting	Christina's World
Title of a Sculpture	The Thinker

The names of individual planes, ships, space vehicles, trains, and cars are also underlined.

19.7 Underlining and Other Uses of Quotation Marks

Underline the names of individual air, sea, space, and land craft.

AIR: the <u>Kitty Hawk</u>   SPACE: <u>Gemini 5</u>

SEA: the <u>Titanic</u>   LAND: the <u>Tom Thumb</u>

Other words, letters, and numbers are sometimes underlined also.

Underline words, letters, or numbers used as names for themselves.

EXAMPLES: The word <u>maybe</u> is not part of her vocabulary.

On this typewriter the <u>o</u> is blurry.

<u>Six</u> is my lucky number.

EXERCISE A: Underlining Titles, Names, and Words.
Each of the following sentences contains a title, name, or word that needs underlining. Write the items that require underlining on your paper and underline them.

EXAMPLE: The Lusitania sank in 1915 off the coast of Ireland.

<u>Lusitania</u>

1. I've seen <u>Doctor Zhivago</u> twice at the movies and once on television.
2. One of the three ships that brought Columbus to the New World was the <u>Santa Maria</u>.
3. <u>Njal's Saga</u> is a long epic poem written in Icelandic.
4. Grant Wood's <u>American Gothic</u> can be seen in the Art Institute of Chicago.
5. Lydia wanted to play the part of Helen Keller in the production of <u>The Miracle Worker</u> done at our school.
6. In the novel <u>The Yearling</u>, Jody learns that he cannot run away from his grief.
7. Many people think the number <u>thirteen</u> is unlucky.
8. <u>Howdy Doody</u> was one of the first television shows for children.

9. The librarian explained that back issues of the <u>Herald Tribune</u> were on microfilm in the periodical room.

10. Charles Lindbergh flew the famous <u>Spirit of St. Louis</u>.

When to Use Quotation Marks

In general, quotation marks are used for short works and works that are a part of a longer work.

Use quotation marks around the titles of short written works.

The following chart contains examples of titles that you should enclose in quotation marks.

WRITTEN WORKS THAT TAKE QUOTATION MARKS	
Title of a Short Story	"The Gift of the Magi"
Chapter from a Book	"The Test Is in the Tasting" from <u>No-Work Garden Book</u>
Title of a Short Poem	"Lucy"
Title of an Article	"How to Build a Birdhouse"

The titles of other short works of art are also placed in quotation marks.

Use quotation marks around the titles of episodes in a series, songs, and parts of a long musical composition.

ARTISTIC WORKS THAT TAKE QUOTATION MARKS	
Title of an Episode	"The Homecoming" from <u>The Waltons</u>
Title of a Song	"Beautiful Dreamer"
Title of a Part of a Long Work of Music	"Waltz of the Flowers" from the <u>Nutcracker Suite</u>

19.7 Underlining and Other Uses of Quotation Marks

Sometimes a long work is mentioned as part of an even longer work.

Use quotation marks around the title of a work that is mentioned as part of a collection.

The play *Uncle Vanya* would normally be underlined. In the following example, however, the title is placed in quotation marks because it is cited as part of a larger work.

EXAMPLE: "Uncle Vanya" in <u>Eight Great Comedies</u>

EXERCISE B: Using Quotation Marks with Titles. Each of the following sentences contains a title that needs quotation marks. Some of the sentences also contain titles that need underlining. Copy the titles onto your paper, either enclosing them in quotation marks or underlining them.

EXAMPLE: My favorite song is Getting to Know You from The King and I.

"Getting to Know You" <u>The King and I</u>

1. "Song of High Cuisine" is a brief poem by Phyllis McGinley that ridicules such delicacies as snails and nightingales' tongues.
2. My favorite song from the musical <u>Brigadoon</u> is "There But for You Go I."
3. Did you see "The Battle of the Clingons" on <u>Star Trek?</u>
4. As do most of Ray Bradbury's short stories, "The Whole Town's Sleeping" has a startling conclusion.
5. While listening to "Sunrise," the first movement of the <u>Grand Canyon Suite</u>, we could almost see the morning light.
6. <u>National Geographic</u> has a fascinating article this month called "The Trouble with Dolphins."
7. Tonight's assignment is to read "The Valley of Humiliation," a chapter in the novel <u>The Mill on the Floss</u>.
8. After reading "I'll Give You Love," a short story by Molly Picon, the class began to discuss its theme.

9. In Friday's English class, we will be reading the play "Twelfth Night" from our textbook <u>The World's a Stage</u>.

10. Edgar Allan Poe's short story "The Tell-Tale Heart" sends chills up and down my spine.

DEVELOPING WRITING SKILLS: Using Underlining and Quotation Marks. Write ten original sentences, each including a specific example of one of the following items. Be sure to punctuate and capitalize correctly.

Answers will vary; samples are given for the first two.

EXAMPLE: The title of a short poem

Reading the poem "Little Boy Blue" always makes me cry.

1. Picasso's <u>Guernica</u> is now in Spain.

1. The title of a painting

2. A book title

3. The name of a specific ship or airplane.

4. A song title

5. A magazine title

6. A short-story title

7. A movie title

8. The title of one work within a collection

9. A newspaper title

10. A letter used as a name for itself

2. Her favorite book is <u>Through the Looking Glass</u>.

19.8 The Hyphen

(pp. 376–382)

OBJECTIVES

After completing this section, students should be able to

- Use hyphens correctly with numbers, word parts, and compound words.
- Divide words correctly at the ends of lines, using hyphens.

19.8 The Hyphen

The *hyphen* is used to combine numbers and word parts, to join certain compound words, and to show that a word has been broken between syllables at the end of a line.

When to Use the Hyphen

Many numbers require a hyphen so that they can be read more easily.

19.8 The Hyphen

Use a hyphen when writing out the numbers *twenty-one* through *ninety-nine*.

EXAMPLES: There were *thirty-four* people at the meeting in the auditorium.

Your paper has *twenty-one* spelling errors.

Sometimes fractions also require hyphens.

Use a hyphen when writing fractions that are used as adjectives.

EXAMPLE: A *four*-fifths majority indicated overwhelming approval.

Notice, however, that a fraction used as a noun, rather than as an adjective, does not need a hyphen.

EXAMPLE: *Two thirds* of the pie has been eaten.

Hyphens are also used to combine certain prefixes and suffixes with other words.

Use a hyphen after a prefix that is followed by a proper noun or adjective.

The following prefixes are often used before proper nouns: *ante-, anti-, mid-, post-, pre-, pro-,* and *un-*.

EXAMPLE: The *pre*-Columbian artifacts were discovered by a team of archeologists.

Three prefixes and one suffix in particular always require a hyphen.

Use a hyphen in words with the prefixes *all-*, *ex-*, and *self-* and the suffix *-elect*.

EXAMPLES: all-powerful   self-determined

ex-leader   governor-elect

Hyphens are also used to join certain compound nouns and compound modifiers.

TEACHING
Getting Started

The ability to use the dictionary to find syllable divisions is a skill linked to the proper use of hyphens to divide words. You will want to ascertain whether your students have this ability and give them practice in locating syllabification information in conjunction with exercises in this section. Point out that not even most adults remember all the rules for use of hyphens. This section is intended not only as a teaching tool but also as a reference point. Discuss with students the value of looking back to check use of hyphens any time in the year as they write compositions, reports, etc. Place on the board several hyphenated words, such as the following, to illustrate rules for hyphenation:

   sixty-two
   two-thirds majority
   son-in-law
   ex-mayor
   all-consuming fear

Guide students to see that the hyphen connects words and word parts whose meaning depends upon their being connected. The hyphen therefore serves as a connector that clarifies meaning.

Text Follow Through

Discuss text pages 376–382.

Assign Exercise A, page 379; Exercise B, page 381; and Developing Writing Skills, page 382.

Less advanced You may want to give students practice in using the dictionary to locate acceptable syllable divisions. Discuss each item in Exercise B as well as the reasons why it can or cannot be divided. Stress the idea that in dividing a word at the end of a line, students must follow its pronunciation, avoiding divisions that break syllables and make it harder for the reader to recognize the word.

Average You will want to stress to students that the dictionary tells whether a specific compound is hyphenated and how a word should be divided. To give students further practice with hyphens, have them follow the instructions for Exercise B with the following items:

1. alone
2. self-explanatory
3. haunted
4. ivory
5. erase
6. lectured
7. oval
8. seventy-seven
9. elect
10. all-encompassing

Advanced Students might be asked to find in newspapers examples of words that have been incorrectly divided (a common phenomenon because of narrow columns and computer typesetting).

Additional Practice

Practice Pages or Practice Book, page 114

Less advanced Exercise Bank, Exercises A and B, pages 174, 175

Average Exercise Bank, Exercises A, B, and C, pages 174, 175

Advanced Exercise Bank, Exercises B and C, pages 174, 175

Use a hyphen to connect two or more nouns that are used as one word, unless the dictionary gives a different spelling.

Some compound nouns are written as one word, and others are written as separate words. The following examples show some of the many compound nouns that are written with hyphens.

EXAMPLES: lady-in-waiting   cave-in

great-grandfather   secretary-treasurer

Modifiers may also consist of two or more words joined by hyphens.

Use a hyphen to connect a compound modifier that comes before a noun.

In each of the following examples, the first part of the modifier describes the second part of the modifier, not the noun. The hyphen shows the connection between the words in each modifier.

EXAMPLES: The teacher told Martin that his *long-winded* essay was unacceptable.

Don't ignore a *once-in-a-lifetime* opportunity such as this one.

No hyphen is necessary when a compound modifier follows the noun it describes.

BEFORE: Nicole has always been a *well-disciplined* person.

AFTER: Nicole has always been *well disciplined.*

BEFORE: An *almost-perfect* term paper is expected of Samantha.

AFTER: Samantha's term paper is *almost perfect.*

However, if a dictionary spells a word with a hyphen, the word must always be hyphenated even when it follows a noun.

TESTING

Test Program
Unit Pretest, page 59
Chapter Test, page 65
Unit Post-Test, page 67

RE-TEACHING

Practice Pages or Practice
Book, page 114

THINKING SKILLS

Application—*Using* hyphens in
numbers, word parts, and
compound words (Exercise A,
page 379)
Showing where words can
and cannot be divided at the
ends of lines (Exercise B,
page 381)

Synthesis—*Writing* sentences
using hyphens for a variety of
purposes (Developing Writing
Skills, page 382)

19.8 The Hyphen

EXAMPLES: This *poor-spirited* horse will never win a race.

This horse is *poor-spirited.*

A few special compound modifiers never take hyphens.

Do not use a hyphen with a compound modifier that includes a word ending in *-ly* or in a compound proper adjective.

INCORRECT: clearly-written

CORRECT: clearly written

INCORRECT: West-Indian music

CORRECT: West Indian music

EXERCISE A: Using Hyphens in Numbers, Word Parts, and Compound Words. Examine the following items and decide where hyphens are needed. If an item does not require a hyphen, write *correct*. If an item does require hyphenation, rewrite the item to make it correct.

EXAMPLE: A newly minted coin

correct

1. nine tenths of the population C
2. anti-Soviet activities
3. self-explanatory letters
4. a never-to-be-forgotten day
5. a jack-in-the-box
6. newly appointed officials C
7. mid-Victorian ideas
8. an all-encompassing study
9. a pre-Babylonian civilization
10. star-shaped designs
11. well-deserved recognition
12. sixty-five employees
13. Jenkins, our president-elect
14. a pro-Mexico delegation

15. an answer quickly determined C
16. a two-thirds majority
17. appetizers before dinner C
18. Miss Humphrey, ex-consultant
19. horse-and-buggy days
20. the North American continent C

Rules for Dividing Words at the End of a Line

Avoid dividing words at the ends of lines whenever possible. Too many divided words can make your writing seem choppy. When it is necessary to divide a word, use the following rules to divide words correctly.

If a word must be divided, always divide it between syllables.

EXAMPLE: You must not feel that a contribution of five dollars is insig-
nificant.

In carrying out this rule, always make sure you place the hyphen at the end of the first line, not at the beginning of the second line.

INCORRECT: These chemicals cause lime particles to dis
-solve.

CORRECT: These chemicals cause lime particles to dissolve.

In addition, take care never to divide one-syllable words, even if they seem long or sound like words with two syllables.

INCORRECT: sch-ool   bru-ised   thro-ugh
CORRECT: school   bruised   through

Another rule points to a major exception to the first rule regarding division of a word between syllables.

Do *not* divide a word so that a single letter stands alone.

The following words are correctly broken into two syllables. However, because the break leaves one letter standing alone, either at the beginning or the end of the word, these words should not be divided at the end of a line.

INCORRECT: a-mid   ver-y   o-kay

CORRECT: amid   very   okay

Also, to avoid awkward pronunciations, you should not place *-ed* at the beginning of a new line.

INCORRECT: halt-ed

CORRECT: halted

Proper nouns and proper adjectives also require a special rule.

Do *not* divide proper nouns or proper adjectives.

INCORRECT: Mar-tin   Lat-vi-a

CORRECT: Martin   Latvia

A final rule applies to words that already have hyphenated spellings.

Divide a hyphenated word only after the hyphen.

INCORRECT: We lost the game in spite of the well-intentioned efforts of all the members of our baseball
team.

CORRECT: We lost the game in spite of the well-
intentioned efforts of all the members of our
baseball team.

EXERCISE B: Using Hyphens to Divide Words. Imagine that you have to decide either to hyphenate each of the following words at the end of a line or to write the complete word on the next line. If you can divide a word, write the part of the word that would appear at the end of the first line on your paper. If you cannot divide the word, write the complete word.

EXAMPLE: old-fashioned

old-

1. ready ready	5. self-serving self-	9. forty for-
2. laugh laugh	6. grocery gro-	10. evasive eva-
3. promised prom-	7. Maryann Maryann	
4. Thailand Thailand	8. handed handed	

DEVELOPING WRITING SKILLS: Using Hyphens in Your Writing. Write ten original sentences, each including a hyphenated word. Divide at least four words at the ends of lines. Try to apply as many of the different rules for hyphenation as you can.
Answers will vary.
EXAMPLE: The ex-governor had once been all-powerful.

19.9 The Apostrophe

The two main uses of the *apostrophe* (') are (1) to show possession in nouns and pronouns and (2) to indicate that letters are left out of contractions.

Apostrophes with Possessive Nouns

Apostrophes are used with nouns to show ownership or possession. The rule for singular nouns is quite simple.

Add an apostrophe and -s to show the possessive case of most singular nouns.

EXAMPLES: The role of the *parent* becomes the *parent's* role.

The sound of the *trumpet* becomes the *trumpet's* sound.

The fur of a *mole* becomes a *mole's* fur.

19.9 The Apostrophe

Even when a singular noun already ends in *-s*, you can usually still add an apostrophe and *-s* to the noun to show possession.

EXAMPLES: The color of an *iris* becomes an *iris's* color.

The blade of a *cutlass* becomes a *cutlass's* blade.

The cow of *Bess* becomes *Bess's* cow.

Sometimes the addition of an apostrophe and *-s* makes it difficult to pronounce a noun ending in *-s*. In this case only an apostrophe is added to show possession.

AWKWARD: Slim Pickens's role was that of a cowboy.

BETTER: Slim Pickens' role was that of a cowboy.

The possessive of a plural noun depends on the ending of the noun.

Add just an apostrophe to show the possessive case of plural nouns ending in *-s* or *-es*.

EXAMPLES: The mother of the *kittens* becomes the *kittens'* mother.

The belief of the *multitudes* becomes the *multitudes'* belief.

Add an apostrophe and *-s* to show the possessive case of plural nouns that do not end in *-s* or *-es*.

EXAMPLES: The squeaking of the *mice* becomes the *mice's* squeaking.

The father of the *children* becomes the *children's* father.

The advice of the *women* becomes the *women's* advice.

The possessives of compound nouns also follow a basic rule.

383

TEACHING
Getting Started

┌─ idea bank ──────────────┐
the smell of the rose
the lapping of the waves
a club for women
the jamboree of the Boy
  Scouts
└──────────────────────────┘

Students will be familiar with the principal uses of the apostrophe, although most will still make errors, especially in the use of apostrophes with possessive nouns. Write the Idea Bank phrases on the board and ask students to rephrase them using apostrophes.

As students place the possessives on the board, ask that they circle the added items. From noting the *'s*, *s'*, or *s's* at the end of each item, ask students to try to formulate a rule for forming the possessive of a singular noun, a singular noun ending in *s*, a plural noun ending in *s* or *es*, a plural noun having no *s* or *es* ending, etc. Later students can compare their rules to those presented in the text.

Text Follow Through

Discuss text pages 382–389.

Assign Exercise A, page 384; Exercise B, page 386; Exercise C, page 388; Exercise D, page 389; and Developing Writing Skills, page 389.

Less advanced   Students may need extra practice in deciding where an apostrophe belongs in singular and plural nouns. They might enjoy taking turns making up sentences that use the possessive case of their classmates' names. Have them use first names to practice

384

singular possessives and surnames to practice plural possessives. Sound-alike pairs such as *their-they're, its-it's, your-you're,* and *whose-who's* give students the greatest difficulty in forming contractions. Give plenty of practice in the use of these words throughout the year.

Average Be sure students understand that a contraction is an abbreviated form of two words. The apostrophe replaces the missing letters. For those students having trouble with contractions, suggest that they say the two words as they write each contraction. As an additional activity, have students write a sentence for each word in the following pairs:

1. who's/whose
2. it's/its
3. you're/your
4. they're/their
5. there's/theirs

Advanced Have students exchange the dialogues they write for the Developing Writing Skills activity and rewrite them to eliminate as many of the apostrophes as possible. Or, if you prefer, have students write paragraphs in which they leave blanks wherever a possessive pronoun or contraction should appear. Students can then exchange papers and fill in the blanks.

Additional Practice

Practice Pages or Practice Book, pages 115, 116

Less advanced Exercise Bank, Exercises A and B, pages 176–179

Average Exercise Bank, Exercises A, B, and C, pages 176–179

Add an apostrophe and *-s* (or just an apostrophe if the word is a plural ending in *-s*) to the last word of a compound noun to form the possessive.

NAME OF A BUSINESS: The Army and Navy Store's sale

NAME OF AN ORGANIZATION: the Girl Scouts' cookie sale

TITLE OF A RULER: the Queen of England's horse

HYPHENATED TITLES: my father-in-law's car
the treasurer-elect's position

In forming the possessive case, you may have trouble deciding where the apostrophe belongs or whether an *-s* is necessary. Use the steps in the following chart.

STEPS FOR DECIDING WHERE AN APOSTROPHE BELONGS

1. Determine the owner of the idea, object, or personality trait. Ask yourself, "To whom or what does it belong?"
2. If the answer to the question is a singular noun, follow the rule for forming the possessive of a singular noun. If the answer is a plural noun, follow the rules for forming the possessive of a plural noun.

In the phrase *the flowers fragrance,* ask yourself, "To what does the fragrance belong?" If the answer is singular, "the flower," then the possessive is *the flower's fragrance.* If the answer is plural, "the flowers," then use *the flowers' fragrance.*

EXERCISE A: Using Apostrophes to Form the Possessives of Nouns. The sentences on the following page contain underlined singular or plural nouns. Copy each underlined noun onto your paper, putting it into the possessive form by adding an apostrophe and *-s* as needed.

384

Advanced Exercise Bank, Exercises B and C, pages 176–179

19.9 The Apostrophe

EXAMPLE: The <u>children</u>/hour at the public library has been a great success.

children's

1. According to legend, a <u>dragon</u> breath was quite dangerous.
2. All of the <u>pencils</u> points were broken. pencils'
3. The pond became the <u>geese</u> home for the summer. geese's
4. Many have benefited from reading <u>Do-It-Yourself</u> advice in the newspaper. Do-It-Yourself's
5. Most designers believe that <u>garments</u> colors attract buyers.
6. This yarn was purchased at the <u>Jack and Jill Craft Store</u> sale. Jack and Jill Craft Store's
7. <u>Ross</u> lizard must be kept on a leash at all times. Ross's
8. Elected officials represent the <u>people</u> choice. people's
9. <u>Chancellor Helmut Schmidt</u> reelection seemed likely. Schmidt's
10. Discard the <u>lettuce</u> outer leaves. lettuce's

1. dragon's 5. garments'

Apostrophes with Pronouns

Both indefinite and personal pronouns can show possession. The possessive case of indefinite pronouns is formed in the same manner as the possessive case of singular nouns.

Use an apostrophe and -s with indefinite pronouns to show possession.

EXAMPLES: another's preference   nobody else's business
anybody's help   no one's ticket
each other's privacy   one's choice
everyone's advice   somebody's hat

The personal pronouns that show possession are treated differently.

Do *not* use an apostrophe with possessive personal pronouns.

None of the following personal pronouns needs an apostrophe to show possession: *my, mine, your, yours, his, her, hers, its, our, ours, their,* and *theirs.*

TESTING

Test Program

Unit Pretest, page 59
Chapter Test, page 65
Unit Post-Test, page 67

RE-TEACHING

Practice Pages or Practice Book, pages 115, 116

THINKING SKILLS

Comprehension—*Distinguishing* between possessive pronouns that do and do not require apostrophes (Exercise B, page 386)

Application—*Using* apostrophes to form the possessives of nouns (Exercise A, page 384) *Showing* how to combine words and use apostrophes correctly to form contractions (Exercise C, page 388) *Demonstrating* special uses of apostrophes (Exercise D, page 389)

Synthesis—*Writing* sentences demonstrating a variety of uses of apostrophes (Developing Writing Skills, page 389)

Some of these pronouns act as adjectives.

EXAMPLES: The spider caught a fly in *its* web.

Our house is for sale.

Others act as subjects, objects, and subject complements.

EXAMPLES: *Mine* is the yellow crayon.

Someone broke *yours*.

The red one is *his*.

The important thing to remember is not to use an apostrophe when these pronouns are used to show possession.

EXERCISE B: Using Apostrophes with Pronouns. The following sentences contain pronouns used as possessives. If all pronouns in a sentence are used correctly, write *correct*. If a pronoun is used incorrectly, rewrite it on your paper to make it correct.

EXAMPLE: When they divided up the property, the lake became his and the island became their's.

theirs

1. Everybody else's favorite dessert is not necessarily yours' or mine.   yours
2. The tools in your garage are our's, not your's.   ours/yours
3. Someones' cat was howling in the alley while our's was sleeping peacefully.   Someone's/ours
4. The veterinarian examined her' parakeet and said it's wing was broken.   her/its
5. Ours is the preferred method, even though their's is almost as good.   theirs
6. Listen to his' idea for a solution before you decide to accept hers.   his
7. Her's is the best solution to our problem.   Hers
8. I will help you finish your math work if you will help Leon with his.   c

9. It is still not too late to file your' tax return. your
10. Their's is always the first yard on the block to have its' leaves raked. Theirs/its

Apostrophes with Contractions

Contractions are shortened forms of words or phrases.

Use an apostrophe in a contraction to indicate the position of the missing letter or letters.

Contractions are used in informal speech and writing both for convenience and to save time. Instead of saying, "Let us go," a person is more likely to say, "Let's go." The following chart shows some other contractions formed with verbs.

COMMON CONTRACTIONS WITH VERBS		
Verb + *not*	are not (aren't) is not (isn't) was not (wasn't) were not (weren't) cannot (can't)	could not (couldn't) did not (didn't) do not (don't) should not (shouldn't) would not (wouldn't)
Pronoun + the Verb *will*	I will (I'll) you will (you'll) he will (he'll) she will (she'll)	we will (we'll) they will (they'll) who will (who'll)
Pronoun or Noun + the Verb *be*	I am (I'm) you are (you're) he is (he's) she is (she's) it is (it's)	we are (we're) they are (they're) who is (who's) where is (where's) Lee is (Lee's)
Pronoun or Noun + the Verb *would*	I would (I'd) you would (you'd) he would (he'd) she would (she'd)	we would (we'd) they would (they'd) who would (who'd) Nancy would (Nancy'd)

An apostrophe is also used to form contractions of years.

EXAMPLE: the 1984 yearbook   (the '84 yearbook)

Still another use of the apostrophe is with the letters *o, d,* and *l. O'* is a shortened version of the longer phrase *of the. D'* in Spanish means *of the,* and *l'* in French simply means *the.* These letters and an apostrophe have become part of certain words and proper names and are always used with them.

EXAMPLES: o'clock (of the clock)

O'Brien (of the Brien family)

d'Agostino (of the Agostino family)

L'Engle (the Engle family)

Although apostrophes are always used in the examples above, you should avoid using most contractions in formal writing.

INFORMAL WRITING: No one could've guessed the outcome.

FORMAL WRITING: No one could have guessed the outcome.

EXERCISE C: Using Contractions in Informal Writing. Each of the following sentences contains one or more word groups that can be written as contractions. On your paper write each of these word groups as a contraction.

EXAMPLE: Where is the new science-fiction book I ordered?

Where's

1. Who is the new student representative? Who's
2. I am not certain whether he is upstairs or downstairs. I'm/he's
3. This pen will write if you will just keep shaking it. you'll
4. You are ignoring what I am saying. You're/I'm
5. Glenda is the one I would like to invite. Glenda's/I'd
6. There cannot be any doubt about who will be invited. can't/who'll
7. You will enjoy looking at these old pictures of the class of 1956. You'll/'56

8. They were not sure who would be on the committee.

9. The school library does not have the book I need.   doesn't

10. Where is the one who said she would be here early?   Where's/she'd

8. They're or weren't/who'd

Special Uses of the Apostrophe

Apostrophes are also used in forming certain plurals.

Use an apostrophe and -s to write the plurals of numbers, symbols, letters, and words used to name themselves.

EXAMPLES: two *5*'s and six *7*'s   three *!*'s

a's first and *z*'s last

Don't begin sentences with *well*'s.

EXERCISE D: Recognizing Special Uses of the Apostrophe. Write five original sentences, each using the plural of one of the following numbers, symbols, letters, or words. Be sure to underline each plural form and use apostrophes where they are needed.

Sentences will vary; plural forms are given.

EXAMPLE: t

Please take greater care in crossing your <u>t</u>'s.

1. 9   2. m   3. huh   4. ?   5. please

1. <u>9</u>'s   2. <u>m</u>'s   3. <u>huh</u>'s   4. <u>?</u>'s   5. <u>please</u>'s

DEVELOPING WRITING SKILLS: Using Apostrophes in Your Writing. Write a brief dialogue between two friends. You can use one of the following topics or make up your own. Apply as many of the rules for apostrophes as you can. If necessary, see Section 19.6 for rules governing the punctuation of dialogue.

Answers will vary.

A discussion of math homework

A discussion of an abstract painting

A discussion of a movie's plot

Checking Your Skills

In the Checking Your Skills assignment, students have corrected punctuation errors in sentences. Discuss with students the variety of punctuation marks needed to punctuate dialogue correctly.

Collaborative Learning

Divide the class into groups of roughly equal ability levels. Each group will create a dialogue that takes place among a number of characters equal to the number in the group. For example, a group of four students would create a dialogue with four characters. Instruct each group member to take the role of a character, contributing all the dialogue spoken by that person. It might be helpful if you advise the groups to first brainstorm for an incident that will be the basis of their dialogues. Once they have decided on an incident, they can create the characters and begin their dialogues. When they have finished, have each group recite their dialogue, with each member taking the role of his or her character.

Using Mechanics Skills in Writing

Publishing You might want to have student volunteers read their adventure stories to the class. If so, have volunteers practice reading their stories first. Encourage them to imitate the way they imagine the characters in their story would speak. Also, they should practice using facial expressions and hand gestures to enhance the telling of their stories.

Skills Review and Writing Workshop

Using Punctuation Marks

1. shark!" 2. "You're/water," 3. serious?" 4. reputation. 5. <u>Jaws</u> 6. 100/

CHECKING YOUR SKILLS

year, 7. shark, . . . fish, 8. However, . . . some documented 9. can, of course,

Rewrite the following paragraph, correcting all punctuation errors. frightening for . . . reasons: its sharp-edged teeth, its great size, and its

(1) "Watch out for the shark" Ernie yelled. (2) Youre not going to get me into the water, he added. (3) "Are you serious" Randy asked. (4) She knew that ⸢the great white shark had an overrated reputation⸥ (5) This reputation had spread probably because of movies such as Jaws that horrified everyone with tales of man-eating sharks. (6) There are actually fewer than 1,00 shark attacks reported worldwide in a year yet white sharks are often the culprits. (7) The white shark which is a meat-eating fish usually stays in warm waters. (8) However there have been some, documented cases of white shark attacks in cold waters. (9) The white shark can of course be very frightening; for the following reasons its sharp edged teeth its great size and its grim reputation. (10) Though sharks rarely attack people you should always be alert when you swim in the ocean.

grim reputation. 10. people,

USING MECHANICS SKILLS IN WRITING:

Writing About an Adventure

Writers know that good dialogue can make an adventure story come alive. Follow the steps below to write a brief adventure story that includes some realistic and exciting dialogue.

Answers will vary.

Prewriting: Plan your adventure story of an actual or fictional event. List the events in chronological order.

Writing: Start with something exciting to get your readers' attention. Build, step by step, to the climax, and then quickly end the story.

Revising: Look at your punctuation to make sure all of it is correct and necessary. Then read the entire story, making other improvements. After revising, proofread carefully.

UNIT IV

Composition
The Writer's Techniques

UNIT IV
**Composition—
The Writer's
Techniques**

(pp. 391–436)

This unit focuses on effective written communication. Chapter 20 considers the writing process itself: prewriting, writing, and revising. Chapter 21 deals with ways for students to improve their use of words by using precise words and by avoiding worn-out and inappropriate words. Chapter 22 focuses on ways students can improve their sentences by adding details and combining; it also discusses ways to simplify long, confusing sentences and to use different sentence openers and sentence structures. Since Chapters 21 and 22 require a knowledge of basic grammatical terminology and sentence structure, you may want to be sure students have studied Unit I before you teach these chapters.

This chapter focuses on the three stages of the writing process and will prove valuable no matter what type of writing your students are doing. Included are prewriting (including exploring ideas, choosing and narrowing a topic, determining an audience and purpose, and developing a main idea and supporting it), writing a first draft, and revising (including revising for sense, editing for word choice and sentences, and proofreading and publishing).

For an additional or alternate writing assignment, see page 405.

20.1 Prewriting
(pp. 392–399)

OBJECTIVES

After completing this section, students should be able to

- Use their interests, experiences, and ideas to explore ideas for writing topics.
- Choose a topic that can be covered effectively in the allotted amount of space.

Chapter **20**

The Writing Process

Usually, much time and preparation goes into anything we do that we care about. For example, a runner does not go out and win his or her first race without months of practice and hard work before the race. That runner follows a specific training program, a process that builds the runner's speed and endurance.

Professional writers also follow a specific course of action to achieve a finished product. This writing process is helpful for students who want to produce quality papers.

The writing process can be divided into three stages: prewriting, writing the first draft, and revising.

20.1 Prewriting

The first step in the writing process is the prewriting or planning stage. It begins with exploring ideas for topics.

Exploring Ideas

Ideas for writing topics come from many sources. They come from books, magazines, television, and the world around you. But the best source for finding ideas is you. You are full of opinions, likes and dislikes, and good and bad experiences. Just take some time to think about yourself. If you have thought out your ideas in advance, it will be easier to write about them.

To explore ideas for writing topics, think about your interests, experiences, and ideas.

When you choose your own topic for a paper, you must think of ideas for topics. There are several methods you can use to help you think of possible topics.

Interview Yourself. To discover topics that interest you, ask yourself questions like the ones in the chart below.

QUESTIONS FOR INTERVIEWING YOURSELF
1. What activities do I enjoy?
2. In what areas do I have special skills or knowledge?
3. What kinds of subjects am I interested in?
4. To whom do I like to speak and about what topics?
5. To whom could I speak to learn about topics that interest me?
6. What has happened to me in the past or is happening to me now that seems of special interest?

Free Writing. Set aside a certain amount of time or a certain number of pages. Write whatever comes into your head for the amount of time or space you have set. When you finish, look over what you have written for topic ideas.

Journal Writing. Good writing takes practice. For this reason, it is a good idea to keep a journal. Write daily on events in your life, the people around you, your emotions, and the scene around you. A journal could be a source for a great many writing topics.

Reading and Saving. Read as much as possible, whenever you can. Read books, novels, newspapers, and magazines. Clip or write down quotes, poetry, lyrics, or anything else that attracts your attention.

- Determine their audience and purpose before writing.
- State a main idea and then gather and organize supporting information to develop it effectively.

TEACHING
Getting Started
Tell students that exploring ideas is as easy as thinking of their interests, experiences, and ideas. Direct students' attention to the chart on page 393. Ask for a volunteer to answer the questions to get other students started. You may want to have two or three students answer the questions in the chart. Continue by reviewing the other methods of exploring ideas: free writing, journal writing, reading and saving, clustering, brainstorming, and cueing.

Text Follow Through
Discuss text pages 392–399.

Assign Exercise A, page 395; Exercise B, page 395; Exercise C, page 395; Exercise D, page 395; Exercise E, page 395; Exercise F, page 396; Exercise G, page 397; Exercise H, page 399; Exercise I, page 399; and Developing Writing Skills, page 399.

Less advanced Use of the journal, inventory, and brainstorming and cueing techniques provide excellent opportunities for these students to gain some fluency in writing without worrying about technical mistakes. They may have difficulty, however, narrowing a topic. Work through one of the topics in Exercise F with the class, from clustering to free writing. Using the overhead projector, you may even wish to spend a class period working up a finished composition into which students have input, but which you have guided in order to illustrate organizing from the basis of notes.

Average Brainstorming with a small group is a valuable tool for students to use; it allows for many ideas and aspects of a topic to emerge. Many students often complain that they do not have enough to say about their topics when in fact they simply have not learned to let go and explore all avenues of the topic before committing the composition to paper. After brainstorming, student groups should then narrow a topic (you may need to help them with this initially) and prepare an outline for a composition. Then each group should select a representative to report to the class on how the process worked. These students should benefit from analyzing some well-constructed short papers using the four methods of organization.

Advanced Have students share their work with classmates as they complete each exercise. Ask them to share with classmates particularly effective methods they use in prewriting. These students might enjoy writing notes for a composition using different audiences and purposes. Assign a high-interest topic to the class, but give different segments each a different audience and purpose. For example, for the topic *best way to read a newspaper*, assign one group the audience of third graders; another group eighth graders; a third group parents; a fourth group newswriters. After

Clustering. Clustering is a method of narrowing a broad topic down to one appropriate for a short paper. Pick a topic (*baseball*, for example) and write it in the center of a piece of paper. Think of words that you associate with that word (*pitching, batting, win, lose)* and write them around the word in the center, the nucleus word. Circle each word and draw a line from that word to the nucleus word. Continue this process until you have a topic narrow enough for a short paper.

Brainstorming. Brainstorming is a way of creating or narrowing ideas. You can brainstorm alone or in a group. You are brainstorming when you and your friends try to decide what to do after school. To brainstorm, start with one idea and build on it. Do not stop to evaluate ideas, just keep adding to them. If you are brainstorming alone, write down your ideas.

Cueing. Cueing devices are another way of stimulating ideas. Use cueing methods like the 5 W's (*Who? What? When? Where?* and *Why?*) or the alphabet to get ideas started. For example, to use the 5 W's, choose a topic. Then ask *Who? What? When? Where?* and *Why?* (or *How?*) about the topic. Journalists use this method to write news stories. Here is an example of 5-W cueing:

Topic: Music
Who: Me
What: piano lessons and practice
When: after school and weekends
Where: at home and school
Why: to improve my skill and talent

Alphabet cueing is a similar process. Start with a letter of the alphabet and list words that come to mind for your topic. If you are writing about a personal experience, the list might contain words like *afraid, Andy, afternoons, achievement.*

The five senses—taste, touch, sight, smell and sound—are good cueing techniques. Five-sense cueing works best with descriptive writing. Place yourself in the situation and concentrate on each sense. Ask yourself questions like: What can I

20.1 Prewriting

see? What can I smell? What sounds can I remember? Explore each sense to discover the situation or refresh your memory. Then write down as many descriptive words as you can.

Try to use all of the prewriting methods with an open mind. The more you let your thoughts flow, the more ideas you will come up with. It is important not to limit your thinking.

EXERCISE A: Taking inventory. Answer the six questions under the heading "Interview Yourself" on page 393.
Answers will vary.

EXERCISE B: Freewriting. Write for ten minutes on any of the following topics. Do not worry about spelling or punctuation. Start with general reactions and move to specific ones. Include any details associated with the subject.
Free writing will vary.

nature	a problem of the day
a favorite movie	a friend
travel	sports
daydreams/nightmares	what I do best
dancing	a favorite holiday

EXERCISE C: Journal Writing. Keep a journal for a week. Describe what you do, think, see, or feel during the day.
Journal entries will vary.

EXERCISE D: Brainstorming. Work in a group of four or five. One person should take notes. Brainstorm for ways of raising money for your class such as having a bake sale. Discuss ideas for about ten minutes without commenting on them. Then choose one, and working on your own, write down why it is a good idea.
Answers will vary.

EXERCISE E: Cueing. Imagine what it would be like to move to Mars. Using the 5 W's or five senses cueing method, write down words or sentences to describe what life on Mars might be like.
Words or sentences will vary.

students have brainstormed, clustered, and organized supporting details, have groups compare the different aspects that have been stressed with each different audience.

Additional Practice

Practice Pages or Practice Book, pages 117, 118
Writing Process Activities, pages 13–20

TESTING

Test Program

    Unit Pretest, page 68
    Chapter Test, page 70
    Unit Post-Test, page 75

Writing Process Activities, Evaluation Sheets, pages 8–12

RE-TEACHING

Practice Pages or Practice Book, pages 117, 118
Writing Process Activities, pages 13–20

THINKING SKILLS

Knowledge—*Stating* an inventory (Exercise A, page 395)

Application—*Using* free writing (Exercise B, page 395)
    Using journal writing (Exercise C, page 395)
    Using brainstorming (Exercise D, page 395)
    Using cueing (Exercise E, page 395)
    Using clustering to narrow a topic (Exercise F, page 396)

Analysis—*Identifying* a purpose and an audience (Exercise G, page 397)

Synthesis—*Planning* a short
paper (Exercise H, page 399)
Compiling and *organizing*
notes for a composition (Exercise I, page 399)
Compiling and *organizing*
notes for a composition
(Developing Writing Skills,
page 399)

Use the following Springboards
for Writing transparencies and
blackline masters for additional
practice:
  Self-Interview, pages 41–45
  Free writing, pages 47–51
  Journal Writing, pages 53–57
  Saving Ideas from Reading,
  pages 59–63
  Clustering, pages 65–69
  Brainstorming, pages 71–75
  Cueing, pages 77–81
  Audience and Purpose, pages
  83–87
  Choosing a Main Idea, pages
  89–93
  Supporting a Main Idea,
  pages 95–99

Choosing and Narrowing a Topic

Now you can see how topics can grow with a little bit of thought. Sometimes it is difficult to limit your papers to one topic or keep to one train of thought.

Choose a topic that you can effectively cover in the allotted amount of space.

You may be assigned a broad topic, such as music, for a short paper, or you may choose that topic when you are given a chance to develop a topic of your own choice. In either case, the topic of music is so broad that it could take several books to cover it satisfactorily. One way to narrow a topic like this is to use the clustering method on page 394. Here's how you could use the clustering technique to narrow the topic of music.

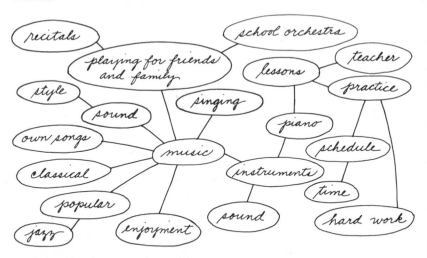

EXERCISE F: Narrowing a Topic. Using the cluster technique, narrow a topic for one of the five broad subjects listed here. Then spend ten minutes freewriting to keep the ideas flowing.

Clusters and free writing will vary.

computers   the importance of exercise   friendship
                   hobbies   seasons

Determining an Audience and Purpose

Before you start writing about any topic, you must know who is going to read your paper and why they are going to read it.

Determine your audience and purpose before you begin writing.

Your audience or readers might be your teacher, classmates, parents, or neighbors. Your purpose for writing might be to inform, to persuade, or to entertain.

The chart below shows audiences and purposes for topics.

Topic	Audience	Purpose
Why daily practice is important	Beginning musicians	to inform
Review of a piano concert	Readers of a local newspaper	To inform
Embarrassing first recital	Classmates	To entertain

Knowing your purpose and audience will help you decide what details to include and what kind of language to use.

EXERCISE G: Determining a Purpose and Audience. Choose one of the five broad topics below and use the clustering technique to narrow the topic to one suitable for a short paper. Then write two possible purposes and audiences for a paper on that topic.
Answers will vary.

sports   hobbies   science   animals   schools

EXAMPLE: babysitting
       1. purpose: to persuade readers of the advantages of hiring a babysitter; audience: parents
       2. purpose: to give tips to babysitters just starting out; audience: friends, classmates

Developing a Main Idea and Support

Once you have a topic, purpose, and audience, you can state your main idea and start to gather support for the main idea.

State a main idea. Then gather and organize supporting information to develop it effectively.

The main idea is a sentence stating the idea you want readers to remember. It does not have to appear in the final paper.

MAIN IDEA: There are many rewards for the time and effort I devote to piano lessons and practice.

Knowing your main idea makes it easier to find information to support it. To find supporting information, use the methods described under Exploring Ideas on pages 392–395.

When you have finished your note-taking, it is time to decide the best way to organize your material. First, think about your purpose and how to present your ideas. Ask yourself how you want your readers to react to what you are writing. For example, if you are trying to convince readers to agree with you, you might want to present your strongest argument first, hoping to grab their attention. You might save it for last, hoping to leave a strong impression in your readers' minds. The chart shows ways of organizing information.

ORGANIZATION OF SUPPORTING INFORMATION	
Chronological order	Information listed in the order in which it happened in time
Order of importance	Information arranged from least to most important, or vice versa
Comparison and contrast	Information arranged according to similarities and differences among items
Developmental	Information arranged so that one point leads logically to the next

Developing Writing Skills

Here is a list of supporting information for a paper on playing the piano. It is numbered in developmental order.

1. Practice
2. What I miss after school
3. A time schedule
4. My teacher, Mr. Reed, and how he helps me
5. The future
6. Rewards of my hard work
7. Recitals
8. How the music makes me feel

EXERCISE H: Developing a Topic. Select topic, purpose, and audience from those listed below. Write a main idea and supporting ideas for developing the topic. Then choose a method of organization. Write the information in that order.
Main ideas, supporting ideas, and methods of organization will vary.

Topics: fixing dinner for a family of eight, my favorite movie, how to meet new people

Purposes: to inform, to persuade, to entertain

Audiences: your classmates, your family, your teachers, young people ages 8–10

EXERCISE I: Prewriting. Practice the prewriting stage of the writing process by choosing your own topic. Then, use whatever techniques you want to narrow that topic down so that you can write a short paper about it. Next, decide who your audience will be and determine what your purpose is. Write down notes about your topic and identify the best method of organization. Number your notes according to the method of organization you choose. Add or subtract any ideas that will improve your work.
Answers will vary.

DEVELOPING WRITING SKILLS: Prewriting. Choose another general topic and follow all the steps of the prewriting stage to create an outline for a short paper.
Outlines will vary.

Writing Across the Curriculum

When students choose their topics, you might suggest that they consider exploring another content area, such as social studies, science, math, sports, or music. For example, students might choose one of the following general topics: the American Revolution, the environment, computers, baseball, or rock music. Once students have chosen a general topic, they should use the clustering technique to narrow the topic. Then they should determine their audience and purpose and develop a main idea and supporting information.

20.2 Writing
(pp. 400–401)

OBJECTIVE

After completing this section, students should be able to

• Use prewriting notes to write a first draft.

TEACHING

Getting Started

Tell students that a first draft is just that—a first try at combining all of their notes and ideas. You might want to have a volunteer share his or her notes for everyone to combine into sentences and paragraphs for a first draft. Have students analyze and improve their suggestions as they go along. You may want to have another volunteer share his or her notes for another group effort in writing a first draft. This should be enough to get all students started in writing their own first drafts.

Text Follow Through

Discuss text pages 400–401.

Assign Exercise, page 400, and Developing Writing Skills, page 401.

Less advanced With some classes, you may want to assign one topic to all students and spend class time asking for input to create a group composition on the board or overhead projector.

Average You may have to work with some students as they organize their notes and write their first drafts. Remind students that this draft is not a final one; their tendency often is to try to write the final draft the first time. Encourage free expression and openness to

20.2 Writing

You are now ready to begin writing your paper.

Writing a First Draft

The first draft just combines all of your notes and ideas. Putting them into sentences and paragraphs is your main goal.

Translate your prewriting notes into sentences and paragraphs, without worrying about punctuation, spelling, grammar, or fine-tuning.

Think of your first draft as free-writing exercise that has a structure and purpose. After you start writing, you may see a new way to express your main idea, or you may come up with a new one. This is the time for you to experiment with any new ideas you may have.

Here is a first draft of a paragraph about music.

When my grandmother sold her house, she gave her old piano to my family. I started taking piano lessons when I was eight years old. It's four years later, and even though I missed some afterschool fun with friends, I don't regret one minute of the time I spend with the piano. The time and effort spent practicing and taking piano lessons are rewarded by appreciation from my family and friends, my own self-confidence, and the way playing makes me feel. With a little determination, some discipline, and a love of music, almost anyone can enjoy playing the piano.

The paragraph contains the main idea from page 398, the first supporting ideas on page 399, and some added specific details.

Once you have a rough draft, you can improve it.

EXERCISE: Writing a First Draft. Write a first draft of a short paper based on your notes from Exercise I on page 399.
Answers will vary.

DEVELOPING WRITING SKILLS: Writing a First Draft.
Write a first draft based on your notes from Developing Writing
Skills on page 399.
Answers will vary.

Revising 20.3

Revising is as important in the writing process as prewriting
and writing are. You now have a chance to read over your
ideas and make them clear, concise, and more interesting.

Revising for Sense

The first stage in revising is to be sure your paper makes
sense.

**Read your paper critically to make sure that all
the ideas support your purpose and that they
are presented logically and connected clearly.**

As you revise, ask yourself the following questions.

REVISING FOR SENSE
1. Have I clearly stated my topic?
2. Will the main idea be clear to my readers?
3. Is there enough supporting information?
4. Are the ideas presented in a logical order?
5. Are the connections between the ideas clear and logical?

EXERCISE A: Revising for Sense. Using the chart on this
page, revise the following paragraph, making sure that it makes
sense.
Revisions will vary.

Basketball is the game that is watched by more people in the
U.S. than any other game. The only thing he had for a goal was
a wooden peach basket, so he called it "basketball." It is

---

added ideas and changes. Their
prepared notes need not be
strictly followed.

Advanced Ask students to
select two of the lists from the
class assignment discussed in
20.1 of this Teacher's Edition,
and prepare two compositions,
varying the tone and sentence
structures to allow for the
audience.

Additional Practice

Practice Pages or Practice
  Book, page 119
Writing Process Activities,
  page 21
Writing Workshop, page 6

TESTING

Test Program
  Unit Pretest, page 68
  Chapter Test, page 70
  Unit Post-Test, page 75

Writing Process Activities,
  Evaluation Sheets, pages
  8–12

RE-TEACHING

Practice Pages or Practice
  Book, page 119
Writing Process Activities,
  page 21

THINKING SKILLS

Synthesis—*Writing* a first draft
  (Exercise, page 400; Developing Writing Skills, page 401)

20.3 Revising

(pp. 401–404)

OBJECTIVES

After completing this section,
students should be able to

• Revise their papers so that
  their ideas support the purpose and are presented
  logically and connected
  clearly.

- Revise their papers for the best word choice and clear, varied sentences.
- Proofread their papers carefully so that their work is ready for publishing.

TEACHING

Getting Started

Tell students that their goal is to revise their writing for sense; their ideas should be presented clearly, concisely, and interestingly. Direct students' attention to the chart on page 401. You might want to have a volunteer share one or two paragraphs of his or her writing for classmates to analyze using the questions in the chart.

Preparation of a class collection of writings is a great motivator. You may wish to tell students they should revise to create a writing of quality high enough for publication in the class book.

Text Follow Through

Discuss text pages 401–404.

Assign Exercise A, page 401; Exercise B, page 402; Exercise C, page 403; Exercise D, page 403; Exercise E, page 404; Exercise F, page 404; and Developing Writing Skills, page 404.

Less advanced Students might benefit from classroom workshop sessions to complete Exercises A, C, and E in this section. Those students who are struggling to grasp the concepts of grammar and usage cannot be expected to edit their compositions effectively for all aspects. Select one or two points that they need to improve in (for example, correcting sentence fragments and run-ons or using correct spelling and subject-verb agreement) and in-

played in almost every country in the world. It did not develop slowly over the years, as some of our other games have. It was invented by one man in 1891. He wanted to provide a game to interest physical-education students at Springfield Training School in Massachusetts. Instead of using a stick, as in lacrosse, or kicking the ball, as in soccer, James A. Naismith devised a game by which the ball is passed from player to player or bounced by one player and shot into a goal. He combined the Indian game of lacrosse and the British game of soccer to make an indoor game.

EXERCISE B: Revising Your Paper. Use the checklist on page 401 to revise the paper you wrote for the exercise on page 400.

Answers will vary.

Editing for Word Choice and Sentences

The second stage in the revision process, often called *editing,* is to check your choice of words and your sentences.

Read your paper several times, making sure that every word is the best possible one to express your thoughts and that the sentences are clear and varied.

When you edit your paper for word choice and sentences, ask yourself the questions in the following chart.

EDITING WORDS AND SENTENCES
1. Does each word mean exactly what I want to say?
2. Does the language sound right for the intended audience?
3. Is the meaning of each sentence clear?
4. Have I used a variety of sentence lengths and structures?

Following is a revised and edited version of the first draft of the paragraph about music that appeared on page 400.

20.3 Revising

When*^* my grandmother sold her house*~ she* ~~gave~~ her old
That is when
piano to my family*~* I started taking piano lessons ~~when I was~~
I *have passed,* *have probably*
~~eight years old.~~ ~~It's~~*^*four years ~~later,~~ an*^*d even though I*^* missed
some afterschool fun with friend*~* I don't regret one minute of
have spent
the time I*~* ~~spend~~ with the piano. The time and effort spent practicing and taking piano lessons are rewarded by appreciation
increased
from my family and friends, my*~*own self-confidence, and the
way playing makes me feel. With ~~a little~~ determination, ~~some~~
my *I'm getting better every*
discipline, and*~*a love of music, ~~almost anyone can enjoy play-~~
day.
~~ing the piano.~~

I was eight years old,
and

EXERCISE C: Editing. Edit the following passage for word
choice and types of sentences.
Editing will vary.

Pyramids are buildings with stones weighing tons. They were
built by the Egyptians from approximately 2600 to 150 B.C. They
were built for religious reasons. They believed after their dead
were buried, they came back to life many times. The Egyptians
prepared the dead body for the afterlife by preserving it in the
coffin-like tomb. A pyramid is not just a coffin. The pyramids
are one of the Seven Wonders of the World.

A pyramid consisted of three different layers. The first layer,
the innermost part, is called the core. The second layer held
the packing rocks, which rested on the steps of the core. They
were carefully carved to fit into place. The third layer had
blocks, called outer blocks, or casing. The casing rested on the
packing blocks. It was cut carefully so that there was only a pa-
per-thin space between each block. The core contained the
body and its belongings. The casing is the part you can see.

EXERCISE D: Editing Your Paper. Use the checklist on
page 402 to edit the paper you wrote for the exercise on page
400.
Answers will vary.

sist that papers be checked
thoroughly for these things. Be
available as a resource person,
but refer students to the dictionary if possible.

Average Students should be
able to complete the exercises
in this section without too
much difficulty. Have students
work in groups to complete Exercises A, C, and E and then
compare their revisions with
those of other groups.

Advanced Collect students'
papers, duplicate them, and put
them into booklet form to be
distributed to the class. Or post
several papers on the bulletin
board as models for class
members.

Additional Practice

Practice Pages or Practice
  Book, page 120
Writing Process Activities,
  pages 22, 23

TESTING

Test Program

  Unit Pretest, page 68
  Chapter Test, page 70
  Unit Post-Test, page 75

Writing Process Activities,
  Evaluation Sheets, pages
  8–12

RE-TEACHING

Practice Pages or Practice
  Book, page 120
Writing Process Activities,
  pages 22, 23

THINKING SKILLS

Evaluation—*Appraising* and
revising a paragraph for sense
(Exercise A, page 401)
Appraising and *revising* a
paper for sense (Exercise B,
page 402)

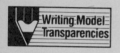
Writing Model Transparencies

Revising for Sense and *Editing Words and Sentences* appear in transparency form. See Checklists, pages 323 and 325.

Proofreading and Publishing

Proofreading is the final step in the writing process. This is your chance to make sure your work is perfect.

Proofreading involves making final corrections in spelling, capitalization, punctuation, and grammar.

When you proofread, do not change the ideas. Just make sure all punctuation, spelling, and grammar is correct.

After proofreading, the only thing left is publishing your paper. Publishing could mean simply handing the final version to your teacher, submitting it to your school newspaper, or passing it around to your family and friends.

Errors are shaded and corrections are given.

EXERCISE E: Proofreading a Paragraph. Proofread the following.

At one time it was difficult for me to give a speech. When I stood in front of an audience, i become very nervous. Once I had to tell a hiking club about my trip to the Rocky Mountains. I perpared my speech, and I hopped that I would be able to get threw it. But something happened that really surprized me. After the initial shock of having people stare at me I started enjoying myself. I have not been afraid to give a speech since.

speech/I/became/prepared/hoped/through/surprised/me, I

EXERCISE F: Proofreading Your Paper. Proofread and recopy the paper you revised for Exercises B and D on pages 402 and 403.

Answers will vary.

DEVELOPING WRITING SKILLS: Revising, Proofreading, and Publishing Your Writing. Use the checklists on pages 401 and 402 to revise the rough draft you wrote for the Developing Writing Skills on page 401. Proofread your final draft; recopy it if necessary. Then think of ways to publish your work.

Answers will vary.

Writing Workshop: The Writing Process

ASSIGNMENT 1

Topic An Overrated (or Underrated) Performer

Form and Purpose An essay that persuades a reader to accept your viewpoint.

Audience Reader of a magazine called *Peopletalk*

Length Four to six paragraphs

Focus Identify the person in your first paragraph and present your opinion in a thesis statement. In the body support your opinion with facts, details, examples, and reasons. Conclude with a restatement of your thesis and a striking thought about the person.

Sources Newspapers, magazines, television, radio

Prewriting Select a public figure whom you feel strongly about. Brainstorm for support. Then prepare an outline.

Writing Follow the outline as you write a first draft.

Revising Use the checklists on pages 401 and 402 to revise edit, and proofread your essay.

Guiding Student Writing

You can use the Writing Workshop assignments either in place of or in addition to the writing assignments in the text. Remind students of the seven techniques for generating ideas in the prewriting stage of the writing process. These techniques will stimulate creativity and help students as they work through the early stages. The groundwork laid in the prewriting stage is a very important part of learning how to write well.

Assignment

Suggestions for Prewriting: Students will probably pick a performer about whom they already have strong feeling and some information. Insist, however, that they check their facts to avoid libel charges.

Suggestions for Revising: Discuss the probable tone of a magazine called *Peopletalk*— breezy and anecdotal rather than serious and scholarly.

For additional practice, use Writing Workshop transparency, page 9.

CHAPTER 21
Improving Your Use of Words
(pp. 406–418)

The first of the two sections in this chapter, Section 21.1, is designed to help students choose appropriate, specific words for sentences they write. The second section, Section 21.2, will help students avoid using clichés and slang in their writing.

For a review of the entire chapter and a related writing activity, see the Skills Review and Writing Workshop on page 418.

21.1 Choosing Precise Words
(pp. 406–414)

OBJECTIVES

After completing this section, students should be able to

• Replace linking verbs and verbs in the passive voice with action verbs in the active voice.
• Use specific, vivid words to enliven sentences.
• Use words with appropriate connotations for a particular context.

Chapter **21**

Improving Your Use of Words

Accurate, interesting writing depends on careful word choices. Words chosen with care can make your ideas seem both clear and fresh to your audience.

21.1 Choosing Precise Words

Whenever you concentrate on what you want to write, you will discover that many possible word choices are open to you. This section will show you how to avoid weak or dull word choices. It will also provide you with some new ways to find the most suitable words to express your ideas.

Using Action Words

Verbs are essential parts of your sentences. As you know from your study of grammar, some verbs are action verbs; other verbs are linking verbs. In addition verbs can be either in the active voice or in the passive voice. In general the more

21.1 Choosing Precise Words

you use *action verbs* in the *active voice*, the more energetic and direct your sentences will be.

Use action verbs in the active voice to express your ideas forcefully.

Action Verbs. Although you will often need to use linking verbs, try to replace linking verbs with *action verbs* in many of your sentences. Note how action verbs make the sentences in the following chart more direct.

With Linking Verbs	With Action Verbs
He *is* a leader in many class projects.	He *leads* many class projects.
We *became* investors in the stock market.	We *invested* in the stock market.

You can rewrite many sentences that have linking verbs by looking for a word in the sentence that suggests an action verb and changing it into a verb. Notice how the use of the word *tutor* changes in the following examples.

LINKING VERB: Sheila *is* a tutor at the elementary school

ACTION VERB: Sheila *tutors* at the elementary school.

Active Voice. You should also avoid using too many verbs in the passive voice. In the following chart, note how verbs in the *active voice* make the sentences more direct.

With Verbs in the Passive Voice	With Verbs in the Active Voice
We *were confused* by the question.	The question *confused* us.
The herd's survival *was threatened* by the plague.	The plague *threatened* the herd's survival.

TEACHING

Getting Started

Review action and linking verbs and the active and passive voices. Then write the following sentences on the board:

1. Jeff is a performer in many school plays.
2. Jeff performs in many school plays.
3. She was really angered by their behavior.
4. Their behavior really angered her.

Ask students what kind of verb sentence 1 contains (linking). Then ask the same question about sentence 2 (action). Elicit that the verb in sentence 3 is in the passive voice and that the one in sentence 4 is in the active voice. Lead students to see that sentences 2 and 4 are livelier and more interesting than sentences 1 and 3. Point out that the reason they are is that 2 and 4 avoid the use of linking and passive-voice verbs. Ask for other examples of sentences containing linking verbs. Write these on the board. Then, where possible, ask students to change the linking verbs to action verbs. Follow the same procedure for turning passive verbs into active ones.

Text Follow Through

Discuss text pages 406–414.

Assign Exercise A, page 408; Exercise B, page 409; Exercise C, page 411; Exercise D, page 413; Exercise E, page 413; and Developing Writing Skills, page 414.

Less advanced Work with students on the revisions required in Exercise A of this section. Point out that each sentence already contains a word that can become the main verb, and remind students that they may have to change more than just the verb. You may also work with them on the first few sentences of Exercise B to be certain they understand the process.

Average Students can compare their answers to exercises D and E and discuss the connotations of each specific word as well as the different senses the connotations give to the sentences.

Advanced Ask students to collect examples of vivid words they encounter in their reading. The words might be compiled into lists or into a card file grouped by categories. An entry might be set up in the following way: Ways of Walking—tiptoe, ramble, hobble, meander. Once the lists are compiled, they can serve as resources when students revise their own writing.

Additional Practice

Practice Pages or Practice Book, page 121

TESTING

Test Program

 Unit Pretest, page 68
 Chapter Test, page 71
 Unit Post-Test, page 75

RE-TEACHING

Practice Pages or Practice Book, page 121

Occasionally you will need to use verbs used in the passive voice. However, a series of sentences with verbs in the passive voice is likely to sound roundabout. In addition the passive voice often adds words to sentences. Whenever you can, use the active voice to make your sentences more direct.

You can rewrite most sentences that have verbs in the passive voice by looking for the performer of the action at the end of the sentence and moving the performer to the beginning. In the following examples, *groom* and *ushers* are the performers of the action.

PASSIVE VOICE: Silver tuxedos *were worn* by the groom and his ushers.

ACTIVE VOICE: The groom and his ushers *wore* silver tuxedos.

EXERCISE A: Replacing Linking Verbs with Action Verbs.

Rewrite each of the following sentences to make it more direct by replacing a linking verb with an action verb.

EXAMPLE: Jed was a student of Greek civilization.

    Jed studied Greek civilization.

Answers will vary; samples are given.

1. Janet's good manners ~~are a pleasure to~~ my grandmother. please
2. Your order must be ~~in the mail~~ by midnight. mailed
3. The map in the bottle ~~was a guide for~~ us to Hammett's Cave. guided
4. Apparently my French tutoring had really ~~been of help to~~ Marilyn. helped
5. Nobody ~~was of the belief~~ that I had actually flown an aircraft. believed
6. The handout sheet ~~was a list of~~ our assignments for the next four weeks. listed
7. Nobody expected that this television show would ~~be successful~~ in the competition for ratings. succeed
8. She ~~was a participant~~ in a number of different club activities. participated

Comprehension—*Rewriting* sentences using action verbs (Exercise A, page 408) *Rewriting* sentences using verbs in the active voice (Exercise B, page 409) *Distinguishing* between connotations of synonyms (Exercise E, page 413)

Application—*Using* specific, vivid words to enliven sentences (Exercise C, page 411)

Synthesis—*Writing* sentences using synonyms containing suitable connotations (Exercise D, page 413) *Rewriting* a passage using direct, suitable, and vivid words (Developing Writing Skills, page 414)

Use the following Springboards for Writing transparencies and blackline masters for additional practice:
Action Verbs, pages 101–105
Specific Words, pages 107–111
Vivid Words, pages 113–117
Connotation and Denotation, pages 119–123

21.1 Choosing Precise Words

9. Ants ~~are the creators of~~ tiny, endless underground tunnels. create
10. The hovering hawk ~~was an observer of~~ our every movement. observed

EXERCISE B: Replacing Verbs in the Passive Voice with Verbs in the Active Voice. Rewrite each of the following sentences to make it more direct by replacing a verb in the passive voice with a verb in the active voice.
Answers will vary; samples are given.
EXAMPLE: The shutters were rattled by the wind.

The wind rattled the shutters.

3. The/hinder store owners who wish to expand their businesses.

1. ~~The barbells were lifted by a~~ man of enormous strength.
2. ~~Mrs. Simpson, our teacher, was annoyed by the builders~~ pounding on the roof. The/annoyed Mrs. Simpson, our teacher.
3. ~~Store owners who wish to expand their businesses are hindered by the~~ new zoning laws.
4. ~~Many species of fish are endangered by industrial~~ wastes.
5. ~~Science students can be helped by the~~ physics review lectures offered on Saturdays. The/can help science students.
6. ~~Many of Leon Uris's novels were inspired by the~~ heroic deeds of World War II. The/inspired many of Leon Uris's novels.
7. ~~The tent was pitched and the fire was built by~~ my father and brothers. My/pitched the tent and built the fire.
8. ~~An article about whales was written by the~~ newest member of our news team, Marion Pratt. The/, wrote an article about whales.
9. The trouble began when the ~~bull was mistakenly released by a~~ gatekeeper. mistakenly released the bull.
10. Finally, ~~her stage fright was relieved by~~ the audience's enthusiasm. relieved her stage fright.

1. A/lifted the barbells.   4. Industrial/endanger many species of fish.

Using Vivid Language

In addition to using action verbs in the active voice, you should try to use words that will paint pictures for your readers. Specific, vivid words can help the reader see what you have visualized in your own mind.

Choose language that is specific and precise rather than general and dull.

In the sentences in the following chart, note the difference between general language and specific language.

Examples of General Language	Examples of Specific Language
A *forest* surrounded the *building*.	*Dense pines* surrounded the *old barn*.
That *motion picture* was *silly*.	That *science fiction movie* was *ridiculously unbelievable*.
The *player moved* across the court.	The *young tennis champion sped* across the court.

The English language offers a great variety of words. You should not always be satisfied with the first words that come to mind. For example, do not write *look* when *glance* or *stare* would be more exact. If you search for the best words, using your memory, a dictionary, or a book of synonyms, you will find words that are both accurate and vivid.

You might begin by giving your verbs a "fitness" test. Ask yourself, "Would another verb help the reader see more clearly the action I am describing?" If the first verb that comes to mind is a common or general one, think about the action you are describing. For example, the verb *run* can be useful and appropriate, but it is general. A more specific verb can make the reader visualize the action exactly as you visualized it.

DULL, GENERAL VERB: Hillary *ran* across the finish line to the wild cheers of spectators.

VIVID, SPECIFIC VERB: Hillary *dashed* across the finish line to the wild cheers of spectators.

You should also examine your nouns and modifiers. Replace dull, general nouns and modifiers with words that will make your writing clearer. In the following example, the word

21.1 Choosing Precise Words

man is vague, and the adjective *loud* is general. *Loud* could describe anything from a sigh to an explosion.

DULL, GENERAL WORDS: The *man* addressed the crowd in a *loud* voice.

VIVID, SPECIFIC WORDS: The *mayor* addressed the crowd in a *booming* voice.

While you are writing, and especially when you are examining what you have written, question your words. Make sure that you have chosen specific and interesting words wherever they can be of help to your reader.

EXERCISE C: Using Specific, Vivid Words to Enliven Sentences.

In the following sentences, the words in parentheses are dull, general verbs, nouns, or modifiers. Replace each item with one or more words that give a more vivid picture.

Answers will vary; samples are given.

EXAMPLE: Lisa (held) her little sister's hand as they crossed the street.

    tightly gripped

1. After a (bad) experience in the dentist's chair, Chuck (said) that he would take better care of his teeth. dreadful/vowed
2. Officer Christie watched the (suspect) dart through the crowd and race around the corner. thief
3. The player (stood) up when the coach called his name. leaped
4. Tyrone was (happy) when he won the basketball scholarship. ecstatic
5. Dancers (moved) to the beat of the drums. swayed gracefully
6. The wrecking ball (hit) the side of the building. smashed
7. With a (loud noise) the entire (structure) crumbled to the ground. thundering crash/tenement
8. The fire spread (fast). quite rapidly
9. The hungry trucker (ate) his food. gobbled
10. After spending three weeks in orbit, the astronaut reported that he was (glad) to be home. delighted

Choosing Words for Their Connotations

The *denotation* of a word is its literal meaning. The word *shivering,* for example, means "shaking." The words *trembling* and *quaking* also mean "shaking." These three words are synonyms because they share the same denotation.

The three synonyms, however, have different *connotations.* The connotation of a word is the set of ideas it brings to mind. *Shivering* generally suggests a physical reaction to cold. *Trembling,* on the other hand, might suggest a number of different emotions—for example, fear, love, anger, or excitement. Of the three words, *quaking* suggests the most violent action. Most people would also associate the act of *quaking* directly with the emotion of fear.

When you are considering synonyms, you should think about their different connotations.

Choose the words with the most appropriate connotations for your sentences.

Whenever you can think of several possible word choices, you are probably considering synonyms with different connotations. Remember that these different connotations can alter the meaning of your sentence. Notice how *shivering, trembling,* and *quaking* all change the idea presented in the following example.

EXAMPLE: *Shivering,* Orin approached the gray cottage.

Trembling, Orin approached the gray cottage.

Quaking, Orin approached the gray cottage.

In the first sentence above, Orin could be going to the cottage to seek shelter from the cold. In the second sentence, the cottage might be Orin's former home or long-sought goal. In the third sentence, the cottage apparently holds something that frightens Orin.

Because their connotations are different, you will generally want to use these words to express different ideas. Note in each of the following sentences that one of the three words is more logical than the other two would be.

EXAMPLE: *Shivering,* Orin approached the icy river.

Trembling, Orin approached his long-lost brother.

Quaking, Orin approached the fiery dragon.

EXERCISE D: Understanding Connotations. List two synonyms for each of the following words. Next to each synonym, write a sentence that suits the connotation of that synonym.
Answers will vary; sample synonyms are given.

1. wide broad/large
2. angry irate/mad
3. hurt injure/damage
4. pleasant pleasing/agreeable
5. strong sturdy/tough

EXERCISE E: Choosing Connotations. Each of the following sentences contains two or more synonyms in parentheses. Consider the different connotation of each synonym in a group. Then choose the word that you think best completes each sentence.
Answers may vary.

EXAMPLE: The baby (chortled, guffawed) at the puppy.

chortled

1. Booster rockets (elevated, <u>lifted</u>) the missile from the launching pad.
2. The radio on the windowsill (<u>blared</u>, bellowed, howled) endlessly.
3. Robert had trouble making friends at first because he was (<u>shy</u>, wary, fearful).
4. After lifting weights for a year, Alfred had (<u>increased</u>, expanded, raised) the size of his arm muscles.
5. Pleasantly (<u>stuffed</u>, bloated) after Thanksgiving dinner, we retired to the living room to watch football on television.

Developing Writing Skills

Have students practice using precise words in their writing by completing the following assignment.

Writing Across the Curriculum

Newspaper reporters are known for their straightforward, concise writing style and their use of precise, forceful language.

Prewriting Imagine that you are a reporter for your school newspaper. Then think of a recent event involving your school that you found especially interesting or important. Next, brainstorm about the details of the event. If you feel that you need additional information, you might consider interviewing teachers or students who were involved with the event. Once you feel that you have gathered enough information, prepare an outline for your article.

Writing When you write your article, try to avoid expressing your own opinions about the event. Instead, focus on presenting facts and details. Use a concise, straightforward, journalistic writing style.

Revising When you revise, make sure that your language is clear, precise, and forceful. Also make sure that you have included enough details to provide readers with a clear understanding of the event.

21.2 Avoiding Worn-Out and Inappropriate Words

(pp. 414–417)

6. The air was still too (icy, frozen, <u>cold</u>) for a light jacket.

7. She (made, shaped, <u>created</u>) more problems by never acknowledging her mistakes.

8. Holding the racket properly, Joni learned to (dominate, <u>control</u>) her serves.

9. State engineers have (invented, <u>designed</u>) a new type of roadway.

10. He made a (<u>clumsy</u>, gawky) attempt to apologize.

DEVELOPING WRITING SKILLS: Choosing the Best Words. Read the following passage carefully, looking for unnecessary linking verbs, verbs in the passive voice, and words that are dull, general, or inappropriate. Then rewrite the passage, using words that are direct, vivid, and suitable.

Revisions will vary; samples are given

(1) Charles Dickens' *The Christmas Carol* is an ~interesting story. (2) The story ~is focused on a man named Ebenezer Scrooge. (3) ~Scrooge is interested only in money. (4) One Christmas Eve, however, ~Scrooge is taught by a scary experience to change his ways.

(5) ~Scrooge is taken by three phantoms—the spirits of Christmas past, present, and future—on a trip through his own past, present, and future. (6) He sees ~things from the future that ~are frightening to him. (7) Scrooge finally ~sees that his love of money can ~be harmful to him and others. (8) Then ~Christmas bells are heard, and ~Scrooge wakes from his ~reverie. (9) Scrooge is ~happy when he ~comprehends that he is still alive and that the future ~can still be changed by him. (10) His life is completely ~revolutionized, and he becomes a ~nice man.

1. entertaining 2. focuses 3. Only money interests Scrooge. 4. a terrifying adventure teaches Scrooge 5. Three/take Scrooge 6. scenes/frighten

21.2 Avoiding Worn-Out and Inappropriate words

Using precise, clear language means choosing words that will be both interesting and clear. For this reason you should guard against two special problems: *clichés* and *slang*. This

7. understands/harm 8. Scrooge hears/he/dreams. 9. thrilled/realizes/he can still change. 10. changed/kind and generous

After completing this section, students should be able to

- Identify and avoid clichés.
- Use precise language in place of slang.

21.2 Avoiding Worn-Out and Inappropriate Words

section will help you replace these words with original words and expressions.

Avoiding Clichés

A *cliché* is an overused expression such as *snug as a bug in a rug.* Your readers will be familiar with clichés—too familiar!

Use precise language in place of clichés.

Watch carefully for clichés. Tired-sounding, ready-made expressions such as *cute as a button* or *fit as a fiddle* will weaken your writing. Language that is more precise and original will convey much more meaning.

Examine the following examples. In each case a cliché makes an idea less precise than it could be. The revised version of each sentence provides a precise expression that makes the idea sharper.

CLICHÉ: The new administrator was afraid *to rock the boat.*

PRECISE   The new administrator was afraid *to make any*
EXPRESSION: *major changes in the organization.*

CLICHÉ: After painting his bedroom, Mike *ate like a horse.*

PRECISE   After painting his bedroom, Mike *devoured two*
EXPRESSION: *hamburgers and a pecan pie.*

EXERCISE A: Recognizing Clichés. Find five clichés by looking in books that discuss clichés, by listening to conversations around you, or simply by using your memory. On your paper list the five clichés, define each one, and write a sentence using the cliché in a way that shows its meaning.
Answers will vary.

EXERCISE B: Revising Clichés. Use the sentences you wrote in Exercise A. Underline the cliché in each. Beneath each sentence write a new version by substituting precise, original language for the cliché.
Answers will vary.

TEACHING

Getting Started

Ask the class if they know what a cliché is. Elicit that it is an overused expression. Write a few examples on the board. These could include *big as a house, quick as lightning,* and *the silvery moon.* Have students give other examples, and write these on the board also. Now elicit that these expressions are so stale and boring that they should not be used in good writing. Point out that clichés are very imprecise. Ask students to replace the clichés on the board with precise and fresh expressions. Write these on the board. You may have to offer help. Have the new expressions used in sentences. Possible replacements for the clichés you wrote on the board are *big as a dinosaur; quick as a frog's tongue snapping up a bug; the milky-white moon.*

Text Follow Through

Discuss pages 414–417.

Assign Exercise A, page 415; Exercise B, page 415; Exercise C, page 416; and Developing Writing Skills, page 417.

Less advanced Work with students as they revise the sentences in Exercise C. Also discuss the clichés and slang expressions these students plan to use when they write the passages called for in Developing Writing Skills. Change the second part of the instructions to omit the exchange of papers.

Average Students might enjoy compiling a class dictionary of clichés and slang. You can have them work in committees, using the sentences they wrote for Exercise A and Developing Writing Skills. Ask students to select the most frequently recurring clichés and slang expressions and give two or three precise revisions for each. They can then enter their results in a notebook or other file, to be placed in a central location and used in revising their own writing. The entries might look something like this:

Cliché/Slang	Precise Writing
1. bite off more than one can chew	• under-take too large a task • overextend oneself
2. go for it	• try one's hardest • don't hesitate
3. chew one's ear off	• chatter aimlessly • babble constantly

Advanced Students might enjoy consulting a dictionary of slang to find outdated slang expressions with which to confuse their classmates.

Additional Practice
Practice Pages or Practice Book, page 122

Avoiding Slang

Slang is made up of words that are popular among certain groups of people at a particular time. Because slang words change over time and vary according to place, however, many people find slang confusing. Only a small percentage of slang words become well-known and permanent parts of the language. Except in very informal writing or in dialogue, slang should be avoided.

Use precise language in place of slang words and expressions.

The following examples are weakened by slang. Notice how more precise word choices clarify the ideas and sound less jarring.

SLANG: *It really blew Scott's mind* to find straight A's on his report card.

PRECISE EXPRESSION: Scott was *astonished* to find straight A's on his report card.

SLANG: The minister's sermon last Sunday morning *was really far out.*

PRECISE EXPRESSION: The minister's sermon last Sunday morning *included a gripping example from daily life.*

EXERCISE C: Replacing Slang. Find the slang word or expression in each of the following sentences. Consult a dictionary of slang if you do not understand some of the expressions. Then write a new sentence, replacing the slang with precise, original words.

Answers will vary; samples are given.
EXAMPLE: His actions showed that he was made of the right stuff.

His actions showed that he was courageous and heroic.

21.2 Avoiding Worn-Out and Inappropriate Words

1. Our team ~~blew them away~~. defeated them soundly.
2. Proving once again that she was ~~an airhead~~, Gina left the apartment without her keys and allowed the door to lock behind her. absent-minded
3. Our neighbor Mr. Sampson ~~chewed my ear off~~ while I was trying to rake our lawn. chattered at me constantly
4. With his ~~wicked~~ curve ball, Jeremy struck out every batter. exceptional
5. When I told Jan to pick up her toys, she ~~got really ticked off~~. became infuriated.
6. The pounding headache ~~bummed me out~~ all day.
7. Yesterday I was ~~nailed~~ by Mrs. DeStefano for not carrying a pass in the halls. reprimanded
8. With a grin on his face, Horace showed that he ~~was wise to~~ their plans. knew of
9. By grabbing the bridge's handrail, David saved himself from a ~~hairy~~ situation. dangerous
10. After rounding the last turn, the horse ~~burned up~~ the final stretch. raced down

6. made me miserable

DEVELOPING WRITING SKILLS: Avoiding Worn-out and Inappropriate Words.
List ten overused or currently popular expressions that are inappropriate in formal writing. Include both clichés and slang. Then complete the following steps.

1. Write a passage using any five of the expressions on your list.
2. Exchange papers with a partner. Then find and underline the five inappropriate expressions on your partner's paper and write a revised version of the passage.

Answers will vary.

TESTING

Test Program
  Unit Pretest, page 68
  Chapter Test, pages 71, 72
  Unit Post-Test, page 75

RE-TEACHING

Practice Pages or Practice Book, page 122

THINKING SKILLS

Application—*Identifying* clichés and *demonstrating* their meanings by using them in sentences (Exercise A, page 415)
  Changing clichés to precise language (Exercise B, page 415)
  Changing slang to precise, original language (Exercise C, page 416)
Synthesis—*Writing* a passage including clichés and slang and *revising* the passage (Developing Writing Skills, page 417)

Writing Model Transparencies

Use the following Springboards for Writing transparencies and blackline masters for additional practice:
  Freshness, pages 125–129
  Improving Sentence Variety, pages 131–135

Checking Your Skills

In the Checking Your Skills assignment, students improved a paragraph by making the language more forceful and precise. To provide students with additional practice in using precise language, have them complete the following activity.

Collaborative Learning

Group students into pairs. Then have each student choose a short story by a distinguished writer, such as Mark Twain, Ray Bradbury, or Langston Hughes. Each student should look through the story he or she has chosen and select three substantial paragraphs in which the language is especially vivid and forceful. Next, the students should rework these paragraphs, replacing action verbs with linking verbs, changing the active voice to the passive voice, and replacing vivid, specific language with general language. The students should then exchange papers with their partners, and they should revise their partners' paragraphs, making the language more forceful and precise. Finally, the students should compare their revisions with the original paragraphs.

Using Composition Skills

Peer Editing Arrange your students into small groups and have them read their paragraphs to one another and suggest ways in which they could be improved. When evaluating the paragraphs, peer editors should make sure that the writers have used action verbs and the active voice and that their language is clear and precise.

Skills Review and Writing Workshop

Improving Your Use of Words

CHECKING YOUR SKILLS

Rewrite the following paragraph, replacing the weak linking verbs with action verbs and using more vivid adjectives and descriptive phrases. Answers will vary.

(1) Davy Crockett is part of the frontier legend. (2) At about age thirteen, Davy was a runaway from home. (3) Later he returned and was a help to his father in paying the elder Crockett's debts. (4) Davy was probably in school only a few months. (5) He was not much of a scholar. (6) In fact, he was somewhat boastful about his illiteracy! (7) He was a scout for Andrew Jackson in the Indian Wars of 1813–14. (8) From 1821–35 he was a member first of the Tennessee legislature and then of the U.S. House of Representatives. (9) The Texan struggle for independence was exciting to him. (10) He was one of the defenders of the Alamo; his death was there in 1836.

USING COMPOSITION SKILLS
Writing About Language

Writers often write articles and books about language. Follow the steps below to write a paragraph about current slang words and expressions. Answers will vary.

Prewriting: Make a list of ten to fifteen current slang words and expressions. Then choose four or five of them that might be used in one single conversation.

Writing: Begin with a general comment about the use of slang in conversation and in formal writing. Then explain what each slang expression means. For each one, suggest a substitute in more precise language that you would use in standard English.

Revising: Check the non-slang words in your writing and replace any that are dull, general, or overused. After you have revised, proofread carefully.

Before students begin this chapter, you will want to be sure that they understand the material on phrases and clauses presented in Chapters 8 and 9. In Section 22.1 students will be asked to use prepositional phrases, verbal phrases, and clauses to expand and combine sentences. Section 22.2 demands a knowledge of compound and complex sentences; so too does Section 22.3, which stresses the need for variety in sentence structure.

For a review of the entire chapter and a related writing activity, see the Skills Review and Writing Workshop on page 436.

Chapter **22**

Improving Your Sentences

Writing style is a term used to describe the way in which a person usually writes. Short, choppy sentences or long, confusing sentences or sentences that repeat the same patterns over and over are signs of poor style. In this chapter you will learn to recognize and avoid each of these problems.

Expanding Short Sentences 22.1

A short, _simple sentence_ sometimes contains too few details to make its idea clear and interesting. Too many short sentences in a series can sound awkward and choppy. By adding details to short sentences and by combining short sentences, you can produce a flowing style that readers are likely to find appealing.

Adding Details

Short sentences often leave out modifying words and phrases that would make ideas come to life.

22.1 Expanding Short Sentences
(pp. 419–425)

OBJECTIVES
After completing this section, students should be able to

- Add details to expand short, choppy sentences.
- Combine short, choppy sentences in a variety of ways.

Improve short sentences by adding details to the subjects, verbs, or complements.

Short sentences are not errors in themselves. Using too many of them, however, can make your writing sound cold and empty, as well as choppy and awkward. Concentrate first on the main parts that are needed in most sentences: the subject, the verb, and the complement. Then add to the main parts any details that will make the idea clearer.

Short sentences below have been expanded by adding details. The additional information makes the idea more vivid.

ADDING DETAILS TO SHORT SENTENCES	
Details Added to the Subject	
A teddy bear sat on the sofa.	A *fuzzy* teddy bear *with only one ear* sat on the sofa.
Details Added to the Verb	
She hurled the javelin.	*In one arching motion,* she *gracefully* hurled the javelin.
Details Added to the Complement	
He found a silver dollar.	He found a *rare* silver dollar *hidden behind a jug.*

EXERCISE A: Adding Details to Short Sentences. Each of the following items contains a short sentence. Beneath each item are details that you can add to the subject, verb, or complement of the sentence. Rewrite each item as a single longer sentence by adding all the details provided.
Answers may vary; samples are given.

EXAMPLE:　The dog chewed a slipper.

　　　　　a. blissfully　　b. lying on the living room floor
　　　　　c. belonging to Mother

　　　　　Lying on the living room floor, the dog blissfully chewed a slipper belonging to Mother.

22.1 Expanding Short Sentences

1. Joey went to camp. b/a/c
   a. basketball   b. full of excitement
   c. with his best friend Emil

2. The sea was calm. c/a/b
   a. bright blue   b. in the still summer air
   c. except for the pencil-thin wake of a passing blue
      speedboat

3. The bishop's silver collection was returned. b/a/c
   a. by the police   b. missing
   c. early in the morning

4. Mrs. Simmons strolled through the corridors. c/b/a
   a. filled with the treasures of foreign lands
   b. of the museum   c. excited and happy

5. The sun set over the horizon a/b/c
   a. golden   b. rapidly   c. distant

6. Sam watched television. b/c/a
   a. absent-mindedly   b. while washing the dishes
   c. the new color

7. The skaters whirled across the ice. a/b/c
   a. with the grace of champions   b. Olympic
   c. from Norway

8. The tiger lunged toward the zebra. a/b/c
   a. with lightning speed   b. solitary
   c. grazing on the tundra

9. We watched the game. c/a/b
   a. football   b. on television
   c. while eating dinner in silence

10. The moonlight shone on the snow. c/b/a
    a. piled on the tree limbs   b. glistening
    c. pale ivory

EXERCISE B: Adding Your Own Details. Rewrite the sentences on the following page to make each one more informative and descriptive. Add at least two different details to each.
Answers will vary; samples are given for the first two.

students to revise the first few groups of sentences in Exercise C and then permit them to work in pairs to combine the remaining groups of sentences.

Average Students will benefit from comparing their revisions of the Developing Writing Skills passage and from discussing which possibilities are smoothest and most interesting.

Advanced Have students use each of the sentence-combining techniques from the chart at least once in revising the sentences in Exercise C. They can then compare their answers to see which seem the smoothest.

Additional Practice

Practice Pages or Practice Book, page 123

TESTING

Test Program
   Unit Pretest, page 69
   Chapter Test, page 73
   Unit Post-Test, page 75

RE-TEACHING

Practice Pages or Practice Book, page 123

THINKING SKILLS

Comprehension—*Rewriting* short sentences by adding details (Exercise A, page 420)

Application—*Producing* new sentences by combining short, choppy ones (Exercise C, page 423)

Synthesis—*Rewriting* short, choppy sentences by adding details (Exercise B, page 421)
Rewriting a passage to make the style smoother by combining choppy sentences and adding details (Developing Writing Skills, page 424)

EXAMPLE: I drank the water.

Hot and thirsty, I drank the cold water shooting out of the drinking fountain.

1. After dinner Mary quickly walked the dog around the block.
  1. Mary walked the dog.
  2. A herd of cattle grazed.
  3. The waves broke violently.
  4. A rainbow appeared.
  5. His uncle spoke on television.
  6. Flowers sprouted.
  7. Our school won every game.
  8. A submarine surfaced.
  9. The scientist made a discovery.
  10. I cut the grass.

2. A small herd of dairy cattle grazed in the open meadow.

Sentence Combining

A series of short sentences can sound choppy and awkward. One way to correct the problem is to use the ideas in some of the short sentences to make a few longer sentences.

Combine two or more short simple sentences to make a longer simple sentence, a compound sentence, a complex sentence, or a compound-complex sentence.

Two short sentences in series often develop the same idea. You can easily join such ideas into one longer sentence. The chart shows different ways of combining ideas from two or more short sentences into one more interesting sentence.

COMBINING SENTENCES FOR VARIETY
Two Simple Sentences
We spent yesterday at the beach. We got burned by the hot sun.
One Sentence Changed to a Modifying Phrase
At the beach yesterday, we got burned by the hot sun.

22.1 Expanding Short Sentences

One Sentence Changed to Make a Compound Verb
We spent yesterday at the beach and got burned by the hot sun.
Two Sentences Joined in a Compound Sentence
We spent yesterday at the beach, and we got burned by the hot sun.
Two Sentences Joined in a Complex Sentence
Because we spent the whole day at the beach yesterday, we got burned by the hot sun.
Two Sentences Joined with a Third Sentence in a Compound-Complex Sentence
Because the sun felt so good, we spent the whole day at the beach yesterday, and unfortunately we got burned.

The ideas in two short simple sentences can be combined to form a variety of new sentences. You might change the independent clause in one sentence to a modifying phrase or to a verb with an object or modifiers and then add the result to the other sentence, as in the second and third examples in the chart. Or you could use a coordinating conjunction to join the clauses in your simple sentences and produce a compound sentence, as in the fourth example. In many cases you can also use a subordinating conjunction to join the two clauses and produce a complex sentence, as in the fifth example. If you choose to expand on or change your ideas, you could write a compound-complex sentence, as in the sixth example.

EXERCISE C: Combining Short, Choppy Sentences. Read each of the following groups of short, choppy sentences and then combine two or more of the sentences in each group. In any group that contains three sentences, you may decide to leave one sentence unchanged. Use your own judgment to make each passage clear and smooth.

Answers will vary; samples are given.

EXAMPLE: Jupiter was once thought to have only ten moons. Scientists have recently discovered new moons around the planet.

Although Jupiter was once thought to have only ten moons, scientists have recently discovered new moons around the planet.

2. strictly because too   5. Because our/country, it

1. ~~The~~ show ͺclosed. ~~Many~~ of the cast members auditioned for daytime soap operas. After the/closed, many

2. The city began to enforce the law against double-parking more ͺstrictly. ~~Too~~ many drivers had been ignoring the law.

3. ~~The~~ sun rose beyond the ͺwater. ~~It~~ cast a pink glow on the lighthouse. As the/water, it

4. I enjoy seeing all the animals at the ͺzoo. ~~The~~ gorillas are my favorites. zoo, but the

5. ͺOur school's choral group is one of the finest in the ͺcoun-try. ~~It~~ requires special auditions for admission.

6. The supermarket was ͺcrowded. ~~People~~ stood in checkout lines stretching back into the aisles. so crowded that people

7. The streets of that city can be quiet and ~~calm. They can be~~ noisy and full of ͺlife. ~~It depends~~ on the time of day.

8. A burglar entered the house through the ͺwindow. ~~He~~ escaped with the jewelry. The jewelry ~~was~~ worth thousands of dollars. window and

9. Hockey is a fast-moving game. Players skate by with great ͺspeed. ~~Hockey~~ pucks can travel at eighty miles per hour.

10. Alexander was a remarkable animal. ~~He could~~ understand words and sign ͺlanguage. ~~He~~ could also invent his own games and tricks. Not only could he/language, but he

7. calm or/life, depending   9. speed, and hockey

DEVELOPING WRITING SKILLS: Expanding Short Sentences. Rewrite the following passage to make the style smoother. You will have to combine several sentences to eliminate choppiness and you should also consider adding some details. Note that you do not need to change every sentence.
Answers will vary; samples are given.

1–2. Because different/varied strengths, people   3–4. horses, which/horse, pulled   5–7. four, harnessed together, could/load, which was   8–9. horses/and

(1) ~~Different~~ breeds of horses have ~~different~~ ~~strengths.~~ (2) ~~People~~ through the years have relied on several different kinds of "horse power." (3) Draft ˄horses are the strongest breed of ~~horse.~~ (4) ~~Draft horses pulled~~ heavy burdens on the American frontier. (5) A team of ˄four could pull a twenty-ton ˄load. (6) ~~They would be harnessed together~~ (7) ~~They could do~~ the work of twenty human beings. (8) Arabians˄ are a very fast˄ breed of horse. (9) ~~Arabian horses~~ ~~are also very spirited.~~ (10) ~~They~~ can cover long ~~distances.~~ (11) ~~They~~ were used most effectively in the past for trips over hundreds of miles. (12) Tennessee Walkers, another popular breed, have a smooth but fast gait. (13) They can maintain a steady˄ running walk for hours. (14) Owners of big farms, particularly in the South, once used many of these ˄horses. (15) ~~They rode them~~ around their˄ property. (16) What if these and other kinds of horses had not existed? (17) The country's˄ growth might have been˄ slower.

very spirited   10–11. Because they/distances, they   14–15. horses for riding/extensive   17. economic/much

Simplifying Long, Confusing Sentences 22.2

The overuse of long sentences can weaken your style just as much as the overuse of short sentences can. Too many ideas strung together can produce an awkward, rambling style. This section shows several basic ways to shorten sentences while maintaining a lively, interesting style.

Shortening Long Compound Sentences

A *compound sentence* contains at least two independent clauses. Too many independent clauses in a compound sentence can sound long-winded.

Recognize compound sentences that ramble, and separate them into two or more shorter sentences.

22.2 Simplifying Long, Confusing Sentences
(pp. 425–429)

OBJECTIVES

After completing this section, students should be able to

- Separate rambling compound sentences into shorter sentences.
- Separate complicated complex sentences into shorter sentences.

TEACHING

Getting Started

Introduce the concept of shortening long compound sentences by writing the following sentence on the board and having students separate it into two or more shorter sentences.

The singers received great praise from all the critics for every performance this week, and on closing night the audience, a group of senior citizens, rose to its feet and gave a standing ovation, and they refused to let the singers leave without an encore.

Ask students to tell you how many independent clauses the sentence contains (three). Help them pick out each such clause. Elicit that the sentence as it stands is long, rambling, and confusing. Work with the class to rewrite the sentence by breaking it into two shorter, but clearer, sentences. The rewritten sentence should look something like this:

The singers received great praise from all the critics for every performance this week. On closing night, the audience, a group of senior citizens, rose to its feet, gave a standing ovation, and refused to leave without an encore.

If time permits, use rambling sentences taken from student writing, put them on the board, and follow the same procedure as above.

Text Follow Through

Discuss text pages 425–429.

Assign Exercise A, page 426; Exercise B, page 428; and Developing Writing Skills, page 429.

When you find a sentence that contains too many independent clauses strung together one after another, look for places where you can end one sentence and begin a new one. In the following example, notice that the sentence is difficult to understand because so many ideas are contained in its three independent clauses. The revised version groups the ideas into two sentences that a reader can absorb comfortably.

RAMBLING COMPOUND SENTENCE: We receive presents from Aunt Amy every year, and this year my gift, a sweater, was a perfect fit, but Leo's gift, a brown leather belt, was too large.

REVISED: We receive presents from Aunt Amy every year. This year my gift, a sweater, was a perfect fit, but Leo's gift, a brown leather belt, was too large.

EXERCISE A: Shortening Compound Sentences. Each of the following compound sentences rambles because it contains too many independent clauses. Rewrite each sentence by breaking it up into shorter sentences.

Answers will vary; samples are given.

EXAMPLE: The batter slugged a line drive to left field and easily made it to first base, and then the ball was thrown to the infield, and he slid into second head first, and the shortstop missed the tag, so the runner was safe with a double.

The batter slugged a line drive to left field and easily made it to first base. Then the ball was thrown to the infield, and he slid into second, head first. The shortstop missed the tag, so the runner was safe with a double.

1. The myths of ancient Greece have inspired writers for ~~cen-~~ ~~turies, and~~ writers have studied the personalities of many Greek characters, and they have followed many of the plots of classical Greek stories. centuries. These

2. A dog can be both an ally and a burden to its ~~master, and~~

22.2 Simplifying Long, Confusing Sentences

2. master. It   4. horizon. Instead

~~it~~ can often be a source of protection and love, but it can also be both an expense and a continuous responsibility.

3. To wire the driftwood as a lamp, you must drill a hole through ~~it, and then~~ you must mount it on a ~~stand, and next~~ you must pull electrical wire through the wood and attach a light socket to the top.   it.Then/stand. Next

4. We had been driving only four hours in Alaska, and already the Cassier Mountains had stopped looking like bumps on the ~~horizon, but instead~~ they began to look like a giant tidal wave of snow, and they seemed to grow steadily in height.

5. Break up six or seven slices of bread into small pieces, and place the pieces in a mixing ~~bowl, and then~~ add two eggs and a quarter cup of milk, and beat the ~~mixture, and finally~~ add a cup of raisins, and salt the entire ~~concoction, and~~ ~~you~~ will then have stuffing for your chicken.

5. bowl. Then/mixture. Finally/concoction. You

Shortening Long Complex Sentences

A *complex sentence* contains one independent clause and two or more dependent clauses. A sentence with too many dependent clauses can become overly complicated.

Recognize complex sentences that are too complicated, and separate them into shorter sentences.

In the following example of a long complex sentence, there are three dependent clauses. Notice in the revised version that the ideas are presented in two separate sentences. Notice also that some of the words have been changed and that the ideas are in a slightly different order. The new sentences express the ideas in a clearer, more logical way.

COMPLICATED
COMPLEX
SENTENCE: Because our washing machine was broken, we took our clothes to the laundromat, which was so crowded, however, that we decided to return home and wash our things by hand.

Less advanced   These students will probably need help in revising the sentences in the exercises and Developing Writing Skills. Work with them as a group on the revisions. In Exercise B, have students identify the most important ideas in each sentence. Then help them structure these ideas into main clauses while placing the relevant supporting information in subordinate clauses.

Average   These students may benefit from working in pairs to revise the exercise sentences.

Advanced   Have students revise sentences from their own work or with unattributed sentences taken from past students' papers.

Additional Practice

Practice Pages or Practice Book, page 124

TESTING

Test Program

Unit Pretest, page 69
Chapter Test, page 73
Unit Post-Test, page 75

RE-TEACHING

Practice Pages or Practice Book, page 124

THINKING SKILLS

Application—*Changing* rambling compound sentences into shorter sentences (Exercise A, page 426)
Changing overly complicated complex sentences into shorter sentences. (Exercise B, page 428)

428

Synthesis—*Rewriting* a passage
to shorten long sentences
(Developing Writing Skills,
page 429)

REVISED: We took our clothes to the laundromat because our washing machine was broken. The laundromat was so crowded, however, that we decided to return home and wash our things by hand.

When you see that too many dependent clauses cause confusion in a sentence, look for different ways to group the ideas into shorter sentences. Try to group together the ideas that are mostly closely related to each other. You may also want to change the order of ideas and add or eliminate some of the words. Your goal should be to clarify the logical relationships among your ideas and to create a pleasant, flowing style.

EXERCISE B: Shortening Complicated Complex Sentences. The complex sentences below are overly complicated. Break each up into shorter sentences by changing the order of ideas and adding or eliminating words as you see fit.

Answers will vary; samples are given.

EXAMPLE: New York is a fast-paced city that can never bore the people who visit it because it contains fascinating museums and historical sights, which tourists can explore, as well as many restaurants, concerts, and plays, which they can enjoy.

New York is a fast-paced city that can never bore the people who visit it. It contains fascinating museums and historical sights, which tourists can explore, as well as many restaurants, concerts, and plays, which they can enjoy.

2. entertainment. As/is left

1. Although Joe had not been fishing in a number of years, he surprised himself by catching a very large ~~swordfish, which, when~~ it was measured, set a local record, which was mentioned in the newspapers. swordfish. When/the fish's size

2. Some of today's television stars seem to worry more about contracts than they do about providing ~~entertainment, which, as~~ a result, ~~leaves~~ the audience wondering which star will disappear next from their favorite shows.

22.2 Simplifying Long, Confusing Sentences

3. My last trip to Africa included my first safari, which was very ~~exciting and which~~ began at sunrise and lasted until the late afternoon when we all sat together and recounted the adventures that we had enjoyed in the bush country.

4. ~~When we~~ heard that school would end early because the storm that was headed our way was closing in sooner than forecasters had ~~thought,~~ we were not very worried until the principal spoke over the public address system to warn us about flooding and electrical power lines that had fallen.

5. Although Liz was a newcomer to Newton, she soon felt at ~~home because~~ neighbors in her apartment building showed her the town, which she found charming, and introduced her to several people, whom she immediately liked. home. The

3. exciting. It   4. We/thought. However,

DEVELOPING WRITING SKILLS: Simplifying Long, Confusing Sentences. Improve the sentence style of the following passage by breaking up each of the five sentences.
Answers will vary; samples are given.

(1) Because accidents are rare, traveling by air is very ~~safe, and, in~~ fact, it is statistically safer than driving a car or taking a shower. (2) In particular, modern equipment enables planes virtually to fly themselves with little assistance from the ~~pilots, who~~ are nevertheless vital to ~~navigation, and who~~ are particularly needed during turbulent weather and for take-offs and landings, when they must guide the aircraft. (3) Pilots and airplanes benefit from the work done by navigation control personnel on the ~~ground, and they depend greatly on these~~ people ~~who~~ monitor airplanes in flight and plan safe routes for planes.

(4) In contrast, the highways are peopled by drivers who act entirely as ~~individuals, and no~~ central control offers them ~~guidance, and instead~~ drivers must guess the next movements of others on the road, a factor that pilots do not usually have to consider. (5) In short, then, it is not surprising that airlines enjoy such an excellent safety ~~record, and people~~ should not be nervous about flying once they realize how much equipment and attention guide the flight of every single craft in the sky.

1. safe. In   2. pilots. However, pilots/navigation. They   3. ground. These
4. individuals. No/guidance. Instead,   5. record. People   **429**

Have students practice varying the length of their sentences by completing the following assignment.

Writing Across the Curriculum

When people are planning trips to foreign countries, it is often helpful for them to learn about the culture and daily lives of the people who live in the places they will be visiting.

Prewriting Imagine that you know someone from a foreign country who is planning to visit the United States. Brainstorm to list facts about the culture and people of the United States that this person might want to know before embarking on his or her journey. Then review your brainstorming notes and underline the most significant ideas and details.

Writing Write a letter to the person, offering information about the culture and people of the United States and suggesting some activities the visitor should include in his or her plans. For example, you might point out that many Americans have a strong interest in baseball and suggest that they attend a baseball game during their visit. Keep your audience in mind as you write, and use an informal, conversational writing style.

Revising Make sure that you have presented your information in a clear, well-organized manner. Also make sure that you have varied the length of your sentences. When you finish revising, proofread your letter and prepare a final draft.

22.3 Using a Variety of Sentences

(pp. 430–435)

OBJECTIVES

After completing this section, students should be able to

- Use a variety of sentence openers in their written work.
- Use a variety of sentence structures in their written work.

TEACHING

Getting Started

Introduce the concept of varying sentence openings by writing the following passage on the board:

Lucy and Mark discovered the space ship while skating on the lake. They spotted a silvery object under a thick grove of trees. They were completely mystified when they first came upon the strange object.

Elicit that the passage is somewhat monotonous because the second and third sentences begin in the same way. Work with the class to replace the subject-first openings of these two sentences with different openers. For the second sentence, the subject-first opening might instead use a prepositional phrase. The sentence would look like this: *Under a thick grove of trees they spotted a silvery object.* The third sentence might have *its* opening changed by moving the clause at the end to the begin-

22.3 Using a Variety of Sentences

Too many sentences that begin in the same way can add up to a dull style. A long series of sentences with similar structures can also be monotonous. To achieve a smooth style, try to vary the beginnings and the structures of your sentences.

Using Different Sentence Openers

One way to avoid monotony in your writing is to avoid using the same kind of sentence opener over and over. If too many of your sentences begin with the most popular sentence opener, a subject, they will soon have a repetitious sound.

Begin your sentences with different openers: subjects, single-word modifiers, phrases, and clauses.

Many of your sentences should begin with subjects because the subject is often the most logical sentence opener. You should, however, avoid the monotony caused by beginning too many sentences with subjects.

SENTENCE OPENERS
Subjects
The *movie* held our interest for only the first hour.
It had been given too much publicity.
One-Word Modifiers
Happy, the child blew bubbles in his milk.
Gently, his mother wiped his face.
Phrases
With great reverence the crowd knelt for the blessing.
Raising his arm, the holy man addressed the crowd.
To record the event, photographers took many pictures.

22.3 Using a Variety of Sentences

Clauses

Because she was pleased with her reception, the violinist played several encores.
When she finished, the crowd clapped for ten minutes.

As you can see, many different kinds of words can replace a subject at the beginning of a sentence. You can use an adjective such as *happy* or an adverb such as *gently*. You can use a prepositional phrase such as *with great reverence*, a participial phrase such as *raising his arm*, or an infinitive phrase such as *to record the event*. Or you can use an adverb clause.

Varying your sentence openers can enliven the style of a whole passage. Look at the two passages in the following chart. The passage on the left sounds monotonous because every sentence begins with a subject. In the passage on the right, the sentence openers are varied, producing a smoother, more interesting style.

Same Sentence Openers	Varied Sentence Openers
Jan and Ed made a valuable discovery during their visit to the attic. They saw an old, rusted chest behind some boxes and old furniture. They had no idea what they would find when they first opened the old chest. They looked excitedly through the crumbling documents and yellowed photographs it contained. They then found beneath the tattered debris an old family Bible showing the birth and death dates of their ancestors.	Jan and Ed made a valuable discovery during their visit to the attic. Behind some boxes and old furniture, they saw an old, rusted chest. When they first opened the chest, they had no idea what they would find. Excitedly, they looked through the crumbling documents and yellowed photographs it contained. Then, beneath the tattered debris, they found an old family Bible showing the birth and death dates of their ancestors.

ning of the sentence. The result would look like this: *When they first came upon the strange object, they were completely mystified.* Have a student read the entire revised passage aloud to give the class a sense of the improved style that results from using a variety of sentence openings. If time and the makeup of the class permit, give examples of sentence-opening variety via the use of phrases and one-word modifiers.

Text Follow Through

Discuss text pages 430–435.

Assign Exercise A, page 432; Exercise B, page 432; Exercise C, page 433; Exercise D, page 434; and Developing Writing Skills, page 435.

Less advanced Supplying additional examples for the chart on pages 430–431 can help these students become more familiar with the varied sentence openers they can use in their writing. Some students may require supervision in completing the exercises in this section.

Average After students have completed the revision called for in the second part of Developing Writing Skills, discuss the need for proofreading as well as for revising. Instruct them to check their work for problems in both mechanics and spelling and to make corrections.

Advanced Ask students to select a passage from their literature text or from a book they are reading outside of class. They should then make a list of the various types of sentence openers (mentioned in the chart on pages 430–431) that are used in the passage. They might also label each sentence in the passage as *simple, compound, complex,* or *compound-complex.*

Additional Practice

Practice Pages or Practice Book, page 125

TESTING

Test Program

Unit Pretest, page 69
Chapter Test, pages 73, 74
Unit Post-Test, page 75

RE-TEACHING

Practice Pages or Practice Book, page 125

THINKING SKILLS

Application—*Modifying* sentences by using a variety of openings (Exercise A, page 432)

Modifying sentences in a passage to achieve variety in sentence openings (Exercise B, page 432)

Modifying a passage by using a variety of sentence types (Exercise D, page 434)

Synthesis—*Writing* original sentences using a variety of sentence openers (Exercise C, page 433)

Writing original sentences using a variety of sentence openers and sentence types (Developing Writing Skills, page 435)

Note that the second sentence on the right moves a phrase from the end of the sentence to the beginning. The third sentence shifts a dependent clause from the end to the beginning, and the fourth and fifth sentences open with modifiers, making the paragraph as a whole flow more smoothly.

EXERCISE A: Using Different Sentence Openers. Each of the following sentences can be rewritten with a different opener. Look for a modifier, phrase, or clause that can be placed at the beginning of the sentence.

Answers will vary; samples are given.

EXAMPLE: The robins used twigs, string, and newspaper to build their nest.

To build their nest, the robins used twigs, string, and newspaper.

1. When the bay became calm, we   2. Usually, we can   3. High above the

1. We ventured out in the boat when the bay became calm.
2. We can usually count on Maxwell's help in the evenings.
3. The planes soared in formation high above the clouds.
4. One must practice diligently to become proficient on a musical instrument. To become proficient on a musical instrument, one
5. The board of trustees made painful cuts in services and personnel, although they avoided bankruptcy.
6. The audience stood from the band's first note to its last.
7. The sound of the collision naturally brought people running from their homes. Naturally, the
8. I met with Dr. Chung at exactly 2:30 p.m. At exactly 2:30 p.m.,
9. Mr. McCauley played basketball while holding one hand behind his back. While holding one hand behind his back,
10. The convoy lost twenty minutes waiting for a slow-moving freight train to pass. Waiting for a slow-moving freight train to pass, the

clouds, the   5. Although they saved the company from bankruptcy, the   6. From the band's first note to its last, the

EXERCISE B: Revising Sentence Openers. The passage contains a series of sentences that all begin the same way. Find different openers for *most* of the sentences. Then rewrite the passage to produce a smoother, more interesting style.

22.3 Using a Variety of Sentences

2. Instantly, all   3. They they   4. As the knock sounded again and again, no

(1) A sharp knock at the door startled everyone in the room. (2) All heads instantly turned toward the door. (3) They then looked upward to the room where General Washington slept. (4) No one spoke as the knock sounded again and again. (5) Margaret rose at last and walked unsteadily toward the door to face the enemy. (6) A captain of the British Army stood motionless, his face hidden in the darkness of the night, when the door swung open. (7) A small cluster of redcoats stood behind him. (8) The captain strode past Margaret without a word and swept into the room. (9) Four other soldiers followed him. (10) They began to search the house at their officer's command.

5. At last   6. When the door swung open, a   8. Without a word the   10. At their officer's command, they

EXERCISE C: Varying Sentence Openers as You Write.
Write five to seven original sentences to complete the story begun in Exercise B. As you write, vary the types of sentence openers you use.
Answers will vary.

Using Different Sentence Structures

A group of sentences that all have the same structure can sound just as monotonous as a group of sentences that all have the same beginning.

Use a variety of sentence structures—simple, compound, complex, and possibly compound-complex—in your writing.

If your writing relies too heavily on *one* kind of sentence, a passage will sound awkward. Too many simple sentences in a series will sound choppy even if some of them are relatively long simple sentences. Too many compound sentences in a series will produce a rambling pattern, and too many complex sentences will sound awkward and difficult. You should try to mix all three kinds of sentences in a passage and, when appropriate, use compound-complex sentences as well.

Look at the following passage. It sounds choppy because all the sentences are simple.

Monotonous passage with all simple sentences

(1) The stage crew for this winter's annual variety show must be commended for a perfect job. (2) Jenny O'Reilly worked the sound effects equipment. (3) Lester Barrio operated the stage lights. (4) Phil Bernstein handled the props and curtains. (5) Supervising this efficient crew of hard workers was Cindy Adamson, the stage manager. (6) At the end of the evening, the entire show received overwhelming approval from the audience. (7) Unquestionably, the stage crew deserves much of the credit for this success.

Now look at the revision. It combines and alters some of these sentences to create several different kinds of sentences. As a result the passage reads more smoothly.

(1) Simple

(2) Compound-Complex

(3) Simple

(4) Compound

(1) The stage crew for this winter's annual variety show must be commended for a perfect job. (2) Jenny O'Reilly worked the sound effects equipment, and Phil Bernstein handled props and curtains, while Lester Barrio operated the stage lights. (3) Supervising this efficient crew of hard workers was Cindy Adamson, the stage manager. (4) At the end of the evening, the entire show received overwhelming approval from the audience, and the stage crew unquestionably deserves much of the credit for this success.

EXERCISE D: Using a Variety of Sentences. The following passage repeatedly uses the same kind of sentence. Rewrite the passage to create a variety of sentences. You may shorten, separate, and combine sentences as you see fit.

Answers will vary; samples are given.

(1) I was glad to arrive home after the long trip was over. (2) However, when I got there, I found the house un-

3. Frightened, 4. Becoming

22.3 Using a Variety of Sentences

locked. (3) ~~When~~ I walked in, ~~I became frightened.~~ (4) ~~As I be-~~ ~~came~~ more and more nervous, I searched the house for signs of a burglary. (5) ~~After I searched and found~~ nothing unusual, I decided to call the police. (6) ~~Although~~ they discovered nothing suspicious, I remained perplexed. (7) After a few days ~~had~~ ~~passed,~~ I finally figured out the mystery. (8) I had simply left the door unlocked when I had left for my trip originally. (9) ~~Because I was relieved,~~ I sank into a chair and sat there numbly for several minutes. (10) After ~~I had thoroughly~~ ~~analyzed~~ the situation, I vowed never to be so careless again.

5. After searching and finding   6. However,/and   9. Relieved,   10. thoroughly analyzing

DEVELOPING WRITING SKILLS: Varying Your Sentences.

Practice writing sentences with different beginnings and a variety of structures by using *one* of the following sets of directions.

Answers will vary.

1. Write a passage of at least seven sentences on any topic that you wish. Make sure it contains different sentence beginnings and varied sentence structures.

2. Take a short composition that you have recently written. Identify the sentence openers and kinds of sentences that you have used. Then make any changes needed to achieve a variety of beginnings and structures.

436

Checking Your Skills

In the Checking Your Skills assignment, your students revised a paragraph to improve sentence variety. To help your students to further understand the importance of sentence variety, have them complete the following activity.

Critical Thinking

Have each of your students choose a short story or essay by a distinguished writer. If your students need guidance in choosing a literary work, you might have them select a work from the following list of selections from *Prentice Hall Literature, Silver:* "The Rule of Names," by Ursula K. Le Guin, page 63; "The Land and the Water" by Shirley Ann Grau, page 119; an excerpt from *I Know Why the Caged Bird Sings* by Maya Angelou, page 403; and an excerpt from *Of Men and Mountains* by William O. Douglas, page 421. Students should then read through the selection they have chosen and choose three substantial paragraphs in which the writer has used a variety of different sentence lengths and structures. Finally, students should write a brief explanation of how the sentence variety contributes to the effectiveness of each paragraph.

Using Composition Skills

Publishing You might want to have student volunteers arrange the paragraphs into a class anthology. In preparing the anthology, the volunteers should also think of a title for the anthology and find photographs or prepare illustrations to accompany the paragraphs.

Skills Review and Writing Workshop

Improving Your Sentences

CHECKING YOUR SKILLS

Rewrite the following paragraph to eliminate the choppiness and increase sentence variety.
Answers will vary.

(1) Gretchen speaks four languages. (2) She speaks French, German, English, and Spanish. (3) She spoke French and German from childhood. (4) She spent her childhood in Germany. (5) Her mother was German. (6) Her father was French. (7) The family moved to this country. (8) Gretchen was seven years old. (9) She spent time with English-speaking children. (10) They were in the neighborhood. (11) Gretchen quickly learned English. (12) She enrolled in junior high. (13) Foreign languages are taught here. (14) Gretchen chose to study Spanish. (15) She learned Spanish easily.

USING COMPOSITION SKILLS
Describing a Sports Event

Sports writers carefully avoid rambling sentences linked by *and* and *then*. They use action verbs and a variety of sentence beginnings. Follow the steps below to write a paragraph describing a sports event.
Answers will vary.

Prewriting: Choose a sports event you recently witnessed or participated in. Write a chronological list of the action.

Writing: Describe the action in chronological order. Combine items from your list in a variety of ways. Use specific action verbs and a variety of sentence lengths and beginnings.

Revising: Examine your writing sentence by sentence. Be sure you have some short and some long sentences and a variety of sentence openers. After you have revised, proofread carefully.

UNIT V

Composition
Forms and Process of Writing

UNIT V
Composition—Forms and Process of Writing

(pp. 437–622)

This unit also focuses on different forms that written communication can take and the steps in the writing process that are needed to create them. Chapter 23 considers the form of paragraphs and ways of organizing them. Chapter 24 discusses the steps in writing effective paragraphs. Chapter 25 deals with three kinds of writing: expository, persuasive, and descriptive. Chapter 26 deals with the form of essays and the prewriting, writing, and revising of them. Chapter 27 considers the form and prewriting, writing, and revising of reports. Chapter 28 deals with the form and prewriting, writing, and revising of book reports. Chapter 29 discusses the forms and creation of journals and autobiographies. Chapter 30 covers the prewriting, writing, and revising of a character sketch and a short short story. Chapter 31 covers the forms of friendly letters, social notes, and business letters. Chapter 32 focuses on taking essay exams successfully.

Chapter 23

Looking at Paragraphs

The three sections of this chapter will help students analyze paragraphs. Section 23.1 presents topic sentences, Section 23.2 discusses supporting information, and Section 23.3 explains unity and coherence. The entire chapter provides a firm foundation for the actual writing of paragraphs, which students will undertake in Chapters 24 and 25.

For additional or alternate writing assignments and a list of topics for writing, see pages 459–461.

Paragraphs are easy to recognize because the first line of a paragraph will generally be indented. You will also find that one sentence usually states the main idea of the whole paragraph. Other sentences follow in logical order to develop the main idea by adding information about it.

Recognizing Topic Sentences

All of the sentences in a paragraph work together to present one main idea. However, one sentence usually tells what the whole paragraph is about.

The Topic Sentence in a Paragraph

Look for the *topic sentence* in a paragraph.

The topic sentence of a paragraph presents the main idea, which all the other ideas in the paragraph support or explain.

23.1 Recognizing Topic Sentences
(pp. 439–442)

OBJECTIVE
After completing this section, students should be able to

• Identify topic sentences in paragraphs.

TEACHING

Getting Started

Tell students that the topic sentence of a paragraph presents the main idea of a paragraph and that it may appear anywhere in the paragraph. Present several paragraphs to students, either by using an overhead projector or by duplicating the paragraphs. Have volunteers identify the topic sentence in each.

Text Follow Through

Discuss text pages 439–442.

Assign the Exercise, page 441, and Developing Writing Skills, page 442.

Less advanced The material in this section should be accessible to all students. You may want to go over the sample paragraphs with these students to be sure they understand why each italicized sentence is a topic sentence. You may want to work through the first two items of Developing Writing Skills with them to be sure they remember appropriate limiting techniques before they create topic sentences.

Average To provide an additional identification exercise, you might ask students to bring to class one of their textbooks from another class. A social studies or science text might be the best choice. They can then choose a chapter or part of a chapter and locate the topic sentence in each paragraph. If a paragraph lacks a topic sentence, students can supply one, as suggested in Developing Writing Skills. Before students complete Developing Writing Skills,

You will usually find the topic sentence at the beginning of a paragraph. In this position the topic sentence provides the reader with an immediate understanding of the paragraph's main idea. The rest of the paragraph will then support or develop this main idea. The following paragraph by a student begins with the main idea, followed by supporting information.

TOPIC
SENTENCE
Supporting
information

The Nile River served as a basis for ancient Egyptian society. It provided the Egyptians with many important resources. One was papyrus, a reed that grew around the banks of the river. It was used to make many things including shoes, mats, ropes, boxes, small boats, and the first form of paper. The Nile also supplied food for the Egyptians. They caught fish in the river. The birds and animals attracted by the water were also a source of food for Egypt's people. Another important purpose the Nile served was transportation. The Egyptians traveled up and down the river for pleasure and for trade. Most important, the Nile provided silt, the fertile mud that overflowed the banks, and water, both of which were crucial for survival. The river gave the Egyptians good farming land and the only water source in the middle of the surrounding desert. Without these resources, ancient Egyptian civilization might never have existed.—Laura Harris

Sometimes a paragraph may offer a few introductory ideas before presenting the main idea. In this case the topic sentence will be found near the middle of the paragraph. The first two sentences in the following paragraph lead up to the topic sentence. Note how the information after the topic sentence answers the question raised by the topic sentence.

TOPIC
SENTENCE

The bird next to me was immature. He still had brown and tawny plumage instead of the predominantly black color of the adult. *But why was he so unafraid?* For one thing, he may never have seen another

23.1 Recognizing Topic Sentences

Supporting information human being. But there is a better explanation: In the remote Galapagos Islands, 600 miles west of Ecuador, there are hardly any land mammals, and the hawk is very nearly the sole predator. With no enemies and almost no competitors, it has nothing to fear and plenty to eat.—Tui de Roy Moore

There is a third possible position for a topic sentence—at the end of a paragraph. When the topic sentence comes at the end of a paragraph, it will generally draw a conclusion or act as a summary. In the following paragraph, the topic sentence follows a series of descriptive details and summarizes them.

Supporting information Dark clouds blocked the sun as it peeked over the farthest mountain. The clouds moved forward and played hide-and-seek with beams of sunlight and slowly overtook them. The clouds began to release large drops of rain. With the clouds a wind made its

TOPIC SENTENCE entrance, and it swirled across the hillsides. *A storm was brewing.*

EXERCISE: Identifying Topic Sentences. Read each of the following paragraphs carefully. Then write the topic sentence of each on your paper. Note that one of the paragraphs has a topic sentence at the beginning, one has a topic sentence in the middle, and one has a topic sentence at the end.

(1) Rynek Glowny is almost as lively at night as during the day. From a window seat in a restaurant on the corner of the square, we could see street musicians strolling about as young boys kicked a soccer ball and couples strolled arm in arm. Every few minutes, a horse-drawn cab would roll by, often with a pretty girl and her date inside. After dinner, we strolled around, delighting in the contrast of old ladies sweeping out dark doorways as the sounds of modern jazz poured into the street from the Klub Pod Jaszczurami.—David Alpern

review with them the concept of narrowing topics. Remind them that a topic sentence must not promise more or less than it can deliver. Once they have thought of a topic sentence, they should mentally list items of support that they could use. If fewer than four come to mind, the topic may be too narrow.

Advanced Students might want to find examples of topic sentences located in different parts of paragraphs in magazine or newspaper articles. Have students bring their examples to class to share with classmates, who can then locate the topic sentences.

Additional Practice

Practice Pages or Practice Book, page 126

TESTING

Test Program

Unit Pretest, page 76
Chapter Test, page 82
Unit Post-Test, page 96

RE-TEACHING

Practice Pages or Practice Book, page 126

THINKING SKILLS

Knowledge—*Identifying* topic sentences (Exercise, page 441)

Synthesis—*Writing* topic sentences (Developing Writing Skills, page 442)

(2) The Virginia Preparatory School lies just off the Shirley Highway between Washington, D.C., and Richmond. It is a small Southern school with dull-red brick dormitories and classroom buildings, quiet old school buildings with quiet old Southern names—Page House, Stuart Hall, Randolph Hall, Breckinridge, Pinckney, and Coulter. The high brick wall that surrounds the school is known as the Breastworks, and the shallow pond behind the football field is the Crater. <u>V.P.S. is an old school, with an old school's tradition.</u>—C.D.B. Bryan

(3) A gleaming silver swan perches majestically on the hood of an old car. Unscarred by the years, the car's body still has its original shiny red coat of paint. Even the trim on the black tires shines a glossy white. <u>Considered by many car fans as a work of art, this 1952 Packard remains in good condition because it is rarely driven.</u> Most of the time the car remains sheltered from heavy snows and winter ice, stored in a garage. Only during the summer months does its owner bring the car into the driveway where sunshine gleams from the finlike fenders and polished chrome. And then the 1950's live again.—Lynn Green

DEVELOPING WRITING SKILLS: Writing Topic Sentences. Write five topic sentences expressing a main idea for a paragraph on each of the following topics. If you wish, you may develop five topics of your own.
Answers will vary.
EXAMPLE: North Carolina has many vacation areas that vary in climate and scenery.

1. sports arenas   3. the art of rug weaving   5. space travel
2. craft show   4. a special collection

23.2 Recognizing Supporting Information

A topic sentence may be supported by many different kinds of information. A paragraph about the items for sale in a cer-

OBJECTIVES

After completing this section, students should be able to

- Identify examples, details, and facts used as supporting information in a paragraph.
- Identify reasons and incidents used as supporting information in a paragraph.

23.2 Recognizing Supporting Information

tain store might offer four or five examples of these items or it might instead give details describing just a few of the most notable items. Some paragraphs will focus mainly on one kind of supporting information; others will offer several different kinds. Every good paragraph, however, must include specific information that thoroughly develops the main idea.

Learning more about the different kinds of supporting information that can be used to develop a main idea will help you write your own paragraphs.

Examples, Details, and Facts

Examples, details, and *facts* are all useful in helping a reader understand the main idea of a paragraph.

Paragraphs may be developed with examples, details, and facts.

Examples show specific instances of some general idea. A paragraph about the dangers of lightning might give three or four examples of the destruction lightning can cause: knocking out the electricity in a town, starting a fire in a building, or causing a forest fire.

Details are pieces of descriptive information. A paragraph that describes a sunset might give details about color, the shapes of the clouds, and the changes that take place in the sky.

Facts are specific pieces of information that can be shown to be true. A paragraph about the results of an election might include such facts as the number of votes for each candidate and the percentage of people who voted.

The following paragraph about Nepal uses all three kinds of support. It contains examples of Nepal's varied geography, details about its animal and plant life, and facts about its location, size, and animals.

TOPIC
SENTENCE

Nepal has one of the world's most remarkable environments. Just half the size of Italy, the country is tucked between the vast plains of northern India and

443

TEACHING

Getting Started

Tell students that paragraphs may be developed with examples, details, and facts. Provide examples showing this kind of paragraph development either by using an overhead projector or by duplicating the paragraphs. Have volunteers identify the main idea of each paragraph and then the supporting information.

Text Follow Through

Discuss text pages 442–447.

Assign Exercise A, page 444; Exercise B, page 446; and Developing Writing Skills, page 447.

Less advanced With these students, you may want to omit the labeling requirement in Exercise A and have them concentrate instead on the need for adequate, specific support.

Average Students may enjoy thinking up paragraph topics and then listing kinds of support, including combinations of different kinds, that could be used for each.

Advanced After students complete Developing Writing Skills, they can be asked to compare the details about your school that they have listed. They might also develop subgroups of details and think of a topic sentence that each subgroup could be used to support. The following are possible subgroups students might consider:

1. Exterior details
2. Setting
3. Courses
4. Athletics
5. Extracurricular activities
6. Student attitudes

Additional Practice

Practice Pages or Practice Book, page 127

TESTING

Test Program

   Unit Pretest, page 76
   Chapter Test, page 82
   Unit Post-Test, page 96

RE-TEACHING

Practice Pages or Practice Book, page 127

THINKING SKILLS

Knowledge—*Identifying* examples, details, and facts used to develop paragraphs (Exercise A, page 444) *Identifying* reasons and incidents used to develop paragraphs (Exercise B, page 446)

Synthesis—*Identifying* types of support and *compiling* support (Developing Writing Skills, page 447)

Supporting information: Examples, details, and facts

rugged, isolated Tibet. But Nepal consists of far more than mountains. In addition to alpine slopes that nourish Norway pines and "edelweiss," it has tropical forests with banyan trees, banana palms, and lush ferns. Within its boundaries are more than 800 species of birds, including the jungle fowl and the Impeyan pheasant, the national bird, which makes its home 12,000 feet above sea level. There are mugger and gharial crocodiles in the low-lying rivers, while the mysterious snow leopard prowls the remote mountain heights and is rarely seen by humans.
—Adapted from Denis D. Gray

EXERCISE A: Recognizing Examples, Details, and Facts. Read the following paragraphs. On your paper make a list of the supporting information in each paragraph. Then indicate whether the supporting information is made up mainly of (a) different examples that all contribute to the main idea, (b) descriptive details that help the reader "see" the point made in the main idea, or (c) specific facts that back up the main idea. Note that the topic sentence in each paragraph is underlined.

Lists of support may vary within reason; basic types of support are given.

(1) Along Greenland's west coast about 100 glaciers reach the sea. <u>Of those, about twenty are the main iceberg makers</u>. Some of the bergs are mammoth. They may be several city blocks long and occasionally a mile or more long. Once a berg several miles long was sighted, but it was exceptionally large. Many tower 200 to 300 feet above the water. Some over 500 feet! Greenland sends out 10,000 to 15,000 good-sized bergs each year and uncountable numbers of smaller ones. The largest are calved from the glaciers along Melville Bay and from Humboldt Glacier farther north in the northwestern part of the island.
—Gwen Schultz facts

(2) <u>The little Pachaug River in southeastern Connecticut is typical of the placid streams near the seacoast that provide a glimpse of marsh life</u>. Near sea level, the Pachaug meanders

through a fairly high-and-dry marsh that can be explored on foot. The marshland is interrupted and bordered by a forest of red oak, pine, and graceful hemlock. Shuttle transportation is unnecessary since the current is so slow that you can paddle effortlessly in either direction. It's a short river, but the miles add up along its twisted path. Near Voluntown, a good day can be spent between Beach Pond and downstream Beachdale and Pachaug Ponds. Lazy bass nibble among the acres of water lilies and ripple away at your approach, while the air is filled with songbird calls.—Jack Waller details

(3) <u>An airport flight departure announcement meant diverse things to those who heard it</u>. To some, it was a routine summons, a prefix to another tedious, work-oriented journey which—had free choice been theirs—they would not have made. For others, a flight announcement spelled a beginning of adventure; for others still, the nearing of an end—the journey home. For some it entailed sadness and parting; for others, in counterpoint, the prospect of reunion and joy. Some who heard flight announcements heard them always for other people. Their friends or relatives were travelers; as to themselves, the names of destinations were wistful not-quite-glimpses of far-away places they would never see.—Arthur Hailey examples

Reasons and Incidents

Other kinds of supporting information can also be used to make a main idea clear.

Paragraphs may be developed with reasons and incidents.

Reasons can be used to answer any questions raised by the main idea. If the topic sentence presents an opinion, reasons can help to defend that opinion. Note how the paragraph on the following page presents and supports an opinion about guitars.

TOPIC SENTENCE	*The guitar leads all fretted instruments in popularity.* It is amazingly versatile. You can play single bass
Supporting information: Reasons	notes, chords, and single melody notes. It's traditional for singing cowboy, hillbilly, and folk songs. It's intimate. "You hold it close and feel its heart beat," says Burl Ives. Its harmony sounds good with a number of instruments, notably the recorder. Its incisive rhythm fits into a dance band.—Adapted from Doron K. Antrim

An *incident* is a brief story or set of events offered to illustrate a main idea. It helps to explain the idea in the topic sentence. The following paragraph is developed by an incident.

TOPIC SENTENCE	*I remember Arthur Rubinstein's return to Poland after World War II....* People stood in line for tickets all night long, and those who did not succeed used
Supporting information: Incident	bribes and every means ingenuity could devise to get in. As a result, the hall was so closely packed that several people fainted and had to be carried out. When the announced program came to an end, the audience simply refused to let Rubinstein go; they shouted titles of pieces they wanted him to play, and the pianist, obviously moved, obliged. Then, when it finally became clear that he wouldn't go on any longer, the audience spontaneously broke into song. "Sto lat, sto lat . . ." they shouted, which means "May he live a hundred years" and is sung on celebratory or joyful occasions.—Eva Hoffman

EXERCISE B: Recognizing Reasons and Incidents. Read the following paragraphs. Either list the reasons used in the paragraph or briefly describe the incident used to develop the paragraph. The topic sentence in each paragraph is underlined.

(1) <u>The main reason why attacks have been increasing has less to do with bears than with people</u>. In recent years, public use

Lists of support and descriptions may vary with reason; basic types of support are given.

of national parks in Canada and the U.S. has exploded. As a result, people-bear confrontations have mushroomed, and the bears have suffered many more provocations. What is surprising, in fact, is not that bear attacks have increased, but that there have not been more of them. Given the amount of people pressure these days, actual bear attacks have been relatively rare.—Paul Grescoe reasons

(2) <u>The first inkling of the earthquake came from a ham radio operator near Seattle, Washington, who happened to be talking to another ham in Anchorage</u>. It was Good Friday. The stores had just closed, and people were homeward bound for the Easter weekend. The man in Anchorage mentioned that it appeared they were having a small earthquake. Then as it worsened, he shouted that the "ground was waving like an ocean." Communications broke off, and the Seattle man phoned the news to a radio station. He and many other amateurs then stayed at their shortwave sets, taking and relaying messages to anxious relatives and friends. There was no doubt that a catastrophe had occurred, but it was impossible to determine the extent till some time afterward.—Norma Spring incident

DEVELOPING WRITING SKILLS: Recognizing Support in Paragraphs. Reexamine the second paragraph in the Exercise of Section 23.1. On your paper list the supporting information used in the paragraph. Identify each piece of supporting information as an example, a detail, a fact, a reason, or an incident. Then, using the paragraph as a model, list *five* pieces of specific information that you could use in a paragraph that describes your school.
Answers will vary.

Recognizing Unity 23.3

A paragraph has *unity* when *all* of the supporting ideas in the paragraph work together to develop the topic sentence.

OBJECTIVE

After completing this section, students should be able to

• Identify unified paragraphs.

TEACHING

Getting Started

To introduce the concept of *unity,* ask students what the word means to them in reference to a team, a country, or a building design. Students may be interested to know that *unity* comes from the Latin word *unus,* meaning "one." Stress with students that "being one" or working together as one is what makes a team, a country, a building, or a written work strong. To illustrate the point in written work, choose several well-organized paragraphs from magazine or newspaper articles. Copy them, adding to each paragraph a sentence that doesn't support the ideas in the paragraph. Present the rewritten paragraphs to students, and have them identify the sentences that don't belong in the paragraphs.

Text Follow Through

Discuss text pages 447–450.

Assign Exercise, page 449, and Developing Writing Skills, page 450.

Less advanced Few students are likely to have any great difficulty in identifying the unrelated supporting ideas in the Exercise and Developing Writing Skills. However, you may wish to have students complete at least one of the items in the Exercise orally as a class exercise before they begin work on their own.

The Unified Paragraph

To tell whether a paragraph is unified, first look for the main idea in the paragraph. Then look at the relationship between the pieces of supporting information and the main idea.

A paragraph is unified if all of the ideas work together to support or develop the main idea.

In a unified paragraph, all of the ideas seem to belong together. For example, if the main idea of a paragraph focuses on the three finalists in a dog show, the supporting material will also focus on the three finalists. The supporting information might offer details describing each winning dog, or it might give the reasons why the judges chose each of these dogs. The paragraph would be unified because all of the supporting ideas would help to develop the main idea.

In order to write good paragraphs, you should also learn to recognize when a paragraph is *not* unified. Unrelated pieces of information or unnecessary details can destroy the unity of a paragraph. The following paragraph about home safety contains two pieces of information that do not support the main idea. The paragraph therefore lacks unity.

TOPIC SENTENCE   The National Safety council warns against letting your home become a dangerous place. Instead, follow some sensible procedures to make your home a safer place. First of all, keep electrical equipment at a safe distance from sinks and bathtubs since contact with water can cause electrical shocks. To reduce the chance of burns—or fires that can result from cooking accidents—keep a dry chemical fire extinguisher in the

Unrelated idea   kitchen. *Many school buildings have fire extinguishers in the hallways, in the cafeteria, and in other key locations.* Check entrance ways and walkways for loose steps, slippery rugs, stray electrical extension cords—

Unrelated idea   anything that someone might trip over. *People fall more in the winter.* Inspect every room for potential hazards:

448

23.3 Recognizing Unity

Does the fireplace have a safety screen? Do staircases have sturdy handrails? Are medicines and harmful chemicals out of the reach of small children?

The paragraph focuses on ways to make your *home* safer. The ideas about fire extinguishers in school buildings and about people falling in the winter do not develop the main idea.

Unrelated ideas can be confusing. Remove any information that will not help the reader understand the main idea.

EXERCISE: Recognizing Unity in Paragraphs. Each of the following items includes a topic sentence and several supporting ideas. Some of these supporting ideas do not belong with the topic sentence. On your paper identify the unrelated idea or ideas in each item.

Unrelated ideas are underlined.

1. A visitor to Philadelphia can see many historical sights.
   a. Independence Hall
   b. The Liberty Bell
   c. Baseball games in the summer
   d. Betsy Ross's House
   e. Great variety of scenery in Pennsylvania

2. A horse requires much care.
   a. Regular brushing and occasional baths
   b. Riding exercise at least once a week
   c. Good idea to walk a dog regularly
   d. Cleaning hooves
   e. Mustangs descended from the horses ridden by Spanish explorers

3. The United States space program has made a great deal of progress.
   a. *Cosmos* and *Nova*, television programs about space
   b. Moon landings began in 1969
   c. America's first manned space flight in 1961
   d. Space shuttle in 1981
   e. Popular movies such as *Star Wars* and *Close Encounters*

Average If you have a file of past compositions, you might wish to select several in which irrelevant details exist, duplicate them without distracting errors in spelling, grammar, and punctuation, and ask students to locate problems in unity and suggest revisions. Do not put any students' names on the compositions.

Advanced If students carried out the grouping activity described in the text follow through for Section 23.2, they can now check the list of details under each of the subgroup headings to ensure that each detail truly supports the topic sentence they have written.

Additional Practice

Practice Pages or Practice Book, page 128

TESTING

Test Program
  Unit Pretest, page 76
  Chapter Test, page 82
  Unit Post-Test, page 96

RE-TEACHING

Practice Pages or Practice Book, page 128

THINKING SKILLS

Knowledge—*Identifying* irrelevant supporting details in paragraphs (Exercise, page 449)

Synthesis—*Rewriting* paragraphs to achieve unity (Developing Writing Skills, page 450)

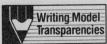
Writing Model Transparencies

For additional practice, use Paragraph Exercises transparency:
  Unity, pages 163 and 165

DEVELOPING WRITING SKILLS: Creating Unity in Paragraphs. Find the three unrelated ideas in each of the following paragraphs. Leaving out these ideas, rewrite each paragraph.
Unrelated sentences are underlined.

(1) I do not enjoy swimming in public pools. Especially on weekends, the pools are crammed with people. Trying to swim any distance results in a collision with someone, and a person can forget about trying to swim in a straight line. In fact, swimming through a crowded pool is much like trying to run an obstacle course that has moving obstacles. <u>Running the hurdles must be an equally frustrating sport. It is probably even more frustrating than trying to ski down a slalom course.</u> Worst of all, I feel, are the people who jump into the pool, ignoring those who are trying to swim. These people should have splashing pools of their own so that they will not interfere with serious swimmers. <u>Tennis courts are also overcrowded.</u>

(2) Backgammon is an easy game to learn but a difficult one to master. It has an element of chance since the players' moves are determined by throwing dice. <u>Dice are often made of ivory.</u> But backgammon also offers many opportunities for using strategy. <u>Checkers, however, is a boring game.</u> Good backgammon strategy usually involves taking risks and playing aggressively. In backgammon the goal is both to advance oneself and to block one's opponent. <u>Football also involves advancing and blocking and is probably the most aggressive of all games.</u> Learning to do both of these things at the same time takes practice.

23.4 Recognizing Coherence

In addition to unity, a paragraph should have *coherence.* In a coherent paragraph, the ideas will be logically organized. They will also be presented in a way that makes the connection between them easy to see. To make a paragraph coherent, you can use one of a number of different logical orders as well as certain connecting words, called *transitions.*

23.4 Recognizing Coherence

(pp. 450–458)

OBJECTIVES

After completing this section, students should be able to

- Identify a number of logical orders that can be used to give a paragraph coherence.
- Identify and choose appropriate transitions to connect ideas.

23.4 Recognizing Coherence

Logical Orders

In order to write coherent paragraphs, you should first become familiar with the different logical orders that can be used to organize information when you write paragraphs.

A coherent paragraph will follow some logical order: chronological order, spatial order, order of importance, comparison and contrast order, or some other logical order suggested by the topic sentence.

Chronological Order. In *chronological order* events or actions are arranged according to their sequence in time. For example, you can write about historical events simply by following the order in which the events took place. Or you can explain a laboratory process in terms of the steps that someone must follow to perform the process.

The following paragraph, written by a student, uses chronological order. Notice that the steps in a process are explained in their proper sequence. The words *first, next, then, after,* and *now* help to point out the sequence.

TOPIC
SENTENCE
Chrono-
logical order
of steps

　　If you like exotic foods, then you might enjoy making one of my banana splits. The only ingredients you need are bananas, ice cream (any flavor), all kinds of syrups, and toppings such as chopped nuts, M and M's, jimmies, and shredded coconut. To make this tasty snack, you *first* slice the banana and put it in a bowl. *Next* you scoop out three scoops of ice cream and put the ice cream on the banana. *Then* (this is the fun part) you pour lots of syrup on top. *After* the syrup, you sprinkle jimmies, chopped nuts, and M and M's on your dessert. *Now* that you have made your banana split, you have the thrill of eating your creation. "A sweet for the sweet" is an old saying; making your own banana split gives this phrase new meaning.—Ethan Kleinberg

Getting Started

Students will take the point of *coherence* more readily if they understand the term. Ask someone to describe an *incoherent* person's speech. (*It is rambling, hard to follow, and does not follow a logical course.*) Tell students that *to cohere* means "to hold together" or "to be logically connected." Both definitions apply to written works. Tell students that to be coherent, a paragraph must follow some logical order: chronological order, spatial order, order of importance, comparison and contrast order, or some other order suggested by the topic sentence. Provide examples of paragraphs developed using these orders, or direct students' attention to the examples in their text. Students might want to supply examples that they find in other texts.

Text Follow Through

Discuss text pages 450–458.

Assign Exercise A, page 454; Exercise B, page 457; Exercise C, page 457; and Developing Writing Skills, page 458.

Less advanced Encourage students to refer to the chart of transitions as they work on Exercise C and Developing Writing Skills.

Average For additional practice, students might work with the second sample paragraph on page 446. Ask students to identify the order used in the paragraph and to locate the transitions used to make this order clear.

Advanced Students might choose one of the items in Exercise C and organize it in two different ways, using different transitions for each order chosen.

Additional Practice

Practice Pages, page 129
Writing Workshops, pages 7–9

TESTING

Test Program
   Unit Pretest, page 76
   Chapter Test, page 82
   Unit Post-Test, page 96

RE-TEACHING

Practice Pages, page 129

THINKING SKILLS

Knowledge—*Identifying* logical orders in paragraphs (Exercise A, page 454)
Identifying transitions in paragraphs (Exercise B, page 457)

Application—*Using* logical order and transitions (Exercise C, page 457)

Synthesis—*Writing* a coherent paragraph (Developing Writing Skills, page 458)

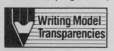
Writing Model Transparencies

For additional practice, use Paragraph Exercises transparencies:
   Chronological Order, pages 167 and 169
   Spatial Order, pages 171 and 173
   Order of Importance, pages 175 and 177
   Comparison and Contrast, pages 179 and 181
   Developmental Order, pages 183 and 185
   Transitions, pages 187 and 189

Spatial Order. In *spatial order* physical details are presented according to their location in a scene. This order is particularly useful in descriptions of people, places, and things. It presents details in a way that a reader might actually see them: from top to bottom, from nearest to farthest, from the inside to the outside, and so forth.

Notice the spatial order of details in the following paragraph, which describes a room. The phrases *from the ceiling, along the walls, in the center,* and *to the floor* help you, the reader, follow the spatial order.

TOPIC SENTENCE
Spatial order of details

After the explosion the room was a shambles. Pieces of plaster curled *from the ceiling. Along the walls* cracks had appeared; pictures hung crookedly; one window had shattered. A cloud of dust floated *in the center* of the room, and some of the furniture had been moved by the blast. A lamp and some dishes had fallen *to the floor* and were now smashed.

Order of Importance. In *order of importance,* supporting information is arranged from least important to most important. Going from the least powerful or least important idea to the most important is effective because it leaves the reader with the strongest idea. You can use order of importance when you are presenting reasons to support an opinion or when you are simply explaining an idea.

The following paragraph gives reasons that support the writer's feeling about a certain day. The first reason presents a minor problem. The second reason shows a more important problem. And the third reason presents the greatest problem. The words *first of all, even more,* and *but worst of all* show this ranking of ideas.

TOPIC SENTENCE
Order of importance for ideas

It was not going to be a good day to play golf. *First of all,* I had awakened late and could not practice my swing in the back yard. *Even more* upsetting was the sore throat that I felt coming on. *But worst of all,* the weather promised to be miserable. Rain had fallen all night, and drizzle greeted me in the morning. The low-hanging fog would reduce visibility, and the soggy, muddy course would have some new water hazards.

Comparison and Contrast Order. The ideas in a paragraph can be arranged in still other ways. Ideas or details can be *compared* because of their similarities, or they can be *contrasted* because of their differences. For example, the following paragraph focuses on the differences between two kinds of watches. The words *on the other hand, whereas,* and *in contrast* highlight the differences.

TOPIC SENTENCE

Comparison and contrast order of ideas

Conventional watches and digital watches both tell time, but they make us see time in very different ways. Conventional watches map time on a round face, with numbers and moving hands. Digital watches, *on the other hand,* simply display the hour, minute, and second in lighted numerals. In other words conventional watches give a picture of time, *whereas* digital watches present time as a series of changing numbers. Time on a conventional watch seems to have a past and a future as well as a present. *In contrast,* time on a digital watch at any moment is an isolated number that is quickly replaced by another isolated number.

Other Logical Orders. Other logical orders can be used to develop a particular topic sentence. For example, a topic sentence might mention three new cars. The paragraph would then discuss the cars in order in which they are listed in the topic sentence. Another kind of logical order might arrange supporting information like a series of building blocks: Each new thought might be based on the idea before it.

The next paragraph follows a single logical arrangement, building idea upon idea to describe the main idea presented in the topic sentence. The word *additionally* helps to link the information at the beginning of the paragraph with the information at the end.

TOPIC
SENTENCE

Logical
order
suited
to topic
sentence

The most unusual gait, perhaps, is the stott, also called the pronk or the spronk. All four legs take off and land nearly together, and during the period of suspension, the legs hang down vertically from the body. Used by many deer and antelope, ranging from wildebeest to small gazelles, it is slower than a gallop but effective in changing direction or climbing hills. *Additionally*, it probably serves as a warning system. A pronking animal jumps so high that it can be seen by others in its group. Some species make a noise while pronking, and others deposit a scent on the ground from glands in the foot.—Anne Innis Dagg

EXERCISE A: Recognizing Logical Orders.

Read the following paragraphs carefully, examining the order of support. Identify the order used in each paragraph as *chronological, spatial, order of importance,* or *comparison and contrast.* If the ideas follow none of these orders, write *other logical order.*

Orders are given; transitions are underlined for Exercise B.

(1) The Egyptian civilization of antiquity visualized the universe as a great box, with Egypt in the center of its long, narrow floor. The top of the box was the sky, from which lamps were suspended by means of ropes. These lamps were the stars. Other lamps, carried in heavenly boats, traveled about the sky and appeared as planets. The Milky Way was supposed to be the celestial equivalent of the Nile, and the regions through which it flowed were populated with dead Egyptians dwelling under the benign supervision of Osiris. At the corners of the universe box were four huge mountains supporting the sky, and joining them around the sides of the box were mountain ranges. Along these mountains a river circumscribed the universe. In this river each morning, in the east, the sun-god Ra was reborn in a boat, appearing as a ball of fire.—Arthur Beiser and Konrad B. Krauskopf spatial

(2) Today, America's hawks, kites, falcons, eagles, ospreys, vultures, and owls are faring much better. Most experts caution

23.4 Recognizing Coherence

that the situation is far from ideal, but they agree real progress is being made. Insecticides such as DDT, which breaks down into another compound that thins the eggshells of bald eagles, peregrine falcons, and other fish- and meat-eaters, have been banned for years and, in some areas, are finally beginning to fade from the environment. <u>But, most important of all</u>, the general public today seems to have a genuine appreciation for the birds, coupled with an understanding of how they fit into the overall scheme of things.—John Neary order of importance

(3) What is most important is an inspection tour of your garden in spring. Check <u>first</u> for any winter damage to tree limbs and branches of shrubs. Prune off anything that is damaged; if a branch is torn, cut it off neatly. Check <u>next</u> to see if the soil mulch is still at an even depth and whether or not it needs a bit of replenishing. <u>Then</u> look for cracks in the masonry of walls, planters, and flooring. Is there damage to the awning or other overhead protection? Snip off dead ends of vines and ground covers. <u>Finally</u>, give the shrubs a "bath" to clean off soot that has accumulated during the winter months.—Adapted from Carla Wallach chronological

Transitions

In the paragraphs presented earlier in this section, certain connecting words, such as *first, next, even more, on the other hand,* and *in contrast,* are printed in italics. These words are *transitions.* Transitions link ideas and guide the reader from one idea to the next.

A coherent paragraph will often use transitions to help connect ideas smoothly and logically.

The chart on pages 456–457 lists some of the most frequently used transitions. Notice that certain ones help to show chronological order. Others are most useful to point out spatial order or order of importance. Still other transitions help to clarify other logical orders of ideas.

COMMON TRANSITIONS

For Chronological Order

after	finally	next
afterward	first	now
at last	formerly	previously
before	last	soon
during	later	then
earlier	meanwhile	until
eventually		

For Spatial Order

above	beneath	in the distance
ahead	beyond	near
around	in front of	next to
away	inside	outside
behind	in the center	to the right
below		

For Order of Importance

also	furthermore	next
another	least	one
even greater	more	perhaps the
finally	moreover	greatest reason
first	most	second
for one reason	most important	third

For Comparison and Contrast Order

also	instead	on the other hand
although	just as	similarly
besides	like	similar to
both	likewise	so also
but	nevertheless	whereas
however	on the contrary	yet
in contrast		

23.4 Recognizing Coherence

For Other Logical Orders		
accordingly	for example	in fact
additionally	for instance	namely
along with	furthermore	therefore
and	in addition	thus
as a result	in conclusion	
consequently	indeed	

Look again at the paragraphs on pages 451 through 455. As you read each paragraph, see how the transitions printed in italics help to connect the ideas.

Not all paragraphs require transitions. Nor do you need to introduce each new idea with a transition. However, you should always check your writing for places where transitions could make your ideas clearer for the reader.

EXERCISE B: Recognizing Transitions. Reread the three paragraphs in Exercise A. On your paper list the transitions used in each paragraph. Some paragraphs may have only one or two transitions; others may have several.
Transitions are underlined in Exercise A. Choices may vary within reason.

EXERCISE C: Choosing Orders and Transitions. In each of the following items, you will find a topic and three or four supporting ideas. Tell which kind of order you would use to organize the supporting information in each item. Then list at least two transitions that you could use to help a reader follow the order that you have chosen.
Answers will vary; probable orders are given along with possible transitions.

1. The beginning of a storm chronological/first, then
   a. Clouds rolling in
   b. Lightning flashing
   c. Sunlight disappearing
   d. Rain beginning to fall
2. A scene in the woods spatial/above, beneath

Developing Writing Skills

Have students practice writing paragraphs by completing the following assignment.

Writing Across the Curriculum

Each state in the United States has its own unique character. For example, Vermont is known for its beautiful mountains, its ski areas, and its maple sugar production.

Prewriting Choose a state other than the one in which you live. Then research this state in an encyclopedia. Next, choose an interesting aspect of the state's history, people, economy, or geography. For example, you might choose to focus on the Vermont maple sugar industry. Finally, develop a main idea and list of supporting information for the topic you have chosen.

Writing Write a first draft of a paragraph about your topic. Make sure that you begin with a topic sentence and that you include enough information to thoroughly support your topic sentence. Also make sure that you present your details in a logical order and that you use transitions to connect your sentences.

Revising When you have finished writing, revise your paragraph, making sure that you have thoroughly supported your topic sentence. After you have finished revising, proofread your paragraph and prepare a final copy. Then share it with your classmates.

a. Birds in the trees
b. Vines hanging from branches
c. Animals on the ground
3. Reasons behind someone's popularity
a. Appearance
b. Friendliness and personality
c. Helpfulness towards others
4. The design of a certain building spatial/in the distance, inside
a. Its appearance from a distance
b. Its details close up
c. Its halls and rooms
5. Steps in preparing for a vacation chronological/earlier, finally
a. Deciding where and when to go
b. Packing and closing the house
c. Loading the car and leaving

3. order of importance/also, furthermore

DEVELOPING WRITING SKILLS: Creating Coherence in a Paragraph. Choose one of the items in Exercise C, and develop a paragraph from it. Write a topic sentence that expresses a main idea. (For example, for the first item you might write, "The beginning of a storm always fascinates me.") Then develop the idea using the list of information for that item and any other related ideas. Your paragraph should follow the logical order you chose in Exercise C and use the transitions you chose to link the supporting ideas. When you finish your paragraph, complete the following steps.

Answers will vary.

1. Identify the logical order you used.
2. Circle all transitions.
3. Read your paragraph again and take another look at the chart on pages 456–457. Decide if you have chosen transitions that make your paragraph flow smoothly and logically. Improve your choices wherever you can.

Writing Workshop: Looking at Paragraphs

ASSIGNMENT 1

Topic   The Most Impressive Movie Villain

Form and Purpose   A paragraph that describes and supports an impression

Audience   Readers of a book entitled *Screen Villains*

Length   One paragraph

Focus   In a topic sentence identify the movie villain and tell why he or she is impressive. Then support your impression with details.

Sources   Films, books about the history of filmmaking

Prewriting   Choose a villain to write about. Write notes about the villain's appearance and behavior.

Writing   Use your notes to write a first draft.

Revising   To improve the connection of ideas, add transition words like those in the chart on page 456. Then proofread your paragraph and prepare a final copy.

Count Dracula

Guiding Student Writing

Students can work together in groups during the prewriting and revising steps to help generate ideas and to evaluate the paper through its developing stages. Students working as peer evaluators might engage in developing standards, such as superior, excellent, fair, and poor. Involved in this evaluation process, students quickly learn the qualities that make a paper good. They can then apply what they have learned to their own writing assignments. However, it is important to supervise peer-evaluation groups, so that students do not reinforce other students' bad writing habits or discourage certain students by being overly critical of their work. For this reason, students need to be given some guidelines before they begin to evaluate each other's papers.

Assignment 1

Suggestions for Prewriting: Bring to class a few books about movie history from the library, preferably ones with photos. Let students scan these, as well as discuss recent possibilities. Record nominees on the board.

Suggestions for Publishing: Actually create *Screen Villains* with student papers. Have a committee design and prepare a cover. Display the book in the library, perhaps in a group with actual books.

Assignment 2

Suggestions for Prewriting: As students list skills, remind them to choose one they can defend to someone who does not agree.

Suggestions for Publishing: Ask students to give their paragraphs to readers who indeed don't share the writers' viewpoint. Readers should be asked to comment on whether they were or were not convinced and why.

ASSIGNMENT 2

Topic Why a Particular Skill Is Important

Form and Purpose A paragraph that explains your viewpoint

Audience A friend who does not share your viewpoint

Length One paragraph

Focus In your topic sentence, state the skill and why you think it is important. Support that main idea with facts, examples, details, and reasons. Present your supporting sentences in order of importance.

Sources Your personal experiences and observations

Prewriting List four or five important skills. Choose one and make notes about its importance. Think of specific facts, examples, details, and reasons.

Writing Using your notes, write a first draft.

Revising Review your draft to make sure that all supporting sentences actually support your topic sentence. Proofread your paragraph and prepare a final draft.

Topics for Writing: Looking at Paragraphs

The above photo may suggest a writing topic about a personal collection or hobby. If so, write a paragraph about it. Other possible topics for a paragraph are listed below.

1. Are Baseball Cards Really Valuable?
2. Old Comics—A Paper Gold Mine!
3. The Rarest Coins
4. How to Preserve a Coin Collection
5. Why People Collect Things
6. An Extremely Valuable Stamp
7. Rating the Condition of Coins
8. The Most Popular Records of the Past
9. Which Records from Today Will Be Valuable in Fifty Years? Why?
10. What Makes a Collector's Item Valuable?

Stimulating Thought

1. "Which are valuable? Why? How much are they worth?"
2. "Which comics are worth the most? Why? How much are they worth?"
3. "How will you organize information—chronologically or from rare to very rare?"
4. Cleaning coins
   Storing coins
   Displaying coins
5. Price in ownership
   The thrill of the find
   Investment purposes
6. "Identify and describe the stamp. Why is it valuable? How many exist?"
7. "What factors does a coin collector consider in judging the coin?"
8. Students are probably most knowledgeable about 1950's nostalgia.
9. Have students brainstorm, but ask the reason for each nominee.
10. Beauty
    Rarity
    Condition

CHAPTER 24
Writing Paragraphs

(pp. 462–495)

This chapter provides students with step-by-step guidance in the prewriting, writing, and revising stages of developing a paragraph. The material builds on what students have learned about sentences in Chapter 22 and about paragraphs in Chapter 23. It also provides a foundation for writing essays and reports as discussed in Chapters 26 and 27.

For additional or alternate writing assignments and a list of topics for writing, see pages 493–495.

24.1 Thinking Out Your Ideas and Writing a Topic Sentence

(pp. 462–469)

OBJECTIVES

After completing this section, students should be able to

- Find and narrow an idea into a good paragraph topic.
- Decide on an audience, main idea, and purpose in order to focus a paragraph topic.
- Prepare a topic sentence for a paragraph.

Chapter **24**

Writing Paragraphs

This chapter presents useful steps you can follow in writing paragraphs. First comes a prewriting, or planning, stage, followed by a writing stage and a revising stage. At every point in this three-part process, you will need to make wise choices that help you write strong, clear, interesting paragraphs.

24.1 Thinking Out Your Ideas and Writing a Topic Sentence

Your first step should be to find a topic that you want to write about. Identify the audience for whom you will write, your main idea, and the purpose behind your writing—to explain, to persuade, or to describe. Finally, express your main idea in a topic sentence.

PREWRITING: Finding and Narrowing a Topic

What should you write about? If you are enthusiastic about a topic and think you can cover it in a paragraph, you are likely to have found a good paragraph topic.

24.1 Thinking Out Your Ideas

Brainstorm for interesting topics. Then find a good paragraph topic by choosing a topic that is small enough to be covered well in a paragraph.

To discover some of the topics that you could write about, you can tap your memories, the things you have learned, and your current interests. You might, for example, think about experiences that have made a big impression on you. You might also think about what you have learned from books or through your work in school. In addition you might think about situations that concern you in your community, your city, the country, or the world. Observations that you have made while riding to school, walking a dog, or visiting a friend can also become topics for writing.

Brainstorming can help you find these ideas. When you brainstorm, you should write down all your thoughts without judging whether or not they are brilliant ones. By letting your mind come up with ideas while you quickly jot them down, you can produce a rough list of possible topics. If one topic particularly interests you, write down other more specific topics under it. The more topics you have jotted down, the more choices you will have. (For other ways of finding possible topics, see Section 20.1.)

When you have a list with some interesting possibilities, you should examine the topics to find one you want to write about. Some of your topics will probably be too general—that is, too big for you to cover well in one paragraph. It might be difficult, for example, to write a single paragraph that covers the topic *Parks* or even the more limited topic *Amusement parks.* On the other hand, you could probably write a very good paragraph on *Ferris wheels* or *The fastest roller coasters* or *The most exciting ride.* After considering each topic on your list, you should choose a topic that you know something about and find particularly interesting. If the topic is too general, like the topic *Parks* or *Baseball,* break it down into smaller topics.

TEACHING

Getting Started

Tell students that the first step in writing is finding a topic and that a good method of finding a topic is brainstorming. Direct students' attention to the text explanation of brainstorming on pages 463–464. Tell students that once they've chosen a topic for a paragraph, they must be sure their topic is narrow enough to be covered in a paragraph. Suggest a topic, such as *Authors,* and have students brainstorm ideas for a paragraph topic. Their suggestions for narrowing the topic might be as follows:

Science-fiction authors, Ray Bradbury, Ray Bradbury's start as an author.

You might want to have students continue to brainstorm until they become adept at choosing and narrowing a topic.

Text Follow Through

Discuss text pages 462–469.

Assign Exercise A, page 464; Exercise B, page 464; Exercise C, page 467; Exercise D, page 468; and Developing Writing Skills, page 469.

Less advanced You can help students develop topics narrow enough to be written about in one paragraph by having them present their paragraph topics from Exercises A and B in class. The class can discuss whether or not the topics are suitable for a paragraph. You can then ask for suggestions to focus those topics that are still too general.

Average It may be helpful to bring a variety of paragraphs to class to demonstrate clearly the need for deciding on audience, main idea, and purpose when preparing a paragraph. The paragraphs you bring can be read aloud and discussed in class. You may wish to present paragraphs of the following types:

1. A persuasive paragraph from an editorial written for a general audience
2. A descriptive paragraph from a book for young children
3. An explanatory paragraph from a scientific journal written for professionals
4. An explanatory paragraph from a textbook your students might use

Advanced Students might want to share with classmates how they chose their paragraph topics, beginning with the broad general topic down to the final narrow topic.

Additional Practice

Practice Pages or Practice Book, page 130
Writing Process Activities, pages 24, 25

TESTING

Test Program

Unit Pretest, page 77
Chapter Test, page 83
Unit Post-Test, pages 96, 97

Writing Process Activities, Evaluation Sheets, pages 8–12

RE-TEACHING

Practice Pages or Practice Book, page 130
Writing Process Activities, pages 24, 25

Then choose a smaller related topic that you think you can develop with specific supporting information.

In your brainstorming for a topic, you might make a list like the one in the following chart. Note that many of the topics that are too large for paragraphs have smaller related topics listed under them. A few of the other topics—*Best fishing spots* and *Making bread*—are probably already small enough to be paragraph topics. With such a list in hand, you should find it relatively easy to choose a topic.

BRAINSTORMING FOR A PARAGRAPH TOPIC	
Subways	Thunderstorms
Best fishing spots	Bears
Radios	—Grizzlies—a threatened species?
—Latest models	—Bears' habits
—Sound pollution	News coverage
Making bread	—Famous reporters
Taking a bicycle trip	—Evening news on television

EXERCISE A: Narrowing General Topics. Write *two* of the following general topics on your paper. Then, under each, list three to five smaller related topics that you or someone else could cover well in a paragraph.
Answers will vary.

Food	Dangerous jobs	Movie
Hobbies	School sports	or television stars

EXERCISE B: Discovering a Paragraph Topic of Your Own. Write the following topics on your paper. Then brainstorm for at least *five* more topics of your own. Choose one topic and then examine it to make sure it is small enough for one paragraph. If it is too big, list two or three smaller related topics under it and choose one of those as a paragraph topic.
Answers will vary.

Music of the 1980's	Famous animals	Fads
New sports	Books	

> ### 24.1 Writing a Topic Sentence

PREWRITING: Deciding on Your Audience, Main Idea, and Purpose

Early in the prewriting stage, generally right after you have chosen a topic, you should make three important decisions that will give a certain direction to your writing. You should decide upon your *audience*—the people with whom you want to communicate in your paragraph. You should determine your *main idea*—what you want to say about your paragraph topic. And you should decide upon your *purpose*—whether you are writing your paragraph to explain, to persuade, or to describe.

Determine your audience, main idea, and purpose in order to focus your paragraph topic.

The order in which you make these decisions will vary depending on the particular writing situation. For instance, sometimes you may know your *audience* from the beginning. If you were asked to write a paragraph on a camp application, you would begin with the knowledge that you were writing to the director or administrator of the camp. Sometimes your *main idea* will come first, either as an assignment or as an obvious point you want to make about your topic.

Sometimes your *purpose* will be clear from the beginning. Your assignment may, for example, tell you to write a paragraph explaining something or a paragraph convincing someone of something.

If none of the three are given, you will have to make your own decisions. One way is to decide on your audience first. You can then use this knowledge to help zero in on a main idea and a purpose. Once you know your audience, you can ask yourself questions about your paragraph topic while thinking about the audience. These questions can help you determine the point of your paragraph. Begin by asking yourself general questions such as these: "What might my audience want to know about the topic?" "What do I think the audience should know about the topic?" "What interests me most about the topic?" From these general questions, you can develop questions that are more directly related to your topic and then answer them. Your answers will give you a number of possible main ideas for a paragraph.

For instance, if you had chosen to write about *Evening news on television,* you might decide to write to a general audience of people who watch the evening news fairly often. You might then ask yourself questions like those in the following chart.

ASKING QUESTIONS TO FIND A MAIN IDEA	
Paragraph Topic: Evening news on television	
Questions	**Possible Main Ideas**
Why are the evening news programs on television so popular?	To attract viewers, television news programs have come up with many new ideas.
What specific things do the different news programs provide?	While some of the news programs focus mainly on news, others provide news as well as many different kinds of special features.
What are the problems, if any, of evening news programs?	Most of the news stories on evening news programs are treated in such a light or rapid way that they lose their impact.

When you examine the possible answers you have written down in response to your questions, you will generally find that they are leading you toward main ideas suitable for different purposes. For example, the first main idea in the chart is a factual statement that you could explain in a paragraph. The second main idea is also a factual statement. The third main

24.1 Writing a Topic Sentence

idea, however, is an opinion that you would have to defend. Your purpose in the third case would be to persuade those members of your audience who have not thought about the issue or who disagree with you that your opinion is right.

After thinking about the possible main ideas and the purposes they suit, decide which one you will choose for your paragraph. For example, if you were writing about television news programs, you might choose the third idea in the chart on page 446 because you thought it was the most interesting.

EXERCISE C: Deciding on a Main Idea. Using the paragraph topic you selected in Exercise B, follow these instructions.
Answers will vary.

1. Decide on an audience and briefly describe it.
2. Write down at least two questions that you think your audience might ask about your paragraph topic.
3. Answer each question briefly with a statement that could be used as a main idea for your paragraph.
4. Examine each of the possible main ideas you have listed. Decide which purpose each suits.
5. Finally, choose the main idea that you would most like to write about, keeping your audience and the purpose related to the main idea in mind.

PREWRITING: Deciding on Your Topic Sentence

Once you have decided upon your audience, main idea, and purpose, you can prepare a topic sentence.

Keep your audience and purpose in mind as you express your main idea in a topic sentence.

To make your main idea as clear as possible to the reader, you should choose the best possible wording for your topic sentence. Think about your audience and purpose as you express your main idea in a well-developed, complete sentence. Choose each word carefully. Even though you can revise your topic sentence at any time throughout the writing process, you will work more confidently and save time if you write a strong topic sentence at this stage. In fact, it is a good idea to write several possible topic sentences, each expressing your main idea in a slightly different way. You can then choose the one that you like best and that best suits your audience and purpose.

POSSIBLE TOPIC SENTENCES

Main Idea: Most of the news stories on evening news programs are treated in such a light or rapid way that they lose their impact.

1. Most of the news stories on evening news programs are treated in such a light or rapid way that they lose their impact.
2. Evening news programs on television skim over the events of the day so quickly that the events lose most of their impact on viewers.
3. Although they try to cover the major events of the day, evening news programs on television often end up by weakening the impact of the information they report.
4. Evening news broadcasts on television weaken the impact of the information they report for a number of reasons—some of which are caused by television itself.

Any of the topic sentences in the chart above would be appropriate for a paragraph about television news programs. All of the topic sentences suit a persuasive purpose, differing mainly in their wording. The first and second are both strong and direct. The third and fourth are more detailed. You might decide to use the third because it sounds the most reasonable.

EXERCISE D: Writing a Topic Sentence. Using the main idea that you chose in Exercise C, write two or more possible

topic sentences that clearly express the main idea. Think about your audience and purpose as you write. Then decide which version of your topic sentence you like best.
Answers will vary.

DEVELOPING WRITING SKILLS: Shaping Ideas for a Paragraph. Practice all of the steps discussed in this section on your own by following these instructions.
Answers will vary.

1. Brainstorm for topics, and jot down a rough list of at least five.
2. Choose a topic that especially interests you. If necessary, break it down into smaller related topics and choose one of those as your paragraph topic.
3. Decide on your audience.
4. With your audience in mind, ask and answer questions about your paragraph topic to find possible main ideas.
5. Decide what purpose suits each main idea.
6. Choose the main idea that you would most like to write about.
7. Write at least two possible topic sentences, and choose the clearest, most suitable one.

Developing Support for a Topic Sentence 24.2

The prewriting steps you have already completed will help you as you gather specific information to develop your main idea. Your earlier work will also help you to organize the supporting information. This section discusses some effective ways to carry out these gathering and organizing steps.

PREWRITING: Brainstorming for Support

When you first chose your paragraph topic and then zeroed in on a main idea, you probably had in mind at least a few

24.2 Developing Support for a Topic Sentence
(pp. 469–475)

OBJECTIVES

After completing this section, students should be able to

- Gather supporting information for a topic sentence.
- Check supporting information for unity and organize it in a logical order to achieve coherence.

TEACHING

Getting Started

Tell students that once they have chosen a topic and decided on a main idea, they should brainstorm for examples, details, facts, reasons, and incidents to support their main idea. Direct students' attention to the chart on page 471. Have students use the chart as a model to find support for a main idea that you or students suggest. You might want to have students brainstorm support ideas for two or three main ideas.

Text Follow Through

Discuss text pages 469–475.

Assign Exercise A, page 472; Exercise B, page 474; Exercise C, page 475; and Developing Writing Skills, page 475.

Less advanced   Students might benefit from a study or review of the material on modified outlines in Section 35.2 before working on Exercise C and Developing Writing Skills.

Average   Students might enjoy an activity based on paragraphs found in magazines. Select at least one paragraph with a clear topic sentence covering a subject with which the students are likely to be familiar. Write the topic sentence on the chalkboard and ask the class to brainstorm for supporting information. Then read the full paragraph.

Advanced   You might ask students to complete the third item in Developing Writing Skills twice, using a different logical order each time. Remind students that a change in the

examples or facts that would help support what you wanted to say about the topic. At this point in the writing process, you should get down on paper as much specific information relating to your main idea as you can.

Brainstorm for examples, details, facts, reasons, and incidents related to your main idea.

Brainstorming for support involves remembering, discovering, and gathering specific information on your paragraph topic. Your goal should be to have a long list of interesting information from which you can select examples, details, facts, and so forth to develop your main idea. You should not throw out or organize information at this point. Instead, gather more information than you can use in one paragraph and plan to sort it later. From your long list, you can then choose the best information.

You can brainstorm in a number of ways. You can brainstorm with another person or by yourself. You can sit quietly and try to come up with things related to your topic, or you can guide your thinking by writing down some questions about your main idea. If you decide to use questions, you should begin by writing your topic sentence at the top of a blank sheet of paper. Then think about your audience and purpose, and jot down some questions that might occur to someone in your audience after reading your topic sentence. What information does your topic sentence indicate that your paragraph will cover? What specific questions should your paragraph answer in order to fulfill the audience's expectations? After you have written down at least two questions, brainstorm for examples, details, facts, reasons, or incidents that will help answer these questions. Your answers should include a fairly long list of specific pieces of information. If you were brainstorming on the topic sentence about television news programs, you might come up with questions and answers like those in the chart on the following page.

24.2 Developing Support for a Topic Sentence

QUESTIONING TO FIND SUPPORT FOR A TOPIC SENTENCE

Topic Sentence: **Although they try to cover the major events of the day, evening news programs on television often end up by weakening the impact of the information they report.**

How do news programs weaken the impact of most stories?
—time is limited
—major stories assigned no more than five minutes
 —often less than a minute
 —average one to two minutes
—need to keep show moving
—appeal to viewers, ratings, with variety, liveliness

—items introduced and developed, finished off neatly
—reporters must use short cuts, avoid heavy analysis
—stories wrapped up with catchy "tag lines"
—stories repeated throughout day, from night to night
—personalities of reporters have become important

Would longer stories improve the situation?
—even these lose impact because mixed in with so many different kinds of lighter material
 —shorter items, human interest stories, humorous notes
 —commercials, announcements, other interruptions, small talk
—constant flow of programs on television—talk shows, news, sitcoms—blend together

—television is often seen mainly as entertainment
 —people tune in for amusement, break from own problems
 —even news is a form of entertainment because it is on television
—therefore, less important, less real than it should be

---

logical order might necessitate changes in the topic sentence and in the supporting information.

Additional Practice

Practice Pages or Practice Book, page 130
Writing Process Activities, pages 24, 25

TESTING

Test Program

 Unit Pretest, page 77
 Chapter Test, page 83
 Unit Post-Test, pages 96, 97

Writing Process Activities, Evaluation Sheets, pages 8–12

RE-TEACHING

Practice Pages or Practice Book, page 130
Writing Process Activities, pages 24, 25

THINKING SKILLS

Application—*Preparing* support for a topic sentence (Exercise A, page 472)

Synthesis—*Organizing* supporting information in a logical order (Exercise C, page 475) *Organizing* support for a paragraph (Developing Writing Skills, page 475)

Evaluation—*Appraising* support (Exercise B, page 474)

This list, like the lists you will probably make, contains more information than you would want to include in a single paragraph. Furthermore, some of the information is not directly related to the main idea. Even so, a list like this can help you see all of the ideas that you could include in your paragraph.

EXERCISE A: Gathering Support for a Topic Sentence. Use the topic sentence you wrote in Exercise D of Section 24.1 to brainstorm for support. Write the topic sentence at the top of your paper and then do one of the following: Jot down every piece of information that comes to mind about your main idea, or write down a few questions that your audience might ask and then answer them as rapidly as you can with as much specific information as you can. However you go about brainstorming, try to list at least a dozen examples, details, facts, reasons, or incidents.
Answers will vary.

PREWRITING: Organizing Supporting Information

The organizing step includes two parts. First, you must evaluate the supporting information to make sure that what you select is clearly related to the topic sentence. Then, you need to find a logical order in which to present that information in your paragraph.

Eliminate unrelated and extra information from your list of support, adding other information, if necessary. Then organize the supporting information so that it follows a logical order.

To start organizing your paragraph, you should examine your list of supporting information for unity and completeness. Think about each piece of information that you have written down. Ask yourself, "Does this information help the reader understand my main idea? Do I need every one of these examples

24.2 Developing Support for a Topic Sentence

and details? Would some other example be better than this one?" Questions such as these can help you weed out weak and unneeded support. For instance, if you have five similar examples, you may want to choose the best three or four. In addition, you may find that you have to revise your topic sentence to fit the supporting information you have gathered.

Look again at the chart of supporting information on page 471. Some of the items listed are not that clearly related to the topic sentence—for example, the point about the way the stories are reported throughout the day. Other items would simply overload the paragraph. You might, for example, choose to skip the point about ratings. From a long list such as the one shown in the chart, you might eliminate about one third of the items, leaving just the best support for the topic sentence.

After evaluating your list of support, you should look at it again to decide on the order you want to use to present your ideas. Your topic sentence may give you some clues. If your topic sentence mentions three or more things in a certain order, your paragraph should develop those things in the same order. For example, if a topic sentence about horses mentions walking, trotting, and galloping, you should discuss those three items in that order in the paragraph. If you are defending an opinion, you may want to rank your information from least convincing to most convincing. Or you may want to use chronological order to show events over time, spatial order to help the reader visualize your topic, or comparison and contrast order to make comparisons.

Once you have chosen an order for your paragraph, you should arrange your information according to that order. You can do this simply by numbering your pieces of support in the appropriate order, or you can make a modified outline of your paragraph. The modified outline on the following page of the paragraph on television news programs lists the problems associated with evening news programs in the order of their importance, ending with the most important.

Topic Sentence: Although they try to cover the major events of the day, evening news programs on television often end up by weakening the impact of the information they report.

Time Limitations of News Programs Weaken Impact
1. Only a few minutes for each item
2. Stories developed without analysis
3. Stories finished off neatly, next item picked up
4. Stories wrapped up with catchy "tag lines"

Mixture of Content on News Programs Weakens Impact
1. Longer, serious items mixed in with lighter material
   —humorous stories,
   —brief announcements
   —commercials
2. Everything blends together

Nature of Television Itself Weakens Impact
1. Television is often seen as entertainment
2. People use it for recreation, as a break from their own problems
3. News less important, less real as a result

Your numbered list of support or modified outline will guide you in writing your paragraph. Of course you may think of more ideas as you write or may find an even better order for your information. Nevertheless, this early thinking and organizing will help you to write a good paragraph. It can even make the actual writing of your paragraph easier and more enjoyable.

EXERCISE B: Evaluating Your Support. Read through the list of supporting information that you made in Exercise A, and examine it for unity and completeness. Cross out information that does not belong with your topic sentence as well as information that would overload your paragraph. If necessary, add new examples, details, and so on. Finally, make sure that your topic sentence fits the supporting information that you have gathered. If it does not, revise it.

Answers will vary.

EXERCISE C: Arranging Supporting Information in a Logical Order. Look again at your revised list of supporting information. Choose a logical order that fits your topic sentence and your list of support. You might choose chronological order or spatial order; you might choose comparison and contrast order or order of importance. Organize your support in the order you have chosen either by numbering the information or by preparing a modified outline.

Answers will vary.

DEVELOPING WRITING SKILLS: Developing Support for a Paragraph. For this exercise use either the paragraph topic you worked with in Developing Writing Skills at the end of Section 24.1 or a new paragraph topic, main idea, and topic sentence of your own. Then follow these steps to develop a paragraph outline.

Answers will vary.

1. Brainstorm for supporting information for your topic sentence, creating a list of examples, details, facts, reasons, or incidents.
2. Check the unity of your support, and cross out any information that might weaken or overload your paragraph. Add to your list or make changes in your topic sentence, if necessary.
3. Decide what order you will use to present your pieces of information. Then make a modified outline of your paragraph.

Writing the Paragraph 24.3

If you have carefully thought out your paragraph, writing it will probably be a satisfying experience. Because of your earlier planning, you will have no reason to worry about what you want to say. Instead, you can concentrate on presenting your ideas in a way that will make them clear and appealing.

24.3 Writing the Paragraph
(pp. 475–478)

OBJECTIVE

After completing this section, students should be able to

• Write the first draft of a paragraph.

TEACHING

Getting Started

Have students use a main idea and the supporting information that they developed by brainstorming in this subsection of TE 24.2. Guide students to help them prepare an outline and write a first draft as a group. Have students use the suggestions in the chart on page 476 as they prepare the first draft. Remind students of the need to create logic and order and to connect ideas appropriately as they make suggestions. You may wish to write a bank of transitional words and phrases on the board from which students may choose.

Text Follow Through

Discuss text pages 475–478.

Assign Exercise, page 477, and Developing Writing Skills, page 478.

Less advanced You might want to work with students to develop the first draft of a paragraph before students write first drafts using their own topics. You can use the work done by one of the students for Developing Writing Skills in Section 24.2, or you can develop another topic of your own choosing.

Average Students can be asked to exchange papers and review each other's first drafts. Students can check to see that the topic, focus for a particular audience and purpose, topic

WRITING: Putting Your Paragraph Together

Your *first draft* should be a complete version of your paragraph, but it will seldom be your final version. In many ways you can think of it as a practice version. Preparing a first draft will give you a chance to try out your ideas and to see the paragraph as a whole, as one unit of thought.

Think about your audience and purpose as you write your first draft, using your outline as a guide and adding transitions where they are needed.

In addition to your outline, you can use the suggestions in the following chart as you prepare your first draft.

SUGGESTIONS FOR DRAFTING A PARAGRAPH
1. Let your awareness of your audience and purpose guide you as you choose your words.
2. Check any new ideas you decide to add against your topic sentence.
3. Feel free to change the order of your ideas if that will make things clearer.
4. Make sure you have used enough transitions to link your ideas clearly.
5. Consider ending your paragraph with a *concluding sentence*— a sentence that wraps up all the ideas in the paragraph.

Keeping your audience and purpose in mind will help you find the right words. It can also help you decide whether you need to add any ideas to make your point clearer, whether you need to make any changes in order, and whether you have used enough transitions. Your audience and purpose can even help you decide whether or not to add a concluding sentence. Simply ask yourself if such a sentence would help your audience understand the point you are trying to make.

24.3 Writing the Paragraph

Below is a final copy of the paragraph about television news programs. The supporting information follows the order of ideas in the modified outline on page 474. The transitions (printed in italics) guide the reader from one idea to the next, while showing that the information is organized in order of importance.

TOPIC SENTENCE

Completed paragraph with unity and coherence

Although they try to cover the major events of the day, evening news programs on television often end up by weakening the impact of the information they report. *First,* because time is limited, only a few minutes can be given to each news item. Therefore, each story is presented without much detail and then finished off neatly with a catchy "tag line." *Even* when a story is reported at greater length, it often loses importance because the broadcast mixes it in with a number of other, lighter stories, as well as with commercials and brief announcements. As a result, everything seems to blend together. *Perhaps the major problem* with broadcast news coverage lies in the fact that television is often seen mainly as entertainment. People turn on their televisions for relaxation. They are looking for a break from their daily routines and problems. Everything they view—even news—becomes somewhat less important and less real under these circumstances. With the problem of time, the blend of many different kinds of stories, and the view of television as entertainment, evening news programs cannot help chopping up and watering down the news of the world into easily digested tidbits that people can enjoy each night with their evening meals.

Concluding sentence

EXERCISE: Writing a First Draft. Pretend that you have prepared the following modified outline for a paragraph to be written for the audience and purpose listed. Referring to the chart on page 476, prepare a first draft of the paragraph.
Answers will vary.

sentence, and support are appropriate. They can then check for unity, logical order, and transitions.

Advanced Students might want to share their first drafts for classmates to analyze using the suggestions in the chart on page 476.

Additional Practice

Practice Pages or Practice Book, page 130
Writing Process Activities, pages 24, 25

TESTING

Test Program
   Unit Pretest, page 77
   Chapter Test, page 83
   Unit Post-Test, pages 96, 97

Writing Process Activities, Evaluation Sheets, pages 8–12

RE-TEACHING

Practice Pages or Practice Book, page 130
Writing Process Activities, pages 24, 25

THINKING SKILLS

Synthesis—*Writing* a first draft from an outline (Exercise, page 477)
   Writing a first draft of an original paragraph (Developing Writing Skills, page 478)

Audience: Friends   Purpose: To explain

Topic Sentence: A bottle of mustard in the wrong hands can easily cause a disaster.

The Situation
1. My family busy packing for camping trip
2. My friend Jack making sandwiches for picnic lunch

What Jack Did
1. Got out plastic mustard bottle, which had not been used in months
2. Lined up slices of bread
3. Squeezed bottle lightly—nothing came out
4. Turned bottle upside down and tapped it
5. Squeezed bottle hard—caused a big pop like a balloon exploding

Results of Jack's Actions
1. Made me laugh and slip in the mustard
2. Splattered mustard everywhere—on the counter, on the refrigerator, on Jack's shirt and jeans, on the floor
3. Took us an hour to clean up the kitchen

DEVELOPING WRITING SKILLS: Drafting Your Paragraph. Using the outline you prepared for Developing Writing Skills at the end of Section 24.2, draft your paragraph. Follow the suggestions in the chart on page 476 as you write.
Answers will vary.

24.4 Revising a Paragraph

Because communicating well in writing is a challenge, it often requires extra time and effort. Even after you have planned and drafted a paragraph, you may not have written exactly what you want to say. Or you may have overlooked problems in your main idea and supporting information that will mislead a reader. For these reasons *revising* is an important

OBJECTIVES

After completing this section, students should be able to

- Identify and correct topic sentences that are too narrow or too general.

- Identify and correct supporting information that provides too little support or that contains generalizations and weak opinions.
- Identify and correct paragraphs that lack unity and coherence.
- Use a checklist to locate problems in paragraphs and correct them.

24.4 Revising a Paragraph

stage. Revising means taking a fresh look at your writing. It means rethinking ideas, seeing your writing as another person would, and often rewriting sentences or even the whole paragraph to make improvements. This section discusses weaknesses you should look for in your paragraphs and ways you can revise to make your paragraphs stronger.

REVISING: Looking at Your Topic Sentence

A topic sentence should always give the reader a clear idea of what the paragraph covers. When you revise, you may discover that your topic sentence does not do this. For one reason or another, it may simply not fit the supporting information you have chosen to use in your paragraph. A topic sentence might be too narrow; that is, it might cover only some of the supporting information. Or it might be too general and suggest that the paragraph will cover much more information than it does. In either case the topic sentence should be revised.

Rewrite a topic sentence that is too narrow or too general by expanding or narrowing its focus to express the main idea of the entire paragraph.

The statements that follow are three possible topic sentences for a paragraph about the different animals and plants on beaches. Read each topic sentence and notice why only one of the topic sentences is suitable for the paragraph.

TOO NARROW: Every type of beach has its own special plant life.

TOO GENERAL: The beaches around the world surprise us with their variety.

CLEARLY FOCUSED: Every type of beach—whether rock or pebble, sand or mud—has its own characteristic group of animals and plants.

TEACHING
Getting Started
Tell students that revising is an important step in their writing. Many students dislike revising, feeling that it reflects badly on what they have created. Stress the fact that professional writers revise constantly. It is not a stage that becomes unnecessary with practice, but rather more valuable.

Explain that, after a first draft is written, the topic sentence can be evaluated in context. If it is too broad or narrow, the paragraph will set up false expectations and confuse the reader rather than setting the stage. To illustrate, have ready to show on an overhead projector several paragraphs with inappropriate topic sentences. Have students locate the topic sentence of each, discuss its problem, and suggest alternatives.

480

Text Follow Through

Discuss text pages 478–492.

Assign Exercise A, page 480; Exercise B, page 484; Exercise C, page 488; Exercise D, page 489; Exercise E, page 492; and Developing Writing Skills, page 492.

Less advanced   This section of the text will prove more useful throughout the year, for reference when problems in writing arise, than when used as a one-time study. Students need to apply the principles to their own work numerous times to be able to use them reasonably well. You may want to help students make the revisions called for in Exercises B and D by discussing in detail the reasons for making the revisions.

Average   Students may benefit from conducting a class revision of one or more unattributed paragraphs written by students in previous years. As a variation of the basic activity, you might divide the class into eight groups, give each group one of the points in the checklist to consider, and then conduct a revision based on the findings of each group.

Advanced   As a challenge for students, prepare a paragraph of comparison and contrast with several extraneous ideas, poor organization, and errors in grammar and sentence structure. Have each student revise the paragraph to make it as unified, coherent, and smooth as possible. Students may then want to read their versions for one another and discuss which changes work best.

Now read the paragraph with the clearly focused topic sentence at the beginning.

Paragraph with a focused topic sentence   Every type of beach—whether rock or pebble, sand or mud—has its own characteristic group of animals and plants. The beach is a world of transition, washed by the ebb and flow of the tides and subject to constant change. The upper reaches are covered by sea water only briefly at high tide, while the lower parts of the beach are rarely exposed. Consequently, the resident animal and plant species vary from top to bottom of the beach, those at the top having little tolerance of salt water, while those lower down being unable to survive for long without it.—Adapted from *Rand McNally Atlas of the Oceans*

If you were to use either of the other two topic sentences, the reader would probably be confused. The topic sentence that is too narrow mentions plant life but not animal life. The topic sentence that is too general prepares the reader for a general discussion of beaches around the world, not for a paragraph on the animal and plant life on beaches.

To find and correct problems in topic sentences, read your paragraph and then check the supporting information against the topic sentence. If the paragraph holds together but the topic sentence does not fit, revise the topic sentence.

EXERCISE A: Improving Topic Sentences. Each of the following underlined topic sentences is either too narrow or too general. Briefly describe why the topic sentence needs to be revised. Then rewrite each topic sentence to fit its paragraph.

(1) You should always practice certain safety measures. Try to figure out exactly where you are going in the city before you set off. Carry street maps, addresses, and important phone numbers with you. Even if you do get lost, try to look as though you know where you are going. It is also a good idea not to

Revisions will vary; problems are identified and sample changes are given.

Additional Practice

Practice Pages, page 130
Writing Process Activities, pages 24, 25
Writing Workshops, pages 10–12

24.4 Revising a Paragraph

wear expensive jewelry, especially gold chains and bracelets. Furthermore, for your own protection, do not act overly friendly or casually start conversations with strangers. Acting purposeful and occupied with your own thoughts will help you blend in safely with the other people in a big city. Too general: When visiting an unfamiliar city, you should practice certain safety measures.

(2) Katherine Sutton, the main character in the fantasy *The Perilous Gard,* has a sharp mind. When Queen Mary of England banishes her to a remote castle for something she did not do, Katherine does not feel sorry for herself. She rides for miles through cold, rainy forests without complaining to her guards. Once settled in the mysterious castle, she explores the nearby countryside alone. Her curiosity is aroused when the townspeople shut their doors in her face and the children run from her. Katherine determines to find the answers to these puzzles and to her questions about the castle. When the People of the Hill imprison the man she loves, she follows him into captivity. Every day she risks her life by going to his cell to talk to him so that he will not go insane. Finally, by speaking the truth in her blunt way, she breaks through the hypnotic trance that threatens to destroy him and saves his life. Too narrow: Katherine Sutton, the main character in the fantasy The Perilous Gard, displays remarkable intelligence, strength, and courage.

REVISING: Looking at Your Supporting Information

You should also examine the supporting information in your paragraphs. There are a number of ways you may be able to strengthen this information.

Revising Paragraphs That Do Not Have Enough Support. Sometimes a paragraph may simply not have enough supporting information to explain its topic sentence or to make the paragraph convincing to a reader.

Revise a paragraph that does not have enough support by adding more information.

When you reread your paragraph, you may discover either that it leaves the reader with unanswered questions or that it

TESTING

Test Program

Unit Pretest, page 77
Chapter Test, page 83
Unit Post-Test, pages 96, 97

Writing Process Activities,
Evaluation Sheets,
pages 8–12

RE-TEACHING

Practice Pages, page 130
Writing Process Activities,
pages 24, 25

THINKING SKILLS

Synthesis—*Rewriting* topic
sentences (Exercise A, page 480)
Rewriting to improve supporting information (Exercise B, page 484)
Revising a paragraph for unity (Exercise C, page 488)
Revising a paragraph for coherence (Exercise D, page 489)

Evaluation—*Appraising* and *revising* someone else's writing (Exercise E, page 492)
Appraising and *revising* an original paragraph (Developing Writing Skills, page 492)

Writing-Model Transparencies

Checklist for Revising a Paragraph appears in transparency form. See Checklists, page 327.

simply seems sketchy. If so, gather a few more examples, facts, or other kinds of supporting information that will help the reader understand or appreciate the main idea. You might also look for words or ideas that readers could find confusing. If you find any of these, add definitions and details that will help clarify your ideas.

The following paragraph is underdeveloped. It barely begins to support its main idea.

Paragraph with not enough supporting information
> Law students face a terrifying world during their first year of law school. Their professors and their textbooks use legal language full of difficult words that the students do not understand. To make matters worse, they must read and remember hundreds of pages of legal material a week.

The preceding paragraph gives only two examples to explain why law students face a "terrifying world." To be clear, the paragraph should have at least two or three more examples, as in the paragraph below.

Paragraph developed with complete supporting information
> Law students face a terrifying world during their first year of law school. Their professors and their textbooks use legal language full of difficult words that the students do not understand. To make matters worse, they must read and remember hundreds of pages of legal material a week. Often, a professor will call on students in class and expect them to discuss in detail the cases they have read. Perhaps the worst part of first-year law school is learning to take the exams. Most college classes require several papers and exams during the semester; in contrast, law school puts more pressure on students by having their grades depend entirely on one exam given at the end of each course. On a single four- or eight-hour exam, students must show how well they have mastered the material covered in an entire course.

24.4 Revising a Paragraph

Revising Paragraphs with Weak Support. The supporting information in a paragraph can also be a problem if it consists mainly of generalizations and weak opinions. A paragraph with weak support will not inform or persuade a reader.

Revise a paragraph made up of generalizations and weak opinions by replacing them with specific examples, details, facts, and reasons.

On rereading your paragraph, you may find that some of your supporting information takes up space without expanding a reader's knowledge. Generalizations will not help the reader grasp your ideas. Similarly, opinions that are not supported with specific information will have little meaning for the reader. You should cross out these pieces of weak support and substitute examples, details, facts, or reasons that will help the reader visualize or understand your main idea. Note how the following paragraph is unclear because it consists mainly of generalizations and weak opinions.

Paragraph with generalizations and weak opinions

My brother's college graduation was a ceremony full of tradition and high spirits. As the audience arrived, a small band played music. Then groups of people in robes and other people carrying flags marched down the center aisle. It was very exciting. Everyone acted proud and important. Next the students filed down to the front of the audience. Then members of the audience cheered as students they knew received their diplomas. The students displayed their enthusiasm when the president awarded their degrees. At the end the procession walked back down the aisle. The ceremony was really meaningful. It was fantastic.

Most likely, the preceding paragraph has failed to convince you that the graduation "was a ceremony full of tradition and high spirits." Simply saying that something is "meaningful" and "fantastic" will not impress most readers. The paragraph could also be made more effective if generalizations such as "groups of people" and "other people" were replaced by specific details and examples.

Paragraph with strong, specific supporting information

My brother's college graduation was a ceremony full of tradition and high spirits. While the audience poured into the rows of chairs on the huge lawn, a small band could be heard playing music from the top of the bell tower right above. Then five graduates of the class of 1923 walked proudly down the center aisle as the audience clapped. Soon robed marshals carried in the multicolored flags that stand for engineering, medicine, humanities, and the other schools of the college. Marching in two by two, the faculty followed in robes and caps, with hoods in the colors of their schools: light blue, copper, purple, lemon, orange, green, salmon, and scarlet. Next the graduate students and the undergraduates streamed in proudly, their black robes and tassels fluttering in the breeze. After several brief speeches, members of the audience applauded as students they knew received their diplomas. When the president of the college declared that the undergraduates had officially graduated, all eight hundred of them tossed their caps into the air and cheered. At the end, while people smiled and waved and cameras clicked, the whole procession swept down the aisle again.

EXERCISE B: Improving Supporting Information. Each of the paragraphs on the following page has problems with its supporting information. Identify the problem in each paragraph as either *not enough supporting information* or *generalizations and weak opinions*. Then revise each paragraph by rewriting it. Either add more specific information or remove the weak support and then add specific information.

Revisions will vary; problems are identified.

(1) Every student who needs economical transportation should consider a bicycle. A bicycle is a great way to get around. It is inexpensive to run. I really enjoy mine. A bicycle is better than a moped or a motorcycle. Most people who ride bicycles regularly recommend them highly.

(2) The arguments for giving away our kitten finally outweighed our reasons for keeping her. At first she was frisky, but eventually she became foul tempered. She scratched us when we picked her up, and she developed the habit of shooting across the room, leaping on us, and clinging with her claws. She started to bite with her little needle teeth.

1. generalizations and weak opinions   2. not enough supporting information

REVISING: Recognizing Problems with Unity and Coherence

During the revising stage, you should also think about the way in which the ideas throughout your paragraphs relate to each other. Do any ideas begin to take off on another topic? Does the paragraph seem disjointed in any way? If so, changes are needed.

Revising Paragraphs That Lack Unity. Occasionally, information that does not add anything or that is definitely unrelated may creep into your paragraphs.

Revise a paragraph that lacks unity by removing unrelated information and unnecessary details.

The following paragraph lacks unity because the writer has gotten sidetracked in a few places and has included some details (printed in italics) that are not needed.

Paragraph with unrelated information and unnecessary details

During our vacation in the White Mountains in New Hampshire, I barely survived the insects. Whenever I stepped outside the cabin, the mosquitoes found me. In just a few hours, I had red itchy mounds on my legs, arms, neck, and even my forehead. *The mosquitoes bother me at home too.* Even when I used mosquito spray, I could hear them whining in my ears when we walked along the lake in the evening. I was not safe from bugs on the water, either. When I tried to slap a horsefly that had circled me for ten minutes, I nearly capsized the canoe. *Horsefly bites can be especially painful, and sometimes these insects carry diseases.* I was particularly disturbed by the assortment of insects that rested on the wall under our cabin's porch light. To enter the cabin, I had to whip open the door and dash inside, slamming the door in the same motion. Even so, a few beetles, mosquitoes, and little moths usually slipped in to buzz and flutter around the lamps. *The lamps are all beautiful, old kerosene lamps, but they are a little unstable.* The giant moths as big as my hand unnerved me most. Like bats they flapped against the screens each night, giving us all nightmares.

If you reread the paragraph above, mentally leaving out the sentences in italics, you will see how much more direct the unified paragraph is. With some paragraphs, such as the preceding one, you can simply cross out unrelated sentences to make the paragraphs unified. With other paragraphs you may need to take out parts of sentences and then rewite the parts of the sentences that are left.

Revising Paragraphs That Lack Coherence. A paragraph may be unified and complete but still not read logically or smoothly. A paragraph that lacks coherence can confuse a reader because its ideas are not clearly organized or well connected. When you revise, you should make sure that your ideas are presented as clearly as possible.

Revise a paragraph that lacks coherence by reorganizing the support in a more logical order, by adding any necessary transitions, and by adding a concluding sentence if you think it will help.

24.4 Revising a Paragraph

When you reexamine your paragraph during the revising stage, you may find that some of your ideas do not follow logically from one to the next. If a reader is likely to have trouble following the order of your ideas, you should reorganize all or some of them for coherence. Maybe a different logical order would be more suitable for your topic sentence and support. If the basic order of your ideas is clear but the reader needs more guidance in following them, you should add transitions. Just one or two transitions can make the order of ideas in your paragraph clearer. With some paragraphs a concluding sentence can also help tie your ideas together. Reading a paragraph aloud and listening for the sense of the sentences will help you decide how you can improve its coherence.

The following paragraph lacks coherence because the writer jumps around too much. Notice how difficult it is to understand the ideas.

Paragraph with poorly organized supporting information

If new skiers follow some simple instructions, they will have few problems using the rope tows on ski slopes. The rope will yank the skiers forward. To get off skiers must head their skis away from the track, release the rope, and push with their bodies away from the tow. By keeping their weight evenly distributed on both skis and by holding both skis parallel in the track, the skiers will find that the rope will pull them steadily to the top of the slope. They should make sure that they have on their gloves or mittens because the moving rope can burn bare hands. When they are ready to get on, they should grab the rope with both hands. One hand should be in front of them and one hand behind. While the skiers get in line, they should loop the straps of their poles around the arm that will be closest to the rope tow. As their turn to get on approaches, they should slide their skis into the smooth track under the moving rope, which is about three feet off the ground.

To make the "simple instructions" listed in the paragraph clear, it needs to be reorganized. When the steps involved in using a rope tow are presented in the order in which a reader would follow them, the paragraph makes more sense. Adding a few transitions and a concluding sentence also helps.

Paragraph with logically organized supporting information and necessary transitions

If new skiers follow some simple instructions, they will have few problems using the rope tows on ski slopes. When the skiers get in line, they should loop the straps of their poles around the arm that will be closest to the tow. They should *also* make sure that they have on their gloves or mittens because the moving rope can burn bare hands. As their turn to get on approaches, they should slide their skis into the smooth track under the moving rope, which is about three feet off the ground. When they are ready to get on, they should grab the rope with both hands. One hand should be in front of them and one hand behind. *At first,* the rope will yank the skiers forward. *But* by keeping their weight evenly distributed on both skis and by holding both skis parallel in the track, the skiers will find that the rope will pull them steadily to the top of the slope. To get off, the skiers must head their skis away from the track, release the rope, and ski away from the tow. The rest is all downhill!

EXERCISE C: Revising a Paragraph for Unity.

Find the three sentences that do not belong in the following paragraph. Then write the new paragraph on your paper.

Revisions may vary; unrelated sentences are underlined.

(1) The city council has approved a number of new measures to beautify the waterfront area. (2) One measure, which will cost the city almost a quarter of a million dollars, involves sandblasting a row of townhouses. (3) The sandblasting will make these dingy brick buildings look fresh and elegant. (4) In cities all over the East, old buildings have been sandblasted and fixed up inside. (5) Then these buildings have been rented

as modern apartments. (6) Another measure calls for the installation of electrified gas lamps. (7) Although these lamps look antique, they will provide enough light to brighten the waterfront. (8) Some street lights can be glaring and ugly. (9) The council also voted money for borders of flowers along the walkways. (10) These changes will make the waterfront one of the most charming sections in the entire city.

EXERCISE D: Revising a Paragraph for Coherence. The following paragraph should describe a scene as taken in by viewers turning in a circle clockwise from north to west. Rewrite the paragraph so the details are logically organized. Consider adding more transitions and a concluding sentence.

Revisions will vary; probable new order of sentences: 1, 6, 3, 2, 7, 5, 4.

(1) The 360° view of the San Francisco Bay area from Mount Tamalpais entranced us. (2) Directly east, the purple cone of Mount Diablo stood out above the folds of the Coastal Range, and nearer to us Berkeley, Oakland, and the other cities spread from the top of the nearest range to the edge of the bay. (3) Nearer still to the east, the Richmond–San Rafael Bridge formed a slender band over the bay. (4) The Pacific Ocean to the west fringed the rocky coast and curled over the horizon. (5) The buildings of San Francisco twinkled to our south, soon to be engulfed by the creeping fog that had already hidden the coastline in that direction. (6) Looking north, we could see a puddle of blue—a reservoir—surrounded by gold hills and forests, and San Pablo Bay spread out to the northeast. (7) The San Francisco–Oakland Bay Bridge in the southeast looked like a chain strung from Oakland to Yerba Buena Island and from that island to San Francisco.

REVISING: Using a Checklist

You should now be familiar with some of the most common weaknesses that a paragraph can have. The practical methods on the following page can help you revise your writing.

Look at your writing after some time has passed, and use a checklist to help rethink your ideas and pinpoint problems.

In order to improve your writing, try to approach it from a new perspective. Leaving some time between writing and revising can help you see things you may have overlooked while writing. Sometimes hearing another person read your writing aloud can also help you be objective.

Once you are ready to take a fresh look at your writing, a checklist can help you find ways to make your writing stronger by pointing out some of the weaknesses discussed in this section. When you use a checklist, you should read each question and then reread your paragraph and think about that specific checklist item.

CHECKLIST FOR REVISING A PARAGRAPH

1. Does the topic sentence clearly express the main idea of the paragraph? If not, should you expand or narrow the focus of the topic sentence?
2. Have you included enough support to develop your topic sentence?
3. Can you find any generalizations and weak opinions that should be replaced with specific supporting information?
4. Are there any unnecessary pieces of information that your paragraph would be stronger without?
5. Would another order be better for your ideas? Would any of the ideas be clearer if they were introduced by transitions? Would a concluding sentence tie your paragraph's ideas together?
6. Could you make your paragraph more suited to your audience and purpose?
7. Could any of the sentences be lengthened, shortened, or combined for smoothness?
8. Are there any mistakes in grammar, usage, mechanics, or spelling?

24.4 Revising a Paragraph

Once you have finished making changes in your paragraph, you should write a neat, final copy of it. You should then proofread the final copy to correct any errors that were made in recopying. Proofreading completes the revising of your paragraph.

The following first draft of a paragraph shows the kinds of changes you should be prepared to make in your own paragraphs. Note that space has been left between all of the lines in the original paragraph. This makes it possible for new words, ideas, and even sentences to be added in the right places throughout.

Both water-skiing and cross-country skiing are good ways
Waterskiing is a good way to exercise. A summer sport, water-skiing depends on the arms and leg muscles to keep the skier riding along the water. *To begin, the* The skier grabs onto a tow line and is pulled up by a motorboat into standing position. Leg muscles and arm muscles help the skier pull up into position and *then* keep balanced as the boat races through the waves. *Like the water-skier, the* The cross-country skier depends on strong arm and leg muscles, too. In the winter, a person can get similar exercise by cross-country skiing. *However, the* The cross-country skier has no outside power pulling him or her along and must rely *even more* on arm and leg strength. The sport is not as much fun because of this extra work. Some people prefer downhill skiing. In cross-country skiing, the *skier* skiier works hard, using the legs to guide and push the skis and using the arms to jab the ski poles into and push off from the snow. *In summer or winter, the person who skis can get plenty of exercise.*

Developing Writing Skills

Have students practice planning, writing, and revising paragraphs by completing the following assignment.

Writing Across the Curriculum

To draw large crowds, professional sports teams must attract the attention of fans by publicizing the qualities that make the team exciting to watch.

Prewriting Imagine that you are the publicity director for your favorite professional team. Brainstorm about the qualities that make the team exciting to watch. As you are brainstorming, record each idea you come up with. Then organize your ideas according to order of importance.

Writing Write a paragraph in which you discuss the team's most exciting qualities. Make sure that you begin with a clear topic sentence and that you thoroughly support your topic sentence in the body of your paragraph. Also make sure that you use transitions to connect your ideas.

Revising Revise your paragraph using the checklist on page 490 of your textbook. When you have finished revising, proofread your paragraph and prepare a final copy. Then share your paragraph with your classmates.

As you can see from the revision, the first draft of the preceding paragraph had a number of problems. Revising has expanded the topic sentence to cover the entire paragraph. A weak opinion and a piece of unrelated information have been eliminated. One piece of supporting information has been moved, and several transitions have been added. Finally, a concluding sentence has been written to tie together the paragraph's ideas.

EXERCISE E: Improving Someone Else's Writing. With another student, exchange first drafts of the paragraphs you wrote for Developing Writing Skills in Section 24.3. Use the checklist on page 490 and the ideas in this section to improve the other student's paragraph. Make your revisions right on your partner's paper.
Answers will vary.

DEVELOPING WRITING SKILLS: Revising Your Own Paragraphs. Use the paragraph that your partner worked with in Exercise E and another paragraph that you have written recently to produce *two* revised paragraphs. First, examine your partner's revisions. If you agree with the changes, keep them. If you think other revisions would be better, make them. Finish your revising by copying your paragraph in its final form and proofreading it for errors. Next, take the other paragraph and use the checklist on page 490 to identify weaknesses. Make your changes right on your paper. Finally, recopy this revised paragraph, and proofread it for errors.
Answers will vary.

Writing Workshop: Writing Paragraphs

ASSIGNMENT 1

Topic   A Peculiar Animal

Form and Purpose   A paragraph that informs a reader about the special qualities of an unusual animal

Audience   Producer of a television program called *Animals*

Length   One paragraph

Focus   Identify and describe the animal. Give details, facts, or examples that explain why this animal is unusual.

Sources   Books, magazines, encyclopedia articles

Prewriting   Narrow the topic to one particular animal by researching and brainstorming. Decide on a main idea and write a topic sentence. Gather and organize support.

Writing   Using your prewriting notes, complete a first draft.

Revising   To help you make changes in your draft, use the checklist on page 490. Then write a complete, final version.

Guiding Student Writing

Encourage students to find their own approach to completing some Writing Workshop assignments. Students can experiment with the planning, writing, and revising steps to find a process that works well for them. For example, instead of preparing an outline, students can organize their supporting information while they are writing by using the cueing technique or by preparing a brainstorming sheet. Students can also try making revisions while writing their first draft.

The writing process needs to be seen as recursive, as looping back on itself. Students are more likely to write several drafts if they know their work will be published, or recognized publicly, in some way. Classroom bulletin boards, occasional oral readings, or printed publications are all ways to recognize and encourage student writers.

Assignment 1

Suggestions for Prewriting: Insist that students do indeed choose a peculiar animal. They should take notes as they seek information. Suggest that they include a picture of the animal, if possible.

Suggestions for Writing: Remind students to keep their audience in mind. The producer is presumably knowledgeable about animals and will be impatient with simplistic information.

Assignment 2

Suggestions for Prewriting: Record the class's suggestions, even silly ones, on the board; then ask students to evaluate which would make a good paragraph. You might require each student to interview one non-family adult in the community.

Suggestions for Publishing: Ask Writers of the better paragraphs to convert them to letters and send them to the local paper.

ASSIGNMENT 2

Topic   Our Town or City Needs _____

Form and Purpose   A paragraph that supports your opinion

Audience   Readers of your local newspaper

Length   One paragraph

Focus   In your topic sentence develop a main idea about something that your town or city needs. Support that idea with facts, examples, and reasons.

Sources   Local newspapers, interviews with neighbors and local political leaders, personal observations

Prewriting   Narrow your topic to an important need in your town or city. Write a topic sentence, and brainstorm for support. Arrange the support in a logical order.

Writing   Write a first draft following your notes.

Revising   Use the checklist on page 490 to make changes and prepare a final draft.

Topics for Writing: Writing Paragraphs

The photo may suggest to you an idea for a writing topic. Plan, write, and revise a paragraph about that topic. If you prefer, choose one of the topics below. You may have to narrow the topic first.

1. Computers: A Threat to Jobs?
2. Computers: A Threat to Privacy?
3. Should All Students Be Required to Take a Computer Literacy Course?
4. Does Everyone Need a Computer?
5. Uses of Computers in Education
6. How the Silicon Chip Changed the Computer
7. Video Games: Exciting or Boring?
8. A Career in the Computer Industry
9. Theft with a Computer: A Serious Threat?
10. The Benefits of Computer Use in a Business

Stimulating Thought

1. Consider both jobs lost and jobs gained.
2. "What about you and your family with a computer? How might it be misused?"
3. Future job use
   Increasing home use
4. Personal finance
   Personal records
   Word processing
5. In science and math
   In English
   In business and courses
6. Size
   Environmental needs
   Speed
   Cost
7. "A fantasy escape or mindless button-pushing?"
8. Computer programming
   Hardware design
   Computer education
9. "Find news reports of actual or attempted thefts. How are they done? What safeguards are there?"
10. Payroll
    Inventory
    Accounts payable and receivable

CHAPTER 25

Kinds of Writing

(pp. 496–512)

Each section in this chapter explores a different kind of writing: expository, persuasive, and descriptive. (Narrative writing is treated separately in Chapter 30.) Within each section students will consider both the special features of and the language appropriate to each of the different kinds of writing. They will also have a chance to plan and write one or more paragraphs of each type.

For additional or alternate writing assignments and a list of topics for writing, see pages 510–512.

25.1 Writing Paragraphs That Explain

(pp. 496–500)

OBJECTIVES

After completing this section, students should be able to

- Identify the features of an expository paragraph, develop a topic sentence and support appropriate for one.
- Use informative language in a paragraph that explains.

Chapter

25

Kinds of Writing

In this chapter you will learn about three different kinds of writing: *expository, persuasive,* and *descriptive.* Each serves a different purpose, and each creates a different kind of relationship between writer and audience. This chapter uses paragraphs as models for discussing the three different types of writing.

25.1 Writing to Explain

Expository writing explains something. In school you may write expository paragraphs for science, social studies, and English. Outside of school you may write expository paragraphs in carrying out club activities, in giving directions, and in letters.

Focusing on an Explanatory Purpose

Whenever you write a paragraph in order to explain some thing or to instruct your reader about something, your purpose will be explanatory. Your goal will be to share information with

25.1 Writing to Explain

an audience. To carry out this purpose, you must make sure that your topic sentence is a factual statement. You should also make sure that the supporting information develops this statement with factual, specific information, arranged so that the reader can grasp it easily.

An expository paragraph explains a factual main idea with factual, specific support that is clearly arranged for the reader.

The topic sentence of an expository paragraph must be a factual statement. It must *not* offer an opinion. It should simply tell the reader what information the paragraph will develop. The first of the following topic sentences would make sense at the beginning of an expository paragraph. The second, which states an opinion, would not.

FACTUAL TOPIC SENTENCE: Many different methods can be used to learn a foreign language.

OPINIONATED TOPIC SENTENCE: The only way to learn a new language is to visit a country where the language is spoken.

The supporting information in an expository paragraph should also be factual, as well as easily understood. You should gather examples, details, and facts about your topic from your own life, from books, and from other sources. Then you should organize your support so that a reader can follow it easily. Consider the logical orders that you studied in Section 23.4, and choose one that suits your topic. As you gather and organize your information, keep in mind your audience's understanding of the topic. A less knowledgeable reader will need more background information than one who is familiar with your topic.

The following expository paragraph explains the history of a musical instrument: the recorder. The explanatory purpose of the paragraph is evident from the topic sentence. The para-

TEACHING

Getting Started

Tell students that their purpose in writing an expository paragraph is to share information with an audience and that the topic sentence of an expository paragraph must be a factual statement. You might want to work with students on statements of fact and opinion. Write the following on the chalkboard:

DDT is a toxic insecticide. All insecticides should be banned.

Have a volunteer tell why one statement is factual and the other is not. Ask for volunteers to suggest other topic sentences for students to identify as fact or opinion.

Text Follow Through

Discuss text pages 496–500.

Assign Exercise A, page 498; Exercise B, page 499; Exercise C, page 500; and Developing Writing Skills, page 500.

Less advanced   You may want to work closely with small groups of students as they complete Exercise B. Then, in place of Exercise C, these students might simply list supporting information they could use to develop one of the topic sentences in Exercise B. Finally, for Developing Writing Skills, they can write that paragraph rather than develop a new one.

Average   Students can exchange their finished paragraphs from both Exercise C and Developing Writing Skills and suggest revisions, checking especially for clarity and logical order.

graph develops the topic with historical facts, presenting the information chronologically so that readers who know little about music can still understand.

TOPIC SENTENCE (Factual statement)

Support in chronological order

The recorder dates back to Shakespeare, who speaks of it in some of his plays. In Elizabethan England, sets of recorders were found in nearly every home. Henry VIII's collection numbered seventy-five of them and Samuel Pepys kept eulogizing this pipe in his writings. The instrument stood foremost among woodwinds until the development of the modern orchestra which supplanted it with the transverse or side-blown flute. A twentieth century revival of the recorder took place in England, the continent, and the United States following the last war. Now more than 250,000 people are playing it over the country and adult evening classes are to be found in some schools.—Doron K. Antrim

EXERCISE A: Examining a Paragraph That Explains.
Read the expository paragraph and answer the questions.

Refinishing old wooden furniture takes time, patience, diligence, and a large supply of sandpaper. Begin by thoroughly cleaning the piece you want to refinish. Then, you can remove old layers of paint or shellac with a commercial solvent, although most experts recommend shaving these layers off carefully with a sharp chisel. Then you can begin refining and smoothing the wood with sandpaper. You should use very coarsely grained paper at first, switching several times to increasingly finer grains. When the surface is perfectly smooth, you can apply a quick-drying stain to protect the wood and bring out its grain. Your old hand-me-down is now something you can show off proudly!

1. What is the topic sentence?
2. List the items of support.
3. How is the support organized?

1. first sentence 2. Answers may vary with reason. 3. chronological order

Use the following Springboards
for Writing transparency and
blackline master for additional
practice:
A Paragraph That Explains,
pages 137–141

25.1 Writing to Explain

EXERCISE B: Planning an Expository Paragraph. Each of
the following topics could be used as the basis for an expository paragraph. Identify a specific audience for each topic.
Then write a topic sentence that states a main idea about the
topic. Be prepared to explain what kind of information you
would use to support each topic sentence.

Answers will vary.

Ways of conserving en-
ergy in the home

What causes a rainbow

Directions from school to
your home

A comparison between
two towns

How to find a book in a
bookstore

Focusing on Informative Language

In expository writing you should use language that teaches
and informs. Your words should be clear, so they will help the
reader grasp your explanation.

**The language in an expository paragraph should
be informative. It should be made up of words
that will help the reader understand each of the
ideas you are presenting.**

Your purpose will help you find the most appropriate language for your expository paragraph. Because you are explaining something, you should choose words that offer facts, not
opinions, as clearly as possible. Try to keep your audience in
mind as you write, explaining those terms that a reader may
not understand. You should also try to choose very specific,
precise language throughout your paragraph.

To help the reader follow the information that you are presenting, you should use transitions as well.

Look at how the expository paragraph about recorders on
page 498 uses language to inform the reader. The paragraph is
simple but factual: It includes several numbers and refers to
familiar historical figures such as Shakespeare and Henry VIII.

It also explains that the term *transverse* means "side-blown." Finally, it explains the history of the recorder in clear, precise words that are easy to follow, and it uses language that makes the historical progression clear: *dates back to, Elizabethan England, modern orchestra, twentieth century, last war,* and *now.*

EXERCISE C: Using Informative Language. Using one of the topic sentences that you wrote in Exercise B, write an expository paragraph using informative language. Keep your specific purpose and audience in mind as you write.
Paragraphs will vary.

DEVELOPING WRITING SKILLS: Writing a Paragraph to Explain. Choose a topic of your own for an expository paragraph. Decide who your audience is. Then write a topic sentence. Finally, write and revise your paragraph, making sure that it clearly explains your topic.
Paragraphs will vary.

25.2 Writing to Persuade

There are many situations in which you may need to write persuasively. You might want to express your opinion about a problem in your school or community. You might be asked to argue for or against a political issue in your social studies class. Or you might someday want to convince an employer to use an idea of yours. Many different writing situations require an ability to persuade. This section will discuss the basic features of *persuasive* writing: a persuasive purpose and reasonable language. It will also give you several chances to use your own persuasive skills.

Focusing on a Persuasive Purpose

Whenever you write a paragraph to convince someone to accept your opinion, take an action of some kind, or simply look at something in a new way, you will need to write persuasively.

25.2 Writing to Persuade

To do this, you must let your persuasive purpose shape your entire paragraph. Your topic sentence should state your opinion. Your support should offer specific and convincing evidence, and the entire paragraph should be presented in an effective order.

A persuasive paragraph attempts to convince a reader to accept the writer's opinion by using specific evidence that is arranged logically.

Your topic sentence should make your persuasive purpose clear by expressing your opinion in strong but reasonable terms. You should state your opinion firmly, but at the same time, you should try not to offend those who disagree with you. The following topic sentences manage to sound reasonable, even while expressing very definite opinions.

TOPIC SENTENCES FOR PERSUASIVE PARAGRAPHS

The proposal to eliminate art and music classes in our school should be vigorously opposed by students and parents because it would deprive students of many valuable experiences.

The major weakness in local news broadcasts is their emphasis on a few sensational stories at the expense of thorough coverage of issues that affect most of the people watching.

Like the topic sentence, the support in a persuasive paragraph should present your case forcefully while taking into account the opposing view. To convince an audience of your main idea, you should provide strong reasons, facts, examples, and other information to support your opinion. You might even try to answer possible objections to your arguments in order to win over readers who oppose your ideas. In addition, you should try to make the most of your evidence by organizing it effectively. One very useful method is to lead your reader up to your strongest argument by organizing your ideas according to the order of their importance.

Getting Started

Tell students that when they write a persuasive paragraph, their topic sentence should state their opinion and that their opinion should be stated in strong but reasonable terms. Direct students' attention to the examples of topic sentences for persuasive paragraphs on page 501. Point out to students that neither of these examples merely makes a value judgment. Rather, both state opinions in a way that makes it possible to provide logical reasons. Write these alternatives on the board and ask students how these topic sentences fail: *The proposal to eliminate . . . because it is crummy and unfair. The major weakness . . . is the stupid way they hype everything from worthless lost kittens to really important sports events.*

Text Follow Through

Discuss text pages 500–504.

Assign Exercise A, page 502; Exercise B, page 503; Exercise C, page 504; and Developing Writing Skills, page 504.

Less advanced If the recommendations for Section 25.1 worked well with students, you may want to follow the same procedure here. Work with students on Exercise B, have them plan in detail for Exercise C, and allow them to use the same topic in place of a new one when they do Developing Writing Skills.

Average You might want to have students bring to class an editorial from a local newspaper or from the school paper. Students can analyze the editorial, noting in writing as many of the following points as you assign:

1. The writer's purpose
2. The topic sentence of one of the paragraphs
3. The pieces of support used
4. An evaluation of the organization
5. Examples of reasonable or, if such is the case, offensive language used

Advanced Students might read to each other the paragraphs they write for Developing Writing Skills, omitting the topic sentences. The listener can then try to write a topic sentence that expresses both the topic and the writer's opinion.

Additional Practice

Practice Pages or Practice Book, page 132
Writing Process Activities, pages 28, 29

TESTING

Test Program

Unit Pretest, page 77
Chapter Test, page 84
Unit Post-Test, pages 96, 97

Writing Process Activities, Evaluation Sheets, pages 8–12

RE-TEACHING

Practice Pages or Practice Book, page 132
Writing Process Activities, pages 28, 29

The following persuasive paragraph offers arguments in support of an opinion about traffic restrictions. Note the firm but reasonable opinion in the topic sentence. Note also that the arguments are arranged in order of importance.

TOPIC SENTENCE (Opinion)

Support in order of importance

This city could solve a number of problems if it began restricting automobile traffic in downtown areas this fall. Our public transportation system is excellent, and yet our streets are usually choked with private cars in addition to buses and taxicabs. This amount of traffic increases the pollution, dirt, and noise in our streets. Furthermore, heavily traveled streets need more frequent repairs, which the city cannot afford. And, most important, the need to regulate automobile traffic spreads our police force too thin to perform its other duties. The protection of lives and property could be improved if fewer police officers were tied up in traffic duty. Limiting people's use of private automobiles would cause some inconvenience, it is true. But this inconvenience would be offset by the benefits of such a move. If automobile traffic were reduced, the city could then direct its human and financial resources toward making our streets cleaner, safer, and more pleasant for all of us.

EXERCISE A: Examining a Paragraph That Persuades. Read the following persuasive paragraph and answer the questions after it.

Despite their aches and pains, old houses have more appeal than modern homes. For one thing old houses, designed before architects began to place a high value on light and space, have many odd corners and surprising little nooks. New houses may be airier and easier to clean, but one seldom finds surprises in their open spaces. Because materials and labor cost less in the past, old houses were built more solidly than their modern counterparts. There seems to be more to an old house—more material, more detail, more rooms, more *house*. Finally, the feeling of time is built into old houses. Newer homes often seem barren and nearly identical. In an old house, the plumbing may be rusting and the wallpaper may be curling away, but its character and atmosphere keep growing over the years.

1. What is the topic sentence? first sentence
2. Identify the major pieces of support in the paragraph.
3. How are these pieces of support arranged in the paragraph?

2. Answers may vary within reason.   3. comparison and contrast order (or order of importance)

EXERCISE B: Planning a Persuasive Paragraph. Each of the following topics could be used as the basis for a persuasive paragraph. Write each topic on your paper and decide what opinion or stand each paragraph might express. Decide on your audience as well. Then write a topic sentence for each topic. Be prepared to explain what kind of supporting information you would provide in the rest of each paragraph.
Answers will vary.

A pass/fail grading system	Eliminating physical education
A particular commercial on television	Using safety belts in cars
Having one's own room or apartment	

Focusing on Reasonable Language

Just as the topic sentence in a persuasive paragraph should be stated firmly without offending those who disagree, the language throughout the paragraph should be both forceful and reasonable.

Persuasive paragraphs should use convincing but reasonable language to win readers over to the writer's viewpoint.

With practice it is not difficult to state opinions strongly but unemotionally. Imagine that you are speaking directly to some-

THINKING SKILLS

Analysis—*Identifying* the features of a paragraph that persuades (Exercise A, page 502)

Synthesis—*Planning* a persuasive paragraph (Exercise B, page 503)
Writing a persuasive paragraph using reasonable language (Exercise C, page 504)

Evaluation—*Planning, writing, appraising,* and *revising* a paragraph to persuade (Developing Writing Skills, page 504)

Writing Model Transparencies

Use the following Springboards for Writing transparency and blackline master for additional practice:
A Paragraph That Persuades, pages 143–147

one who disagrees with you but who is willing to listen to reason. To win over such a listener, you should find specific language that establishes your point clearly and directly without overstating it. If your arguments are good, they do not need to be pumped up with emotion-charged words. Above all you should avoid name-calling and other offensive references to opposing opinions. It only does your argument harm to make a remark such as "Any idiot could see that I am right."

Take another look at the persuasive paragraph on page 502 arguing in favor of limiting automobile traffic. Note that although the issue is important, the writer has used simple, specific words, letting the arguments speak for themselves. The writer does not ridicule or blame drivers of automobiles and even admits that the proposal would cause them some inconvenience. Note also how smoothly the transitions lead the reader to the writer's final and strongest argument.

EXERCISE C: Using Reasonable Language. Using one of the topic sentences that you developed for Exercise B, write a persuasive paragraph using reasonable language.
Paragraphs will vary.

DEVELOPING WRITING SKILLS: Writing a Paragraph to Persuade. Choose a topic of your own for a persuasive paragraph. Decide on both your opinion and your audience. Then write a topic sentence. Finally, write and revise your paragraph, making it as persuasive as possible while using reasonable language.
Paragraphs will vary.

25.3 Writing to Describe

You probably write *descriptive* paragraphs often—in letters, on postcards, in notes to friends—in short, whenever you want your readers to appreciate how something appears to you. This section will discuss the basic features of descriptive writing: a descriptive purpose and descriptive language. It will also give you a chance to exercise your creativity in writing descriptive paragraphs of your own.

Focusing on a Descriptive Purpose

The purpose of any descriptive paragraph is to provide a sharp, vivid picture for the reader. The descriptive paragraphs you write will naturally be based on your own powers of observation: your ability to note the exact details of your topic and to share them with your reader. Your choice of details and your organization of details are also important. Your goal should be to make it possible for your reader to form a specific *dominant impression* of your topic, to "see it with your eyes."

A descriptive paragraph creates a dominant impression of a person, place, or thing through the use of vivid details arranged so that the reader can also see or experience the thing described.

A descriptive paragraph should give the reader a single dominant impression of your topic. This dominant impression will be the main idea of your paragraph, the idea that holds your description together. The dominant impression in a descriptive paragraph can be a particular quality of what you are describing. For example, in describing your brother, you might emphasize his weird sense of humor. The dominant impression you create can also be a *mood,* an emotion that runs throughout your description. For example, you might describe a quiet room in such a way that the reader feels tranquil and secure.

The dominant impression will generally be the topic sentence of a descriptive paragraph. In some cases, however, the dominant impression may not be expressed easily in a topic sentence. Instead, the various details of the paragraph may add up to a dominant impression that is implied rather than stated.

OBJECTIVES

After completing this section, students should be able to

- Identify the features of a descriptive paragraph, and develop a topic sentence offering a dominant impression and support appropriate for a descriptive paragraph.
- Use a number of different kinds of descriptive language in a paragraph that describes.

TEACHING

Getting Started

Tell students that the purpose of a descriptive paragraph is to provide a sharp, vivid picture for the reader, who should be able to form a dominant impression of the topic. Direct students' attention to the examples of topic sentences for descriptive paragraphs on page 506. Using the second topic sentence as an example, make columns on the board headed by the words *Sounds, Sights, Smells, Sensations,* and *Textures.* Ask students to list details they think would vividly support this topic sentence. Encourage specificity of word choices and use of figurative language.

Text Follow Through

Discuss text pages 504–509.

Assign Exercise A, page 507; Exercise B, page 507; Exercise C, page 509; and Developing Writing Skills, page 509.

Less advanced Students might benefit from studying or reviewing Section 21.1, particularly the material on vivid language and connotations. These students could also base their paragraphs for the present section on one of the sentences in Exercise C of Section 21.1. Using that sentence as a topic sentence for a descriptive paragraph, students can make up vivid descriptive details, decide on the arrangement of the details, and then write the paragraph.

Average Students can bring to class a descriptive paragraph from their outside reading and discuss any vivid modifiers or figures of speech used by the writer. The various examples of descriptive language can then be compared and evaluated.

Advanced To emphasize the creation of mood in a descriptive paragraph, you might suggest the following. Have students choose a specific place and write a paragraph describing how it would look on a bright sunny day from the point of view of someone who has just received some good news. They can then write a second paragraph describing the same place on a dismal, dreary day from the point of view of someone who has just suffered a disappointment. If students need help deciding on a place, you might suggest the following:

1. The street on which a student lives
2. The school grounds
3. A familiar room
4. A beach or lakefront

Additional Practice

Practice Pages or Practice Book, page 133
Writing Process Activities, pages 30, 31
Writing Workshops, pages 13–15

Each of the following sentences expresses a dominant impression in a topic sentence.

TOPIC SENTENCES FOR DESCRIPTIVE PARAGRAPHS

In his black trenchcoat and dark glasses, Father became an altogether different—almost glamorous—personality.
After a few days, the normally comforting sound of rain drumming steadily on our roof grew more and more maddening.

Support in a descriptive paragraph should be made up of details based on careful observation. You should always try to select the most vivid details you can find. Include specific details of shape, color, size, and texture to make the picture clear. Use sensory impressions—sights, sounds, smells, tastes, and sensations—to bring your topic to life. If you are describing a thing, you will probably concentrate on physical appearance. If your topic is a person, you can describe behavior and movement as well as physical appearance. And if you are recreating a scene, you can write about the people involved as well as the surroundings. You should arrange your details in the order that best conveys your dominant impression. For physical descriptions spatial order will often give your reader the best idea of what you are describing.

The following paragraph gives a vivid picture of Simon Rodia's Watts Towers, a landmark in Los Angeles. The dominant impression of the structure is expressed in the first sentence. Note the numerous visual details that the writers use to recreate the towers for the reader. Note also the use of spatial order to tie all these details together.

TOPIC SENTENCE (Dominant impression)   It was not until the late 1960's that people began to realize that Simon Rodia's towers were not only unique, but possibly Southern California's most distinctive architectural landmark. The Watts Towers are certainly the tallest thing around. They spiral upward

Test Program
  Unit Pretest, page 77
  Chapter Test, pages 84, 85
  Unit Post-Test, pages 96, 97

Writing Process Activities,
  Evaluation Sheets,
  pages 8–12

RE-TEACHING

Practice Pages or Practice
  Book, page 133
Writing Process Activities,
  pages 30, 31

THINKING SKILLS

Analysis—*Identifying* the
  features of a paragraph that
  describes (Exercise A, page
  507)

Synthesis—*Planning* a descriptive paragraph (Exercise B,
  page 507)
  Writing a paragraph using
  descriptive language (Exercise
  C, page 509)

Evaluation—*Planning, writing,
  appraising,* and *revising* a
  paragraph to describe
  (Developing Writing Skills,
  page 509)

Use the following Springboards
for Writing transparency and
blackline master for additional
practice:
  A Paragraph That Describes,
  pages 149–153

25.3 Writing to Describe

Support in
spatial
order

like tall mosaic cages, or primitive twin Eiffel Towers. Below the two major spires are several smaller ones, two or three fountains, a thronelike entrance pavilion, a bejewelled concrete ship, and a scalloped wall that runs along the street. Everything seems connected to everything else, making the whole environment into a great enclosing web, sparkling with shells, glass, pottery, and tile. Etched into the wall by the main gate are the words "Nuestro Pueblo," which can mean "Our Town" or "Our People." It is Rodia's name for his very personal work, which has now been adopted by his neighbors as a symbol of community spirit.—Adapted from Jane and Michael Stern

EXERCISE A: Examining a Paragraph That Describes.
Read the paragraph and answer the questions after it.

The car is jet black, swooping low to the ground. Its wheels are fully covered and its tiny windows are darkened so that none may gaze inside. It is rounded and streamlined, a front sweep of chrome bumper the only flash in the glossy blackness. It appears to have an expression, like a fierce and silent warrior rearing back on its haunches, coiled, ready to spring. It looks as though it hardly needs a human driver to come to life. The doors are flush and invisible. The tiny windshield is like two lidded eyes.—Adapted from Jane and Michael Stern

1. Answers may vary.   2. Answers may vary within reason.   3. spatial order

1. This paragraph's dominant impression is implied through its details rather than stated directly in a single sentence. What dominant impression does the paragraph build up for you?
2. Identify three especially vivid details.
3. In what order are the details in the paragraph arranged?

EXERCISE B: Planning a Descriptive Paragraph. Each of the following topics could be used as the basis for a descrip-

tive paragraph. Write each topic on your paper, and decide on the dominant impression that you would like to create for it. Then, for each topic, write a topic sentence that expresses this impression. Be prepared to identify supporting details that you would provide to develop each impression.
Answers will vary.

A stranger that you once observed

The ugliest animal you have ever seen

A memorable Halloween costume

The atmosphere of a certain street

Inside your refrigerator

Focusing on Descriptive Language

The language in your descriptive paragraph should bring your dominant impression to life for your reader. It should be full of sharply drawn images and strong sensory impressions. You might also appeal to your reader's imagination by comparing your topic to another item. If you show how your topic resembles something else familiar to the reader, you will help the reader imagine your topic more vividly.

A descriptive paragraph should bring its topic to life with colorful and precise language, sensory impressions, and striking comparisons.

The language of description consists of strong verbs, precise nouns, and vivid modifiers. You should avoid general and colorless modifiers such as *large* and *nice* and instead find more exact and vivid words that will tell your reader more about your topic. For example, *brawny, bloated,* and *mountainous* are all more precise and vivid ways of saying *large.* Which modifier you choose will depend on the actual characteristics of your topic.

Your choice of language can also increase the descriptive power of your paragraph by involving your reader's senses. Find words that create vivid sensory impressions as in the examples on the following page.

25.3 Writing to Describe

EXAMPLES: the silky feel of a petal

the screech of chalk on the blackboard

the sweet, penetrating smell of honeysuckle

Occasionally you will be able to help your reader see (and possibly hear, feel, taste, and smell) your topic much more sharply by comparing it to something else that your topic in some way resembles. Such comparisons are called *similes* and *metaphors*. Similes are comparisons that include the word *like* or *as*.

SIMILES: His painting was like a crazy quilt.

She moved as swiftly as an arrow.

Metaphors create comparisons without *like* or *as* and suggest a closer identification between the items they compare.

METAPHORS: The electric clock was a buzzing insect.

The clown darted into the studio, a rainbow streaking through the gray corridor.

The paragraph about the Watts Towers on pages 506–507 includes a simile and a metaphor: *like tall mosaic cages* and *making the environment into a great enclosing web.*

EXERCISE C: Using Descriptive Language. Using one of the dominant impressions that you developed for Exercise B, write a descriptive paragraph. Use vivid modifiers, sensory impressions, and at least one simile or metaphor in your description.
Answers will vary.

DEVELOPING WRITING SKILLS: Writing a Paragraph to Describe. Choose a topic of your own for a descriptive paragraph. Decide on the dominant impression you want to create for your audience. Then write a topic sentence expressing that impression. Finally, write and revise your paragraph, using precise and vivid language.
Paragraphs will vary.

Developing Writing Skills

If you feel that your students need additional guidance in completing this assignment, have them follow the steps outlined below.

Writing Across the Curriculum

Throughout history writers and artists have tried to capture the beauty and energy of nature in their works.

Prewriting Think of an especially beautiful natural scene, such as a cold stream rushing down the side of a mountain, a single deer hurrying across a clearing in the wilderness, or waves crashing onto an empty beach at sunset. Prepare a list of details that could be used in describing this scene. Then arrange your details in either chronological or spatial order.

Writing Using your list of details, write a first draft of a paragraph describing the scene you have chosen. Try to create a clear picture of the scene by using vivid words that appeal to the reader's senses. Also make sure that you use transitions to indicate relationships among details in your paragraph.

Revising When you revise your paragraph, make sure that you have included enough details to provide readers with a clear picture of the scene. Replace any general words with more specific words and make sure that the modifiers you have used are as vivid as possible. Also check that you have varied the length and structure of your sentences.

Guiding Student Writing

Once students have narrowed their topics and decided upon their main ideas, direct their attention to the necessity of considering a particular audience when they write. Using student topics, discuss the following questions: Who is the audience? What do they know about the topic? How might I need to help them? How do they feel about the topic?

As they revise their first drafts, have students once again consider their audience. Will the audience be interested in what they have written? Have they included all the information the audience will need? Have they explained the topic clearly? Students might tape record their paper and have their peers listen to the recording, assuming the role of the intended audience. The listeners can then indicate whether they feel the paper adequately addresses that audience.

Writing Workshop: Kinds of Writing

ASSIGNMENT 1

Topic   An Item for a Time Capsule

Form and Purpose   An expository paragraph that explains the importance of an object or artifact

Audience   People living in the year 3000

Length   One paragraph

Focus   Identify the item and tell why you selected it. Explain its importance in today's world, how it is used, and what it might reveal about us to people living in the year 3000.

Sources   Magazine and newspaper articles, personal observations and thoughts

Prewriting   Make a list of items that may not exist in the year 3000. Choose one and make notes explaining its use, importance, and how it symbolizes our society.

Writing   Use your notes to write a first draft.

Revising   The checklist on page 490 will help you focus your revision. Then prepare a corrected, final copy.

Toaster Oven

Calculator

Food Processor

Compact Cassette Player

Electric Can Opener

Digital Clock

Jim Rice

ASSIGNMENT 2

Topic A Talented Athlete

Form and Purpose A descriptive paragraph that conveys a dominant impression of a person

Audience Someone who has not seen that athlete perform

Length One paragraph

Focus Tell your dominant impression of this athlete. Then support that impression with details of his or her appearance, athletic movements, and behavior.

Sources Athletic events, action pictures, sports magazines

Prewriting Select an athlete and decide what quality most impressed you about the athlete's performance. Make a list of descriptive details.

Writing In a topic sentence state your dominant impression. In the remainder of your first draft, use vivid language to describe the athlete's appearance, movements, and behavior.

Revising Use the checklist on page 490 to revise your paragraph. Write a final draft.

Assignment 1

Suggestions for Prewriting: Students should avoid choosing a personally important object unless they can show its significance in our society. Also remind them to be precise in their description, since by 3000 the audience may be unfamiliar with the object.

Suggestions for Publishing: Have students organize a school-wide display case of their time capsule—the objects they have chosen and their paragraphs written on large index cards.

Assignment 2

Suggestions for Prewriting: Encourage students to use very specific details rather than backing up the abstract quality (dominant impression) with more abstracts.

Suggestions for Writing: Remind students to choose precise, vivid verbs when writing about sports.

Stimulating Thought

1. Describing it in motion will be more dramatic than picturing it at rest.

2. Students can focus on private fishers or boats that take out groups.

3. "Is there pollution? What is the source? What are the effects?"

4. Even students with a decided opinion probably need to do research.

5. Ask why "Save the whale" efforts are needed now. Suggest writers seek out Greenpeace literature.

6. Suggest that students affix a labeled picture with their paragraph.

7. Consider both natural forces and the effects of human activity.

8. Suggest writers focus on a particular time of day.

9. To start, the city paper probably lists arrivals, departures, and cargoes.

10. "What was the process? When did this occur? How stable are the oceans now?"

Topics for Writing: Kinds of Writing

Vineyard Haven harbor, Martha's Vineyard, Massachusetts

The above ocean setting may suggest a topic for writing. Plan, write, and revise either an expository, persuasive, or descriptive paragraph on that topic. Other possible writing topics are listed below. You may have to narrow and research your topic further.

1. The Beauty and Grace of a Sailboat: A Description
2. The Big Business of Ocean Sportfishing
3. Pollution: A Threat to the Oceans?
4. Regulation of the Fishing Industry: Yes or No?
5. The Whaling Industry: Why It Died
6. The Life Cycle of a Lobster
7. The Process of Beach Erosion
8. Saltmarsh Splendor: A Description
9. How Important Is a Large City's Harbor?
10. How the Oceans Formed

Chapter 26 Writing Essays

Chapter 26 gives students a chance to analyze and write a longer, more detailed composition—an essay. Section 26.1 describes the parts and the organization of an essay. Section 26.2 provides step-by-step prewriting guidelines for developing a thesis statement for an essay. Section 26.3 takes students through the prewriting steps for the body of the essay. Section 26.4 offers concrete suggestions for writing and revising an essay.

For additional or alternate writing assignments and a list of topics for writing, see pages 538–540.

An *essay* is a composition made up of several paragraphs that work together to present and develop one main point for a particular audience and purpose. Because of its greater length, an essay covers its topic in greater depth and detail than would be possible in a paragraph.

In this chapter you will learn to follow some helpful steps for planning and writing essays of your own.

Looking at Essays 26.1

You should learn to recognize the parts of an essay. Every essay should have a title, an introduction with a thesis statement, a body, and a conclusion.

Recognizing the Parts of an Essay

An essay begins with a *title*, which attracts the reader's attention and suggests the topic of the essay. After the title the structure of an essay parallels that of a paragraph. In a paragraph the topic sentence presents the writer's main idea. In an essay, the *introduction* leads up to and includes the writer's main point. The main point is presented in a *thesis statement*, which

26.1 Looking at Essays
(pp. 513–521)

OBJECTIVES

After completing this section, students should be able to

• Identify the parts of an essay.
• Identify how the parts of an essay work together.

513

TEACHING

Getting Started

Explain step by step the parts of an essay: title, introduction with thesis statement, body, and conclusion. Have students refer to the chart on page 514 for visual reinforcement. Then read aloud a brief, well-organized essay from a text or a previous year's sample, asking students to pinpoint where each part begins and ends. You might want to have students read the examples of essay titles (page 515) and introductions with thesis statements (page 516) and suggest what facts they might expect each essay to contain based upon the titles and thesis statements.

Text Follow Through

Discuss text pages 513–521.

Assign Exercise A, page 517; Exercise B, page 520; and Developing Writing Skills, page 520.

Less advanced You might ask students to take notes on the explanatory material in this section; they can then refer to these notes as they answer the questions in Exercise B and Developing Writing Skills. You might also have them prepare a modified outline of the annotated model essay. This activity may help them see more clearly the relationship between the ideas in the essay and the way in which the essay is developed.

Average To provide students with further practice in analyzing essays, ask them to bring in essays that appear in weekly news magazines. They can then use as many of the Exercise B

usually comes at the end of the introduction. A paragraph has supporting information; in the same way, an essay has information that develops the thesis statement. This supporting information is presented in paragraphs called *body paragraphs*. Just as a paragraph often has a concluding sentence that presents a closing idea, an essay ends with a *conclusion* that brings the essay to a satisfying close.

The following diagram can help you see the similarities between an essay and a paragraph.

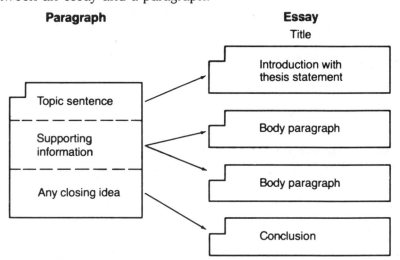

In the following pages, you will take a closer look at each of the parts of an essay.

The Title. The first thing that you see when you read an essay is the *title*. The title indicates the topic of the essay and often suggests the writer's main point. A good title should also capture the reader's interest.

The title of an essay suggests what the essay will be about while attracting the reader's attention.

A good essay title will be both accurate and interesting. It should provide a brief preview of what the writer has said in the essay and encourage the reader to read further. Titles can be straightforward or clever. But they should not simply state the topic flatly, nor should they be so creative that the reader is misled about the essay's content.

The chart lists sample topics and titles. All the titles give information about the essay's content and make the reader curious.

SAMPLE ESSAY TOPICS WITH TITLES	
Topics	**Titles**
Basic ice hockey shots	What Every Hockey Player Needs to Know
Behind the scenes at a circus	Greasepaint, Spangles, and Sawdust
The making of ancient maps	Charting the Ends of the Earth

The Introduction and Thesis Statement. Unlike the title, which suggests the topic of an essay, the *introduction* and *thesis statement* tell the reader exactly what the essay is about.

The introduction presents the essay's topic in an interesting, informative way. It also presents the thesis statement, which expresses the main point of the essay.

The introduction can offer incidents or examples to draw the reader into the essay. It may also provide any background information necessary for the reader to understand the writer's main point. In addition, the introduction should suit the writer's audience and purpose. It should let the reader know whether the essay is going to be serious or funny, formal or informal, explanatory or persuasive. Most important of all, the introduction gradually zeroes in on the writer's main point, which is presented in the thesis statement.

The thesis statement generally comes at the end of the introduction so that it will stand out. Because it focuses the essay's topic into one main point that the essay will develop or prove, the thesis statement is the single most important part of the es-

questions as possible in analyzing the essays they bring in.

Advanced Students might want to write an essay based on one of the thesis statements in Exercise A.

Additional Practice
Practice Pages or Practice Book, page 134

TESTING
Test Program
   Unit Pretest, page 78
   Chapter Test, page 86
   Unit Post-Test, page 97

RE-TEACHING
Practice Pages or Practice Book, page 134

THINKING SKILLS
Analysis—*Identifying* an audience for thesis statements and writing subtopics (Exercise A, page 517) *Identifying* the features of an essay (Exercise B, page 520)

Synthesis—*Planning* and *writing* parts of an essay (Developing Writing Skills, page 520)

Writing Model Transparencies

For additional practice, use Models transparencies:
   Introductory Paragraph, pages 193–197
   Concluding Paragraph, pages 199–203

say. The rest of the essay works to support this main point.

Like the other sentences in the introduction, the thesis statement should suit the writer's audience and should be written with a particular purpose in mind.

SAMPLE THESIS STATEMENTS	
Thesis Statements	**Audience/Purpose**
To achieve precision as well as power in offensive action, hockey players must master three basic shots: the wrist shot, the slap shot, and the backhand shot.	To explain to an audience unfamiliar with ice hockey the three basic shots
One effect of television has been to break down some of the variety in American life.	To persuade a general audience to consider the writer's opinion about television

The Body. The *body* of the essay, which follows the introduction, will generally contain two or more paragraphs. These paragraphs present the supporting information.

The body paragraphs develop the thesis statement with specific and logically organized information—examples, details, facts, reasons, and incidents.

The body paragraphs should develop two or more *subtopics* of the main point. If a thesis statement makes a point about three different problems, then these problems would become the subtopics. The body paragraphs should also be clearly related to each other. A writer can show the relationship among subtopics by ordering them logically (for example, in chronological order, order of importance, or spatial order) and by using transitions. The simplest way to write the body of an essay is to devote one paragraph to each subtopic.

26.1 Looking at Essays

Each body paragraph should also have its own main idea, generally one of the subtopics of the thesis statement. In addition, each body paragraph should be unified, and each should be organized logically.

The Conclusion. The *conclusion* is the essay's ending. It can be a few sentences within the last paragraph of the body. But it is usually the entire final paragraph.

The conclusion ends the essay by recalling the thesis statement and completing the writer's thoughts.

The conclusion should tie the essay together. It should remind the reader of the thesis statement in some way without repeating the thesis statement word for word. It should also complete the essay with fitting and possibly memorable examples, statements, quotations, or incidents. Sometimes a writer will use a particularly interesting observation or incident that is related to the topic or a forceful or witty statement to end the essay. Such endings are called *clinchers* because they clinch the essay in the reader's memory.

EXERCISE A: Understanding Thesis Statements. Each of the sentences below is a thesis statement for an essay. For each statement identify the most likely audience and purpose. Then suggest two or three subtopics that the body paragraphs might develop. Answers will vary; possible audiences and purposes are given; stated subtopics are underlined.

1. Learning to make your own clothes is <u>easy</u>, <u>fun</u>, and, best of all, <u>inexpensive</u>.
2. <u>Television game shows</u>, <u>variety shows</u>, and <u>crime dramas</u> all appeal to different needs of viewers.
3. Although no summer would be complete without a vacation, winter vacations offer special pleasures.
4. There are a number of precautions that people can take to avoid being robbed.
5. Basketball is an exciting sport to watch.

1. people unfamiliar with sewing/to persuade   2. gen aud/to explain   3. gen aud/to persuade   4. people who have not been robbed/to persuade   5. people who are not yet fans/to persuade

Recognizing How the Parts of an Essay Work Together

Because an essay is made up of a number of parts and paragraphs, the parts must work together and flow smoothly.

The title, introduction with thesis statement, body, and conclusion of an essay must all work together to present and develop the main point for the reader's understanding and enjoyment.

The best way to see how the parts of an essay work together is to read an essay. The following essay about hockey contains five paragraphs: an introduction, three body paragraphs, and a conclusion. As you read the essay, you will see how the paragraphs fit together logically and smoothly.

Title	What Every Hockey Player Needs to Know
Intro- duction	When an ice hockey player sends a speeding puck past a heavily padded goaltender, the player creates one of the most exciting moments in sports by scoring a goal. Hockey means both entertainment and tension for the spectators. For the players it is a game of skillful motion. Defensive and offensive movements in hockey are fast paced and sometimes dangerous. Hockey players act like speeding machines on the ice,
Thesis statement with three subtopics	delivering shots that can reach 100 m.p.h. To achieve precision as well as power in offensive action, players must master three basic hockey shots: the wrist shot, the slap shot, and the backhand shot.
Body Paragraph 1 (Develops the first subtopic)	The easiest shot for players to learn is the wrist shot. Since this shot is often used when the puck—a small, hard disk—is traveling slowly, a player can aim quite accurately. The shot is taken by sweeping the puck with the stick while turning the wrists quickly. This movement lets the player guide the puck in any

direction. A wrist shot is especially practical when a player is close to the other team's net. It is a shot of accuracy and power, one that can make a goal.

Body Paragraph 2 (Develops the second subtopic)

A more difficult shot, the slap shot, is perhaps the most explosive move a player can make. In one motion the player pulls the hockey stick back off the ice to about waist level and then swings it forward and through, "slapping" the puck with the end of the stick. The shot sends the puck across the ice at a tremendous speed but is not always accurate, certainly not as accurate as the wrist shot. Players cannot easily direct the puck with a slap shot; therefore, this shot is often used by those who are far away from the goal. A player who does not have a chance of scoring will often use this shot to forward the puck to teammates closer to the opponent's net.

Body Paragraph 3 (Develops the third subtopic)

By far the most difficult of the three shots is the backhand shot. Players cannot plan to take such a shot. Instead they must decide upon it instantaneously at the moment that the puck is about to travel past them. To reach the puck, they must sweep the hockey stick across and behind their bodies, in much the same movement that tennis players make for a backhand shot. Then they must pull the puck across in front of them to propel it across the ice. Mastering the backhand shot can be a great asset to a forward, who plays near the opponent's net. Often forwards will have a chance to pick up a puck that rebounds off the goalies. The forward can then backhand the puck for a quick second attack against the goal.

Conclusion with reminder of thesis statement

These three shots are the most important moves of good offensive action in ice hockey. Players will generally use one of these shots to catch and deliver the puck. Because forwards are positioned close to the goal in the offensive zone, they will generally find wrist shots and backhands most useful. Defensive players, on the other hand, should concentrate on the slap shot because they are positioned farthest away from their goal. Of course, all players will use each of these shots at one time or another. This variety adds to the thrill and suspense of the game of hockey.

EXERCISE B: Understanding an Essay. Take another look at the preceding essay on ice hockey and answer the following questions.

1. attention-getting remarks and thesis statement   2. wrist shot, slap shot,

1. What information does the introduction provide?
2. What are the three subtopics?
3. How are the subtopics ordered in the body of the essay?
4. Which sentence reminds the reader of the thesis statement?
5. What other information does the conclusion provide?

backhand shot   3. order of importance (or order of difficulty)   4. first sentence in last paragraph   5. which players use each shot

DEVELOPING WRITING SKILLS: Planning and Writing Parts of an Essay. Choose one of the following thesis statements and then follow the instructions below. If you wish, you may develop a thesis statement of your own in place of the ones given below.

Answers will vary.

a. Keeping physically fit is the best gift I can give to myself.
b. Not everyone has the qualities to be an excellent baby sitter.
c. There are disadvantages to watching a movie on a VCR.

1. Decide on your audience and purpose. Is it a general audience? Is your purpose to explain something? Is it to persuade an audience to agree with an opinion you are expressing?
2. Think of a title for the essay and write it down. If the title is too general, make it more specific.
3. Write a short introduction that ends with your thesis statement.

4. List at least five major pieces of supporting information that could go in the body paragraphs.
5. Write a conclusion that refers to the thesis statement and ends the essay with a final example, incident, or clever statement.

Thinking Out Your Ideas and 26.2 Writing a Thesis Statement

Now that you are familiar with essays, you can practice writing your own. Following a few special steps can help you get started and can make writing easier. This section discusses the first steps in the prewriting stage of an essay: discovering something to write about, narrowing your topic to a suitable essay topic, deciding on your audience, main point, and purpose, and writing your thesis statement.

PREWRITING: Finding and Narrowing a Topic

First, you must think carefully about topics for an essay.

Brainstorm for appealing topics and then find a suitable essay topic by narrowing down a general topic into smaller topics.

You should begin looking for an essay topic by jotting down a number of general topics that interest you. Jot down on a blank paper anything that occurs to you. You might think about your skills, hobbies, recent experiences, and daily activities. Any of these can provide you with an essay topic. Your classes and the books you have read might also offer ideas for topics. Movies, television shows, records, and news stories might give you topics. You might also try looking in a new way at familiar things or at things you have taken for granted. For example, you might think about why leaves fall in autumn, why dogs

26.2 Thinking Out Your Ideas and Writing a Thesis Statement
(pp. 521–527)

OBJECTIVES

After completing this section, students should be able to

- Find and narrow an idea into a suitable essay topic.
- Decide on an audience, main point, and purpose.
- Prepare a thesis statement.

TEACHING
Getting Started

Tell students that the first step in writing an essay is finding a suitable topic. Have students brainstorm ideas for essay topics as you write their suggestions on the board. If students' suggestions are far too broad and general, remind the class that an essay typically contains six or fewer paragraphs, of which two are devoted to the introduction and closing. Ask whether the topics suggested can be fully explored in this space. If not, students should revise appropriately.

Text Follow Through

Discuss text pages 521–527.

Assign Exercise A, page 523; Exercise B, page 525; Exercise C, page 526; and Developing Writing Skills, page 526.

Less advanced For these students, finding and narrowing a topic can be a difficult task. As the text suggests, these students can brainstorm to find topics. One student can then write the suggested topics on the board. After you have explained ways of narrowing down a topic, with the help of the chart on page 522, you can use one of the suggested topics to demonstrate the narrowing down process. Students should then be able to complete Exercise A. You might also use the same topic for demonstration purposes when students move on to the chart on page 524, thus helping your students with the task presented in Exercise B. With your guidance, students should then be able to complete Exercise C and Developing Writing Skills.

Average Give students extra practice in preparing suitable thesis statements by providing them with broad topics, like those listed below, and asking that they narrow them, shape them for a particular audience and main point. Finally, as a group, have students suggest appropriate thesis statements.

1. Learning to swim
2. Holidays
3. Intelligent animals

howl at sirens, why people become nervous before performing in front of an audience, or why escalators were invented. (For other ways of discovering possible topics, see Section 20.1.)

Once you have jotted down a number of topics, you should examine your rough list to find one or more that particularly catch your interest. Then you should figure out if these topics are too general for one essay. For instance, it would be difficult to write a good essay on a topic as general as *Airplanes,* but you could probably write a very good essay about *The first passenger plane.* If a general topic interests you, you should think about it more and list smaller related topics under it.

The chart below shows a list similar to the one you should make. Some of the topics are narrow enough already while other more general topics have been broken down into smaller, more suitable topics.

BRAINSTORMING FOR AN ESSAY TOPIC	
Yardwork as good exercise	Twenty years from now
Dinosaurs	—My career
—Why they became extinct	—Telephones of the future
—Dinosaurs in North America	Shopping
—How to make a dinosaur model	—Food budgets in 1960 and today
—A day in the life of Tyrannosaurus Rex	—Shopping malls
Plants	Cats
—Plants with unusual needs	—Persian cats
—Terrariums	—Caring for cats
—Flower arranging	—Cat shows
	The curfew in our community
	Learning to handle a sailboat

Your list of topics should give you a number of possibilities. Choose a topic that interests you greatly as well as one about

Advanced Students may be able to see the importance of purpose more clearly if they are asked to rewrite the thesis statements they have prepared for Developing Writing Skills to show another purpose entirely.

which you have something to say. If terrariums were one of your hobbies, you might choose that topic.

EXERCISE A: Thinking of Suitable Essay Topics. Add to the following list of general topics by thinking of *five* topics of your own. Then, from the total list of fifteen topics, choose five topics and write them on your paper. Beneath each general topic, list at least three smaller essay topics. Finally, choose three topics that are suitable for an essay that you might write.

Topics will vary.

A musical instrument	Electronic games/gadgets
Automobiles	Friends
Status symbols	Cultural differences
Humor	Faces
Political campaigns	Oceans

PREWRITING: Deciding on Your Audience, Main Point, and Purpose

Once you have a topic, you should make three important decisions. You should decide for whom you are writing—who will make up your audience. You should also decide what main point you want to make about your topic. And you need to decide why you are writing: to explain, to persuade, or to describe. The order in which you make these decisions may vary, but you should give some thought to each.

Focus an essay topic by deciding on your audience, main point, and purpose.

One good way to find a main point on which to base your essay is to think about your audience first. Will you be writing for other students in your class or school, for the adults in your community, for the staff of a local newspaper, for students who graduated from your school, or for a general audience made up of people of all ages and backgrounds? Will your audience

Additional Practice

Practice Pages or Practice Book, page 135
Writing Process Activities, pages 32, 33

TESTING

Test Program

Unit Pretest, page 78
Chapter Test, page 86
Unit Post-Test, page 97

Writing Process Activities, Evaluation Sheets, pages 8–12

RE-TEACHING

Practice Pages or Practice Book, page 135
Writing Process Activities, pages 32, 33

THINKING SKILLS

Application—*Producing* suitable essay topics (Exercise A, page 523)
Preparing a thesis statement (Exercise C, page 526)

Analysis—*Selecting* a main point for an essay (Exercise B, page 525)

Synthesis—*Compiling* ideas for an essay (Developing Writing Skills, page 526)

be familiar with your topic beforehand? Will your audience agree with you?

Suppose, for example, that you were planning to write about terrariums, and you had chosen other students in your class as your audience. You would then be ready to explore possible main points for your essay. Thinking about your topic and your audience, you might ask some questions about your topic. Questions can help you discover what your audience might be interested in and help you focus your topic.

ASKING QUESTIONS TO FIND A MAIN POINT	
Essay Topic: Terrariums	
Questions	**Possible Main Points**
Why are terrariums interesting?	Terrariums are miniature plant worlds that show scientific principles in action.
Are terrariums better than other house plants?	Terrariums are better than house plants because they are easier to care for and more fun to observe.
How do you make a terrarium from scratch?	Making a terrarium is a three-step process.

When you ask yourself a series of questions with your audience in mind, the questions will lead you to possible main points. When you look at the points you have listed, you will see that they most likely suit different purposes. In the preceding chart, the first and third main points are factual and would be suitable if you wanted to explain an idea to your audience. The second main point is an opinion that you would have to persuade your audience to agree with.

At this stage you can decide on both your purpose and your main point. If you decided to teach other students how to make a terrarium, you would choose the last main point.

EXERCISE B: Coming Up with a Main Point for Your Essay. Choose *one* of the three topics that you selected in Exercise A. Then follow these instructions.

Answers will vary.

1. Write a sentence telling who your audience is.
2. Think about your topic and audience. Then write down at least three questions that your audience might ask about your topic.
3. The answers to your questions will be your main points.
4. Decide which purpose each of the main points would suit.
5. Finally, choose a main point to use in your essay.

PREWRITING: Deciding on a Thesis Statement

Your main point is actually a rough version of your thesis statement. To prepare a thesis statement, simply rewrite your main point to make it as clear and complete as possible.

Keeping your audience and purpose in mind, write a thesis statement by expressing your main point in a clear and complete sentence.

Your thesis statement should present your main point clearly and accurately. It should suit your audience and purpose. Although you can revise your thesis statement once or many times throughout the writing of your essay, finding a thesis statement that you like now can speed up your writing. You may want to write several thesis statements expressing your main point. Try using different words in each.

The chart on the following page presents several possible thesis statements for an essay on making a terrarium. It begins with the main point itself.

Developing Writing Skills

When students choose their topics, they should not hesitate to draw upon what they have learned in their other classes, such as social studies, health, science, or art. For example, if they are studying the dangers of cigarette smoking in their health class, they might consider focusing on this topic. They can then review the notes from their health class to help them develop their thesis statement and come up with supporting information.

POSSIBLE THESIS STATEMENTS

Main Point: Making a terrarium is a three-step process.

1. Making a terrarium is a three-step process.
2. There are three steps involved in making a terrarium.
3. To make a terrarium, all you need to do is select the ingredients, prepare the soil, and root the plants you have chosen.
4. Making a terrarium is a three-step process: selecting the ingredients, preparing the soil, and rooting the plants.

After comparing the different versions, you might decide that the third version of the thesis statement is the clearest. By listing the three subtopics—the three steps in making a terrarium—you can help the reader see that the process is not difficult. This short but clear thesis statement might appeal particularly to students who have never made a terrarium.

EXERCISE C: Preparing a Thesis Statement. Use the main point that you chose in Exercise B, and write three practice versions of a thesis statement. Then decide which version appeals to you most.
Thesis statements will vary.

DEVELOPING WRITING SKILLS: Shaping Ideas for an Essay. Apply the thinking steps in this section by practicing them on your own, following these instructions.
Answers will vary.

1. Brainstorm for topics and jot down a rough list of at least five.
2. Choose one or two topics that especially interest you. If a topic is too large for an essay, break it into smaller topics. Then choose one topic for your essay.
3. Decide on your audience.
4. To find two or more possible main points, ask and answer at least two questions that your audience might have about your topic.

5. Decide which purpose suits each of your main points.
6. Choose the main point that you want to use in your essay.
7. Write at least two versions of your thesis statement, and choose the one you like best.

Developing Support for a 26.3 Thesis Statement

Your thesis statement sets the boundaries of your essay. It also makes it possible for you to begin planning the body of your essay. To plan the body, you will need to carry out two more prewriting steps: finding supporting information and then organizing it so that it will clearly develop your thesis statement.

PREWRITING: Brainstorming for Support

The first step after you have written your thesis statement is to find the best information you can to support and develop that statement.

Brainstorm for examples, details, facts, reasons, and incidents that will develop your thesis statement.

Brainstorming is not difficult, but it does require concentration. You might begin by simply writing down thoughts on your thesis statement as they occur to you. List as much specific information as possible. Do not weed out any information. Instead, try to come up with more support than you will actually use in your essay. The more you have on paper, the better your chances will be of finding the best information.

Another way to begin brainstorming is to write your thesis statement at the top of your paper. Then write down a few questions that your audience might ask after reading your thesis statement. The questions will help you come up with the

527

26.3 Developing Support for a Thesis Statement
(pp. 527–532)

OBJECTIVES
After completing this section, students should be able to

• Gather supporting information to develop a thesis statement.
• Organize supporting ideas for an essay.

TEACHING
Getting Started
Tell students that after they have found a suitable essay topic, the next step is finding supporting information and then organizing it. The best way to find supporting information is to brainstorm for examples, details, facts, reasons, and incidents that will develop their thesis statements. Direct students' attention to the chart on pages 528–529. Have students use the questions in the chart as a model as they brainstorm for support for a thesis statement suitable for development into an expository essay.

Text Follow Through

Discuss text pages 527–532.

Assign Exercise A, page 529; Exercise B, page 531; and Developing Writing Skills, page 532.

Less advanced   A study or review of the material in Sections 23.2 and 23.4 on supporting information and coherence is vital for these students. Before beginning Exercise A, students can benefit greatly from thinking about the different kinds of support they can use, as discussed in Section 23.2. Before completing Exercise B, they can benefit equally from a discussion of the logical orders presented in Section 23.4.

Average   These students, too, will benefit from a study or review of the material in Sections 23.2 and 23.4 on supporting information and coherence. After students have completed Developing Writing Skills, you may want to try to schedule time for individual conferences during which you can discuss the modified outlines they have prepared. Improvements discussed at this point can help students greatly when they actually begin to write their essays.

Advanced   Review with students the modified outlines they have prepared for Developing Writing Skills.

Additional Practice

Practice Pages or Practice Book, page 135
Writing Process Activities, pages 32, 33

information your audience needs to know in order to understand the thesis statement. Then brainstorm by listing examples, facts, and other information that answer the questions.

The following chart shows how you might use the second method to brainstorm for information to support the thesis statement about making a terrarium.

QUESTIONING TO FIND SUPPORT FOR A THESIS STATEMENT

Thesis Statement: **To make a terrarium, all you need to do is select the ingredients, prepare the soil, and root the plants you have chosen.**

What is a terrarium?
—enclosed collection of plants
—small world
—self-sufficient—doesn't need to be watered or fertilized
—miniature—from a few inches to several feet

—plants create own environment
—can be attractive, decorative—different plants, shapes, colors
—educational value— chance to observe plant life

What are the ingredients for a terrarium?
—a clear container
  —fish tank or bowl
  —large jar
—soil and sand
—charcoal (optional)

—pebbles
—small plants
—ferns
—mosses
—tree seedlings

How do you prepare the soil?
—line container with gravel 2 inches deep
—put in a layer of charcoal (optional)—holds water, nutrients

—put in a layer of sand
—put in a layer of soil 1 inch deep
—make soil deeper in center (easier to add plants)

TESTING

Test Program
　Unit Pretest, page 78
　Chapter Test, page 86
　Unit Post-Test, page 97

Writing Process Activities,
　Evaluation Sheets,
　pages 8–12

RE-TEACHING

Practice Pages or Practice
　Book, page 135
Writing Process Activities,
　pages 32, 33

THINKING SKILLS

Application—*Preparing* support-
　ing information (Exercise A,
　page 529)

Analysis—*Outlining* an essay
　(Exercise B, page 531)

Synthesis—*Planning* and
　organizing support for an
　essay (Developing Writing
　Skills, page 532)

26.3 Developing Support for a Thesis Statement

How do you root the plants?
—dig holes 1 inch deep—far
　enough apart to allow
　plants to grow
—press plant roots into holes
— pack dirt

—moisten soil
—place terrarium near
　window—should get some
　but not too much light

EXERCISE A: Gathering Supporting Information. Use the thesis statement you wrote in Exercise C of Section 26.2 to brainstorm for support. Write down three questions your audience might ask about the main point in the thesis statement. Then brainstorm for information to answer the questions.
Answers will vary.

PREWRITING: Organizing Your Ideas

The next prewriting step is to use your brainstorming list to organize the body of your essay.

Choose the best pieces of support from your brainstorming list and organize them logically, first making a rough plan of subtopics and then making a modified outline.

Your list of support should give you more than enough information. You should now select the information that you will use in your essay. Look at your list. Cross out any ideas that are not closely related to your main point and add any new ideas. You might want to put aside a few pieces of support to use in your introduction and conclusion. At this time, however, you should concentrate mainly on the information you will present in the body of your essay.

After you have crossed out and possibly added some information, look again at your brainstorming list. Try to find logical groupings for the pieces of support that you plan to use. These groupings will be your subtopics. In some cases your thesis statement and the questions you asked while brainstorming will help you divide up your supporting information into subtopics. In other cases you will have to choose your subtopics now. For the essay on making a terrarium, the most logical subtopics would be the three steps of the process.

Next, decide on a logical organization for your subtopics. In the terrarium essay, the three most logical subtopics—the three steps—would naturally follow a chronological order. The subtopics in another essay might naturally follow some other logical order.

You should now see the body of your essay taking shape. Making a rough plan at this point can help. The following chart shows a possible plan for the essay on making a terrarium. The introduction and thesis statement make up the first paragraph. Each subtopic can be developed in one body paragraph although sometimes you may want to use more than one paragraph for a subtopic. The conclusion can be a paragraph at the end.

POSSIBLE PLAN FOR AN ESSAY	
First paragraph	= Introduction with thesis statement
Second paragraph	= Subtopic 1: Finding ingredients
Third paragraph	= Subtopic 2: Preparing the soil
Fourth paragraph	= Subtopic 3: Rooting the plants
Fifth paragraph	= Conclusion

With your subtopics in order, you can now begin to organize the information under each subtopic. To show your final plan, you may find it helpful to make an outline. The following is a modified outline for the body of the essay on making a terrarium.

Thesis Statement: To make a terrarium, all you need to do is select the ingredients, prepare the soil, and root the plants you have chosen.

26.3 Developing Support for a Thesis Statement

Subtopic 1: <u>Selection of Basic Ingredients</u>
1. Finding a suitable container
   —glass-covered fish tank or bowl
   —wide-mouth gallon jar
2. Finding soil
   —rich, dark forest soil
   —gravel and sand, possibly charcoal and pebbles
3. Choosing plants
   —ferns
   —mosses
   —tree seedlings

Subtopic 2: <u>Preparation of Soil</u>
1. Lining bottom with two-inch layer of gravel or pebbles
2. Adding equal amounts of sand and soil on top of stones
3. Making sand and soil slope down on all sides

Subtopic 3: <u>Rooting of Plants</u>
1. Digging holes
2. Pressing roots into holes
3. Adding stones and bark for realism
4. Moistening soil, placing near a window (not too much light)

EXERCISE B: Organizing an Essay. Look again at the brainstorming list you made in Exercise A and follow these instructions.

Modified outlines will vary.

1. Cross out any ideas that now seem to be unrelated to the main point.
2. Add any new information you think of.
3. Examine your list of support and decide on subtopics.
4. Decide on a logical order for your subtopics, and make a plan for the essay like the one in the chart on page 530.
5. Organize the supporting information under each subtopic by making a modified outline of the body of the essay.

DEVELOPING WRITING SKILLS: Developing Support for an Essay. Using the thesis statement you wrote for the Developing Writing Skills at the end of Section 26.2, follow the prewriting steps that you have learned in this section. First brainstorm for support, then select and group your supporting information, and finally prepare a modified outline for the body of your essay.
Modified outlines will vary.

26.4 Completing Your Essay
(pp. 532–537)

OBJECTIVES

After completing this section, students should be able to

- Prepare an effective introduction, conclusion, and title for an essay.
- Write a first draft using transitions for a smooth flow of ideas.
- Revise an essay.

TEACHING

Getting Started

Tell students that the introduction to their essay is especially important because it accomplishes three tasks:

1. Catches the reader's interest.
2. Presents the topic.
3. Leads up to the thesis statement.

Have on hand the introductions to several essays, either published or written by students in other classes, and present them to students either by using an overhead projector or by duplicating them. Have stu-

---

DEVELOPING WRITING SKILLS: Developing Support for an Essay. Using the thesis statement you wrote for the Developing Writing Skills at the end of Section 26.2, follow the prewriting steps that you have learned in this section. First brainstorm for support, then select and group your supporting information, and finally prepare a modified outline for the body of your essay.
Modified outlines will vary.

26.4 Completing Your Essay

All of your planning up to this point will make it possible for you to write your essay with confidence. Because you know what you plan to say, you can concentrate on presenting the information in the clearest and most interesting way. You may find it useful to begin by thinking of ideas for the beginning and end of your essay. Then you can use your brainstorming list, rough plan, and modified outline as guides for producing a complete first draft. Finally, you should go over your essay carefully to make any improvements you can in the ideas, organization, and writing.

WRITING: Preparing Your Introduction, Conclusion, and Title

The writing of your essay will go more quickly if you first jot down ideas for your introduction, conclusion, and title.

Think of different possible ideas to introduce and end your essay. Give some thought to a title as well.

Your introduction should accomplish several very important tasks: grabbing the reader's interest, presenting the topic, and leading up to the thesis statement. As you prepare your introduction, think about getting the reader interested. You might begin with a vivid example. You might start off by presenting a short incident. You might use a memorable quotation or ask an intriguing question about your topic. Use your imagination and check your brainstorming list to find ideas. Once you have found a "hook" to catch the reader's attention and have given any background information the reader will need to understand your topic, you can present the thesis statement.

Just as the introduction draws the reader into the essay, the conclusion leads the reader out. Its basic purpose is to tie together the thoughts that you have explored in the essay. A conclusion generally begins by referring to the thesis statement without repeating it word for word and then wraps up the essay in some interesting or memorable way. You may not want to write your conclusion before writing the body of the essay. However, it helps to have ideas in mind for the ending. You might think of a way to mention your main point using different words. You might also jot down examples, unusual facts, or incidents that expand upon your main point. Try to find something to help make your essay stick in the reader's mind.

Finally, think about a few possible titles. Finding a good title can help spark your imagination.

EXERCISE A: Finding Ideas for an Introduction, Conclusion, and Title. Use the list and outline developed in Exercises A and B of Section 26.3, and follow these instructions.
Answers will vary.

1. Jot down ideas for an introduction to the essay.
2. Jot down ideas that you could use in a conclusion.
3. Write down the possible titles for the essay.

WRITING: Creating a First Draft

You now have everything needed to write a first draft.

Write a first draft of your essay following your rough plan and outline. Include transitions to make your thoughts flow smoothly.

Text Follow Through

Discuss text pages 532–537.

Assign Exercise A, page 533; Exercise B, page 534; Exercise C, page 537; and Developing Writing Skills, page 537.

Less advanced Before students begin to write, you may want them to study or review the material on transitions in Section 23.4. You can then have a chart drawn on the board, showing the five orders discussed in Section 23.4 with appropriate transitions listed under each. As students revise their essays, they can refer to the chart when they need help in making logical transitions from paragraph to paragraph.

Average After students have completed Developing Writing Skills, you may want to ask them to share essay assignments they have prepared for another class. Have them exchange and revise the assignments as they did for Developing Writing Skills.

Advanced Students may want to share their essays with classmates. Have them make a duplicate copy on which they label the parts and highlight each transition they used. These essays could then be posted on a bulletin board and serve as models.

Your rough plan and outline should guide you in developing your main point logically. Try to make the main point and supporting information in your essay clear and connected. As you express your ideas in complete sentences, use transitions to move from one idea to another.

You should feel free to make both little changes and big changes as you write. If an idea no longer seems to fit, leave it out. Similarly, add any new examples or facts that you wish. If you decide to change the order of your ideas, you should check the outline to make sure the new order works as well as the old.

EXERCISE B: Writing a First Draft. Write a first draft of the essay with which you worked in Exercise A. Use your rough plan and your outline as a guide and connect your ideas with transitions.
First drafts will vary.

REVISING: Polishing Your Essay

After you have written your first draft, there is still one major stage to be completed: the revising stage.

Revise your first draft by looking for areas that could be improved.

Revising is an important part of the writing process. Few writers produce their best work the first time they try. Once you have your ideas down on paper in a first draft, you can usually find many ways to improve your essay. You might change words, rewrite sentences, or even add and take out ideas to make your essay clearer and more interesting.

In order to get a fresh perspective on your first draft, put it aside for a little while before you revise it. Pretend that someone else wrote it and has asked you for your suggestions. Make any changes right on the first draft. As a final check, answer the questions in the following checklist and make any additional changes that seem necessary.

26.4 Completing Your Essay

CHECKLIST FOR REVISING AN ESSAY

1. Do you have a good title for your essay?
2. Is there any way you could make your introduction more interesting or informative?
3. Does the thesis statement fit the essay? Is it clear?
4. Are there any pieces of supporting information in the body of the essay that are not really needed?
5. Are there any examples, details, facts, reasons, or incidents that should be added to the body paragraphs to make the essay clearer or more interesting?
6. Would another order for the subtopics make the essay clearer?
7. Are there any transitions that you could add to make the essay read more smoothly?
8. Does the conclusion tie the essay together by referring to the main point? Are there ways in which you could make the conclusion more interesting for the reader?
9. Are there any mistakes in grammar, usage, mechanics, or spelling?

When you have expressed your ideas as clearly as you can, you should recopy your essay. Before you hand it in, you should also proofread it for mistakes that may have been added in recopying.

The following is the revised version of the essay about making a terrarium. Notice the transitions (printed in italics) that guide the reader through the steps in the process.

Title · · · · · · · · · · · · · · · Making a Small World

Introduction · · · · · · · · A terrarium is a self-sufficient, miniature world for a group of plants. If you would like to have a terrarium to decorate a room or to observe for scientific purposes, you can learn to make one. It is not difficult. To

Thesis statement with three subtopics · · · · · · make a terrarium, all you have to do is select the ingredients, prepare the soil, and root the plants that you have chosen.

Subtopic 1   *To begin,* you must find a suitable container, good soil, and plants. You can use a glass-covered fish tank or bowl or a wide-mouth gallon jar, which usually comes with a tightly fitting lid. You should thoroughly clean any container you choose. *In addition* to a container, you will need soil. You can use rich, dark forest soil as well as gravel and sand. You may want to collect charcoal and pebbles as well. You can use nearly any small plant, but assorted ferns, mosses, and even tree seedlings are especially good choices. However, you should avoid soil and plants that show any signs of having insects or parasites.

Subtopic 2   *After* you have chosen the outside of your terrarium and what will go into it, you are ready to prepare the soil. *First* line the bottom of the container with a two-inch layer of gravel or pebbles, which helps prevent root rot by allowing water to drain. You may want to place charcoal bits the size of peas in a one-inch layer on top of the pebbles. Charcoal is not necessary, but it will absorb moisture and supply nutrients. *Next* top the stones or charcoal with equal amounts of sand and soil. Try to make the sand and soil slope down on all sides so that the plants will be easy to see.

Subtopic 3   *When* you have finished placing the layers of soil in the terrarium, you can add the plants. You should root your plants with care. *First* dig holes that are an inch or so deep and far enough apart so that the plants will not be crowded. *Then* gently press the roots of the plants into the holes. Cover the roots with dirt and pack the dirt firmly with a fork or with your fingers. No part of the roots should be exposed. *When* the plants are in place, you can add stones and pieces of bark to make the scene realistic. *Finally,* you should moisten the soil thoroughly but gently by spraying or sprinkling water to avoid making holes in the soil. *After* you have completed this step, place the top firmly on your terrarium. *Then* place your terrarium near a window that has filtered light—that is, light that comes through a shade, blinds, or opaque glass. Too much light will encourage algae to grow on the glass.

Conclusion with reminder of thesis statement

When you have performed the three main steps, you can leave your terrarium on its own with little care. The water is prevented from escaping and will be used and reused by the plants in an endless process known as the water cycle. Filtered sunlight will provide the energy that the plants need for nourishment. With your work done, you can sit back and enjoy watching nature in action.

EXERCISE C: Revising an Essay. Reread the essay you prepared in Exercise B silently and aloud and note any changes that should be made. Then use the questions in the checklist on page 535 to examine the essay for further changes. Make all changes that are needed. Then, recopy your essay and proofread it to catch any mistakes that have been added in recopying.
Revisions will vary.

DEVELOPING WRITING SKILLS: Drafting and Revising an Essay. Using the outline you prepared and organized in the Developing Writing Skills at the end of Section 26.3, follow the steps you have learned in this section for completing an essay. Think up ideas for your introduction, conclusion, and title. Then draft the essay. Finally, exchange first drafts with another student in your class. Read the other student's essay carefully. Go over the essay using the checklist for revision on page 535. Circle any problems and make suggestions for improvements on the student's first draft. Then reread your own essay and the student's comments. Revise your essay according to the helpful comments you have received. As a final step in revising, recopy your essay and proofread it.
First drafts and revisions will vary.

Guiding Student Writing

To help students improve their writing styles, you can have them discuss ways to vary their sentences and improve word choice. The revision stage is the best time to consider the use of different sentence lengths, sentence structures, and sentence openers.

Sharing their work with classmates in peer-editing groups can help students discover ambiguities and imprecise wording in their writing. Students can encourage each other by telling why specific word choices are particularly effective. They might even choose the best sentence in the paper and the sentence that most needs improvement. This kind of specificity will help students learn to evaluate their own work better. You might also suggest a thesaurus to help students choose precise words and supply vivid word choices.

Writing Workshop: Essays

ASSIGNMENT 1

Topic   A Method of Transportation that Significantly Changed People's Lives

Form and Purpose   An essay that informs

Audience   People attending a special exhibit, "The History of Transportation," at a science museum

Length   Four to five paragraphs

Focus   Your thesis statement should identify the transportation method and emphasize its historical significance. The remainder of your essay should present facts, details, and examples that explain its significance.

Sources   Books, magazine articles, encyclopedias, museums

Prewriting   Select a method of transportation. Research information about it. Develop a thesis statement, make notes about supporting details, and prepare an outline.

Writing   Use your notes and outline to write a first draft.

Revising   The checklist on page 535 will guide you during revision. Then write a complete, final draft of your essay.

FOURSCORE AND SEVEN YEARS AGO OUR FATHERS BROUGHT FORTH ON THIS CONTINENT A NEW NATION CONCEIVED IN LIBERTY AND DEDICATED TO THE PROPOSITION THAT ALL MEN ARE CREATED EQUAL NOW WE ARE ENGAGED IN A GREAT CIVIL WAR TESTING WHETHER THAT NATION OR ANY NATION SO CONCEIVED AND SO DEDICATED CAN LONG ENDURE. WE ARE MET ON A GREAT BATTLEFIELD OF THAT WAR. WE HAVE COME TO DEDICATE A PORTION OF THAT FIELD AS A FINAL RESTING PLACE FOR THOSE WHO HERE GAVE THEIR LIVES THAT THAT NATION MIGHT LIVE. IT IS ALTOGETHER FITTING AND PROPER THAT WE SHOULD DO THIS. BUT IN A LARGER SENSE WE CANNOT DEDICATE, WE CANNOT CONSECRATE, WE CANNOT HALLOW THIS GROUND THE BRAVE MEN, LIVING AND DEAD WHO STRUGGLED HERE HAVE CONSECRATED IT FAR ABOVE OUR POOR POWER TO ADD OR DETRACT. THE WORLD WILL LITTLE NOTE NOR LONG REMEMBER WHAT WE SAY HERE, BUT CAN NEVER FORGET WHAT THEY DID HERE. IT IS FOR US THE LIVING RATHER TO BE DEDICATED HERE TO THE UNFINISHED WORK WHICH THEY WHO FOUGHT HERE HAVE THUS FAR SO NOBLY ADVANCED. IT IS RATHER FOR US TO BE HERE DEDICATED TO THE GREAT TASK REMAINING BEFORE US-THAT FROM THESE HONORED DEAD WE TAKE INCREASED DEVOTION TO THAT CAUSE FOR WHICH THEY GAVE THE LAST FULL MEASURE OF DEVOTION - THAT WE HERE HIGHLY RESOLVE THAT THESE DEAD SHALL NOT HAVE DIED IN VAIN, THAT THIS NATION UNDER GOD SHALL HAVE A NEW BIRTH OF FREEDOM AND THAT GOVERNMENT OF THE PEOPLE, BY THE PEOPLE, FOR THE PEOPLE, SHALL NOT PERISH FROM THE EARTH

BRUCE SHANKS

ASSIGNMENT 2

Topic   What Freedom Means to Me

Form and Purpose   An essay that informs readers about your definition of freedom

Audience   Readers of the "Personal Viewpoint" column

Length   Four to five paragraphs

Focus   At the end of your introduction state your main idea. Support that thesis statement in body paragraphs with specific facts, examples, details, incidents, and/or reasons. Re-emphasize your thesis in the conclusion.

Sources   History books, magazine articles, newspapers, television documentaries, personal observations

Prewriting   Narrow your topic to a specific aspect of freedom. Write a thesis statement that clearly reflects your viewpoint. Brainstorm for support. Develop an outline.

Writing   Use your outline to write a first draft.

Revising   Polish your draft by using the checklist on page 535. Prepare a corrected, final copy.

Assignment 1

Suggestions for Prewriting: Since students will be using similar sources, you might have them work in small groups for the notetaking stage. Students could choose their groups, or you could assign them. Suggest that one group work on the domestication of the horse. Each student, however, should write his or her own essay.

Suggestions for Publishing: Reform the groups and have them compare essays.

Assignment 2

Suggestions for Prewriting: Check that student notes include very specific points; they may tend to be abstract. Help them move from "I can be what I want" to " I can be an astronaut or a pianist or a carpenter." Also remind students to consider how they will organize their supporting points—order of importance will work well with most papers.

Stimulating Thought

1. Ask about local examples as well as national chains.

2. Ask why banks and restaurants have thrived while movies have declined.

3. An illustrated chart would be a nice touch.

4. Suggest research in business journals, which have studied this topic.

5. Ask students about their frustrating experiences. Suggest a humorous essay.

6. Ask students to list what they think are the methods and interview a manager to check the list.

7. Ask students to compare the scene in fast-food and fine restaurants.

8. Hamburgers
   Pizza
   Mexican food

9. Survey the class: how often they are customers and how many have siblings who are employees.

10. Have students do a skit of a family in a car—with no fast-food restaurants.

Topics for Writing: Essays

W. Miller, © 1975, The New Yorker Magazine, Inc.

"Man, it really tears me to think that some squares want to pull down these lovely, beautiful signs!"

If the above cartoon suggests a writing topic to you, plan and write an essay about the topic. If not, write about one of the folowing related topics

1. Fast-Food Avenue: Visual Pollution

2. The Drive-In Culture

3. Fast Foods and Nutrition

4. The Great Hamburger War

5. But I Don't Want Onions on My Burger!

6. Efficiency in a Fast-Food Restaurant

7. The Effects of Fast-Food Gobbling on Dining Behavior and Taste

8. Explosive Growth of the Fast-Food Industry: 1955–1985

9. The Teenager, Employee and Customer: An Important Factor in the Fast-Food Industry

10. A Humorous View of Life Without Fast-Food Restaurants

Chapter 27

Writing Reports

The first section in Chapter 27 covers sources of information and crediting of sources in a report. The second section presents the three stages of writing a report: prewriting, writing, and revising.

For additional or alternate writing assignments and a list of topics for writing, see pages 555–557.

In many of your classes, you are asked to find information about a topic and to present it in a *report*. Learning to prepare effective reports will help you be a more successful student.

As you write reports, you can use the skills you have already developed for writing paragraphs and essays. However, reports also have special features of their own. This chapter will look at these special features and will guide you through the steps you should follow to plan, write, and revise reports.

Looking at Reports 27.1

27.1 Looking at Reports
(pp. 541–548)

In many ways, preparing a *report* is similar to planning and writing an essay. Like an essay, a report develops a main point with facts and ideas. However, a report, unlike an essay, is based on information that has been gathered from various sources. Much of the information is made up of facts and ideas from sources such as books and magazine articles. Your job is to put these facts together in a clear and interesting way.

Sources of Information

Because a report is based on information from other sources, it contains two special features that are not in an es-

OBJECTIVES

After completing this section, students should be able to

- Identify sources of information in footnotes and a bibliography.
- Identify the basic structure of a report based on research.

TEACHING

Getting Started

Have available a report done by a former student or one from a different class, any level. Also ask the librarian for a copy of a journal that prints formal research. If possible, enlarge the pages of these or prepare them for the overhead projector. Explain that while a report is similar to an essay, it identifies where the writer found information. Point out a footnote number in the text, read the information it is connected to, and point out the footnote. Then display and explain the bibliography.

Text Follow Through

Discuss text pages 541–548.

Assign Exercise A, page 544; Exercise B, page 547; and Developing Writing Skills, page 548.

Less advanced You will almost definitely want to begin with a study or review of Sections 38.1 and 38.2. Ideally, this review should be conducted in the library so that students can use the card catalog, locate books on the shelves, and handle various kinds of reference books. Before assigning Exercise A in the current section, you may also want to give students information about several kinds of sources and have them prepare footnotes and bibliography entries under your guidance.

Average These students, too, may benefit from review on the use of the library. You may also want to discuss question 2 in Exercise B very carefully to make sure students understand

say. One feature is the addition of *footnotes* throughout the paper to show where different pieces of information came from. The second feature, a *bibliography,* must be added at the end to give the reader a list of all the outside sources used. In writing a report, you will need to add these two features. You will also need to combine the ideas from your sources with your own ideas to produce a clearly organized and unified paper.

Footnotes. Because so much of the information in a report is taken from outside sources, a special system has been developed for giving credit to these sources.

A report should contain footnotes giving credit to all outside sources.

You will need to use *footnotes* both when you quote someone else's words exactly and when you put someone else's ideas or words into your own words. You should also use footnotes for unusual facts.

Whenever you repeat, word for word, what someone else has said, enclose the statement in quotation marks and use a footnote to give credit to the speaker. You should also use a footnote when you state someone else's ideas in your own words; this will make it clear to the reader that the ideas are not your own but those of some authority. Well-known facts that are generally accepted do not need footnotes. For example, you would not need to cite the source for a famous baseball record such as Hank Aaron's homerun total. But you *would* need to mention a source for a lesser-known record—such as the longest game ever played in the major leagues.

To write a footnote, you should place a small number right after and just above the quotation, idea, or fact you are borrowing. This number will refer the reader to the footnote itself, which you can place either at the bottom of that page of your report or in a list at the end of the report. The footnote will tell the reader where you found the information you have used.

You may have to use footnotes for a number of different kinds of sources: books by one or two authors, magazine articles with and without authors, and so forth. The following chart will help you decide what information to include in each.

FOOTNOTES FOR DIFFERENT SOURCES

Kind of Source	Footnote
Book with one author	[1]Veronica Ions, <u>Indian Mythology</u>, p. 47.
Book with two authors	[2]Jane Stern and Michael Stern, <u>Amazing America</u>, p. 186.
Magazine article (signed)	[3]Marguerite Johnson, "Delay with Diplomacy," <u>Time</u>, May 18, 1981, p. 30.
Magazine article (unsigned)	[4]"Toys for Tots," <u>Time</u>, December 14, 1981, p. 68.
Encyclopedia article (signed)	[5]<u>The World Book Encyclopedia</u>, 1981 ed., "Berlin, Irving," by Ethan Mordden.
Encyclopedia article (unsigned)	[6]<u>The Random House Encyclopedia</u>, 1977 ed., "Hollywood."

Bibliography. In addition to using footnotes throughout the report, you must also include a *bibliography* at the end listing all the sources you have used.

At the end of a report a bibliography should list all the sources that were used in the preparation and writing of the report.

Your bibliography will give a general view of your research. If readers want to explore your topic further, your bibliography helps them find your sources. List complete information about each source, whether or not you actually used information from that source.

A bibliography entry differs from a footnote. In a bibliography entry for a book, list each author's last name first. Also

that all borrowed information, not just direct quotations, should be cited.

Advanced Even if students have not done a formal report before, they should have little difficulty with this section. Even students who have done a formal report, however, will benefit from a review of the conventions and from the analysis of an actual report.

Additional Practice

Practice Pages or Practice Book, page 136

TESTING

Test Program

Unit Pretest, pages 78, 79
Chapter Test, pages 88, 89
Unit Post-Test, page 98

RE-TEACHING

Practice Pages or Practice Book, page 136

THINKING SKILLS

Application—*Demonstrating* correct citations by writing footnotes and a bibliography (Exercise A, page 544)

Analysis—*Identifying* the features of a report (Exercise B, page 547)

Synthesis—*Writing* a paragraph about a report (Developing Writing Skills, page 548) list your sources alphabetically, according to first letters. Finally, use a reverse indent as in the following chart. Use the samples in the chart as guides.

BIBLIOGRAPHY ENTRIES FOR DIFFERENT SOURCES

Kind of Source	Bibliography Entry
Book with one author	Ions, Veronica. Indian Mythology. London: Paul Hamlyn Limited, 1967.
Book with two authors	Stern, Jane and Stern, Michael. Amazing America. New York: Random House, 1977.
Magazine article (signed)	Johnson, Marguerite. "Delay with Diplomacy." Time, May 18, 1981, p. 30.
Magazine article (unsigned)	"Toys for Tots." Time, December 14, 1981, p. 68.
Encyclopedia article (signed)	The World Book Encyclopedia, 1981 ed., "Berlin, Irving," by Ethan Mordden.
Encyclopedia article (unsigned)	The Random House Encyclopedia, 1977 ed., "Hollywood."

EXERCISE A: Practicing Citation of Sources. Select as a topic a person, event, or place that interests you. Use the library card catalog and *The Readers' Guide to Periodical Literature* to find one or more books and a magazine article about your topic. Write a footnote for each source you find. Then write a bibliography of all your sources, using the chart above. Footnotes and bibliographies will vary.

The Basic Structure of a Report

A complete report includes a title, an introduction that ends with the main point (the thesis statement), two or more body paragraphs, and a conclusion. A report should also contain footnotes and a bibliography. All of this is on one topic only.

A report is a unified paper on a single topic, based on information gathered from research. It has a title, an introduction with a thesis statement, a body, a conclusion, footnotes, and a bibliography.

Your paper should not be simply a collection of all the information you found in your research. Rather, it should be a clearly organized presentation about the topic, following in logical order. Every piece of information should support and develop your thesis statement. The title and introduction should help lead up to the main point. The body should present subtopics logically. The conclusion should tie the discussion together by referring to the main point. The footnotes and bibliography should tell how much research went into developing your main point.

The following report illustrates the features and structure of a report. Note the way in which the footnotes are abbreviated when a source is used a second time.

Title	Brazil: The Growing Republic
Intro-duction	Brazil, the fifth largest country in the world, covers nearly half of South America and contains an untold wealth of natural resources.[1] In a sense Brazil is two different countries. Most of its population is concentrated in the east along a narrow coastal strip, while the vast jungles and plains of the interior remain, for the most part, unexplored and unpopulated. During the twentieth century, however, Brazil has made significant technological
Thesis statement with two subtopics	and economic progress and has begun to develop the resources of its vast interior. This development, however, has been made without adequate environmental safeguards and has already exacted a cost

which may spell trouble in the future.

Subtopic 1: industrial rate of growth

Brazil possesses enormous industrial potential. A wealth of minerals lies untouched under the Guiana highlands in the northern part of the country.[2] The mining state of Minas Gerais contains nearly ten percent of the world's iron. São Paulo, the largest city in Brazil, hosts a wide range of industries and at present accounts for one third of the nation's income.[3] Other cities are catching up with São Paulo. According to Herbert Wendt, "in the past decade a number of major steel plants have been built in Minas Gerais in the vicinity of Santos."[4] Volkswagen, Incorporated, manufactures cars in Brazil because the country has a healthy market for cars.[5]

Subtopic 2: cost of this development

Yet this development has taken place at serious environmental and human cost. There is a severe problem of urban air pollution, erosion has claimed arable land, and landslides have taken human lives. The northeastern section of Brazil has been virtually deforested to make room for sugar and coffee plantations and ranches, and loggers have continually moved further south.[6] Although Brazil produces more than a third of the world's coffee, and its range of climates allows a variety of crops,[7] future agricultural expansion may depend on proper environmental controls.

Conclusion

Fortunately Brazil has not ignored its problems. In June of 1985, concern for the environment led to the designation of a 450-mile-long section of the Atlantic forest in the northeast as a protected national landmark.[8] If Brazil can protect its environment, and at the same time find a way to develop such resources as the potential of the Amazon River for hydroelectric power,[9] the country may someday become a major industrial and agricultural power.

27.1 Looking at Reports

[1]National Geographic Atlas, 1975 ed., "Brazil."
[2]The Random House Encyclopedia, 1977 ed., "Brazil."

[3]Rose Brown, The Land and People of Brazil, p. 64.

[4]Herbert Wendt, The Red, White, and Black Continent, p. 421.

[5]The Random House Encyclopedia, "Brazil."

[6]"In Brazil, Environmentalists Enjoy a Rare Taste of Success," The New York Times, July 23, 1985, pC3.
[7]The Random House Encyclopedia, "Brazil."

[8]"In Brazil, Environmentalists Enjoy a Rare Taste of Success," p. C3.

[9]National Geographic Atlas, "Brazil."

BIBLIOGRAPHY

Brown, Rose. The Land and People of Brazil. Philadelphia: J. B. Lippincott Company, 1972.

"In Brazil, Environmentalists Enjoy a Rare Taste of Success." The New York Times, July 23, 1985.

National Geographic Atlas, 1975 ed., " Brazil."

The Random House Encyclopedia, 1977 ed., "Brazil."

Wendt, Herbert. The Red, White, and Black Continent. Garden City, N.Y.: Doubleday and Company, Inc., 1966.

The World Book Encyclopedia, 1981 ed., "Brazil," by Manoel Cardozo.

EXERCISE B: Examining a Report. Read the report on Brazil again and then answer the following questions.

1. How many footnotes does the report contain? 9
2. Which footnotes refer to facts and ideas? Which footnote is used for a quotation? 1-3, 5-9/4
3. How many entries are listed in the bibliography? In what order are they listed? 6/alphabetical order

4. What kinds of sources has the author used?

5. List as bibliography entries two additional sources on Brazil that your school library or public library contains.

4. books, newspaper, atlas, encyclopedias   5. Answers will vary but should follow bibliography form.

DEVELOPING WRITING SKILLS: Looking at Reports.
Use the topic you selected for Exercise A and find an article on the topic that cites sources and has a bibliography. You may wish to ask the school librarian to help you, or use one of the articles already in your bibliography. Write a short, well-organized paragraph answer to one of the following questions.
Answers will vary.

1. How many sources did the author use? What kinds of sources are they?

2. Choose one fact or direct quotation from a source and tell how it supports the main point of the thesis statement.

3. How well does the conclusion sum up the report?

27.2 Writing a Report

Now that you are familiar with the features and structure of a report, you can begin to plan and write one of your own.

PREWRITING: Planning Your Report

Following a few special prewriting steps can help you to plan, research, write, and revise your report. The prewriting steps make the writing and the revising steps go smoothly.

Finding a Good Topic. A good topic is one that appeals to you and for which you can find solid information.

Choose a topic that interests you and one for which you can find at least three good sources of information.

You will probably work best on a topic that you would like to know more about. If the topic is too general, use library

---

27.2 Writing a Report

(pp. 548–554)

OBJECTIVES

After completing this section, students should be able to

• Plan a report by identifying a workable topic, preparing bibliography cards, taking notes, and outlining information.

• Draft and revise a report.

27.2 Writing a Report

sources to narrow it down. Then, check to see how much information you can find on this narrower topic.

In the library you can look up your topic in encyclopedias, the card catalog, and *The Readers' Guide to Periodical Literature.* The encyclopedias will give you general information and suggest ideas for more specific topics. The card catalog will tell you what books the library has on a number of subjects. It will also list subcategories of larger subjects. *The Readers' Guide* will list magazine articles on a number of topics. Using these sources and your own imagination, find a topic that you want to write about and that you can cover in your report. Then you can use the same general sources to see if there is enough information about your topic. You should be able to locate at least three different sources for your topic. Try to find five or six. If possible, you should also gather information from different kinds of sources. In addition to encyclopedias and other books, try to use magazines as well.

Making Bibliography Cards. To help keep track of the books and articles that you find, you should make a bibliography card for each of your sources.

For every book or article that you plan to use, make a bibliography card that lists the information you will need to know about each source.

Even before you begin to read through your sources, you should make a bibliography card for each of them. You can prepare many of your cards directly from the card catalog or *The Readers' Guide* Your bibliography cards should list the call number and complete publishing information for each book and article that you plan to use. Making these cards will help you keep your research in order as you gather more and more information. The cards will also give you the information that you will need when you write your footnotes and bibliography. The chart on the next page offers guidelines for preparing bibliography cards.

Getting Started

Again have available an actual report and the bibliography and note cards the author used. (Prepare a few of each based on the report if the originals are not available.) Before showing students the cards, ask how they think the author collected information. Demonstrate the cards and explain the advantages of this method compared to the paper method.

Text Follow Through

Discuss text pages 548–554.

Assign Exercise A, page 552; Exercise B, page 552; Exercise C, page 553; and Developing Writing Skills, page 554.

Less advanced Students will probably need step-by-step guidance through this process. So that you can give individual help as needed, you may want students to do most of the actual research, note-taking, and organizing in class, with several sessions held in the library. The librarian may be willing to work with students as well.

Average If students are working on their reports outside of class, you may want to post a calendar specifying dates when certain activities are to be accomplished. Setting aside time on due dates to check students' progress will help you decide if they need more guidance.

Advanced Students may enjoy organizing the reports from all your classes on a classroom reference shelf. Have them use the Dewey Decimal System to assign location numbers and then make up subject, author, and title cards. A shoebox can be used as a file.

Additional Practice

Practice Pages, page 137
Writing Process Activities,
pages 34, 35
Writing Workshops, pages
19–21

TESTING

Test Program
Unit Pretest, pages 78, 79
Chapter Test, pages 88, 89
Unit Post-Test, page 98

Writing Process Activities,
Evaluation Sheets,
pages 8–12

RE-TEACHING

Practice Pages, page 137
Writing Process Activities,
pages 34, 35

THINKING SKILLS

Application—*Narrowing* a general topic and *preparing* bibliography cards (Exercise A, page 552)

Analysis—*Preparing* note cards and *outlining* a report (Exercise B, page 552)

Evaluation—*Writing, appraising, revising,* and *proofreading* a report (Exercise C, page 553) *Planning, writing, appraising, revising,* and *proofreading* a report (Developing Writing Skills, page 554)

Writing Model Transparencies

For additional practice, use Models transparencies:
Report, pages 217–239

GUIDELINES FOR PREPARING BIBLIOGRAPHY CARDS

1. Use one note card for each source.
2. On each card write all of the information that you will need when you write the bibliography entry.
3. In addition, write down the call number, if the source has one, so you can find the source in the library.
4. Finally, note whether or not the source includes any illustrations or charts that you might want to use.

Taking Notes on Your Sources. Now you can begin to gather your information.

Begin your research by jotting down several questions about your topic and writing a rough thesis statement. Use these to decide what to focus on when you take notes.

Do some planning before you actually start reading and taking notes. Jot down four or five questions about your topic that you think your report should answer. In addition, think about a main point you might want to develop. Write down a rough thesis statement expressing this main point. Your research will now have a focus that can help you to take meaningful notes.

SUGGESTIONS FOR TAKING NOTES

1. Take notes on note cards, using one card for each aspect of your topic in each book or article.
2. In the upper left-hand corner of each card, write the author and title of the source as well as any other information that may be useful.
3. In the upper right-hand corner, write a subject heading that describes the information on that card.
4. Be sure to note the page number for each quotation, idea, or fact that you write down on your card. Record quotations exactly using quotation marks.

Checklist for Revising a Report appears in transparency form. See Checklists, page 331.

27.2 Writing a Report

> 5. Keep the note cards from each source together, organized by subject headings.

Begin your note-taking with the source that seems to cover your topic most fully. Skim the material first; then read it carefully and take notes. Plan on several different note cards for each book or article. From some sources you may take exact quotations and detailed notes. From others you may take only short summaries. Use your judgment, but limit your notes to items related to the questions you have written about your topic and your rough thesis statement.

The following sample note cards for a report on Halley's comet show notes taken from two different kinds of sources.

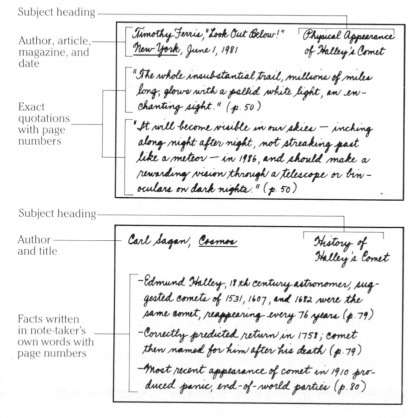

Subject heading

Author, article, magazine, and date

Exact quotations with page numbers

Timothy Ferris, "Look Out Below!" *New York*, June 1, 1981 — Physical Appearance of Halley's Comet

"The whole insubstantial trail, millions of miles long, glows with a pallid white light, an enchanting sight." (p. 50)

"It will become visible in our skies — inching along night after night, not streaking past like a meteor — in 1986, and should make a rewarding vision through a telescope or binoculars on dark nights." (p. 50)

Subject heading

Author and title

Facts written in note-taker's own words with page numbers

Carl Sagan, *Cosmos* — History of Halley's Comet

—Edmund Halley, 18th century astronomer, suggested comets of 1531, 1607, and 1682 were the same comet, reappearing every 76 years (p. 79)

—Correctly predicted return in 1758; comet then named for him after his death (p. 79)

—Most recent appearance of comet in 1910 produced panic, end-of-world parties (p. 80)

Organizing the Report. After you have found the information you need, arrange it so the main point develops logically.

Find a logical order for your information and write a modified outline for the report body.

You may want to review the information on organizing an essay in Chapter 26.

STEPS FOR ORGANIZING A REPORT
1. From your note cards, decide which aspects of your main point you want to develop. These will be your subtopics.
2. Group your note cards according to your subtopics.
3. Decide on a logical order for presenting the subtopics and the information under each.
4. Write a modified outline that shows the organization of the body of your report by subtopic.

EXERCISE A: Finding a Topic and Preparing Bibliography Cards. Choose one of the following general topics or use one of your own. Then narrow it down to a topic suitable for a report. Finally, find at least three possible sources of information in the library, and make a bibliography card for each.

Answers will vary.

Aviation	Local history	American customs
Cartoons	Predatory animals	Women in sports
Language	Astronomy	Musicians/Composers
The Olympics		

EXERCISE B: Taking Notes and Organizing the Report. After preparing a few questions and a rough thesis statement, take notes on each source that you have found in Exercise A. Make different cards for the different parts of your topic. Group your cards according to subtopics, and find a logical organization for your information. Then write a modified outline.

Answers will vary.

WRITING AND REVISING: Creating a First Draft and Polishing Your Paper

You are now ready to write a first draft, using the outline you have developed and following the basic structure of an essay. When you have finished your first draft, you should look for any improvements you can make. You should also check your footnotes and bibliography to make sure you have used the correct forms. Finally, you should make a final copy and proofread it.

Using your outline, write a first draft of your report with footnotes and a bibliography. Then revise your report, paying special attention to the form of your footnotes and bibliography.

As you write, keep in mind the basic essay structure you are following: an interesting title, an interesting introduction with thesis statement, body paragraphs that develop the thesis statement, and an effective conclusion. Remember to use transitions to link your ideas throughout. When you have finished a first draft complete with footnotes and bibliography, look at the checklist for revising an essay on page 535. The questions below will also help you to revise your report.

CHECKLIST FOR REVISING A REPORT

1. Does your report include footnotes from at least three different sources?
2. Are all quotations, borrowed ideas, and little-known facts clearly credited?
3. Do your footnotes follow the appropriate form?
4. Are all sources listed correctly in the bibliography?
5. Is your bibliography in alphabetical order?

EXERCISE C: Drafting and Revising Your Report. Using your note cards and outline, write a first draft of your report

Developing Writing Skills

If you feel that your students need additional guidance in planning, writing, and revising their reports, you might want to have them use the topic and follow the steps outlined below.

Writing Across the Curriculum

The contributions of important historical figures often have a major impact on the lives of many generations of people.

Prewriting Think of a historical figure whom you especially admire. Then research the accomplishments of this person in reference books and biographies. Make sure that you record on note cards the bibliographic information for each source you consult. Once you have finished your research, review your notes and prepare a thesis statement. Then organize your notes into an outline.

Writing Write the first draft of a report in which you examine the accomplishments of the person you have chosen and discuss the impact of his or her accomplishments. Include your thesis statement in your introduction and end your report with a conclusion that sums up your ideas. Make sure that you cite the sources of any quotations or borrowed ideas that you use. When you have finished writing, decide on a title and prepare a bibliography.

Revising You may want to make revisions in your first draft before having your report evaluated by one of your classmates. If so, use the checklist on page 553 to guide your revision.

including footnotes and a bibliography. Revise your report following the checklists on pages 535 and 553. Complete your revision by writing a final copy of your paper and proofreading it to catch any errors added in recopying.
Drafts and revisions will vary.

DEVELOPING WRITING SKILLS: Evaluating and Writing a Report. Choose a new topic for a report. Follow the planning, writing, and revising steps provided in this section to complete the new report. Working with another student, exchange reports. Evaluate the other student's paper, using the following questions. Write the evaluation and offer suggestions for improvement. Return the paper to the other student. Revise your own report by responding to the suggestions you have been given. Then write out a final copy of your report and proofread it.
Answers will vary.

1. How many footnotes does the paper contain?
2. What kinds of sources (books, magazines, and so on) have been used?
3. Are all the footnotes complete and correct?
4. How many sources has the writer used in all?
5. Are all the bibliography entries complete and correct?
6. What is the thesis statement? What are its subtopics?
7. How many body paragraphs are used to develop each of the subtopics in the report?
8. What logical order is used to arrange the subtopics in the report?
9. What are the strong points of the report?
10. What improvements could be made?

Writing Workshop: Writing Reports

ASSIGNMENT 1

Topic An Important Scientist

Form and Purpose A report that informs readers of a particular scientist's contribution to the quality of life

Audience Readers of a science reference text

Length Four to six paragraphs

Focus Your report should explain what a scientist's major accomplishments were and what their effects were.

Sources Books, biographies, science reference encyclopedias, general encyclopedias, magazine articles

Prewriting Select a scientist whom you admire. Conduct research, taking notes on bibliography cards. Follow the steps on page 552 to organize your report.

Writing Follow your outline notes to write a first draft.

Revising Use the checklist on page 553 to revise and to prepare a final copy of your report.

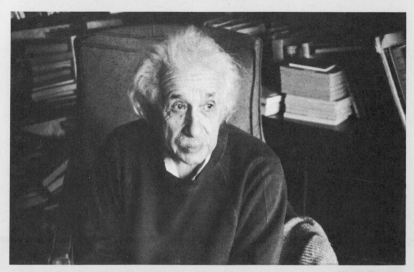

Albert Einstein

555

Guiding Student Writing

Students can work together in groups during the prewriting and revising steps to help generate ideas and to evaluate the paper through its developing stages. Students working as peer evaluators might engage in developing standards such as superior, excellent, fair, and poor. Involved in this evaluation process, students quickly learn the qualities that make a paper good. They can then apply what they have learned to their own writing assignments. However, it is important to supervise peer-evaluation groups, so that students do not reinforce other students' bad writing habits or discourage certain students by being overly critical of their work. For this reason, students need to be given some guidelines before they begin to evaluate each other's papers.

Assignment 1

Suggestions for Prewriting: If students cannot suggest enough names, have them check with the librarian or with science teachers. Then, as students collect information, ask them to decide whether order of importance or chronological order will work better with this subject.

Assignment 2

Suggestions for Prewriting: Point out to students that if they are working with one animal, each support paragraph must discuss a different aspect of intelligence or of the animal's behavior, while if they work with several animals, each support paragraph will deal with a different example.

Suggestions for Publishing: Hold the conference, each student orally presenting his or her report. See if the class can come to any conclusions about the topic question.

ASSIGNMENT 2

Topic   Animal "Intelligence"

Form and Purpose   A report that informs, explains, and persuades a reader of your view on animal intelligence

Audience   Other students attending a conference entitled "Animal Behavior: Instinct vs. Intelligence"

Length   Five to six paragraphs

Focus   Your report should apply a definition of the term "intelligence" to animal behavior or an animal's learning ability. You may choose to focus on one animal or several animals that demonstrate a particular learning skill.

Sources   Books, encyclopedias, magazines, wildlife conservation organizations, science museums, aquariums

Prewriting   Conduct research to narrow your topic. As you research it further, take notes on bibliography cards. To plan and organize your report follow the steps on page 552.

Writing   Write a first draft that follows your outline.

Revising   Review and revise your first draft by following the checklist on page 553. Write a clean, corrected final draft.

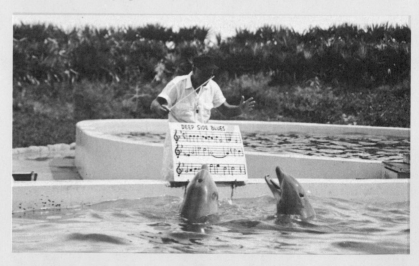

1. Suggest interviewing older community members.

2. Hazardous wastes
   Acid rain
   Power generation

3. Water
   Oil
   Farmland and wilderness

4. Underground?
   Under the sea?
   In space?

5. Suggest focusing on one country: the United States, Mexico, China, etc.

6. "Which countries have faced famines? Why? Which routinely have to import food? Why?"

7. Have students seek out statistics and reasons.

8. Effects on building
   Economic effects
   Crime

9. One possibility: illegal immigration here.

10. Cram desks as close as possible. Conduct class as if this were usual, but reserve the last ten minutes for discussion.

Topics for Writing: Writing Reports

The above chart indicates both past and predicted future population growth in the world. It may suggest a topic for a report. If so, research, plan, and write your report. Other possible report topics are listed below. You may have to narrow one for a report.

1. Population Growth: Its Effect on Your Town or City

2. The Population Explosion and Pollution

3. Population Growth and Its Effect on One Natural Resource

4. The Future: Where Will Everyone Live?

5. Recent Developments in the Population Explosion

6. Excess Population and the Problem of Food

7. The Changing Landscape of the United States: A Population Shift from the Rural to the Urban

8. The Gold Rush and San Francisco: The Effects of an Instant, Massive Human Migration

9. Population Growth and International Tension

10. People Need Space: A Report on Population Growth and Human Stress

CHAPTER 28
Writing Book Reports
(pp. 558–567)

The two sections of this chapter teach students to recognize the basic features of a book report and to plan, write, and revise a book report.

For an additional or alternate writing assignment, see page 567.

28.1 Looking at Book Reports
(pp. 558–562)

OBJECTIVES

After completing this section, students should be able to

- Identify the basic parts of a book report and the elements of literature that can be discussed in a book report.
- Analyze a book report.

Chapter 28

Writing Book Reports

A book report is a form of writing that allows you to describe a book that you have read and to tell others what you think about it. As a student, you will often need to write book reports. In this chapter you will learn that book reports share some features with other kinds of writing, but that they also differ in some important ways.

Most book reports contain a few basic features designed to give the reader a good understanding of the book. The following section will discuss these basic features and give you some specific things to think about when you write book reports.

28.1 Looking at Book Reports

The book reports you write will vary depending on the kind of book you are writing about and your teacher's requirements. Every book report, however, needs to have several basic features.

The Format of a Book Report

A book report identifies the book by title and author and gives the reader some idea of the contents. It also shows the

28.1 Looking at Book Reports

writer's understanding of the book by focusing on some elements that are particularly interesting. Finally, it gives some idea of how the writer feels about the book. Although these features can be arranged in many different ways, a simple three-part format can be used to cover all of the basic features.

One particularly useful format for a book report has the following three parts: an introduction that identifies the book and gives a short summary of it, body paragraphs that focus on specific elements of the book, and a conclusion that makes a recommendation.

When you write a book report, you should generally assume that your reader has not read the book you are discussing. Therefore, it makes sense to begin your report by clearly identifying the book by title and author. You should also give your reader some idea of what the book is about. If you are writing about a work of nonfiction, you can simply mention the subject of the book. If you are discussing a novel, you should mention that the book is a work of fiction and give a capsule version of the story. Do not, however, write more than a sentence or two about the story.

Once you have given your reader some background information, you can present a few thoughtful ideas or opinions about the book and support them with evidence from the book itself. You can usually explore any of a number of topics, especially if you are writing about fiction. Every work of literature has certain basic elements, such as characters and setting. Since you will probably use one or more of these elements in the book reports you write, you can benefit from taking a few moments to become more familiar with them now. The chart on the following page lists and briefly explains some of the most important elements you will find in books, particularly in fiction. There are other topics—for instance, a book's language—that you can also write about.

TEACHING
Getting Started
Have available some professional book reviews from newspapers or magazines. Pass these around. As students look at them, explain that book reports serve two purposes: they help the writer of the report understand a book better by forcing a closer look, and they help readers of the report decide whether this is a book they might like.

Text Follow Through
Discuss text pages 558–562.

Assign Exercise A, page 560; Exercise B, page 562; and Developing Writing Skills, page 562.

Less advanced Before having students analyze the sample book report in the text, you might want to write and distribute one on a book or even a short story students have already read this year. They will enjoy recognizing the characters and more easily see how a writer selects information for a report.

Average If your school paper publishes book reports, you might ask students to use the questions in Exercise B to analyze a couple of these or of professional reviews of juvenile or young adult books. (You can find these in many Sunday papers and in certain library journals to which the librarian probably subscribes.)

Advanced Ask each student to find and bring to class a copy of a professional book review that each finds personally appealing. Then the class could use the questions in Exercise B to analyze a few of these. Of course, you could also recommend that students then read these books to see if their expectations are fulfilled.

Additional Practice

Practice Pages or Practice Book, page 138

TESTING

Test Program

Unit Pretest, page 79
Chapter Test, page 90
Unit Post-Test, page 98

RE-TEACHING

Practice Pages or Practice Book, page 138

THINKING SKILLS

Knowledge—*Describing* the features of a book report (Exercise A, page 560)

Analysis—*Identifying* the features of a sample book report (Exercise B, page 562)

Synthesis—*Writing* a one-paragraph response to a book report (Developing Writing Skills, page 562)

IMPORTANT ELEMENTS IN BOOKS	
Element	**Explanation**
Theme	A general truth or observation about life— the author's main point. It might not be stated directly in the book, but it is the idea that holds the work together.
Character	A person in a story. Characters are presented to the reader through their actions, dialogue, other characters' reactions to them, and sometimes through the author's comments on them.
Plot	The planned ordering of events in a story. The plot usually involves some *conflict*, a problem or struggle faced by the characters in the story. The conflict builds toward a *climax*, or turning point, when the conflict is resolved.
Setting	The time and place of the story. A story might take place in the past, present, or future. It might be set in a particular area of this country or in another country or even in another galaxy.

After you have discussed different elements of the book, it makes sense to give your own opinion of the book as a whole. This can be done in a concluding paragraph.

EXERCISE A: Looking at Book Reports. Although book reports differ they all share some features. Answer the following questions about the basic features of book reports.

1. by title and author

1. How should you identify a book on which you will report?

2. How would you describe what the book is about?

2. as fiction or nonfiction and 1 or 2 sentence capsule summary

3. Should you include your opinions? Why or why not?

4. What three parts belong in every book report?

5. What elements of books can be discussed in book reports?

3. Yes/to advise readers   4. introduction, body, conclusion   5. theme, character, plot, setting

Examining a Sample Book Report

The following is a book report on the novel *Watership Down* by Richard Adams. After a short introductory paragraph, the book report focuses on two different elements of the novel. The book report then concludes with a paragraph that gives an evaluation of the book as a whole.

Report on *Watership Down*

Intro-
duction

Watership Down, a fantasy novel by Richard Adams, follows the heroic struggles of a group of rabbits who journey through unknown territory in search of a new home. Along the way the rabbit characters must fight against overwhelming difficulties and danger.

First
element

One of the most interesting things in the story is the way in which all of the rabbits work together to achieve their goal. The value of cooperation is stressed throughout. All of the rabbits seem to understand how they can best serve the group. The hero Hazel uses his courage and resourcefulness to lead the other rabbits to their new home. Even though he is not the largest rabbit, the others recognize that he is their leader. Big-wig, the largest rabbit, is clearly the best fighter, but he soon accepts his position as Hazel's lieutenant. Black-berry, the smartest rabbit, is given the job of figuring out strategy at various points in the journey. Fiver, Ha-zel's brother, is a small, weak rabbit, but he has the gift of second sight and so is regarded as the group's prophet. All of these individual rabbits and their com-panions are united by a deep sense of community, an instinct that goes beyond self-preservation.

Second element   The author also gives the reader a feeling for the special society of the rabbits by creating a special language for them. For example, *frith* means "sun," "day," and "God" to the rabbits while its opposite, *inle,* means "moon," "night," and "death." To *silflay* means to feed above ground, one of the rabbits' favorite activities. This language makes the book come alive. The reader soon begins to think in a kind of rabbit language. The special language also makes the adventures more believable.

Conclusion   It is difficult to put this book down after living through a few of these gripping rabbit adventures. By sympathizing with the struggles of the rabbit characters in *Watership Down,* the reader may even develop a feeling of kinship with real-life rabbits.

EXERCISE B: Examining a Book Report. Read the book report on *Watership Down* on page 561 and above again carefully, and then write the answers to the following questions on your paper.

3. the roles of four specific rabbits in the society/the use of three words of the rabbit

1. Where does the writer of the book report identify the title, author, and basic content of the novel? first paragraph
2. What elements of the novel do the two body paragraphs focus on? theme/language
3. What specific pieces of support are used in each body paragraph?
4. What is the writer's opinion of the book as a whole? positive
5. Would you like to read this novel? Why or why not?

language   5. Answers will vary. Students might present opinions in a class discussion.

DEVELOPING WRITING SKILLS: Writing About a Book Report. Write a paragraph in response to the book report on *Watership Down.* What elements does it discuss? Do you feel that the report gives you a good idea of the book? Tell whether or not the report makes you want to read the book and why.

Writing a Book Report 28.2

Writing a book report involves many of the same steps that writing an essay does, such as planning, organizing, drafting, and revising. However, when you write a book report, you must begin by choosing the elements of the book that you will examine, deciding what you will say about each one, and then find support for your statements in the book itself.

Develop what you have to say about the elements in the book using specific information from the book. Then follow the basic steps for organizing, writing, and revising an essay.

PREWRITING: Planning Your Book Report

The following chart shows some of the questions you can use to examine the elements in a book.

EXAMINING THE ELEMENTS OF BOOKS
Theme
1. In what way has the book changed your mind about something or made you see something in a new light?
2. Why do you think the author wrote the book?
3. What general idea seemed to hold the book together?
Character
1. Which character is your favorite? Why?
2. Which character did you like least? Why?
3. In what special ways did any of the characters change?
Plot
1. What was the most amusing, exciting, or moving incident?
2. What was the major problem faced by the characters?
3. How did the writer create suspense?

28.2 Writing a Book Report
(pp. 563–566)

OBJECTIVES

After completing this section, students should be able to

- Plan a book report by focusing on certain elements of a book.
- Write and revise a book report.

TEACHING

Getting Started

Point out the chart of elements of books on page 563. Explain to students that the same concepts that are used in a class discussion of a book are used in a written report on it. Emphasize that a book report is not just a summary of the plot; point out that even the questions about plot call for judgment, not just a simple recitation of events.

Text Follow Through

Discuss text pages 563–566.

Assign Exercise A, page 564; Exercise B, page 565; and Developing Writing Skills, page 566.

Less advanced For students' first report, you may want to use a book with which they are familiar in order to give step-by-step demonstrations of all the points covered in the section. Students could first discuss all the questions in the chart, then decide what to focus on and brainstorm as a group for supporting details.

Average For their first report these students, too, may benefit from a general discussion of a single title. After this discussion, however, they should be able to proceed with the planning and writing of their individual reports. You might simultaneously have them reading individually chosen books for a second report. If you cover this section relatively early in the year, you can have students use the same process for outside reading throughout the year.

Advanced For students' first report you could assign a title to each of several small groups, who could meet when reports are finished to read and compare each other's treatment of the book. Students might also enjoy organizing a way for students in all your classes to share their reports. If the reports are put into a binder, for example, students can be encouraged to check there when looking for a good book to read.

Additional Practice

Practice Pages or Practice
  Book, page 139
Writing Process Activities,
  pages 36, 37
Writing Workshop, page 22

TESTING

Test Program
  Unit Pretest, page 79
  Chapter Test, page 90
  Unit Post-Test, page 98

Writing Process Activities,
  Evaluation Sheets,
  pages 8–12

Setting
1. What influence did the time or place of the story have on the plot and characters?
2. Would you like to live in the world created in the book? Why or why not?
3. Was the setting believable?

Answers to these questions should give you ideas for the body paragraphs of your report.

Once you have decided which elements you want to write about and what you want to say about them, you should gather supporting information. In order to develop your ideas, you should look through the book you have read for specific information: examples, details, incidents, and statements made by the author or the characters. If you are discussing theme, for instance, you might mention specific ideas about characters, plot, setting, or language since all of these elements can help to present the book's central idea. If your topic involves character, you should look for examples of the character's thoughts, words, and actions. If you are focusing on plot, you could look at how events are related to each other in the story.

You should be able to find plenty of support for your ideas. Try to select the most interesting and significant information. If you decide to quote a description or something that a character says, write the words from the book exactly, enclose the statement in quotation marks, and indicate in parentheses the page on which it appears.

EXERCISE A: Planning a Book Report. From the books that you have read recently, choose one that you would like to write about. Use the list of questions on page 563 and above to find something to say about at least two of the elements in the book. Find as much specific support in the book as you can, and then choose the best support. Finally, organize the information for your body paragraphs using a modified outline. Modified outlines will vary.

RE-TEACHING

Practice Pages or Practice
Book, page 139
Writing Process Activities,
pages 36, 37

THINKING SKILLS

Analysis—*Outlining* a plan for a
book report (Exercise A, page
564)

Evaluation—*Writing, appraising,
revising,* and *proofreading* a
book report (Exercise B, page
565)
Planning, writing, appraising,
and *revising* a book report
(Developing Writing Skills,
page 566)

Writing Model Transparencies

For additional practice, use
Models transparencies:
Book Report, pages 241–251

*Checklist for Revising a Book
Report* appears in transparency
form. See Checklists, page 333.

28.2 Writing a Book Report

WRITING AND REVISING: Creating a First Draft and Polishing Your Paper

Once you have chosen your support and organized it, you can write your first draft. The first paragraph should identify the book for your reader and say enough about it so that your report will make sense to someone who has not read the book. The next few paragraphs should discuss the elements you have chosen. The last paragraph should end the report by giving an evaluation.

When you have completed your first draft, revise your book report carefully. The following chart suggests a few questions that you might use to improve your first draft.

CHECKLIST FOR REVISING A BOOK REPORT

1. Is there additional information that you could include to make your ideas clearer?
2. Is there any unnecessary information that you could take out?
3. Are there any examples that would be better than the ones you have used?
4. If you have used quotations, are they accurate?
5. Are there any transitions that you could add to make the book report read more smoothly?
6. Are there any ways in which you could make the introduction and the conclusion to your book report clearer or more interesting?
7. Does the report contain any mistakes in grammar, usage, mechanics, or spelling?

EXERCISE B: Writing and Revising a Book Report. Write a first draft of your book report. Be sure that it includes all of the basic features discussed in this section. Then revise your book report using the checklist on this page. As a final step in revising, make a clean copy, proofread it, and correct any mistakes that were added in recopying.

First drafts and revisions will vary.

Developing Writing Skills

To provide your students with additional guidance in preparing their book reports and to expose them to books from other content areas, you might want to have them follow the steps outlined below.

Writing Across the Curriculum

Choose a book about music, sports, social studies, or science. For example, you might choose *The Summer Game* by Roger Angell, *These Were the Sioux* by Mari Sandoz, *Of Men and Mountains* by William O. Douglas, or *A Circle of the Seasons* by Edwin Way Teale.

Prewriting When you read the book you have chosen, take note of the book's most important elements, characteristics, and details, and look for the overall message that the book conveys about its subject. After you have finished reading, look over your notes and highlight the information you want to include in your report. Then organize your information into an outline.

Writing Following your outline, write a first draft of your report. Make sure that you thoroughly examine two or three major elements or characteristics of the book in your body paragraphs. Also make sure that you offer your overall evaluation of the book in your conclusion.

Revising You may want to make revisions in your first draft before having your report evaluated by one of your classmates. If so, use the checklist on page 565 to guide your revision.

DEVELOPING WRITING SKILLS: Planning, Writing, and Revising a Book Report. Choose another book to read and write about. Use the list of questions on pages 563 and 564 to find at least two of the elements in the book that you would like to discuss. Then follow the steps presented in this section to plan and write the first draft of a second book report. When your draft is completed, follow these instructions.

First drafts, evaluations, and revisions will vary.

1. Exchange book reports with another student.
2. Read the other student's report carefully, checking it with the revision checklist on page 565. Answer in writing each question on the checklist. Also write a brief evaluation that will help the other student to improve future book reports.
3. When you receive back your own book report, revise it, taking the other student's comments into account. Make any changes that you believe will improve it.
4. If you disagree with any points in the evaluation, write your reasons on a separate sheet of paper.
5. Make a clean final copy. Hand in the clean copy together with the marked first draft and the evaluation of the report.

Writing Workshop: Writing Book Reports

The Trojan Horse

ASSIGNMENT

Topic   Reporting on a Historical Novel

Form and Purpose   A book report that informs, evaluates, and persuades a reader about a historical novel

Audience   Readers of a book review column in a newspaper

Length   Four to five paragraphs

Focus   Concentrate on the major character(s) and the plot. In the conclusion, state your opinion of the book and tell if it accurately depicts the historical period and events.

Sources   Historical novels, history texts

Prewriting   After reading the novel, research the period and events. Develop a thesis statement and make notes about the character(s) and events. Develop an outline.

Writing   Use your notes and outline to write a first draft.

Revising   To help you make changes, follow the checklist on page 565. Then write a final draft.

Guiding Student Writing

You can use the Writing Workshop assignments either in place of or in addition to the writing assignments in the text. If students have difficulty writing their book reports, encourage them to refer back to the instruction in this chapter. You might also want to have students work in pairs when revising their reports. If you take this approach, stress the need for peer editors to make positive, constructive suggestions.

Assignment

Suggestions on Sources: Depending on your library's resources, you might require students to choose a novel set in the era covered by the eighth-grade social studies curriculum.

Suggestions for Prewriting: Remind students to focus on character and plot aspects that make this a historical novel.

CHAPTER 29
Personal Writing
(pp. 568–578)

This chapter focuses on personal writing. Section 29.1 covers the purposes for keeping journals and how to write journal entries. Section 29.2 covers the form of an autobiography and the prewriting, writing, and revising steps in creating an autobiography.

For additional or alternate writing assignments and a list of topics for writing, see pages 576–578.

29.1 Journals
(pp. 568–572)

OBJECTIVES

After completing this section, students should be able to

- Identify different reasons for keeping journals.
- Plan a journal and write a journal entry.

TEACHING

Getting Started

idea bank
Got up at 6:30. Went to school. Came home. Ate. Studied and then watched TV. Went to bed.

Chapter # 29

Personal Writing

Personal writing tells about your own life. Most of it takes the form of *journals* and *autobiographies.* In a journal you record events, thoughts, and impressions. In an autobiography you write about some part of your life or your whole life.

29.1 Journals

A journal is a day-to-day account of your life. Some people allow no one else to read their journals. This section is about journals written for others, besides the writer, to read.

Understanding Journals

Even though journals vary widely in form and style, they all relate details of a person's life.

A journal is an ongoing record of important experiences, events, and personal observations.

Kinds of Journals. Some writers begin a journal by keeping a record of a trip or similar experience. The writer may enjoy rereading the journal and may continue it on a daily or weekly basis. Others prefer only to record special occasions.

29.1 Journals

KINDS OF JOURNALS

Purposes of Journals	Probable Writing Time
To summarize everyday experiences	Daily
To express personal feelings and insights	Daily or several times a week
To record important events	Several times a week
To record experiences in an area of special interest	As each occasion arises

Journal Entries. Some journal entries are like stories or essays. Others are brief observations about books, movies, or conversations.

Journal entries can be of any length, but they all include facts about activities, people, and events and the writer's feelings. The best journals help readers understand the writer through vivid impressions and personal views.

The journal entry below tells about a familiar event, but the writer's eye for detail brings the scene to life.

Descriptive details Around four the sky was bruised-looking and the
Personal sheet lightning began, silent and eerie. I went to the
Observation back porch and watched it, wondering if I would ever
see this again, the mountains grape purple and the
fields glowing dull yellow until the second of the
white, white lightning that came from nowhere and
Event had no shape; even as you tensed for the thunder you
knew that none was coming, and still a slight tightening happened inside your ear, and your back automatically got stiff, shoulders hunched against the imagined blow. The metallic smell of ozone was sweet and
heavy on the air.
Action Around five, when the wind began and the leaves

Write the Idea Bank on the board and ask students to identify it. Someone will probably say it is a diary entry. Discuss the fact that this entry has little point, either for the writer or anyone else. Explain what a journal is and the fact that journals are often not as private as diaries. Explain, too, that a well-written entry will generate a far more memorable record than the sample will, regardless of whether the writer intends it to be public or not.

Text Follow Through

Discuss text pages 568–572.

Assign Exercise A, page 570; Exercise B, page 570; Exercise C, page 571; Exercise D, page 571; and Developing Writing Skills, page 572.

Less advanced Before asking students to choose a journal style, you might want to set aside a block of time over several days for in-class writing. Focus students' writing by asking a different question each day, such as "Write about yesterday. What do you want to remember about yesterday?" or "What were your feelings about [some event that recently occurred at school]?" If you intend students to keep journals regularly, you will probably want to monitor their writing, perhaps through weekly checks by you or occasional oral readings.

Average Students may begin by writing fairly predictable entries. If you read early entries and respond with pointed questions ("What did the stranger look like?" or "Tell me more about your dog."), you may stimulate students to more specificity.

Advanced After students have kept journals for about a month, you might ask them to find and publish excerpts that seem in some way to go together. You could display these on the bulletin board or have students read them aloud.

Additional Practice

Practice Pages or Practice Book, page 140

TESTING

Test Program

Unit Pretest, page 79
Chapter Test, page 91
Unit Post-Test, page 99

RE-TEACHING

Practice Pages or Practice Book, page 140

THINKING SKILLS

Application—*Discovering* a purpose for a journal; *preparing* notes for an entry (Exercise C, page 571)

Analysis—*Identifying* the features of a journal entry (Exercise A, page 570; Exercise B, page 570)

Synthesis—*Writing* journal entries (Exercise D, page 571; Developing Writing Skills, page 572)

---

swirled around in square-dance fashion, and the sky fell so low the birds wouldn't fly, I went inside and tried to breathe. The house was eerie, lit by a yellow-purplish cast. It was a great relief when the rain started and the real lightning and thunder.—Katie Letcher Lyle

EXERCISE A: Understanding a Journal. Reread the excerpt from Katie Letcher Lyle's journal above and answer the following questions.

1. How much time does this entry cover? one hour
2. What event does the entry describe? an approaching thunder storm
3. Why do you think the writer chose to write this entry?
4. Pick three descriptive details that help you see the scene.
5. What do you learn about the writer's feelings? Answers will vary.

3. Answers will vary. 4. Answers will vary.

EXERCISE B: Looking at Journal Entries. Find a published journal. Answer the questions from Exercise A about an entry.

Keeping a Journal

In your journal you can keep details of thoughts, feelings and ideas about the events that happen to you and the people you meet.

Record ideas, events, and impressions in chronological order, and include clear and memorable details.

Journal writing is less formal than other kinds of writing. Think about why you are writing. If you are recording a trip, include facts about places, sights, and travel arrangements, as well as the people you meet and your impressions of the trip. If you are keeping a daily record, take notes, and write for a few minutes each evening or morning.

PLANNING A JOURNAL

1. Determine the purpose of your journal. Decide whether you want to express ideas and feelings, record daily events or important happenings, or keep a record of special experiences.
2. Decide how often you will write entries. Your purpose will help you make this decision, but also consider your own habits: How serious are you about keeping a journal?
3. Take notes about the things that happen to you. Try to answer questions such as Who? What? When? Where? and Why?
4. Brainstorm for descriptive details about the people, places, and things in your notes. Add these details to your notes.

Remember the purpose of your journal as you prepare the entries. The chart below offers help to a writer planning an entry on the school holidays.

PREPARING TO WRITE A JOURNAL ENTRY

When?	During school holidays
Who?	My sister and me
Where?	In Yosemite Park
What?	New experiences: train ride, first impression of the ranch, people we met, trail rides

Using the information you have gathered for your journal entry, write the events in chronological order, adding interesting details.

EXERCISE C: Planning Your Journal. Decide on the purpose of your journal and how frequently you will write your entries. Then take notes for your first journal entry.
Answers will vary.

EXERCISE D: Writing a Journal Entry. Using your notes from Exercise C, write a first entry. Try to make your descriptions come alive by adding colorful details.
Entries will vary.

OBJECTIVES

After completing this section, students should be able to

- Identify the features of an autobiography.
- Plan, write, and revise an autobiography.

TEACHING

Getting Started

Have students read an autobiography in a literary anthology or read one to them. Discuss its similarity to a short story and point out that while stories are presented as fictional even if they are based on true events, an autobiography is presented as true. Also explain that our own lives are a rich source for writing, even if we are not famous.

Text Follow Through

Discuss text pages 572–575.

Assign Exercise A, page 573; Exercise B, page 574; Exercise C, page 575; Exercise D, page 575; and Developing Writing Skills, page 575.

DEVELOPING WRITING SKILLS: Keeping a Journal. Add new entries to the journal you started in Exercise D. If you miss a day or two, just make an entry on the following day.
Entries will vary.

29.2 Autobiographies

An *autobiography* is a story of the writer's own life. It can be a few pages long or as long as a book. It can cover many years or only short periods in a life.

Understanding Autobiographies

Autobiographies have a first-person point of view.

An autobiography is a writer's account of his or her life.

Autobiographies have beginnings, endings, settings, characters, and related incidents similar to the plot of a short story.

FEATURES OF AN AUTOBIOGRAPHY	
Features	**Use in an autobiography**
Point of View	The writer tells his or her own story using *I, me, we,* and *us.*
Setting	In a brief autobiography, the writer often focuses on an arrival at a new place. In longer autobiographies, the setting shifts as the person moves about.
Incidents	A brief autobiography focuses on a period in the writer's life. Events follow chronological order.
Characters	Vivid characters help avoid the monotony of focusing only on personal thoughts and feelings.

29.2 Autobiographies

Dialogue	Dialogue tells readers about the writer's relationship to other characters.
Descriptive Details	Details about setting and characters help readers to visualize the writer's world.

This excerpt from an autobiography captures vivid details of the writer's early life and some of his personal views.

Time span

Descriptive detail

Characters

Personal reaction

Personal observations

At New Street we lived on coffee and talk. Talking was the great Depression pastime. Unlike the movies, talk was free, and a great river of talk flowed through the house, rising at suppertime, and cresting as my bedtime approached before subsiding into a murmur that trickled along past midnight, when all but Uncle Charlie had drifted off to bed, leaving him alone to reheat the pot . . . and settle down with his book.

If my homework was done, I could sit with them and listen until ten o'clock struck. I loved the sense of family warmth that radiated through those long kitchen nights of talk. There were many chords resonating beneath it, and though I could not identify them precisely, I was absorbing a sense of them and storing them away in memory. There was longing for happy times now lost, and dreaming about what might have been. There was fantasy, too, which revealed itself in a story to which they returned again and again, about the time Papa made his wonderful trip to England in search of the family's great lost fortune.—Russell Baker

EXERCISE A: Understanding an Autobiography. Answer the following questions about the selection by Russell Baker.

Less advanced You will probably want students to plan their autobiographies in class so you can encourage use of specific details.

Average You may want to combine this work with reading of additional autobiographies. You can use those in anthologies or ask students to bring to class a copy of the excerpt they chose for Exercise B. Have different students read their excerpts aloud for comment by the class.

Advanced In conjunction with this section, you might want to require students to read a book-length autobiography. If you have covered Chapter 28, you could also assign a book report on this book. Or you could have students give oral reports on the individual they have read about.

Additional Practice

Practice Pages or Practice Book, pages 141, 142
Writing Process Activities, pages 38, 39
Writing Workshops, pages 23–25

TESTING

Test Program
    Unit Pretest, page 79
    Chapter Test, page 91
    Unit Post-Test, page 99

Writing Process Activities, Evaluation Sheets, pages 8–12

RE-TEACHING

Practice Pages or Practice Book, pages 141, 142
Writing Process Activities, pages 38, 39

574

1. evenings during the Depression when he was a boy   2. the Depression   3. his

1. What period of the author's life does the section cover?
2. What event in American history plays a part in it?
3. Who else besides the author is part of the story?
4. What did the author like about the events he relates?
5. List three descriptive details he uses. Answers will vary.

family, including Uncle Charlie and Papa   4. sense of family warmth

EXERCISE B: Examining Autobiographies. Read parts of two or three autobiographies. Select a passage that you like and answer the questions in Exercise A.
Answers will vary.

PREWRITING, WRITING, AND REVISING: Creating an Autobiography

Careful writing, planning, and revising will help you to produce interesting autobiographical writing.

Prewriting. Before you start writing, decide on the key elements of the autobiographical account you will write.

Choose a time span, setting, incidents, and characters for your brief autobiography.

Plan to write two or three pages to cover a time span of a day or a week. Longer periods will require greater length. Include details about incidents, people, places, and events.

PLAN FOR AN AUTOBIOGRAPHY	
Time span and setting: First day in Nancy, France	
Incidents	Walks around town on Sunday, observes the handsome old church, nods to the flower seller
Characters	Churchgoers, flower woman

Writing. With your plan ready, you can begin to write about the events you listed. Follow chronological order. Use details and descriptions, transitions, and any other helps to a reader.

29.2 Autobiographies

Use your plan to write a first draft.

The following part of an autobiography covers a brief part of the writer's life, starting with a setting and an incident.

Setting	Hardly anyone was in the village street when I started out that Sunday morning, but before I had walked two blocks, the doorway of the fine seventeenth-century cathedral filled with people. They spilled onto the cobbled street and down the steep hill.
Incident	At the corner of the square, a gnarled old woman was selling fresh flowers. She stared at me, forgetting her wares, then smiled a toothless smile. I nodded, pleasantly I hope, and walked on as best I could among the homebound worshippers. They chattered in musical French and paid no attention to me.

Revising. Reread your first draft and improve it, using the following checklist for guidance.

CHECKLIST FOR REVISING AN AUTOBIOGRAPHY

1. Have you used the first-person point of view throughout?
2. Do you present the time span and the setting clearly?
3. Do your events follow in chronological order?
4. Have you used vivid descriptive details?
5. Have you included interesting personal observations?

EXERCISE C: Planning an Autobiography. Gather and organize information about a part of your life.
Answers will vary.

EXERCISE D: Writing About Yourself. Use your work from Exercise C to write, revise, and proofread an autobiography.
Autobiographies will vary.

DEVELOPING WRITING SKILLS: Writing an Autobiography. Following the steps you have learned, continue your autobiography with another event in your life.
Autobiographies will vary.

Developing Writing Skills

To provide students with additional guidance in completing this assignment, you might want to have them follow the steps outlined below.

Writing Across the Curriculum

Technological developments and scientific discoveries often have a major impact on the way people live their lives. For example, when television was developed, many families began spending their evenings in front of their television sets.

Prewriting Think of a technological development or scientific discovery that has had an impact on your life. For example, you might think of how the development of personal computers has affected you. Then free write about an event in your life in which the impact of this development is apparent. Next, review your free writing and underline the most interesting ideas.

Writing Using your list of ideas and details, write a first draft of an autobiographical account of the event you have chosen. Do not hesitate to include any additional ideas and details that you think of while you are writing. Make sure that you include a clear description of the event and that you discuss how the event reflects the impact of a particular scientific or technological development.

Revising Revise your autobiographical account using the checklist on page 575. After you have finished revising, proofread your account and prepare a final copy.

Guiding Student Writing

Students can work together in groups during the prewriting and revising steps to help generate ideas and to evaluate the paper through its developing stages. Students working as peer evaluators might engage in developing standards, such as superior, excellent, fair, and poor. Involved in this evaluation process, students quickly learn the qualities that make a paper good. They can then apply what they have learned to their own writing assignments. However, it is important to supervise peer-evaluation groups, so that students do not reinforce other students' bad writing habits or discourage certain students by being overly critical of their work. For this reason, students need to be given some guidelines before they begin to evaluate each other's papers.

Writing Workshop: Personal Writing

ASSIGNMENT 1

Topic Developing an Awareness of the Big Sell

Form and Purpose Journal entries that describe the steady bombardment of advertising and its effect on you

Audience Yourself

Length At least one entry each day over a two-week period.

Focus. Each journal entry should focus on advertising pitches you heard or saw during a particular day. After two weeks, review your entries and write a one-paragraph summary of your impressions.

Sources Radio, television, magazines, billboards, junk mail

Prewriting Each day carry a notebook and jot notes about ads you hear or see.

Writing At the end of each day, use your notes to record a journal entry. After a two-week period, review your notes and write a one-paragraph summary.

Revising Review your summary with this thought in mind: Does it precisely and clearly summarize my observations?

Assignment 1

Suggestions for Prewriting: Urge students to take notes not on a single ad each day, but on the many contacts they have. This will highlight the importance of carrying a journal. Entries, since they will be based on specific experiences, will then be more pointed.

Suggestions for Publishing: Students might enjoy a round-table discussion at the end of the two-week period.

Assignment 2

Suggestions for Prewriting: Hold a general discussion before directing students to take notes: What is friendship? What experiences fulfilled students or made them realize friendship? The discussion will help students to focus on a particular aspect of friendship and to use a specific event to illustrate it.

ASSIGNMENT 2

Topic Friendship Is More Than a Word

Form and Purpose An autobiography that narrates an experience and conveys an idea about friendship

Audience Yourself and your friend

Length Two to four pages

Focus Develop a narrative account of an incident that showed you the true meaning of friendship. Use description and dialogue to recreate the incident.

Sources Memories of personal experiences

Prewriting Develop a plan that lists notes about the event: time span, setting, incidents, and people involved.

Writing Use a first-person point of view and chronological order as you write a first draft.

Revising The checklist on page 575 will help you review and revise your draft. Then prepare a final copy.

Stimulating Thought

1. "What overall made the trip memorable? What happened to make this so?"

2. "Was the disaster caused by your own mistakes or by external factors?"

3. "Describe the scene as well as telling your narrative about skiing."

4. "Why do photographers and writers routinely keep journals as they travel?"

5. "Where to? Under the sea? To a distant planet? To the past?"

6. "Does the title mean mountain hiking, having a hiking adventure, or making an adventure of any hike?"

7. Remind students to include description with the narration.

8. "Build from frustration to victory—or to defeat."

9. "Unforgettable because of newness, beauty, adventure? Some combination?"

10. "Visit the same spot at several times of day and during different weather."

Topics for Writing: Personal Writing

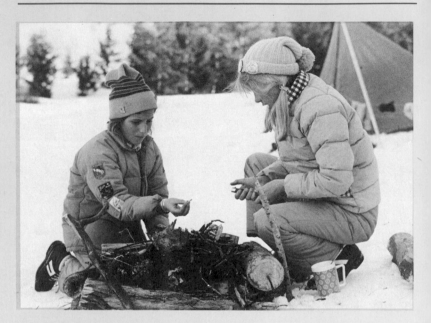

The scene depicted above may suggest a similar outdoor or wilderness experience you have had. Write about that experience in an autobiographical narrative. If you prefer, select one of the topics below for an autobiography or as the focus in a series of journal entries.

1. A Memorable Fishing Trip
2. A Disastrous Camping Experience
3. Skiing in the Mountains
4. A Journal of a Vacation
5. An Imaginary Voyage
6. High Adventure Hiking
7. Adventures on a City Street
8. First Time on Skates
9. A Canoe/Boat/Raft Trip That I'll Never Forget
10. Observing the Many Moods of Nature: A Journal

Chapter 30

Writing Short Stories

If students have studied Section 28.1, they will already have encountered the elements of character, plot, and setting in their consideration of book reports. In this chapter, they will explore the development of these elements in original writing. Section 30.1 is devoted to the character sketch, while Section 30.2 brings all the narrative elements into play in developing a short short story.

For additional or alternate writing assignments and a list of topics for writing, see pages 595–597.

You probably enjoy reading fiction—novels and short stories—more than any other type of literature. You will probably enjoy writing fiction as well, since fiction, more than almost any other form of writing, gives you a chance to make full use of your experiences, your knowledge of people, and your imagination.

Fiction usually grows out of characters. In fiction the personalities and actions of the characters are often used to present the writer's views about life to the readers. For this reason the first section in this chapter focuses on character sketches. In the second section, you will have a chance to expand your creative writing skills by writing *short* short stories with dialogue between different characters.

Writing a Character Sketch 30.1

30.1 Writing a Character Sketch
(pp. 579–586)

A *character sketch* is much like an artist's sketch. But instead of using paint, you must use words. The goal is to present a dominant impression of a person through the use of a few well-chosen details.

OBJECTIVES

After completing this section, students should be able to

- Identify the basic features of a character sketch.
- Choose a subject for a character sketch and focus on a particular dominant impression to be conveyed.
- Develop and organize a character sketch.
- Write and revise a character sketch.

TEACHING

Getting Started

Display an interesting non-stereotypical photograph of a person and engage the class in brainstorming: "Who is this? How old is she? Where does she live? What does she enjoy doing?" Build up as complete a biography as your students' interest allows. If disagreements arise ("She's a good student." "No, she hates school."), force the class to make a decision. Now ask about this person's personality: "What is her dominant characteristic? How do you know? Give me an example of that." Explain that characters are the heart of a story and that the ability to create a character like this is fundamental to writing a story.

Text Follow Through

Discuss text pages 579–586.

Assign Exercise A, page 582; Exercise B, page 583; Exercise C, page 584; Exercise D, page 585; and Developing Writing Skills, page 585.

Recognizing the Basic Features of a Character Sketch

To create an interesting picture of another person, you must give the reader a strong, single impression of your character.

A character sketch should focus on a dominant impression of a person. It should use lively details and exact language to support this impression, and it should end with a strong concluding idea.

The subject of your sketch can be a person you know, a character you have read about, or someone you have created in your imagination. The only real requirement is that it be someone whom you can write about in a vivid way.

The sketch should center on your *dominant impression* of this person. The person might have some outstanding quality, or you might have a special feeling or idea about the character, which could become your dominant impression. Your sketch can develop this impression in several ways. Physical descriptions that go beyond simple height, weight, and hair color can help you reveal your character. The person's actions and words can also help develop the impression.

A character sketch does not need to have a specific introduction, body, and conclusion. But it *should* have a strong, definite direction. It should build up more and more revealing details that create a sharper and sharper picture. A "telling" final detail can make your character memorable to the reader.

The following character sketch develops an impression of a young woman through examples, details, and an incident.

Dominant impression	Lucy Graham has had more hair-raising adventures than anyone else I have ever met. With a quick smile and a toss of her curly, red hair, she will launch into
Examples	the story of her latest escapade the minute anyone asks. Her blue eyes flashing with memories, she will

30.1 Writing a Character Sketch

describe, without taking a breath, anything from her latest rock-climbing adventure to a white-water kayak race. Every weekend finds Lucy enjoying the excitement of the world she loves best—the outdoors.

Examples and details

Lucy's room is a monument to her life style. In the corner a gray backpack that smells of campfire smoke leans against worn hiking boots and a battered tent. The rest of her gear—cooking equipment, bicycle helmet, rain poncho, and more—is stashed in a closet too small to hold it. Each time the door is opened, a stray pan or flashlight escapes with a loud crash. On the walls colorful posters and carefully cut out magazine photographs of forests, mountains, and rushing rivers cover almost all of the paint, along with bumper stickers that proclaim the joys of rock climbing and hiking. Several well-marked books on wilderness survival line the bookshelf above the desk, which is covered with travel and adventure magazines.

Incident

To Lucy every chance to explore the outdoors is a learning experience. Each trip she takes, she learns something new about herself and what she can do. Once, because she had misjudged a river's length, a white-water canoe trip stretched for over ten long hours. Hungry and exhausted, Lucy missed seeing a rock hidden beneath the river's surface and was suddenly catapulted into the swiftly moving current. As she was swept downstream, she kept calm, remembering that she would be safest from rocks if she kept her feet aimed downstream. Bruised and battered, Lucy called on her last reserves of strength as the current carried her near a large boulder, which she grasped to pull herself to safety. It was a terrifying experience and one Lucy did not forget. She made sure not to make the same mistakes the next time she went canoeing on that river—the following weekend!

Less advanced Before assigning Exercise A, you might want to point out a character sketch in a current reading. Then before assigning original character sketches, you might want to work further with the character created in Getting Started. As a whole class or in small groups, have students study the chart on page 583, decide what to include in the sketch, and write it up.

Average You may want to relate this section to a story or book the class is reading. Students may also enjoy identifying their own favorite characters from literature or movies, making a class tally of favorites, and discussing why these are memorable. Each student can be asked to write a few sentences giving his or her dominant impression of these popular characters.

Advanced You might ask students to develop two character sketches—both of the same person but written to focus on contrasting aspects of the person.

Additional Practice

Practice Pages or Practice
  Book, pages 143, 144
Writing Process Activities,
  pages 40, 41

TESTING

Test Program

  Unit Pretest, page 80
  Chapter Test, page 92
  Unit Post-Test, page 99

Writing Process Activities,
  Evaluation Sheets,
  pages 8–12

RE-TEACHING

Practice Pages or Practice
Book, pages 143, 144
Writing Process Activities,
pages 40, 41

THINKING SKILLS

Analysis—*Identifying* features
of a character sketch (Exercise A, page 582)
Discovering a subject for a
character sketch and *selecting* a dominant impression to
present (Exercise B, page 583)

Synthesis—*Organizing* a
character sketch (Exercise C,
page 584)

Evaluation—*Writing, appraising,*
and *revising* a character
sketch (Exercise D, page 585)
Planning, writing, appraising,
and *revising* (Developing
Writing Skills, page 585)

Writing Model Transparencies

For additiional practice, use
Models transparencies:
Character Sketch, pages
265–275

*Checklist for Revising a
Character Sketch* appears in
transparency form. See Checklists, page 337.

EXERCISE A: Recognizing a Good Character Sketch.
Look through novels, short stories, and magazines for character sketches, and choose two examples. For each one write a few sentences about (1) the author's dominant impression of the character and (2) the kind of descriptive material used to develop this impression.
Answers will vary.

PREWRITING: Choosing a Subject and Focusing Your Ideas

The first step in planning your own character sketch is choosing a subject.

Choose a character who really interests you and decide on the particular impression of that person that you want to express.

Before selecting a character to write about, think over a number of possibilities. Think about characters from literature as well as people you know in real life. Search your imagination for other characters who may not be real but who appeal to you for some reason. Try to find a character about whom you feel strongly. Strong feelings—either positive or negative—will help you find things to say about your character.

Once you have chosen your character, you should focus on *one* major idea about that person. Your dominant impression can be a special feeling that you have about the character. It can be an unusual trait of the character. It can even be a combination of the physical appearance and the personality of your subject. Whatever your impression, it should be something *specific.* Never simply say that your character is "interesting" or "exciting" or "admirable." Instead, give your reader a clear idea of what makes your subject special.

WEAK IMPRESSION: My aunt is the most interesting person I know.

STRONGER IMPRESSION: Aunt Thelma was never willing to accept an obvious explanation.

30.1 Writing a Character Sketch

EXERCISE B: Choosing a Character. Choose a real or imaginary character, using the following items as suggestions. Identify an outstanding characteristic of the person and write one or two sentences introducing the character and expressing a dominant impression.
Answers will vary.

1. A distant friend
2. A mysterious stranger
3. A memorable character from a book or play
4. A well-known person in your city or home town
5. Yourself (from another person's point of view)

PREWRITING: Developing and Organizing Your Sketch

You can now begin to develop your sketch.

List physical details, incidents, and other information that will help develop the dominant impression you have chosen for your character. Then arrange your ideas in an order that will help your reader see the character vividly.

In much the same way that you prepare paragraphs and essays, brainstorm for information to support your character sketch. The chart below lists ideas that can help you develop support.

IDEAS FOR DEVELOPING A CHARACTER SKETCH
1. Describe the person's physical characteristics, including clothing, movements, and facial expressions.
2. Mention important facts about your character's past.
3. Use the character's own words if these help you focus on an aspect of the character's personality.
4. Describe the character's opinions and typical activities.
5. Show the character in action.
6. Describe the feelings of others about the character.

After you have listed a number of ideas, sort and arrange them. Look over your list and weed out the less effective or less important details. You should now be ready to arrange your best supporting items into a character sketch that will clearly present your dominant impression to the reader. If you want to show the character's development over time, chronological order will probably work best. On the other hand, if your sketch includes examples and details about your subject's appearance, habits, or ideas, the best way of organizing the support might be by order of importance. For example, if you were describing different habits of your character, you might plan three paragraphs, each describing a different habit, with the most unusual habit of all in the final paragraph.

EXERCISE C: Developing a Character Sketch. Beneath the dominant impression you wrote in Exercise B, list as many supporting details as you can think of, including physical details, incidents, and other information that supports your dominant impression. Eliminate weaker items, and arrange the details in the order most likely to create a vivid picture.
Lists will vary.

WRITING AND REVISING: Completing Your Sketch

You are now ready to begin your first draft of the sketch. While you write, you should concentrate on making your subject come alive on paper. Assume that the reader does not know your character. Your task is to make your character into a recognizable and familiar individual.

Use vivid language as you draft your character sketch. Then make any changes that will strengthen your sketch.

Because your purpose is to create a sharp picture of your subject, you must choose words that will let your reader see

30.1 Writing a Character Sketch

your character as you see him or her. Use strong action verbs, specific nouns, and lively modifiers as you write. You might also want to review the sections on word choice on pages 406–418.

When you have completed your first draft, reread it. Then make improvements wherever you can. The following checklist should help.

CHECKLIST FOR REVISING A CHARACTER SKETCH

1. Could your opening sentence establish a sharper impression of the person?
2. What additional details might strengthen your impression?
3. Would another arrangement of details make your sketch clearer or more interesting for your reader?
4. Are there places where more vivid word choices could be used to help make your subject come to life?
5. Is there any better way of closing your sketch?
6. Are there any mistakes in grammar, usage, mechanics, or spelling?

When you have made all the improvements you can, write a final copy. Then finish your revising by proofreading your sketch to catch any errors added in recopying.

EXERCISE D: Writing and Revising a Character Sketch. Using the list you developed in Exercise C, write a first draft of your character sketch. Then revise your draft, using the checklist on this page.
First drafts and revisions will vary.

DEVELOPING WRITING SKILLS: Evaluating a Character Sketch. Write another character sketch, following the steps you learned in this section. Then exchange sketches with another student, and answer the questions on the following page. Finally, revise your own sketch, taking into consideration your partner's comments.
Answers will vary.

1. What is the dominant impression of the sketch? Could it be established more sharply?
2. Should the sketch have included more details? What kinds?
3. Are the writer's feelings about the person clear? What are they?
4. What, if anything, would have made the sketch more interesting to you?
5. Could the language be more vivid? Where?

30.2 Writing a Short Short Story

Just as a character sketch is like a picture, a *short short story* is like a short but complete scene in a movie. A short short story introduces a character or characters involved in an interesting or difficult situation. Then it shows what happens as a result of the characters' words or actions.

Recognizing the Basic Features of a Short Short Story

A short short story must include a number of different features in order to be convincing.

A short short story should describe characters and setting clearly, present and resolve a conflict, be told from a consistent point of view, follow a chronological order, and include dialogue where appropriate.

Characters and setting are the basic elements of any short short story. As you did in your character sketch, you will need to see these people and places in your mind and find ways of making them come alive for the reader.

The action in a short short story is usually based on some central *conflict,* or problem, that must be resolved. The conflict is usually between two or more characters, but it can also be

---

30.2 Writing a Short Short Story

(pp. 586–594)

OBJECTIVES

After completing this section, students should be able to

- Identify the basic features of a short short story.
- Plan a short short story.
- Write dialogue that helps develop characters and the plot.
- Write and revise a short short story.

TEACHING

Getting Started

Reintroduce the character the class created in Section 30.1. Explain that to move beyond a character sketch, a writer must let a character face a conflict. Ask what conflict this person is facing; insist on specific details—not "She's jealous of her sister" but "She's jealous of her older sister Diane because Diane is a better student than she is."

Text Follow Through

Discuss text pages 586–594.

Assign Exercise A, page 589; Exercise B, page 591; Exercise C, page 592; Exercise D, page 594; and Developing Writing Skills, page 594.

Less advanced You may want to present a short story for class analysis before assigning Exercise A. You may also want to continue the discussion begun in Getting Started before assigning original stories. Students can brainstorm for setting and incidents and experiment with point of view. Before assigning Exercise C, you may want to review Section 19.6.

Average After students plan their stories in Exercise B, you might ask them to present them orally in small groups. Listeners can jot down the characters, setting, conflict, point of view, and suggestions for dialogue. Each student can use these notes to improve his or her story.

Advanced To increase students' range of expression, you might ask that they write one serious and one humorous story. Students might also enjoy organizing and displaying the stories written by all your classes.

Additional Practice

Practice Pages or Practice Book, pages 145, 146
Writing Process Activities, pages 42, 43
Writing Workshops, pages 26–28

30.2 Writing a Short Short Story

within one character. The characters should think and act in order to work out the conflict.

In writing a short short story, you will also have to make a choice about who is telling the story. The teller of the story is called the *narrator.* The way in which the narrator tells the story is called the *point of view.* You can choose to tell the story through a first-person or "I" narrator, as if you were a character and the story were happening to you. Or you might use a third-person narrator, who does not take part in the story but is able to tell about one or several characters' thoughts as well as their actions. Whichever point of view you use, it must remain consistent throughout the story.

The following two passages tell the same story, first from a first-person point of view and then from a third-person point of view. Note the differences between the two points of view.

Passage with a first-person narrator

I walked into the cottage and saw that no one was home. Well, this didn't look too promising. Then I noticed that everything was covered with millions of coarse brown hairs. I definitely was not looking forward to meeting these people. Worst of all, there were three of everything—beds, chairs, bowls of porridge, you name it. I hate the number three. It always means that something weird is going to happen to me.

Passage with a third-person narrator

Goldilocks entered the cottage and soon realized that no one was home. This made her very uncomfortable. Then she noticed the coarse brown hairs that covered every inch of the room and wondered what sort of people lived there. But she was most upset by the fact that everything was in sets of three—three beds, three chairs, three bowls of porridge. Goldilocks had always hated the number three. She believed that it brought her bad luck.

Whatever the point of view, most short short stories will follow a chronological order, showing the action as it unfolds.

Writing Model Transparencies

For additional practice, use
Models transparencies:
  Short Story, pages 277–289

*Checklist for Revising a Short
Story* appears in transparency
form. See Checklists, page 339.

Transitions such as *next, then, later,* and *soon* can help you show the order of events as well as the passing of time.

Finally, a short short story often includes dialogue between the characters. Dialogue helps to make both the events and the people involved in them more vivid.

The following short short story with a first-person narrator shows how these different elements work together.

First-person narrator

Character's actions and thoughts

When a note was brought into my algebra class requesting my immediate appearance in the principal's office, my mouth became paste, my palms got wet, and my heart fluttered. As I walked the long, long corridors to the main office, my mind jumped back a week to April Fools' Day. Surely no one knew that I was the one who had rearranged the lane markers in the swimming pool so that they looked like a huge duck. I had done it after swim practice—who had seen me?

Explanation of conflict

Finally, I reached the office. Mrs. Coveney, the secretary, looked at me over her glasses and said, "Have a seat, please. Mrs. Howard will be with you shortly." She was missing her normal friendly smile.

Dialogue

Description

Minutes ticked by on the large oak regulator clock as my world hung suspended. At last the door to the principal's office opened, and Mrs. Howard signaled for me to come into her office. She sat. I sat. Another moment passed. Then she broke the silence.

Dialogue

"Gerald," she began. Her voice locked my attention. "Gerald, the faculty is planning a little surprise party in honor of Mr. Burdett, who, as you probably know, is retiring after twenty years of coaching the swimming team."

Did she know? I searched her face for a hint of sarcasm. Nothing. She went on.

"So. We've decided to ask you, as a member of the team, to organize a committee to decorate the pool for

30.2 Writing a Short Short Story

Character's thoughts

the party. Can you manage that without his knowledge, do you think?"

What was going on here? Was she trying to trick me into a confession? I decided to stay innocent until proven guilty. I would go down fighting.

Dialogue

"Uh, sure. I'd be happy to." And I waited for the blow to fall.

It didn't. She just handed me a folded paper and said, smiling, "Fine. Now, I've jotted down a few of the things we have in mind for the party. Take a look when you get a chance." She nodded for me to go.

Character's actions and thoughts

Relieved, I walked out of the office. This had certainly been a close one. But I had made it. In the safety of the hall, I smiled. Decorations? They probably want a bunch of crepe-paper streamers and other junk. Then I took a look at the sheet. This is what it said:

Resolution

Dear Gerald,

Be good to your school.
Don't mess with the pool.
(Next time *won't* be cool.)

April Fool.

Sincerely,
Mrs. Howard

EXERCISE A: **Examining a Short Short Story.** Find a short short story in a book or magazine. Then answer the following questions.

Answers will vary.

1. Who are the characters?
2. What is the central conflict and how is it resolved?
3. From what point of view is the story told?
4. What transitions are used to guide the reader through the events of the story?
5. What role does dialogue play in the story?

PREWRITING: Planning and Organizing Your Short Short Story

Writing your short short story calls for a good deal of creativity. Whether you make up the entire story or tell about something that really happened, you must think through the whole story in advance. A number of prewriting steps can help you plan your story.

Deciding on Characters, Setting, Conflict, and Point of View. You can begin by letting your imagination take over. Has something happened to you that you can develop into a story? Is there a setting that seems ripe with possibilities? Can you imagine two or more specific characters—a customer and a clerk, two drivers, or perhaps two neighbors—involved in some interesting conflict?

> **Brainstorm for ideas about interesting characters, settings, and conflicts. When you know what story you will tell, choose the point of view you will use.**

If you have a clear idea of either the characters, setting, or conflict, you can begin to fill in the other elements. Use your own experiences and those of people you know as ideas. Maybe you remember two customers arguing over a piece of merchandise. Or maybe a favorite family story can give you ideas for your own story. Your point of view is likely to grow naturally out of your choices of characters, setting, and conflict. Do you see yourself as a character in the story, or will you tell the story as a narrator removed from the story?

Developing and Shaping Your Story. Once you have a specific story in mind, you should list the key events of the story and begin thinking of specific details to enliven the story.

> **Make a chronological list of events and then brainstorm for specific details that will make the characters and happenings in your story come alive for the reader.**

At this point you should give your story flesh and bones. Jot down the main things that happen, especially the actions of your characters. Then try to list as many details about the characters and the setting as you can. Just as you listed details for a character sketch, you should think of physical characteristics, gestures, expressions, or thoughts that will help the reader visualize and get to know your characters. Try to make the setting of your story clear by using revealing details, sights, sounds, and smells to capture the exact place.

Once you have a number of details to enliven your story, you will need to find a place for them in your outline of events. Although you will want to set the scene and sketch the characters at the beginnning, be sure to save some details for later to give your reader a feeling of greater and greater understanding.

EXERCISE B: Choosing the Story You Will Tell. Think of ten different characters, five specific settings, and five conflicts or problems that need to be resolved. Then choose two or three characters, one specific setting, and one appropriate conflict. Decide what point of view you will use. Then develop an outline of events. Finally, brainstorm for specific details and add them to your outline in appropriate places.
Answers will vary.

PREWRITING: Thinking About Dialogue

Dialogue is not necessary in all short short stories. It can, however, add considerable interest if you use it well.

If you plan to write dialogue for your characters, choose words and phrases that suit each personality and make sure that the dialogue helps move the action forward.

Dialogue breathes life into your characters when the words that you place in their mouths sound like things these people would actually say. An older person's words will be different from those of a ten year old. A police officer's phrasing is likely to differ greatly from that of a disc jockey. The situation can also have an effect on a character's words. If your character is nervous about something, for example, you should write dialogue that sounds anxious. Even slang and jargon may be appropriate if they are truly connected to the characters who use them.

Notice the difference between the following examples of dialogue, both written as the words of a young child who has just been scolded.

UNNATURAL: "It was truly an accident. The trash bag is enormous and I have difficulty handling it."

MORE NATURAL: "Okay, I'm sorry. But it wasn't my fault. The dumb bag is too big."

Dialogue should also contribute to the ongoing action of a story. You can use it to show the characters trying to resolve their problems. Or you can use it to help draw the reader from one event to the next. In the story about the April Fools' prank, the dialogue between the principal and the main character is an important part of the action. It shows the conflict between Gerald and the principal. It builds suspense, gives Gerald a false feeling of relief, and prepares the reader for Mrs. Howard's own April Fools' joke.

When you write dialogue, make sure the words of different characters are separated into different short paragraphs. You might also review the material on quotations in Section 19.6.

EXERCISE C: Developing a Short Short Story with Dialogue. Using the outline you prepared in Exercise B, decide on at least one place where dialogue might help to develop the characters or carry the action. Write three to five short paragraphs of dialogue, trying to make your characters sound as natural as possible.
Paragraphs of dialogue will vary.

WRITING AND REVISING: Completing Your Short Short Story

With an outline of events that shows where you will include description and dialogue, you can begin to write your short short story. When you have finished the first draft, revise it by making improvements where possible, recopying it, and proofreading it.

Following your basic plan, write your first draft. Use a consistent point of view, and make your characters act, talk, and think to resolve the conflict. Then revise your draft using a checklist.

Writing the first draft gives you a chance to put all the parts together. Drafting your story should be fun. Play with your descriptions and dialogue. Try different ways to sharpen them and make them interesting. Do not be afraid to experiment with language, but remember to keep your story's point of view consistent. Add and take out events in your story line if such changes will help hold the reader's interest. Try not to leave out any necessary information, and make sure that the ending grows naturally out of the story.

When you read over your story, you may find many things to improve. Reading it aloud is a particularly good way to find awkward phrases, unnatural dialogue, and other weak spots. The following checklist can also help.

CHECKLIST FOR REVISING A SHORT SHORT STORY

1. Are the characters and setting clearly described? Will the reader see them as you do?
2. Have you presented and resolved some interesting conflict or problem?
3. Have you kept a consistent point of view throughout?
4. Does any dialogue you have included help make the story interesting and realistic?
5. Will the ending of your story leave the reader satisfied?

Developing Writing Skills

As an alternative, you might have your students complete the following assignment.

Writing Across the Curriculum

Many writers have written novels and short stories based on important historical events or set during the period in which an important historical event occurred. For example, Stephen Crane's novel, *The Red Badge of Courage,* is set during the Civil War.

Prewriting Choose a historical event that interests you. Then brainstorm about the types of people who were involved in this event and about the types of experiences that these people might have had. Next, review your brainstorming notes and choose an idea that would make a good topic for a short story. Prepare a list of ideas and details that you can use in your story. Then organize your ideas and details into a plot outline.

Writing Following your plot outline, write a first draft of your short story. Make your dialogue seem natural and realistic, and describe places and events as vividly as possible. Also make sure that you use transitions to indicate the order in which the events occur and that you maintain a consistent point of view.

Revising Revise your short story using the checklist on page 593. Finally, after you have proofread your story and prepared a final draft, consider submitting it to your school's literary magazine.

EXERCISE D: Writing a Short Short Story. Using the outline and dialogue you have developed, write the first draft of your short short story. Then use the preceding checklist to revise your work. Finish your revising by writing a clean copy and proofreading it.

Short short stories will vary.

DEVELOPING WRITING SKILLS: Writing and Evaluating a Short Short Story. Choose one of the following ideas or make up one of your own. Then write a short short story, following the steps you have learned in this section. When you have finished, revise your draft by making necessary changes, recopying it, and proofreading it. Then exchange stories with another student. Finally, write a brief evaluation of your partner's story, identifying the conflict and point of view and commenting on the strongest and weakest parts of the story.

Short short stories and evaluations will vary.

1. A baby sitter encounters unusual children
2. A young person tries to gather enough courage to ask someone to dance
3. A family of very strong individuals has a hard time finding a vacation plan that will suit everyone
4. Two friends argue over reporting a possible UFO sighting
5. Confusion reigns in a school during a power blackout

Writing Workshop: Writing Short Stories

ASSIGNMENT 1

Topic Developing a Tall-Tale Character

Form and Purpose A character sketch that entertains a reader with a description of an invented tall-tale character

Audience Children of ages 4–8

Length Three to four paragraphs

Focus Describe a dominant impression of a character with a special skill or power. Present details and examples that support the dominant impression. Conclude with a narrative paragraph that tells how that character uses the special skill or power to solve a major problem.

Sources Legends and tall tales, your imagination

Prewriting Invent a character with a special skill or power. Write descriptive notes about the character. The ideas checklist on page 583 will help you develop details.

Writing Using your notes, write a first-draft character sketch.

Revising Use the checklist on page 585 to revise your draft.

Guiding Student Writing

Encourage students to find their own approach to completing some Writing Workshop assignments. Students can experiment with the planning, writing, and revising steps to find a process that works well for them. For example, instead of preparing an outline, students can organize their supporting information while they are writing by using the cueing technique or by preparing a brainstorming sheet. Students can also try making revisions while writing their first draft.

The writing process needs to be seen as recursive, as looping back on itself. Students are more likely to write several drafts if they know their work will be published, or recognized publicly, in some way. Classroom bulletin boards, occasional oral readings, or printed publications are all ways to recognize and encourage student writers.

Assignment 1

Suggestions for Prewriting: Before students create their own characters, brainstorm as a class to create one, recording the notes on the board. If there is an artist among the students, have him or her sketch as the description is refined.

Suggestions for Writing: Remind students that their audience will have an effect on their vocabulary.

Suggestions for Publishing: Ask students to provide a picture of their character.

Assignment 2

Suggestions for Prewriting: Again have the class brainstorm as a group to build a story around the character developed above.

Suggestions for Publishing: Students could illustrate their tall tales, bind them together, and send them to a primary school in your system. If possible, ask for comments from the younger students.

ASSIGNMENT 2

Topic   Writing a Tall Tale

Form and Purpose   A tall tale that entertains readers

Audience   Children of ages 4–8

Length   Two to four pages

Focus   In your tall tale develop a central conflict, or major problem, that is resolved by the main character's heroic action. Use a third-person narrator and include dialogue.

Sources   Assignment 1 notes or a character sketch for a different tall-tale character.

Prewriting   Using the character sketch from Assignment 1 or a sketch plan for another character, develop a story plan. Determine a setting, a conflict, and a resolution.

Writing   Follow your story plan, and write a first draft.

Revising   Review your tall tale and add dialogue where it will help make your characters more believable. The checklist on page 593 will help you revise. Then write a complete, final copy and share it with a younger audience.

Topics for Writing: Writing Short Stories

Charles Adams, © 1954, *The New Yorker Magazine, Inc.*

If the cartoon gives you an idea for a story, plan and write a short story that develops that idea. As an alternative, you may wish to choose one of the story ideas below.

1. Captured by a U.F.O.
2. A confrontation with the Abominable Snowman.
3. Seeing the Ghostly Ship *The Flying Dutchman* While Sailing
4. A Friend Who Becomes a Werewolf
5. Squash and Zucchini Plants Threaten to Overtake a City
6. Discovering a Prehistoric Beast While on a Camping Trip
7. The Ghost of a Famous Person Appears in a Recent Photo
8. A Dream Becomes a Reality
9. You Visit the Past and Find Yourself in a Position to Change the Course of History
10. A Pet Begins to Communicate with You, But No One Else Can Hear It

Stimulating Thought

1. Ask students to brainstorm to develop a list of features and character traits for the aliens.
2. Have students list details describing the Abominable Snowman.
3. Have students research the story of The Flying Dutchman. Then have them share stories of other mysterious ships.
4. Have students discuss movies they have seen in which a human being becomes a werewolf.
5. Ask students to discuss the methods they think these plants would use to overtake a city.
6. Have students discuss trips that they have taken to a natural history museum. Ask them what they think would happen if the skeletons of the prehistoric animals there were suddenly to come alive.
7. Have students brainstorm to form a list of the people from the past they would most like to meet.
8. Have students free write about their dreams.
9. Have students make a list of *what ifs.* To start with write the following *what ifs* on the chalkboard: What if the British had won the Revolutionary War? What if the wheel had never been invented? What if Abraham Lincoln had not been assassinated?
10. Survey the class: What pets do they have?

Writing Letters

(pp. 598–617)

Section 31.1 discusses the form of different types of letters and envelopes, while Section 31.2 emphasizes content. Each section deals with both social and business letters. If you prefer, you may work back and forth from one section to the other, discussing both form and content for each type of correspondence at the same time.

For additional or alternate writing assignments and a list of topics for writing, see pages 615–617.

31.1 Looking at Friendly Letters, Social Notes, and Business Letters

(pp. 598–607)

OBJECTIVES

After completing this section, students should be able to

- Set up friendly letters and social notes and prepare them for mailing.
- Set up business letters and prepare them for mailing.

Chapter **31**

Writing Letters

This chapter will explain the forms and purposes of *friendly letters*, *social notes*, and *business letters*, and will give you practice in writing all three.

31.1 Looking at Friendly Letters, Social Notes, and Business Letters

A clear form is important to any letter. Both personal letters and business letters should have certain expected parts and should follow a consistent style.

Setting Up Friendly Letters and Social Notes

There are many different reasons for writing a friendly letter or a social note: to correspond with a friend, to offer an invitation, to accept or decline an invitation, to offer congratulations, or to offer sympathy. Whatever your purpose in writing, you should include certain basic parts and follow a consistent

31.1 Looking at Friendly Letters and Social Notes

style to make the letter look neat and orderly. In addition, the letter should be folded and the envelope prepared in a proper fashion.

The Basic Parts of a Friendly Letter or Social Note. To write a personal letter, you must be familiar with its five basic parts.

A friendly letter or social note should include a heading, a salutation, a body, a closing, and a signature.

The *heading* should include your own address and the date on which you write the letter. The first line should contain your street address. The second line should contain your city or town, state, and ZIP code. The date on which you write the letter should appear in the third line.

HEADINGS: 141 Dogwood Drive
Clearwater, New York 11794
December 14, 1981

120 North 14th Street, Apt. 4A
Phoenix, Arizona 85005
May 20, 1982

The *salutation* is the part that greets your reader. You should generally use a formal salutation if you are not very familiar with the person to whom you are writing or if he or she is older than you. For a friend or close relative, you may want to use an informal salutation. Note in the following examples that a comma comes after each salutation.

FORMAL SALUTATIONS: Dear Thomas,   Dear Mrs. Henry,
Dear Uncle Ed,   Dear Ms. Ryan,

LESS FORMAL SALUTATIONS: My good friend,   Hi, Brian,
Hello, pal,   Greetings,

The *body* is the main part of your letter. In it you should write your basic message. You might share personal informa-

Advanced Depending on students' experience, you may want simply to review letter forms, skipping Exercises A through D, and move directly to Developing Writing Skills. You could also ask students to exchange their letters and to respond as the person to whom the letter was addresed.

Additional Practice

Practice Pages or Practice Book, pages 147, 148

TESTING

Test Program
   Unit Pretest, pages 80, 81
   Chapter Test, page 93
   Unit Post-Test, page 100

RE-TEACHING

Practice Pages or Practice Book, pages 147, 148

THINKING SKILLS

Application—*Demonstrating* forms of friendly letters (Exercise A, page 603)
Demonstrating the forms of envelopes for friendly letters (Exercise B, page 603)
Demonstrating the forms of business letters (Exercise C, page 607)
Demonstrating the forms of envelopes for business letters (Exercise D, page 607)
Synthesis—*Writing* friendly and business letters (Developing Writing Skills, page 607)

For additional practice, use Models transparencies:
   Friendly Letter, pages 291–301

---

tion with a friend, you might invite people to a party, or you might give any of a number of other kinds of information. Depending on the kind of information you wish to send, the body of your letter can vary in length. In a letter to a friend, the body may be several pages long. In an invitation the body will generally contain only a few sentences giving such things as the date and the location.

The *closing* of your letter should tell the reader that the message is finished. It may be only one word, or it may be a brief phrase. Note in the following examples that the first word of a closing is capitalized and that the closing is followed by a comma.

CLOSINGS: My best wishes,   Love,

   Sincerely,   Very truly yours,

The *signature* signals the end of the letter. In writing your signature, you should use the name that the reader normally uses to address you. Always write your signature in ink, even if you have typed the rest of the letter.

You may also include a sixth part—an *R.S.V.P.*—in a letter of invitation. This abbreviation tells the reader to respond soon so that you will know if he or she plans to attend. Often a phone number is given for this purpose.

Two Styles for Friendly Letters and Social Notes. To set up your friendly letters and social notes, you must also know where each of the basic parts goes on the paper. The heading goes in the upper right-hand corner of the letter, and the salutation follows several lines beneath it along the left margin. The body is the middle of the letter. The closing follows in the lower right-hand section of the letter two or three lines beneath the body, and the signature follows beneath the closing. If you include an *R.S.V.P.*, write it in the lower left-hand corner of the letter. Although the basic positions are always the same, you can choose from two styles to present these parts of your letter.

Social Note, page 303–307
Business Letter, pages
309–319

31.1 Looking at Friendly Letters and Social Notes

To write the basic parts of a friendly letter or social note, use either the indented style or the semiblock style.

If you use the *indented style,* you must indent the lines of the heading and the signature as shown in the following example. If you use the *semiblock style,* the heading, the closing, and the signature should all be lined up one beneath the other.

Indented Style   **Semiblock Style**

Heading

Salutation

Body

Closing

Signature

Envelopes for Friendly Letters and Social Notes. If you have used special stationery for your letter, you should use a matching envelope. In addition, if you have typed the letter, you should plan to type the envelope as well. Finally, you should write the mailing information on the front of the envelope using the same style that you used in the letter itself.

On the envelope include your full return address and a complete mailing address, using the same style as you used in the letter, either indented or semiblock.

On the envelope the first line of your return address should contain your full name. The second line should give your street address. The third line should give your city or town, state, and

ZIP code. The mailing address should provide exactly the same information about the person to whom you are sending the letter. When preparing an envelope, you should also keep in mind a few additional guidelines.

GUIDELINES FOR ENVELOPES FOR PERSONAL LETTERS

1. Do not use titles—Mr., Miss, and Ms.—in writing your own name in the return address.
2. Avoid unclear abbreviations in both addresses.
3. Include ZIP codes in both addresses.
4. Be sure to use envelopes that are large enough to meet postal service regulations. Write the return address on the back of small envelopes.

The following examples show envelopes using each of the two styles.

Indented Style   **Semiblock Style**

        Return
                            address

                            Mailing
                            address

Mailing the Letter. To mail your letter, follow a simple but important procedure.

Fold your letter properly and place it inside its envelope.

If you are writing on relatively small-size stationery, you will probably be able to fold the paper in half and slip it into the envelope. With some stationery you may even be able to fit it into an envelope without folding. With large paper you will generally need to fold your letter into thirds, creating a double-fold as shown in the following diagram.

31.1 Looking at Business Letters

Letter   **Letter Folded Once**   **Letter Folded Twice**

EXERCISE A: Setting Up the Parts of Friendly Letters and Social Notes. Use two separate sheets of paper to set up one letter in indented style and one letter in semiblock style. On each letter use your own address and today's date for the heading. Choose a different salutation for each letter, and draw lines for the body. Then add the proper closing and signature.
Answers will vary.

EXERCISE B: Preparing Friendly Letters and Social Notes for Mailing. Following the style of each letter that you prepared in Exercise A, write an envelope for each letter. Use the information in each letter's heading to write a return address. Make up a mailing address to suit each salutation. Then fold each letter properly, and place it inside its envelope.
Answers will vary.

Setting Up Business Letters

You may need to write business letters to order merchandise, to register a complaint or opinion, to answer an advertisement, or for any of a number of other purposes. As you will see, business letters contain many of the same parts that friendly letters and social notes contain, with a few additional features. The styles used for business letters are also similar to those used for personal letters, with a few minor changes.

The Basic Parts of a Business Letter. To write a business letter, you must become familiar with its six basic parts.

A business letter should include a heading, an inside address, a salutation, a body, a closing, and a signature.

The *heading* of a business letter should contain the same information as the heading of a friendly letter: your street address, town or city, state, ZIP code, and the date you write the letter, arranged in three lines.

The *inside address,* placed two to four lines beneath the heading, should begin with the name of the person or business that you are writing to, sometimes including a title such as *President* or *Director.* The address of the person or business goes beneath the name.

INSIDE ADDRESSES: Mrs. Joanne Burns, Editor
The <u>Appleton Sun-Times</u>
Appleton, Illinois 60771

Meyer's Discount Drugs, Inc.
1200 Turnpike Access
Hamilton, New York 10615

The *salutation* of a business letter, which should go two lines beneath the inside address, is your greeting to the reader of the letter. It should be formal and should be followed by a colon.

SALUTATIONS: Dear Mrs. Ryan: Dear Sir or Madam:

   Dear Sir: Gentlemen:

The *body* of the letter should give whatever information you need to include to achieve your purpose in writing. If you have written a business letter to order merchandise, for example, the body should contain your specific requests and provide all required information. The body can be any length—a few sentences or several paragraphs—but it should always be precise.

31.1 Looking at Business Letters

The *closing* of a business letter is a formal sign-off. It begins with a capital letter and ends with a comma.

The *signature* must be written in ink, even if the letter has been typed. If you have typed the letter, you should type your full name beneath your signature. In typed business letters, women sometimes write in parentheses before their name the title by which they wish to be addressed. The following are examples of closings and signatures from typed business letters.

CLOSING: Yours truly,   Sincerely,

            Harrison Martin *Betty Randolph*

NAME: Harrison Martin   (Mrs.) Betty Randolph

Two Styles for a Business Letter. The parts of a business letter are arranged in much the same fashion as a friendly letter. However, the exact position of a few of the parts depends on which of two different styles you decide to use.

To write the basic parts of a business letter, use either the block style or the semiblock style.

The following examples show both styles.

Block Style   **Semiblock Style**

Block Style	Labels	Semiblock Style
	Heading	
	Inside address	
	Salutation	
	Body	
	Closing	
	Signature	
	Name	

If you use the *block style,* you must line up all parts of the letter along the left margin of your paper. Do not indent any lines—not even the first lines of paragraphs. If you use the *semiblock style,* place the heading, the closing, and the signature on the right just as in the semiblock style for the friendly letter. As in the friendly letter, paragraphs are indented.

If your business letter is long enough to have a second page, write the name of the person receiving the letter, the page number *(Page 2),* and the date at the top of the second page.

Envelopes for Business Letters. Most business letters are written on white, business-size stationery. Your envelope should also be white and of a standard business size.

On a business envelope, include your full return address and a mailing address that matches the inside address of the letter exactly.

All business envelopes should follow the style of the following example, regardless of the style you chose for the letter.

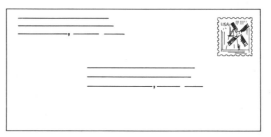

You should also follow a few additional guidelines when addressing business envelopes.

GUIDELINES FOR ENVELOPES FOR BUSINESS LETTERS

1. Do not use titles—Mr., Miss, and Ms.—in writing your own name in the return address.
2. Avoid unclear abbreviations in both addresses.
3. Include ZIP codes in both addresses.

31.1 Looking at Business Letters

Mailing the Letter. You should fold most business letters into thirds by making a double-fold, as shown on page 603.

Fold your letter properly and place it inside its envelope.

EXERCISE C: Setting up the Parts of Business Letters. Use two separate sheets of paper to set up one letter in block style and one letter in semiblock style. On each letter use your own address and today's date for the heading. Use the following information to write an inside address. Choose a salutation, draw lines for the body, and add a closing and signature. Answers will vary.

Mr. Harris Fontaine, the President of Comptons Stores, located at 500 Main Street, Ocala, Florida, ZIP code 32668

EXERCISE D: Preparing Business Letters for Mailing. Write a business-size envelope for one of the letters in Exercise C. Then fold the letter and place it inside the envelope. Answers will vary.

DEVELOPING WRITING SKILLS: Writing Personal and Business Letters. Choose two ideas from those listed below or use ideas of your own and write one personal letter and one business letter. Include all the necessary parts for each type. Use your own name and address for the heading. Personal and business letters will vary.

1. Write a letter to Key Computer Camp, 63 Willow Corner, Calhoun Falls, SC 29628. Ask for information about courses, schedules, and costs of tuition, room, and board.
2. Assume that you had ordered a red desk lamp with a long extension arm from the Brant's Store catalog. You received a white clip-on lamp instead. Write to the store at 222 Marden Avenue, Kittery, ME 03904, asking for an adjustment.
3. Write a letter congratulating a friend who made the winning home run when your team became state champions.

Developing Writing Skills

To provide students with additional practice in writing letters, have them complete the following assignment.

Writing Across the Curriculum

Politicians are generally eager to learn about the needs and concerns of the people who live in their districts. For this reason, it is important for people to send letters expressing their thoughts and feelings about issues that concern them to their political representatives.

Prewriting Think of a local or national issue about which you have a strong opinion. Then free write about your thoughts and feelings concerning this issue. Next, review your free writing and underline the ideas that you would like to include in a letter to one of your political representatives.

Writing Using the ideas from your free writing, write a letter to the politican you have chosen. Follow the six-part structure of a business letter, including a heading, inside address, salutation, body, closing, and signature. Use a precise, formal, and respectful writing style.

Revising When you revise your letter, make sure that you have presented your ideas clearly. After you have finished revising, proofread your letter and, if necessary, prepare a final copy. Then mail your letter to the politician.

31.2 Writing Different Kinds of Letters

(pp. 608–614)

OBJECTIVES

After completing this section, students should be able to

- Write friendly letters and social notes.
- Write business letters.

TEACHING

Getting Started

Engage students in a discussion of what they like to read in letters they receive. Guide them toward the realization that specific information about the writer's life and thoughts is far more interesting than general remarks. Ask for examples of things that have happened recently that would be of interest to a former classmate.

Text Follow Through

Discuss text pages 608–614.

Assign Exercise A, page 611; Exercise B, page 614; and Developing Writing Skills, page 614.

Less advanced To get students started, you might want to propose a situation and have them brainstorm to write an appropriate letter. For example, they can pretend that a classmate was absent and missed an interesting field trip. They can then collaborate on a

31.2 Writing Different Kinds of Letters

Once you know the basic parts of letters, where they should be placed, and what styles can be used to present them, you can begin concentrating on the writing itself. This section will give you suggestions for writing a number of different kinds of personal and business letters.

Writing Friendly Letters and Social Notes

Many different kinds of personal letters are possible. Different social occasions often require special responses. No matter what kind of friendly letter or social note you are writing, however, it should be well organized and clearly written.

Learn the characteristics of friendly letters, invitations, letters of acceptance and regret, and other kinds of social notes.

Understanding the different kinds of letters you may need to write will help you respond appropriately in different situations. Keep in mind that you should make all letters clear and accurate, possibly by revising them, and always by proofreading them.

The Friendly Letter. Of all correspondence a friendly letter is usually the least formal. The purpose of such a letter is to share current personal news with friends and family members, to continue the communication of an earlier letter, or simply to maintain relationships with people. Your letter should show an interest in the reader by asking questions about his or her activities. You should also answer questions that the reader has asked you.

When you write a friendly letter, you can use either of the two styles for the parts of a friendly letter. The only requirement is that you be consistent within each letter. In the body

31.2 Writing Different Kinds of Letters

you should also follow the rules of grammar, usage, mechanics, and spelling. Try to make the content of the letter specific, interesting, and enjoyable to read. You might include vivid descriptions and relate incidents of interest to the reader. Finally, you should always try to make your letter neat, and you should always proofread it for mistakes before you send it.

The following sample shows the basic characteristics of a friendly letter.

18 Sunrise Avenue
Miami, Florida 32986
June 1, 1986

Dear Sam,

How have you been? How do you like your new home? I hope the weather in Anchorage hasn't been too cold for you. This week the air here was so humid that it felt like a hot, wet towel. I'm beginning to wish that I could switch places with you.

Our baseball team is doing well. We beat Oscala's B-team the other day with a run-scoring single in the bottom of the seventh inning. Although we lost the next game to Granite Springs, I believe we have a chance for a spot in the sectionals.

I hope you've found some new friends in Alaska. Have you gone fishing on a salmon boat yet? Do you think that your family will stay there for more than a year? Frankly, I hope you return soon because the team needs you. Keep me informed.

Your friend,
D. J.

letter describing the day's events. You might also want students to write more than the one letter specified in Exercises A and B. Perhaps you could assign one per week over several weeks.

Average Once again, students could review each other's work for form, content, and mechanics. Encourage students to suggest constructive improvements in word choice and sentence structure.

Advanced If your students need additional review, you could again have them exchange and respond to the letters written for Exercises A and B.

Additional Practice

Practice Pages or Practice Book, page 149
Writing Workshops, pages 29–31

TESTING

Test Program
   Unit Pretest, pages 80, 81
   Chapter Test, page 94
   Unit Post-Test, page 100

RE-TEACHING

Practice Pages or Practice Book, page 149

THINKING SKILLS

Synthesis—*Writing* friendly letters or social notes (Exercise A, page 611)

Evaluation—*Writing, appraising, revising,* and *proofreading* a business letter (Exercise B, page 614; Developing Writing Skills, page 614)

Invitations and Letters of Acceptance and Regret. An *invitation,* like any other social note, should be relatively short and precise. Within a few sentences, however, it should present a number of specific details: the date and time of the event, the location and nature of the event, and possibly what the person invited should bring or wear. When writing an invitation, try to put yourself in the reader's place and anticipate any questions that the reader might ask about the event. If you need a speedy reply to your invitation in order to complete your plans, you should also include an *R.S.V.P.*

---

10 Sanbar Place
Fresno, California 94182
June 16, 1986

Dear Liam,

My family is hosting a party to celebrate our graduation. The party will begin at 5:00 p.m. on June 30, and dinner will be served at approximately 7:00 p.m. Please dress casually and bring a Frisbee and baseball equipment.

I hope that you can attend.

Yours truly,
Sue Kiley

R.S.V.P.

31.2 Writing Different Kinds of Letters

A *letter of acceptance or regret* is a social note used to reply to an invitation. In a letter of acceptance, you should repeat the date, time, place, and any other information needed to prevent confusion. In a letter of regret, be sure to offer a reason why you cannot attend. Whether you accept or decline, you should express your appreciation for the invitation.

Other Social Notes. There are also a number of other occasions for writing social notes. You might want to write a thank-you note for a present. You might decide to write to a friend to offer your congratulations on a special award or honor. You might wish to send your sympathy to someone who has suffered a loss or an injury. Whenever writing, follow the guidelines in this chapter, and write clearly and precisely.

EXERCISE A: Writing Friendly Letters and Social Notes.
Choose any one of the following ideas to write a friendly letter or social note. Be sure to include all five parts of the letter, and use your own name and address for the heading and envelope. Focus on the purpose of the letter and the person to whom you are writing. Then prepare an envelope for the letter, and place the letter inside the envelope.
Answers will vary.

1. Write a friendly letter to a friend who is vacationing somewhere far away. Include personal news as well as the details of some interesting events. Use any of these ideas:
   a. You struck out with bases loaded in the championship game.
   b. At a local resturant you saw someone walk out without paying.
   c. You had a surprise visitor.
   d. You attended a party.
   e. A camera crew has just arrived to shoot a movie in your neighborhood.
2. You have decided to gather a group of friends to attend a concert in a nearby city. Write a letter of invitation to one

of these friends, supplying all of the information that your friend will need to know in order to reply.

3. You have received the invitation that was written following the idea in the second item. Write a letter of acceptance or a letter of regret in response to the invitation you have received.

4. Your cousin is away at school. You hear that she was named to the school's honor society. Write to congratulate her.

5. A friend is sick in the hospital. Write a letter wishing your friend a speedy recovery.

Writing Business Letters

Business letters can be used to achieve many different goals.

Learn the characteristics and purposes of a number of different kinds of business letters.

Because they serve specific business needs, business letters are usually more formal than personal letters. Focusing on the specific purpose of such a letter will help you make it a good letter. You should also develop the habit of revising and proofreading your business letters for clarity and accuracy.

Order Letters. Perhaps the most common kind of business letter is the *order letter.* It can be used to order almost any kind of merchandise through the mail. When you prepare an order letter, you should include all six parts of a business letter and take special care to make sure that the company address is accurate. The body of the letter should begin by stating your specific request. If the items are from a catalog and have order numbers, include these as well as sizes, prices, amounts, and so on. Think about any questions that the person filling your order may have, and provide all the information needed for billing and mailing. If you send a check or money order with your letter, be sure to state the amount in the letter.

The following order letter fills all the basic requirements.

```
                          3 Bagshot Row
                          Cleveland, Ohio   45201
                          October 30, 1986

Lesley Herman, Inc.
140 Main Street
Port Chester, New York   10850

Dear Sir or Madam:

   I would like to order three items from your 1982

Christmas catalog. I have enclosed a money order

for $25.25, which includes postage and handling

costs.

Amount   Item                 Price

1        Silver anniversary   $19.25
         dish
         No. 5492

2        German/English         6.00
         dictionaries
         No. 9910            _____

TOTAL                        $25.25

   Thank you for filling my order.

                          Sincerely,

                          Ann Hoag

                          (Miss) Ann Hoag
```

Other Business Letters. At times you may have to write other kinds of business letters. If you need information for writing reports or planning trips, you may need to write to a business or agency, asking for specific information. At other times you may have to write a letter of complaint about faulty merchandise or services. You might also want to write a letter of opinion to a newspaper or a television station.

In writing any of these letters, you should try to keep the reader in mind at all times. In letters requesting information, you should state your purpose clearly and directly. In letters of complaint or opinion, you should be persuasive, including information that will help support the point you are making. Try to convince your reader to agree with you and to take action.

EXERCISE B: Writing Business Letters. Use any of the following ideas to write a business letter. Include all six parts of a business letter. Use your own address for the heading, and for the inside address, invent a person, business, or organization. Then write the letter, focusing on the reader and your purpose. When you have written, revised, recopied, and proofread your letter, prepare an envelope for it.
Answers will vary.

1. Obtain a mail-order catalog and identify two or three items that you would like to purchase. Write an order letter, paying attention to necessary ordering and billing information.
2. Write to a local travel agency or a tourist office, requesting information about a place you would like to visit.
3. Write to the manager of a radio station, requesting changes in or additions to the kinds of music played.

DEVELOPING WRITING SKILLS: Writing a Friendly Letter, Social Note, or Business Letter. Identify a real purpose that you have for writing a friendly letter, social note, or business letter at this time. Review the characteristics of that kind of letter as presented in this section. Then write the letter, revise it, proofread it, and prepare an envelope for it.
Answers will vary.

Writing Workshop: Writing Letters

ASSIGNMENT 1

Topic Giving Advice to a Friend

Form and Purpose A friendly letter that advises and persuades a friend to make a change in her or his life

Audience A friend

Length One to two paragraphs

Focus Adopt an informal yet serious tone in your letter. Offer some advice about a serious problem or issue.

Sources A personal relationship and observations

Prewriting Identify your audience, a specific purpose, and make notes about the advice you will offer.

Writing Write a first draft of your letter.

Revising Check capitalization, punctuation, spelling, and letter parts positions. Prepare a corrected final version.

Guiding Student Writing

To help students improve their writing styles, you can have them discuss ways to vary their sentences and improve word choice. The revision stage is the best time to consider the use of different sentence lengths, sentence structures, and sentence openers.

Sharing their work with classmates in peer-editing groups can help students discover ambiguities and imprecise wording in their writing. Students can encourage each other by telling why specific word choices are particularly effective. They might even choose the best sentence in the paper and the sentence that most needs improvement. This kind of specificity will help students learn to evaluate their own work better. You might also suggest a thesaurus to help students choose precise words and supply vivid word choices.

Assignment 1

Suggestions for Prewriting: Urge students to write to a real friend with a real problem. Assure them that the letters can be private.

Suggestions for Writing: Students could conceal the identity of the friend in the draft of the letter.

Suggestions for Publishing: Tell students to consider sending the letter to the friend.

Assignment 2

Suggestions for Writing: Remind students that they will be more persuasive if they are quite specific about why they admire this person and why they seek an interview. Be sure they include a suggested setting for the interview and some comment about willingness to adjust to the addressee's schedule.

Suggestions for Publishing: As a follow-up, you could have students exchange letters and respond in the persona of the addressee.

ASSIGNMENT 2

Topic Requesting an Interview with Someone You Admire

Form and Purpose A business letter requesting an interview

Audience Your choice

Length Two to three paragraphs

Focus Your letter should begin with an explanation of why you admire the person. Conclude with a reason why you want to interview the person. Include suggestions for a date, time, and place for the interview.

Sources Newspapers, magazines, television programs

Prewriting Identify the intended recipient of the letter and write notes about why you admire that person.

Writing Write a first draft of your letter.

Revising Check all letter parts and their positions. Correct any errors in capitalization, punctuation, and spelling. Prepare a final copy.

Bill Cosby

Chris Evert

1. "What is your opinion? What examples demonstrate this? What do you recommend?"

2. Remind students to ask this audience about local possibilities—which do include production, though on a limited scale—rather than about network possibilities. Students may ask about the training for various jobs, as well as about opportunities.

3. Students may need research to find out what the ratings are, how they are compiled, and how they are used.

4. Point out that if the friend lives abroad, a more complete description of the show will be necessary. In any event, writers should include reasons and examples that indicate why this is their favorite.

5. Brainstorm for reasons and, where appropriate, for examples.

Topics for Writing: Writing Letters

If the cartoon above suggests a writing idea, plan and write a friendly letter or a business letter on the topic. Decide on a specific audience and purpose. If you wish, choose one of the related letter purposes and audiences that are listed below.

Purpose	Audience
1. Conveying an Opinion About the Quality of Children's TV Programs	TV Station Manager
2. Requesting Information About Careers in the Television Business	Personnel Director of a Local TV Station
3. Telling Your Views on Television Ratings	Publisher of a Television Guide
4. Describing Your Favorite Television Program	A Friend
5. Explaining the Dangers of Watching Too Much TV	Parent Group

CHAPTER 32
Essay Exams
(pp. 618–622)

This chapter focuses on the essay exam: how to prepare, plan, and write answers to essay exam questions.

For an additional or alternate writing assignment, see page 622.

32.1 Preparing Answers to Essay Exams
(pp. 618–621)

OBJECTIVES

After completing this section, students should be able to

- Identify the kind of information an essay exam question is asking for.
- Plan and write essay exam answers.

TEACHING

Getting Started

Ask students if they have ever studied well for an essay exam, yet done poorly. Explain that when this happens, the fault often lies with their test-taking skills. Explain, too, that these skills can be practiced so that

---

Chapter **32**

Taking Essay Exams

In an essay examination, you must write short paragraphs or essays as answers to specific questions. Your answers must be prepared and written in a limited amount of time.

32.1 Preparing Answers to Essay Exams

Planning and budgeting your time is the first step.

Plan your time for essay exams and pace yourself to make sure you stay on schedule.

Read all instructions and questions first to make certain that you understand them. Use half your time in planning and outlining answers, and half writing and proofreading them.

Understanding the Question

To answer a question, you need to know what it is asking.

Read the question carefully to see exactly what information it asks for.

There are key words in essay exam questions that can help you understand them. The chart on the following page lists them.

32.1 Preparing Answers to Essay Exams

KEY WORDS IN ESSAY EXAM QUESTIONS

Kind of Questions	Key Words	What You Should Do
Comparison	*compare, similarities*	Look for and explain likenesses.
Contrast	*differ, contrast*	Look for and explain differences.
Definition	*define, explain*	Tell what something is or means, give examples.
Description	*describe*	Give the main features with specific examples.
Diagram	*diagram, draw, chart*	Make a drawing or chart, label and explain it.
Discussion	*discuss, explain*	Give facts and examples to support a general statement.
Explanation	*explain, why, what, how*	Give information that tells why, what, or how.
Opinion	*in your opinion, what do you think*	State your opinion and support it with reasons and examples.

EXERCISE A: Understanding Essay Exam Questions.
Identify the key words and explain how to answer each question.

EXAMPLE: Describe the effects of a drought.

   description   Give examples of drought areas and explain what happens in those areas.

1. discuss/facts and examples to show importance   2. define/tell what *rhyme*

1. Discuss the importance of the Panama Canal.
2. Define the term *rhyme scheme.*
3. Show how primary colors combine to form other colors.
4. Contrast cross-country and downhill skiing.
5. Describe the main street of your town.

scheme means and give examples   3. explain/examples of combining colors   4. contrast/name and explain differences   5. describe/give main features of the street

Text Follow Through

Discuss text pages 618–621.

Assign Exercise A, page 619; Exercise B, page 620; Exercise C, page 621; Exercise D, page 621; and Developing Writing Skills, page 621.

Less advanced   You will probably want to discuss Exercise A very carefully. Then have various students write the modified outlines prepared for Exercise B on the board for comparison and comment. It is probably advisable to have covered Chapter 24 before dealing with the current section.

Average   Careful work on this section can make a significant difference in students' performance. You might want to administer essay exams in your course, the first time guiding students step by step through the process, then allowing them to work independently with you circulating to monitor their work and offer help when needed. You might also want to combine this section with work on Section 37.2, Taking Tests.

Advanced You might ask students in small groups to outline one another's answers to an actual essay test, yours or from some other course. If they then discuss each in turn, their ability to distinguish good topic sentences and relevant support should be sharpened.

Additional Practice

Practice Pages or Practice Book, pages 150, 151
Writing Workshop, page 32

TESTING

Test Program

Unit Pretest, page 81
Chapter Test, pages 94, 95
Unit Post-Test, page 100

RE-TEACHING

Practice Pages or Practice Book, pages 150, 151

THINKING SKILLS

Comprehension—*Explaining* essay exam questions (Exercise A, page 619)

Application—*Outlining* an essay exam answer (Exercise B, page 620)

Synthesis—*Writing* an essay exam answer (Exercise C, page 621)

Evaluation—*Appraising* an essay exam answer (Exercise D, page 621)
Planning, writing, appraising, and *revising* an essay exam answer (Developing Writing Skills, page 621)

Planning Your Answer

When you understand the question, you are ready to plan an answer.

Plan an answer by listing your ideas in a modified outline.

Write a summary of your main idea for your topic sentence. List the supporting information that will lead you to your conclusion. (Modified outlines are discussed in Chapter 35.)

The following modified outline relates to the question, "Why were the Articles of Confederation a poor basis for the new American government?"

MAIN IDEA   The Articles of Confederation were weak.

MAJOR DETAILS   1. No central government to settle disputes or deal with other nations
               2. States would not cooperate
               3. Other governments took advantage of U.S.

EXERCISE B: Outlining Answers. Using one question from Exercise A, prepare a modified outline for the answer.
Outlines will vary.

Writing Your Answer

With your outline for a guide, you can now write your answer.

Let your modified outline guide you as you start writing your answer to the question.

Your answer may be one or more paragraphs in length. Notice how the parts of the answer below follow the outline.

TOPIC SENTENCE   The Articles of Confederation were too weak to become the basis for the new government. There were three main reasons why this was so.

     Americans mistrusted central authority, associating it with the repression that had led to the revolution. As a result, the articles did not set up a central government.

32.1 Preparing Answers to Essay Exams

This meant that there was no authority responsible for settling disputes or dealing with the outside world.

Power remained in the hands of the states, which had never been able to cooperate with each other. Even during the revolution, constant disputes had arisen. Other governments took advantage of the division among the states to occupy American territory.

Clearly, America needed a stronger government to see that the states cooperated with one another and to protect itself from other nations.

EXERCISE C: Writing Your Answer. Write an essay answer, one paragraph long, based on your outline for Exercise B.
Answers will vary.

Checking Your Answer

Before you hand in an examination, check your answers. **Proofread your answer for accuracy and clarity.**

The following list will guide you as you check your answers.

CHECKING YOUR ANSWERS
1. Did you respond to the question directly and clearly?
2. Did you write a topic sentence or thesis statement?
3. Did you offer enough supporting information?
4. Did you use correct grammar, spelling, and mechanics?

EXERCISE D: Proofreading Your Answer. Use the checklist to recheck the paragraph you wrote for Exercise C.
Answers will vary.

DEVELOPING WRITING SKILLS: Preparing Answers to Essay Exams. Following the steps in this chapter, write an essay-length answer to a question from another of your classes.
Answers will vary.

Developing Writing Skills
Writing Across the Curriculum

As an alternative, you might have each student think of one essay question that focuses on one of the following content areas: science, social studies, or music. You can then hold a simulated essay exam in which the students each answer one or two of the questions submitted by their classmates. Before your students take the simulated exam, remind them to follow the steps outlined in this chapter.

Guiding Student Writing

To help students improve their test-taking skills, you may want to have them complete this assignment in class within a limited time period. Remind them that it is important for them to start by reading the question carefully, looking for key words, such as *explain, describe,* or *discuss.* Also remind them that they should take some time to plan their answer before they begin writing.

Assignment

Suggestions for Topics: You could require each student to choose a different topic by having a sign-up list in the classroom.

Suggestions for Prewriting: Check that students have organized information in stages subdivided by steps rather than in a multitude of discrete steps.

Suggestions for Publishing: Where appropriate, students could include a sketch.

ASSIGNMENT
Answers will vary.

Topic   Explaining a Scientific or Technical Process

Form and Purpose   An essay-exam answer that explains a process

Audience   Your science teacher

Length   One to three paragraphs

Focus   At the beginning of your essay, identify the process. Then explain the process.

Sources   Science texts, science and technical reference books, magazines, science museum exhibits

Prewriting   Select a scientific or technical process and write an explanation-type essay-exam question about it. Plan an answer by outlining the specific stages of the process.

Writing   Use your outline to write a first draft.

Revising   Use the checklist on page 621 to review and revise your answer. Then prepare a final draft.

UNIT VI

Vocabulary and Spelling

UNIT IV
Vocabulary and Spelling
(pp. 623-670)

Although mastering the content of this unit is critical to success in everyday life as well as in school, the concepts covered are not directly related to those in any other units and may, therefore, be taught at any time during the year. You might, in fact, find it helpful to present Sections 33.1 and 34.1 quite early in the year so that students can set up vocabulary notebooks and personal spelling lists and add to them at regular times throughout the year. In addition, you may wish to set aside a short time each week for students to share additions to their lists of vocabulary and spelling words. This device will ensure that students are using these tools and will also provide an opportunity for their classmates to consider possible additions to their own lists.

The other sections in the unit may also be worth covering early. The vocabulary lessons presented in Sections 33.2 through 33.4 and the spelling rules presented in Section 34.2 can help the students carry out their other course work in English as well as in other areas.

CHAPTER 33
Building Your Vocabulary
(pp. 624–648)

Chapter 33 begins with a general strategy for building vocabulary and then looks more closely at specific aspects of vocabulary building. Section 33.1 gives students a number of concrete suggestions that they can use to learn new words. Section 33.2 explains how to use context clues and provides a variety of selections for practicing this skill. Section 33.3 presents structural analysis as a way to expand one's vocabulary, and Section 33.4 demonstrates how to approach words from the standpoint of etymology, or word origin.

For a review of the entire chapter and a related writing activity, see the Skills Review and Writing Workshop on page 648.

33.1 Ways to Enlarge Your Vocabulary
(pp. 624–629)

OBJECTIVES

After completing this section, students should be able to

- Record new words and their definitions in a vocabulary notebook.
- Use vocabulary notebook, flash cards, tape recorder as aids to developing vocabulary.

Chapter **33**

Building Your Vocabulary

As your vocabulary grows, your pleasure in reading and your ease in writing will grow also. This chapter will suggest various methods for learning and remembering the meanings of new words so that the words become part of your vocabulary.

33.1 Ways to Enlarge Your Vocabulary

The most important tool in vocabulary building is a good dictionary. There you will find the meaning of a word, its pronunciation and part of speech, and often information about its history.

Setting Up a Vocabulary Notebook

You may find it useful to set up a vocabulary notebook with separate sections for each of your subjects. Whenever you are reading or studying, jot down on a piece of paper any words

33.1 Ways to Enlarge Your Vocabulary

that are new to you. When you have finished reading, write the words in your notebook. Then use a dictionary to find out the meaning of each word.

Set up a vocabulary notebook and use a dictionary to add new words to your vocabulary.

A good plan is to divide each page of your vocabulary notebook into three columns. Label the first column "Words" and use it for new words and, if you wish, their pronunciations. Label the second column "Bridge Words" and use it for hints or helping words that will make it easier for you to remember the meanings of new words. Label the third column "Definitions" and use it to write the meanings of new words.

	Words	Bridge Words	Definitions
1.	tempestuous (tem pes′choo wəs)	a tempest = a violent storm	violent

1   2   3

This three-column format will make it easier for you to learn the meanings of the new words you list. When you study, cover the third column with a piece of paper or fold the page back so you can test yourself on the definitions. The bridge words in the middle column will give you hints. When you think you have learned a word, you can cover the middle column as well as the third column and then try to give the word's definition. Study four or five words at a time using this method. You might

Additional Practice

Practice Pages or Practice
Book, page 152

TESTING

Test Program

Unit Pretest, page 101
Chapter Test, page 104
Unit Post-Test, page 108

RE-TEACHING

Practice Pages or Practice
Book, page 152

THINKING SKILLS

Application—*Preparing* a
vocabulary notebook (Exercise
A, page 626)
Preparing and *using* flash
cards or tapes to learn new
vocabulary (Exercise B, page
628)
Demonstrating vocabulary
skills by *using* new words in
original sentences (Developing Writing Skills, page 629)

want to write the definitions on a piece of paper and then compare these with the definition column. Each time you define a
word correctly, place a check in your notebook next to the
word. Three checks should mean that you are gaining familiarity with the word and that it has become part of your
vocabulary.

EXERCISE A: Working with Your Vocabulary Notebook.
Set up a vocabulary notebook with separate sections for each
of your subjects. For each subject go over your corrected papers or look through the reading assignments in your textbooks and choose five words whose meanings you are not
sure of. Using the three-column format, list the vocabulary
words you have chosen in your notebook.
Notebook entries will vary.

EXAMPLE:	Words	Bridge Words	Definitions
	amendment	to mend	a change for
	(ə mend′ mənt)		the better

Using Other Study Methods

Frequent review of the words in your vocabulary notebook is
an excellent way of improving your vocabulary. Other study
methods, however, might also work well for you and can be
used together with your vocabulary notebook.

**Use a variety of methods for studying and re-
viewing new words.**

Try each of the following three methods to see which works
best.

Reviewing New Words with Flash Cards. A good way to
expand your vocabulary is to review words using a set of flash
cards. Just as a vocabulary notebook can act as your personal
dictionary, so can flash cards be tailored to meet your own vocabulary needs. The steps on the following page can help you
prepare flash cards.

33.1 Ways to Enlarge Your Vocabulary

MAKING FLASH CARDS

1. Using index cards, make a flash card for each word in your vocabulary notebook.
2. Write or print the word on one side of the card. If the word is hard to pronounce, copy the phonetic spelling given for it in the dictionary.
3. In the lower right-hand corner of the card, pencil in one or more bridge words that will give you a hint about the meaning of the word. These words can later be erased when you find that you no longer need them.
4. On the back of the card, write the definition of the word. You may also want to note in the upper left-hand corner whether the word is from a particular subject area or from your general reading.

The following illustration shows the front and back of a card you might make.

Front

solidify
(sə lid'ə fī')
solid = firm
or hard

Back

Science
to make or become
solid, firm, hard

You can carry your flash cards with you and flip through them whenever you have time. If you feel sure of the definition of a word, put that card aside in a "review set." Go through the review set from time to time to make sure you have not forgotten any words.

Reviewing New Words with a Tape Recorder. Some people learn new words more easily by hearing them than by reading them. If you have access to a tape recorder, you may find the procedure on the following page helpful.

REVIEWING WITH A TAPE RECORDER

1. Read a vocabulary word into the tape recorder.
2. Leave approximately five seconds of blank space on the tape and then give the definition.
3. Follow the definition with a sentence using the word. The sentence is to help you remember the word and its meaning.
4. Leave another blank space of about five seconds.
5. Record the rest of the words in the same fashion.
6. Study the words by replaying the entire tape, filling in the first blank space with a definition spoken aloud and the second blank space with the vocabulary word spoken aloud.
7. Rerun the tape until you are able to give all of the definitions and words without hesitation.

If you listen to your tape several times a week, the new words will soon become a permanent part of your vocabulary.

Reviewing New Words with a Partner. All the methods described so far work well when done with a partner. You can alternate between using your vocabulary notebooks, your flash cards, or a tape recorder. One person can read the words listed in one of your notebooks while the other defines the words. If the person defining the words hesitates, the reader can offer bridge words. You might also drill each other on difficult words by using the flash cards. In either case, you might use the tape recorder as a final review.

EXERCISE B: Making Flash Cards or Tapes. Using the preceding instructions as a guide, make a set of flash cards or a tape. Use five of the following words, concentrating on those whose meanings you do not know.
Answers will vary.

1. context	5. fanatic	9. plausible
2. disperse	6. intolerant	10. sardonic
3. elongate	7. koala	
4. evade	8. malice	

DEVELOPING WRITING SKILLS: Using New Vocabulary Words in Sentences. Select five words from the notebook you made in Exercise A and five words from Exercise B. For each word write an original sentence that will give a reader a clear understanding of the meaning of the word.
Sentences will vary.

EXAMPLE: disperse

The pigeons gathered from all directions waiting for him to disperse the bread crumbs.

Using Context 33.2

If *context* was one of the words you looked up in Exercise B of Section 33.1, you now know that it refers to the sentence, the surrounding words, or the situation in which a word is used. The context of a word can be very useful in learning new words.

Use context clues to guess the meanings of unfamiliar words.

Often, without even realizing it, you will guess at the meaning of an unfamiliar word as you read. Context clues are what enable you to figure out the meaning of a word in this way. For example, look at the word *muffed* in the following sentence and then see how you arrive at the word's meaning.

SENTENCE: Jon was on his way to becoming an instant hero when he *muffed* an easy fly ball.

CLUES: The reader knows that something happened to keep Jon from becoming a hero. The word *easy* is another clue.

GUESS: Jon must have missed the ball.

DEFINITION OF *MUFF*: to fail to catch, to fumble

The chart on the following page gives steps to follow when using context clues.

33.2 Using Context
(pp. 629–635)

OBJECTIVES

After completing this section, students should be able to

- Infer the meaning of words from context clues in daily reading.
- Infer the meaning of words from context clues in science assignments.
- Infer the meaning of words from context clues in social studies assignments.

TEACHING

Getting Started

Introduce the class to the concept of context clues by writing the following sentence on the board:

After a week in a lifeboat, the sailor was so *enervated* that he could not even wave to the passing ship.

Ask the class to read the sentence twice, leaving out the underlined word during the second reading. Then help them examine the surrounding words to see if these provide any clues. Next, tell them to guess the meaning of the word. Write their guesses on the board.

Have them read the sentence again, substituting the various guesses. Then have them check the guesses in a dictionary. Last, they should write the word *enervated* and the dictionary definition in their notebooks. Ask the class if they can name the method they just used to find the meaning of *enervated.* Follow the same procedure using sentences suggested by students.

Text Follow Through

Discuss text pages 629–635.

Assign Exercise A, page 631; Exercise B, page 633; Exercise C, page 634; and Developing Writing Skills, page 635.

Less advanced To ensure that these students are actually using context clues and are not just guessing the answers, go over the exercises with them in small groups and have them pinpoint the context clues they have used to arrive at meanings.

Average Ask students to bring in passages from their texts in science or social studies that contain difficult or unfamiliar terms surrounded by particularly good context clues. Ask students to exchange passages and identify the unfamiliar terms. They should then supply short definitions from the context. Words should be checked in a dictionary and added to their vocabulary notebooks.

> ### USING CONTEXT CLUES
>
> 1. Reread the sentence, leaving out the unfamiliar word.
> 2. Examine the surrounding words to see if they provide any clues.
> 3. Use the clues to guess the meaning of the word.
> 4. Read the sentence again, substituting your guess.
> 5. Check your guess by looking up the word in a dictionary.
> 6. Write the word and the dictionary definition in your notebook.

Using Context in Daily Reading

The following passage contains the kind of material you might read in a newspaper or a magazine. Although the paragraphs describe an experiment, the words used are not scientific or technical; they are general words such as those you are likely to meet when you read for pleasure.

Read the paragraphs and try to determine the meaning of each underlined word from its context. On a separate piece of paper, write down what you think each of the words means.

EXAMPLE: Michel Siffre entered a <u>subterranean</u> cave near Del Rio, Texas, on February 14, 1972. His goal was to learn how long he could live without human companionship. Michel brought supplies, including food, water, a radio, and a lamp, to the floor of the cave, where he set up a shelter about one hundred feet below the surface of the earth. The cave was completely silent and, except for the small circle of light cast by his lamp, totally dark. It seemed like a suitable <u>retreat</u> for the experiment.

In the beginning Michel spent much of his time reading, but after a few weeks this activity became <u>tedious</u>. Except for occasional radio contact with friends on the surface, he was completely alone. As time passed, his isolation began to affect him. After ninety-four days his behavior was quite changed. He spoke to his friends rarely, and then in a <u>disjointed</u> and expressionless way. His condition continued to <u>deteriorate</u>.

After four months in the cave, Michel was <u>reduced</u> to a <u>passive</u> existence, sitting motionless for hours in darkness. His friends urged him to <u>terminate</u> the experiment, but he refused.

After more than five months, Michel spotted a tiny mouse. Now he would have a companion to <u>alleviate</u> his loneliness! He managed to trap the mouse, but his <u>exaltation</u> was short-lived. Soon after Michel had caught the mouse, it died. Once again, Michel was completely alone in the cave.

On August 10 Michel finally left the cave. He had proven to his own satisfaction that an important element in life is companionship.

EXERCISE A: Defining Words. Use your list of guessed meanings from the preceding passage to answer the following questions. For each word choose the definition that most closely matches the meaning of the word as it was used in the passage. Then check your answers in a dictionary and record in your notebook any words that you missed.

EXAMPLE: cave   (a) ditch; (b) capsule; (c) cavern;
                  (d) hill

                  (c)

1. alleviate   (a) share; <u>(b) lessen</u>; (c) alter; (d) destroy

2. deteriorate   (a) improve; (b) be dejected; <u>(c) get worse</u>; (d) prevent

3. disjointed   (a) dissatisfied; (b) slow; (c) angry; <u>(d) disconnected</u>

Additional Practice

Practice Pages or Practice Book, page 153

TESTING

Test Program

   Unit Pretest, page 101
   Chapter Test, page 104
   Unit Post-Test, page 108

RE-TEACHING

Practice Pages or Practice Book, page 153

THINKING SKILLS

Comprehension—*Inferring* word meaning from context clues and checking the meaning in a dictionary (Exercise A, page 631; Exercise B, page 633; Exercise C, page 634)

Synthesis—*Writing* original sentences that incorporate context clues for selected words (Developing Writing Skills, page 635)

4. exaltation   (a) feeling of joy; (b) great discovery; (c) anticipation; (d) honor

5. passive   (a) sad; (b) unreal; (c) inactive; (d) former

6. reduced   (a) made smaller; (b) brought to a poorer state; (c) took off weight; (d) divided

7. retreat   (a) quiet place; (b) signal; (c) enemy; (d) go back

8. subterranean   (a) train; (b) overground; (c) underground; (d) below

9. tedious   (a) long; (b) difficult; (c) boring; (d) technical

10. terminate   (a) end; (b) continue; (c) determine; (d) transfer

Using Context in Science

The material presented in science textbooks often includes technical words as well as ordinary words used with a special meaning. The following passage is similar to material you might read in a science textbook. At first glance it might seem difficult, but if you pay attention to context as you read, you will find hints about the meanings of the unfamiliar words.

After you read through the paragraphs, try to determine the meaning of each underlined word by its context. Write down what you think each word means.

EXAMPLE: Although water constitutes over 70 percent of the earth's surface, there are some areas of extreme aridity. For example, neither the Great Basin nor the Mojave Desert receives enough rainfall to support abundant plant growth. The plants and animals of those areas have all had to adapt to the harsh desert environment.

In contrast to the deserts of the Southwest, the Ozark Plateau has a <u>mild</u> climate with warm summers, cold winters, and abundant rainfall spread over the entire year. As a result vast, dense forests flourish there. The leaves dropped every fall by <u>deciduous</u> trees create decaying matter that becomes a rich, fertile soil on the forest floor. The several layers of this material provide an excellent environment for a variety of wildlife. Plant- and grass-eaters such as deer, rabbits, and small birds find plentiful food in the forest, and these in turn support such <u>carnivorous</u> creatures as birds of prey, foxes, and weasels.

EXERCISE B: Defining Words. Use your list of guessed meanings to answer the following multiple choice questions. For each word choose the definition that most closely matches the meaning of the word as it was used in the passage. Then check your answers in a dictionary and record in your vocabulary notebook any words that you missed.

EXAMPLE: desert   (a) swamp; (b) cake; (c) garden;
(d) wasteland

(d)

1. adapt   (a) make one's own; (b) give in; (c) skillful; (d) <u>adjust</u>

2. aridity   (a) humidity; (b) <u>dryness</u>; (c) temperature; (d) area

3. carnivorous   (a) <u>flesh-eating</u>; (b) fiesta; (c) very large; (d) grass-eating

4. constitutes   (a) presses together; (b) settles (c) <u>makes up</u>; (d) contracts

5. deciduous   (a) poisonous; (b) dishonest; (c) <u>leaf-shedding</u>; (d) definite

Using Context in Social Studies

The following passage includes material that you might find in a social studies textbook. After you read the paragraphs, look back at the underlined words and try to determine their meanings from the context. Write down what you think each word means.

EXAMPLE: The first settlers faced <u>unprecedented</u> physical hardships after they stepped onto the rocky New England shores in the winter of 1620. Never in a <u>quandary</u> about their spiritual mission, the small band of men and women faced the problem of earthly survival in a harsh land. They erected temporary shelters, later replacing them with sturdy log cabins, filling in the <u>crannies</u> between the logs with a mud plaster made of dirt, water, grass, and leaves. At the same time, they cleared the land and prepared it for cultivation.

There was little <u>deviation</u> from the basic pattern of life in the settlement: work and worship, worship and work; every man, woman, and child had tasks to complete. They had little time for <u>revelry</u> since all their energy was directed toward living from day to day.

<u>Steadfast</u> of purpose, the settlers endured their first year. Each week and month that passed saw their lives become less and less <u>vulnerable</u> to the forces of nature. In the fall they <u>affirmed</u> their belief in the <u>omnipotence</u> of God by setting aside a day of praise and thanksgiving for a <u>bountiful</u> harvest.

EXERCISE C: Defining Words. Use your guessed meanings to answer the following multiple choice questions. For each word choose the definition that most clearly matches the meaning of the word as it was used in the passage. Then check your answers in a dictionary and record in your vocabulary notebook any words that you missed.

EXAMPLE: settler   (a) old inhabitant; (b) new inhabitant; (c) dog; (d) nomad

(b)

1. affirmed   (a) denied; (b) suggested; (c) declared firmly; (d) strengthened greatly

2. bountiful   (a) reasonable; (b) plentiful (c) prayerful; (d) bordering on

3. crannies   (a) plasters; (b) windows; (c) narrow openings; (d) bark shelves

4. deviation   (a) turning away; (b) acceptance; (c) good; (d) evil

5. omnipotence   (a) lack of power; (b) great power; (c) knowledge; (d) angry feeling

6. quandary   (a) mistake; (b) amount; (c) state of uncertainty; (d) sailing vessel

7. revelry   (a) competition; (b) merrymaking; (c) act of vengeance; (d) revelation

8. steadfast   (a) firm; (b) unsure; (c) hopeful; (d) endurance

9. unprecedented   (a) usual; (b) infrequent; (c) unpleasant; (d) unheard of

10. vulnerable   (a) impolite; (b) strongly defended; (c) open to injury; (d) affectionate

DEVELOPING WRITING SKILLS: Using Words in Context. Choose any ten vocabulary words from the passages you have read. For each word write an original sentence that will give a reader a clear understanding of the meaning of the word.

Sentences will vary.

EXAMPLE: affirmed

She affirmed her belief in his words by staking her life on them.

Developing Writing Skills

To provide students with additional practice in using vocabulary words in their writing, have them complete the following assignment.

Writing Across the Curriculum

Reading books from other content areas, such as social studies and science, is an excellent way of developing your vocabulary.

Prewriting Read a chapter in one of your other textbooks and jot down each unfamiliar word you come across. If you cannot determine the meaning of a word from its context, look it up in your dictionary. When you have finished reading the chapter, prepare an outline for a paragraph about one of the topics you have just learned about. Then look over your list of vocabulary words and select five words that you could include in your paragraph.

Writing Following your outline, write the first draft of a paragraph about the topic you have chosen. Make sure that your paragraph has a clear topic sentence and that you support your topic sentence in the body of the paragraph. Also make sure that you include each of the vocabulary words you have chosen.

Revising When you have finished writing, revise your paragraph using the checklist on page 490. Then proofread your paragraph and prepare a final copy.

33.3 Using Structure
(pp. 636–641)

OBJECTIVES

After completing this section, students should be able to

- Determine the meaning of a word using the meaning of its prefix and a known root.
- Determine the meaning of a word using the meaning of its root.
- Determine the meaning of a word using the meaning of its suffix and a known root.

TEACHING

Getting Started

Ask the class to define the word *prefix.* Refine the answers and then write the following definition on the board: *A prefix is one or more syllables added at the beginning of a root.* Follow the same procedure with *root.* Write its definition on the board. *A root is the base of a word.* Next, ask for and write on the board examples of prefixes and of roots. Elicit how a knowledge of the meaning of certain prefixes and roots can provide clues to the meanings of unfamiliar words. Demonstrate this technique by writing some words that contain a select group of the prefixes and roots suggested by students at the beginning of this Getting Started. Have students guess the meanings of these words and then verify their guesses in a dictionary. Write the defini-

33.3 Using Structure

Another way to expand your vocabulary is to use the *structure* of words to get an idea of their meanings. For example, the word *intervention* has three parts whose individual meanings add up to the meaning of the word itself.

WORD PARTS: inter- + -ven- + -tion

MEANING OF PARTS: between + come + the act of

MEANING OF WORD: intervention = the act of coming between

The three word parts in English are *prefix, root,* and *suffix.* A prefix, such as *inter-* , is one or more syllables added at the beginning of a root. A root, such as *-ven-*, is the base of the word. A suffix, such as *-tion*, is one or more syllables added at the end of a root. Thousands of English words are made up of one or more of these word parts. Knowing only a small number of word parts and their meanings will make it easier to figure out the meanings of a great many difficult words.

Use prefixes, roots, and suffixes as clues to the meanings of unfamilar words.

Some words consist of a root alone *(pay)*, some words have a prefix and a root *(repay)*, some words have a root and a suffix *(payment)*, and some have all three word parts *(repayment)*. Not all roots, however, can stand by themselves. Such roots as *-dic-*, which means "to say," and *-spec-*, which means "to see," must be combined with a prefix or a suffix in order to make a complete word.

Using Prefixes

An easy way to enlarge your vocabulary is to learn the meanings of a few common *prefixes*. Once you have learned them, you can add these prefixes to words you already know to make new words.

33.3 Using Structure

TEN COMMON PREFIXES			
Prefix	**Meaning**		**Example**
ad-	to, toward	ad-+-here	to stick to
com-	with, together	com-+-pile	to gather together
dis-	away, apart	dis-+-grace	to lose favor
ex-	from, out	ex-+-port	to send out
mis-	wrong	mis-+-lead	to lead in a wrong direction
post-	after	post-+-war	after the war
re-	back, again	re-+-occupy	to occupy again
sub-	beneath, under	sub-+-merge	to place under water
trans-	across	trans-+-oceanic	across the ocean
un-	not	un-+-beatable	unable to be defeated

As you combine these prefixes with words or roots, you will notice that some of them change their spelling when they are joined to certain roots.

EXAMPLES: *ad-* becomes *ac-* in accept, *ap-* in apply, and *as-* in assume

com- becomes *co-* in cooperation, *con-* in confess, and *cor-* in correct

sub- becomes *suc-* in succeed, *suf-* in suffix, and *sup-* in support

EXERCISE A: Working with Prefixes. Divide your paper into two columns. Then use the preceding chart to find a prefix you can join to each of the following words. In the first column, labeled "Words," write the word you form. In the second

tions next to the words. Ask the class to suggest words that contain some of these prefixes and roots. Follow the same procedure as with the words *you* supplied.

Text Follow Through

Discuss text pages 636–641.

Assign Exercise A, page 637; Exercise B, page 639; Exercise C, page 640; and Developing Writing Skills, page 641.

Less advanced Encourage these students to use the charts on pages 637, 638–639, and 640 as they complete the exercises.

Average Have students use a dictionary to find two additional words that use each prefix in the chart on page 637. They can then quiz each other on the meanings of the new words.

Advanced Have students exchange the papers they write for Developing Writing Skills and write short definitions for the key words in each other's sentences. They should then make a master list of all the words they constructed in Developing Writing Skills, grouping them by root.

Additional Practice

Practice Pages or Practice Book, pages 154–156

TESTING

Test Program

Unit Pretest, page 102
Chapter Test, page 105
Unit Post-Test, page 108

RE-TEACHING

Practice Pages or Practice Book, pages 154–156

THINKING SKILLS

Comprehension—*Using* roots to define words (Exercise B, page 639)

Application—*Using* prefixes to build and define words (Exercise A, page 637)
Using suffixes to change one part of speech to another (Exercise C, page 640)

Synthesis—*Writing* original sentences from words made by combining word parts (Developing Writing Skills, page 641)

column, labeled "Definitions," write a brief definition, using your knowledge of the prefixes and the information in the chart. Check your definition in the dictionary. If you have chosen a valid word but the wrong definition, write the word in your vocabulary notebook, giving its correct definition.
Answers will vary; sample words are given.

EXAMPLE: take

Words	Definitions
mistake	something that is understood or done incorrectly

1. press
2. read misread
3. play replay
4. arm disarm
5. form reform
6. change
7. marine
8. venture adventure
9. reliable unreliable
10. place

1. compress   6. exchange   7. submarine   10. replace

Using Roots

Of the three word parts, the *root* is the most important because it carries the basic meaning of the word. In the chart are only a few of the roots in the English language, but you can combine them with other word parts to make many words. Notice that each of these roots has more than one spelling. A variant spelling for each root is shown in parentheses.

TEN COMMON ROOTS		
Root	**Meaning**	**Example**
-cap- (-capt-)	to take or seize	capt- + -ivate to take or hold
-dic- (-dict-)	to say or point out in words	pre- + -dict to foretell
-mit- (-mis-)	to send	re- + -mit to send back
-mov- (-mot-)	to move	mov- + -able able to be moved
-pon- (-pos-)	to put or place	com- + -pose to put together

-spec- (-spect-)	to see	spec- + -tator	one who sees or watches
-ten- (-tain-)	to hold	de- + -tain	to hold back
-ven- (-vent-)	to come	con- + -vene	to come together
-vert- (-vers-)	to turn	in- + -vert	to turn upside down
-vid- (-vis-)	to see	vis- + -ible	able to be seen

EXERCISE B: Using Roots to Define Words. Match the words in the first column with their meanings in the second.

EXAMPLE: postpone

to put off until later

1. prospect f
2. inversion d
3. diction a
4. mobility j
5. intervention b
6. transpose i
7. submission c
8. supervise e
9. attain h
10. captive g

a. way of using words
b. the act of coming between
c. something sent for approval
d. a turning upside down
e. to oversee
f. future outlook
g. someone taken as a prisoner
h. to reach
i. to change places
j. ease of movement

Using Suffixes

A *suffix* is one or more syllables added at the end of a root to form a new word. The chart on the following page shows seven suffixes, their meanings, and a word using each one. It also tells you the part of speech formed by each suffix. Using these suffixes together with the prefixes and roots you have been learning, you can form many words. In addition, when you come upon a new word you can analyze its various parts and get clues as to its meaning and part of speech.

SEVEN COMMON SUFFIXES			
Suffix	**Meaning**	**Example**	**Part of Speech**
-able (-ible)	capable of being	comfort-+-able	adjective
-ance (-ence)	the act of	confid-+-ence	noun
-ful	full of	joy-+-ful	adjective
-ity	the state of being	senior-+-ity	noun
-ly	in a certain way	firm-+-ly love-+-ly	adverb or adjective
-ment	the result of being	amaze-+-ment	noun
-tion (-ion, -sion)	the act or state of being	ten-+-sion	noun

EXERCISE C: **Using Suffixes to Change Words from One Part of Speech to Another.** Using the suffixes in the preceding chart, change each of the following words to the part of speech indicated. Because the spelling of some of the words will change slightly, you will need to use a dictionary. Then write a brief definition of each new word. Check your definition, again using the dictionary. Enter in your vocabulary notebook any words whose definitions you missed.

Answers may vary; sample words are given.

EXAMPLE: Change *grace* to an adjective.

       graceful   full of grace

1. Change *perform* to a noun. performance
2. Change *regret* to an adjective. regrettable
3. Change *act* to a noun. action
4. Change *like* to an adjective. likable
5. Change *timid* to a noun. timidity

DEVELOPING WRITING SKILLS: Using Structure to Form New Words. Try your hand at combining word parts to form words. Choose from among the prefixes, roots, and suffixes in the charts in this section. Combine the parts to make ten words. Then write ten sentences using the words.

Answers will vary.

EXAMPLE: transmit

They will transmit the message at dawn.

Exploring Word Origins 33.4

You can use words to tell stories, but many words have interesting stories of their own. Some words have traveled here from other lands, including familiar words such as *chowder* (taken from a French word), *dollar* (from a Dutch word), and *algebra* (from an Arabic word). Some words acquire new meanings over the years; others team up to form new words with new meanings. *Magazine* is an example of the first type of word; *spacewalk* and *southpaw* are examples of the second. Other words have been made up, or *coined*, because scientists and inventors needed names for things that were unknown or that never existed before. Some examples of coined words are *laser, scuba,* and *quark.*

This section will examine the origin and development, or *etymology*, of a number of interesting words in all of these different categories.

Loanwords

Many English words are borrowed from other languages. Although you use some of these words everyday, it probably never occurs to you that they came from another language.

Loanwords are words in the English language that have been borrowed from other languages.

OBJECTIVES

After completing this section, students should be able to

- Identify words that have been borrowed from other languages.
- Identify ways in which old words may acquire new meanings.
- Identify ways in which new words are coined.

TEACHING

Getting Started

Discuss with the class the concept that the English language has always, and is still, acquiring new words in a variety of ways. Elicit the three major ways this process occurs. Write these terms—*Borrowed Words, Old Words with New Meanings,* and *Coinages*—as the headings of three columns on the board. Under each heading should be some examples of each category. Examples to use if your class needs help getting started:

Borrowed Words—*delicatessen* (German); *opera* (Italian); *algebra* (Arabic)
Old Words with New Meanings—*hardware* (the steel or plastic components of a computer); *satellite* (a manmade object in space, used for communication purposes)
Coinages—*NATO* (North Atlantic Treaty Organization); *bus* (from *omnibus*); *dahlia* (from the name of a botanist)

Text Follow Through

Discuss text pages 641–647.

Assign Exercise A, page 642; Exercise B, page 643; Exercise C, page 643; Exercise D, page 645; Exercise E, page 646; Exercise F, page 647; and Developing Writing Skills, page 647.

Less advanced Be sure these students are able to find etymologies in a dictionary before assigning the exercises. Consider dividing the students into several groups and assigning each group a different exercise. Then allow class time for each group to share its work with the others.

Average Have these students compare their answers to Exercise C and compile a master list.

Advanced Ask students to keep a running list of words that have been taken into English exactly as they exist in another language: *en route, pasta, tortilla, sauerkraut,* and so forth.

Of all the *loanwords* in the English language, by far the greatest number can be traced back to Latin and French. The Latin words are usually words that refer to philosophy, religion, and other intellectual topics. Many of the French words describe literature, the arts, and government. By contrast, many of the simple words you use daily, such as *sky, house, mother, winter,* and *summer*, can be traced back a thousand years to the Scandinavian influence that began with the Viking conquests of England. Loanwords have also come into English from other European languages—Spanish, Italian, and German—and from the languages of the East and of Africa.

Along with all the words borrowed from various foreign languages, there are a number of loanwords that were borrowed from the languages of the Native Americans. Many of these words name foods, plants, and animals that were unknown to the early settlers and for which they thus had no words. Some examples of these loanwords are *squash, succotash, skunk,* and *moccasin*. Of the words borrowed from the Native American languages, perhaps the most important are those used as place names. For example, Kansas, itself a Siouan tribal and river name, has for its capital Topeka, another Siouan name that means "good place to dig potatoes." Among the counties of Kansas are Chautauqua, a Seneca word that means "one has taken out fish there"; Cheyenne, a Dakota work meaning "to speak unintelligibly"; and Shawnee, an Algonquian word for "southerners."

EXERCISE A: Discovering the Sources of Borrowed Words. In a dictionary that provides etymologies, look up each of the underlined words in the following paragraph. On your paper write the language of origin next to the number for each word. When more than one origin is given for a word, use the first. If your dictionary uses abbreviations for languages, use the guide to abbreviations in the front or back of the dictionary to find the full name of each language.

Additional Practice
Practice Pages or Practice
Book, page 157

TESTING
Test Program
  Unit Pretest, page 102
  Chapter Test, page 105
  Unit Post-Test, page 109

RE-TEACHING
Practice Pages or Practice
Book, page 157

THINKING SKILLS

Knowledge—*Identifying* the
sources of borrowed words
(Exercise A, page 642)
Discovering words from
specific foreign languages
(Exercise C, page 643)
Using a dictionary to find
definitions and origins of
words (Exercise E, page 646)
Using a dictionary to find the
origins of clipped words,
blends, and brand names (Exercise F, page 647)

Comprehension—*Selecting*
origins of words from a given
list (Exercise B, page 643)
Forming new words by combining two words (Exercise D,
page 645)

Synthesis—*Writing* original
sentences incorporating loanwords and coinages (Developing Writing Skills, page 647)

33.4 Exploring Word Origins

EXAMPLE: loyal

      French

1. Fr 2. Hebrew 3. Irish 4. Fr 5. Algonquian 6. Narragansett 7. Fr 8. Fr

On their way to the (1) <u>concert</u>, (2) <u>Sarah</u> and (3) <u>Kevin</u> stopped at a (4) <u>restaurant</u>. (5) <u>Squash</u> and (6) <u>succotash</u> were on the (7) <u>menu</u>, but the couple decided to order an (8) <u>omelet</u>, (9) <u>spaghetti</u>, and a salad of (10) <u>tomatoes</u>, lettuce, and (11) <u>mayonnaise</u>. For (12) <u>dessert</u>, they had (13) <u>tapioca</u>, (14) <u>chocolate</u> cake, and (15) <u>coffee</u>. Sarah was wearing a (16) <u>shawl</u> and a new (17) <u>denim</u> skirt. Kevin was wearing a (18) <u>parka</u> and (19) <u>dungarees</u>. Fortunately, they had an (20) <u>umbrella</u>, because on the way to the concert, it was raining.

9. It 10. Sp 11. Fr 12. Mid Eng 13. Port 14. Fr 15. It 16. Urdu 17. Fr
18. Aleut 19. Hindi 20. It

EXERCISE B: Matching Words with Their Origins. On your paper match the words in the first column with their origins in the second column. Since many of the words have changed in meaning over the years, you may have to look some of them up in a dictionary that provides etymologies.

EXAMPLE: powwow

      a conference (Algonquian)

1. escape c	a. great water (Algonquian)
2. radical h	b. brotherly love (Greek)
3. janitor g	c. out of one's cloak (Latin)
4. plaid f	d. an arm (Latin)
5. geometry j	e. to tremble (Latin)
6. pretzel d	f. blanket (Gaelic)
7. Lake Michigan a	g. doorkeeper (Latin)
8. prairie i	h. root (Latin)
9. Philadelphia b	i. meadowland (French)
10. tremendous e	j. to measure the earth (Greek)

EXERCISE C: Finding Loanwords in the Dictionary. In a dictionary that provides etymologies, find words from any five of the following languages. For each word that you find, give yourself points for the word according to the number in parentheses after each language. A total score of 25 would be considered excellent for this exercise.

Answers will vary; samples are given.

EXAMPLE: Hindi (7)

bungalow   7 points

1. French (1)   chrome
2. Italian (2)   balcony
3. German (3)   noodle
4. Spanish (3)   ranch
5. Yiddish (4)   schlep
6. Chinese (4)   tea
7. Japanese (4)   sushi
8. Native American (5)   opossum
9. Sanskrit (7)   sutra
10. Arabic (7)   candy
11. Persian (7)   shah
12. Hindi (7)   lathi

Old Words with New Meanings

Another way speakers of English have expanded the language is by giving new meanings to existing words. Sometimes the original meaning falls into disuse and is forgotten. *Camera,* for example, originally meant "chamber" or "room." More often a word simply gains one or more additional meanings. *Rig,* for example, still means "the arrangement of sails and masts on a ship." Today, however, *rig* also means "oil drilling equipment" and "a tractor-trailer."

The English language grows by giving new meanings to existing words.

Think of all the different meanings for words that describe parts of the body. Look up the words *head, arm, elbow, hand,* and *heart,* for example. Each has many meanings, both old and new. In addition, all but one of the five words can easily be used as either a noun or a verb.

Existing words also take on new meanings by working together. From the time of its origin, the English language has combined words to create new words with new meanings. Common examples are *lion-hearted, breakfast,* and *freeway.*

33.4 Exploring Word Origins

EXERCISE D: **Combining Words to Create New Words.**
Match each word in the first column with the appropriate word
in the second column and write the words you have formed on
your paper.

EXAMPLE: waste   paper

   wastepaper

1. hitch	a. book	1. hitchhike
2. copy	b. sick	2. copycat
3. text	c. way	3. textbook
4. home	d. pack	4. homesick
5. search	e. hike	5. searchlight
6. free	g. ball	6. freeway
7. back	g. tack	7. backpack
8. basket	h. weight	8. basketball
9. thumb	i. light	9. thumbtack
10. feather	j. cat	10. featherweight

Coinages

In addition to borrowing words and adding new meanings to
existing words, the English language grows through the creation of new words called *coinages*.

**The English language grows through the addi-
tion of newly coined words.**

New words are needed for new things. There are several different methods of inventing new words.

Acronyms. An acronym is a word coined from the first letter or first few letters of a series of words. Many acronyms were
invented to describe scientific advances. The words *radar* (*ra*-
dio *d*etecting *a*nd *r*anging) and *sonar* (*so*und *na*vigation and
*r*anging) were formed this way. Others were invented as abbreviations for organizations or acts of government. The word *SAC*
(*S*trategic *A*ir *C*ommand) falls into this category. Like other
similar words, it is made up of capital letters.

1. equipment worn by divers for breathing under water, an acronym for *self-contained underwater breathing apparatus*
2. unreasoning devotion to one's country, after a soldier of Napoleon named Chauvin
3. a poisonous alkaloid in tobacco, after a French ambassador named Nicot who first introduced tobacco into France
4. a distant, starlike celestial object, an acronym for *quasi* and *stellar*
5. a system to speed mail deliveries, an acronym for *Zoning Improvement Plan*
6. an acronym for *National Aeronautics and Space Administration*
7. to destroy bacteria in milk by heating, after a French scientist named Pasteur who developed the process
8. a type of engine, after a German inventor named Diesel
9. an acronym for *Organization of Petroleum Exporting Countries*
10. a sweater that opens down the front, after the seventh Earl of Cardigan

"People" Words. A surprising number of words have their origin in the name of a person. When you speak of eating a sandwich, driving along a macadam road, or wearing sideburns, you are memorializing the Earl of Sandwich, a Scottish engineer named McAdam, and a Civil War general named Burnside.

Clipped Words. Some new words are simply shortened versions of old words. Examples are *ad* (advertisement), *hi-fi* (high fidelity), and *bike* (bicycle).

Blends. Some words are formed by combining parts of other words. For example, *motel* was formed when someone wanted to describe a hotel intended for people traveling by motor car. *Chortle* was invented by Lewis Carroll to describe the way a character could chuckle and snort at the same time.

Brand Names. The brand names created by companies to describe new products are another fertile source of new words. Often, one of these names eventually becomes the word used for the whole group of products, even though some of them may be manufactured by other companies. The word *Kleenex* is a good example. If you look up *Kleenex* in the dictionary, you will find that the word is used to refer to tissues in general.

EXERCISE E: Finding the Origins of Acronyms and "People" Words. In a dictionary that provides etymologies, look up each of the following words. On your paper write the definition and the origin of the word next to the appropriate number. Answers are in the margin.

EXAMPLE: mackintosh

raincoat, named after a Scottish inventor named Mackintosh

1. scuba	5. ZIP code	9. OPEC
2. chauvinism	6. NASA	10. cardigan
3. nicotine	7. pasteurize	
4. quasar	8. diesel	

33.4 Exploring Word Origins

EXERCISE F: Finding the Origins of Clipped Words, Blends, and Brand Names. In a dictionary that provides etymologies, look up each of the following words. On your paper write the word or words from which each of the clipped words or blends was derived. If the name was coined by a manufacturer, write *brand name* next to the appropriate number.

EXAMPLE: stereo

   stereophonic record player

1. motor pedal   2. taxicab   3. brand name   4. breakfast lunch   5. omnibus

1. moped
2. taxi
3. Band-Aid
4. brunch
5. bus
6. splurge
7. zoo
8. Xerox
9. Levi's
10. sci-fi

6. splash surge   7. zoological garden   8. brand name   9. brand name
10. science fiction

DEVELOPING WRITING SKILLS: Writing Sentences with Loanwords and Coinages.

Follow the instructions below to write five sentences of your own that contain words with a variety of origins. Look back through this section or use a dictionary to help you find word origins. Underline the words that fit the instructions.

Answers will vary.

EXAMPLE: Write a sentence that contains a word borrowed from Latin and a "people" word.

When I had a <u>virus</u>, I wore a <u>cardigan</u> sweater to stay warm.

1. Write a sentence that contains a word borrowed from a Native American language and a combination word.
2. Write a sentence that contains a blend word and a word borrowed from Latin.
3. Write a sentence that contains a word borrowed from French and a "people" word.
4. Write a sentence that contains a person's name borrowed from Hebrew and a person's name borrowed from Latin.
5. Write a sentence that contains a brand name, a clipped word, and an acronym.

648

Checking Your Skills

In the Checking Your Skills assignment, students used context clues to determine the meanings of unfamiliar words. To provide students with additional practice in using context clues, have them complete the following assignment.

Collaborative Learning

Have each student look through short stories and articles to come up with ten sentences that each contain one unfamiliar word. Then have students look up the definition of each unfamiliar word. Next, divide your class into two teams. Then play a game in which members from each team take turns writing their sentences on the chalkboard and underlining the unfamiliar words. The members of the opposing team should then try to use context clues to determine the meaning of each underlined word.

Using Vocabulary Skills in Writing

Publishing You might want to make copies of your students' compositions and arrange them into an anthology that you can distribute to the class.

Answers for Checking Your Skills, page 648

1. impressive display of people or things 2. to keep in existence 3. path taken by a heavenly body in a revolution around another body 4. burned to ashes 5. to solidify or thicken 6. gaseous envelope surrounding the earth. 7. to judge or determine 8. risky; dangerous 9. unbelievable 10. one and only

Skills Review and Writing Workshop

Building your Vocabulary
CHECKING YOUR SKILLS

Use context clues to write a definition for each underlined word in the following paragraph.
Definitions will vary; answers are in the margin.

(1) Despite the vast <u>array</u> of science fiction movies, scientists know that life could not exist on any of Earth's planets. (2) None of them provides the conditions necessary to <u>sustain</u> life as we define it. (3) Most of the other planets have <u>orbits</u> around the sun that are either too long or too short for living creatures. (4) Several planets have temperatures so high that any life would be instantly <u>incinerated</u>. (5) The temperatures on planets far from the sun are low enough to <u>congeal</u> any living matter. (6) Only the earth has enough oxygen in its <u>atmosphere</u> to sustain life. (7) We know this because astronomers can <u>estimate</u> the amount and kinds of gases surrounding each planet. (8) The gravitational pull on most planets is so different from that on earth that any prolonged stay would be <u>hazardous</u> to living beings. (9) The <u>incredibly</u> intense pressure on many planets would crush the life out of any creature who ventured there. (10) Some people conclude that life may be <u>unique</u> to the earth.

USING VOCABULARY SKILLS IN WRITING
Writing a Science Fiction Description

Follow these steps to write a description of an imaginary place in outer space.
Answers will vary.
Prewriting: Write about what you have seen, heard, smelled, tasted, and touched. Note any events that occurred.

Writing: Begin with a description of the place. Include details that make the scene vivid for your reader.

Revising: Look over your words and change any that could be more descriptive or accurate. Proofread carefully.

648

The first of the two sections in this chapter, Section 34.1, suggests general techniques for identifying and solving spelling problems. It also provides practice in working with one hundred common spelling demons. Section 34.2 identifies basic spelling rules and gives the students a chance to practice applying them.

For a review of the entire chapter and a related writing activity, see the Skills Review and Writing Workshop on page 670.

Chapter **34**

Improving Your Spelling

The ability to write effectively has always been recognized as a valuable skill. One of the first steps in improving your writing is to improve your spelling.

The first section of this chapter describes several techniques for learning the spelling of problem words. The second section focuses on specific types of spelling errors and provides rules to help you avoid them.

Solving Your Spelling Problems 34.1

Before you can begin a successful program of spelling improvement, you must identify the words that you most frequently misspell. This section will give you useful suggestions about how to correct your spelling problems.

Your Personal Spelling List

One of the best ways to improve your spelling is to keep a personal spelling list. Set aside a special section in your notebook to list words that you use often but have trouble spelling.

34.1 Solving Your Spelling Problems
(pp. 649–657)

OBJECTIVES

After completing this section, students should be able to

- Set up and use a personal spelling list.
- Use study strategies to analyze problem words.
- Use memory aids to learn the spelling of difficult words.
- Use a list of spelling demons to correct personal spelling problems.

TEACHING

Getting Started

Discuss with students the problems they have with spelling. Mention the value of keeping a personal spelling list. Elicit how such a list can help them improve their spelling. (It will gather in one place the words *they* most frequently misspell.) Tell students that in this section they will learn how to set up and use their personal spelling list. They will also find out which of one hundred common spelling demons are also *their* demons.

Text Follow Through

Discuss text pages 649–657.

Assign Exercise A, page 651; Exercise B, page 652; Exercise C, page 653; Exercise D, page 655; Exercise E, page 655; Exercise F, page 657; Exercise G, page 657; and Developing Writing Skills, page 657.

Less advanced Work closely with these students to help them set up their personal spelling lists. Check their notebooks at regular intervals to see that they are keeping the lists up to date.

Average Hold a spelling bee based on the list of demons. Students who miss words can add them to their personal spelling lists.

Advanced Have these students practice their spelling skills by proofreading each other's written work. Misspelled words should be corrected and added to students' personal spelling lists.

To start your list, gather together a group of corrected papers from all of your courses. A quick review of your spelling errors on these papers should supply you with enough words for a small list.

Make a list of words that you misspell, write the list in your notebook, and review it regularly.

The example shows one useful way of setting up a spelling list. Each page of the list is divided into four columns. Each entry includes a spelling word, its correct pronunciation, a simple definition, and a short sentence using the word. The fourth column can also be used for memory aids, which are described later in this section. Note that troublesome letters have been underlined in the first column and the fourth column of the spelling list to make the problem areas stand out.

Spelling List			
Word	Pronunciation	Definition	Sentence / Memory Aid
accept	әk sept'	to take or receive willingly	Carla was asked to accept the trophy for the basketball team.
cafeteria	Kaf'ә tir'ē ә	a self-service restaurant	Meet me in the cafeteria for lunch.
necessary	nes' ә ser'ē	required	Plenty of sun and rain are necessary for a good crop.
schedule	sKej' ool	a list of details or times when certain things will happen	Do you have a schedule for every school day?

34.1 Solving Your Spelling Problems

To prepare your own list begin by looking up each word in a dictionary and entering it in the first column. If you have difficulty finding the word, you can refer to the chart on page 740 of Section 38.3. In the same section, under the heading "Understanding Main Entries," there is an explanation of pronunciation. Since dictionaries differ slightly in the pronunciation symbols they use, the symbols used on page 650 may vary from those in your dictionary. It will be useful for you to become familiar with the pronunciation symbols used in your own dictionary since those are the ones you should use in the second column of your notebook. Finally, add a definition and a short sentence for each entry.

When you have completed your list, proofread each spelling entry to be sure that the information you have written is correct. Proofreading, incidentally, is a good way to check the spelling in all of your written work. When you proofread your papers, check a dictionary for the spelling of any words you are not sure of. Every student who is serious about spelling improvement should acquire the "dictionary habit."

To carry out a spelling improvement program, you must also keep your personal spelling list. Once a week review your written work and spelling tests for new words to add to your list.

EXERCISE A: Starting Your Personal Spelling List. Select at least five words that you have trouble spelling and enter them into a special spelling list in your notebook. Follow the model given on page 650. Consult a dictionary to find the correct spelling, pronunciation, and definition of each word.

Spelling lists will vary.

EXAMPLE: secretary

Word	Pronunciation	Definition	Sentence/ Memory Aid
secretary	sek′ rə ter′ ē	a person who carries out clerical duties	Her secretary was excellent.

TESTING
Test Program
   Unit Pretest, page 102
   Chapter Test, page 106
   Unit Post-Test, page 109

RE-TEACHING
Practice Pages or Practice
Book, pages 158, 159

THINKING SKILLS
Knowledge—*Identifying* misspelled words and finding their correct spelling in a dictionary (Exercise B, page 652)
Identifying and correcting misspelled words (Exercise C, page 653)

Application—*Using* misspelled words to start a personal spelling list (Exercise A, page 651)
Using spelling demons in sentences (Exercise G, page 657)
Demonstrating mastery of spelling demons (Exercise F, page 657)
Designing memory aids for a given list of spelling words (Exercise D, page 655)
Designing memory aids for a personal spelling list (Exercise E, page 655)

Synthesis—*Writing* a short story containing ten spelling demons and ten words from one's personal spelling list (Developing Writing Skills, page 657)

EXERCISE B: Adding to Your Personal Spelling List. Rewrite each sentence correcting the misspelled word. You and a classmate should then correct each other's papers. Check a dictionary and add to your spelling list any words that you misspelled.

EXAMPLE: The lines were separate but paralel.

The lines were separate but parallel.

1. Sarah loves to do experiments in the science <u>labratory</u>. laboratory
2. Nate <u>accidentaly</u> spilled his glass of milk. accidentally
3. The detective just received an <u>anonimous</u> tip. anonymous
4. How many books did you borrow from the <u>libary</u>? library
5. The camel is well adapted to <u>dessert</u> life. desert
6. The magician made the rabbit <u>dissappear</u>. disappear
7. Do you have an extra pair of <u>scissers</u>? scissors
8. The twins had spaghetti at the <u>resturant</u>. restaurant
9. Our teacher was absent, so we had a <u>substatute</u>. substitute
10. <u>Tomorow</u> is Terry's birthday party. Tomorrow
11. Bart has a brother in the <u>eigth</u> grade. eighth
12. Some people are afraid of thunder and <u>lightening</u>. lightning
13. <u>Mathmatics</u> is Rosa's favorite subject. Mathematics
14. Did you bring me back a <u>souvenier</u> from your trip? souvenir
15. I wonder <u>wheather</u> Jennifer will win the race. whether
16. The jury found the <u>defendent</u> not guilty. defendant
17. Mark was <u>dissappointed</u> with his test grade. disappointed
18. Who was the <u>villan</u> in the play? villain
19. Tina went to the beauty salon for a <u>permanant</u>. permanent
20. Bill is my next-door <u>neighber</u>. neighbor

A System for Improving Your Spelling

Review the words on your spelling list frequently.

Use the following method to study the words on your personal spelling list.

34.1 Solving Your Spelling Problems

The method given in the chart can be very helpful if you use it regularly.

A METHOD FOR LEARNING PROBLEM WORDS

1. *Look* at each word. Does it have a pattern of letters that you could memorize? For example, the word *committee* has two *m's,* two *t's,* and two *e's.* Notice how the letters are arranged in the word. Then cover the word and try to get a mental picture of it.
2. *Pronounce* the word, syllable by syllable. If, for example, you pronounce *library* carefully, you will note that there is an *r* after the *b.*
3. *Write* the word on a sheet of paper. Say each syllable aloud as you are writing it down.
4. *Compare* the word that you wrote on the paper with the word in your notebook. If you spelled the word correctly, put a small check in front of the word in your notebook. If you misspelled the word, circle the letter or letters on your paper that are incorrect and start over again with the first step.

Once a week you might have a member of your family or a friend read your spelling words to you. As each word is read, write it. Try to use these words in any writing assignments that you have. Using the words will help you to master them more quickly. You may consider a word mastered when you have spelled it correctly at least three times in your own written work.

EXERCISE C: Spelling Difficult Words. Look carefully at each underlined word in the sentences on the following page. If the word is spelled correctly, write *correct* next to the appropriate number on your paper. If the word is misspelled, write the correct spelling of the word. When you are finished, check each underlined word in a dictionary. Add to your personal spelling list the correct spellings of any words you misspelled. Review these words using the Look, Pronounce, Write, and Compare method.

EXAMPLE: Missing our train was just the first event in an <u>extrodinary</u> day.

extraordinary

1. The <u>captain</u> of the ship wore a blue uniform. c
2. Grandma served warm apple pie for <u>dessert</u>. c
3. Molly Pitcher was a <u>couragous</u> figure during the Revolutionary War. couragous
4. Jason wrote the address on the <u>envelope</u>, using invisible ink. c
5. Check the <u>calender</u> to see when spring vacation begins.
6. The school band marched to the <u>rythm</u> of the drums. rhythm
7. Dale, an expert gymnast, excels on the <u>parallel</u> bars. c
8. The principal gave awards for perfect <u>attendence</u>. attendance
9. Do you know the <u>capital</u> of Alaska? c
10. Someone left a blue <u>hankerchief</u> on the desk. handkerchief
11. The ambulance drove up to the <u>emergency</u> entrance. c
12. Debbie's cat, Penelope, was <u>particularly</u> fond of fish. c
13. What mystery book would you <u>reccommend</u>? recommend
14. The cashier forgot to put my <u>receipt</u> in the bag. c
15. Friday morning the <u>superintendant</u> spoke to us. superintendent
16. The glee club stayed after school to <u>rehearse</u>. c
17. Have you ever seen a <u>prairie</u> dog? c
18. <u>Occassionally</u> my grandfather drives me to school. occasionally
19. This car needs a <u>thorough</u> cleaning. c
20. What <u>foriegn</u> language can you speak? foreign

5. calendar

Developing Memory Aids

If, after several practice sessions, there are some words that you are still misspelling, you can make up a short memory aid for each word.

Use memory aids to help you remember the spelling of words that are difficult for you.

You can often associate some of the letters in troublesome words with the same letters in related words.

34.1 Solving Your Spelling Problems

EXAMPLES: The lib*rary* has *rare* books.

Station*ery* is another word for lett*er* pap*er*.

Sometimes you may find a shorter word within the problem word.

EXAMPLES: The *air* smells fresh on the pr*air*ie.

There is a *mile·* in *mile*age.

A *law*yer studies the *law*.

A *rat* is in the labo*rat*ory.

Did you *hear* the band re*hear*se?

EXERCISE D: Writing Memory Aids. Write a memory aid for each of the following spelling words.
Answers will vary; samples are given for the first two.
EXAMPLE: There's <u>iron</u> in the envi<u>ron</u>ment.
1. An <u>ally</u> should not be chosen accident<u>ally</u>.   2. Her <u>mate</u> is an a<u>mateur</u> actor.

1. accidentally	5. clothes	9. mathematics
2. amateur	6. criticize	10. secretary
3. attendance	7. foreign	
4. believe	8. handkerchief	

EXERCISE E: Making Your Own Memory Aids. Select five words from your personal spelling list. In your notebook write a short memory aid for each word.
Answers will vary.
EXAMPLE: A princip<u>le</u> is a ru<u>le</u>.

Studying Common Spelling Demons

When you have mastered most of the words on your personal spelling list, it is time to expand your spelling program. Studying a list of words that people frequently misspell can help you further improve your spelling skills. Words that are often misspelled are commonly called *spelling demons*.

Study the words on a list of spelling demons to find out which ones you need to work on.

The following chart of spelling demons contains one hundred words that students often misspell. Divide this list into groups of ten words. Use the Look, Pronounce, Write, and Compare method described on page 653 to study each group of words. When you find a word that you have trouble spelling, add it to your personal spelling list and review it along with the other words on your list.

100 COMMON SPELLING DEMONS

absence	courageous	knowledge	receipt
accidentally	criticize	laboratory	recommend
achieve	curious	lawyer	rehearse
acquaintance	deceive	library	restaurant
aisle	defendant	lightning	rhythm
amateur	desert	mathematics	scissors
analyze	desperate	mileage	secretary
anniversary	dessert	misspell	separate
anonymous	disappear	naturally	similar
appearance	disappoint	necessary	sincerely
argument	dissatisfied	neighbor	souvenir
athletic	eighth	nuisance	spaghetti
attendance	embarrass	occasion	straight
awkward	emergency	occasionally	substitute
barrel	envelope	opinion	succeed
behavior	environment	parallel	superintendent
believe	exercise	particularly	suspicious
calendar	explanation	permanent	technique
capital	extraordinary	physician	temporary
capitol	familiar	possession	thorough
captain	foreign	prairie	tomorrow
cemetery	guarantee	preparation	unnecessary
clothes	handkerchief	privilege	vacuum
committee	independence	probably	villain
condemn	interfere	pronunciation	whether

34.1 Solving Your Spelling Problems

EXERCISE F: Adding the Missing Letters. Each of the following spelling demons has one or more letters missing. Write the complete words on your paper. Then check your answers against the chart of common spelling demons. Add to your personal spelling list any words that you misspelled.

EXAMPLE: mi _ _ pell

misspell

1. ach _i_ _e_ ve
2. bel _i_ _e_ ve
3. calend _a_ r
4. capt _a_ _i_ n
5. courag _e_ _o_ _u_ s
6. ei _g_ _h_ th
7. emergen _c_ y
8. lab _o_ _r_ atory
9. lib _r_ _a_ ry
10. light _n_ ing

11. perman _e_ nt
12. prep _a_ ration
13. privil _e_ ge
14. re _c_ ommend
15. r _h_ _y_ thm
16. s _c_ _i_ ssors
17. sep _a_ rate
18. spa _g_ _h_ etti
19. vac _u_ _u_ m
20. vill _a_ _i_ n

EXERCISE G: Using Spelling Demons. From the chart on page 656, choose ten spelling demons that you need to practice. On your paper write a sentence for each word. Then proofread your work carefully.

Sentences will vary.

EXAMPLE: dissatisfied

We were dissatisfied with the test results.

DEVELOPING WRITING SKILLS: Using Spelling Words in a Story. Write a short story using at least ten words from the chart of spelling demons on page 656 and ten additional words from your own personal spelling list. Underline each of the words that you have chosen from the chart and your list. Then proofread your story carefully for misspelled words.

Answers will vary.

EXAMPLE: Although we had <u>rehearsed</u> the play for weeks, the opening night held a number of surprises for us all.

658

34.2 Following Spelling Rules
(pp. 658–669)

OBJECTIVES

After completing this section, students should be able to

- Spell the plural forms of most words correctly.
- Add prefixes to root words and spell the resulting words correctly.
- Add suffixes to root words and spell the resulting words correctly.
- Spell *ie* and *ei* words correctly.
- Spell words that end in *-cede*, *-ceed*, and *-sede* correctly.

TEACHING

Getting Started

Introduce the concept of forming plurals by asking if the class knows what a *regular plural* is (a word that forms the plural by adding either *-s* or *-es* to the singular form of the noun). Ask for examples of such nouns, and write them on the board in both their singular and plural forms. Try to get at least one example of each kind of regular plural. Now ask if the class has heard of irregular plurals of nouns. Elicit some examples of such nouns, and write them on the board in both their singular and plural forms. Follow the same procedure with the plurals of compound nouns, if time permits.

34.2 Following Spelling Rules

Certain kinds of spelling errors are very common. Some people have difficulty forming plurals. Others make mistakes when adding a prefix or a suffix. Still others have problems with certain combinations of letters such as *ie* and *ei* or *-cede* and *-ceed*. This section will help you find out which of these situations cause problems for you. It will also provide you with one or more rules for each situation in order to help you avoid misspelling the problem words.

Forming Plurals

When you change a noun from its singular to its plural form, you may be unsure about what ending to add. This is because the plural ending is not always the same. Most nouns in English form their plurals according to a few simple rules. The plurals of nouns that do not follow these rules are called *irregular plurals*. Recognizing the differences between these two types of plurals can help you find the right endings, as can a knowledge of two simple rules that cover compound nouns.

Regular Plurals. Most nouns in English form the plural by adding *-s* or *-es*.

A regular plural is one that is formed by adding either -s or -es to the singular form of the noun.

Most regular plurals are formed simply by adding *-s*.

EXAMPLES: bell   bells

opinion   opinions

athlete   athletes

A number of other regular plurals, such as the plurals of *mix* and *wish*, are formed by adding *-es*. In other cases you may need to change the spelling of the singular before adding the plural ending. The following chart will help you to form regular plurals correctly.

658

34.2 Following Spelling Rules

FORMING REGULAR PLURALS

Word Ending	Rule	Examples
-s, -ss, -x, -z, -ch, -sh	Add -es.	gas, gases success, successes fox, foxes waltz, waltzes branch, branches ash, ashes
-o preceded by a consonant	Add -es.	hero, heroes potato, potatoes EXCEPTIONS: alto, altos soprano, sopranos piano, pianos (and other muscial terms)
-o preceded by a vowel	Add -s.	rodeo, rodeos
-y preceded by a consonant	Change y to i and add -es.	berry, berries party, parties story, stories
-y preceded by a vowel	Add -s.	toy, toys monkey, monkeys
-f	Add -s. OR Change f to v and add -es.	roof, roofs half, halves loaf, loaves
-ff	Add -s.	staff, staffs sheriff, sheriffs
-fe	Change f to v and add -s.	knife, knives wife, wives

Text Follow Through

Discuss text pages 658–669.

Assign Exercise A, page 661; Exercise B, page 662; Exercise C, page 662; Exercise D, page 664; Exercise E, page 665; Exercise F, page 667; Exercise G, page 668; and Developing Writing Skills, page 668.

Less advanced Permit these students to refer to the charts as they complete the exercises.

Average These students can make lists of words to add to those contained in the charts.

Advanced Conduct a spelling bee that focuses on individual sets of rules or on all of the rules in this section. Call out directions such as the following:

1. Spell the plural form of *thief*.
2. Add the suffix -y to *fun*.
3. Spell *intercede*.

Words for the bee can be taken from section charts and exercises.

Additional Practice

Practice Pages or Practice Book, page 160

TESTING
Test Program

Unit Pretest, pages 102, 103
Chapter Test, pages 106, 107
Unit Post-Test, pages 109, 110

RE-TEACHING
Practice Pages or Practice Book, page 160

THINKING SKILLS

Irregular Plurals. Some words have irregular plurals. They do not follow the rules in the preceding chart.

Use your dictionary to check the correct spelling of words with irregular plurals.

The following chart gives examples of some common irregular plurals.

FORMING IRREGULAR PLURALS		
Singular Form	**Rule**	**Plural Form**
ox	Add -*en*.	oxen
child	Add -*ren*.	children
foot	Change vowels.	feet
mouse	Change vowels and one other letter.	mice
moose	Make the plural the same as the singular.	moose
radius	Change -*us* to -*i*.	radii
crisis	Change -*is* to -*es*.	crises
medium	Change -*um* to -*a*.	media

If you are unsure about spelling the plural form of a word that does not appear in the charts, look it up in a dictionary. If no plural form is listed, then the plural is regular: Simply add -*s* or -*es* to the word. If a spelling change is necessary, the plural form will be listed after the entry word.

You should also know that some words have two ways to spell the plural. The plural of *mosquito,* for example, can be spelled either *mosquitoes* or *mosquitos*. In such cases the preferred form is listed first in the dictionary.

Plurals of Compound Nouns. Some compound nouns are written as one word *(handbook)*, some are hyphenated

34.2 Following Spelling Rules

(father-in-law), and some are written as separate words *(left field)*.

Most compound nouns written as single words form their plurals regularly.

EXAMPLES:　driveway　　driveways

armchair　　armchairs

If a compound noun is written with hyphens or as separate words, use the following rule.

Compound nouns written with hyphens or as separate words generally form the plural by making the modified word plural.

EXAMPLES:　mother-in-law　　mothers-in-law

field mouse　　field mice

EXERCISE A: Writing Plural Forms. On your paper write the plural for each of the words in the list below. If you are not sure of the spelling, refer to your dictionary. Add to your personal spelling list the plural form of any words that you had to look up.

EXAMPLE:　station wagon

station wagons

1. veto es	11. piano s	21. shelf shelves
2. house s	12. tractor s	22. beach es
3. ax es	13. tomato es	23. magnet s
4. tariff s	14. raspberry raspberries	24. baseball s
5. thief thieves	15. leaf leaves	25. emergency
6. turkey s	16. loss es	26. rodeo s
7. crisis crises	17. woman women	27. deer deer
8. wolf wolves	18. handkerchief s	28. dollar sign s
9. activity activities	19. ferry ferries	29. tooth teeth
10. crash es	20. boardwalk s	30. chimney s

25. emergencies

EXERCISE B: Using Plurals in Sentences. Write ten sentences of your own, each using the plural form of one of the following words.

Sentences will vary; plurals are given.

EXAMPLE: child

> The children were eager to see what was inside the package.

1. sheep _{sheep}
2. loaf _{loaves}
3. cherry _{cherries}
4. sandwich _{sandwiches}
5. igloo _{igloos}
6. goose _{geese}
7. axis _{axes}
8. starfish _{starfish or starfishes}
9. echo
10. cliff _{cliffs}

9. echoes

Adding Prefixes

A prefix is one or more syllables added at the beginning of a word to form a new word.

When a prefix is added to a root word, the spelling of the root word stays the same.

When a familiar prefix such as *un-* is added at the beginning of a root word that you already know, you should be able to spell the new word without any trouble. Misspellings sometimes occur, however, when the last letter of a prefix is the same as the first letter of the root word. Remember to keep both letters when you are forming the new word.

EXAMPLES: re- + -cover = recover

un- + -necessary = unnecessary

dis- + -satisfied = dissatisfied

mis- + -spell = misspell

EXERCISE C: Using Prefixes. Combine the prefixes and root words in the following twenty items to form new words.

EXAMPLE: mis- + -lead

mislead

1. in- + -complete incomplete
2. mis- + -read misread
3. dis- + -solve dissolve
4. un- + -usual unusual
5. re- + -fill refill
6. dis- + -appear disappear
7. un- + -fortunate unfortunate
8. in- + -visible invisible
9. dis- + -appoint disappoint
10. un- + -noticed unnoticed
11. re- + -gain regain
12. mis- + -place misplace
13. dis- + -agree disagree
14. con- + -serve conserve
15. in- + -numerable innumerable
16. re- + -play replay
17. in- + -expensive inexpensive
18. mis- + -manage mismanage
19. dis- + -cover discover
20. re- + -paint repaint

Adding Suffixes

A suffix is one or more syllables added at the end of a word to form a new word.

Be aware of spelling changes needed in some root words when a suffix is added.

When a suffix is added to a root word, the spelling of the root word often changes. In these situations misspellings can easily occur.

SPELLING CHANGES TO MAKE WHEN ADDING SUFFIXES		
Word Ending	**Rule**	**Examples**
-y preceded by a consonant	Change *y* to *i*.	lazy, laziness EXCEPTIONS: When the suffix begins with *i*: deny, denying fry, frying
-y preceded by a vowel	Make no change.	play, playful EXCEPTIONS: day, daily gay, gaily

-e	Drop the final *e* if suffix begins with a vowel.	like, likable value, valuable EXCEPTIONS: courage, courageous foresee, foreseeable notice, noticeable
-e	Make no change if suffix begins with a consonant.	grace, graceful sincere, sincerely EXCEPTIONS: argue, argument, true, truly
One-syllable word ending in a single consonant preceded by a single vowel	Double the final consonant if suffix begins with a vowel.	bat, batted plan, planning EXCEPTIONS: Words ending in *-x* or *-w:* fix, fixed tow, towing
Word accented on the final syllable and ending in a single consonant preceded by a single vowel	Double the final consonant if suffix begins with a vowel.	begin, beginner EXCEPTIONS: Words in which the accent changes when the suffix is added: confer', con'ference

EXERCISE D: Making New Words with Suffixes. Make a new word to complete each sentence below by combining the words and suffixes in parentheses. Write each new word on your paper, spelled correctly. Then check the spelling of the new words in a dictionary.

EXAMPLE: When the check finally arrived, he thought his
____(happy-+-ness)____ was assured.

happiness

34.2 Following Spelling Rules

1. We spent a ___(peaceful-+-ful)___ Saturday afternoon in the country. peaceful
2. The ___(shop-+-er)___ had too many packages to carry.
3. The manager of the local hardware store had a very ___(response-+-ible)___ job. responsible
4. Does this rocking chair seem ___(comfort-+-able)___ to you? comfortable
5. Lisa ___(benefit-+-ed)___ from the art lessons she took.
6. Jack enjoys his new job at the lake, and he likes his ___(employ-+-er)___, too. employer
7. Is the ___(amplify-+-er)___ working? amplifier
8. Do you think that the story Gerry told us Monday is ___(believe-+-able)___? believable
9. ___Play-+-ing)___ softball has always been Jody's favorite activity. Playing
10. I think a letter has been ___(omit-+-ed)___ from that word.

2. shopper   5. benefited   10.omitted

EXERCISE E: Using Suffixes. Combine the following root words and suffixes to form twenty new words. Then write twenty sentences, using one of the new words in each sentence. Underline each new word in your sentences and check the spelling of each new word in your dictionary.
Sentences will vary; spellings for new words are given.
EXAMPLE: wax-+-ing

        waxing   <u>Waxing</u> the floor by hand took hours.

1. value-+-able valuable
2. grow-+-ing growing
3. imagine-+-ary imaginary
4. hope-+-ful hopeful
5. rely-+-able reliable
6. scarce-+-ly scarcely
7. rever-+-ence reference
8. busy-+-ness business
9. beauty-+-ful beautiful
10. pay-+-ment payment
11. slip-+-ery slippery
12. lucky-+-ly luckily
13. perform-+-ance performance
14. plenty-+-ful plentiful
15. final-+-ly finally
16. love-+-able lovable
17. amuse-+-ment amusement
18. guide-+-ance guidance
19. break-+-able breakable
20. reside-+-ence residence

Deciding on *ie* or *ei*

A major source of difficulty for many spellers is deciding whether to use *ie* or *ei* in a number of common words. Following these few general rules can help you to make your choice.

When a word has a long e sound, use *ie*.

When a word has a long a sound, use *ei*.

When a word has a long e sound but is preceded by the letter c, use *ei*.

The following chart lists a few common words that follow the above rules.

COMMON *ie* AND *ei* WORDS		
Long *e* Sound Use *ie*	Long *a* Sound Use *ei*	Long *e* Sound Preceded by *c* Use *ei*
brief	eight	ceiling
chief	freight	deceive
niece	reign	perceive
piece	sleigh	receipt
relieve	vein	receive
shield	weight	
yield		

However, a few words are exceptions to these rules. The most important of these are shown in the next chart.

SOME EXCEPTIONS TO THE RULES		
either	neither	seize

When you are in doubt about how to spell a word that does not appear in the preceding charts, consult your dictionary.

EXERCISE F: Working with *ie* and *ei* Words. Write the incomplete word from each of the following sentences on your paper, filling in either *ie* or *ei* in the blanks. You may refer to the rules as you work. Then check each word in your dictionary and add to your personal spelling list any words that you misspelled.

EXAMPLE: He asked the clerk for a rec __ __ pt.

    receipt

1. The c _e_ _i_ ling in Aunt Grace's living room was powder blue.
2. We noticed that the farmer was in his f _i_ _e_ ld plowing the soil.
3. May I have a p _i_ _e_ ce of watermelon?
4. Tom is giving a report about nutrition today in hyg _i_ _e_ ne class.
5. We stopped at a Chinese restaurant for shrimp chow m _e_ _i_ n.
6. How many cars did you count as that fr _e_ _i_ ght train went by?
7. Sally's Irish setter likes to retr _i_ _e_ ve sticks when we throw them.
8. Queen Victoria had a long r _e_ _i_ gn.
9. Dennis forgot to bring a clean handkerch _i_ _e_ f with him.
10. How much does a full-grown Indian elephant w _e_ _i_ gh?

Using -*cede*, -*ceed*, and -*sede*

Many spellers find the words that end in -*cede*, -*ceed*, and -*sede* confusing. Fortunately, there are relatively few words that end this way.

Memorize the words that end in -*cede*, -*ceed*, and -*sede*.

The chart on the following page lists those words ending in -*cede* that you are most likely to meet.

Developing Writing Skills

To provide students with additional practice in using spelling rules in writing, have them complete the following assignment.

Writing Across the Curriculum

People often have strong opinions about movies they have seen. However, only film critics get an opportunity to express their opinions about movies to a large audience.

Prewriting Imagine that you are a film critic for your school newspaper. Then either watch a current film at a local theater or watch a television broadcast of an earlier commercial film. As you watch the film, focus on the performances of the actors, the quality of the script, and the use of special effects, as well as the overall effectiveness of the film. If possible, jot down your opinions of the various elements of the film.

Writing Write a first draft of a review of the film, trying to be as objective as possible. Make sure that you support each of your opinions with details from the film. If you find that you have difficulty writing your review, you might find it helpful to look at a number of movie reviews in newspapers or magazines and to model your own review after the ones you have read.

Revising Revise your review, making sure that your review is as objective as possible and that you have supported each of your opinions with details from the film. Then proofread your review, making sure that it does not contain any spelling errors.

WORDS ENDING IN *-cede*		
concede	precede	secede
intercede	recede	

In contrast only three common words end in *-ceed: exceed, proceed,* and *succeed.* Only one word ends in *-sede: supersede.*

EXERCISE G: Spelling Words Ending in *-cede, -ceed, and -sede.* Some of the words in the following paragraph have missing letters. Write each word next to the appropriate number on your paper, with the letters correctly filled in. Then check the words in your dictionary and add to your personal spelling list any words that you misspelled.

EXAMPLE: Suc _ _ _ _ ing in an exploration of arctic regions can be difficult.

Succeeding

The tiny village (1) re c e d e d in the distance as explorer Colin Irwin set off across the ice. Irwin (2) super s e d e d the original leader, who had been removed from command even though Irwin had (3) inter c e d e d for him. (4) Pre c e d e d by his guide, the explorer and his team headed for Point Barrow, Alaska. Although Colin had not (5) suc c e e d ed in earlier attempts, he was not ready to (6) con c e d e defeat. Despite the fierce wind, the group (7) pro c e e d ed to make their way across the frozen bay. Their speed (8) ex c e e d ed that of any previous group.

DEVELOPING WRITING SKILLS: Using Spelling Rules in Writing a Story. Write a story using words that follow the spelling rules you have learned in this section. Use at least three words that represent rules for plurals, three words that represent rules for prefixes and suffixes, and three words that

34.2 Following Spelling Rules

represent rules for *ie* and *ei* words. Also include at least one word that ends in *-cede* or *-ceed*. Underline the words that you choose to represent the spelling rules you have learned. Proofread your story for misspelled words.

Stories will vary.

EXAMPLE: Good <u>stories</u> often begin with good characters.

Checking Your Skills

In the Checking Your Skills assignment, your students read about an important and influential American woman, Abigail Adams. Have your students think of other important and influential American women. List on the chalkboard each woman that the students suggest.

Speaking and Listening

Have your students review the list on the chalkboard and choose the influential woman that most interests them. The students should then research the woman they have chosen. Using the notes from their research, students should prepare an oral report describing the life of the woman they have chosen. Finally, students should deliver their reports to their classmates.

Using Spelling Skills in Writing

Peer Editing Divide your class into groups of three or four. Then have the members of each group take turns reading their compositions to one another and suggesting ways in which the compositions could be improved. When evaluating their classmates' compositions, students should keep the following questions in mind: Does the writer include enough facts and details to create a clear portrait of the historical figure? Are the facts and details organized in a logical manner? Does the writer clearly express his or her opinion about the figure? Does the writer support his or her opinion?

Skills Review and Writing Workshop

Improving Your Spelling

CHECKING YOUR SKILLS

Rewrite the following paragraph, correcting all spelling errors.

1. courageous, influential, government 2. mismanage, absence 3. believed,

(1) A couragous woman who was influentiel during the early days of our goverment was Abigail Adams, wife of John Adams. (2) He had to leave his business affairs in her hands, and never did she missmanage them in his absense. (3) She beleived it necessery to write to her husband often. (4) Her letters discuss important principals of the American Revolution as well as domestic crisises. (5) She worried about the arguements taking place in the new nation, and sometimes reccommended cources of action. (6) Many times she wondered if the dissagreeing factions would ever acheive unity. (7) She asked that the new legal code ". . . remember the ladies . . ." and pass laws more favoreable to them. (8) She reminded her husband that ". . . all men would be tyrents if they could" and urged that the new laws not put so much power into the hands of already priviledged husbands. (9) Unfortuneately, her advise was not followed. (10) Not until 1920 were all women granted the right to vote by a constitutionel amendmant.

necessary 4. principles, crises 5. arguments 6. recommended, courses 7. disagreeing, achieve

USING SPELLING SKILLS IN WRITING

Writing About a Historical Figure

Follow the steps below to write about a historical figure whom you admire.

Answers will vary.

Prewriting:

List details why the person is especially appealing to you.

Writing:

Identify the person and what he or she did. Conclude with a statement that sums up your opinion.

Revising:

Proofread carefully, checking your spelling.

8. tyrants, privileged 9. Unfortunately, advice 10. Constitutional, Amendment

UNIT VII

Study and Research Skills

This unit covers skills that are useful both in English class and in other subject areas. Since it does not depend directly on any other material in the text, it can be taught at any time during the year. You may, for example, choose to teach Chapter 35, Basic Study Skills, early in the year to enable students to establish good study habits and note-taking skills from the start. Similarly, you may decide to cover Chapter 38, Library and Dictionary Skills, at a point in the curriculum where students begin work on writing a report or a research paper.

CHAPTER 35
Basic Study Skills

(pp. 672–684)

It is advisable that students be assigned this chapter early in the school year so that they can practice the study skills throughout the year. You will then be able to reinforce and test the skills at regular intervals.

The first section of this chapter, Section 35.1, deals with general study methods: creating a distraction-free study area, developing good study habits, scheduling study time, and recording assignments. More specific study skills are covered in Section 35.2, including methods for recording assignments and using modified and formal outlines to take notes.

For a review of the entire chapter and a related writing activity, see the Skills Review and Writing Workshop on page 684.

35.1 Establishing Good Study Habits

(pp. 672–676)

OBJECTIVES

After completing this section, students should be able to

- Evaluate their study settings.
- Establish a schedule for regular studying.
- Set up an assignment book.

Chapter # 35

Basic Study Skills

Study skills are tools you can use to build a solid foundation in all the subjects you study. They can help you to understand, remember, and apply what you read or learn in class.

35.1 Establishing Good Study Habits

To become consistently good at studying, you must have good study habits. That way, you will study well without having to think about it all the time. In this section, you will learn how to create a useful study setting, schedule your study time, and keep track of your assignments.

Choosing a Study Setting

Make a habit of studying in the same place every day. Your study area should be equipped with everything you need, so you won't have to hunt for pencils, erasers, paper, and so on.

Establish a study area that works well for you.

35.1 Establishing Good Study Habits

It is best to be able to study in the same place every day. A special area set aside for studying should be off-limits to other people so that you can be free from interruptions. If it is both comfortable and attractive, you will find it easier to work in. The table or desk should be at a good height for reading and writing. The chair should be comfortable, but not made for lounging. Be sure the study area is well lit. You may not be able to create an ideal study area, but knowing what one contains can help you make your study area better.

Having the right supplies and materials available is an important part of creating an efficient study area. Make sure your study area is equipped with everything you need and want.

EQUIPMENT MY STUDY AREA MUST HAVE	
pencils	stapler and staples
pens	paper clips
pencil sharpener	markers and/or colored pencils
eraser	ruler
paper and/or notebooks	wastepaper basket
tape	index cards
scissors	folders
glue	dictionary

In addition to the items on the chart, you may want to include other supplies and equipment in your study area. These items may include a compass, a protractor, templates, a slide rule, a calculator, a typewriter, a thesaurus, other reference books, and other art supplies.

EXERCISE A: Rating Your Study Area. List all the items and qualities your ideal study area would have. Then write two paragraphs. In the first compare your present study area to your ideal. In the second paragraph describe how you could improve your study area.
Paragraphs will vary.

revise their schedules each month or whenever outside activities change.

Advanced You could ask students to try different methods of recording assignments and to report on which work best for them. Students may also want to develop symbols that show at a glance which assignments are most time-consuming or most important.

Additional Practice

Practice Pages or Practice Book, page 163

TESTING

Test Program

Unit Pretest, page 111
Chapter Test, page 114
Unit Post-Test, page 123

RE-TEACHING

Practice Pages or Practice Book, page 163

THINKING SKILLS

Application—*Preparing* a study schedule (Exercise B, page 675)
Preparing an assignment book (Exercise C, page 676)

Synthesis—*Writing* a paragraph to describe levels of success in using study skills (Developing Writing Skills, page 676)

Evaluation—*Appraising* study habits (Exercise A, page 673)

Scheduling Study Time

A study schedule that fits your personal needs is an important tool to help you make the best use of your time.

Schedule regular periods for studying.

Draw up a chart like the following sample. List after-school hours down the left-hand side, divided into half-hour segments. Next to the times, write the activity you are going to do then. First, write in regularly scheduled, after-school activities such as sports practice, family chores, and dinner. Second, schedule at least two hours for homework divided into two blocks. Finally, fill in the remaining time with leisure activities. Allow at least half an hour before bedtime for pleasure reading.

SAMPLE SCHEDULE	
Time	**Activity**
3:30–4:00	Dance Class
4:00–4:30	Dance Class
4:30–5:00	Homework
5:00–5:30	Homework
5:30–6:00	Chores
6:00–6:30	Dinner
6:30–7:00	Homework
7:00–7:30	Homework
7:30–8:00	Relaxation
8:00–8:30	Television
8:30–9:00	Pleasure Reading
9:00–9:30	Pleasure Reading

If you have different activities on each day of the week, you may have to write up more than one study schedule. Be sure to schedule study time at nearly the same hour every day and to follow your plan until it becomes a habit. Keep one copy of your study schedule in your notebook and post one near your study area.

EXERCISE B: Preparing Your Own Study Schedule. Plan your own study schedule. If you have different after-school activities on different days of the week, you may have to write more than one schedule. Follow your plan for one week and then evaluate it. Did it help you complete your work on time? Did you follow it every day? Revise the schedule based on your evaluation and follow the revised version.
Answers will vary.

Keeping Track of Assignments

Another useful tool is an assignment book or a special assignment section in your notebook. You can use this to keep track of all your reading and writing assignments as well as tests for which you must study. Keeping track of assignments will help you to plan what to work on when you study, to complete each assignment on time, and to be prepared for any in-class discussions or tests.

Use an assignment book to record homework assignments and due dates.

A useful format for setting up an assignment book is to make five columns on each page. In the first column write the date you received the assignment; in the second write the subject; in the third write the assignment itself, as well as any directions the teacher gave on how to do it; in the fourth write the date the assignment is due; and in the fifth place a checkmark when you have completed the assignment. Look over your assignment book before leaving school for the day so you can take home the books you will need.

Notice the information in each column of the following sample from an assignment book.

Date	Subject	Assignment	Due	Completed
11/19	English	Read Ch. 9, pp. 126–136 Answer questions on page 137	11/21	X
11/19	Math	Prepare for test on decimals	11/20	
11/20	Science	Report on fruit fly experiment in class	11/30	X

EXERCISE C: Setting Up an Assignment Book. Set up an assignment section in your notebook or in a separate assignment book by following the directions on the previous pages. Use it for a week, and revise it if necessary (for example, you may want to leave more room for writing down assignments, use a red marker to indicate tests or quizzes, and so forth). Answers will vary.

DEVELOPING WRITING SKILLS: Improving Your Study Habits. Write a paragraph describing your efforts to create an efficient study area, schedule study time, and keep an assignment book. Discuss whether you studied more efficiently, completed all your assignments on time, had more or less leisure time, and if you could improve your study habits even more. Paragraphs will vary.

35.2 Developing Your Note-Taking Skills

Taking notes is one of the best ways to remember what you hear and what you read. Note-taking will also help you concentrate better. When you take notes, you must constantly make decisions. As you listen or read, you must decide what infor-

OBJECTIVES

After completing this section, students should be able to

- Organize and maintain their own notebooks.
- Use modified and formal outlines for taking notes.
- Use summaries to record main ideas.

TEACHING

Getting Started

Show students a well-organized three-ring notebook, your own or a student's. Demonstrate how dividers make for easy use and how items can be added or deleted logically. If students defend their typically paper-crammed spiral notebooks, ask for one and demonstrate the difference.

Text Follow Through

Discuss text pages 676–683.

Assign Exercise A, page 678; Exercise B, page 679; Exercise C, page 682; Exercise D, page 683; and Developing Writing Skills, page 683.

Less advanced You may want to deal with this section early in the year. You may, however, want to skip or de-emphasize formal outlining in favor of additional work on modified outlines and summaries. Before assigning Exercise B, you could put the following words in mixed order on the board and have students pick out the main headings, group remaining items, and prepare a modified outline.

35.2 Developing Your Note-Taking Skills

mation is important and what is not. Then, you must write down the important material clearly and quickly.

In this section you will learn how to keep your notes in order by organizing your notebook. You will also learn two methods for taking notes. These are the modified outline and the formal outline.

Keeping an Organized Notebook

A neat, well-organized, and complete notebook is the foundation of all your studies. Your notebook can remind you what went on in class on any particular day. You can also use it to keep track of notes you take while reading or studying at home. A good notebook provides useful material for studying for tests, writing papers, or preparing a class report.

Keep a neat, well-organized, and complete notebook.

TEN STEPS TO A WELL-ORGANIZED NOTEBOOK

1. Use a three-ring looseleaf binder, so you can remove, replace, and rearrange your notes as necessary.
2. Keep a good supply of looseleaf paper in your binder, so you always have enough to take notes.
3. Use dividers to separate each subject in your notebook. (Note: Dividers with pockets in them are very useful for keeping class handouts and tests on that subject which may not be three-hole punched.)
4. Keep all notes on the same subject in the section you have marked for that subject.
5. Label all notes by subject and write the date when they were taken.
6. Rewrite any notes that are messy or hard to read and throw away the messy copy when you are finished.
7. Use gummed reinforcements on any torn pages, so they don't fall out of your notebook.

Dogs: Dachshunds, Cocker Spaniels, Irish Setters, Poodles
Fish: Goldfish, Guppies
Cats: Siamese, Persians, Tabbies, Angoras
Birds: Canaries, Parakeets, Parrots

Average   Using the items above, you could ask students to prepare a formal outline, adding more detailed subcategories covering such information as color and size. Students could also practice writing summaries of articles or of classroom notes and then work in pairs to compare these summaries for clarity and content.

Advanced   You could put students in pairs or trios and ask each group to consult an encyclopedia or other source in order to prepare a single formal outline classifying some kind of animal—dogs, cats, birds, etc. Each group must therefore agree on content and organization. These students, too, may benefit from writing and comparing summaries.

Additional Practice

Practice Pages or Practice Book, page 164

TESTING

Test Program

Unit Pretest, page 111
Chapter Test, page 115
Unit Post-Test, page 123

RE-TEACHING

Practice Pages or Practice Book, page 164

---

8. Keep tests or homework assignments in their subject section. They may be useful for future studying.
9. Include a special section to keep track of homework assignments, or keep a separate assignment book.
10. Place a copy of your class and study schedules on the inside front cover of your notebook for easy reference.

Taking notes is part of the process of learning and remembering, so it is best to take your own notes. However, to keep your notebook complete and up-to-date, be sure to get notes from a classmate if you must miss a class. You can also ask your teacher how to make up what you missed.

Neatness is also important in keeping a good notebook. It allows you to reread what you have written easily and quickly. A neat notebook allows you to concentrate on your studying.

EXERCISE A: Evaluating Your Notebook. Look at your notebook carefully. Then rate it in comparison to the chart on page 677 and above. Give yourself 1 point if you rarely follow the suggestion; 2 points if you sometimes follow it; 3 points if you follow a suggestion often or always. A score of 25 or more means you have a notebook that really works for you. Use your score to guide you to the areas that need improvement.
Answers will vary.

Making Modified Outlines

A *modified outline* is a method of taking notes quickly and easily. It can help you to recall the main points from class or your reading. It can also be used to organize ideas for a short essay or writing assignment. In a modified outline, main points are underlined, and information related to each main point is listed underneath, preceded by numbers or letters.

Use a modified outline to take notes while listening or reading.

THINKING SKILLS

Application—*Preparing* a modified outline using given items (Exercise B, page 679) *Summarizing* information (Exercise D, page 683) *Preparing* a formal outline for the contents of a textbook chapter (Exercise C, page 682)

Synthesis—*Writing* original paragraphs that describe note-taking skills (Developing Writing Skills, page 683)

Evaluation—*Appraising* student's notebook by comparing it to items in a chart (Exercise A, page 678)

35.2 Developing Your Note-Taking Skills

Read the passage and study the modified outline. Notice how the main point is underlined and major details are numbered.

PASSAGE: There are many different parts that make up the human eye. Each part plays a different role, and they all work together to produce the sense of sight.

The iris (the colored part of the eye) acts as a filter to cut out excess light. In the center of the eye is the pupil (the black spot). It is actually a hole, which, like the aperture of a camera, can open wide or close down to vary the amount of light coming in. In bright light the pupil closes down, because enough light can get in through a small opening. When it is dark, the pupil opens wide, to let in more light.

The cornea and the lens help focus light entering the eye. They make an upside-down image on the retina—which is like a screen on which a movie is projected. Nerves transmit this image to the brain, which interprets it.

MODIFIED OUTLINE:
<u>Many parts of human eye</u>   Main idea
1. Iris—colored part, filters out excess light
2. Pupil—black spot (hole) opens wider or closes as more or less light comes in
3. Cornea and lens—help focus   Major Details
   light, project upside-down image on retina
4. Retina—like movie screen, image projected on it; NERVES transmit image to BRAIN, which interprets it

EXERCISE B: Making a Modified Outline. Arrange the following words into three groups, using a modified outline. Decide which three words are the main points and underline them. Then, under the headings, list the words that are related details.

Outlines will vary; main points are underlined.

1. <u>movie</u>	6. cassette deck	11. <u>stereo</u>
2. keyboard	7. projector	12. director
3. speakers	8. modem	13. <u>computer</u>
4. screen	9. receiver	14. turntable
5. disc drive	10. camera	15. monitor

Making Formal Outlines

A *formal outline* is a useful tool for organizing ideas and information for a lengthy report or for taking detailed notes from textbooks that have headings for each section and subsection. A formal outline is more complete and exact than a modified outline and follows strict rules of organization.

Use a formal outline to arrange ideas when preparing major written and oral assignments.

Roman numerals (I, II, III) are used to label main ideas in a formal outline. Major details that support a main point are indented under it and labeled with a capital letter (A, B, C). Minor details that relate to a major detail are further indented and labeled with numbers (1, 2, 3). Subdetails are indented still further and labeled with small letters (a, b, c).

RULES FOR MAKING FORMAL OUTLINES

1. Every level of importance must have at least two items. An outline must have a I. and a II.; an A. must have a B; a I. must have a 2.; and so on.
2. Every new level of information must be indented.
3. All roman numerals should be lined up vertically, all capital letters should line up, and so on.
4. The first word in each item should be capitalized.
5. A period should be placed after each number or letter.

35.2 Developing Your Note-Taking Skills

There are two kinds of formal outlines: *sentence outlines* and *topic outlines*. Both follow the five rules for formal outlines, but in a sentence outline, each piece of information is written as a complete sentence. In a topic outline, each item is written as a word or phrase. In general, topic outlines are more useful for note-taking and organizing your compositions.

Look at the following formal topic outline on the passage about the eye on page 679. This outline is similar to the modified outline on the same passage, but it breaks the information down into more detail and arranges it according to its level of importance. Numbers and letters, as well as indentations, are used to label the bits of information. Which type of outline you choose to use depends on the amount of detail and organization you require in your notes.

The Eye

I. Parts of the Eye
    A. Many different parts of eye
    B. Each plays different role
    C. All work together

II. Iris
    A. Colored part of eye
    B. Acts as filter to cut out excess light

III. Pupil
    A. Black spot (actually a hole)
    B. Acts like aperture of camera
        1. Can open wide or close down to vary amount of light
            a. Closes down in bright light
            b. Opens wide in darkness

IV. Cornea and Lens
    A. Helps focus light that enters eye
    B. Makes an upside-down image on retina
        1. Retina is like projector screen
        2. Nerves transmit this image to brain
            a. Brain interprets image
            b. Tells us what the picture is we see

EXERCISE C: Writing a Formal Outline from a Textbook.
Write a formal outline of the contents of this chapter. Use the section titles that are numbered 35.1 and 35.2 as your main ideas and label them I and II. Then look for major details for each main point and indent them under each heading, labeling them with capital letters. Continue looking for minor details and subdetails, indenting and labeling them according to the rules you have learned in this section.
Outlines will vary.

Writing Summaries

You can also take notes by making summaries. A *summary* is a shortened version of a longer body of information. For example, a summary of a chapter or a lecture might be a few sentences or a paragraph long. A summary includes only main ideas and a few major details, all presented in complete sentences. You can use summaries to help remember information or to gather the information you need for compositions.

Use a summary to take notes when you need to remember only the main ideas.

A summary should be brief, well written, and informative. It should be much shorter than the original, generally not more than a few sentences. You should also write and record only the information mentioned in the original material. Do not add your own opinions or ideas when writing a summary.

STEPS FOR WRITING SUMMARIES

1. Pay attention to the important words and main ideas as you hear or read them.
2. Write down these main ideas and important words.
3. Combine the important information into general statements.
4. Write these statements in sentences, using your own words.
5. Remember not to add any ideas or opinions of your own.

35.2 Developing Your Note-Taking Skills

Summaries are useful in a number of ways. They can be used to gather information in a concise form for study and test preparation. You can also use them when you only want to remember main points or when you cannot take notes, such as at a movie or a play.

EXERCISE D: Writing a Summary. Write a summary of the passage about the eye on page 679. Follow the suggestions on the chart on how to write a good summary.
Summaries will vary.

DEVELOPING WRITING SKILLS: Writing About Your Notebook. Write two or three paragraphs describing the different methods for taking notes you learned in this chapter: modified outlines, formal topic outlines, formal sentence outlines, and summaries. Also comment briefly on the importance of keeping a neat, well-organized, and complete notebook.
Answers will vary.

Developing Writing Skills

Have students practice taking notes and writing summaries by completing the following assignment.

Writing Across the Curriculum

When we watch a political speech on television, it is important for us to be aware of the main ideas and major details that the speaker conveys.

Prewriting Watch a political speech on television. As you are watching the speech, take notes using a modified outline. Make sure that you record each of the main ideas and major details that the speaker conveys.

Writing Using your outline, write a short summary of the speech. Try to make your summary as clear and concise as possible and make sure that you include all of the speaker's main ideas.

Revising Revise your summary, making sure you have not omitted any main ideas or major details. When you have finished revising, proofread your summary and prepare a final copy.

Checking Your Skills

In the Checking Your Skills assignment, your students read about the process through which dead trees turn into petrified wood. Have students explore other natural processes by completing the following assignment.

Speaking and Listening

Have each student choose a natural process, such as photosynthesis, ocean tides, or the creation of soil. If students have difficulty thinking of a natural process on which to focus, you might encourage them to ask their science teacher to offer some suggestions. Next, students should research their topics in the encyclopedia or other reference books. Using the information from their research, students should then prepare an oral report about the topic. Once students have finished preparing their reports, they should deliver their reports to the class; students should be prepared to answer any questions that their classmates may have.

Using Study Skills in Writing

Peer Editing Divide your class into small groups. Then have the members of each group read their summaries to one another and comment on ways in which the summaries could be improved. When listening to their classmates' summaries, the peer editors should focus on whether the writer has clearly and concisely captured the main ideas of the article.

Skills Review and Writing Workshop

Using Basic Study Skills

CHECKING YOUR SKILLS

Take notes on the following passage, using either a modified outline or a formal topic outline.

When most trees die, they simply decay and become part of the soil. Under special conditions, however, a dead tree can turn into stone, or petrified wood.

Wood starts to petrify when buried in sand, mud, or ash from a volcano. The ground water in the area must be rich in minerals. This water seeps down to the tree. Layers of minerals build up in the tree as the water continues to seep into the ground. Finally, completely filled by the dried-up minerals, the tree becomes solid stone.

Petrified wood is a special kind of fossil. Like most fossils, it is very old. Some of the wood in Arizona's Petrified Forest National Park is 150 million years old.

USING STUDY SKILLS IN WRITING
Summarizing a News Article

News reporters and broadcasters often summarize the news for their readers and listeners. Follow the steps below to write a summary of a news article.
Answers will vary.

Prewriting: Read a news article in a newspaper or news magazine, writing down the most important words and ideas as you read.

Writing: Write a summary of the article by combining the important words and ideas into general statements. Use your own words, but be careful not to include your own ideas.

Revising: Read your summary and make sure it is well written, informative, accurate, and brief. Revise it checking grammar, spelling, and punctuation. After you have finished, proofread it.

Chapter **36**

Critical-Thinking Skills

This chapter is designed to help students apply critical-thinking skills to material that they read or listen to. Section 36.1 helps students analyze and evaluate fact and opinion statements to determine whether information is reliable, and to use inference and generalization to draw valid conclusions. Section 36.2 teaches students to analyze language to determine whether it is being used to communicate or distort information.

This chapter teaches thinking skills that students need to learn before they are assigned the Reading Critically section in Chapter 37, and the Listening Skills section in Chapter 39.

For a review of the entire chapter and a related writing activity, see the Skills Review and Writing Workshop on page 692.

When you think critically, you analyze, apply, and evaluate information. You can get this information from reading and listening. This chapter will help you develop skills for thinking in a clear and reasonable way.

Forms of Reasoning 36.1

When you think critically, you first determine if the information you are given is *reliable* or *unreliable* and then if the author's position or argument is *valid* or *invalid*.

Using Fact and Opinion

The first step in thinking critically is to determine whether or not the information you have is *reliable*. Is it based on proven facts, or is it merely someone's unsupported opinion?

Analyze your material to determine whether or not it is based on reliable information.

In order to determine if your material is reliable, you must be able to tell statements of fact from statements of opinion.

685

36.1 Forms of Reasoning
(pp. 685–690)

OBJECTIVES

After completing this section, students should be able to

- Analyze fact and opinion statements to determine whether information is reliable.
- Analyze inferences and generalizations to draw valid conclusions.

TEACHING

Getting Started

Direct students' attention to the definitions of fact and opinion on page 686. Emphasize that facts can be verified, or proved true. Tell students that although opinions cannot be verified, they can be validated, or supported by related facts from authoritative sources. Write the following on the board:

PERSONAL FEELING Workaholics ruin their health.
JUDGMENT Workaholics are people with Type A personalities, whose behavior often leads to heart attacks.
PREDICTION If a person has a Type A personality, he or she will likely die of a heart attack.

Discuss the statements above; if students seem perplexed by the difference between the personal feeling and the judgment statements, ask them which statement can be backed up by going to a factual source such as an encyclopedia. Ask for volunteers to supply other examples of valid opinions for classmates to analyze.

Text Follow Through

Discuss text pages 685–690.

Assign Exercise A, page 687; Exercise B, page 689; and Developing Writing Skills, page 690.

Less advanced Students will need extra help to distinguish between facts and opinions, and between valid opinions and invalid opinions. You may want to have students complete the exercises in this section in

---

Fact. Facts can be *verified,* or proved true. You can verify a statement of fact by personal observation or experimentation; by consulting sources such as a dictionary, encyclopedia, or other reference book; or by consulting an authority.

FACT: President Carter was involved in the signing of a peace treaty between Israel and Egypt.

The statement of fact above can be verified by research on the Carter Administration in newspapers or magazines.

Opinion. Opinions cannot be verified, but they can be *validated,* or supported by related facts from authoritative sources. Opinions may express a person's feelings, judgments, or predictions about a given situation. Remember that opinions may be based on facts, but they are *not* facts.

PERSONAL FEELING: Jimmy Carter was a great President.

JUDGMENT: President Carter's success in the signing of a peace treaty between Israel and Egypt indicates that he was an able negotiator.

PREDICTION: Jimmy Carter will run for President again.

The first statement is a personal feeling without any related facts, so it is an *invalid opinion*. The second statement is a judgment, supported by related facts, so it is a *valid opinion*. The third statement is a prediction and cannot be proved or disproved until the event takes place.

The following chart lists questions you should ask yourself to help you distinguish between fact and opinion statements.

QUESTIONS TO ASK TO TELL FACTS FROM OPINIONS

1. Can the statement of fact be checked to *verify,* or prove that it is true? How? (dictionary, reference book, human authority, personal observation, or experimentation)

2. If the statement cannot be verified as fact, it is opinion. Are there supporting facts to make the opinion *valid*?

36.1 Forms of Reasoning

EXERCISE A: Analyzing Fact and Opinion Statements.

First, identify each of the following statements as *fact* or *opinion*. Then analyze whether each fact statement is *true* or *false,* and give your sources for verification. Then analyze whether each opinion statement is *validated* by supporting facts.

1. Fact/True 4. Fact/True 6. Fact/False

1. Carl is a talented artist who has won three painting prizes.
2. John Steinbeck wrote *Two Gentlemen of Verona*. Fact/False
3. Donna has been training hard all year. She will win first place in the track competition. Opinion (prediction)/Valid
4. William Shakespeare wrote *A Midsummer Night's Dream*.
5. There are nine planets in this solar system. Fact/True
6. Texas has the largest land area of any state in the U.S.
7. Chocolate pudding tastes terrible. Opinion/Invalid
8. My cousin Sarah makes chocolate pudding out of water, flour, instant cocoa, and beef broth. It tastes terrible.
9. The coach said that our school basketball team won all of the home games last season. Opinion/Valid
10. Because his plays and poetry form a respected part of English Literature, William Shakespeare is a famous author.

8. Opinion/Valid 10. Opinion/Valid

Using Inference and Generalization

In order to think critically, you must think logically and reasonably about the information you are examining. When you think logically, you draw valid conclusions from the details of the material you have been given.

Think logically to draw valid conclusions.

Two forms of reasoning that can be used to draw valid conclusions are *inference* and *generalization*. They can also be misused to draw invalid conclusions. Following is a discussion of these two forms of reasoning.

Inference. Sometimes the main idea of what you read or hear is stated directly by the author. More often, this main idea is *implied,* or hinted at. One aspect of critical thinking is the

---

classroom workshop sessions. You may opt to omit Developing Writing Skills with these students.

Average   Have students write ten statements for a partner to identify as fact or opinion, and if opinion, as valid or invalid. Students can then discuss their responses. You might want to post some of the papers as examples for other students.

Advanced   Have students write five generalizations for a partner to identify as valid or hasty. Students can then discuss their responses. You might want to post these papers as examples for other students.

Additional Practice

Practice Pages or Practice Book, page 165

TESTING

Test Program

Unit Pretest, page 112
Chapter Test, page 117
Unit Post-Test, pages 123, 124

RE-TEACHING

Practice Pages or Practice Book, page 165

THINKING SKILLS

Analysis—*Distinguishing* between fact and opinion statements to determine truth or validity (Exercise A, page 687) *Distinguishing* between inferences and generalizations and *identifying* conclusions as valid or invalid (Exercise B, page 689)

Synthesis—*Writing* an original paragraph describing conclusions and the methods used to arrive at them (Developing Writing Skills, page 690) ability to examine details in the writing and to make *inferences* about the main idea. Any conclusions you draw must be based on the details of the information you are given. You can also use inference to predict logically or reasonably what will happen in the future, given specific information.

A *valid inference* is a logical or reasonable conclusion (or prediction) drawn from the information given. An *invalid inference* is an interpretation or statement that does not follow from the information given.

INFORMATION GIVEN: Joey works hard delivering sixty-two papers on his paper route every day.

VALID INFERENCE: Joey probably earns a fair amount of money per week.

INVALID INFERENCE: Someday Joey will be the editor of the newspaper.

The second statement is a *valid inference* because one can draw the conclusion that Joey earns money from the information given—that he works hard at a job. The third statement is an *invalid inference* because the conclusion drawn is not based on the facts given. Just because Joey works hard delivering papers is no indication that he has either the desire or the ability to be the editor of a newspaper someday.

The following chart lists questions to help you draw valid inferences from the materials you are analyzing.

QUESTIONS TO ASK TO DRAW VALID INFERENCES

1. What details give clues to the main idea of the material?
2. What main ideas do you conclude from these details?
3. Does your conclusion follow reasonably from the inferences you have made?
4. Are there other conclusions you could draw from the same details? What are they?

36.1 Forms of Reasoning

Generalization. A *valid generalization* is a conclusion based on a large number of examples, taking into account any exceptions or qualifying factors. A *hasty generalization* is one based on an insufficient number of examples, or one that ignores exceptions or qualifying factors.

VALID: Average height for boys, age twelve, is 149 centimeters; for girls, 152 centimeters. Therefore, at age twelve, most girls are taller than boys.

HASTY: Anita is taller than Larry. Therefore all girls are taller than boys.

The second statement is a *hasty generalization* because it is based on only one example.

The following chart lists questions you can ask yourself to help you make valid generalizations.

QUESTIONS TO ASK TO MAKE VALID GENERALIZATIONS
1. What facts or cases are presented to make the generalization?
2. Will the generalization you make hold true for all or most cases? Are there any exceptions to the statement?
3. Are enough cases given to make a valid generalization?

EXERCISE B: Analyzing Forms of Reasoning. Identify whether *inference* or *generalization* is used in each of the following statements. State if each conclusion is *valid* or *invalid*.

1. Jo plays the piano well; she will become a concert pianist.
2. We should travel on foot more often to lower the accident rate. Generalization/Invalid
3. My father's car got stuck in the snow twice last winter, so people should not drive during snowy weather. Generalization/Invalid
4. Seat belts save lives, so all drivers should wear them.
5. Since Governor DeLeo was elected the state population has declined. Therefore, the governor should not be reelected.

1. Inference/Invalid   4. Generalization/Invalid   5. Inference/Invalid

36.2 Language and Thinking

(pp. 690–691)

OBJECTIVES

After completing this section, students should be able to

• Analyze language for its use of denotation, connotation, and jargon.

• Use language so that it communicates honestly, simply, and directly.

TEACHING

Getting Started

Direct students' attention to the explanation of denotation and connotation on pages 690–691. Write the following on the chalkboard:

DENOTATION She plays the violin for the senior citizens' enjoyment.

CONNOTATION She scratches on that old fiddle while the old folks giggle.

Discuss how each statement uses words, one in a neutral tone and the other in a negative tone. Have volunteers point out words with negative connotations and explain why they cause a negative reaction. Volunteers may suggest other pairs of sentences for classmates to identify as the use of denotation or connotation. Continue in this way to review the use of jargon.

Text Follow Through

Discuss text pages 690–691.

Assign the Exercise, page 691, and Developing Writing Skills, page 691.

Less advanced Students will benefit from additional practice in analyzing the uses of denotation and connotation. Provide

DEVELOPING WRITING SKILLS: Analyzing Writing. Analyze all statements of *fact* and *opinion* in the following passage and explain whether they can be verified or validated. Then, make *inferences* and *generalizations.* Write a paragraph about the conclusions you have drawn and the methods you used. Answers will vary.

Americans became aware of the huge toxic waste problem in about 1980. At that time the Surgeon General declared "an environmental emergency." The Environmental Protection Agency called it "a ticking time bomb primed to go off." Over the years poisonous chemicals had been stored in steel drums and buried underground in every state in the country. Today those drums have begun to corrode and leak their contents into the ground. This leakage presents a most serious threat to America's water supplies. Moreover, it is the most dangerous public health problem to strike the nation in years.

36.2 Language and Thinking

People think mostly by using language. We express thoughts to ourselves and explain them to other people in words. We also use words to help us express our feelings to one another. Critical thinking includes analyzing how words are used to express thoughts and feelings. This can help us evaluate an author's or speaker's purpose.

Uses of Language

Thinking critically involves understanding what language is being used for. Words can be used to communicate information honestly or to distort it in order to manipulate people.

Learn to identify different uses of language.

Word Meanings. Words can be used in a *denotative* manner, in which they present facts or describe a situation objectively in a neutral tone. Words can also be used in a *connotative* manner, in which they imply a particular point of view and convey a positive or negative tone. The connotations of words can affect a person emotionally and thus cause a particular response to the material.

DENOTATION: The novel contains a lot of descriptive language.

CONNOTATION: The book is loaded with flowery language.

The first statement uses words in a denotative manner, describing the book in a neutral tone. The second statement uses words to imply that one would not enjoy reading the book.

Jargon. Jargon is the use of words with specialized meanings in a particular trade or profession. Jargon is meant to have precise meaning, but it is often used to obscure ideas that anyone could understand if they were stated simply and directly.

JARGON: Student dialoguing facilitates idea networking.

DIRECT LANGUAGE: It is helpful for students to share ideas.

EXERCISE: Analyzing Uses of Language. Analyze each pair of sentences below for uses of *denotation/connotation*, and *jargon/clear language*.

1. Denotation/Connotation   3. Connotation/Denotation

1. The girl wore a pink and yellow dress.
   The young girl was dressed in shades of rose and lemon.
2. Declining sales made a negative impact on our base line. Jargon
   Lower sales have caused us to lose money. Direct language
3. The Senator's petty questioning dragged on interminably.
   The Senator's interrogation lasted for two hours.
4. At preschool, children interface with their peer group.
   At preschool, children play with their classmates.
5. The candy has a cloying, sickeningly sweet taste. Connotation
   The candy has an overly sweet flavor. Denotation

4. Jargon/Direct Language

DEVELOPING WRITING SKILLS: Using Critical-Thinking Skills in Writing. Rewrite the passage from Developing Writing Skills on page 690 to communicate honestly and directly.
Answers will vary.

691

pairs of words such as the following, and ask students to identify the word whose connotation is negative. Then have students use each word in a sentence.

1. dog, mongrel
2. janitor, custodian
3. slim, skinny
4. uninhabited, desolate
5. morose, unsmiling

Complete Exercise and Developing Writing Skills in classroom workshop sessions.

Average Students should be able to complete the exercises in this section without any difficulty. You might want to have students share their work in Developing Writing Skills for classmates to analyze. With these students, too, additional practice in identifying connotative uses is valuable. Provide words in groups of three: one neutral, one negative, and one positive. Ask students to label each, then use each in the same sentence to give a different emotional feel.

1. peddler, salesman, field representative
2. plump, overweight, fat
3. small, petite, undersized
4. trash, waste, disposed units
5. stern, mean, disciplined

Advanced Have students bring to class editorials in which they have highlighted the uses of denotation, connotation, and jargon. They can then read the editorials to classmates for them to identify the uses of language.

Additional Practice

Practice Pages or Practice Book, page 166

(continued on page 692)

Checking Your Skills

In the Checking Your Skills assignment, students used their critical-thinking skills to examine a piece of writing. To provide your students with additional practice in using their critical-thinking skills in reading, have them complete the following assignment.

Critical Thinking

Have students find an interesting editorial in a local newspaper. Then have them critically examine the article, making sure that the writer has supported each of his or her opinions and generalizations. The students should also note any examples of denotation, connotation, and jargon. When students have finished examining the article, they should write a short summary of their findings.

36.2 cont'd
TESTING

Test Program

  Unit Pretest, page 112
  Chapter Test, page 117
  Unit Post-Test, pages 123, 124

RE-TEACHING

Practice Pages or Practice Book, page 166

THINKING SKILLS

Analysis—*Pointing out* the uses of denotation, connotation, and jargon in sentences (Exercise, page 691)

Synthesis—*Rewriting* a passage so it communicates honestly and simply (Developing Writing Skills, page 691)

Skills Review and Writing Workshop

Critical-Thinking Skills
CHECKING YOUR SKILLS

Read the following paragraph and make lists of the following: facts, opinions, denotation, connotation, and jargon. Use inference and generalization to draw conclusions and write a sentence or two describing its main idea. Explain whether the information presented is reliable and the reasoning in it is valid.
Answers will vary.

Jimmy Connors will be viewed in years to come as the best tennis player of his generation. Connors was one of the first professional tennis players to use a two-handed backhand. This, together with his left-handedness, has made him a tough man to beat. In addition, his hard-hitting style and outstanding return of serve have enabled him to win numerous tournaments. He was champion of Wimbledon twice and the U.S. Open four times. As one of Connor's fans once said, "Some like McEnroe. Some liked Borg. But it's always been Connors for me. Even in the days of his quick temper and outlandish outbursts, Jimmy has always been Number One!"

USING CRITICAL-THINKING SKILLS IN WRITING
Writing an Editorial

Follow the steps below to write an editorial that uses honest thinking and valid reasoning to persuade readers about your point of view.
Answers will vary.

Prewriting. Choose and issue you feel strongly about and state your opinion. Then list several facts to support your opinion.

Writing. Begin by stating the main facts and showing how they support your opinion. Then discuss how the facts relate to opposing points of view. Write a strong conclusion.

Revising. Rework the editorial to eliminate unsupported opinions, invalid arguments, and inappropriate use of language. After you have revised, proofread carefully.

Chapter 37

Reading and Test-Taking Skills

Different types of reading material require different reading skills. This chapter will help you develop skills that are useful when you read textbooks. In this chapter you will also develop your ability to prepare for tests confidently and to take tests successfully.

Developing Your Reading Skills 37.1

Knowing how to read well is important to your success in school and in life. Learning special reading skills to use in different situations can help you improve as a student.

Examining Textbooks

Most textbooks have special features to help you get the most out of your reading and study time. You should become familiar with these features.

Identify and make use of the special sections at the front and back of your textbooks.

This chapter is designed to help students improve their textbook-reading skills and their test-taking skills. Section 37.1 treats both literal-level reading skills and higher-level critical reading skills. Section 37.2 covers strategies students can use as they prepare for and take objective tests.

It is advisable to assign this chapter early in the school year so that you can monitor students' progress in the use of the reading and test-taking skills during the year. Before students begin work with Reading Critically in Section 37.1, they need to study Chapter 36, Critical-Thinking Skills, to give them a foundation for the reading section.

For a review of the entire chapter and a related writing activity, see the Skills Review and Writing Workshop on page 711.

37.1 Developing Your Reading Skills
(pp. 693–705)

OBJECTIVES

After completing this section, students should be able to

- Use the special sections of their textbooks.
- Use the organization of a textbook to study more effectively.
- Use different reading styles—phrase reading, skimming, and scanning—for specific purposes.

• Read critically in order to distinguish between fact and opinion; make valid and invalid inferences; recognize an author's attitude by examining connotative and denotative uses of language.

TEACHING

Getting Started

Explain to students that their school work will be easier if they understand the resources and organization of their textbooks. Guide students through an examination of this book, first reviewing or discussing the purpose of the various parts, then analyzing chapter organization, including the use of headings and subheads and the treatment of rules.

Text Follow Through

Discuss text pages 693–705.

Assign Exercise A, page 696; Exercise B, page 698; Exercise C, page 700; Exercise D, page 700; Exercise E, page 704; and Developing Writing Skills, page 705.

Less advanced This chapter, covered early in the year, may help your students off to a good start. For Exercise A, which asks students to examine textbooks, you might group those students that take the same courses. You could also guide students through the suggestions on pages 697–698 as you cover the first substantive section of this textbook. If your students are not taking reading as a separate course, you may want to ask the reading teacher for materials students could use to practice the various reading styles.

Most textbooks have some or all of the following special features: a table of contents, a preface or an introduction, an index, a glossary, an appendix, and a bibliography.

The special features of a textbook are meant to be used. Once you have examined your textbook to find out what kind of special features it offers, you will want to use those features to help you in your studying and reading of the textbook. Descriptions of the special features found in most textbooks follow. Included are the location of the features in textbooks, what they contain, and some suggestions on how to use them.

Table of Contents. Located at the front of the textbook, the table of contents lists the sections and chapters of the book in order and the pages on which each section begins. It can be used to help you locate general information or a particular section.

Read through the table of contents when you first receive a textbook to get an overview of what it covers. You can also use the table of contents to test yourself at the end of a chapter by looking at the listings and seeing how much detail you can remember about each section.

Preface or Introduction. The preface or introduction is also located at the beginning of the book. It states the author's purpose, format, and use of the textbook's special features.

Read this when you first get your textbook to become familiar with its contents.

Index. The index is at the back of the book. It lists all the subjects covered in the book in alphabetical order, and tells on which page they can be found.

Use the index to find all the references to a particular topic in the entire textbook or to help you find one particular entry on that topic.

Glossary. You will find the glossary at the back of the book. It lists and defines a number of words or special terms that are used in the textbook.

Reading the glossary first will help you understand the terms as they come up in your reading. Also, if you run across a term

37.1 Developing Your Reading Skills

you do not understand or do not remember while you are reading, you can flip to the glossary in the back of the book and look it up.

Appendix. If the textbook has an appendix it will be located at the back of the textbook. An appendix may contain information such as documents, charts, graphs, maps, and essays. The author has included this material because he or she thinks it will be helpful to students. The material supports and amplifies the material in the book itself.

Use the additional information contained in an appendix to save time. Otherwise you would have to look for outside reference books and materials on your subject.

Bibliography. A bibliography may be located at the back of the textbook. Sometimes, however, a bibliography may appear at the end of each chapter or unit of the book. A bibliography is a list of books, pamphlets, magazines, and other publications and reference materials. In some books the bibliography is made up of a list of materials that the author recommends for you to read for more information on the subject.

If you have questions on the material you are studying that are not answered in your textbook or if you want to write an in-depth report, use the bibliography to find additional material to read and study.

Other features of your textbooks can also help you in your studying. *Chapter titles, headings,* and *subheadings* are usually printed in large, bold, heavy, or colored type. Headings divide each chapter into smaller, easier-to-read sections and give you an overview of what that section will cover.

You can skim through the chapter reading only headings and subheadings to help you locate, preview, or review the material. Also, as you read, you can turn each heading into a question and then read the following material to answer the question. This helps you remember what you read.

At the end of each chapter or section, there are usually *questions* and *exercises.* They are designed to help you test your knowledge and skills.

Average These students, too, may benefit from your guidance with the suggestions on pages 697–698 as they cover a unit. You could also give additional practice with the three types of reading. For example, you could ask students comprehension questions that require a close reading of, say, a short story; allow students a few minutes to skim their notes before one of your tests; and ask them to scan a newspaper article for specified information.

Advanced You may want to move through the first two subsections quickly, but since some advanced students over-read and some rely too much on skimming, you should probably work with reading styles, having students practice in various situations as described above.

Additional Practice

Practice Pages or Practice Book, pages, 167, 168

TESTING

Test Program

Unit Pretest, page 112
Chapter Test, pages 118, 119
Unit Post-Test, pages 124, 125

RE-TEACHING

Practice Pages or Practice Book, pages 167, 168

THINKING SKILLS

Knowledge—*Identifying* reading styles (Exercise C, page 700)

Comprehension—*Distinguishing* reading styles (Exercise D, page 700)

Application—*Demonstrating* ability to use the special features of a textbook by answering questions about those features (Exercise A, page 696)

Using a set of suggestions for studying a textbook chapter and *showing* three ways in which the suggestions were helpful (Exercise B, page 698)

Using a set of questions to apply critical-reading skills to a newspaper or magazine article (Exercise E, page 704)

Synthesis—*Writing* a paragraph evaluating reading skills by answering a set of questions (Developing Writing Skills, page 705)

You can glance at the questions and exercises before reading the chapter itself to see what you are expected to master by the end of it. When you finish reading, use them to see how much you remember and how well you can use your new skills.

Pictures and *captions* are often located throughout the book. Pictures may be artwork, photographs, maps, diagrams, charts, graphs, or any visual image. The captions explain the meaning or use of the pictures in words. Pictures are used to illustrate or to add information to the text in which they are found. They can help you focus what you have read into a single image in your mind, making the knowledge easier to remember.

You can flip through a chapter looking only at pictures and captions and see how much you remember of what you have read by asking yourself questions such as What is this picture here for? What does it illustrate or explain?

The aim of each chapter is usually presented in a *chapter introduction*. It is useful to help guide and focus your attention while reading the chapter.

Chapter summaries may be located at the end of each chapter. A summary is a brief review of the main ideas and major details of the entire chapter. Use summaries to check your knowledge. If something mentioned in the summary is vague or unclear to you, go back and reread the section on that topic in detail.

EXERCISE A: Examining Your Textbooks. Examine one of your textbooks to become acquainted with its special sections. Answer the following questions about the book.
Answers will vary.

1. According to the table of contents, how many units and chapters does the text have? Are chapters divided into smaller sections in the table of contents? What additional facts can you learn from the table of contents?

2. If there is a preface, what does it contain?

3. What are two specific pieces of information you can learn from the index?
4. Does the text have a glossary? If so, what are two pieces of information you can learn from it?
5. Does the text have an appendix? If so, what kind of information does it contain?

Using Textbooks to Study

Once you are familiar with the features of your textbook, you will want to use its organization to help you study. Most texts use *titles, headings, subheadings,* and other devices to help make your studying easier.

Use the organization of your textbooks to help you study them effectively.

The suggestions in the following chart can guide you in this task.

SUGGESTIONS FOR STUDYING TEXTBOOKS

1. *Think* about the assignment or about why you are reading the textbook. Remember reasons such as class discussions or tests for which you will need the information in your textbook. You will remember more if you are aware of what and why you want to learn.
2. *Preview* the material you want to cover. Skim through the chapter and decide what you will read at one sitting. Take note of chapter headings and subheadings, words printed in boldface or in color, pictures and captions, and so on. These will give you clues as to what is important in the chapter.
3. *Read* through the material with close attention. Set yourself a time limit (minimum one-half hour; maximum one hour) and do not be distracted. Say "I will read for 45 minutes, and during that time I will not think about anything else." This will help you focus your attention on the immediate goal of completing the reading.

4. Make *questions* out of what you are reading. When you reach a chapter heading or subheading, turn it into a question. Then read the paragraph beneath it to answer the question. For example, if you reach a boldface heading, **Parts of the Eye,** ask yourself the question, "What are the parts of the eye?" Then read the paragraph to answer your question.

5. Take *notes* on what you are reading. As you think about your assignment and ask yourself questions, take notes on the main ideas and major details of what you are reading. The action of note-taking itself helps you remember what you have read. You can also review the notes later to refresh your memory before writing a paper or taking a test.

6. *Recite* important sections of the textbook or the notes you have taken out loud. Hearing the information in this way will help to fix it in your mind.

7. *Review* your notes at the end of your reading period. Check what you have learned. You may wish to skim through the material once more to make sure you haven't skipped anything important. This immediate review will help you when you use the notes again at a later date. If you wait too long to review your notes, they may seem unfamiliar to you and be less useful than they could be.

EXERCISE B: Using a Textbook Effectively. Choose a chapter from one of your textbooks or use a chapter that has been assigned to you. Follow the suggestions in the chart on page 697 and above to study the chapter. Then list three ways in which the suggestions helped you to study the chapter effectively.

Answers will vary.

Using Different Reading Styles

Knowing what style of reading to use for different purposes is an important skill. For example, you do not read a magazine the same way you read a poem or read a comic book the same

37.1 Developing Your Reading Skills

way you read a cookbook. A textbook should be read in yet other ways.

Learn to choose the style of reading suitable to your purpose and material.

The three reading styles discussed in this section are *phrase reading, scanning,* and *skimming.*

Phrase Reading. Use phrase reading when you are reading information in detail for the first time. In phrase reading, your eyes carefully take in small groups of words at a time. The individual words become part of larger groups of words. This allows you to read more quickly and to understand the material you are reading better.

Words have more meaning in groups, so your understanding as well as your reading speed will increase when you use phrase reading. Look at the following sentence. It has been divided into phrases for easier reading.

EXAMPLE: During the Middle Ages/ /gruesome epidemics/ / swept across the earth.

Reading this sentence in phrases takes only three eye stops, whereas reading each word by itself would take ten stops. Also, reading phrases makes the meaning of the sentence clear much faster.

Skimming. Use skimming to preview material that you are about to read carefully or to review material that you have already read. In skimming, your eyes skip over many words, stopping only at key words or phrases. You should move through the material rapidly, looking only for a general idea of what the material contains.

You can skim through material a few minutes before class to refresh your memory about important points or questions you want to discuss. You can skim through a textbook to gain essential information that will help you focus your attention when you read it closely. You can skim through an article in a magazine to see if it contains the information you require. If you wish to go more deeply into the material you are skimming, use phrase reading.

Scanning. In scanning you read even less material than in skimming. All you do is run your eyes over the page in search of a single piece of information. Use scanning to review, to do research work, or to find references to one specific topic, idea, statistic, fact, or date.

Scanning is very useful when you are looking for details you cannot remember when studying for a test or writing an essay. You can scan a history book for the date of the invention of the printing press, a science book for facts about the digestive system, or a work of literature for all references to one specific character or theme. When you find the material you are looking for, use phrase reading to take it in.

EXERCISE C: Identifying Different Reading Styles. Identify the reading style of each of the following items as *phrase reading, skimming,* or *scanning*.

1. Gives general idea of what material is about skimming
2. Read groups of words without leaving any out phrase reading
3. Requires least amount of actual reading scanning
4. Stop only at key words or phrases scanning
5. Use to read material completely phrase reading
6. Stop only when you find the one piece of information you were looking for scanning
7. Use to read material in detail for the first time phrase reading
8. Use to preview or review material you have already read closely skimming
9. Increases both reading speed and comprehension phrase reading
10. Use to search for a specific fact, date, or statistic scanning

EXERCISE D: Choosing a Reading Style. Write the reading style (phrase reading, skimming, or scanning) that is most suited to each of the reading situations on the following page.

37.1 Developing Your Reading Skills

1. Reading and taking notes on a chapter in a textbook
2. Looking through a magazine article to see if it interests you
3. Looking over your notes before a class discussion skimming
4. Reading a novel for pleasure phrase reading
5. Looking up a specific word in a dictionary scanning

1. phrase reading   2. skimming

Reading Critically

The first step in reading is to understand and remember the main ideas and major details of what you read. The second step is to read critically to understand the material more fully. When you read critically, you ask yourself questions so that you can analyze and evaluate what you read.

Read critically in order to question, analyze, and evaluate what you read.

Reading critically is really thinking critically because you must think logically about what you are reading. A full discussion of critical thinking is found in Chapter 36.

The following chart describes the five main skills you need to be able to read critically.

CRITICAL-READING SKILLS

1. Understanding the difference between statements of *fact* and statements of *opinion*
2. Making *inferences* from the material presented to come to a conclusion about the main idea in the writing
3. Recognizing the *tone* the author uses in writing and noticing how it gives clues to the author's purpose
4. Recognizing any *persuasive techniques* used and what effects they have

Fact and Opinion. After you have read to get a basic grasp of the material, you need to read critically to tell factual statements from opinion statements. You can *verify* a statement of fact, or prove it to be true, by written or human authority, direct personal observation, or experimentation.

The chart below gives examples of statements given as fact and the sources to verify them.

Fact Statement	Sources to Verify
It takes the earth 24 hours to make one revolution on its axis. (True)	Science textbook, personal observation, encyclopedia
Jessamyn West is the author of *The Friendly Persuasion*. (True)	Library, biographical dictionary
The term of the President of the United States is five years. (False)	Social studies textbook, encyclopedia

You cannot prove a statement of opinion to be true. However, you can *validate* it, or find material that supports it, such as related facts or an authoritative source. The chart below gives examples of valid and invalid opinion and sources to validate.

Opinion Statement	Sources to Validate
Research scientists believe nuclear fallout causes cancer as reported in the *Journal of the American Medical Association*. (Valid opinion)	This opinion has been validated by authoritative sources.
Nuclear fallout causes cancer. (Invalid opinion)	This opinion is not validated by facts or authority.

Inference. Sometimes an author states exactly what he or she means in direct language. More often, however, ideas are not stated directly. In this case, you must uncover the meaning. You must act like a detective to observe clues and draw logical conclusions from the material that is presented. This is called making *inferences*. An inference is valid if it is supported by information in the material you are working with. Below are examples of inferences drawn from the same information.

INFORMATION GIVEN: The teacher asked Tim to help correct math tests for the younger students.

VALID INFERENCE: The teacher asked Tim to help correct math tests, so Tim probably gets good grades in math and does careful work.

INVALID INFERENCE: The teacher asked Tim to help correct math tests, so Tim should be the class treasurer.

To infer that Tim is interested in being class treasurer or popular enough to be elected does not follow from the information given. The information given implies only that he is good in math and does careful work.

Denotation and Connotation. An author chooses words to reveal a particular attitude toward the subject. The author's attitude toward the subject affects your response to each.

STATEMENT ONE: The student sat in his desk and looked out the window.

STATEMENT TWO: The lazy student slouched in his desk and stared out the window.

Statement one above presents a neutral attitude toward the subject. The author uses words *(sat, looked)* that have a *denotative,* or literal meaning, to describe the boy in his desk. Statement two presents a negative attitude toward the subject. The author uses emotional words *(lazy, slouched, stared)* that have a *connotative,* or implied meaning, to describe the boy in a negative way.

Persuasive Techniques. An author can use the connotative effect of words to make you think or feel a certain way about a subject. Politicians and advertisers, in particular, use words in this way to convince you that their policies are right or to sell you their product. Since a skilled writer can bend the truth to fit his or her purpose, it is important to read critically to recognize the persuasive techniques being used.

Two common persuasive techniques are *jargon* and *slanting*.

Jargon is language that seems to be technical or scientific but is really vague and confusing. Below are examples of sentences that contain the same information but said in two different ways.

JARGON: The conflict at the border rendered the enemy installation inoperative.

DIRECT LANGUAGE: The border war destroyed the enemy camp.

Slanting is the use of loaded or prejudiced words that have strong connotations to the reader. An author may use loaded words to slant facts in such a way as to support his or her point of view. Slanting can be used to persuade the reader to make conclusions based on emotion rather than reason.

SLANTING: The Secretary of State brushed rudely past the group of faithful supporters.

OBJECTIVE LANGUAGE: The Secretary of State walked quickly past the group of people.

EXERCISE E: Applying Critical-Reading Skills. Look in a newspaper or a magazine and find an article that interests you. Answer the following questions, using that article as your source.
Answers will vary.

  1. Find one statement of fact and one statement of opinion. Note if each statement is verified or validated.

2. What inferences or conclusions did you draw about the main idea or ideas of the article?

3. What was the author's attitude toward the subject matter? List examples of sentences that contain words with a connotative meaning.

4. Did the author use any persuasive techniques, such as jargon or slanting? If so, quote them and rewrite them in direct language.

5. What is the author's purpose in writing? Use the answers to the four questions above to help you come to your conclusion.

DEVELOPING WRITING SKILLS: Evaluating Your Reading Skills. After a week of practice, write a paragraph about your reading skills. Include the answers to the following questions.

Answers will vary.

1. Have you been using the special sections of your textbooks?

2. Which of the suggestions for studying textbooks have you found most helpful?

3. What have you read recently that required you to use critical-reading skills?

4. What were some of the critical-reading questions that you asked to help you analyze and evaluate what you read?

5. What do you need to focus on in the future to improve your reading skills?

Taking Tests 37.2

Students are often nervous at the prospect of taking tests. If you practice the suggestions and exercises in this chapter, you will gain confidence about taking tests. To improve your performance on tests, you must prepare properly for the tests, budget your time during the test, and master the different kinds of questions found in tests.

Developing Writing Skills

Writing Across the Curriculum

Encourage your students to read books and articles that focus on other content areas, such as current events, history, science, sports, and music. For example, students might read articles in a variety of magazines, including *Time, Rolling Stone, Science Digest,* and *Sports Illustrated.* From their reading, students should develop a file of potential writing topics. They can then look through this file whenever they must come up with their own topic for a writing assignment.

37.2 Taking Tests
(pp. 705–710)

OBJECTIVES

After completing this section, students should be able to

- Prepare effectively for a test.
- Budget their time while taking a test.
- Proofread their test answers.
- Evaluate their test-taking skills.

TEACHING

Getting Started

Ask students how they feel when a test is announced and when they are actually confronted with it. Also ask them precisely what they do when the test is distributed. Explain that the dislike and nervousness they feel can be reduced if they both prepare effectively before the test and use their time well during it.

Text Follow Through

Discuss text pages 705–710.

Assign Exercise A, page 707; Exercise B, page 710; and Developing Writing Skills, page 710.

Less advanced Students will probably benefit from careful work on this section. You might want to guide them through the process using a test of your own on a reading project. Use class time to monitor students' first review and assign a second review for homework. Then cue students as they take the test, using the chart on pages 708–709.

Average Again you could use one of your own tests as application practice, allowing students to use the chart on pages 708–709 as they work. You can then circulate to guide those who seem to need help.

Advanced Students probably use the suggestions in this section intuitively, but you may want to cover it briefly anyway, with the specific purpose of helping to relax those who overstudy or who suffer too much test tension.

Preparing for Tests

Preparation is the most important part of test-taking. Be sure to set aside enough time to study for a test for several days beforehand. Effective studying for a test requires time, organization, and concentration.

Schedule time for several days before a test in order to prepare for it.

To use your test preparation time wisely, you must be well organized. Schedule the time for test preparation on your regular study schedule. This ensures that you will have enough time to review and memorize all the material you need to know for the test.

The first thing you should do to prepare for a test is to find out what material the test will cover. It will also be helpful to know what sorts of questions it will have. This will help you direct your studying. It will also take away some of the nervousness about not knowing what the test will be or what will be on it.

Next, review any class or reading notes that relate to what you are going to be tested on. This aspect of test preparation actually begins much earlier. You should review your notes three times altogether: once on the day you take them, once a few days later, and once the night before a test.

Checking your knowledge is also important. Make up questions on the material you will be tested on and write out the answers. Any weak spots will show you where you need to do additional studying. It is useful to work with a friend on this. You can make up questions for each other, and if one of you knows more on the subject, that one can help the other learn what he or she does not know.

Memorize material by going over it repeatedly for several days before the test. This helps to fix it in your mind. Have someone quiz you on the material to make sure that you know it and to test yourself before the actual test.

Additional Practice
Practice Pages or Practice
Book, page 169

37.2 Taking Tests

Memorization techniques can be very useful. You can use rhymes, acronyms, or sentences to help you remember information you will need. An acronym is a word formed from the first letter (or few letters) of a series of words. One example of a technique to help you remember the colors of the spectrum is *ROY G. BIV,* which is an acronym of the colors of the spectrum in order: Red, Orange, Yellow, Green, Blue, Indigo, Violet.

Doing all your studying at the last minute, which is called *cramming*, is not a useful method of preparing for a test. It will leave you tense, tired, and confused. This can hurt your test performance a lot. You should be relaxed and rested when you sit down to take a test. Also, if you cram, the test will not really be a measurement of *your* knowledge. Instead, it will test only your short-term memory. Most likely, if you cram, you will forget whatever you did manage to remember within the next few days, and it will be of no long-term value to you.

Test preparation is the last part of your studying. If you practice all your other study skills diligently and make an effort to be active in class, preparing for tests will be much easier. You will be building on work you have already done, rather than trying to memorize information you never really learned.

EXERCISE A: Checking Your Knowledge About How to Prepare for Tests. Write a short answer for each of the following questions. Answers will vary; samples are given.

1. Find out what material and what kinds of questions the test will include   2. on

1. What do you do to help reduce nervousness and direct your studying for a test?
2. When should you schedule time to study for a test?
3. How do you check whether or not you have learned something while preparing for a test?
4. How do you memorize material for a test?
5. Which memory technique do you use?
6. Why is cramming not a useful method for preparing for a test? It will leave you tense, tired, and confused

several days before a test   3. make up questions about the material and try to answer them   4. go over it repeatedly for several days; use rhymes acronyms and sentences

TESTING

Test Program

Unit Pretest, page 113
Chapter Test, page 119
Unit Post-Test, page 125

RE-TEACHING

Practice Pages or Practice
Book, page 169

THINKING SKILLS

Knowledge—*Describing* test-preparation skills (Exercise A, page 707)

Synthesis—*Writing* a paragraph about how to improve test-taking skills (Developing Writing Skills, page 710)

Evaluation—*Appraising* test-taking skills by answering questions about a recent test (Exercise B, page 710)

Taking Objective Tests

There are three steps you should follow in taking an objective test. The first step is to look over the test to get an overview of its content and format. The second is to answer the questions. The third step is to proofread your work to make sure you have not made any careless mistakes. Budget the time during your test period so you can do each of these steps well.

Budget your time among looking over the test, answering the questions, and proofreading.

Arrive at the test on time or early, if possible. This will help cut down on any nervousness you may feel. Arriving on time or early will also help you be mentally ready to take the test.

Be sure to bring a watch, pens, pencils, erasers, and paper with you. If you have been instructed to bring any books or other materials with you, be sure to do so. Sit down, arrange your things, and wait for the test to be handed out.

Looking over the test and proofreading should take no more than 15 percent to 25 percent of your time. You will want to allow most of your time for answering the questions.

Once you receive the test and are told to begin, start looking over the test immediately.

The following chart lists steps you may follow when you look over an objective test.

STEPS FOR LOOKING OVER A TEST

1. Put your name on each sheet of paper you will hand in.
2. Skim through the entire test to get an overview of the arrangement of the test and the types of questions you will have to answer.
3. Decide how much time to spend answering the questions in each section of the test. Make a small mark next to the most difficult questions and those that are worth the most points. Allow the most time for answering those questions.

After you have looked over the entire test and have decided how you are going to work on it, begin to answer the questions.

ANSWERING QUESTIONS ON A TEST

1. If you are allowed to use clean scratch paper, begin by writing down any notes or information that will be useful to you in answering questions on the test. Use the scratch paper freely for making outlines, calculations, and so on.
2. Answer all the easy questions first. This leaves the bulk of your time for tackling the difficult questions. Put a mark beside difficult questions that you will want to come back to later.
3. Get to work on the tough questions. Concentrate on one question at a time. If you have difficulty remembering certain information, try to relax your mind and see if it comes back to you. If it does not, answer the question to the best of your ability and move on. If the material comes to you later, you can go back to that question.
4. Be sure to follow the directions carefully and completely.

Once you have answered all the questions, take a few minutes to go over your work and proofread it. This allows you to catch and correct any careless mistakes you may have made out of nervousness or rushing. It also permits you to double-check that you have answered all the questions and followed all the directions completely.

PROOFREADING TEST ANSWERS

1. Check to see that your name is on each sheet of paper used.
2. Make sure you have followed the directions accurately and completely and that you have answered all the questions.
3. Read all the test questions and your answers. Correct any errors and add any answers you were not sure of before.

EXERCISE B: Evaluating Your Test-Taking Skills. Give short answers to the following questions about a test you have taken recently.

Answers will vary.

1. Did you give yourself enough time to study beforehand?
2. How could you have improved your test score by better use of your study time?
3. Did you come on time or early?
4. Did you bring all the materials you needed with you?
5. Did you look the test over carefully?
6. Did you make marks next to the hard questions so that you could come back to them later?
7. Did you answer all the easy questions first?
8. Did you allow enough time for difficult questions or for questions that were worth more points?
9. Did you proofread carefully, catching all mistakes and making sure you answered all the questions?
10. Did you miss any questions or give wrong answers you could have corrected if you had proofread it more thoroughly?

DEVELOPING WRITING SKILLS: Evaluating Your Test-Taking Skills. Write a brief paragraph about how you can strengthen your test-taking skills. Use your answers to the questions above to help you guide your evaluation of previous test performance and how it could be improved.

Answers will vary.

Skills Review and Writing Workshop

Reading and Test-Taking Skills

CHECKING YOUR SKILLS

Read the following paragraph, first by skimming and then by phrase reading. Then write the main idea or ideas and the major details of the paragraph.

Main idea is shaded; major details are underlined.

When the subway was first proposed to be built under Manhattan in the 1890's, most New Yorkers did not consider it practical. Their reason was that most of Manhattan island is composed of granite. Critics said that the effects of tunneling through this rock would be disastrous. Property owners claimed that their buildings would collapse. Protests came from city water board members who claimed that construction would destroy underground water pipes. However, the first subway was completed without mishap in 1904. Three miles of track were laid. Today the New York City subway system extends much farther—about 230 miles. In 1973 two subway buffs decided to set a record by riding all 230 miles, just as a British rider had done in the London subway. The two New York subway riders visited 462 stations altogether.

USING STUDY SKILLS IN WRITING

Making Up an Objective Test

Follow the steps below, using a social studies, literature, or science textbook chapter to make up your test.

Answers will vary.

Prewriting: Read the material in the chapter, using the skimming and phrase reading. Take detailed notes on the main ideas and major details.

Writing: Write your test questions, using the main ideas and major details. Use many types of questions: fill-in, multiple-choice, and short answer. Word each question clearly.

Revising: Imagine that you are taking the test by answering each question. Rewrite unclear questions. Proofread carefully.

Checking Your Skills

In the Checking Your Skills assignment, students used skimming and phrase reading to grasp the main ideas and major details in a paragraph. To provide your students with additional practice in using different reading styles, have them complete the following assignment.

Collaborative Learning

Have each student scan a single encyclopedia volume to find articles that interest them. Whenever they find an interesting article, they should phrase read the article. Using information from the article, students should form a question that can be answered with a single word or phrase. Once each student has developed ten questions, divide the class into two teams. Then have members take turns asking their questions, and have the members of the opposing team try to answer each question that is asked.

Using Study Skills in Writing

Peer Editing Group your students into pairs. Then have the students read their test questions to their partners and have their partners try to answer them. The students should then revise any questions that their partners find unclear and difficult to answer.

CHAPTER 38
Library and Dictionary Skills
(pp. 712–750)

This chapter discusses some of the valuable learning resources found in both school and public libraries and explains how to use them. Section 38.1 explains how works of fiction, nonfiction, and biography are listed in the card catalog and arranged on the library shelves. Section 38.2 focuses on the use of reference books. Section 38.3 gives detailed explanations of how students can benefit from the many special features of a dictionary.

You may teach this chapter at any time during the year, but may find it useful to cover Sections 38.1 and 38.2 when students begin work on report and research-paper writing.

For a review of the entire chapter and a related writing exercise, see the Skills Review and Writing Workshop on page 750.

38.1 Using the Library
(pp. 712–724)

OBJECTIVES

After completing this section, students should be able to

- Use the card catalog to find information about books.
- Identify alphabetical order in a card catalog.
- Locate fiction, nonfiction, biographies, and special materials in the library.

Chapter # 38

Library and Dictionary Skills

You have probably been using the books and other materials in libraries for years. You are also likely to be very familiar with dictionaries. You may not, however, be getting as much value out of these sources as you could.

The purpose of the first two sections in this chapter is to explain the resources of the library and show you how to find and use these resources. The third section explores the contents and special features of dictionaries.

38.1 Using the Library

Libraries exist to help you and everyone else in your school and community. Because so many people use libraries, it is important for all users to follow a few useful rules. First, be considerate of the other people by trying to be as quiet as possible. Second, return books and materials that you check out on time, and take care of them while you are using them. This way other people will have a chance to use the materials, and you can avoid paying fines. Third, be careful with the copying machines, microfilm readers, and other equipment available in the library. If you do not know how to use these machines, ask someone to show you. Fourth, when you are puzzled about finding the information you need, ask a librarian to help you. The librarian is trained to guide people to the materials they want. Finally, learn about the contents and organization of libraries in general and your own library in particular so that you will know where to find things.

This section will explain the card catalog—the major key to the contents of the library—and then guide you to the shelves to find the books you want.

The Card Catalog

Often one of the first objects you see when you enter a library is the *card catalog.* It is important for you to learn to use it properly. Using the card catalog, you can locate any book.

Use the card catalog as a key to finding books in the library.

The card catalog is made up of small file drawers that contain alphabetically arranged cards. Each drawer has a label on the outside that tells you what part of the alphabet is in that drawer. For example, a label that says BE—BRI means that the card headings in that drawer begin with words that start with BE and go through words that start with BRI. Inside the drawer are *guide cards.* Guide cards have tabs that stick up above the rest of the cards. These tabs can help you find the words you want. Between these guide cards, the catalog cards are filed alphabetically.

Kinds of Catalog Cards. Each nonfiction book in the library will have at least three cards in the catalog: an *author card,* a *title card,* and a *subject card.* Each fiction book will have an author card and a title card. For any single book, all the cards are identical except for the top line of each card.

Use the card catalog to find a book by author, title, or subject.

Less advanced   After they have toured the library, ask these students to draw a map of the floor plan, complete with labels.

Average   Give more practice with the Dewey Decimal System by listing topics such as the following on the board:

1. Musical theater
2. Baseball
3. Sailing
4. Dance
5. U.S. political parties
6. American authors

Have pairs of students working together on a topic examine library books on their topic and note the Dewey Decimal category in which their topic belongs. They can then answer the following questions:

1. In which main class does the topic belong?
2. What is the number of this class?
3. What are some of the other topics covered by books in this main class?

Advanced   Some of these students might want to research and report to their group (or to the entire class) on the Library of Congress System.

Additional Practice

Practice Pages or Practice Book, page 170

TESTING

Test Program

Unit Pretest, page 113
Chapter Test, pages 120, 121
Unit Post-Test, pages 125, 126

You can find any book by looking under the author's last name. For instance, if you had read a book by Cipriano and wanted to read other books written by him, you could look in the card catalog under C and find a card that looks like this one.

AUTHOR CARD:

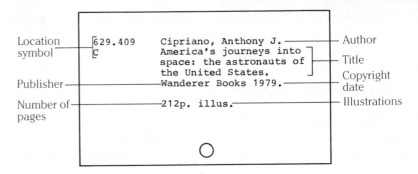

If you do not know or remember the name of an author, you can find a book by looking under the title. Locate the book in the card catalog by looking under the first letter of the first word of the title. If you wanted the book *America's Journeys into Space,* you would look under A.

TITLE CARD:

```
629.409    America's Journeys into Space
C          Cipriano, Anthony J.

           America's journeys into
           space: the astronauts of
           the United States.
           Wanderer Books  1979.

           212p. illus.
```

You can also find books by looking under the subject. If you have to write a report, you will probably be interested in finding as much information as you can about one specific subject. In such a case, you might begin by looking up the subject.

RE-TEACHING
Practice Pages or Practice
Book, page 170

38.1 Using the Library

If your paper were on astronauts, you might look under that word.

SUBJECT CARD:

```
629.409    ASTRONAUTS--UNITED STATES--
C          BIOGRAPHY

           Cipriano, Anthony J.
           America's journeys into
           space: the astronauts of
           the United States.
           Wanderer Books  1979.

           212p. illus.

                    ◯
```

If you can not find a subject card in the card catalog, you may find *cross-reference cards* helpful. There are two kinds of cross-reference cards. The first is called a *see* card. A *see* card tells you that the library does not file cards under the subject you have looked up. The card directs you instead to a subject that the library does use. If you were looking for books about the American Army and found the following card, you would then have to look under the subject heading *United States, Army*.

CROSS-REFERENCE
CARD:

```
           AMERICAN ARMY

                See

           United States, Army




                    ◯
```

The second kind of cross-reference card is a *see also* card. If you want additional books on a subject, a *see also* card can be useful. This card lists subjects related to the subject you have looked up. The following example of a *see also* card

THINKING SKILLS
Knowledge—*Listing* information contained on a catalog card (Exercise A, page 718)
Listing items alphabetically in card catalog order (Exercise B, page 719)
Listing items in special card catalog order (Exercise C, page 719)
Listing fiction books in the order in which they would appear on the shelves (Exercise D, page 723)
Listing call numbers in the order in which they would appear on the shelves (Exercise E, page 723)
Listing biographies in shelf order (Exercise F, page 723)

Synthesis—*Writing* about information gained from researching a topic in the library (Developing Writing Skills, page 724)

would be found under the subject heading *Moving pictures.* The card lists related topics, such as *Moving picture projection.*

CROSS-REFERENCE CARD:

```
                  MOVING PICTURES
                    See also
        Moving picture projection
        Moving picture theaters
        Moving pictures in education
        Puppet films
        Science fiction films
        Vampire films
        War films
        Western films
                            ◯
```

What Catalog Cards Tell You. In addition to giving you the author, title, and subject, catalog cards include other helpful information.

Consult catalog cards to find publishing information, a description of features, related subject headings, and the location symbol for each book.

You should be aware of how the information on catalog cards can be useful to you. Most cards will give you the book's publisher and the copyright date right after the title. For some subjects it is important to know how up-to-date the information in a book is. A card will also tell the number of pages and will indicate if the book has illustrations, a bibliography, or an index. Furthermore, it may be important for you to have pictures on your topic, and a bibliography can help you find additional information. Some cards also include a summary of the contents of the book, sometimes called an *annotation.* At the bottom of the card, subject headings may be listed. There will be a card for the book filed under each of these headings. Finally, in the upper left-hand corner, you will find a *location symbol.* This code of numbers or letters will help you find the book on the shelf.

38.1 Using the Library

Title
Author
Location symbol
Publisher
Copyright date
Number of pages
Illustrations
Description of contents
List of books on the same topic
Subject headings
Index

973.4
P
Phelan, Mary Kay
The story of the Louisiana Purchase.
Crowell 1979.
149p. illus.

SUMMARY: An account of the events leading to the United States' purchase of a huge tract of land from France in 1803.
Includes bibliography and index.

1. Louisiana Purchase   2. United States--History--1801-1809

Arrangement of Cards. To use the card catalog effectively, you also need to know how the library alphabetizes cards.

Use word-by-word alphabetizing and a few additional rules to find cards in the catalog.

A library may alphabetize author, title, and subject cards together or it may alphabetize author and title cards together and subject cards separately. Most smaller libraries alphabetize author, title, and subject cards together.

There are two basic ways of alphabetizing: *word by word* and *letter by letter.* Letter-by-letter alphabetizing means that you look only at the order of the letters, regardless of the number of words. Letter-by-letter alphabetizing is used in dictionaries. Word-by-word alphabetizing is used in the card catalog. This method requires that you look first at the order of the letters in the first word of a group of words and then at the letters in the succeeding words. Thus, in letter-by-letter alphabetizing, *newspaper* would come before *New York.* However, in word-by-word alphabetizing, *New York* would come first because all groups of words beginning with the word *new* are listed before words that begin with the letters *new.* Look at some other examples.

TWO WAYS OF ALPHABETIZING	
Library's Method: By Word	**Other Method: By Letter**
New Deal	New Deal
New Jersey	newer
New York	New Jersey
newer	newsletter
newsletter	New York

In addition to this general rule for alphabetizing, you should keep in mind the points in the following chart.

SPECIAL METHODS OF ALPHABETIZING IN THE CARD CATALOG

1. *A, an,* and *the* at the beginning of an entry are not used in alphabetizing; *The Enemy* would be alphabetized under *E.*
2. Abbreviations and numbers are alphabetized as if they were spelled out; *Dr.* is treated as *Doctor* and *100* as *one hundred.*
3. All *Mc's* and *Mac's* are alphabetized as if they were *Mac;* the following are in the correct order: *McBrien, MacDonald, machine, McInerney.*

EXERCISE A: Examining a Catalog Card. Use the following catalog card to provide each of the ten pieces of information requested after the card.

```
909.0492  Banks, Lynne Reid
B            Letters to my Israeli sons: the
           story of Jewish survival.
           F. Watts 1980.

           276p. maps

           Includes bibliography and index.

           1. Jews--History  2. Zionism--
           History  3. Palestine--History--
           1917-1948
                   O
```

1. The location symbol 909.0492
B
2. The author Lynne Reid Banks
3. The title *Letters to my Israeli Sons: The Story of Jewish Survival*
4. The copyright date 1980
5. The publisher F. Watts
6. The number of pages in the book 276
7. Any information about illustration maps included
8. Any information about bibliography or index both included
9. Subject headings under which the book is listed
10. The kind of card this is author card

9. Jews—History/Zionism—History/Palestine—History—1917–1948

EXERCISE B: Alphabetizing Using the Library's Word-by-Word Method. Arrange the items in card catalog order.

1. Santa Anna 7
2. Sanskrit 6
3. Sandwich Islands 3
4. San Juan 2
5. Sapphire 10
6. San Andreas Fault 1
7. Santiago 9
8. Sanitation 5
9. Sanhedrin 4
10. Santa Fe Trail 8

EXERCISE C: Following Special Rules for Alphabetizing. Arrange the following items in card catalog order.

1. Mt. Rainier 5
2. *100 Story Poems* 7
3. *An African Treasury* 1
4. McCullers, Carson 3
5. St. Catherine 9
6. *The Outsiders* 8
7. Mt. St. Helens 6
8. *A Wrinkle in Time* 10
9. MacLeish, Archibald 4
10. MacArthur, Douglas 2

Finding Books on the Shelves

Using the card catalog is the first step to finding books. The second step is letting the card catalog guide you to the books on the shelves. Usually a library divides and shelves books according to whether they are *fiction* or *nonfiction*. Works of fiction are made-up storics that may be based on facts but are created mainly from the authors' imaginations. Works of nonfiction are factual. A library may also categorize and shelve separately two subgroups of nonfiction—biographies and reference books—and various other materials as well.

Finding Fiction. The simplest shelving system in the library is the one used for *fiction.*

Fiction is arranged on the shelves alphabetically by the last name of the author and then by the title of the book.

The card catalog tells you that a book is fiction by the marking in the upper left-hand corner of the card. The location symbol for fiction usually consists of the letter *F* or the letters *Fic* along with the first few letters of the author's last name. You must go to the shelves that hold fiction and look under the first few letters of the author's last name, which will often be printed at the bottom of the spine of the book. For example, a book by Marjorie Kellogg would be shelved before a book by John Knowles. If there are several books by the same author, the books will be in alphabetical order by title.

Finding Nonfiction Using Call Numbers. *Nonfiction* books are arranged differently. On many catalog cards, you will find a location symbol that is a number and the first letter or letters of the author's last name. This number and letter make up the book's *call number.*

Nonfiction is arranged on the shelf in call-number order.

The call number also appears on the spine of the book. Libraries have agreed on a way to arrange all their books so that people can find books the same way in every library. There are two systems in general use: the Dewey Decimal System and the Library of Congress System. This section will focus on the Dewey Decimal System because the Library of Congress System is primarily used in college libraries and very large public libraries.

38.1 Using the Library

The Dewey Decimal System attempts to classify all knowledge. It does this by first breaking all knowledge down into ten main classes.

MAIN CLASSES OF THE DEWEY DECIMAL SYSTEM

Numbers	Subjects
000–099	Generalities
100–199	Philosophy and related disciplines
200–299	Religion
300–399	Social sciences
400–499	Language
500–599	Pure sciences
600–699	Technology (applied sciences)
700–799	The arts
800–899	Literature
900–999	General geography and history

Each main class is then subdivided into a number of smaller divisions. The second digit in a call number gives the division breakdown. For example, 320 means political science and 324 means the political process.

In call numbers there are often numbers beyond the decimal point as well. These divide the categories of knowledge into still more specific groups. For example, 324.2 is the number for political parties.

Although you do not have to memorize the Dewey Decimal System, understanding it will give you two advantages: (1) You will know that you can find more books about a subject by looking at books with the same call number; (2) you will know that a subject not covered in books with one number, say 324, might be talked about in chapters of a more general book having, for example, the number 320.

The call number of a book guides you to the book on the shelf. Call numbers appear on the spines of all nonfiction books, and books are arranged on the shelves in call-number order. Often a label on a row of shelves will indicate the range of numbers in that row. Knowing that the books are grouped numerically will help you find them. A book with the call number 300 will come before a book with the call number 310. A book numbered 312.1 will come before one numbered 312.12, and both of these will come before one numbered 312.2. When books have the same number, they are arranged alphabetically by the letters of the authors' last names: for instance, 312.3 will come before 312.3.

A

B

Finding Biographies and Special Materials. Besides grouping books on the shelves by fiction and nonfiction, libraries may use special location symbols and special sections for biographies, reference books, and young-adult books.

Biographies, reference books, young-adult books, and other materials may be given special symbols and grouped separately.

Many libraries have a separate section for biography. This section includes biographies, which are factual books written about a person by another person, and autobiographies, which are factual books written by a person about himself or herself. The location symbol for biographies will generally be *B* or *92* followed by the first letter, the first few letters, or the entire last name of the person who is the subject of the biography. Biographies are arranged alphabetically by subject, not by author. For example, the book *First Woman Doctor: The Story of Elizabeth Blackwell, M.D.* by Rachel Baker would be labeled *B* (for biography) and *B* (for Blackwell). It would be placed on the shelf before *Kit Carson: Trail Blazer and Scout* by Shannon Garst, labeled *B* (for biography) and *C* (for Carson).

Another special collection in most libraries is the reference collection. A reference book is usually indicated by the letter *R* before the call number. (See Section 38.2 for a discussion of reference books.)

Some libraries also have a separate section for young-adult books, which are books used primarily by junior high school students. The location symbol is usually *YA* followed by the proper call number or location symbol for fiction. For example, *YA 324* means that the book is shelved in the young-adult collection.

In addition to knowing about these common markings, find out what special markings your library uses.

EXERCISE D: Locating Fiction. Arrange the following books in library shelf order.

1. *Mystery at Crane's Landing* by Marcella Thum 9
2. *The Martian Chronicles* by Ray Bradbury 2
3. *High Wind in Jamaica* by Richard Hughes 7
4. *Little Women* by Louisa May Alcott 1
5. *Summer of the Swans* by Betsy Byers 3
6. *Old Yeller* by Fred Gipson 6
7. *Lisa, Bright and Dark* by John Neufeld 8
8. *Sea Glass* by Laurence Yep 10
9. *The Pistachio Prescription* by Paula Danziger 4
10. *Johnny Tremain* by Esther Forbes 5

EXERCISE E: Locating Nonfiction. Arrange the following call numbers in library shelf order.

1. 150.1 G 1
2. 301.42 A 5
3. 746.4 A 10
4. 600 G 6
5. 150.2 A 2
6. 301.415 F 4
7. 629 A 7
8. 300 F 3
9. 629 M 8
10. 745 M 9

EXERCISE F: Locating Biographies. Arrange the following biographies in library shelf order.

1. *The Story of Eleanor Roosevelt* by Jeanette Eaton 5
2. *Loretta Lynn* by Robert K. Krishef 4
3. *Jack London: The Pursuit of a Dream* by Ruth Franchere 3

4. *Trumpeter's Tale: The Story of the Young Louis Armstrong* by Jeanette Eaton 1

5. *Arthur Ashe: Tennis Champion* by Louie Robinson 2

DEVELOPING WRITING SKILLS: Using Your Knowledge of the Library. Pick a topic. Go to your school or local library and use the card catalog to choose three or four books about your topic. Then, go to the shelves and find the books. Examine the books to see how well they cover your topic. List the books you have found. Finally, in a few brief sentences, explain how you found them and describe how well they cover your topic.

Answers will vary.

38.2 Finding Reference Books in the Library

The cards for reference books are marked with an *R* before the call number. These books are generally kept in a separate area and usually may not be borrowed.

A good way to describe a reference book is to say that it is a book to be consulted for information. A reference book may be an index that leads you to information in other books or in magazines, or it may be a fact book that contains a large collection of information. Both indexes and fact books can be either general or specialized. A general reference book covers many subjects in broad outline. A specialized reference book covers one subject in greater detail. In this section you will learn how to use general and specialized reference books as well as magazines and journals.

General Reference Books

General reference books include encyclopedias, almanacs, atlases, and dictionaries. (See Section 38.3 for a detailed discussion of dictionaries.)

38.2 Finding Reference Books in the Library
(pp. 724–737)

OBJECTIVES

After completing this section, students should be able to

- Use general reference books.
- Use specialized reference books.
- Use magazines and journals to find information.

TEACHING

Getting Started

Ask the class to name some general reference books other than a dictionary. Elicit encyclopedias, atlases, almanacs, and so forth. Write each item named on the board. Follow by asking what kind of information is available in each reference listed on the board. Tell the

38.2 Finding Reference Books in the Library

Encyclopedias. *Encyclopedias* contain basic facts on a great many subjects.

Use encyclopedias for basic facts, background information, and bibliographies.

If you need a piece of information quickly, you can find the answer in an encyclopedia. If you have to write a report on a subject you know little about, a general encyclopedia can give you an overview of the subject.

Most encyclopedias consist of volumes arranged alphabetically. The volume number and the portion of the alphabet covered are marked on the spine. The pages of each volume also have guide words at the top to show you the first and last subjects included on those pages.

To aid you further, most encyclopedias have an index volume. An index is especially helpful if your subject does not have a complete article devoted to it. Notice the articles listed under the following subject in *The World Book* index.

INDEX ENTRY:

— Volume
— Page Number

Space travel Sc:560 *with pictures and maps*
See also the Reading and Study Guide on this topic
Air Force, United States (The Air Force in Space) A:185
Altitude A:372b
Astronomy (Space Exploration) A:813
Computer (In Engineering) Ci:742 *with picture*
Cosmic Rays (Effects of Cosmic Rays) Ci:857
Guided Missile (Postwar Developments) G:413-414
Life (The Search for Life on Other Planets) L:245
Mercury (Flights to Mercury) M:340
Moon (Man's Future on the Moon) M:651
Radar (In Space Travel) R:66
Research (Mathematics and Physical Sciences) R:236 *with picture*
Rocket (Space Travel) R:358 *with pictures;* (The Space Age) R:360c
Television *picture on* T:85
Thermocouple T:192
United States, History of the (Space Exploration) U:123 *with picture*
World, History of (Modern Times) W:360d-360e
See also the list of Related Articles in the Space Travel article

---

class that they will be learning about both general and specialized reference books in the section they are about to study.

Text Follow Through

Discuss text pages 724–737.

Assign Exercise A, page 728; Exercise B, page 729; Exercise C, page 733; Exercise D, page 733; Exercise E, page 736; Exercise F, page 736; and Developing Writing Skills, page 736.

Less advanced Offer a step-by-step explanation of exactly how to use *The Readers' Guide to Periodical Literature.* Ask students to pick a subject, to find an article on that subject, and to write a step-by-step explanation of how they found the article by using *The Readers' Guide.* Their explanations should include a copy of *The Readers' Guide* entry used and a translation of the entry.

Average Have these students follow the same assignment as the less advanced students, but omit some of the procedural details and instead read the article that they find and write a summary of it. Ask them to make a photostatic copy of the page from *The Readers' Guide* and attach it to their article précis.

Advanced Have students use almanacs to write five to ten trivia questions and their answers (for example, "Who is the governor of Arkansas?"). Use these questions to set up a game. Organize the group into two teams and give the first member of each team an almanac. Using the students' trivia questions, ask one question of the first member of both teams. Both must find the answer quickly in the almanac—the first to raise his or her hand with the answer receives one point for the team. The book is then passed on to each of the next team members for the next question. At the end of the game, the team with the most points wins.

Additional Practice

Practice Pages or Practice Book, page 171

TESTING

Test Program

Unit Pretest, page 113
Chapter Test, page 121
Unit Post-Test, pages 125, 126

RE-TEACHING

Practice Pages or Practice Book, page 171

THINKING SKILLS

Comprehension—*Rewriting* an excerpt from *The Readers' Guide,* using complete words for all abbreviations (Exercise E, page 736)

Application—*Using* encyclopedias and almanacs to find the answers to specific questions (Exercise A, page 728)
Using atlases to find answers to specific questions (Exercise B, page 729)
Using specialized dictionaries and encyclopedias to find specific pieces of information (Exercise C, page 733)
Using biographical reference books to find answers to specific questions (Exercise D, page 733)
Using The Readers' Guide to find articles on a specific topic (Exercise F, page 736)

As you can see, the first heading directs you to a main entry, giving the letters of the volume and the page of the article. In addition, volume letters and page numbers are given for a number of related articles on a variety of topics.

To be a valuable source of information, an encyclopedia must be kept up-to-date. The people who publish encyclopedias update their books in different ways. One way is continuous revision. Articles on subjects that change rapidly—subjects such as medicine and politics—are constantly revised to keep the facts current. Most encyclopedias also publish yearbooks. Yearbooks contain information about the events of the year and about new developments in many fields.

Your library is likely to have many encyclopedias. As you use the different encyclopedias, you will discover the strengths and special features of each set. For example, *The World Book* has good pictures and is useful for short, clear explanations. The *Encyclopedia Americana* is excellent for information about places in America.

Almanacs. *Almanacs* should be the first place you look for minor facts or certain types of specific information.

Use almanacs to find a number of different kinds of miscellaneous information.

Almanacs contain a wealth of specific information on a wide range of subjects—science, government, world history, religion, literary and motion picture awards, and sports, among others. Like encyclopedia yearbooks, almanacs include a summary of the events of the year. Unlike encyclopedias, however, they are not good for thorough background information. The information they include is generally sketchy, covering only a few key facts.

Almanacs are not arranged alphabetically. Instead, you must use the index at the front or back of each volume. The following entry from the index of the 1984 *World Almanac and Book of Facts* refers you to information about ice hockey.

Evaluation—*Appraising* reference books to find the best ones for specific information to answer given questions (Developing Writing Skills, page 736)

38.2 Finding Reference Books in the Library

INDEX ENTRY:

```
Hockey, ice—
    Addresses, teams . . . . . . . . . . . . 829
    All-Star team (1983) . . . . . . . . . . 792 ————— Page number
    Arenas . . . . . . . . . . . . . . . . 802
    Canadian intercollegiate . . . . . . . . 811
    NCAA champions . . . . . . . . . . . 793
    National Hockey League (1983) . . 789-793
    Olympic records . . . . . . . . . . . . 782
    Smythe Trophy . . . . . . . . . . . . 792
    Stanley Cup . . . . . . . . . . . . . . 789
    World Hockey Association . . . . . . . 793
```

If you wanted to find information about the 1983 National Hockey League's all-star hockey team, you would turn to page 792 of the 1984 *World Almanac and Book of Facts.* There you would find lists of the players on the first and second teams for 1983.

The two best known almanacs are *The World Almanac and Book of Facts* and the *Information Please Almanac.* Each is published annually.

Atlases. *Atlases* give geographical information about the countries of the world. From the maps that make up most *atlases,* you can gather many different kinds of facts.

Use atlases to find information from maps.

There are many different kinds of atlases, each of which has a certain emphasis. Most general atlases focus primarily on *political maps,* which show the boundaries of countries and the locations of cities, towns, rivers, and oceans. General atlases may also include *topographical maps,* which show the surface features of a region, and *economic maps,* which present information about the types of industry and the population.

Use an atlas by turning to the index at the back. The index at the back lists all cities, towns, countries, bodies of water, and other geographical locations that are shown in the atlas. The following entry from the index to Hammond's *World Atlas* shows you where to turn to look for maps of Hawaii.

INDEX ENTRY:

```
Havertown, Pa., 294
Havířov, Czech., 41
Havre, Mont., 262
Havre de Grace,
    Md., 245
Havre-Saint-Pierre,
    Que., 174
Hawaii (isl.), Hawaii, 218 ————— Page number
Hawaii (state), U.S., 218
Hawaiian (isls.), 218
Hawaii Volcanoes Nat'l
    Park, Hawaii, 218
Hawarden, Iowa, 229
```

If you turn to page 218, you will find various maps of Hawaii. Each map also gives a scale of miles and kilometers so that you can figure out the distance between the different places.

Other atlases that you may find useful are *The Prentice-Hall Great International Atlas*, the *National Geographic Atlas of the World*, and *Goode's World Atlas*.

In preparing reports you may also want to make use of atlases that provide historical information. A historical atlas is arranged to show the changes over time in the boundaries of territories, countries, and empires. Some examples are *Shepherd's Historical Atlas*, the *Atlas of American History*, and the *American Heritage Atlas of American History*.

EXERCISE A: Using Encyclopedias and Almanacs. Use the encyclopedias and almanacs in your school or public library to find the following information. Write the information and the book you used to find it. Specific sources will vary; information is given.   2. chills and fever, spleen enlargement, anemia, jaundice

1. The average temperature in Phoenix, Arizona, in March 60°F

2. The symptoms of malaria

3. The fourth fastest animal in the world and its speed lion/50mph

38.2 Finding Reference Books in the Library

4. "conductor" on Underground Railroad; led over 300 slaves to freedom; worked

4. Three accomplishments of Harriet Tubman

5. The name of the mayor of Honolulu, Hawaii, in 1982

6. The cartoonist who created Dennis the Menace Hank Ketchum

7. The legend of the Blarney Stone

8. Three countries in NATO Belg, Can, Den, etc

9. Two painters of the Hudson River School Durand, Kensett, etc.

10. The winner of the Heisman Trophy in 1950 Vic Janowicz

with Union forced in South, etc.   5. Eileen R. Anderson   7. those who kiss it acquire skill at flattery

EXERCISE B: Using Atlases. Use atlases to find the following information. Write each piece of information and the book you used to find it.

Specific sources will vary; information is given.   1. USSR and US   3. VT, KY, TN,

1. The two mainland countries nearest Wrangel Island

2. The states that border on Lake Erie NY, PA, OH, MI

3. The states admitted to the Union between 1791 and 1803

4. The countries that border on Bolivia

5. The countries that border the Mediterranean Sea

OH   4. Chile, Peru, Braz, Para, Arg   5. Sp, Fr, It, Yugo, Alban, Gr, Turk, Syr, Leb, Isr, Eg, Libya, Tun, Alg, Mor

Specialized Reference Books

A specialized reference book covers one topic in great depth. Many specialized reference books are available on a wide range of topics.

Specialized Dictionaries. *Specialized dictionaries* provide definitions and background information on words and terms that have a particular meaning in one field.

Use specialized dictionaries to find detailed information about words.

One kind of specialized dictionary you are likely to use often focuses on synonyms—words with similar meanings. A dictionary of synonyms can help you find other words that have approximately the same meaning as a particular word. Some dictionaries of synonyms are *Funk and Wagnall's Modern Guide to Synonyms, Roget's International Thesaurus, Roget's Pocket Thesaurus,* and *Webster's New Dictionary of Synonyms.*

Some dictionaries of synonyms are arranged alphabetically. Others are arranged by categories and approached through an alphabetical index. If you wanted to find a synonym for *nourish* in one of these, you would look under that word in the index and find references to various meanings of the word, each with a category number and a paragraph number.

INDEX ENTRY:

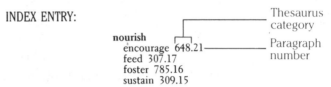

If you were interested in words that mean "to encourage," you would then look for category 648, paragraph 21, in the body of the book. The guide number at the top of the page would tell you that you were on the right page. There you would find the following list of words from which you could choose.

GUIDE NUMBER: 648.1–648.22

TEXT ENTRY: **.21 encourage,** give encouragement, pat *or* clap on the back; **invite,** ask for; **abet,** aid and abet, countenance, keep in countenance; **foster, nurture,** nourish, feed.

Other specialized dictionaries are devoted to foreign languages. Still others cover particular fields or topics, such as rhyming words or dialects.

OTHER SPECIALIZED DICTIONARIES

The Dictionary of American Slang
A Dictionary of Contemporary American Usage
The Harvard Dictionary of Music

James' Mathematical Dictionary
The Pocket Dictionary of American Slang
Steen's Dictionary of Biology

38.2 Finding Reference Books in the Library

Specialized Encyclopedias. Some *specialized encyclopedias* are multivolume with extensive information; others are single volumes. All deal with particular fields and treat topics more thoroughly than general encyclopedias do. Usually, however, they are organized alphabetically, just as general encyclopedias are.

Use specialized encyclopedias to find detailed information on a topic.

Some multivolume sets specialize in subjects related to your school courses. For example, *The Book of Popular Science* gives good basic information on all areas of science and can thus be useful in preparing science reports. *Peoples of the Earth* provides information about people all over the world and can be used for many social studies assignments. Other single and multivolume works focus on subjects such as sports, art, music, and medicine.

Biographical Reference Books. When you need information about famous people, living or dead, you can consult reference books that specialize in people.

Use biographical reference books to find information about people.

One of the best *biographical reference books* is *Current Biography,* a multivolume set started in 1940. Each bound volume covers one year. *Current Biography* includes articles on athletes, politicians, scientists, and other famous people living at the time of publication. It is published eleven times a year, and at the end of the year all the monthly issues are combined into one volume. The long illustrated articles end with bibliographies that can suggest other sources of information.

To find articles in *Current Biography,* you should use one of the indexes. *Current Biography* has an index at the end of each volume. The indexes in the latest volumes can help you find articles on people who have been in the news recently. You can look in the 1980 ten-year index for people who have been important over a longer period of time. For someone whose fame stretches back over a number of decades, you can check the cumulated index volume, covering the years 1940–1970.

In the index of the 1980 volume of *Current Biography*, you would find the following entry for Alice Walker, giving the month and year in which the article was published.

INDEX ENTRY:

Subject —————— Walker, Alice Mar 84 —————— Volume year

Walcott, Derek (Alton) Apr 84
Walesa, Lech Apr 81
Walker, Alice Mar 84
Wallace, DeWitt obit May 81
Wallace, Lila (Bell) Acheson
    obit Jul 84
Wallenstein, Alfred obit Mar
    83
Walton, Sir William Turner
    obit May 83
Wang Shih-chieh obit Jun 81
Ward, Barbara (Mary) obit Jul
    81
Waring, Fred obit Sep 84
Warren, Harry obit Nov 81

Then, looking in the volume listed, under Walker, you would find the article. Here is an excerpt from the article.

TEXT ENTRY: **Walker, Alice**

Feb. 9, 1944– Writer; social activist. Address: b. c/o Wendy Weil, Julian Bach Literary Agency, 747 Third Ave., New York City, N.Y. 10017.

Alice Walker is not only an essayist, poet, and award-winning novelist and short-story writer but also a social activist and an ardent "womanist"—that is, a black feminist. Although some reviewers have faulted her work for its unflattering portrayal of men, her ability to capture dialect and to evoke life in the rural South and the passionate intensity of her social concerns, as demonstrated in such books as *Revolutionary Petunias*, a collection of poems, and her Pulitzer Prize-winning novel, *The Color Purple*, have prompted many critics to rank Alice Walker among the best of contemporary American writers.

Alice Malsenior Walker was born on February 9, 1944 in Eatonton, Georgia, the youngest of the

38.2 Finding Reference Books in the Library

The many *Who's Who* publications cover a number of different fields. These books are primarily helpful because they include so many people. For example, *Who's Who in America* is a book of basic facts about prominent living Americans. *Who Was Who in America* covers prominent people who have died. The articles in these books are very short. In addition, because the information is obtained directly from the people covered, it may not be totally objective. Even so, the *Who's Who* volumes can give you some useful information.

A good source for information on people no longer living is the *McGraw-Hill Encyclopedia of World Biography*. It is international in scope and gives short illustrated articles on a number of different people.

The following chart lists biographical works you might use.

OTHER BIOGRAPHICAL REFERENCE BOOKS	
Contemporary Authors	*Modern Men of Science*
Dictionary of Scientific Biography	*Notable American Women*

EXERCISE C: Using Specialized Dictionaries and Encyclopedias. Use specialized reference books in your school or public library to find the following information. Write each piece of information and the book you used to find it.

Sources will vary; information is given. 1. absurdity, foolishness, senselessness,

1. Four synonyms for the word *nonsense* outrageousness, etc.

2. The meaning of the slang term *big cheese* self-important person

3. The diameter of the planet Mars 4,200 mi (6800 km)

4. The titles of two paintings by Mary Cassatt

5. Three kinds of nonpoisonous snakes garter, black, king, etc.

4. *Mother and Child, Lady at the Tea Table,* etc.

EXERCISE D: Using Biographical Reference Books. Use the biographical reference books in your school or public library to answer the questions on the following page. Write each piece of information and the book you used to find it.

Specific sources will vary; information is given.

1. When did Black Hawk live? 1767–1838
2. Who is Toni Morrison? black writer, author of *Song of Solomon*
3. What awards did Marie Curie receive? Nobel Prize, etc.
4. Who is Katharine Meyer Graham?
5. When and where was Scott Joplin born? 1868 in Texarkana, TX

4. former publisher of *Washington Post*

Periodicals

Periodicals are publications that are issued at regular intervals during the year. They may be published daily, weekly, monthly, every two months, or every three months.

A *magazine* is a periodical with articles of general interest written for the general public. A *journal* is a more scholarly periodical with information on a special field. While a book will give you clear and often detailed information, a magazine or journal can provide information that is both concise and very recent. In these periodicals you can find information on new discoveries, recent happenings, and people in the news.

Use magazines and journals to find concise, current information.

The next question is, "How do you find specific information in periodicals?" Just as you used the card catalog to find books, so you can use indexes to find magazine articles. The most important index is *The Readers' Guide to Periodical Literature*, which indexes more than 180 popular magazines. In the front of every volume of *The Readers' Guide*, you will find an alphabetical list of the magazines indexed and a list of the abbreviations used in the index. Throughout most of the year, *The Readers' Guide* is published twice a month. At the end of each year, all the monthly volumes are collected into one volume for that year.

The Readers' Guide is an author and subject index. You can find articles if you know either the author or the subject. Usually you will be looking for articles on a particular subject. To find the most recent information, you can begin with the most recent volumes of *The Readers' Guide* and work backwards. By first looking under general subjects and then looking under the more specific subheadings, you will be able to find articles on almost any subject.

The following entry shows the information you can expect to find in *The Readers' Guide*. Note that the entries give you the names of the articles, the authors, the titles of the magazines, the volume and page numbers, the dates, and whether there are illustrations. There are *see* and *see also* references.

ENTRY FROM *THE READERS' GUIDE:*

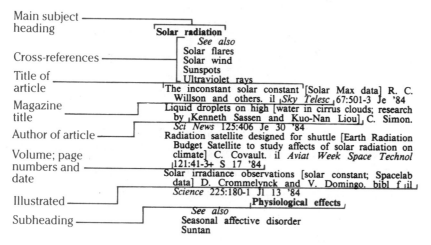

Once you have found an article covering your subject, there are several ways to find the magazine. Some libraries keep separate issues of the magazines. Others bind them together in volumes, and still others keep them on microfilm or microfiche. If your library stores magazines as single issues, you should write out the title of the magazine, the volume, and the date on a slip of paper and give it to the librarian. The librarian will go to where the periodicals are stored and find the one you have requested. If periodicals are bound and shelved, you can locate them on the shelves yourself. At other times you may have to use a machine called a *reader* to read the articles that are on microfilm (rolls) or microfiche (sheets).

Developing Writing Skills

Have students work on strengthening their research skills by completing the following assignment.

Writing Across the Curriculum

Because the condition of the environment affects the entire human race, it is important for everyone to have an awareness of the environmental issues that are currently facing us.

Prewriting Choose an environmental issue that you feel you should learn more about. For example, you might choose the disposal of toxic waste or the destruction of tropical rain forests. If you have difficulty coming up with a topic, you might ask your science teacher to make some suggestions. Next, research the topic in reference books and periodicals. Make sure that you record the bibliographic information for each source you consult. Once you have finished your research, review your notes and prepare a thesis statement about your topic. Then organize your ideas into an outline.

Writing Referring to your outline and your notes, write the first draft of a report about your topic. Include your thesis statement in your introduction, and end your report with a conclusion that sums up your ideas. Make sure that you cite the sources of any quotations or borrowed ideas that you use.

Revising Revise your paper, following the checklist on page 553. When you have finished revising, proofread your report and prepare a final draft.

EXERCISE E: Interpreting *The Readers' Guide*. Examine the following excerpt from *The Readers' Guide*. Then, using complete words for all abbreviations, write out each of the five entries in the excerpt. Include the titles of the articles, the names of the authors when they are given, the titles of the magazines, the volume numbers when they are given, the page numbers, and the dates. Then explain the procedure you would follow to find one of these articles.

Complete words are given for abbreviations.

> **Friendship**
> *See also*
> Pen pals
> Being friends with a beautiful woman. R. Smoodin. *Mademoiselle* 90:146-7+ F '84 February
> Best friends. H. Johnson. il *Vogue* 174:232-7+ Jl '84 illustrated/July
> Best friends: why is 3 a crowd? [teenage girls] S. S. Soria. *Teen* 28:34-5+ Ja '84 January
> Between friends: that special chemistry [women] J. Levine. *Mademoiselle* 90:188-9+ Ap '84 April
> Can you ever be friends with an old love? *Glamour* 82:121-2 Jl '84 July

EXERCISE F: Using *The Readers' Guide*. Use a recent volume of *The Readers' Guide* in your school or public library to find two other articles on friendship. On your paper, write the information you would need to locate the magazines.

DEVELOPING WRITING SKILLS: Using the Research Tools in Your Library. Choose the best reference book to find information on each of the following items. Then use the book to find the information requested. Try to use as many different kinds of reference books as you can. Write each piece of information and the book you used to find it in a complete sentence.

Specific sources will vary; information is given; sentences will vary.

1. Who won the 1977 World Series? NY Yankees
2. Find a synonym for the word *mess* when it means "eat." dine
3. What are the effects of too little vitamin A in a human's diet? night blindness, susceptibility to infection
4. When was Nikki Giovanni born? For what is she known?
5. Who was Kublai Khan? Emperor of China 1259–1294 A.D.
6. How many square miles are covered by the Pacific Ocean?

4. 1943/writing poetry   6. 64,186,300

7. What is the capital of Paraguay? Asuncion
8. What was Jacques Cousteau's first major achievement?
9. What is the best treatment for lead poisoning?
10. What was the population of Texas in 1980? 14,228,383

8. invented scuba equipment with Emil Gagnon in 1943   9. injections of metal-attracting compounds

Using the Dictionary 38.3

Professional writers and people who read widely usually make it a practice to keep a dictionary handy. For them it is the first place to look for quick answers to questions they may have about the spelling and meaning of words.

As a student you may find it very useful to develop a similar habit. If you want to use words correctly when you write and wish to understand what you read, you should never be reluctant to consult a dictionary. The trick is to be able to find what you are looking for quickly and easily. As with any other skill, quickness and ease come with practice.

This section will explain how you can use a dictionary to find a great variety of information. As you read, apply what is said here to the particular dictionary that you use most often at school or at home.

A Dictionary for Everyday Use

Not all dictionaries are the same. Different writers and publishers offer a variety of dictionaries, each with a particular audience in mind. Some dictionaries are made for scholars. Others are designed for the special needs of college students. Still others are made for students in high school or elementary school. There are even dictionaries for children who are just learning to read. Since there are many kinds of dictionaries, the dictionary you use every day should be one that is right for you.

Use a dictionary that best suits your present needs.

38.3 Using the Dictionary
(pp. 737–749)

OBJECTIVES

After completing this section, students should be able to

- Choose a dictionary that suits their needs.
- Use a dictionary to check spelling quickly and easily.
- Find words in a dictionary, using the letter-by-letter alphabetizing method.
- Identify and use the different parts of dictionary entries.

TEACHING

Getting Started

Ask the class to mention some uses for a dictionary. Write these on the board. Obvious uses should include spelling, syllabification, pronunciation, parts of speech, origins, and definitions. Point out that a dictionary contains many other kinds of information, and that the section they are about to start will inform them of some of these. It will also help them find the kind of information they are looking for quickly and easily.

Text Follow Through

Discuss text pages 737–749.

Assign Exercise A, page 738; Exercise B, page 739; Exercise C, page 741; Exercise D, page 741; Exercise E, page 748; and Developing Writing Skills, page 749.

Less advanced These students may need additional practice in alphabetizing. If so, give them the following list before assigning Exercise C. Point out that the words in the list are arranged in word-by-word order, as in a card catalog. Direct students to place the words in letter-by-letter order. Students can check their answers in a dictionary when finished.

1. New Bedford
2. New Brunswick
3. New England
4. New Year's Eve
5. newborn
6. newcomer
7. newfangled
8. news
9. news conference
10. newscast

Average Have students use a dictionary both to define the following words and to research their etymologies. Students should give the language or languages from which each word is derived and cite and define the words given in the etymology that help explain the basis for the word's present-day meaning.

1. Mayday
2. discothèque
3. nostalgia
4. temerity
5. winnow

Advanced Have students examine copies of different student dictionaries, looking for variations.

Additional Practice

Practice Pages or Practice Book, page 172

Such a dictionary should be neither too easy nor too difficult for you. It should contain all the words you are likely to come upon in your schoolwork and should explain these words in language you can understand.

DICTIONARIES RECOMMENDED FOR STUDENTS
The Macmillan Dictionary
The Scott, Foresman Advanced Dictionary
Webster's New World Dictionary, Students Edition

Once you have found a dictionary that you think will suit your needs, use it often—even browse through it occasionally to see what new things you can discover. The more you use your dictionary, the easier it will be to use.

EXERCISE A: Examining Your Dictionary. Examine the dictionary that you use most often at home, in school, or in the library. Answer the following questions about it.
Answers will vary.

1. What is the complete title of your dictionary?
2. What company published it and when?
3. For what kind of audience was it made? (You should find the answer to this question in the preface or foreword at the beginning of the dictionary.)
4. Does the dictionary have an introduction that explains how to use the book? If so, how many pages are in this section?
5. List three technical terms that you have had to learn in science, history, English, or some other subject. Does your dictionary define them?

Using Your Dictionary to Check Spelling

A common complaint of students is, "How can I find the word if I can't spell it to begin with?" Checking the spelling of a word *can* sometimes be difficult because English often has many different spellings for the same sound.

TESTING

Test Program

Unit Pretest, page 113
Chapter Test, pages 121, 122
Unit Post-Test, pages 125, 126

RE-TEACHING

Practice Pages or Practice
Book, page 172

THINKING SKILLS

Knowledge—*Listing* words in
alphabetical order (Exercise
C, page 741)

Application—*Using* a dictionary
to find answers to a list of
questions (Exercise A, page
738)
Using a dictionary to find correct spellings (Exercise B,
page 739)
Using the three-step method
for finding words in a dictionary quickly and easily (Exercise D, page 741)
Using information from a dictionary page to answer specific questions about information in an entry (Exercise E,
page 748)

Synthesis—*Writing* complete
sentences to answer ques-
tions by using information
found in a dictionary
(Developing Writing Skills,
page 749)

38.3 Using the Dictionary

Become familiar with the different spelling patterns of the sounds in English words.

Always begin with your best guess. The odds are that you will find the word you are looking for after a few tries. The more spelling patterns you know, the better your chances are of finding the word quickly.

Some dictionaries have a chart or list that shows the different ways a sound can be spelled in English. The following is part of such a chart. It is from *Webster's New World Dictionary,* Student Edition.

WORD FINDER CHART		
If the sound is like the . . .	try also the spelling . . .	as in the words . . .
a in fat	ai, au	pl*ai*d, dr*au*ght
a in lane	ai, ao, au, ay, ea, ei, eigh, et, ey	r*ai*n, g*ao*l, g*au*ge, r*ay*, br*ea*k, r*ei*n, w*eigh*, sach*et*, th*ey*
a in care	ai, ay, e, ea, ei	*ai*r, pr*ay*er, th*e*re, w*ea*r, th*ei*r
a in father	au, e, ea	g*au*nt, s*e*rgeant, h*ea*rth
a in ago	e, i, o, u	ag*e*nt, san*i*ty, c*o*mply, foc*u*s
ch in chin	tch, ti, tu	ca*tch*, ques*ti*on, na*tu*re
e in get	a, ae, ai, ay,	*a*ny, *ae*sthete, s*ai*d, s*ay*s,

Suppose, for example, that you had written the sentence "As I entered the barn, the horse nayed" and your teacher has noted that "nayed" is misspelled. An educated guess, however, would tell you that the problem is with the *a* sound. After checking the letters given for the *a* sound, you would look up these spellings in the dictionary. You would then find that *neighed* is correct.

EXERCISE B: **Correcting Spelling with Your Dictionary.**

Using the dictionary, write the correct spelling for each of these misspelled words.

1. agravated aggravated   5. vanaty vanity   9. tishue tissue
2. rythm rhythm   6. lisense license   10. ajency agency
3. recroot recruit   7. emfasize emphasize
4. hymm hymn   8. hygene hygiene

Finding Words Quickly

Most of the time you will know how a new word is spelled because you will have just come across it in your reading. At these times you will want to find the word's meaning quickly and get back to your reading.

Learn to use alphabetical order to find words quickly in the dictionary.

Thumbing aimlessly through a dictionary to find a word wastes time. Here are three steps to help you find any word in the dictionary quickly.

STEPS FOR FINDING WORDS QUICKLY
1. Use the Four-Section Approach.
2. Next use the guide words.
3. Then follow strict, letter-by-letter alphabetical order.

The Four-Section Approach. Most dictionaries can be mentally divided into four roughly equal sections.

FOUR SECTIONS: ABCD
EFGHIJKL
MNOPQR
STUVWXYZ

Knowing the section of the dictionary in which a word will be found can help you open to that general area right away. The word *kinkajou,* for example, will be near the middle of the book, whereas *springbok* will be toward the end, near the beginning of the fourth section.

Guide Words. Once you narrow your search to a general area, begin using the *guide words*. These are the two words printed at the top of each page. The guide word at the left tells you the first word on that page. The one on the right tells you the last word on that page. If, for example, the guide words are *glower* and *go*, you know that *glucose* will be on that page.

Letter-by-Letter Alphabetical Order. All items in a dictionary are in *strict alphabetical order*—that is, letter by letter right to the end of the entry. This rule holds even if the item has more than one word.

EXAMPLES: okra *before* Olaf

Olaf *before* olden

olden *before* old hand

EXERCISE C: Alphabetizing. Put the following items into the order you would find them in a dictionary.

1. riprap 4
2. rise 7
3. ripen 2
4. rival 10
5. riptide 5
6. ritual 9
7. ripe 1
8. risk 8
9. Rip van Winkle 6
10. ripple 3

EXERCISE D: Finding Words Quickly. Using the three steps for finding words quickly, look up the following items in your dictionary. Write the guide words on the page where each item is found.
Answers will vary.

1. tomahawk
2. impassive
3. paradox
4. biopsy
5. shilling

Understanding Main Entries

In a dictionary the words you look up and the information given about them are known as *main entries*. The words themselves are called *entry words*. The chart on the following page shows different kinds of entry words.

KINDS OF ENTRY WORDS	
Single Word	**la·goon** (lə goon′) *n.* [< Fr. *lagune* & It. *laguna* < L. *lacuna*, lake] **1.** a shallow lake or pond, esp. one connected with a larger body of water **2.** the water enclosed by a circular coral reef **3.** shallow salt water separated from the sea by dunes
Compound Word	**national bank 1.** a bank or system of banks owned and operated by a government ☆**2.** in the U.S., a member bank of the Federal Reserve System, chartered by the Federal government
Abbreviation	**nat. 1.** national **2.** native **3.** natural
Prefix	**an·ti-** (an′ti; *also variously* -tē, -tī, -tə) [< Gr. < *anti*, against] *a prefix meaning:* **1.** against; hostile to [*antilabor*] **2.** that operates against [*antiaircraft*] **3.** that prevents, cures, or neutralizes [*antitoxin*] **4.** opposite; reverse [*antimatter*] **5.** rivaling [*antipope*]
Suffix	**-ant** (ənt, 'nt) [Fr. < L. -*antem* or -*entem*, acc. prp. ending] *a suffix meaning:* **1.** that has, shows, or does [*defiant, radiant*] **2.** a person or thing that [*occupant, accountant*]
Person (Family Name Usually First)	**An·tho·ny** (an′thə nē; *also, for 1 & 2,* -tə-) [< L. *Antonius*, name of a Roman gens] **1.** a masculine name: dim. *Tony;* var. *Antony* **2. Mark,** *see* ANTONY **3. Susan B(rownell),** 1820–1906; U.S. leader in the women's suffrage movement
Place	**La·gos** (lā′gäs, -gəs) capital of Nigeria; seaport on the Atlantic: pop. 665,000

As you can see in the chart, the information following an entry word varies depending upon the kind of word it is.

Learn to recognize and use the different kinds of information contained in a main entry.

Explanations of the different kinds of information that you can expect to find in a dictionary follow.

Spelling. Most words have only one correct spelling, as

shown by the entry word. Some words, however, can be spelled in more than one way. The one most commonly used, called the *preferred spelling,* is listed first. Less commonly used spellings are called *variant spellings.* If the form of a word you are looking up is a variant spelling, the entry will refer you to the main entry that begins with the preferred spelling.

VARIANT SPELLINGS:

> **la-di-da, la-de-da** (lä′dē dä′) *adj.* [Colloq.] affected in speech, manners, etc.; refined in a showy way

PREFERRED SPELLING FIRST:

> **lah-di-dah, lah-de-dah** (lä′dē dä′) *adj. same as* LA-DI-DA

Syllabification. Centered dots, spaces, or slashes in an entry word indicate where the word may be divided if it is to be broken at the end of a line. In the following example, the centered dots indicate that the word *parliament* has three syllables.

EXAMPLE:

> **par·lia·ment** (pär′lə mənt) *n.* [< OFr. *parlement* < *parler:* see prec.] **1.** an official conference or council concerned with public affairs **2.** [P-] the national legislative body of Great Britain, composed of the House of Commons and the House of Lords **3.** [P-] a similar body in other countries ——— Syllabification

Pronunciation. Pronunciations are given after most entry words. Exceptions are sometimes made for entries—such as abbreviations, prefixes, and suffixes—that are not complete words. Pronunciations are also avoided with compound words when pronunciations have already been given for the individual words that make up the compounds.

The dictionary tells you how a word is pronounced by respelling it in a *phonetic alphabet.* This is a set of special symbols. Each symbol is assigned one sound. Since phonetic alphabets vary from one dictionary to another, it is important for you to become familiar with the one in the dictionary you use. A *pronunciation key* at the front or back of your dictionary lists and explains all the symbols used throughout the book. Study this carefully. Most dictionaries for students also print short pronunciation keys on every other page to help you pronounce the words.

The dictionary also shows you which syllables are stressed. The syllable that gets the most emphasis has a *primary stress,* usually shown by a heavy mark after the syllable (′). Words of more than one syllable may have a *secondary stress,* shown by a shorter, lighter mark (′) after the syllable. Unstressed syllables have no stress marks. Again, symbols may vary from one dictionary to another, so check the introduction of the book you use.

PRIMARY STRESS ONLY:

par·ley (pär′lē) *vi.* [< Fr. *parler*, to speak < LL. < *parabola*, PARABLE] to hold a talk or conference, esp. with an enemy —*n., pl.* **-leys** a conference; specif., a military conference with an enemy to discuss terms

PRIMARY AND SECONDARY STRESSES:

an·ti·dote (an′tə dōt′) *n.* [ME. & OFr. < L. < Gr. < *anti-*, against + *dotos*, given < *didonai*, to give] **1.** a remedy to counteract a poison [milk and olive oil are common *antidotes*] **2.** anything that works against an evil or unwanted condition [education is a good *antidote* for prejudice] —**an′ti·dot′al** *adj.*

When two or more pronunciations of a word are given, the pronunciation shown first is the one most frequently used. Any others are usually abbreviated.

MORE THAN ONE PRONUNCIATION:

par·tic·u·lar·ly (pər tik′yə lər lē, pär-) *adv.* **1.** in detail **2.** especially; unusually **3.** specifically

Part-of-Speech Labels. The *part-of-speech labels* in a dictionary tell you whether a word can be used as a noun, verb, or some other part of speech. This information is given in abbreviated form, usually after the pronunciation, but sometimes at the end of the entry. When a word can be used as more than one part of speech, the word's meanings are grouped accordingly under each part-of-speech label.

After the appropriate part-of-speech label, the dictionary may also show the plural forms of certain nouns, the various forms of irregular adjectives or adverbs, or the principal parts of certain verbs. As the following example illustrates, such information is often shown in bold type.

EXAMPLE:

fo·cus (fō′kəs) *n., pl.* **fo′cus·es, fo′ci** (-sī) [ModL. < L., hearth] **1.** the point where rays of light, heat, etc. or waves of sound come together, or from which they spread or seem to spread; specif., the point where rays of light reflected by a mirror or refracted by a lens meet **2.** *same as* FOCAL LENGTH **3.** an adjustment of the focal length to make a clear image [to bring a camera into *focus*] **4.** any center of activity, attention, etc. **5.** a part of the body where an infection is most active **6.** *Math. a*) either of the two fixed points used in determining an ellipse: see illustration at ELLIPSE *b*) any similar point for a parabola or hyperbola —*vt.* **-cused** or **-cussed, -cus·ing** or **-cus·sing 1.** to bring into focus [to *focus* light rays] **2.** to adjust the focal length of (the eye, a lens, etc.) so as to make a clear image **3.** to concentrate [to *focus* one's attention] —*vi.* to come to a focus —**in focus** clear; distinct —**out of focus** indistinct; blurred —**fo′cus·er** *n.*

— Noun
— Plural forms of noun
— Principal parts of verb
— Intransitive verb
— Transitive verb

Etymologies. The origin and history of a word is called its *etymology.* This information usually appears in brackets near the beginning of the entry.

Etymologies are printed in a code of symbols, abbreviations, and different kinds of type. The meaning of the code is explained at the front of the dictionary.

EXAMPLE:

aq·ua·ma·rine (ak′wə mə rēn′, äk′-) *n.* [L. *aqua marina,* sea water] **1.** a transparent, pale bluish-green mineral: a variety of beryl, used in jewelry **2.** its color —*adj.* bluish-green

— Etymology

The etymology for *aquamarine* tells you that the word comes from the Latin (L.) words *aqua marina,* which means "sea water."

Definitions. Many words have more than one meaning. Each meaning of a word is called a *definition.* When a word has two or more definitions, they will be numbered and grouped according to their part of speech. Related definitions may be divided even further and indicated by a series of small letters, as in the following example.

EXAMPLE:

Definition with
two lettered parts

Numbered
definitions

Example of
word in use

lag (lag) *vi,* **lagged,** **lag′ging** [? akin to MDan. *lakke,* to go slowly] **1.** (*a*) to fall, move, or stay behind; loiter [the tired hikers *lagged* behind] (*b*) to move or develop more slowly than expected, hoped for, etc. [the assembly line was *lagging* in production] **2.** to become gradually less strong, energetic, etc.; wane; flag [her interest in sports was *lagging*] —*n.* **1.** a falling behind or being slowed or delayed in motion, development, etc. **2.** the amount of such falling behind [a great *lag* between social behavior and scientific knowledge] —**lag′ger** *n.*

As you can see in this example, many definitions are followed by a helpful phrase or sentence showing the word in use.

Special Labels. A definition may sometimes begin with a label that restricts that meaning of the word to a particular area of language. *Usage labels,* such as *Slang, Dialect,* and *Informal* (or *Colloquial*), tell you that a certain meaning is not generally used in formal, standard English. *Field labels,* such as *Biology, Mathematics,* and *Photography,* tell you that the word has a meaning that is limited to the particular occupation, activity, or branch of knowledge.

EXAMPLE:

Field label

Usage label

wid·ow (wid′ō) *n.* [OE. *widewe*] **1.** a woman whose husband has died and who has not remarried ☆**2.** *Cards* a group of cards dealt into a separate pile, typically for the use of the highest bidder ☆**3.** [Colloq.] a woman whose husband is often away taking part in a certain sport, hobby, etc. [a golf *widow*] —*vt.* to cause to become a widow [*widowed* by the war] **wid′ow-hood′** *n.*

Idioms. *Idioms* are expressions such as *down at the heels* and *in the pink* that have meanings different from what the words would literally suggest. Most dictionaries for students list idioms near the end of the main entry. The example on the top of the following page shows the idioms that one dictionary lists for the word *peg.*

EXAMPLE:

peg (peg) *n.* [prob. < LowG. source] **1.** a short pin or bolt used to hold parts together, close an opening, hang things on, fasten ropes to, mark the score in a game, etc. **2.** a step or degree *[the promotion moved me up a few pegs]* **3.** any of the pins that hold the strings of a violin, etc. and are used to tighten or loosen them: see illustration at VIOLIN **4.** [Colloq.] the foot or leg *[it knocked his pegs out from under him]* **5.** [Colloq.] a throw *[a good peg from the outfield]* —*vt.* **pegged, peg′ging 1.** to put a peg or pegs into so as to fasten, mark, etc. **2.** to maintain (prices, etc.) at a fixed level **3.** [Colloq.] to identify or put in a category *[she quickly pegged him as a fool]* **4.** [Colloq.] to throw *[to peg the ball to first base]* —*vi.* to move quickly (with *along*, etc.) —peg away (at) to work hard and steadily (at) — round peg in a square hole one in a position, etc. for which he is unfitted: also square peg in a round hole — take down a peg to make less proud or vain; humble ———— Idioms

Derived Words. Words formed by adding a common suffix, such as *-ly* or *-ness*, to an entry word are called *derived words*. Such suffixes change the word from one part of speech to another. Most dictionaries list derived words at the end of a main entry and do not give definitions for them. A derived word simply appears with its part-of-speech label and, sometimes, with its pronunciation.

EXAMPLE:

☆**pep·py** (pep′ē) *adj.* **-pi·er, -pi·est** [Colloq.] full of pep, or energy; brisk; vigorous —**pep′pi·ly** *adv.* —**pep′pi·ness** *n.* ———— Derived words

Synonyms. A word that is closely related but not identical in meaning to another word is called a *synonym*. After certain main entries you may find a block of words labeled *SYN*. Here the differences in meaning among synonyms are explained. Some dictionaries list *antonyms*—words that are opposite in meaning—right after the synonyms to the entry word, usually without defining them.

EXAMPLE:

pen·i·tence (pen′ə təns) *n.* the state of being penitent
SYN.—**penitence** implies sorrow over having done wrong and a willingness to make up for one's wrongful act; **repentance** implies a full understanding of one's wrongs and a will to change one's ways; **contrition** implies a deep sorrow for one's wrongs, with a firm determination to change for the better; **compunction** suggests a sharp but passing feeling of uneasiness about one's wrongdoing; **remorse** implies a deep and torturing sense of guilt; **regret** may refer to sorrow over any unfortunate happening as well as over a fault or act of one's own

Synonyms ————

EXERCISE E: Understanding the Parts of Main Entries.
Read the following main entries carefully from a dictionary excerpt. Then, on your paper, write the answers to the ten questions on the following page.

char·ac·ter·is·tic (kar'ik tə ris'tik) *adj.* that gives the basic quality or character to someone or something *[the characteristic sound made by an owl] —n.* **1.** a trait, feature, etc. that makes a person or thing different from others **2.** the whole number, or integral part, of a logarithm, as 4 in the logarithm 4.7193: see also MANTISSA **—char'ac·ter·is'ti·cal·ly** *adv.*
SYN·—characteristic suggests a quality that is typical of, and helps identify, a certain person or thing *[her characteristic honesty; the characteristic taste of honey]*; **individual** and **distinctive** refer to a quality that makes something different from others of its kind, **distinctive** often implying excellence *[an individual, or distinctive, style]*

char·ac·ter·ize (kar'ik tə rīz') *vt.* **-ized', -iz'ing** **1.** to describe or show as having particular qualities or traits *[Tennyson characterized King Arthur as wise and brave]* **2.** to be the distinctive character of; distinguish *[bribery characterized her term in office] —char'ac·ter·i·za'tion n.*

character sketch a short piece of writing describing a person or type of person

cha·rade (shə rād') *n.* [Fr. < Pr. *charrada* < *charrar,* to gossip] *[often pl.]* **1.** a game in which the players try to guess a word or phrase that another player is acting out without speaking, often syllable by syllable **2.** an action, show of feeling, etc. that is easily seen as misleading or insincere

char·coal (chär'kōl') *n.* [ME. *char cole,* prob. < *charren,* to turn + *cole,* coal] **1.** a form of carbon produced by partially burning wood or other organic matter in large closed containers from which air is kept out **2.** a pencil made of this substance **3.** a drawing made with such a pencil **4.** a very dark gray or brown, almost black *—vt.* to draw with charcoal

chard (chärd) *n.* [Fr. *carde* < L. *carduus,* thistle] a kind of beet whose large leaves and thick stalks are used as food

Char·din (shàr dan') **1. Jean Si·mé·on** (sē mä ōn'), 1699-1779; Fr. painter **2. Teilhard de,** *see* TEILHARD DE CHARDIN

chare (cher) *n.* [OE. *cierr,* a turn, job < *cierran,* to turn] a chore, esp. a household chore *—vi.* **chared, char'ing** **1.** to do chores **2.** *same as* CHAR[2]

charge (chärj) *vt.* **charged, charg'ing** [< OFr. *chargier* < VL. *carricare,* to load < L. *carrus,* CAR, wagon] **1.** to load or fill with the required material *[a firearm charged with gunpowder]* **2.** to saturate with another substance *[air charged with steam]* **3.** to add carbon dioxide to (water, etc.) ☆**4.** to add an electrical charge to (a battery, etc.) **5.** to give as a task, duty, etc. to *[the nurse is charged with giving medicine to the patients]* **6.** to give instructions to or command authoritatively *[the judge charged the jury]* **7.** to accuse of wrongdoing; censure *[the state charged her with murder]* **8.** to set as a price or fee *[barbers used to charge a dollar for a haircut]* **9.** to have recorded as a debt one is to pay later *[he charged his purchases]* **10.** to attack vigorously *[our troops charged the enemy] —vi.* **1.** to ask payment *(for)* *[to charge for a service]* **2.** to attack vigorously or move forward as if attacking *—n.* **1.** the amount, as of fuel, gunpowder, etc., used to load or fill something **2.** *a)* the amount of chemical energy stored in a battery to be a source of electrical energy *b)* a change from the condition of electrical neutrality by the gaining of electrons *(negative charge)* or by the loss of electrons *(positive charge)* ☆**3.** [Slang] a thrill **4.** responsibility or duty *(of)* *[she took nurses' *charges]* **7.** instruction or command, esp. instructions given by a judge to a jury **8.** accusation; indictment *[charges of cruelty]* **9.** the cost or price of an article, service, etc. **10.** a debt or expense ☆**11.** *same as* CHARGE ACCOUNT **12.** *a)* an attack, as by troops *b)* the signal for this **13.** *Heraldry* a bearing —see **SYN.** at COMMAND —**charge off 1.** to regard as a loss **2.** to think of as due to a certain cause; ascribe *[charge off her mistake to inexperience]* —**in charge (of)** having the responsibility or control (of) —**in the charge of** in the care of or under the control of —**charge·a·ble** (chär′jə b'l) *adj.*

4. gossip   6.a. to set as a price or fee   6.c. accusation; indictment
8. in (or out of) character, charge off, in the change of/Sentences will vary.

1. In which quarter of the dictionary would these entries be found? first

2. Of the main entries given, which entry word has the most syllables? characteristic

3. Which syllable is stressed in the word *charade?* second

4. According to its etymology, what does *charade* mean?

5. As how many different parts of speech can *charcoal* be used? two—verb and noun

6. Write the definition that explains the meaning of *charge* as it is used in each of the following sentences:

   a. The carpenter *charged* us $10 for the shelf. to set as a price or fee

   b. The British cavalry *charged* at dawn. to attack vigorously

   c. The *charges* brought against him were false. accusation; indictment

7. Which definition of *charge* is not considered formal English? a thrill

8. List three idioms found in the excerpt. Use them in sentences. characteristically, characterization, changeable

9. List three derived words that can be found in the excerpt.

10. List the synonyms that are explained in the entry for *characteristic.* individual distinctive

9. characteristically, characterization, changeable

DEVELOPING WRITING SKILLS: Using a Dictionary to Answer Questions.
Use a dictionary to answer the following questions. Write your answers in complete sentences.
Some answers will vary; samples are given. Sentences will vary.

1. What is the first meaning of the word *key?*

2. According to its etymology, what does *gospel* mean? good news

3. In what country would you find *curb* spelled *kerb?* Gr Brit

4. What idioms are listed under the word *fall?*

5. What are some synonyms of the word *fatal?*

1. an instrument, usually of metal, for moving the bolt of a lock   4. -(all) over oneself, -among, -away, -back, -back on, etc.   5. deadly, mortal, lethal, etc. **749**

Checking Your Skills

In the Checking Your Skills assignment, your students read about postal service in the United States. To help students learn about other governmental services, have them complete the following speaking and listening activity.

Speaking and Listening

Have each student select a governmental service, such as the social security system, the welfare system, or the Occupational Safety and Health Administration. If students have difficulty thinking of governmental services, you might encourage them to ask their social studies teachers to provide suggestions. Next, students should research the topic in the encyclopedia and other reference books. Using the information from their research, students should then prepare an oral report about their topic. Finally, they should deliver their reports to the class.

Using Study Skills in Writing

Peer Editing Divide your students into groups of three or four. Then have them read their reports to one another and suggest ways in which they could be improved. When evaluating their classmates' reports, peer editors should use the revision checklist on page 553.

Skills Review and Writing Workshop

Library and Reference Skills

CHECKING YOUR SKILLS

Take notes on this selection from a magazine.
Answers will vary.

The worst postal service in America's history occurred during the Revolution. The war resulted in postal rates four thousand percent higher than those under the British mail system. After the war, however, postage soon became much cheaper. And mail was distributed more widely. However, rates were still exorbitant by today's standards. The shortest letter cost as much to send as a package. Home delivery was rare. The addressee more often than not had to pay the postage. In those days, Americans were reluctant to trust the post office with delivery of money. The most popular solution was to mail half of a bill and wait until the addressee got it before sending the other half.

USING STUDY SKILLS IN WRITING
Writing a Report

When you are assigned a written report, you must use the library to find information. Use the steps below to write a report about a famous American who is still living.
Answers will vary.

Prewriting: Decide who you want to write about. Include information from the following sources: a general encyclopedia, *Current Biography*, and *Who's Who in America*. Take notes and make an outline for your report.

Writing: Begin your report by giving general information about the person such as date of birth, place of birth, and accomplishments for which the person is noted. Then clearly present the facts that led up to the person's becoming famous. Then explain the effect the person's achievements have had on his or her life and on other people.

Revising: Read over your report to see if you have covered all the points in your outline. After you have revised, proofread carefully.

UNIT VIII

Speaking and Listening

39 Speaking and Listening Skills

UNIT VIII
Speaking and Listening
(pp. 751–768)

This unit covers the essential speaking and listening skills that students need in order to communicate effectively both in school and outside of school. This unit, consisting of one chapter, does not depend on prerequisite learning of material in other units. You may, however, choose to teach this unit early in the year so that students can use and reinforce the skills during the year.

CHAPTER 39
Speaking and Listening Skills
(pp. 752–768)

The three sections of this chapter are designed to help students develop basic speaking and listening skills that are invaluable tools to help them learn. A useful way to begin work in this chapter is to explain how speaking and listening are part of the communication process—both a speaker and a listener are needed in order to share feelings and ideas.

Section 39.1 covers informal speaking skills such as speaking in class discussions, giving directions, making introductions, and making announcements. Section 39.2 treats formal speaking skills including the major kinds of speeches as well as practice in planning, preparing, and delivering a speech. Section 39.3 helps students develop effective listening strategies for selecting and remembering information.

For a review of the entire chapter and a related writing activity, see the Skills Review and Writing Workshop on page 768.

39.1 Informal Speaking Skills
(pp. 752–757)

OBJECTIVES

After completing this section, students should be able to

- Participate in class discussions.
- Give clear, complete directions.
- Make good introductions.
- Make clear, complete announcements.

Chapter **39**

Speaking and Listening Skills

Listening and speaking are two activities that everybody does every day. Both activities are part of one process. When one person speaks, another listens. Someone who speaks well can express ideas clearly. Someone who listens well can remember more of what he or she hears. Good speaking and listening skills can help you be successful both in and out of school.

39.1 Informal Speaking Skills

You use speaking skills every day in informal situations: in conversations, in class discussions, while giving directions, making introductions, and making announcements. This section can help you improve your informal speaking skills.

Speaking in Class Discussions

You will have many opportunities in the classroom to practice your informal speaking skills. Every time you answer a

39.1 Informal Speaking Skills

question or make a comment about the topic being discussed, you are practicing informal speaking skills.

Some people feel uneasy about speaking in front of a group. If you are one of these people, preparation and practice can help you overcome your anxiety.

Develop confidence about participating in class through preparation and practice.

Usually, some preparation is useful to participate in a class discussion. The more well prepared you are, the more you will be able to contribute to your class and benefit from it.

The chart below offers suggestions to follow.

SUGGESTIONS ON HOW TO TAKE PART IN CLASS DISCUSSIONS

1. Set a goal for yourself about taking part in class. For example, you might decide to speak at least once during each class.
2. Do required homework and reading so that you are well prepared. Extra reading on the subject you are studying can help you say something of special interest to the class.
3. If possible, plan what you might say before the discussion begins.
4. Do not wait for the teacher to call on you. Raise your hand and volunteer to contribute your thoughts.
5. Listen to the discussion carefully so that what you say will be to the point.
6. Observe other students who make good contributions to the class, and learn from their example.

As you put these suggestions into practice, you will develop your speaking skills and build your self-confidence about speaking in front of others. This, in turn, will enable you to contribute more freely and regularly to class discussions in the future, and will improve the quality of your classes, both for yourself and for others.

Getting Started

Ask students what speaking/listening situations they have been involved in during the last twenty-four hours. List these on the board. Elicit specific responses: a conversation at the dinner table, a class discussion in history, planning a class trip, etc. The number of items on the board should by itself help students realize the importance of speaking and listening skills. Explain that these can be improved by practice.

Text Follow Through

Discuss text pages 752–757.

Assign Exercise A, page 754; Exercise B, page 755; Exercise C, page 756; Exercise D, page 757; and Developing Writing Skills, page 757.

Less advanced You may want to work on the various subsections over time, one per month perhaps. If you use the first subsection early, you could help students apply the suggestions in your own class. If you assign Exercise A, you will probably need to monitor students' charts

Average Again, you may want to introduce the activities in this section over time. Then if you introduce students to using a tape recorder in these non-threatening situations, they may be more comfortable with its use when you work on formal speeches. If PA announcements are made in your school by students, you could encourage some of yours to volunteer.

Advanced Since most students probably participate well in class, you may want to work individually with any who need encouragement. You can probably work quickly through other subsections, using them as an icebreaker before more extensive work on formal speaking.

Additional Practice

Practice Pages or Practice Book, page 173
Speaking and Listening Activities, pages 22–27

TESTING

Test Program

    Unit Pretest, page 127
    Chapter Test, page 128
    Unit Post-Test, page 130

Speaking and Listening Activities, Evaluation Sheets, pages 8, 9

RE-TEACHING

Practice Pages or Practice Book, page 173
Speaking and Listening Activities, pages 22–27

THINKING SKILLS

Application—*Preparing* a record of class participation (Exercise A, page 754)
Demonstrating speech skills (Exercise B, page 755; Exercise C, page 756; Exercise D, page 757)

Synthesis—*Writing* a paragraph about the importance of speech skills (Developing Writing Skills, page 757)

EXERCISE A: Improving Your Class Participation. For each of your classes, make a chart with columns like the sample below. Try to increase the number and the quality of your comments for a one-month period.

Answers will vary.

CLASSROOM DISCUSSION CHART: ENGLISH			
Date	Topic	Number of Contributions	Evaluation of Comments
Oct. 15	"Casey at the Bat"	2	Being both a player and a fan helped
Oct. 16	"Casey at the Bat"	2	OK. Could have been better if paid more attention to discussion
Oct. 17	"Casey at the Bat"	1	Good. Reviewed book right before class.

Giving Directions

People often ask for directions on how to get somewhere or how to do something. For example, someone may ask how to get to your house or how to play a certain game. To be followed easily, directions must be clear and complete.

When giving directions, be as clear and accurate in your language as possible.

Look at the difference between the two examples below.

VAGUE DIRECTIONS: To make scrambled eggs, put mixed-up eggs and milk in a pan and cook them until done.

CLEAR DIRECTIONS: For each serving of scrambled eggs, use a fork to beat two eggs and two tablespoons milk together in a bowl. Melt two teaspoons butter in a skillet until hot enough to make a drop of water sizzle.

Then, pour in the egg mixture and turn the heat low. Stir gently as the eggs start to get firm so the uncooked portion goes to the bottom. Cook until the eggs are all firm but moist.

The chart gives suggestions for giving clear directions.

SUGGESTIONS FOR GIVING DIRECTIONS
1. Take a moment before you speak to think through the directions carefully.
2. Speak slowly so that your listeners can follow your directions without difficulty.
3. Choose your words carefully, being as specific as you can. Give only one step of the directions in each sentence.
4. Give the most important details, but do not confuse your listener with unnecessary information.

EXERCISE B: Giving Directions. Take turns giving a partner directions to another location in the school or in your community. See if each partner can reach the destination that he or she has been given. After following the directions, each partner should evaluate whether they were given clearly and accurately.
Answers will vary.

Making Introductions

You have probably introduced one person to another many times. You may have introduced two of your friends to each other or a friend to your parents or other relatives.

When you introduce one person to another or to a group, you should try to make the people involved feel at ease. Practice will help you learn to make introductions smoothly. The most important thing is to remember the person's full name and to pronounce it correctly. You should also add something of interest about the people you are introducing.

Introduce people by their full names and tell something of interest about them.

Look at the difference between the following two introductions.

INTRODUCTIONS: Mrs. Soares, this is Jim. He's new.

Mrs. Soares, I'd like you to meet Jim Hyatt. He's a new student here. Jim just transferred from Fairdale High, where he was in the Honor Society and played on the basketball team. Jim, this is Mrs. Soares, our English teacher.

This sort of detailed introduction will help make the person you are introducing feel comfortable with a new group of people right away.

EXERCISE C: Making an Introduction. Do this exercise with a partner. Take turns pretending to be a new student in your school, and introduce each other to the class. Be sure to include the full name as well as interesting information about the person you are introducing.
Answers will vary.

Making Announcements

Announcements provide factual information that answers six key questions: who, what, when, where, why, and how. Although every announcement will not answer all six questions, you can use them as a checklist to ensure that you cover all the important details.

When making an announcement, supply answers to the questions who, what, when, where, why, and how.

The information in an announcement should be easy to understand and remember. When you make an announcement, speak loudly and clearly, so your listeners can hear what you are saying.

39.1 Informal Speaking Skills

The following example of an announcement that might be given in your school answers the six key questions in the following way.

ANNOUNCEMENT: This is an announcement about the talent show that will be held in the auditorium on Friday, October 15, at 7:30 p.m. Tickets will be sold at the door and will cost $2.00. After the show a bake sale will be held in the lobby. Proceeds from the tickets and the bake sale will be used to help pay for new band uniforms. Anyone interested in doing an act, providing baked goods, or helping with set-up or clean-up should speak to Elizabeth Ann Hirschfeld. She will be available during lunch period and after school today and tomorrow in Room 19.

EXERCISE D: Making Announcements Write an announcement for a real or imaginary event that would be of interest to the students in your class. Read it to the class, and ask one or two people to repeat the important details. Did you present all the necessary information? Did you present it clearly? Did you leave unanswered any questions about the event that your classmates might have?
Answers will vary.

DEVELOPING WRITING SKILLS: Writing About Informal Speaking Skills. Write two paragraphs about why you think informal speaking skills are important for you to have. In the first paragraph, write about speaking with friends or family, participating in class discussions, giving directions, making introductions, and making announcements. In the second paragraph, write about ways in which informal speaking situations skills prove useful to you in a career when you become an adult. What kinds of jobs require good speaking skills?
Answers will vary.

39.2 Formal Speaking Skills

(pp. 758–763)

OBJECTIVES

After completing this section, students should be able to

- Identify three kinds of speeches: explanatory, persuasive, entertaining.
- Plan and deliver a short speech.
- Evaluate a speech.

TEACHING

Getting Started

If your school has videotape facilities, tape a segment of a news show, a commercial monologue, and a humorous monologue. Play the tape one segment at a time, asking students in each case what the speaker's purpose seems to be. Explain that speakers need to understand their own purpose as they plan and deliver a speech. (If your school does not have videotape, describe the suggested situations.)

Text Follow Through

Discuss text pages 758–763.

Assign Exercise A, page 758; Exercise B, page 761; Exercise C, page 762; Exercise D, page 763; and Developing Writing Skills, page 763.

39.2 Formal Speaking Skills

Formal speaking skills are used when speaking to an audience. The audience may be a small group, such as a club meeting or a school class, or it may be a large group, such as a school assembly. Formal speaking requires more preparation than informal speaking does. Many people are nervous about speaking before a group. This can be overcome by having experience in speaking in front of others and by being well prepared to give your speech.

Recognizing Different Kinds of Speeches

There are three main kinds of speeches: *explanatory* speeches, *persuasive* speeches, and *entertaining* speeches. The kind of speech you give will depend on why you are giving the speech and the age and background of your audience.

Choose the kind of speech you will give by considering both the purpose of the speech and your audience.

An *explanatory* speech explains an idea, an object, or an event. In an explanatory speech, you present the facts.

A *persuasive* speech is used to get your audience to agree with your point of view or to take some action. In a persuasive speech you state your position on an issue and then defend your opinion in a logical, orderly way.

An *entertaining* speech is given to amuse the audience. A good speaker will often use humorous and entertaining material to enliven an explanatory or persuasive speech. This relaxes the audience and allows them to listen to the informative or convincing material more readily.

EXERCISE A: Identifying Kinds of Speeches. Label each of the speech topics as *explanatory, persuasive,* or *entertaining.* Then identify who the audience might be for each speech.
Kinds of speeches and two samples for audience are given.

758

1. How to survive with four-year-old twin brothers entertaining
2. What is modern art? explanatory; art class
3. The importance of eating a balanced diet persuasive
4. How to build a bookcase explanatory
5. Why soccer is a better sport to watch than football persuasive
6. How to get a part-time job after school explanatory
7. How to become a brain surgeon in three easy lessons
8. Why we need a new school gym persuasive
9. What to do with one sock left from a pair entertaining
10. The best way to study for an exam explanatory

1. entertaining; classmates   7. entertaining

Planning Your Speech

Preparation is the most important part of giving a speech. When you are asked to give a speech in class or before some other group of people, begin by thinking carefully about both the purpose of your speech and the audience you will be speaking to. This will help you choose the kind of speech you will give, the topic of the speech, and the way in which you will present your material.

Choose a subject that you know or like in order to interest your audience.

After choosing your topic, gather all the information you need and then organize it in outline form. The outline should contain only main ideas and their supporting details. If you need to review outlining, see the samples for modified and formal outlines given in Chapter 35.

Study your outline, and write note cards to use when you deliver your speech. The brief headings and major details on the note cards can be read quickly and easily while you are speaking. Note cards help you present your speech in order without skipping important details.

The chart on the following page can help you prepare note cards for a speech.

Less advanced You may want students to work on the planning of their speeches in class so that you can give individual help. The librarian or media aide might also be available for work with individual students. It might be preferable not to grade students' first speeches.

Average You will probably want to introduce students to the advantage of practicing a speech on tape, audio or video. Depending on the importance of speech in your curriculum, you may want to have students give speeches regularly, perhaps once every month or two. In this case, you will again probably want to avoid grading the first speech.

Advanced Students will benefit from giving speeches from time to time. For the first speech you may want to direct one third of the students to choose an explanatory topic, one third persuasive, and one third entertaining. For succeeding speeches you can rotate these assignments.

Additional Practice

Practice Pages or Practice Book, pages 174, 175
Speaking and Listening Activities, pages 28–34

TESTING

Test Program

Unit Pretest, page 127
Chapter Test, page 129
Unit Post-Test, page 130

Speaking and Listening Activities, Evaluation Sheet, page 10

RE-TEACHING

Practice Pages or Practice
  Book, pages 174, 175
Speaking and Listening
  Activities, pages 28–34

THINKING SKILLS

Knowledge—*Identifying* given
  topics for speeches as explanatory, persuasive, or
  entertaining (Exercise A, page
  758)

Application—*Preparing* a
  speech (Exercise B, page 761)

Synthesis—*Delivering* a speech
  (Exercise C, page 762)

Evaluation—*Appraising* a
  speech (Exercise D, page 763;
  Developing Writing Skills,
  page 763)

SUGGESTIONS FOR ORGANIZING MATERIAL TO GIVE A SPEECH

1. Use only a few $3'' \times 5''$ index cards.
2. Print all information neatly.
3. Write out quotations or facts that you want to remember exactly.
4. Write out beginning and ending statements if you think they will be useful.
5. Rely mainly on key words and phrases or clear abbreviations to jog your memory.
6. Use a clear outline form and indent all of the details under the ideas they support.
7. Use underlining and capital letters to make important information stand out.
8. Number your cards to help keep them in order.

The following note cards have been developed for a speech demonstrating how to make a paper hat.

①   <u>Making Newspaper Hats</u>
Need a quick hat that anyone can make in a matter
of seconds? Try a newspaper hat!
I. USES
    A. Costumes
    B. Boat - it floats
    C. Container for snacks
II. MATERIALS
    A. Newspaper (double sheet)
    B. Pencil & ruler

② C. Paint
   D. Seals (optional)
III. HOW TO <u>FOLD</u>
    A. Hold sheet with <u>short length facing you</u>
    B. Fold top ½ <u>down</u> to meet bottom
    C. On front, draw line <u>2"</u> from bottom
    D. Fold <u>left corner</u> to line
    E. Fold <u>right corner</u> to line
    F. Separate <u>2" margin</u> at bottom
    G. Fold front & back margins <u>up</u>

③ · H. Open up △ part of hat & place on head
IV. DECORATE
    A. Paint
    B. Add seals or stickers
    C. Add fringe
Newspaper hats may not be the most attractive
of hats, but their price is right and materials
are usually available.

EXERCISE B: Planning Your Speech. Prepare a three-minute speech. Select a topic of interest to you from the following list or choose one of your own, think about the nature of your audience, gather any information you will need, organize it in outline form, and write note cards for the speech.
Answers will vary.

How to make an apple pie	Free activities in our town
What is a sonnet?	
The best TV program this season	What to do about daydreaming
Our most successful President	
What is a mammal?	Why fish make the best pets
How to avoid stage fright	
Why study?	

Delivering Your Speech

Practice giving your speech at home as you plan to give it in class. Use the note cards you have prepared and deliver your speech several times. The more practice you get, the more confidence you will have when you deliver your speech.

Practice your speech to gain confidence.

The suggestions below will help you give a speech.

SUGGESTIONS FOR GIVING A SPEECH

1. Do not read to your audience. Refer to your note cards and speak in a natural, relaxed manner.
2. Pronounce your words clearly, and speak steadily.
3. Be aware of nonverbal language, such as your movements, posture, facial expressions, and gestures, while you practice and deliver your speech.
4. Stay within the time limit you were given for your speech.
5. Be prepared to answer questions from your audience.

Work on these suggestions as you practice your speech. When the time comes to actually deliver your speech, they will come naturally. Then you will be able to focus on the content of your speech, rather than on the manner of your presentation.

EXERCISE C: Practicing and Delivering a Speech. Take the note cards you wrote for a speech in Exercise B on page 761. Practice giving the speech several times, following all the suggestions given. Look at your note cards as little as possible, speak naturally, stand comfortably, and be aware of your nonverbal language. Then deliver your speech in class, putting all your skills to use.
Answers will vary.

Evaluating a Speech

When you evaluate another person's speech, you do two things. First, you give constructive criticism that the speaker can use to improve his or her speaking skills. Second, you think about how you can improve your own speaking skills.

Evaluate a speech in a way that offers benefits both to the speaker and to yourself.

Never criticize someone's speech without saying something good about it first. Then give constructive criticism.

CHECKLIST FOR EVALUATING A SPEECH

1. What type of speech was given—expository, persuasive, or entertaining?
2. Did the speaker introduce the topic clearly, develop it well, and end in a conclusive manner?
3. Did the speaker support main ideas with details?
4. Was the speaker's voice loud enough? Was the rate of speaking varied? Were words pronounced clearly and correctly?
5. Did the speaker appear confident and support his or her verbal delivery with appropriate nonverbal language?

EXERCISE D: Evaluating a Speech. Using the checklist on page 762, make a detailed evaluation of a speech given in class. Then, find two or more skills that the speaker used effectively and practice using them in a speech of your own.
Answers will vary.

DEVELOPING WRITING SKILLS: Writing a Speech Evaluation. Write a paragraph evaluating a speech you have given. Discuss what you said as well as how you said it.
Answers will vary.

Listening Skills 39.3

Listening is something we do every day. But there are so many sounds around us every day that we must be selective in what we actually listen to. It is important, however, to distinguish between *hearing* (what happens automatically when sounds reach your ear) and *listening* (actively paying attention to and attempting to understand and retain what you hear). Being able to listen well is important for your development as a student and as a human being.

Preparing to Listen

Nearly seventy-five percent of your time in school is spent listening. You listen to teachers, friends, announcements, movies, tape recordings, records, instructions, and so on. There are so many different speakers you must listen to, that you must be prepared to listen well. To listen well, you must give the speaker your complete attention.

Prepare to listen by giving the speaker your complete attention.

Listening effectively requires concentration and attention. The ability to concentrate and pay attention must be developed by practice.

The chart on the next page gives suggestions that will help you learn to concentrate and pay attention if you practice them daily.

39.3 Listening Skills
(pp. 763–767)

OBJECTIVES
After completing this section, students should be able to

- Focus attention for listening.
- Listen for the main idea and major details.

TEACHING
Getting Started

Engage students in a discussion about the difference between hearing and listening. Ask them what sorts of things distract them while they are listening and what happens when their attention wanders. Ask them why being able to really listen when we choose to is important. Explain that understanding listening can help not only in school but also in life situations.

Text Follow Through

Discuss text pages 763–767.

Assign Exercise A, page 764; Exercise B, page 766; and Developing Writing Skills, page 766.

Less advanced Students will probably need work on listening, but will have more or less difficulty depending on how cooperative the class is. You might want to combine work on Exercises A and B in order to make the suggestions on page 764 more concrete.

Average To give students more practice in listening, you can borrow from the library recordings of well-known speeches. Play short selections for the class, telling students to jot down the main idea and major details as they listen. Afterwards, have students discuss their notes to compare what each considered important.

Advanced While students' listening skills are probably good, they may tend to take too many notes. The comparison described above can help refine their skills.

Additional Practice

Practice Pages or Practice
  Book, page 176
Speaking and Listening Activities, pages 35, 36

TESTING

Test Program

  Unit Pretest, page 127
  Chapter Test, page 129
  Unit Post-Test, page 130

RE-TEACHING

Practice Pages or Practice Book, page 176

SUGGESTIONS FOR PREPARING TO LISTEN

1. Start with a positive attitude. Say to yourself, "I am going to concentrate and pay attention." Avoid daydreaming by actively trying to listen, understand, and remember what is being said.
2. Don't look around at your friends in class, out the window, and so on. Focus your eyes and ears on the speaker.
3. Concentrate on *what* the speaker is saying and try not to be distracted by his or her looks or manner of speaking.
4. Block out any distractions such as noises inside or outside the classroom or any concerns or thoughts you had earlier in the day. Don't try to think of questions or answers now—put all your energy into listening and taking in what is being said.
5. Put away anything that may detract from your paying attention to the speaker, such as books, magazines, homework schedules, and so on.
6. Keep a pencil and paper handy in case you want to take notes, but avoid doodling or writing things unrelated to the discussion.
7. Try to find out in advance what main topic will be discussed. That way you have some idea of what to focus on while you are listening. However, do not ignore the speaker because you think you already know what he or she is going to say. You might be surprised if you really pay attention.

It is important to note that your physical condition also greatly affects your ability to pay attention. Therefore, you should be sure to get enough rest, to eat properly, and to exercise. Otherwise, you will be distracted by your body saying "I'm tired! I'm hungry! I want to run around!" and so on—and you won't be able to concentrate on what's being said.

EXERCISE A: Developing Your Listening Skills. Before one class actively prepare yourself to listen by following the suggestions in the chart above. After class evaluate whether

THINKING SKILLS

Application—*Preparing* to listen
(Exercise A, page 764)
Demonstrating listening skills
(Exercise B, page 766)

Synthesis—*Writing* about listening (Developing Writing Skills,
page 766)

39.3 Listening Skills

your preparing to listen helped. Did you understand and remember more than usual? Did you take notes? Did you avoid
doodling, daydreaming, and looking around the room?
Answers will vary.

Selecting Information to Remember

Learning how to listen also involves learning what to listen
to. It is important to be able to identify main ideas and major
details while listening to a speaker so you know what you want
to remember and what is unnecessary.

**Identify and remember the main points and ma-
jor details while you are listening to the speaker.**

Asking yourself the questions in the following chart can help
you identify main ideas and major details. Study them and ask
yourself these questions when you are listening in class.

IDENTIFYING MAIN IDEAS AND MAJOR DETAILS

1. What is the general topic?
2. What important points are being made about the topic?
3. What needs to be remembered about each point?
4. What examples or facts relate to each point?
5. What clues is the speaker giving about something's importance? Does he or she begin by saying "Remember . . . ,"
   "Most of all . . . ," "Importantly . . . ," or "To sum up. . . ."
6. Does the speaker repeat an idea or phrase a number of times
   or emphasize its importance by his or her tone of voice or by
   using gestures?
7. What is written on the blackboard? What do the visual aids or
   supporting materials (if any) tell me about the main idea and
   major details of what I am listening to?

If you practice asking yourself these questions while you are
listening attentively, you will eventually become an active and
effective listener. You will find that you can get much more out
of a class by developing your listening skills.

Developing Writing Skills

To help students further develop their listening skills, have them complete the following assignment.

Writing Across the Curriculum

Television documentaries convey important and interesting information about a wide array of subjects.

Prewriting Watch a television documentary, such as a program about a scientific development or an artistic movement. As you watch, take notes about the main ideas and major details that the program conveys. Also make sure that you follow the listening suggestions on page 764 of your textbook.

Writing Using your notes, write a short summary of the documentary. Try to make your summary as clear and concise as possible, and make sure that you include all of the program's main ideas.

Revising Revise your summary, making sure that you have not omitted any main ideas or major details. When you have finished revising, proofread your summary and prepare a final copy.

EXERCISE B: Developing and Practicing Listening Skills. Work with a partner on this exercise. One of you should read the first paragraph aloud while the other listens for the main idea and major details, writing them down after the reading is completed. Then switch roles and repeat the process with the second passage.

Main ideas are underlined; major details are shaded.

1. The arctic environment changes radically with the seasons. In the winter, there are months of darkness and cold. Snow and ice transform the polar world into an endless white wasteland. Even the boundaries between land and sea become invisible. But in the early spring, there are 24 hours of daylight. The warmth of the sun melts the ice and streams splash through the landscape. Many beautiful flowers spring up in the surface soil. Young animals such as hares, foxes, caribou, and muskoxen grow with incredible speed. These contrasts between the seasons, so different than any other in the world, make the Arctic a unique place.

2. The pine barrens of New Jersey is an unusual area in North America. It covers about 650 thousand acres, nearly as large as Yosemite National Park or Grand Canyon National Park. The pine barrens area, in the center of the state, is so undeveloped it can truly be called wilderness. It has only 15 people per square mile. This is quite remarkable when you realize that the state of New Jersey as a whole has nearly 1,000 people per square mile—the greatest population density anywhere in the United States. The natural vegetation and unusual beauty of the pine barrens area, as well as its location in the heart of the Northeast industrial corridor, make it a special place.

DEVELOPING WRITING SKILLS: Writing About Developing Your Listening Skills. Practice preparing to listen in class for one week. Refer to the suggestions given in this section often. At the end of the week, write a paragraph describing any changes you have noticed in your ability to listen effectively. Include in your paragraph answers to the following questions.

Answers will vary.

1. Were you able to concentrate and put distractions aside so that you were ready to listen to each speaker?

2. Were you able to identify the main ideas and major detail in each listening situation?

3. What areas do you still need to work on to listen more effectively? What specific steps should you take to improve?

Checking Your Skills

In the Checking Your Skills assignment, students answered questions about their speaking skills. To help students improve both their speaking skills and their listening skills, have them complete the following assignment.

Speaking and Listening

Have each student research an important historical event in the encyclopedia or another reference book. Then have them prepare a brief oral presentation in which they outline the details of the event and discuss any known causes or effects of the event. Next, the students should take turns delivering their presentations to the class. When listening to their classmates' presentations, students should write down the main ideas and major details. Students should also feel free to ask questions if any of the details of the event are not clear to them.

Using Study Skills in Writing

Publishing After students have finished revising their essays, you might want to have student volunteers read their essays to the class.

Skills Review and Writing Workshop

Speaking and Listening Skills

CHECKING YOUR SKILLS

To keep track of your progress using informal and formal speaking skills, answer the following questions:
Answers will vary.

1. What goals have you set for your participation in class discussions? Do you raise your hand in class? Have your contributions increased? Why or why not?

2. If you have had to give directions, or make an announcement, or make an introduction recently, did you present the information accurately? Did you speak clearly, slowly, loudly? Were people confused by anything you said? Did they have to ask questions?

3. If you have given a speech recently, did you schedule enough time to plan it well and to practice it several times before actually delivering it? Did you use note cards? Were they clear and well-organized? Did you just glance at them and speak naturally, or did you read to your audience?

USING STUDY SKILLS IN WRITING

Writing a Personal Essay

Write a brief, personal essay based on your answers to the questions above.
Answers will vary.

Prewriting: Look over your answers. Construct an outline using the main ideas.

Writing: When writing your essay, include examples of successes and difficulties you have encountered in trying to improve your speaking skills.

Rewriting: Look over what you have written. Is it an interesting essay? Does it show a clear picture of your efforts to master these skills? Correct any spelling, grammar, or punctuation errors. After you have revised, proofread carefully.

Preparing Papers

This short section on preparing papers will give you a style to use in setting up your papers. It will also suggest questions you can ask if you are having problems with grammar, usage, mechanics, or spelling. Finally, it will give you a few useful symbols that you can use when you revise and proofread.

Setting Up Your Papers

Neatness counts. It may sometimes be a part of your grade, and it will almost always have a favorable effect on your reader. If you use the suggestions in the following charts, your reader will be able to concentrate on your ideas, not on the physical appearance of your paper.

Setting Up a Handwritten Paper. Use the following guidelines for a handwritten paper.

HANDWRITTEN PAPERS
1. Use white, lined, notebook-sized paper. Do not, however, use pages ripped from a spiral binder.
2. Use either blue or black ink.
3. Leave a margin of space on the right side.
4. Indent each paragraph.

Setting Up a Typed Paper. Use these guidelines for a typed paper.

TYPED PAPERS
1. Use white, unlined, notebook-sized paper.
2. Use a clear black ribbon.
3. Leave a margin of space on all sides.
4. Double-space all lines and indent each paragraph.

Identifying Your Papers. Your teacher may have a form for you to follow in identifying your papers. If not, use one of the two forms below. The example on the left shows a full title page for long papers. The example on the right works best for short papers.

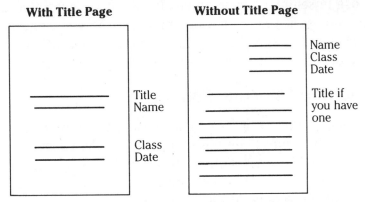

The second page and all additional pages should carry your name and the page number in the upper right-hand corner.

Checking for Errors

In revising papers look for errors in grammar, usage, mechanics, and spelling. The following charts will help.

Errors in Grammar. Common errors in grammar are fragments, run-ons, and modifiers.

Problems	Questions to Ask	Sections in Text
Fragments	Does each sentence have all of the necessary sentence parts?	10.1
Run-ons	Are any of your sentences really two sentences?	10.2
Misplaced Modifiers	Are all modifiers as close as possible to the words modified?	10.3

Errors in Usage. Agreement causes problems in usage.

Problems	Questions to Ask	Sections in Text
Subject-Verb Agreement	Do subjects and verbs agree in number?	14.1 and 14.2
Pronoun-Antecedent Agreement	Do all the pronouns agree in person and number with their antecedents?	14.3
Special Problems with Verbs, Modifiers, and Other Words	Have you chosen the wrong verb from certain troublesome pairs? Have you chosen the wrong adjective or adverb? Have you used the wrong word?	12.5 for Verbs 15.5 for Modifiers 16.2 for Words in General

Errors in Mechanics. Capitals and a few widely used punctuation marks cause the most widespread problems in mechanics.

Problems	Questions to Ask	Sections in Text
Capitals	Are all proper nouns and adjectives capitalized correctly?	17.2 for Nouns 17.3 for Adjectives
End Marks	Does every sentence have the correct mark at the end?	19.1
Commas	Do you have a good reason for every comma used?	19.2 and 19.3
Apostrophes	Are apostrophes used incorrectly in personal pronouns such as *its*?	19.9

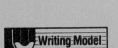
Errors in Spelling. Misspellings are common errors.

Problem	Question to Ask	Sections in Text
Misspelled Words	Have you used a dictionary to check every word you are not sure of?	34.1 and 34.2

Using Correction Symbols

Correction symbols are special marks that make it easier to show where changes are needed in a paper. The following chart shows some of the most common.

Symbol and Meaning	Corrected Example	Final Version
— take out	Randy admired the ~~the~~ lake.	Randy admired the lake.
∧ add	It was a ∧ blue color. *(deep)*	It was a deep blue color.
¶ paragraph	¶ Along the lake four hikers were walking.	Along the lake four hikers were walking.
frag fragment	Very hungry and tired. *(frag)*	They looked very hungry and tired.
ro run-on	The group had left camp at dawn, *(ro)* they had hiked for hours.	The group had left camp at dawn, and they had hiked for hours.
mod misplaced modifier	Distant, Randy pointed to the campsite. *(mod)*	Randy pointed to the distant campsite.
sp spelling	They headed down the trale. *(sp)*	They headed down the trail.

Index

Bold numbers show pages on which basic definitions and rules can be found.

776

778

Acknowledgments

The authors and editors have made every effort to trace the ownership of all copyrighted selections found in this book and to make full acknowledgment for their use.

The dictionary of record for this book is *Webster's New World Dictionary*, Second College Edition, Revised School Printing, copyright © 1983 by Simon & Schuster, Inc. The basis for the selection of vocabulary words appropriate for this grade level is *Living Word Vocabulary: A 43,000 Word Vocabulary Inventory* by Edgar Dale and Joseph O'Rourke, copyright © 1979.

Citations follow, arranged by unit and page for easy reference.

Composition: Forms and Process of Writing.   Pages 440-441 Tui de Roy Moore, "Ruler of the Island Sky," Copyright 1979 by the National Wildlife Federation. Reprinted from the July-August issue of *International Wildlife* Magazine. **441** David Alpern, "City at the Edge of Time," in *Travel/Holiday Magazine*, March 1981. **442** C.D.B. Bryan, "So Much Unfairness of Things," *Ten Top Stories*, edited by David A. Sohn (New York: Bantam Books, Inc., 1977). **443-444** Denis D. Gray, "Crossroads in Katmandu," Copyright 1980 by the National Wildlife Federation. Reprinted from the July-August issue of *International Wildlife* Magazine. **444** Gwen Schultz, *Icebergs and Their Voyages*, (New York: William Morrow and Company, 1975). **444-445** (first item) Jack Waller in *Travel and Leisure Magazine* (June 1981). **445** (second item), Arthur Hailey, *Airport* (New York: Doubleday & Company, 1968). **446** (first item), **498** Doron K. Antrim, *Having Fun with Music* (New York: Thomas Y. Crowell Company, 1958). **446** (second item), Adapted from Eva Hoffman, "Poland," GEO Magazine (April, 1981). **446-447** Paul Grescoe, "Learning to Live With Old Grizz," copyright 1980 by the National Wildlife Federation. Reprinted from the July-August issue of *International Wildlife* Magazine. **447** Norma Spring, *Alaska: Pioneer State* (New Jersey: Thomas Nelson & Sons, 1966). **454** (first item) Anne Innis Dagg, "Legs, Legs, Legs," copyright 1978 by the National Wildlife Federation. Reprinted from the November-December issue of *International Wildlife* Magazine. **454** (second item) Arthur Beiser and Konrad B. Krauskopf, *Introduction to Earth Science*, (New York: McGraw-Hill Book Company, 1975). **454-455** John Neary, "Hawks and Eagles," copyright 1980 by the National Wildlife Federation. Reprinted from the August-September issue of *National Wildlife* Magazine. **455** Adapted from Carla Wallach, *Gardening in the City* (New York: Harcourt, Brace, Jovanovich, 1976). **480** Adapted from *Atlas of the Oceans* © Mitchell Beazley 1977. Published in the U.S. by Rand McNally & Company. **506-507** Adapted from Jane & Michael Stern, *Amazing America* (New York: David Obst Books/Random House, 1977). **573** Adapted from Russell Baker, "Growing Up," copyright © 1982 by Russell Baker (New York: Congdon & Weed, Inc.).

Study and Research Skills. **Pages 725** Excerpted from *Research Guide/Index*, Volume 22 of *The World Book Encyclopedia* © 1981 World Book-Childcraft International, Inc. **727** (first item), *The World Almanac & Book of Facts*, 1984 edition, copyright © Newspaper Enterprise Association, Inc., 1983, New York, N.Y. 10166. **727** (second item), **728** (map) *Hammond Citation World Atlas*, Hammond, Inc., Maplewood, N.J., 1980. **730** (index entry, text entry) From *Roget's International Thesaurus*, Fourth Edition, by Robert Chapman. Copyright © 1977 by Harper & Row Publishers, Inc. Reprinted by permission of the publisher. **732** (both items) From *Current Biography*, 1984. Copyright © 1984 by the H.W. Wilson Company. Material reproduced by permission of the publisher. **735** *Readers' Guide to Periodical Literature* Copyright © 1984 by the H.W. Wilson Company. Material reproduced by permission of the publisher. **736** *Readers' Guide to Periodical Literature* Copyright © 1984, 1985 by the H.W. Wilson Company. Material reproduced by permission of the publisher. **739, 742** (chart), **743-749** With permission. From *Webster's New World Dictionary*, Students Edition, Copyright © 1981 by Simon & Schuster, Inc. Reprinted by permission of Simon & Schuster, Inc.

Art Acknowledgments. **Pages 459** Culver Pictures. **460** Marilyn Sanders, Peter Arnold, Inc.; Will Blanche, DPI. **461** Michael Hayman, Stock Boston. **495** Christina Thomson, Woodfin Camp. **511** Ira Kirschenbaum, Stock Boston. **512** Peter Simon, Stock Boston. **538** Culver Pictures. **539** Bruce Shenks, Buffalo Evening News. **540** W. Miller, *The New Yorker*, 1975. **555** Sanford Roth, Photo Researchers. **556** Monkmeyer Press. **567** Culver Pictures. **577** Ellis Herwig, Taurus Photos. **578** George Bellerose, Stock Boston. **597** Charles Addams, *The New Yorker*, 1954. **615** Alice Kandell, Photo Researchers. **616** Steven E. Sutton, Duomo; Ben Weaver, Camera 5. **617** Amy Krieg, Curtis Publications.

GRAMMAR USAGE MECHANICS